CREATIVITY
IN THE CLASSROOM

Schools of Curious Delight

Third Edition

CREATIVITY
IN THE CLASSROOM

Schools of Curious Delight

Third Edition

Alane Jordan Starko

2005

LAWRENCE ERLBAUM ASSOCIATES, PUBLISHERS

Mahwah, New Jersey   London

Copyright © 2005 by Lawrence Erlbaum Associates, Inc.
All rights reserved. No part of this book may be reproduced
in any form, by photostat, microform, retrieval system, or
any other means, without prior written permission of the
publisher.

Lawrence Erlbaum Associates, Inc., Publishers
10 Industrial Avenue
Mahwah, New Jersey 07430

Cover design by Kathryn Houghtaling Lacey
Cover art by David Jernigan, used with permission.

Library of Congress Cataloging-in-Publication Data

Starko, Alane J.
Creativity in the classroom : schools of curious delight / by Alane
Starko.—3rd ed.
p. cm.
Includes bibliographical references and index.
ISBN 0-8058-4791-X (pbk. : alk. Paper)
1. Creative thinking. I. Title.

LB1062.S77 2004
370.15'7—dc22   2004046922
                                                        CIP

Books published by Lawrence Erlbaum Associates are printed on acid-
free paper, and their bindings are chosen for strength and durability.

Printed in the United States of America
10 9 8 7 6 5 4 3 2

Contents

Preface

WHY CREATIVITY IN THE CLASSROOM?

At many points in the writing process an author asks him- or herself, "Why am I doing this? Why write this book?" For me, the answer has two components: belief in the importance of creativity in the constant reshaping of the world in which we live and, more specifically, belief in the importance of creativity in the schools. It is easy to consider the essential role of creativity in bringing joy and meaning to the human condition—without creativity we have no art, no literature, no science, no innovation, no problem solving, no progress. It is, perhaps, less obvious that creativity has an equally essential role in schools. The processes of creativity parallel those of learning. Recent calls for authentic activities, teaching for understanding, and real-world problem solving all require engaging students with content in flexible and innovative ways. Students who use content in creative ways learn the content well. They also learn strategies for identifying problems, making decisions, and finding solutions both in and out of school. Classrooms organized to develop creativity become places of both learning and wonder, the "curious delight" of the book's title.

WHY THIS BOOK?

Creativity in the Classroom: Schools of Curious Delight is a book about creativity written specifically for teachers. It was designed for a graduate course that helps teachers incorporate important aspects of creativity in the daily activities of classroom life. Teachers who understand the creative process can choose content, plan lessons, organize materials, and even grade assignments in ways that help students develop essential skills and attitudes for creativity. To do this well, teachers need both a firm grounding in research and theory regarding creativity and a variety of strategies for teaching and management that tie research to practice. This book is designed to do both.

This is not another book on research regarding creativity, although research and theory are important components of the book. It is not a book of creative activities or "What do I do on Monday?" lessons, although it contains numerous examples and strategies for teaching and classroom organization. It does build bridges between research and practice, providing the reflective teacher with appropriate strategies for today and enough background to develop effective strategies for tomorrow.

WHAT'S HERE?

The book has two parts. The first part, Understanding Creative People and Processes, provides the theoretical framework for the book. It has four chapters. Chapter 1 is an introduction that considers the nature of creativity and how it might be recognized in students. Chapter 2 reviews theories and models of creativity, including creativity across cultures, and chapter 3 reviews the characteristics of creative individuals. Chapter 4 examines research on talent development, identifying key ideas and research used to organize the remainder of the book. Although the purpose of the first part is to build understanding of research and theory, it considers each from the viewpoint of teachers and schools, examining how theories may be applied to young people and considering the implications for classroom practice.

The second part of the book, Creativity and Classroom Life, deals directly with strategies for teaching and learning. Chapter 5 teaches techniques developed specifically to teach creative thinking and examines how they may be applied to the classroom. Chapter 6 describes approaches to teaching major content areas—language arts, social studies, mathematics, and science—that support and encourage creativity. Rather than approaching creativity as a supplement to classroom content, this chapter concentrates on creativity as an organizing strand that shapes the core curriculum. Both chapters 5 and 6 include lesson ideas developed by teachers with whom I have been privileged to work. Their contributions immensely improve the work. Chapter 6 also includes standards-based lesson ideas from the state of Michigan, demonstrating how teaching to standards and teaching for creativity can happen simultaneously. Chapter 7 addresses classroom management and organization, showing how they may hinder or support the intrinsic motivation underlying creativity. The chapter examines recent trends such as cooperative learning, authentic assessment, and teaching for independence, and how they may be implemented in ways that enhance the opportunities for student creativity. Chapter 8 discusses assessment of creativity both formally and informally.

Each chapter includes periodic Thinking About the Classroom activities that help the reader tie material to a particular teaching situation. Also included are Journeying and Journaling questions that assist the reader in reflecting on how content may affect his or her life as a teacher and as an individual. Through Journeying and Journaling, the reader is encouraged to engage in creative activities, reflect on creative processes, and experiment with developing skills and habits of mind that may enhance creativity. Through them, I hope readers may not only develop creativity in their classrooms and plan creative opportunities for students, but find creativity in their own lives as well. Perhaps they may find, there, a source of curious delight.

WHAT'S NEW IN THIS EDITION?

In addition to the usual updating, there are a few changes and additions in this third edition. In the first chapter there is a section addressing the appropriateness of teaching for creativity in a time of increased emphasis on teaching to content standards. This is supported in chapter 6 by examples of content lessons developed for the MI (Michigan) CLiMB (Clarifying Language in Michigan Benchmarks) that also support creativity. Created for the Michigan Department of Education, MI CLiMB provides clarification and teaching examples for Michigan standards and benchmarks. It includes many fine examples of lessons that teach to content standards and creativity simultaneously. In chapter 1 the reader will also find an expanded section on learning, brain research, and creativity.

In chapter 2 there are expanded sections on creativity across cultures and collaborative creativity. It seems, as with many important things, the more I learn about creativity, the more complex and interesting it becomes—and the more humbled I am by the limits of our understanding.

ACKNOWLEDGMENTS

It is always impossible to acknowledge fully the many individuals whose contributions, critiques, support, and friendship allow a publication to evolve from dream to reality. Certainly that is true for this work. I do, however, express my gratitude publicly to a few individuals whose assistance was particularly essential.

First, I acknowledge the contributions of Jared Chrislip and David Jernigan, two talented young men who, as high school students, created the illustrations for the first edition of this book (with one assist from David's brother Nathan). For the second and third editions we retained half the original illustrations and created new ones for the other half. As will be obvious, Jared and David have grown into extraordinary talented young adults. Their imagination, energy, and professionalism have been a joy to watch and an enormous asset to the book. They are fine human beings as well as fine artists, and I am grateful to work with them.

Second, I thank the students in CUR 510, Developing Creativity in the Classroom, for their assistance in the development of my ideas, their practical insights, and their helpful critiques of the manuscript. Perhaps most of all, I appreciate their patience as we struggle together to understand the complexities of this topic. Thanks also to the many professionals at Lawrence Erlbaum Associates who helped keep this book alive in a third edition. In particular, thanks to Lane Akers, Bonita D'Amil, and Sarah Wahlert. I am also grateful for the faculty and staff in the Department of Teacher Education at Eastern Michigan University—especially Heather Shelton, Karen Metz, Brandi Wilkins, and Kris Futrel—who help me keep sane while trying to manage a department and a manuscript simultaneously. I could not do either without them.

I express gratitude for, and a warning about, the three black cats who have been my companions at the keyboard during almost all the hours of my writing. Any strange sets of letters appearing in the manuscript can be attributed to their wandering paws. Their purrs remind me it will all work out.

Finally, as always, I must acknowledge that my work would be impossible and my life a lot less fun without the constant love, support, and confidence of my husband, Bob. When I'm looking for an example of creativity, I never have to look very far. For more than 30 years his creativity has been a wonder to me, a joy to watch, and a privilege to share. What could be better?

part I

Understanding Creative People and Processes

chapter **1**

What Is Creativity?

In 1905 an unknown clerk in the Swiss patent office published a paper in which he advocated abandoning the idea of absolute time. This fundamental postulate of the theory of relativity suggested that the laws of science should be the same for all observers, regardless of speed. The clerk's name was Albert Einstein (Hawkins, 1988).

Vincent van Gogh began painting in 1880. His adaptations of the impressionist style were considered strange and eccentric, and his personal life was complicated by illness and poverty. He sold only one painting before his death in 1890 (Fichner-Rathus, 1986).

In a quiet space under an ancient tree, the Storyteller recounts a familiar tale. The audience listens carefully to each nuance, appreciating both the well-known story line and the new turns of language and elaboration that make the characters come to life.

In first grade, Michelle was given an outline of a giant shark's mouth on a worksheet that asked, "What will our fishy friend eat next?" She dutifully colored several fish and boats, and then wrote the following explanation. "Once there was a shark named Peppy. One day he ate three fish, one jellyfish, and two boats. Before he ate the jellyfish, he made a peanut butter and jellyfish sandwich."

At 19, Juan was homeless and a senior in high school. One cold evening he thought that a warm space inside the school would be a more appealing sleeping place than any he could see. Getting into the building was no problem, but once he was inside, a motion detector would make him immediately detectable to the guard on the floor below. Juan entered a storage room and carefully dislodged a pile of baseball bats. In the ensuing commotion he located a comfortable sleeping place. The guard attributed the motion detector's outburst to the falling bats, and Juan slept until morning.

Who is creative? What does creativity look like? Where does it originate? What role do our classrooms play in the development or discouragement of creativity? The word "creativity" suggests many powerful associations. In some contexts it seems almost beyond the scope of mere mortals—few of us can imagine treading in the footsteps of Einstein or Curie, Picasso or O'Keeffe, Mozart or Charlie Parker. Their accomplishments are stunning in originality and power, not just contributing to their disciplines, but transforming them.

On the other hand, many of us have created a new casserole from ingredients in the refrigerator, jury-rigged a muffler to last to the next service station, or written a poem or song for the enjoyment of a loved one. What about Michelle and her peanut butter and jellyfish sandwich or Juan and his decoy bats? Were they creative? Can there be creativity in recounting a familiar story? Are we all creative? How do we know creativity when we see it? What does it have to do with education?

The word "creative" is used frequently in schools. Virtually all of us, as teachers or students, have had experiences with creative writing. Teacher stores abound with collections of creative activities or books on creative teaching of various subjects. Such sources frequently provide interesting and enjoyable classroom experiences without tackling the fundamental questions: What is creativity? Where does it originate? What experiences or circumstances allow individuals to become more creative? Although collections of activities can be useful, without information on these more basic issues it is difficult for any teacher to make good decisions on classroom practices that might encourage or discourage creativity in students.

University libraries contain theoretical texts and research studies that address basic questions about creativity, but the authors of these books seldom extend their investigations to explore implications of research and theory for daily classroom life. Few theorists examine what their theories mean for the language arts curriculum or consider how the research on motivation and creativity might affect methods of grading, evaluation, or reward. Even more rarely are such implications explored with school-age students.

This book brings these two points of view together, examining the basic questions, theories, and research with an eye to classroom practice. Although the investigation of a phenomenon as complex and elusive as creativity will, of necessity, raise more questions than it answers, it provides a place to begin. I hope that thoughtful teachers who raise these questions will go far beyond the strategies suggested in this book to experiment, try new ideas, and observe what happens. Only through such efforts can we expand the body of knowledge on the development of creativity, its impact in classrooms, and its manifestations in children.

GETTING STARTED: DEFINING CREATIVITY

There are many definitions of creativity (e.g., Parkhurst, 1999, Sternberg, 1988, 1999). Some definitions focus on characteristics of individuals whose work is determined to be creative (What is a creative person like?), whereas others consider the work itself (What makes this creative?). In either case, most definitions have two major criteria for judging creativity: novelty and appropriateness. For example, Perkins (1988) defined creativity as follows: "(a) A creative result is a result both original and appropriate. (b) A creative person—a person with creativity—is a person who fairly routinely produces creative results" (p. 311). Although Perkins' propositions are broad, they tie together the concepts of creative people and creative activities in a neat practical package. Even so, each aspect of this simple definition poses questions.

Novelty and originality may be the characteristics most immediately associated with creativity. Works of literature that imitate those before them or scientific discoveries that are merely a rehash of earlier work are seldom considered creative. To be creative, an idea or product must be new.

The key dilemma is, new to whom? If a researcher at the University of Michigan works for years to engineer a gene transfer to cure a particular disease only to discover that a researcher at Stanford published the same techniques only 2 weeks before, is the Michigan researcher's work no longer creative? Must elementary school children devise ideas that are unique in the world before their efforts can be considered creative? Either of these questions becomes, in the end, a semantic or a value issue. Some researchers—including some of the most active today—are focused on high-level creativity, creativity that changes some aspect of our world in dramatic ways. For them, only ideas new to a particular discipline or culture are designated creative. It is the purpose of this book to describe the development of creativity in the classroom. Therefore, the following definition seems most reasonable for our purposes: To be considered creative, a product or idea must be original or novel to the individual creator. By this standard, Michelle's peanut butter and jellyfish sandwich can be considered original, as can the unhappy researcher's discoveries, because both efforts were new to their creators, if not to the world. But although we can select this standard as reasonable for educational practice, it is important to recognize that the issues regarding novelty are not ultimately resolved.

Thinking About the Classroom

With a friend, examine the same set of student papers or products. Do you both agree on which are the most original? Why or why not?

The second aspect of creativity is appropriateness. If I am asked the time and I reply, "The cow jumped over the computer yesterday," my response would certainly be novel—but would it be considered creative or simply inappropriate? Again, the definition can be fuzzy. Was Juan's late-night entrance to the school appropriate? Because van Gogh's works were not accepted by the public of his time, were they inappropriate? If they had never been accepted, would they have been creative?

One important factor in determining appropriateness is the cultural context in which the creativity is based. Just as intelligence is viewed differently in various cultures (Lubart, 1999; Sternberg, 1990), so the vehicles and focus of creativity vary from culture to culture and across time. Works by van Gogh or Manet that 19th-century audiences rejected are considered masterpieces today. The expressive individualism of some African American young men can take the form of creative stances, walks, and gestures that can go unnoticed or misunderstood by those outside their culture. Contemporary artists see beauty and power in graffiti that escape much of the general public.

Cultures in fact, differ in their conceptions of the nature of creativity itself (Liep, 2001; Lubart, 1990, 1999; Weiner, 2000). The product-oriented, originality-based phenomenon emphasized in this book is a Western orientation, whereas some Eastern or traditional cultures conceptualize creativity as a process of individual growth, spiritual journey, or evolution (rather than revolution) in shared community culture. Additional information on conceptions of creativity across cultures is found in chapter 2.

It is interesting to think about which areas in our culture are most tied to our cultural values and how that may affect our openness to creativity. It seems likely that the types of problems and modes of expression will vary in any multicultural society such as the United States. Certainly, the dulcimer music of Appalachia differs from New Orleans jazz. In a similar fashion, the styles of art and language as well as the modes and themes of expression show great diversity. In facilitating creativity in schools, it is important for the teacher to consider the cultural contexts of students' lives. It is necessary to provide multiple vehicles or strategies to appeal not just to students' varied abilities or learning styles, but also to their diverse social and cultural values. This varied sense of appropriateness perhaps makes defining creativity more complicated, but it also allows richness and diversity in the types of creative efforts that are attempted and appreciated.

I consider a definition of appropriateness here that is nearly as broad as the term itself: An idea or product is appropriate if it meets some goal or criterion. Creativity is purposeful and involves effort to make something work, to make something better, more meaningful, or more beautiful. In much adult creativity, criteria are set by the culture and the discipline. Most paintings, for example, must have some balance and composition. The question becomes much trickier as the norms change in a discipline. Although styles of painting vary and evolve, works of art are seldom considered creative unless they are eventually appreciated by some audience. Van Gogh was originally considered dysfunctional. Our revised standards consider him creative.

Each culture and discipline sets standards for creative activities. In many Western cultures a story has a beginning, middle, and end, as well as an identifiable conflict and climax. In other cultures with elaborate oral traditions, the shape of a story may be very different, embracing multiple side roads and circles. Criteria for judging African ceremonial masks are very different from those for evaluating Italian *commedia dell'arte* masks. Nonetheless, the creative efforts in each case are eventually considered to meet some standard and be accepted by some audience.

Adult standards of appropriateness, however, are generally not suitable for children. Few expect elementary school students' paintings or stories to match those of Cassatt or Fitzgerald. We can consider children's efforts appropriate if they are meaningful, purposeful, or communicative in some way. If students successfully communicate an idea or endeavor to solve a problem, their efforts can be considered appropriate. If they do so in a way that is original, at least to them, we can consider the efforts creative.

Even such broad parameters can be difficult to translate into reality. Consider the following cases. Which behaviors would you consider creative or not creative?

1. In the middle of a discussion on plants, 6-year-old Toshio raises his hand. "Do you think the plants would grow taller and stronger if, instead of watering them, we milked them?"

2. Jane dressed for the first day of eighth grade in long underwear with a black half-slip over the top, a purple satin blouse, and grapes hanging as earrings.

3. Maria wrote the best essay on federalism her teacher had ever seen. It was clear, well documented, and thorough, including implications of federalism seldom considered by high school students.

4. Eduardo's first-grade class has been taught to subtract by taking away the designated number. Numerous manipulatives are available for students' use. Eduardo refuses to use the method he has been taught. Instead, he uses his fingers to count up from the smaller to the larger number.

5. Sam is wearing a baseball cap on hat day. Unbeknown to his teacher, he has installed a mirror under the brim. When the hat is cocked at the correct angle, he can see the desk next to his. This will be handy during the sixth-period quiz.

6. Karin has recently become captivated by *Leave It to Beaver* reruns. She frequently uses her journal to write new adventures of Wally, Eddie, and the Beaver.

7. Susan is asked to illustrate a scene from the biography of Frederick Douglass her second-grade teacher is reading. Having heard that he traveled through England and Wales, she draws Frederick Douglass walking across a row of smiling whales.

8. Max's music class has been given the assignment of composing a short piece in the style of one of the classical composers they have studied to date. Max creates a rap about Beethoven's hair (and its lack of style) using the rhythms of Beethoven's *Fifth Symphony*.

9. Tzeena is known for her caricatures. During English class, she has at times passed around sketches in which she has drawn her teacher's head attached to the body of an ostrich.

Whose behavior did you consider creative? When Toshio wonders about the possibility of milking rather than watering plants, it is almost certainly an original idea. It is unlikely he has seen or heard of anyone

Creative ideas are new and appropriate.

putting milk on plants. Because the idea of plants' growing stronger with milk is perfectly consistent with what Toshio has been taught about children needing milk to grow strong, it is also appropriate and can be considered a creative response.

Jane's case is a little trickier. Attire is not necessarily novel simply because it is unusual. Did Jane originate the grape earrings? Is she the first to wear a slip over her long underwear? If so (and because it certainly meets the adolescent criterion of being different from her parents' fashions), her dress can be considered creative. In many cases, however, clothing that may appear innovative to an outsider may be the latest craze in some groups. Jane may not be creative in her dress at all, but may be conforming completely to unwritten standards.

Maria's report on federalism, although appropriate, is probably not creative. Although it is thorough, well written, and unusual for her grade level, we have no clear indication that she has developed any new ideas on the subject. If her assessment of the implications of federalism represents an unusually careful analysis or logical extensions of her sources, she should be commended for her efforts, but her work probably is not original. However, if she is able to approach the idea in a new way (perhaps using parallels to classrooms in a school) or to derive new and unusual implications from her reading, it is possible that her efforts can be considered creative. It is important to note, however, that even unusually well-written and documented analyses and summaries generally are not considered creative when they are a representation of someone else's ideas.

Eduardo's subtraction method may be creative if he has devised the method for himself. It is certainly appropriate because he is able to derive the correct answers by using it. If, however, Eduardo was taught the method elsewhere (e.g., at home, on the school bus), it cannot be considered creative.

What about Sam? If his mirrored cap is original, we must (perhaps grudgingly) consider it creative. It may not be considered appropriate by his sixth-period teacher, but it is purposeful to its creator. The same standard can be applied to Juan, the young man described at the beginning of the chapter, whose tumbling-bat distraction allowed him into the school after hours. Although breaking and entering are not appropriate as measured by legality, the strategy is purposeful. Juan is able to stay warm for most of the night because of his creative action. Although allowing the creator to be the primary judge of appropriateness poses some difficulties (e.g., should people with mental illnesses determine whether their responses are appropriate?), it still seems the most reasonable standard for children, whose ideas of purposeful behavior may be meaningful to them, but not to adults.

Karin's *Leave It to Beaver* stories probably are creative if they are original stories consistent with the characters she chooses. If, however, they are a reprise of televised adventures, they cannot be considered original. The same criterion can be applied to student artists who while away the hours sketching countless *Nickelodeon* or *Lord of the Rings* characters. Elaborate drawings of well-known characters, however technically impressive, are not creative unless the content of the drawings is original. A standard pose of a familiar character cannot be considered creative, no matter how well it is drawn. If, however, the drawings represent characters in new and unusual settings, tell a story, or portray an original message, they may be creative.

Susan's illustration of Frederick Douglass walking across whales probably is novel. It is unlikely that she has seen a similar drawing! However, if the originality resulted from a misunderstanding or lack of prior knowledge of the difference between Wales and whales, the drawing is not a clever visual pun; it is a mistake. Although mistakes often can provide stimulus or inspiration for creative endeavors, they usually are not considered creative. In creative endeavors, the originality must be purposeful. In very young children, it is possible to confuse originality with immature understanding. If a toddler begs for a new jumper so she can jump higher, it is not a purposeful, novel thought if the child thinks that is what jumpers do. He or she is not being creative, but is making a logical connection with familiar uses of the word "jump," just as an adult might accidentally misuse new vocabulary.

Max's response to the composition assignment is certainly original. However, is it appropriate? If we gauge appropriateness as meeting the criterion for the assignment, probably not. Max, after all, created a piece about the style of Beethoven rather than in his style. However, if appropriateness is judged from Max's point of view—"How can I use music I value to do this assignment?"—the effort falls closer to the mark. Perhaps we can view Max's composition as falling short of the criterion for the assignment while still demonstrating considerable creative thought. It might also be relevant to ask whether it is good rap. That is, does it meet criteria in its own domain?

Tzeena's caricatures can probably be considered creative, if not kind. The idea of teacher-as- ostrich is probably original, and the drawings certainly portray a meaningful message. As with Max's music, it is important to remember that creativity is not necessarily channeled into school-appropriate behaviors. Although we can certainly endeavor to change students' vehicles for creativity, it is important to recognize creativity in a variety of forms.

Thinking About the Classroom

Creativity is not always expressed in school-appropriate ways. For 1 week, pay careful attention to students causing disturbances in your room. Do you see evidence of creativity in their behavior? Perhaps that originality can be channeled in other ways.

WHY DO PEOPLE CREATE?

Why did Emily Dickinson write? What prompted Scott Joplin to compose or Edison to invent or Pacific island people to tell stories with dance? Examining the forces that motivate individual creativity may be crucial to encouraging those behaviors in school settings. Consider the statements of these creative individuals.

I think I teach people how to find meaning. I write about the most chaotic, tragic, hard-to-deal-with events, and these events are sometimes so violent and so horrible that they burst through bounds of form and preconceptions. I'm hoping that readers will find how to get the meaning out of these events. How do you find beauty and order when we've had this bloody horrible past? (Maxine Hong Kingston, in Moyers, 1990, p. 11)

... to try to get something on the page and see that it's not working or that it's only half there or that some people would think it's there but you know it isn't. When we fantasize in our daily lives, that's easy, because fantasy by definition is sufficient and compensating. But, the writer's fantasy is not complete until he can transmit it to somebody else .... Where it flows, where you find yourself going on and the writing generates more writing—there's your book. (E. L. Doctorow, in Ruas, 1984, p. 203)

I drew them several times and there was no feeling in them. Then afterwards—after I had done the ones that were so stiff—came the others .... HOW IT HAPPENS THAT I CAN EXPRESS SOMETHING OF THAT KIND? Because the thing has already taken form in my mind before I start on it. The first attempts are absolutely unbearable. I say this because I want you to know that if you see something worthwhile in what I am doing, it is not by accident but because of real intention and purpose. (Vincent van Gogh, in Ghiselin, 1985, p. 47)

In each case, individuals created works of art or literature because they had something to communicate. The message was not always easy to express. The ideas were sometimes difficult or the forms hard to manage. Despite the difficulties, the creators persisted. They wished to allow the audience to make meaning in new ways or share a vision of the world. The process of making meaning and shared vision can be seen in the efforts of visual artists, storytellers, musicians, dancers, myth makers, playwrights, and other creators throughout history. Such an observation almost seems so obvious as to be meaningless: Of course writers and artists strive to communicate. Yet this most basic process of creativity, the effort to communicate, is missing in many so-called creative school activities. How often does a student in school write or paint or use another form of expression not because it has been assigned, but because he or she has something to say? Others use creative processes in slightly different ways. Consider the forces that motivated these creators.

In 1873, Chester Greenwood received a pair of ice skates for his 15th birthday. Unfortunately, Chester was unable to enjoy the skates, because each time he ventured on the ice, the chill Farmington, Maine, air made his sensitive ears uncomfortable enough that he was forced indoors. The earmuffs Chester designed to solve this problem were sold across New England by the time Chester was 19 (Caney, 1985).

In Chicopee, Massachusetts, a group of middle-school students read about the city's sludge problem. The state had ordered Chicopee to stop burning sludge because doing so violated air-quality regulations. In the winter, the sludge froze before it could be hauled away to a landfill. (Another difficult New England winter!) Officials suggested constructing a brick building around the sludge to keep it from freezing, but the city did not have the necessary $120,000. Students at the Bellamy Middle School brainstormed numerous solutions and sent them to the chief operator of the sludge plant. Their suggested solar green-house successfully kept the sludge warm and was constructed for $500 (Lewis, 1991).

In 1924 Kimberly-Clark began to market Cellucotton sheets as dis-posable cloths for removing makeup. In 1929 they patented the pop-up box and renamed the product Kleenex. Sales were still only moderate. A marketing survey revealed that over half the people purchasing Kleenex were using them, not to remove makeup, but as disposable handkerchiefs. A new marketing strat-egy and slogan, "Don't put a cold in your pocket," led to a 400% sales increase in 2 years (Caney, 1985).

In these cases, individuals exercised creative thinking not only to com-municate, but also to solve problems. The inventors of modern lighting, heating, and cooling devices used creative thinking to address the prob-lems of comfort in their homes. Mail-order catalogues are full of devices de-signed to address less dramatic problems. Products that locate the end of the masking tape, clean the venetian blinds, or protect the shoe that works the gas pedal from scuffing all resulted from someone's creative thinking about a particular problem or annoyance.

Many times, the more important part of this process is realizing that a problem exists. Until their marketing survey, sales personnel at Kimberly-Clark had no knowledge of a need for a disposable handkerchief. It is hard to imag-ine now that a few years ago no one thought offices needed the now indispens-able stick-on, pull-off notes. In a similar fashion, someone realized that there was a need (or at least a market) for frozen dinners, facsimile (fax) machines, and digital video disk players (DVDs) before those products existed. In scien-tific research, it may be at least as important to select a potent research ques-tion as it is to solve it. The researcher who first wondered whether it was possible to alter the structure of genes opened up new worlds of medical re-search and treatment. Imagine the impact of the first human being to realize that the inability to record language was a problem. Identifiying a problem to solve rather than solving a preset problem is called *problem finding*.

Problem finding, in its broadest sense, underlies all types of creativity. Some of the most basic research in problem finding was done with visual artists (Getzels & Csikszentmihalyi, 1976). In those studies, artists were considered to be problem finding as they manipulated materials to find ideas for their paintings. Finding the idea or theme to communicate, as well as finding a societal problem or need, can be considered problem finding. I consider both of these themes as the underlying (and overlapping) purposes of creativity in Western cultures. Within the primary culture in which I work and teach, individuals are often creative in their efforts to communicate an idea or to find and solve problems. Extending these processes into classroom situations can allow creative activities to occur there naturally. Introducing these procedures also holds implications for classroom learning because the purposes of creativity have much in common with key attributes of learning theory.

Thinking About the Classroom

Try giving two assignments on the same general topic, one demanding accuracy and one requiring originality. For example, if the class is studying the Civil War, the one assignment may ask students to develop a time line of key events or describe the causes of the war, and the other may ask students to describe our lives today if the South had won the war. Do the same students give the most accurate and the most original responses? Are the original responses also appropriate?

A QUICK LOOK AT LEARNING THEORY

Early theories of learning were often based on what might be termed a connectionist or behaviorist perspective. In this perspective, researchers observed, in carefully controlled conditions, the behaviors of various learners in response to certain stimuli. The learner was perceived as a passive receptor of stimuli—as outside forces directed, so the learner learned. The basic processes of learning were considered to be uniform across species. "It does not make much difference what species we study .... The laws of learning are much the same in rats, dogs, pigeons, monkeys, and humans" (Hill, 1977, p. 9). A poet writing a poem was considered to be as controlled by prior stimuli during that act as a chicken laying an egg (Skinner, 1971).

This view of the learner as a passive absorber of stimuli appears to have little in common with processes or purposes of creativity. However, contemporary learning theory acknowledges human learning to be a more complex, constructive process than previously thought. Increasing consensus among researchers suggests that learning is a goal-oriented process (Jones, Palincsar, Ogle, & Carr, 1987; Resnick & Klopfer, 1989). Activities undertaken in pursuit of a meaningful goal offer more fertile ground for learning than activities undertaken without an obvious cause. Learning as a constructive process implies that learners build their own knowledge as a contractor builds a house, not as a sponge absorbs water or a billiard ball bounces off the table. Processes associated with this vision of learning are organizing information, linking new information to prior knowledge, and using metacognitive (thinking about thinking) strategies to plan the accomplishment of goals (Bransford, Sherwood, Vye, & Rieser, 1986; Carey, 1986; Resnick, 1985; Schoenfeld, 1985).

Learning in pursuit of a goal makes the learning purposeful. Tying information to prior knowledge, understanding, and affect makes it meaningful. Because the ties created by each unique student must be original, and because goal-oriented learning must, by definition, be appropriate (if it meets the goal), the processes of learning themselves can be viewed as creative. In fact, some cognitive theorists studying creativity believe that creativity is only a special case of the same processes we use to construct new ideas—and even new sentences—daily (see chap. 2). Each learner builds an individual cognitive structure different from all others and full of unique personal associations. "Meaningful learning ... is essentially creative. All students must, therefore, be given permission to transcend the insights of their teachers" (Caine & Caine, 1991, p. 92).

The processes of building cognitive structures underlie all learning. The development of expertise in an area might be seen as developing spaces or ties in the cognitive structure into which new information can fit. An expert's framework parallels the structure of his or her subject, allowing the expert to fit new information easily in the appropriate place, just as a builder with framing in place and a blueprint in hand deals more easily with a new piece of plasterboard than a builder newly arrived on the construction site. Helping students become more expert entails assisting them in putting up the framework.

> Expertise ... involves much more than knowing a myriad of facts. Expertise is based on a deep knowledge of the problems that continually arise on a particular job. It is accumulated over years of ex-

perience tackling these problems and is organized in the expert's mind in ways that allow him or her to overcome the limits of reasoning. (Prietula & Simon, 1989, p. 120)

To me, it is fascinating that multiple paths seemingly lead to very similar recommendations. Our understanding of neuropsychology is in its infancy, yet it appears to lead us to conclusions very similar to those derived from learning theory.

Studies in this area begin with the brain and its development. Many of our neural pathways are already established at birth (e.g., those that control breathing and heartbeat) but many more are created through interaction with our environment. Each interaction uses and strengthens neural connections. The more we use particular connections, the stronger they become. As we create new connections, we build the capacity for more flexible thought.

We always have the ability to remodel our brains. To change the wiring in one skill, you must engage in some activity that is unfamiliar, novel to you but related to that skill, because simply repeating the same activity only maintains already established connections. To bolster his creative circuitry, Albert Einstein played the violin. Winston Churchill painted landscapes. (Ratey, 2001, p. 36)

The brain was designed for survival (Pinker, 1997). Survival is based on the brain's ability to make meaning of the outside world and respond appropriately. The brain constantly receives sensory input and builds neural connections based on the way the input relates to prior experiences. In its efforts to make sense of the deluge of information presented moment by moment, the brain creates patterns. If input fits neatly into an existing pattern, it is accepted and the pattern is reinforced. If input is so foreign that it fits no existing pattern, it can be rejected without meaningful learning. If input is novel but can be connected to some existing pattern, new connections are established, with the old pattern both stretched and reinforced. Psychiatrist John Ratey (2001) stated:

Every time we choose to solve a problem creatively, or think about something in a new way, we reshape the physical connection in our brains. The brain has to be challenged in order to stay fit, just as the muscles, heart, and lungs must be deliberately exercised to become more resilient. (p. 364)

It is precisely such stretching of patterns that we hope to achieve when we teach in a way that enhances creativity. Students think about content from different points of view, use it in new ways, or connect it to new or unusual ideas. These associations strengthen the connections to the content as well as the habits of mind associated with more flexible thinking. In fact, creative thinking is one core component of contextual teaching and learning, a system of instruction designed to help students see meaning in academic material then learn and retain it by connecting it to their daily lives (Johnson, 2002). In this system, creative thinking is promoted as one of the key strategies to help students learn.

Other educators studying neural research also have attempted to draw conclusions regarding classroom teaching and learning. Although it is important to recognize the tentative nature of such inferences, many recommendations made by writers addressing "brain-based curriculum" are consistent with the constructivist approaches to learning rooted in cognitive psychology: students' active engagement in learning, clear organization of content, and involvement in complex activities (Caine & Caine, 1997; Jensen, 2000; Scherer, 2000). Similar recommendations are made based on studies directly investigating teaching methods.

When researchers attempt to delineate teaching strategies that are most effective in supporting student learning, such lists typically include the activities required for finding and solving problems. For example, generally conservative William Bennett (1986) included the use of experiments in his list of "What Works," along with more traditional strategies such as direct instruction and homework. Marzano (2003) attempted to synthesize multiple meta-analyses of effective instructional strategies into nine categories of effective practice. One those is "generating and testing hypotheses" (p. 83). Additionally, several of his other categories include activities that reflect strategies recommended in this text. For example, his "nonlinguistic representations" category (p, 82) includes visual imagery and role play. The category of "identifying similarities and differences" (p. 82) includes the use of metaphors and analogies. All of these strategies are discussed in chapter 5.

How, in the end, do these recommendations tie to creativity? Simply stated, if we want to teach effectively, the strategies that support creativity will help us do so. Giving students opportunities to be creative requires allowing them to find and solve problems and communicate ideas in novel and appropriate ways. Learning takes place best when learners are involved in setting and meeting goals and tying information to their experiences in unique ways. Students develop expertise by being immersed in problems of a discipline. Creativity aside, we know that raising questions, solving problems, tying information to personal and original ideas, and communicating results all help students learn. How much better it is, then, to find and solve problems in ways that facilitate original ideas, and to give students tools for communicating novel thinking. Structuring education around the goals of creativity is a wonderful two-for-one sale—pay the right price for the learning and you may get creativity free.

Thinking About the Classroom

If you teach young children, watch your students on the playground. Look for behaviors that use novel or original ideas for play activities. If you teach older students, observe their interactions during extracurricular or other social activities. Look for evidence of originality. Do you also see evidence of learning?

TEACHING FOR CREATIVITY VERSUS CREATIVE TEACHING

Structuring teaching for creativity can be a slippery goal. I once attended a class in which graduate students demonstrated lessons designed to enhance creative thinking. One activity particularly stands out in my memory. The teacher of the lesson took the class outside, a welcome break from the stuffy college classroom. She then brought out a parachute and proceeded to show us how the chute could be used to create various forms—a flower, an ocean wave, and other shapes. We were taught a specific, tightly choreographed series of moves to tie one form to the next in a story line. As the teacher narrated, we marched and ducked and raised our arms so that the parachute was transformed into various shapes to accompany the story. We acquired an audience of passersby, and the striking visual effect we created earned us hearty applause. We enjoyed the exercise and activity, especially the break from the usual routine and the enthusiastic acceptance by our audience. When we finished, however, I was struck by a clear question. Who was being creative? The living sculpture of the parachute activity certainly seemed original, and it communicated in novel and effective ways. Yet, as a participant, my thoughts were not on communication or originality, but on counting my steps and remembering when to duck—hardly the chief ingredients of creative thought. A teaching activity that produces an enjoyable, or even creative, outcome does not necessarily enhance creativity unless the students have the opportunity for creative thinking. The parachute activity might be considered creative teaching because the teacher exercised considerable creativity in developing and presenting the exercise. However, creative teaching (the teacher is creative) is not the same as teaching to develop creativity.

This distinction becomes clearer when books of so-called creative activities are examined. In some cases, the illustrations are adorable and the activities unusual, but the input from students is fairly routine. For example, a color-by-number dragon filled with addition problems may have been an original creation for the illustrator, but completing the addition problems and coloring as directed provide no opportunities for originality among the students. A crossword puzzle in the shape of a spiral was an original idea for its creator, but it still requires students only to give accurate responses to the clues and fill in the correct spaces. In these cases, those who created the materials had the opportunity to be creative. The students do not. In other cases, classroom teachers may use enormous personal creativity in developing activities that allow few opportunities for students to be original.

Teaching to enhance creativity has a different focus. The essential creativity is on the part of the students. If the students develop parachute choreography or a new form of crossword puzzle, they have the opportunity to exercise creative thinking. Creativity also can be developed as students devise their own science experiments, discuss Elizabethan England from the point of view of a woman at court or a farm woman, or rewrite "Snow White" as it might be told by the stepmother. When teaching to enhance creativity we may well be creative as teachers, but we also provide students the knowledge, skills, and surroundings necessary for their own creativity to emerge. The results may not be as flashy as those in the parachute story, but they include real problem finding, problem solving, and communication by students.

Thinking About the Classroom

Examine a book on creative activities or creative teaching. For each activity, identify the person who has the opportunity for original or innovative thought. Is it primarily the author, teacher, or student?

AUTHENTIC PROBLEMS AND PROCESSES

Structuring education around the goals of creativity involves shifting our visions of teachers and learners. Learning activities designed to foster creativity cast students in the roles of problem solvers and communicators rather than passive acquirers of information. Teachers, in turn, are transformed from founts of all wisdom to problem setters, problem seekers, coaches, audience, and sometimes publicity agents. If students are to solve real problems, teachers have the responsibility not only to teach them the necessary knowledge and skills, but also to set problems for which the teachers have no answers and to work together with students to find the solutions. If students are to communicate, teachers must help them find ideas worth sharing and audiences with whom to share them. These are fundamentally different processes from those most of us experienced as learners in school. This type of restructuring also has major implications for the content in curriculum areas to be addressed.

It is essential to understand that restructuring curriculum does not mean eliminating it. Students can and should learn required content while also enhancing their creative thinking—the two should be inextricably entwined. One cannot solve problems involving plants without knowledge of botany, and teachers have the responsibility to help students gain that knowledge. Contrary to some quickly turned phrases, sometimes the sage should be on the stage. In fact, the processes of identifying and solving problems form an effective context in which to gain content knowledge. But students who are to be taught strategies for finding and solving problems and for communicating information must be taught not just the *what*, but also the *how* of the disciplines in the curriculum. For example, students who are to be problem solvers in history must know not only facts, concepts, and generalizations about history, but also how history works and what historians do. How does a historian decide on an area for study? What types of problems do historians find and solve? How do they gather information? Learning as much as possible about the authentic methodology of the disciplines allows students to become seekers and solvers of real or authentic problems while learning content about history in more complex ways.

The investigation of authentic problems was espoused by educators such as Dewey (1938) and Renzulli (1977) throughout much of the 20th century. Such problems were emphasized in literature on authentic learning (Brandt, 1993), situated learning (Brown, Collins, & Duguid, 1989), and problem solving ranging from opportunities for astronomical data gathering (Bollman, Rodgers, & Mauller, 2001) to solving dilemmas of real-world businesses (Holt & Willard-Holt, 2000). Although more complete discussions on the nature of problem types and authentic learning are included in chapters 4 and 6, for now, a simple definition will suffice. An *authentic problem* (a) does not have a predetermined answer, (b) is personally relevant to the investigator, and c) can be explored through the methods of one or more disciplines. Students who are to address authentic problems must be provided with the knowledge and tools that allow them to be successful. In a parallel fashion, students who are to be effective communicators not only must have an idea worth communicating, but also must be taught the skills of communication in a variety of formats.

As you can see, this book does not view teaching for creativity as something to be pulled out on Friday at 2 p.m. or when students are restless after an indoor recess. Teaching for creativity entails creating a community of inquiry in the classroom, a place in which asking a good question is at least as important as answering one. Building this climate includes organizing curriculum around the processes of creativity, providing students with content and processes that allow them to investigate and communicate within disciplines, teaching general techniques that facilitate creative thinking across disciplines, and providing a classroom atmosphere that supports creativity.

TEACHING FOR CREATIVITY IN A TIME OF STANDARDS

One of the most important educational trends of the early 21st century is the increased emphasis on teaching to specific state and national standards (Chatterji, 2002; Elmore & Fuhrman, 1994; Glatthorn, Carr, & Harris, 2001; Kendall & Marzano, 1997). This has been associated with increases in high-stakes testing. In many areas, required content is increasing both in quantity and in complexity while test scores are viewed as the public standard for educational quality. Debate over the viability of state versus national standards continues, spurred by the requirements of federal legislation titled "No Child Left Behind." As I have met with teachers and discussed barriers to teaching for creativity, the most common response is some variation of "there are no standards for creative thinking" or "it isn't on the test."

"Creative teaching" itself has come under fire. In a speech in Stockton, California, U.S. Assistant Secretary of Education, Susan Newman, said that the federal No Child Left Behind Act, if implemented correctly, will "put an end to creative and experimental teaching methods in the nation's classrooms" (Balta, 2002). Here again, it is extremely important to make the distinction between teaching for creativity and creative teaching. We should also draw a clear line between creative teaching and irresponsible professional behavior.

It is true that no responsible teacher should devote significant amounts of time to activities that will not enhance students' opportunities for success, both on high-stakes tests and on the often more complex challenges of life and continued intellectual growth. If teaching for creativity were simply an add-on of cute activities, teachers should question its value. However, teaching for creativity is not additional curriculum. It is a set of strategies for designing curriculum so that both content learning and creative thinking are enhanced. Used in conjunction with careful curriculum alignment, teaching to enhance creativity can help students identify and solve problems, see from multiple points of view, analyze data, and express themselves clearly in multiple genres. These are the very activities that will enhance students' learning and (assuming reasonably designed assessments) are highly likely to enhance their test scores as well.

In the current education climate, this point can not be made too often: Activities that engage students in problem solving, meaningful communication, questioning, and original representations of ideas enhance learning. When such activities are planned around core curriculum goals, they constitute effective curriculum alignment. Good teaching is not dull, rote, or constantly repetitious. Good teaching finds multiple ways to help students think about important content. If we use content standards wisely, the biggest change in teaching is that we will more clearly delineate the content about which we want students to think.

Because I live in the state of Michigan, I am most familiar with the standards and benchmarks there. One of the most interesting curriculum alignment projects here is Michigan (MI) CLiMB (Clarifying Language in Michigan Benchmarks). In chapter 6, I use several examples from MI CLiMB to illustrate the potential links between standards-based teaching and recommendations in this text

Created by statewide educators in conjunction with the Michigan Department of Education, MI CLiMB was designed to supplement the Michigan curriculum standards and benchmarks in language arts, science, social studies, and mathematics. It explains each benchmark and gives examples of instruction and assessment that clarify how the benchmarks appear in action. Examples from MI CLiMB serve as illustrations showing that state-designed standards-focused activities can enhance creativity as well. The state of Michigan also has created a Web site of sample curriculum for each grade level in core subject areas, Sample Curriculum and Plans for Education (SCoPE). While not designed to be mandated, it clearly is having a significant impact on state curricula. Many of the lessons enhance creativity as well, whereas others could easily do so with minor adaptations. As you review your own state's standards and benchmarks, consider how your voice may be important in helping educators see that curriculum designed in flexible ways can enhance both critical and creative thinking within content learning. The Michigan projects are located at www.miclimb.net/index.html and www.michigan.gov/scope.

IS CREATIVITY GOOD FOR US?

Given the fact that I have invested time and energy in writing a book on developing creativity, it would be reasonable to assume that if someone were to ask me if creativity is a good idea, I would answer yes. In truth, I would answer, "It depends." It depends on the definition of creativity and on how the power of creativity is used.

History has taught us that creativity can be used for good or evil, in ways both large and small. We celebrate beautiful art and discoveries that allow us to live healthier and more productive lives. Yet it is possible to use creative thought to devise new and original ways to do terrible things. As with all kinds of education, teaching for creativity demands a context of shared human values. Teaching about and for creativity brings with it the responsibility to discuss the ways new ideas bring joy and benefit to others in our collective community.

Bowers (1995) called creativity, "one of the most overused words in the educator's vocabulary" (p. 41). He described creativity as a guiding metaphor that brings with it key and dangerous aspects of modern consciousness. Bowers' goal is education for an ecologically sustainable culture. His response to the construct of creativity is grounded in the ties between creativity and the changes associated with progress in contemporary culture. In particular, the idea that creativity is based on the individual needs and values of single individuals without concern for their impact on others is, to Bowers, problematic. He stated that "creativity, along with all the other cultural promises that accompany its use, leads to the forms of hubris that either ignores or damages [sic] the environment .... Creativity in the areas of technology and even the visual arts has a visible history of contributing to a spectator and manipulating relationship with the environment" (p. 50).

Bowers (1995) is concerned that in our efforts to help students express their individual thoughts and plan individual actions, we risk undermining their sense of responsible self-questioning and care for their community. He calls for a view of creativity that is not centered in individuals, but in a part–whole relationship between individuals and community. Creativity would be aimed not at individual self-expression or accomplishment, but at the well-being of society and the environment.

Renzulli (2002) examined his definition of giftedness, which includes creativity, and asked:

> What causes some people to use their intellectual, motivational, and creative assets in ways that lead to outstanding creative productivity, while others with similar assets fail to achieve high levels of accomplishment: What causes some people to mobilize their interpersonal, political, ethical, and moral lives in such ways that they place human concerns and the common good above materialism, ego enhancement, and self- indulgence? (p. 36)

A parallel question needs to be asked. How do we help students develop creativity in ways that sustain and support their fellow human beings and the places they live? How to we develop caring creators? The idea of creativity as a vehicle for renewing and sustaining communities brings a new layer of responsibility for teachers, one that seems particularly apt in the early years of the new millennium. In the forward to John-Steiner's (2000) book on creative collaboration, David Feldman described the 20th century as the "century of the individual" (p. ix). From the developmental theories of Piaget through most of the century, psychologists focused on individuals as autonomous beings interacting with the world and creating their own cognition. With the reemergence of Vygotsky's work (see chap. 2), we have come to understand that learning and creativity occur within communities. Feldman dubbed the 21st century as the "Era of Community" (p. xiii) in which the dominant challenge will be striking a balance between individuality and social connectedness. This balance echoes the part–whole relationship sought by Bowers (1995). If we are to continue on the planet, particularly if we are to continue in cultural richness and natural balance, new kinds of thinking about creativity may be required. John-Steiner (2000) begins her work:

> We have come to a new understanding of the life of the mind. The notion of the solitary thinker still appeals to those molded by the Western belief in individualism. However, a careful scrutiny of how knowledge is constructed and artistic forms are shaped reveals a different reality. Generative ideas emerge from joint thinking, from significant conversation, and from sustained, shared struggles to achieve new insights by partners in thought. (p. 3)

Helping students find their way to creativity that lives in the balance between self and others, individuality, and community will require experiences both new and familiar.

STRUCTURE OF THE BOOK

Each of the dimensions of teaching for creativity are addressed in this book. The text is divided into two parts: part I: Understanding Creative People and Processes and part II: Creativity and Classroom Life. Part I concentrates on research and theory about creativity in an effort to tie research to classroom practice, whereas part II deals directly with classroom activities, organization, and practice. As you read, you will find two types of activities that can be used to explore the ideas presented. Throughout the book, Thinking About the Classroom activities will help you apply material to your particular teaching situation. At the end of each chapter, Journeying and Journaling suggestions are provided to assist your reflections on each aspect of the creative process. You may find it helpful to keep a journal as you read, recording your thoughts, questions, and ideas. Do not feel limited to the suggestions at the end of each chapter. Use your journal to explore your own experiences with creativity, ideas that puzzle you, classroom observations, dilemmas, and solutions.

Finally, this book has two goals. First, I hope you will leave the book with an understanding of theories of creativity, the characteristics of creative individuals, and aspects of the creative process that reflect the status of contemporary research. The second (admittedly lofty) goal is that you will use these ideas to transform the ways you think about and act toward education. Teaching to develop creativity touches the very heart of the educational process, the ways that we, as teachers, interact with our students. I hope you may find here some ways to interact that are both powerful and empowering, ideas that help your students find the curious delight of creativity. I cannot imagine a more valuable investment than time spent helping students learn in ways that allow them to solve problems, create, and share.

JOURNEYING AND JOURNALING

1. One of the most interesting and effective ways to explore creativity is to undertake a creative project of your own. In my course, Developing Creativity in the Classroom, graduate students must iden-

tify a problem and invent something to address it. Their inventions have ranged from an enormous version of a dentist's mirror that allows the user to check leaves in building gutters without climbing a ladder to a device that signals forgetful teenagers to retrieve their wet laundry. You may want to try a similar activity. Look around you for everyday annoyances or dilemmas that you might solve. What things around you might be improved, simplified, or elaborated? Alternatively, you might want to undertake a creative writing project, artistic endeavor, or other creative task. Whatever you choose, record your thoughts, feelings, and activities in your journal. As you read, compare the research, theories, and techniques to your own experiences. How do you feel as you contemplate such a project?

2. Examine today's newspaper. What evidence of creative thought do you see in the stories or advertisements? Look for original ideas appropriate to the situation. Are all creative ideas socially appropriate?

3. Think about the influence of culture on your conception of creativity. Do you consider some forms of expression or activity more creative than others? Why? What forms of creative expression are most valued by the cultures of the students in your classroom? Are they the same as those you value?

REFERENCES

Balta, V. (2002). End creative teaching, official says. (2002, October 25). *Stockton* [California] *Record.* Available: www.recordnet.com/articlelink/102502/news/articles/102502-gn- 2.php

Bennett, W. J. (1986*). What works: Research about teaching and learning.* Washington, DC: U.S. Department of Education.

Bollman, K. A., Rodgers, M. H., & Mauller, R. L. (2001). Jupiter Quest: A path to scientific discovery. *Phi Delta Kappan, 82*(9), 683–686.

Bowers, C. (1995). *Educating for an ecologically sustainable culture.* Albany, NY: State University of New York Press.

Brandt, R. (Ed.). (1993). Authentic learning [Theme issue]. *Educational Leadership, 50*(7).

Bransford, J. D., Sherwood, R., Vye, N., & Rieser, J. (1986). Teaching thinking and problem solving. *American Psychologist, 41,* 1078–1089.

Brown, J. S., Collins, A., & Duguid, P. (1989). Situated dognition and the culture of learning. *Educational Researcher, 18*(1), 32–42.

Caine, R. N., & Caine, G. (1991). *Teaching and the human brain.* Alexandria, VA: Association for Supervision and Curriculum Development.

Caine, R. N., & Caine, G. (1997). *Educating on the edge of possibility.* Alexandria, VA: Association of Supervision and Curriculum Development.

Caney, S. (1985). *Steven Caney's invention book.* New York: Workman.

Carey, S. (1986). Cognitive science and education. *American Psychologist, 41,* 1123–1130.

Chatterji, M. (2002). Models and methods for examining standards-based reforms and accountability initiatives: Have the tools of inquiry answered pressing questions on improving schools? *Review of Educational Research, 72,* 345–386.

Dewey, J. (1938). *Experience and education.* New York: Macmillan.

Elmore, R. F. & Huhrman, S. H. (Eds.) (1994*). The governance of curriculum.* Alexandria, VA: Association for Supervision and Curriculum Development.

Fichner-Rathus, L. (1986). *Understanding art.* Englewood Cliffs, NJ: Prentice-Hall.

Getzels, J., & Csikszentmihalyi, M. (1976). *The creative vision: A longitudinal study of problem finding in art.* New York: Wiley.

Ghiselin, B. (1985). *The creative process.* Berkeley, CA: University of California Press.

Glatthorn, A. A., Carr, J. F., Harris, D. E. (2001*). Planning and organizing for curriculum renewal: A chapter of the curriculum handbook.* Alexandria, VA: Association for Supervision and Curriculum Development.

Hawkins, S. (1988). *A brief history of time.* New York: Bantam.

Hill, W. E. (1977). *Learning: A survey of psychological interpretations* (3rd ed.). New York: Harper & Row.

Hughes, L. (Ed.). (1968). *Poems from black Africa.* Bloomington, IN: Indiana University Press.

Holt, D. G., & Willard-Holt, C. (2000). Let's get Real. *Phi Delta Kappan, 82*(3), 243–246.

Jensen, E. (2000). Brain-based learning: A reality check. *Educational Leadership, 57*(7), 7–80.

Johnson, E. B. (2002). *Contextual teaching and learning.* Thousand Oaks, CA: Corwin Press.

John-Steiner, V. (2000). *Creative collaboration.* New York: Oxford University Press.

Jones, B. F., Palincsar, A. S., Ogle, D. S., & Carr, E. G. (1987). *Strategic teaching and learning: Cognitive instruction in the content areas.* Alexandria, VA: Association for Supervision and Curriculum Development.

Kendall, J. S., & Marzaho, R. J. (1997). *Content knowledge: A compendium of standards and benchmarks for K-12 education* (2nd ed.). Alexandria, VA: Association for Supervision and Curriculum Development.

Lewis, B. A. (1991). *The kid's guide to social action.* Minneapolis, MN: Free Spirit.

Liep, J. (Ed.). (2001). *Locating cultural creativity.* Sterling, VA: Pluto Press.

Lubart, T. I. (1990). Creativity and cross-cultural variation. *International Journal of Psychology, 25,* 39–59.

Lubart, T. I. (1999). Creativity across cultures. In R. J. Sternberg (Ed.). *Handbook of creativity* (pp. 339–350). New York: Cambridge University Press.

Ludwig, A. M. (1992). Culture and creativity. *American Journal of Psychotherapy, 46,* 454–469.

Marzano, R. J. (2003). *What works in schools: Translating research into action.* Alexandria, VA: Association for Supervision and Curriculum Development.

Moyers, B. (1990). *A world of ideas II.* New York: Doubleday.

Parkhurst, H. B. (1999). Confusion, lack of consensus, and the definition of creativity as a construct. *Journal of Creative Behavior, 33*(1), 1–21.

Perkins, D. N. (1988). Creativity and the quest for mechanism. In R. J. Sternberg & E. E. Smith (Eds.), *The psychology of human thought* (pp. 309–336). New York: Cambridge University Press.

Pinker, S. (1997). *How the mind works.* New York: W.W. Norton.

Prietula, M. J., & Simon, H. A. (1989). The experts in your midst. *Harvard Business Review, 1,* 120.

Ratey, J. J. (2001). *A user's guide to the brain.* New York: Vintage Books.

Renzulli, J. S. (1977). *The enrichment triad model.* Mansfield Center, CT: Creative Learning Press.

Renzulli, J. S. (2002). Expanding the conception of giftedness to include co-cognitive traits and promote social capital. *Phi Delta Kappan, 84,* 1, 33–58.

Resnick, L. B. (1985). Cognition and instruction: Recent theories of human competence and how it is acquired. In B. L. Hammonds (Eds.), *Psychology and learning: The master lecture series* (Vol. 4, pp. 123–186). Washington, DC: American Psychological Association.

Resnick, L. B., & Klopfer, L. E. (Eds.). (1989). *Toward the thinking curriculum: Current cognitive research.* Alexandria, VA: Association for Supervision and Curriculum Development.

Ruas, C. (1984). *Conversations with American writers.* New York: McGraw-Hill.

Scherer, M. (Ed.) (2000, November). *Educational Leadership, 58*(3).

Schoenfeld, A. H. (1985). *Mathematical problem solving.* New York: Academic Press.

Skinner, B. F. (1971). *Beyond freedom and dignity.* New York: Knopf.

Sternberg, R. J. (1988). *The nature of creativity.* New York: Cambridge University Press.

Sternberg, R. J. (1990). *Metaphors of the mind: Conceptions of the nature of intelligence.* New York, NY: Cambridge University Press.

Sternberg, R. J. (1999). *Handbook of creativity.* New York: Cambridge University Press.

Wang, P. W. (1990). How to appreciate a Chinese painting. *Vision, 2,* 1.

Weiner, R. P. (2000). *Creativity and beyond: Cultures, values and change.* Albany, NY: State University of New York Press.

chapter 2

Theories and Models of Creativity

When I am, as it were, completely myself, entirely alone, and of good cheer—say, travelling in a carriage, or walking after a good meal, or during the night when I cannot sleep; it is on such occasions that my ideas flow best and most abundantly. Whence and how they come, I know not; nor can I force them .... Nor do I hear in my imagination the parts successively, but I hear them, as it were, all at once. What a delight this is I cannot tell! All this inventing, this producing, takes place in a pleasing lively dream .... This is perhaps the best gift I have my Divine Maker to thank for. (Wolfgang Amadeus Mozart, in Ghiselin, 1985, pp. 34–35)

Generally speaking, the germ of a future composition comes suddenly and unexpectedly. If the soil is ready—that is to say if the disposition to work is there—it takes root with extraordinary force and rapidity .... In the midst of this magic process it frequently happens that some external interruption wakes me from my somnambulistic state: a ring at the bell, the entrance of my servant, the striking of a clock .... Dreadful, indeed, are such interruptions. Sometimes they break the thread of inspiration for a considerable time .... In such cases cool headwork and technical knowledge have to come to my aid. Even in the works of the greatest master we find such moments, when the organic sequence fails

*and a skillful join has to be made …. But it cannot be avoided. If
that condition of mind and soul, which we call inspiration, lasted
long without intermission, no artist could survive it. (Peter Ilich
Tchaikovsky, in Vernon, 1975, pp. 57–58)*

*Molly wanted to write a song for an upcoming church musical.
She had never written a song before, but she played several instruments and was convinced that if she could manage the task, the
musical would be much improved. For several days she was frustrated with her efforts. Her ideas seemed either stiff and mechanical or very similar to popular songs she enjoyed. One evening, in
the shower, she found herself singing a new, interesting chorus to
her song. Hair still dripping, she ran to write it down. With this
new beginning, the rest of the song followed easily.*

Individuals who have created music, told stories, solved problems, and
dreamed dreams have probably been the objects of curiosity and wonder
from the earliest times. From the beginnings of recorded history, scholars
have speculated about the source creativity, how it works, and how individuals identified as creative differ from others. Studies, theories, and models
of creativity usually center on three areas. Some examine characteristics of
the creative person. They investigate personal characteristics, family dy-
namics, or essential abilities of individuals who have been identified as creative. Other theories and models are organized around the creative
process. They examine the processes by which individuals generate creative ideas. Still others study and theorize about the creative product itself.
They answer such questions as what makes something creative or how creative ideas are different from other ideas. Many theories of creativity, especially contemporary theories, examine all three areas.

Just as theorists have emphasized different aspects of creativity, they
also have examined it through different lenses (e.g., Sternberg, 1988a,
1999). Each individual views the creative process from the perspective of a
specific culture. Psychologists espousing particular theories of human
learning and development have viewed creativity in those frameworks. This
chapter examines models and theories of creativity from several vantage
points. First, I examine varied cultural perspectives on the concept of creativity. Next, I discuss models of the creative process and then theories
about the origin, nature, and systems of creativity. As you read, you may find
it helpful to consider how each theory fits with others of a similar orientation, which aspects (person, product, or process) it emphasizes, and how
the theory fits with your experience. Finally, it is helpful to consider how

each theory might influence classroom practice. Ask yourself, "If this theory is valid, how might it affect the way I teach—or perhaps the way I live?"

CREATIVITY ACROSS CULTURES

The definition of creativity presented chapter 1 held that one of the keys to defining creativity was appropriateness. Creative responses are appropriate to the context in which they appear. Cultures across the world today vary in the types of creativity that are valued and the means used to display them. Some cultures have powerful oral traditions that are difficult to translate into written form. For example, much African poetry is only spoken or sung. Its rhythms are closely related to those of music and dance, and it often uses tone and pitch as well as words to express meaning (Hughes, 1968). Such art could hardly be evaluated by counting the iambs or looking for Western style imagery. Cultures vary enormously in the style and materials of their visual arts. Chinese paper cutting and calligraphy, Native American sand painting, and Ashanti wood carvings all express creativity in visual arts that demand measures of appropriateness different from those used for impressionist paintings.

Cultures, however, do not differ only in their standards of appropriateness, but also in the ways they conceptualize novelty and the processes of creativity itself. The notion of creativity as an original contribution has deep roots in the Western tradition of individualism. Since the Renaissance, Western thought has upheld the ability of individual artists, writers, and inventors both to imitate and to improve nature. By the late-19th century, the word "creative," which had been used primarily to reference art and poetry, began to be applied to the wonders of a dawning technical age as well. The word "creativity" first entered the English at the same time, although it was not in common usage until well into the 20th century (Weiner, 2000). Particularly in the United States, the image of a creative individual changing the face of the nation with a new invention became part of a national culture of individual enterprise and constant seeking for expansion and change.

The notion of originality and inventiveness as both good and necessary for progress is deeply embedded in our culture. Our history of individual rights as part of a natural inheritance supports the image of rugged individuals struggling against cultural norms to bring forth progress. Liep (2001) noted the connection between the growth of interest in creativity and the processes associated with modernity: "Instead of being placed in a timeless order, which came about through the original creation of the world by God, humanity finds itself in a condition where creation has moved into the present. The life trajectory of the individual and the course and shape of society are becoming a consciously human project" (p. 3). This can lead to implicit definitions of creativity suggesting that something new or original is intended to change society, move forward, and be significantly different from that which has gone before. Is not that what "original" means?

In contrast, many non-Western and traditional cultures have very different basic assumptions about the role of individuals in society as well as the nature and purposes of creativity. In the Western perspective, "modern" society is considered dynamic and progressing, whereas "traditional" cultures are viewed as static. In fact "creative" and "traditional" can be used as opposites. Tradition, after all, does not change, whereas creativity is inherently novel.

The reality is not that simple. Each society determines the domains in which creativity will be more restricted and those in which it will be allowed more flexibility. These constitute, for each society, the parameters of appropriateness. Many of these parameters are shaped by religion. For example, the religious traditions of Orthodox Jews' limit creativity in the visual arts while encouraging thoughtful and creative interpretations of religious texts. Of course, the same society offers multiple opportunities for creativity in business, writing, and other domains. Religion also shapes creativity in traditional societies across the globe, wherein many works considered art by outsiders are sacred objects with invariable forms. Their anonymous makers seek worship above artistry, yet create beauty.

For many Hindu and Buddhist cultures, the notion of an individual striving to create something new to the world runs counter to the central goal of suppressing ego. Lubart (1999) described creativity within Hinduism as spiritual expression rather than innovation. Time and history are seen as cyclical. To make traditional truths come alive by finding a new interpretation—rather than by seeking to break with tradition—is the focus of such creative activity. From that perspective, differences in Eastern and Western conceptions of creativity can be visualized through the metaphors used in creation stories. Lubart (1999) stated: "If Eastern creation (and human creativity) can be characterized as a circular movement in the sense of successful reconfiguration of an initial totality, then the Western view of both creation and human creativity seems to involve a linear movement toward a new point" (p. 341).

One fundamental goal of many traditional or non-Western societies is to preserve core cultural traditions. This goal shapes but does not eliminate opportunities for creativity within those cultures. A more accurate description would suggest that a traditional society manages to circumscribe the realms and manner of creativity by handing down largely determinative structures from generation to generation. This happens in part because traditions are sufficiently revered that they serve as models for future work. The traditions also provide a crucial framework for comprehending and integrating all kinds of new developments. Repetition and reinterpretation of inherited practices are therefore hallmarks of successful traditional cultures. Continuity and cultural identify go hand in hand. (Weiner, 2001, p. 148)

Wiener used the example of contemporary Balinese culture, with its rich tradition of art, music, and dance. Outsiders are struck by the extent to which the whole population is involved in these apparently creative endeavors. Yet almost all the artistic activity is devoted to following classical patterns rather than forging new structures, exemplifying Lubart's (1999) circular model of cultural regeneration.

This is but one example of the ways that the basic concepts in the definition of creativity can vary across cultures. The concept of newness or novelty, particularly dramatic changes from previous ideas or practices, flies in the face of traditional cultures, in which the dominant social need may not be change but conservation. Without care, the traditions of many generations can be swallowed up in Westernization. In such circumstances, creativity may take a different form. Weiner (2000) suggested:

When we examine traditional society more carefully, we might recognize that the opposite of creativity is not tradition, but thoughtless habit and routine. Within a traditional framework, repetition of a pattern may or may not be a routine, mechanical process; it could also be an opportunity for personal interpretation of the pattern. (p. 153)

Many traditional cultures have types that are used for sacred religious symbols. These images not only represent the creativity of the maker, but also provide impetus for diverse interpretations and insights on the part of those who view them. In cultures with rich oral traditions, the retelling of a familiar story may provide continually changing opportunities to elaborate and expand the tale. Although the story itself is not new or original, important richness is added to the cultural tradition with each new interpretation.

Of course, creativity within repetition is not limited to traditional cultures. In the Western performing arts, repeated interpretations of the same script, piece of music, or choreography offer new opportunities for creativity within often classic forms. All creativity recognized by any society falls within some social rules, patterns, or definitions. Otherwise, it would not be recognized. However, definitions of creativity requiring that it be focused on transforming the society in which it operates limit our ability to appreciate creativity that enriches and preserves existing social systems.

In a multicultural society such as that in the United States, creativity situated in individual cultures can present mixtures of elements that hold fast to specific traditions and elements that draw from the outside. For example, the tradition of stepping, a contemporary dance form rooted in African American culture, draws from African dance forms, slave dance, Motown, and contemporary music and dance forms. Fine (2003) cited historian James Clifford, who described African American identities that "no longer presuppose continuous cultures or traditions. Everywhere, individuals and groups improvise local performance from (re)collected pasts, drawing on foreign media, symbols, and languages" (p. 21). Yet stepping represents an important tie to a collective past. Stepping both preserves and energizes African American culture. If it strayed too far from its roots, it would lose its power.

Courlander (1996) described the influence of African culture on the songs, stories, customs, and humor across the Western hemisphere. As the cultures came together, new forms of blended creativity emerged, from Haitian drumming to American railroad songs shaped by the rhythm of hammers. Similarly, American artists working within a host of individual cultures today often strive for a balance between preserving traditional forms and values and stretching the boundaries to find individual expression for contemporary experiences.

Cultures use creativity to express their values. For example, Native American cultures use imagery to reinforce the interrelationships between humans and nature. "Because Indians see themselves as part of nature, and not apart from it, their stories use natural images to teach about relationships between people, and between people and the earth. To the Indians, what was done to a tree or a rock was done to a brother or sister (Caduto & Bruchac, 1988, p. xxiii)." Traditional Chinese paintings emphasize simplicity, spontaneity, and natural forms. These images are used to create a visual statement of a philosophy of life. Distilling the constant changing natural lights and shapes into something simple and permanent emphasizes the power of stable natural law (Wang, 1990). Although both cultures find meaning in nature, the forms and messages are culture specific. Each creator is bound in complex ways to the culture in which he or she develops. Chinese artist Xu Bing (2001) described the complex relationships among his culture, his art, and himself.

> Art has value because it is genuine, not false. If you create art, the material "you" will mercilessly reveal you in all your complexity. Perhaps in life you can hide, but in art it is impossible .... That which belongs to you is yours. You may wish to get rid of it, but you cannot. Then there are those things that do not belong to you and, regardless of your effort, will never belong to you. All of this is decided by fate. This might sound fatalistic, but it is what I have experienced. In reality, this "fate" is what you experience: It is your cultural background and your life. It determines the inclination and style of your art. Your background is not of your own choosing; this is especially true for mainland Chinese artists As far as I am concerned, artistic style and taste are not man-made; they are heaven- sent. (p. 19)

Cultural appropriateness also can be constrained by politics. In the 1980s, the (presumably egalitarian) Soviet style art instruction imported to mainland China demanded that all students be able to render the same object or scene in the exactly the same way (Xu Bing, 2001). It is interesting to contemplate whether artistic creativity could function under such circumstances, or whether it could be held in abeyance until more flexible opportunities emerged.

Cultural values affect whose creative efforts will be accepted and the areas in which creativity is and is not encouraged. Ludwig (1992) suggested that cultures are least likely to encourage creativity in areas affecting deep cultural patterns and described creativity in Bali: "The more serious the art form, like sculptures of gods or ritual dances, the less the permitted change, and the less serious the art form, like carvings of kitchen gods, the theatrical performances of clowns, the playing of instruments or the weaving of containers, the greater the originality can be" (p. 456).

Cross-Cultural Creative Processes

Differing conceptions of nature of creativity itself (Lubart, 1990, 1999) make the study of creativity across cultures both a challenge and a joy. Most of the processes and theories described in the remainder of this chapter (and this book) are part of the individually focused Western orientation that emphasizes originality and problem solving. It is important to consider whether the processes and theories encompass the myriad ways creativity can be conceptualized, experienced, and expressed.

Campbell (1996) described the concept of unique individual creativity as antithetical to the artistic and spiritual goals in much of Asia, particularly in traditional Indian art. The Indian artist must not seek individual self-expression. Such a thing would be inconceivable in a culture that sees the quenching of the individual ego as the goal of spiritual progression. Yet that culture has produced countless beautiful works of art.

Instead of seeking their own goals, traditional Indian artists have sought to open their minds through study and meditation in hope that the god they hope to portray will reveal itself in vision. Campbell described much great Indian art as literal renditions of visions. The artist would not conceive of the image as his or her idea, but as a much-appreciated gift.

Understanding creativity as literal visions from the gods is not limited to Eastern or ancient peoples. Norval Morrisseau (1997) is a shaman and one of Canada's most famous contemporary native artists. He described his creativity as emanating not from his own mind, but from the House of Invention.

> Now what we're going to talk about is where and when did I get my creativity. Maybe twenty-five years ago, on one of my many visits to the astral plane [in dream], I came upon a group of beings who talked to me .... One of the spiritual helpers, who was called the Inner Master, said, "What's up above is down below. So while you're up here, we want you to go into the House of Invention and look over your artistic record and the picture you're going to bring down to your waking state, to bring down an art form for the people, for society in general. Your Shamans have done the same thing by recording their pictographs on the walls of the caves near and around the lakes. So now you're going to do the same thing. This will give an idea to the ones that will follow you, so it will give them an idea of where you are getting your picture, your images, where your image path would be."(p. 17)

Morrisseau continued to describe the pictures and colors experienced in the House of Invention and how they are to be brought to earth. He said, "Now, when I paint a picture I just allow myself to be used. I pick up the pencil and the canvas. I allow the interaction with soul to reflect in the mind" (p. 19).

Contemporary Native American cultures can reflect conceptions of creativity in both art and science that are more communal than individualistic.

Cajete (2000) described the "primacy of a lived and creative relationship with the natural world" (p.20) as essential to native science.

> There is no word for education, or science, or art in most Indige-nous language. But, a coming-to-know, a coming-to-understand, metaphorically entails a journey, a process, a question for knowl-edge and understanding. There is then a visionary tradition in-volved with these understandings that encompasses harmony, compassion, hunting, planting, technology, spirit, song, dance, color, number, cycle, balance, death, and renewal. (p. 80)

Cajete described native science as rooted in the understanding that cre-ativity is the universe's ordering principle and process. Human creativity, whether it be in art or science, is part of the greater flow of the creativity in nature. He describes three basic concepts of creativity. First, chaos and cre-ativity are the generating forces of the universe, with new patterns and truths constantly emerging. All things in the universe are related. Second, we experience and are experienced by the world. By participating in the world with heightened awareness, we can receive gifts of knowledge. Third, the metaphoric mind, rather than the rational mind, is the facilitator of creative processes. This type of thinking is particularly vital as knowledge comes in literal journeys or vision quests. Journeys and stories provide al-ternative ways to understand both the world and the creative process.

To outsiders, the idea of metaphoric journeys or seeking for oneness with the studied may seem strange, or perhaps quaint. Yet, Barbara McClintock, Nobel prize winning biologist, credited her success to investi-gating and understanding key processes from the corn's perspective. A fun-damental mystery of quantum mechanics is the apparent truth that at subatomic levels measurement affects reality. Objectivity appears to vanish, and the observer helps to determine the outcome. "The observer is inescap-ably promoted to participator. In some strange sense, this is a participatory universe" (Wheeler, 1982, p. 18). It may be that the key to creative discover-ies in the next stages of physics is, after all, understanding our impercepti-ble connections to the natural world. This sense of connection parallels the Navaho sense of beauty and creativity.

> Understood is the principle that an event is nothing without hu-man participation: There can be no beauty without our creative role in it .... Humans breathe into the world the proper sustaining songs and stories; man and woman keep the world in motion in

dance, in ceremony and ritual. All to maintain the luster, the life, of sheer beauty .... The Navajo define themselves chiefly as artists. Cosmic artists. (Martin, 1999, pp. 24–25)

One of the great questions in studying traditional or non-Western conceptions of creativity is whether just the descriptions or the processes themselves differ. If individuals set out to investigate a scientific principle using analytic investigative strategies, will they use the same mental processes to generate new ideas as individuals who have a similar knowledge base, but whose concept of creativity leads them to seek heightened awareness and receive gifts from the natural world? Are those who claim their ideas come from the gods experiencing the same phenomena as those who believe their ideas to be their own? As yet we have no answers to such questions.

It is interesting to contemplate the degree to which culture-specific concepts of creativity will continue, or to consider whether our global communication will render the concept of creativity so Westernized that, like MacDonald's, it has similar meaning, but widely varied levels of appreciation, around the world. For example, Rudowicz and Yue (2000) questioned undergraduates across four different Chinese populations regarding characteristics associated with creative people and characteristics important for a Chinese person. They found some differences across the samples, but most of the characteristics associated with creative individuals were similar to those identified in Western conceptions. Interestingly, two characteristics consistently rated low by Chinese students were sense of humor and aesthetic appreciation. The most striking finding of the study, however, was that most of the characteristics associated with a creative person were considered as having a relatively low value for a Chinese person. A number of "specifically Chinese personality traits" (p. 187), such as following tradition or concern with face, were perceived as the least indicative of creativity. Does this mean that no creativity is valued by these audiences, or that the characteristics associated with Western creativity are not valued? If the same students had been questioned about the characteristics of great Chinese writers or artists, what might they have said? Only further study will tell us.

Yet, there is evidence that understanding the differences in creativity across cultures can help students learn. Boykin (1994) identified nine cultural styles manifested in the learning preferences of African American children: spirituality, harmony, movement, verse, oral tradition, expressiveness, individualism, affect, communalism, and social time perspective. In school activities that build on these strengths, students are more successful (Boykin & Bailey, 2000; Boykin & Cunningham, 2001).

Harmon (2002) analyzed the creative strengths associated with each preference. For example, expressive individualism may be manifested in personal style, independence, risk taking, or "cool pose." It can provide evidence of bodily kinesthetic intelligence and opportunities for flexibility and originality. Oral tradition can provide strength in metaphoric language, embellishment in phrasing, and facile code switching. It may be manifested in storytelling or in the rhythmic creative insults called dozens, snaps, or capping. In classrooms that build on these cultural strengths, students not only have more opportunities to be creative, but they may also be more academically successful.

Studying creativity across cultures poses numerous challenges. Current measures of creativity have been developed by and for contemporary Western populations. When such assessments are used to compare creativity in Western and non-Western or traditional and "contemporary" samples, it is difficult to determine whether identified differences reflect actual differences in creative thinking, differences in cultural responses to the instrument, or a missed opportunity to measure a different form of creativity. For example, Khaleefa, Erdos, and Ashria (1997) found differences on three creativity measures between Sudanese students educated in traditional schools and those trained in "modern" schools. Measures on two tests of divergent thinking favored the modern education, whereas a listing of creative activities actually practiced by the students favored the traditional education. Because the latter measure was developed in Egypt and emphasized verbal creativity, it is impossible to know whether the differences reflected real variations in the types of creativity displayed, greater familiarity with the cultures in which the instruments were developed, or both.

Despite the challenge involved, it is important to recognize and examine differences in the ways human beings conceptualize and experience creativity. There is danger in assuming that the ways that seem most logical or contemporary are the only views we must understand. The linear path may not be the one we need. Understanding multiple perspectives may allow us insight into our students' lives and thoughts, and perhaps into the nature of creativity itself.

THE CREATIVE PROCESS

Probably the most common source for models of the creative process can be found in the experiences of individuals who have developed creative ideas or products. Much of the information on these experiences comes from writings or interviews of individuals whose creativity is generally accepted, such as the letters of Mozart and Tchaikovsky excerpted at the beginning of this chapter. It also is likely that most scholars have been influenced by their own experiences in generating new and appropriate ideas. Certainly, if Molly, whose composing in the shower was cited earlier, were to describe the creative process, she would want to develop a model that rang true, not just with outside sources but with her own experiences. Thus, traditional models of creativity tend to be based on descriptions of experienced creativity, as seen through the lens of the creator.

Think for a moment about a time you had a new idea, solved a problem, or created a piece of art or literature that was particularly meaningful to you. It might have been the time you planned a new interdisciplinary unit, fixed an appliance with a paper clip, or finally painted the picture that expressed your frustration with the pain some children bring to school. How did your idea happen? Did it come all at once, as Mozart described his inspiration, or did it demand the "cool headwork" of Tchaikovsky? As you read the descriptions of the creative process, consider how they fit with your experienced creativity.

Dewey and Wallas: To Incubate or Not to Incubate

One of the earliest contemporary models of creativity can be found in Dewey's (1920) model of problem solving. Dewey described the process of problem solving in five logical steps: (a) a difficulty is felt; (b) the difficulty is located and defined; (c) possible solutions are considered; (d) consequences of these solutions are weighed; and (e) one of the solutions is accepted.

Wallas (1926), Dewey's contemporary, studied the writings of creative people and generated a series of four steps that probably is the classic description of the creative process. In it, Wallas went beyond Dewey's logical sequencing to include unconscious processing and the experienced "Aha!" described by many creators. The first step in the process is *preparation*. During this stage, the creator is gathering information, thinking about the problem, and coming up with the best possible ideas. Molly, whose experience is described at the beginning of the chapter, must have gathered ideas and experimented with melodies and lyrics as part of her preparation. The second stage, *incubation*, is the heart of the Wallas model. During incubation, the individual does not consciously think about the problem. He or she goes about other activities while, at some level, the mind continues to consider the problem or question. Molly may have been incubating while in the shower. How incubation functions (and whether it exists) is one of the key debates among theorists in creativity. Whatever the means, the third stage in Wallas's model is *illumination*, the "Aha!" experience. It is the point at which ideas suddenly fit together and the solution becomes clear. In Molly's case, the melody for the finale ran through her mind. This is followed by *verification*, in which the solution is checked for practicality, effectiveness, and appropriateness. During this stage, the solution may be elaborated and fine-tuned as necessary. Molly may have needed to rework lyrics and write a melody for the verse before the song was complete. If the solution is found to be unsatisfactory, the cycle may begin again.

One of the examples frequently used to illustrate the Wallas model is Kekulé's description of his discovery of the benzene ring, a basic structure in organic chemistry. Kekulé had been working on the problem of how the carbon atoms fit together when his oft-quoted experience occurred.

> I turned my chair to the fire and dozed. Again, the atoms were gamboling before my eyes. This time, the smaller groups kept modestly to the background. My mental eye, rendered more acute by repeated vision of this kind, could now distinguish larger structures,

Sometimes creative ideas need incubation.

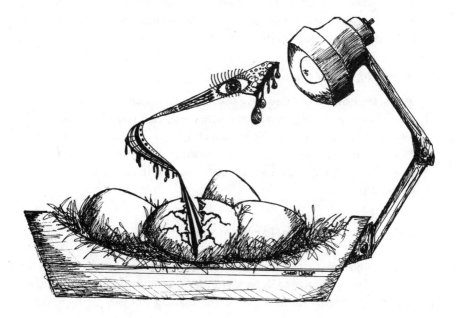

of manifold conformation, long rows, sometimes more closely fitted together, all twining and twisting in snakelike motion. But look! What was that? One of the snakes had seized hold of its own tail, and the form whirled mockingly before my eyes. As if by a flash of lightning I awoke. (Wiesberg, 1986, p. 32)

Kekulé's early work provided preparation. His incubation occurred during his doze (also translated "reverie") and ended on his awaking with illumination. Subsequent thought and experimentation provided verification. Interestingly, several of the stages Catjete (2000) described as typical in the creation of ceremonial art in indigenous societies parallel Wallas' stages. The process begins with personal preparation (purification) and attention to materials, suitable time and place, and the like. This stage also includes a self-effacing "letting go and becoming" (p. 50) necessary for the artist and the artifact to become one. It involves seeking the appropriate will and integrating the intention for creating work with the necessary planning, vigilance, and devotion. Only when both physical and spiritual preparation are complete can the work be brought into physical existence.

Although Catjete's description of the processes of ceremonial art is much more complex and integrated than the Wallas stages, it is noteworthy that the concepts of preparing, "letting go," and eventual creation are present, although in very different forms.

Understanding the four steps of the Wallas model, particularly the incubation and illumination stages, provides a key to understanding the differences among many theories of creativity.

Thinking About the Classroom

Consider how incubation may (or may not) operate in your classroom. Try giving two assignments: one that must be completed immediately and one for which there is incubation time between the assignment and the activity. Do you notice any differences? You may want to experiment with different amounts of incubation time.

Torrance and the Osborn–Parnes Model

Torrance (1988) put forth a definition or process model of creativity as the basis for research. Similar to Dewey's model, it is made up of logical stages: (a) sensing problems or difficulties; (b) making guesses or hypotheses about the problems; (c) evaluating the hypotheses, and possibly revising them; and (d) communicating the results. The final stage, which implies actually doing something with the idea, is missing from both the Dewey and Wallas models. It raises an interesting question. Is an idea less creative if it is never used or shared? If Emily Dickinson's poems had never been discovered or valued, would that have affected their creativity? Such concerns are part of some theories of creativity.

The Osborn–Parnes model of Creative Problem Solving (CPS) was developed over more than 50 years by several theorists. It differs from many other models of creativity in that it was designed not just to describe or explain the creative process, but also to allow individuals to use it more effectively.

The CPS model was developed originally by Osborn (1963), who also originated brainstorming and was highly successful in advertising. He was interested not just in theorizing about creativity, but also in finding ways to use it well. The process was developed and elaborated by Parnes (1981), and later by Isaksen and Treffinger (1985). Each version of the process includes a number of steps that involve both divergent (finding many ideas) and convergent (drawing conclusions and narrowing the field) stages of problem solving. Early versions were represented in a linear form with alternating periods of convergent and divergent thought. The processes were designated as finding the ideas needed at each state: (a) Mess-finding, (b) Data-Finding, (c) Problem-Finding, (d) Idea-Finding, (e) Solution-Finding, and (f) Acceptance-Finding. In the early 1990s a more fluid model was suggested that divided the stages into three general components: Understanding the Problem, Generating Ideas, and Planning for Action (Treffinger & Isaksen, 1992; Treffinger, Isaksen, & Dorval, 1994). This view presented the states not as a prescribed sequence, but as a set of tools that can be used in the order and to the degree necessary for any problem.

The most recent version of CPS continues this evolution (Isaksen, Dorval, & Treffinger, 2000; Treffinger, Isaksen, & Dorval, 2000; Treffinger; Isaksen, & Dorval, 2003). It reframes the components (specifying four), and renames stages and components to clarify functions (Fig. 2.1). In addition, the newest model makes the fluidity of the process explicit by incorporating the decisions about the ways CPS should be used into the model itself.

For the purposes of illustration, I will assume that I am concerned about a situation near and dear to the heart of those who frequent university campuses: the lack of available parking. Given the complexity of the situation and my inability to generate any immediate solutions, I decide to consider each stage. In reality, I would select and use only the components I

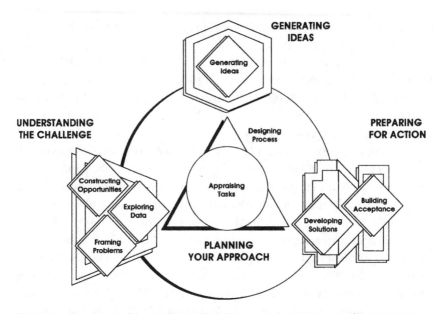

FIG. 2.1.   Creative Problem Solving (CPS) Framework, CPS Version 6.1, © 2003 Center for Creative Learning, Inc. and Creative Problem Solving Group, Inc. Reproduced by permission of authors.

need, but because I want the opportunity to describe each possible stage, I assume here that I need them all.

The first component I describe, Understanding the Challenge, involves investigating a broad goal, opportunity, or challenge and clarifying thinking to set the principal direction for work. Notice how the more inclusive language shifts the focus from the traditional view of understanding a problem. Within that component, I am likely to begin with the stage, Constructing Opportunities. In that stage, I state a broad, brief, and beneficial goal. In this case, I might start with the goal "I want to improve the parking situation on campus."

The second stage in Understanding the Challenge, Exploring Data, entails examining many sources of information from different points of view and focusing on the most important elements. In my parking problem, I might gather data about the number of spaces available, the number of classes held at various times of the day, and so on. I also might interview students and staff to find out whether the frustration with parking differs for different groups of people, at different times, or in different situations. The most important data can be used at the third stage in this component, Framing Problems. In this stage, alternative problem statements are generated, usually starting with "In what ways might we ..." (IWWMW). The intent is to identify ways to state the problem that will open the door to creative ideas. If the challenge to be considered is lack of adequate campus parking, the problem statements might include the following:

IWWMW build more parking lots?

IWWMW create more parking spaces on campus?

IWWMW limit the number of students parking on campus?

IWWMW limit the number of vehicles on campus?

IWWMW match the number of vehicles to the number of spaces available?

IWWMW provide students who live outside walking distance easy access to campus?

Clearly, the problem statement selected will affect the types of solutions considered. The broader the problem statement, the broader the range of possible solutions. The first problem statement, which is limited to creating traditional parking lots, offers limited options. The second might lead us to consider parking underground, in elevated structures, or on top of buildings. The last problem statement could lead to a range of possibilities—from traditional lots to bus routes, off- campus classes, or helicopter pads!

The second general component of CPS, Generating Ideas, has only one stage. In it ideas are generated for the selected problem statement(s) using a variety of tools. These may include brainstorming or any of the other tools for divergent thinking described in chapter 5.

The third component is Preparing for Action. This involves exploring ways to make the promising options into workable solutions—translating ideas into action. It has two stages. The first, Developing Solutions, applies deliberate strategies and tools to analyze, refine, and select among ideas. Often developing solutions entails using criteria to evaluate each of the proposed ideas systematically. In the case of the parking dilemma, possible criteria might include these:

How much would it cost?

Is it legal?

Is the technology available?

Would it be convenient for students?

Would it be convenient for staff?

Would it be acceptable to the university administration?

Criteria often are presented in a grid (Fig. 2.2) that allows each idea to be evaluated by each criterion.

The final stage in this component is Building Acceptance. In this stage, plans are made for the implementation of the chosen solution. Possible difficulties are anticipated and resources identified. This stage usually results in an action plan, with steps, resources, and individual responsibilities outlined.

The fourth component of CPS Version 6.1 is Planning Your Approach. This component reflects the need to monitor your thinking throughout the problem-solving process to make sure that you are moving in the desired direction and using an appropriate selection of CPS stages. One aspect of this component, Appraising Tasks, involves determining whether CPS is a promising choice for this situation. If a situation is open-ended and would benefit from thinking about a number of possible options, CPS is an appropriate method. However, if the problem at hand truly has only one correct answer and the task is to identify that answer, CPS may not be the best option. A second aspect, Designing Processes, involves selecting from among

	How much would it cost?	Is it legal?	Is the technology available?	Would it be convenient for students?	Would it be convenient for staff?	Is it acceptable to the administration?
Build a new parking structure						
Build a lot at the edge of campus with a shuttle						
Run a shuttle from parking lot near the highway						
Create car pool lots for cars with 3 passengers						

FIG. 2.2.   Solution-finding grid.

the CPS options the components and stages most likely to be helpful. Planning Your Approach can be considered the metacognitive facet of the CPS process that operates throughout the entire process.

Clearly, the CPS model is designed to be used, and programs and possibilities for teaching with it are presented in chapter 5. At this point, however, we consider how well it and other process models fit with various theories of creativity.

Early Views

Both Plato and Aristotle described the creative process, but in very different ways. In *The Ion*, Plato writes about Socrates' responses to questions concerning the creative process in poetry. He describes the poet as under the influence of a divine madness that carries him out of his senses.

> The lyric poets are not in their senses when they make these lovely lyric poems. No, when once they launch into harmony and rhythm, they are seized with the Bacchic transport, and are possessed .... A poet is a light and winged thing, and holy, and never able to compose until he has become inspired and is beside himself, and reason is no longer in him .... It is not they who utter these precious revelations while their mind is not within them, but ... it is god himself who speaks, and through them becomes articulate to us. (Rothenberg & Hausman, 1976, p. 32)

Plato's emphasis on a mystic and external source of inspiration might ring true for Mozart. Both men saw the inspiration for creative activities as coming from outside, beyond the control of the creative individual, perhaps in the same way that Morrisseau (1997) saw his ideas as originating in the House of Invention. Creativity was considered unexplainable and outside normal human abilities. In fact, many of us listening to the music of Mozart may find it easier to attribute such beauty to divine intervention than to the powers of a fallible, vain, and possibly crass human being.

In contrast, Aristotle argued that creative processes must obey understandable natural laws.

> All makings proceed either from art or from a faculty or from thought. Some of them happen also spontaneously or by luck just as natural products sometimes do .... Anything which is produced is

produced by something ... and from something .... The artist makes, or the father begets, a "such" out of a "this"; and when it has been begotten, it is "this such." (Rothenberg & Hausman, 1976, pp. 35–36)

Aristotle did not believe that creative products came through mystical intervention or unique creative processes. He believed that just as plants and animals produced young in a rational, predictable fashion, so art, ideas, and other human products derived from logical steps of natural law. His approach may have appealed to Tchaikovsky, for whom much of the creative process was the result of "cool headwork and technical knowledge" (Vernon, 1975, p. 58).

Although their arguments are complex, the basic contrast between Plato's and Aristotle's positions continues into modern psychology. Some theorists emphasize inspiration, insight, or other processes unique to creativity that may occur in ways not discernible to the conscious mind. Others emphasize the similarities between creativity and other cognitive processes and postulate, as did Aristotle, that there is nothing unique in the creative process. From that perspective, with enough understanding, we should be able to dissect creativity and understand how it works.

Beginning in the nineteenth century, psychologists have presented a variety of theories to explain creativity. Each author brings to the task a specific theoretical perspective, the lens through which he or she views a range of human behaviors. A theorist who believes human behavior is largely the result of subconscious forces will view creativity differently from one who believes behavior can better be explained by conscious learning through experience. For the clusters of theorists presented in this chapter, think about how each theory of creativity fits into a broader perspective of thinking about human thought and behavior.

PSYCHOANALYTIC THEORIES

Psychoanalytic theories explain human behavior, development, and personality traits as shaped by powerful unconscious processes. Such theories attempt to uncover the unseen needs that motivate individuals' actions, often looking to childhood events to comprehend adult behavior.

Freud's Approach

Of course, the granddaddy of psychoanalytic theory is Sigmund Freud. Freud believed that human behavior could be explained by examining conflicts between unconscious desires and acceptable outward behavior. He postulated three aspects of human personality: the ego (logical conscious mind), the id (primitive unconscious drives), and the superego (a con-science- like force that acts as mediator between the other two). Freud tied creativity and much other behavior to the sublimation of drives deriving from the id. If an individual cannot freely express his or her desires, those desires must find release in other ways or be sublimated. Freud believed that beginning in childhood, a person must repress his or her sexual desires in order to fit into conventional society. Thus he saw these sexual urges as particularly powerful forces that must be countered by psychic defenses. Many of the defense mechanisms, he postulated, resulted in unhealthy be-haviors and various neuroses. Creativity, on the other hand, represented a healthy form of sublimation, using unfulfilled unconscious drives for pro-ductive purposes. In discussing creative writers, he stated:

> We may lay it down that a happy person never phantasies, only an unsatisfied one. The motive forces of phantasies are unsatisfied wishes, and every single phantasy is the fulfillment of a wish, a cor-rection of unsatisfying reality. These motivating wishes vary accord-ing to the sex, character and circumstances of the person who is having the phantasy; but they fall naturally into two main groups. They are either ambitious wishes, which serve to elevate the sub-ject's personality, or they are erotic ones. In young women the erotic wishes predominate almost exclusively, for their ambition is as a rule absorbed by erotic trends. In young men egoistic and am-bitious wishes come to the fore clearly enough alongside of erotic ones. (Rothenberg & Hausman, 1976, p. 50)

Although we may speculate about the effects of Victorian society on Freud's assessment of the differing genders' needs, it is clear that he viewed fantasy and creative writing as the results of unfulfilled wishes, a continua-tion of childhood play. Heroic characters may express the need for con-quest, and romantic heroines may express the need for love in a representation of the writers' daydreams. Personal desires for sex or power are cloaked in story, allowing writer and reader to experience pleasure without unacceptable guilt.

Kris and Kubie

Later psychoanalysts developed variations on Freud's theories. Kris (1952/1976) asserted that the basic process of creativity is regression, that creative individuals are able to recreate a childlike state of mind in which unconscious ideas are more accessible to the conscious mind. Kris believed that freely wandering fantasy may serve the id in relieving unconscious desires, but unlike Freud, he emphasized regression in service of the ego. That is, he believed that the childlike state involved in reflective thinking, problem solving, and creativity may be undertaken purposefully, under the control of the creator. He postulated two phases of the creative process: an inspirational phase deriving from uncontrolled unconscious processes and an elaborational phase directed by the conscious ego.

Kubie (1958) extended psychoanalytic theory in two major breaks with Freud. First, Kubie postulated that creativity has its roots, not in the unconscious, but in the preconscious system flowing between the conscious and unconscious. In his view, both the conscious and unconscious are rigid functions distorting or disrupting creativity. The symbolic processes in the conscious mind are limited to the recall of past experiences shaped by our use of language. Without the limitations of language, he postulated, our memories could be richer in sensory and emotional data. The processes of the unconscious are seen as similarly rigid, frozen by unconscious needs and desires. The painter who paints the same picture over and over again was seen as expressing an unconscious need, but as unable to find the flexibility necessary for true creativity. This flexibility, according to Kubie, is found in the preconscious state on the fringe of consciousness. This is the state we experience between sleep and wakefulness or during daydreams. He believed that to encourage creativity, we must strengthen preconscious processes.

> The goal is to free preconscious processes from the distortions and obstructions interposed by unconscious processes and from the pedestrian limitation of conscious processes. The unconscious can spur it on. The conscious can criticize and evaluate. But creativity is a product of preconscious activity. This is the challenge which confronts the education of the future. (Kubie, as cited in Rothenberg & Hausman, 1976, p. 148)

Kubie also broke with Freud on the role of neuroses in creativity. Whereas Freud believed that powerful unconscious desires and neuroses could be expressed through creative activity, Kubie believed that neuroses distort creativity. If unconscious needs are so powerful that they predominate, flexible preconscious processes are blocked and individuals are stuck in repetitious behavior that may mimic creativity but is not truly creative. Mountains of paintings or volumes of stories that all are essentially the same may release tension by placing conflicts in acceptable form, but according to Kubie, they are not creative.

Jung's Theories

Carl Jung (1972), an associate of Freud, also believed in the importance of personal experiences and the unconscious mind in framing creative production. However, he believed that important creative ideas come from influences greater than those in the mind of a single individual. Jung examined the patterns in human behavior, story, and myth that transcend time or culture. He believed that such patterns can be explained by postulating a human collective unconscious, "a sphere of unconscious mythology ... [that is] the common heritage of humankind" (p. 80). The collective unconscious was seen as a series of inherited patterns that evolved through human history, predisposing individuals to think in particular forms.

> There are no inborn ideas, but there are inborn possibilities of ideas that set bounds to even the boldest fantasy and keep our fantasy activity within certain categories: a priori ideas, as it were, the existence of which cannot be ascertained except from their effects. They appear only in the shaped material of art as the regulative principles that shape it; that is to say, only by inferences drawn from the finished work can we reconstruct the age-old original or the primordial image. (Jung, 1972, p. 81)

The images, figures, and characters of the collective unconscious are seen to be remnants of the experiences of our ancestors. According to Jung, they explain the similarities of earth-mother figures, creation myths, and resurrection and flood stories found in widely separated cultures. Jung believed that the greatest creativity taps these archetypal images, or images that provide the foundation for beliefs across cultures.

> The impact of an archetype ... stirs us because it summons up a voice that is stronger than our own. Whoever speaks in primordial images speaks with a thousand voices; he enthralls and overpowers, while at the same time he lifts the idea he is seeking to express out of the occasional and the transitory into the realm of the ever-enduring. (Jung, 1972, p. 82)

Jung believed that the individuals most adept at tapping into the collective unconscious are those most capable of high-quality creative activity.

Contemporary Psychoanalysts

Similar to Kubie, Rothenberg (1990) and Miller (1990) were particularly interested in the relationships among trauma, neuroses, and creativity. Miller studied the childhood of creative individuals and sought information on repressed childhood traumas that might give clues to their creative development. For example, in Picasso's painting *Guernica*, she identified images she believed are linked to an earthquake in Málaga during which Picasso, a terrified 3-year-old boy, escaped with his family through the crumbling city. She believed that the roots of Buster Keaton's creativity were his efforts to escape childhood abuse, and that much creativity is the result of individual efforts to deal with unconscious childhood pain. Although Miller's writings called for an end to child abuse, it is not clear whether the elimination of early trauma and abuse would eliminate or merely change the focus of creative efforts.

Rothenberg (1990) examined the creative process through extensive psychiatric interviews and experiments with artists and scientists, including Nobel and Pulitzer prize winners, poets laureate of the United States, and recipients of numerous other honors. He emphasized that, unlike the subjects of many other psychoanalytic researchers, his subjects were not patients in therapy, but willing participants in a research effort.

Rothenberg (1990) identified specific thought processes that he believed are used by creative people across disciplines. These processes, he said, "distinguish creative people from the rest of us" (p. 11). The first of these he called the janusian process (after Janus, the Roman god of doorways and beginnings, whose two faces look in opposite directions). Contrary to much psychoanalytic thought, he viewed the janusian process as a conscious, rational procedure. In the janusian process, opposites are conceived simultaneously, a leap that transcends ordinary logic. Although not necessarily represented in the finished product, the idea of opposites being equally true represents an important stage in the creative process. For example, playwright Arthur Miller described coming up with the idea for his play *Incident at Vichy* while traveling in Germany. As he was driving on the Autobahn, he was struck with how beautiful Germany had become and the contrast between that beauty and Hitler's destruction. Rothenberg believed that Miller's ability to conceptualize the beauty and the horror simultaneously was central to his writing. Nobel laureate Edwin McMillan was able to conceive of accelerating particles having simultaneously too much and too little energy, which led to the idea of phase stability and the development of the synchrotron, a high-energy particle accelerator. In each case, opposites provided the key to innovation.

The second of Rothenberg's creative processes is the homospatial process, conceiving of two or more entities occupying the same space at the same time. This, he believed, is the process leading to the development of metaphors. A poet interested in the similar sound of the words "handle" and "branch" was able to bring these ideas together in a mental image leading to the phrase "the branches were handles of stars."

In an interesting series of experiments, Rothenberg created a set of slides in which subjects could be presented with images either side by side or superimposed (the superimposed pictures representing the homospatial process). Some writers and artists were shown a picture of soldiers next to a picture of a bed. Others were shown the two pictures superimposed, as if in a double- exposed photograph. A third group saw the photos with one on top, blocking part of the other. He found that in all three groups, significantly more creative products came from the subjects who had seen the superimposed photographs, suggesting that the homospatial process may, in part at least, be learned.

Thinking About the Classroom

If you have access to two projectors, you may want to experiment with Rothenberg's homospatial process. In one exercise, project two images side by side and use them to stimulate a writing or art activity. In the next class, try projecting two images on top of each other. See if you notice any differences in the originality of responses.

Finally, Rothenberg examined the relationship between mental illness and the processes he identified as underlying creativity. He determined that although creative processes differ from logical everyday thinking, as do those in mental illness, there are vast differences between the two. Whereas people engaged in the creative process may use ideas outside logic to facilitate their thinking, people affected by psychosis are more likely to believe contradicting or illogical ideas, to have no control over them, and to be unable to use them for creative purposes.

> The truly creative person is oriented toward producing something outside of himself, is rational, and is completely aware of logical distinctions. His emotional energy is not directed toward himself, as in psychosis, and he knowingly formulates unusual conceptions in order to improve on reality and to create .... Unlike psychotic episodes, in which bizarre thinking develops because of the person's inability to tolerate extreme anxiety ... the creative process requires an ability to tolerate high levels of anxiety .... In sum, although creative people may be psychotic at various periods of their lives, or even at various times during a day or week, they cannot be psychotic at the time they are engaged in a creative process, or it will not be successful. (Rothenberg, 1990, pp. 35–36)

Although Rothenberg, like other psychoanalysts, is interested in unconscious mental processes, his description of creative processes characterizes them as being under the conscious control of the creator—healthy, logical control of illogical mental connections. This view parallels that of Hershman and Lieb (1998) who investigated the role of manic–depressive disorder in the lives of creative people. While describing characteristics of this disorder in prominent creators such as Beethoven and Isaac Newton, the authors concluded that whereas mild instances of both depression and mania can enhance creativity, severe forms of the disease diminish it. They believe it is important for creative individuals with manic–depressive disorder to understand that they can maintain—and enhance—their creativity while seeking treatment for the destructive phases of the illness.

BEHAVIORIST OR ASSOCIATIONIST THEORIES

Psychoanalytic theorists consider human behavior to be determined primarily through the interaction of conscious and unconscious drives. Associationist psychologists, on the other hand, view human activities as resulting from a series of stimuli and responses. The most famous advocate of this position was B. F. Skinner. The "Father of Behaviorism," Skinner believed that individuals' actions were determined solely by their history of reinforcement. If actions were followed by pleasant consequences, they were likely to be repeated. If the consequences were unpleasant, it was less likely the individual would try a similar action again. Theorists from this perspective focus on observable behaviors rather than internal drives or desires.

Skinner and the Chickens

In a famous paper entitled "A Lecture on 'Having' a Poem," Skinner (1972) stated that a poet is no more responsible for the content or structure of a poem than a chicken is responsible for laying an egg. Each action is seen as a result of the creator's history, the stimuli and responses each one has experienced. In this view there can be no truly original behavior or ideas, except as they are an inevitable product of a unique individual's experiences. Presumably, another person who experienced every aspect of Shakespeare's life would have had no choice but to write the same plays. According to this theory, those who would influence creativity can do so through reinforcement. The more creativity or activities approaching creativity are reinforced, the more they should occur.

Mednick's Associative Theory

Another associationist theorist, Mednick (1962), also viewed the production of ideas as the result of stimuli and responses, but he theorized that creative ideas result from a particular type of response, the bringing together of remote, unrelated ideas. Individuals who frequently bring remote ideas together should be more likely than others to produce creative ideas. This process may be influenced by several factors. First, individuals must have the needed elements in their repertoires. The person who invented the beanbag chair must have had some experience with beanbags or similar objects. Second, individuals must have a complex network of associations with the stimulus. Those who are able to make multiple associations with a given idea are more likely to make unusual associations than those who give only a few stereotyped responses. This hypothesis was supported in Mednick's research using word-association tests with creative and less-creative research scientists.

According to Mednick, individuals who have had many experiences with a given stimulus in a familiar setting are less likely to make remote associations with that stimulus; their patterns of responses are too well defined. The greater the number of diverse associations with a given stimulus, the greater is the probability that remote ideas may be connected. An individual who has used a hair dryer to inflate a hot-air balloon, warm a bottle, dry a shirt, and play balloon catch will probably generate more ideas for its use or improvement than one who has used it simply to dry hair. Mednick developed a test designed to measure the number of associations individuals form with specific stimuli and used it to assess creativity.

Others investigating from a behaviorist or associationist perspective examined the effects of reward on novel behavior. Glover and Gary (1976) manipulated the reinforcement, practice, and instructions given to fourth- and fifth-grade students, listing all the possible uses for an object. Specific types of creative thinking (fluency, flexibiliy, originality, and elaboration) increased when they were rewarded. Holman, Goerz, and Baer (1977) found that the diversity of children's paintings or block structures could be increased through reward. From this perspective, a teacher who wants students to generate more elaborate or original ideas should reward students for that behavior. Eisenberger and Cameron (1996) and Eisenberger, Armeli, and Pretz, (1998) used a behaviorist perspective to argue for the positive influence of reward on creativity, at least in divergent-thinking tasks. This contradicts the current prevailing view regarding the negative impact of reward on intrinsic motivation and creativity (see chap. 7).

HUMANIST THEORIES

Humanist theorists do not emphasize either neuroses or reinforcement as predominant forces in human psychology. Instead, they focus on normal growth and the development of mental health. Humanist theorists view creativity as the culmination of well-adjusted mental development.

Maslow's Theories

Maslow (1954), founder of the humanist psychology movement, postulated a hierarchy of human needs that can be met in a generally ascending order, beginning with physical needs and progressing to needs for safety and security, love and belonging, self-esteem, and self- fulfillment. At the top of the hierarchy, one has the opportunity for self-actualization as a fully functioning human being. In examining the relationship between this development and creativity, Maslow found he had to reexamine his hypothesis that mental health, talent, and creative productivity went hand in hand. He could not match his ideas about creativity and healthy mental development with the apparently unhealthy behaviors of such great creators as Wagner or van Gogh.

To deal with this conflict, Maslow (1968) postulated two types of creativity. The first, *special talent creativity*, is "independent of goodness or health of character" (p. 35) and functions in creative geniuses. He concluded that we know very little about this type of ability except that we sometimes can recognize it when we see it.

The second type of creativity, *self-actualizing creativity*, is the basis for most of Maslow's writings on this topic. He believed that creativity of this type is a manifestation of mental health and movement toward self-actualization. It may be applied not just to the traditional creative arts, but to any aspect of human behavior. Perhaps his most famous statement on the topic concerned a subject from whom he learned that "a first-rate soup is more creative than a second-rate painting ... cooking or parenthood or making a home could be creative while poetry need not be; it could be uncreative" (Maslow, 1968, p. 136).

According to Maslow, people with a high level of self-actualizing creativity tend to do everything creatively. They are characterized as more spontaneous and expressive than average, more natural, and less controlled or inhibited. He believed that the ability to express ideas freely without self-criticism is essential to this type of creativity, and that this ability paralleled the innocent, happy creativity of secure children. Creativity was described as "a fundamental characteristic, inherent in human nature, a potentiality given to all or most human beings at birth, which most often is lost or buried or inhibited as the person gets enculturated" (Maslow, 1968, p. 143).

Maslow described the personality characteristics of subjects he identified as displaying self- actualized creativity. He considered them to be relatively unfrightened of the unknown, more self-accepting, and less concerned with others' opinions. These personality characteristics provide the essence of self-actualizing (SA) creativity.

> SA creativeness stresses first the personality rather than its achievement, considering these achievements to be epiphenomena emitted by the personality and therefore secondary to it. It stresses characterological qualities like boldness, courage, freedom, spontaneity, perspicuity, integration, self-acceptance, all of which make possible the kind of generalized SA creativeness, which expresses itself in the creative life, or the creative attitude, or the creative person. (Maslow, 1968, p. 145)

Rogers' Approach

This emphasis on personality variables is also found in the work of Rogers (1961), another humanistic psychologist, who also viewed creativity as the product of healthy human growth. He identified specific factors that allow or enhance creativity: "The mainspring of creativity appears to be the same tendency which we discover so deeply as the curative force in psychotherapy—man's tendency to actualize himself, to become his potentialities" (Rothenberg & Hausman, 1976, p. 298). Rogers viewed creativity as the emergence of novel products through the interaction of an individual and the environment. The characteristics associated with creativity allow this interaction to take place.

The first characteristic identified by Rogers is openness to experience. He believed that creative individuals are free of psychological defenses that would keep them from experiencing their environment. (Notice how this contrasts with Freud's idea that creativity is a psychological defense.) Openness to experience implies that an individual is willing to view experiences outside traditional categories, to consider new ideas, and to tolerate ambiguity if ambiguity exists.

The second characteristic is an internal locus of evaluation—that is, reliance on one's own judgment, particularly in gauging creative products. My actor-husband demonstrates this characteristic in his attitude toward his performances. After a performance, he does not judge his success by the volume of applause, the standing ovations, or the enthusiastic comments of audience members. Only when he judges his performance to be satisfactory is he happy. On the other hand, unfavorable reviews for a performance with which he was pleased also have little impact. With the exception of a few knowledgeable friends, other people's opinions have little to do with how he evaluates his achievements. His own (admittedly critical) judgment is the one he cares about.

Rogers's third characteristic is the ability to toy with elements and concepts. He believed creative individuals must be able to play with ideas, to imagine impossible combinations, and to generate wild hypotheses. This characteristic is associated with the same type of openness and lack of rigidity found in the first characteristic. When these three characteristics are present, according to Rogers, the natural human trait of creativity can develop.

DEVELOPMENT OF CREATIVITY AND SOCIAL INTERACTIONS

Surprisingly little research and theory has examined the longitudinal development of creativity across time. One of the most interesting writers in this area was Lev Vygotsky. For years Vygotsky's work was unavailable to Western readers. In 1992, Smolucha reconstructed Vygotsky's theory of creativity from three translated papers. Originally written in the 1930s, the papers are part of Vygotsky's sociocultural analysis of human thought, emphasizing the social and cultural interactions that underlie human thought and understanding. As such, they foreshadow the complex interactions among individuals and society that characterize the systems theories of creativity discussed later in this chapter. However, Vygotsky also characterized creative thought and activity in three major stages, so I consider his work first as a developmental approach.

Vygotsky believed that creative imagination originates in child's play. In particular, he saw the use of objects in symbolic play as key to the development of imagination. An often-cited example is a child using a stick as a play horse. The child at play is able to imagine a horse, creating an animal where none exists. Vygotsky distinguished between *reproductive imagination*, in which the individual imagines things from memory, and *combinatory imagination*, in which he or she combines elements of previous experience into new situations or behavior that characterizes creativity. The little child on the stick horse reproduces much of the experience from his or her prior understanding of horses, but the child may use and combine parts of this in new ways. Symbolic play experiences are influenced (and perhaps directed) by social interactions, such as an adult's suggesting that the stick might be a horse.

Despite the importance of early childhood experiences, Vygotsky saw them only as a beginning stage, not as the pinnacle of creativity. Because children have fewer interests, less complex understandings, and less diverse thoughts than adults, they are considered to be capable of less mature creativity. "The child's imagination is not richer, but poorer than the imagination of an adult; in the process of child development imagination also develops, reaching maturity only in the adult" (Vygotsky, 1930/1967, cited in Smolucha, 1992, p. 54). Vygotsky saw adult creativity as a consciously directed thought process in which individuals change and combine ideas in specific social conditions to create works of art, inventions, or scientific conclusions.

According to Vygotsky, the transition between the child's imagination and the adult's mature, thoughtful creativity occurs in the middle stage, adolescence. Before adolescence, imagination and thought are portrayed as separate strands of development. During adolescence, the strands come together. As adolescents develop the ability to manipulate abstract concepts, they begin to develop a more active and volitional creativity than that of childhood. Whereas children's actions in symbolic play may be mainly imitative or suggested by others, mature creativity is purposefully used and controlled. Vygotsky believed that the development of this type of creativity is influenced by inner speech, formal schooling, and thinking in concepts. Speech allows individuals to think about, represent, and communicate things that are not present. School also requires considerable thought about ideas and objects not in the immediate environment. Thinking in concepts allows individuals to process and combine experiences in new, more complex ways. In a parallel fashion, imagination is viewed as "a necessary, integral feature of realistic thought" (Smolucha, 1992, p. 65). We can think about things not present or ideas not yet achieved only if we can imagine them.

Thus, Vygotsky proposed a developmental theory in which creative imagination begins in children's symbolic play and develops into a consciously regulated mental function influencing and influenced by inner speech and concept development. According to this theory, the linking of imagination and thought begins in adolescence, but does not reach maturity until adulthood.

Vygotsky also foreshadowed contemporary systems theories by situating creativity in a particular time and place. "Any inventor, even a genius, is always a plant growing in a certain time and environment. His creativity issues from needs, which are given to him. He operates on the possibilities that exist around him" (Vygotsky 1030/1967 cited in Smolucha, 1992, p. 54). Vygotsky continued to explain that the availability of resources explains the disproportionate distribution of innovators and artists in privileged classes. Such individuals have much greater access to the problems and processes of the disciplines.

Vygotsky emphasized that creativity, like other learning, emerges through interactions with other individuals. This occurs both at a micro level, as when an adult interacts with a child in imaginative play, and at a macro level in which societies grow through the collective efforts of countless individuals. He used the analogy of electricity to describe the relationship between easily recognized creativity in genius and the important creative contributions of unknown citizens.

> Electricity is not only present in a magnificent thunderstorm and dazzling lightning, but also in a lamp, *so also, creativity exists, not only where it creates great historical works, but also everywhere human imagination combines, changes, and creates anything new* [italics original]. Turning our attention to the collective creativity which unites all these insignificant fragments, comes the realization of what a great part belongs to the collective work of unknown inventors. (Vygotsky, 1030/1967 cited in Smolucha, 1992, p. 54)

A contemporary theorist influenced by Vygotsky is Vera John-Steiner. Her (2000) study of creative collaborations presented the idea that creative processes or ideas do not develop within individuals but in interactions among individuals within a sociocultural context. Feldman, in the forward to John-Steiner's book, pointed out that the notion of creativity as a collaborative activity and Vygotsky's commitment to relationship as the "central ingredient in human development" (p. xi) are in marked contrast to the focus on individual responsibility for cognitive development and activity described by Piaget. He viewed the shift in thinking as representative of society's shift from the "Age of the Individual" to the "Era of Community" (p. xiii). Additional information on collaborations are considered in the section on systems theories.

Thinking About the Classroom

Vygotsky suggested that symbolic play is crucial in the development of creative imagination. Symbolic play may be influenced by social interaction—for example, an adult commenting that a box could be used as a boat. Observe a parent or teacher with young children. Note any comments that encourage symbolic play.

CREATIVITY, INTELLIGENCE, AND COGNITION

The relationship between creativity and intelligence might best be described as "it depends." It depends on the definition and measures used to assess both creativity and intelligence. Perhaps the most common relationship postulated is the threshold theory. According to this theory, below a certain threshold (approximately 120 IQ) there is a strong, positive relationship between creativity and intelligence; the more intelligent the person, the more likely he or she is to be creative. Above the threshold level, however, the relationship is seen as weaker; a highly intelligent person may be highly or only moderately creative. At that point, intelligence no longer predicts creativity. The threshold theory is discussed further in chapter 3. In this section we examine theories that treat creativity as part of intelligence or as comprising many of the same components as intelligence.

Guilford's Structure of the Intellect

Guilford's (1959, 1986, 1988) Structure of the Intellect (SOI) model is a complex model of intelligence including, in its most recent form, 180 components. The components are formed through combinations of types of content, operations, and product (Fig. 2.3). Each type of content can be matched with each operation or product to form a separate cell of the cube

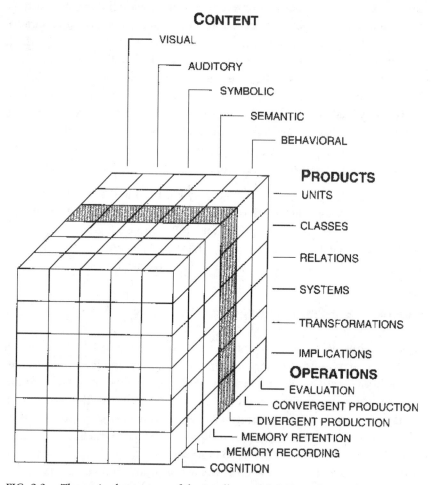

FIG. 2.3. The revised structure of the intellect model. From Some Changes in the Structure-of- Intellect Model, by J. P. Guilford, 1988, *Educational and Psychological Measurement, 48*, p. 3. Copyright © 1988 by *Educational and Psychological Measurement.* Reprinted with permission.

associated with a particular intellectual ability. For example, intellectual abilities include the cognition of semantic relationships and the transformation of figural units.

Unlike previous models of intelligence, the SOI model includes *divergent thinking,* or thinking of many possible responses to a given question, as one of the basic processes of intelligence. Guilford identified components of divergent production that have formed the backbone of much research and assessment of creativity. They include fluency (generating many ideas), flexibility (generating different types of ideas or ideas from different perspectives), originality (generating unusual ideas), and elaboration (adding to ideas to improve them). Guilford identified two categories of abilities associated with creativity. The first is the divergent thinking "slab." You might picture this as a slice cut out of the cube containing all the cells involving divergent production. The second is associated with transformations, the ability to revise what one experiences or knows to produce a new form. Transformations are part of the product dimension of the SOI model. Guilford also recognized the importance of sensitivity to problems and evaluation in generating and assessing creative ideas.

Whichever cells are identified as critical, the key to this perspective on creativity is that it is an intellectual function. Guilford did not portray creativity as rooted in conflict and childhood trauma or as a manifestation of mental health. Similar to any other aspect of intelligence, it represented to him a pattern of cognitive strengths that include, but are not limited to, the abilities to produce diverse responses to varied tasks. Similarly, several contemporary psychologists have attempted to identify cognitive processes underlying creativity. Although they may also identify personality or motivational characteristics associated with creativity, they do not. view creativity itself as a mysterious force unlike other human experiences, but rather as a manifestation of the same sorts of processes found in other types of thought.

Perkins, Weisberg, and Myth Busting

Perkins (1981, 1988, 1994) examined ties between ordinary cognitive processes and the extraordinary processes sometimes postulated for creativity. He noted that many theories and ideas about creativity have their roots in the self-reports of creative individuals, such as the statements by Mozart and Tchaikovsky at the beginning of this chapter. Such reports are likely to be unreliable. Criminologists attest that eyewitness accounts of any event are likely to be contradictory, incomplete, and inaccurate. If the self-reports of creative individuals are to be believed, we must be convinced that the individuals remember the experience in sufficient detail at the time the report is made, understand the experience themselves, and are honest about the experience. It is not unreasonable to think that some individuals may be tempted to report their creative efforts in a manner that adds to their mystique or enhances their reputation. For example, Perkins (1981) noted that Coleridge, who reported an opium dream in which the poem "Kubla Khan" appeared to him, also wrote several earlier versions of the work. Even if no deliberate misrepresentation took place (a possibility that must be considered given other examples of Coleridge's inaccuracies in reporting his own work), his opium dream statement was made 16 years after the poem was written, leaving ample opportunity for selective or incomplete memory.

Perkins (1981, 1994) also examined the effectiveness of physical evidence documenting the history of a creative effort (such as early drafts or revisions) in helping one to understand the creative process. Although it is possible to learn from such records, they also conceal much. A study of preliminary drawings leading up to Picasso's *Guernica* shows the artist's experimentation with varied images and the gradual evolution of the piece. It cannot, however, tell why Picasso made the changes he did, why he kept some images and not others, or what alternatives he considered but did not record.

Perkins suggested that a more complete and accurate source for gaining understanding of the creative process is immediate self-reports—descriptions of the creative process given by creators while the process is taking place or immediately thereafter. Such descriptions were obtained from poets writing in a laboratory situation, who verbalized their thought processes as they wrote. Perkins used these records and reviews of other research as evidence for his theories.

Perkins (1981, 1988, 1994) did not find evidence to support the traditional view of incubation (creative leaps after extended unconscious activity) or unique creative thought processes. Rather, he viewed the creative process as made up of ordinary mental processes used in extraordinary ways. The key to creativity, according to Perkins, is not the process but the purpose. People involved in creative activities are trying to be creative. They are not seeking a mundane solution, but an original (and perhaps elegant) one. He postulated that creativity, rather than being a specific thought process, may be a trait made up of abilities, style, values, beliefs, and tactics.

The abilities that may be essential for creativity are yet to be determined. Although Perkins did not find a sufficient research base to defend any specific abilities, he did leave the possibility open that some may yet be identified. Cognitive style refers to the ways a person approaches problems and processes information. Some such patterns (e.g., searching for problems and reserving judgment) facilitate creativity. The influence of values and beliefs is fairly straightforward: Individuals who value creativity also are more likely to be creative, as are those who believe that creative solutions are possible. Finally, there are specific tactics that may enhance creativity. These may be tied to a particular discipline or to general heuristics such as "set the work aside for a while." These abilities, styles, values, beliefs, and tactics enhance the possibility that an individual will use the ordinary resources of his or her mind (noticing, remembering, and realizing) to select an original idea or solution from the many possible ideas or solutions. Although Perkins's theory involves both affective and cognitive components, it essentially equates the cognitive processes of creativity with the processes involved in other mental activities.

Weisberg (1986, 1988, 1993, 1999) attempted to demystify the creative process by debunking familiar myths about creative genius and examining research that ties creativity to familiar cognitive processes. As did Perkins, he questioned the validity of self-reports of creativity and used several classic examples to illustrate their fallibility. The Mozart letter at the beginning of this chapter is one of the most commonly cited reports of an individual widely acknowledged to be creative. Weisberg noted that there is, among musicologists, doubt as to whether Mozart wrote the letter at all. It may be a forgery. If it is authentic, there remains the question of whether it is (intentionally or unintentionally) accurate. Mozart's notebooks contain compositions never completed and compositions started and revised, indicating that his report of music emerging fully formed was, at best, only sometimes true.

Kekulé's dream is also subject to scrutiny. The word translated "doze" can also be translated "reverie," so Weisberg (1986) suggested that Kekulé was not dreaming, but was lost in thought. Because the images Kekulé considered were described as "snakelike" and not as "snakes," Weisberg rejected the idea that an unconscious analogy allowed Kekulé's discovery. Rather, he believed that Kekulé thought about the problem, considered images in his visual imagination, and used the description of snakes to clarify the image.

In addition to the myth of the unconscious as a source of complete creative products, Weisberg (1986) examined several other prominent ideas and theories about creativity. He questioned the idea of creative leaps or flashes of insight by citing research showing that solutions to problems come, not in a sudden change of direction, but in gradual increments based on experience. For example, in the candle problem, a person given a candle, a book of matches, and a box of tacks is instructed to attach the candle to the wall. (You might want to stop and think a moment about how you might approach this task.) Most subjects either tried to tack the candle to the wall or tried to glue it with melted wax. The simplest solution is to use the box as a candle holder and tack it to the wall. Because this method involves using the box in a novel way, it is sometimes viewed as requiring creative insight. Weisberg examined verbal protocols (blow-by-blow descriptions of subjects' thought processes as they worked) and noted that all of the subjects who came up with the box solution started out by trying more common methods. Only when those failed did they experiment with other options, each building on the previous idea. One subject went from trying to put a tack through the candle to putting tacks next to the candle to using the box. Weisberg believed that this type of progression indicated that the solution came, not as a creative leap, but as an extension of past experiences.

Weisberg (1986, 1993) also tackled the idea of divergent thinking. He cited research indicating that divergent thinking is not associated with creativity in scientific research and reported studies that call into question the effectiveness of the traditional rules for brainstorming. He examined records of both artistic and scientific efforts ranging from *Guernica* to Beethoven's *Ninth Symphony* to the discovery of deoxyribonucleic acid (DNA). In each case, incremental steps (preliminary drawings, experimental themes, or unsuccessful models) can be identified leading from one idea (or theme or image) to the succeeding one. Ideas that appear to be new and original emerge, not fully formed from the depths of genius, but bit by bit as part of a long, constantly evolving effort.

In one sense, Weisberg's theory of creativity is that creativity does not exist, at least not as a unique process. He believed that every human action takes place in a unique time and environment, and hence could be considered novel.

> No two responses will ever be exactly alike because no two situations will be exactly alike .... Because novel output can be considered normal, the question again arises whether a distinction can be made between the creative and noncreative. (Weisberg, 1986, p. 147)

He described creative products as beginning with "an individual using personal experience as the basis to approaching some problem" (1988, p. 169). In this view, although the processes of creativity are not novel, the novelty may emerge from the interaction of an individual's past experiences and the problem at hand. Creativity might, in fact, be compared with the proverbial straw that broke the camel's back. The straw itself was not extraordinary; the extraordinary result was the effect the straw had on the camel. Similarly, creativity might, although composed of very ordinary processes, have extraordinary effects (Weisberg, 1993).

According to Weisberg (1988, 1993), creativity can be enhanced in two basic ways: by increasing expertise (allowing the individual to build more broadly on what has gone before) and by increasing commitment and persistence (allowing the individual to keep on building when initial attempts fail). Weisberg (1999) focused on the impact of knowledge on creative behaviors. Citing the 10-year rule, in which data suggest many years of learning and practice before masterworks are achieved in a variety of fields, he postulated that immersion in a discipline is key to highly creative behavior. In fact, he suggested that if we had access to all the knowledge available to a creative thinker, we would be able to see quite clearly where the new ideas originated. In fact, from that perspective, a new idea may not seem new at all, but may merely be a logical extension of existing ideas. According to Weisberg, it is only our limited knowledge that makes it appear that an idea represents a new conceptual leap. He also suggested that experience with a wide variety of problems or instruction on how analogies or other external triggers facilitate solutions may allow individuals to apply their experiences to new situations more fruitfully. Strategies based on these ideas are discussed in chapter 6.

Creative Cognition

Other cognitive psychologists have investigated how fundamental cognitive structures and processes result in creative thinking. From this perspective, creativity occurs along a wide range of activities, beginning with the very ordinary processes of language use and concept development and extending to ideas representing fundamental shifts in various domains. Although few of us will exhibit earthshaking creativity, each time we express ourselves in a new sentence, we have created a new example within our linguistic framework. Each time we come to understand another idea, we have created a new cognitive structure. In this view, the generativity, or ability to produce new ideas, associated with everyday thought uses cognitive processes similar to those used in thinking more commonly recognized as creative (Ward, Smith, & Finke, 1999).

Ward (2001) stated, "The creative cognition approach concentrates primarily on the cognitive processes and conceptual structures that produce creative ideas" (p. 350). An important characteristic of this approach is its focus on basic conceptual processes rather than global thinking strategies. For example, instead of considering divergent thinking or the use of metaphors (two commonly sited examples of creative thinking), the creative cognition approach would ask, "How does divergent thinking work? What basic component processes such as retrieval, combination, or mapping are used in divergent thinking?" In general, these processes are seen as similar to those used in other cognitive processes. Similarly, Fauconnier and Turner (2002), while not focusing on creativity per se, identified the operations of identity, integration, and imagination as keys to both everyday meaning and exceptional creativity.

Ward, Smith, and Vaid (1997) divided the processes of creative cognition into four general categories. Conceptual combination is the bringing together of diverse ideas in new ways. Conceptual expansion is the stretching of existing concepts to accommodate new experiences or challenges, or inventions based on previous experience. Metaphors, analogies, and mental models use existing ideas to understand, interpret, or extend seemingly diverse concepts. These authors' later work (Ward, Smith, & Finke, 1999) added insight, imagery, and response to recently activated knowledge to the list of processes that may affect creative thinking (Ward, 2001). This perspective does not claim that cognition alone can explain creative productivity. Motivation, culture, and timing are among the factors that can be used to explain why some individuals make creative contributions to the world around us. But creative cognition theory suggests that if, indeed, an intrinsically motivated person is more likely to persist long enough to find a new and interesting idea, he or she still uses the same cognitive processes used to generate more mundane ideas.

The Ultimate Mechanics: Creativity and Computers

To most of us, the idea of a creative computer may seem at best absurd and at worst frightening. It summons forth images of mechanical poems or science fiction machinery gone awry, using intelligence in new and dangerous ways. Separating creativity from the uniquely human personality characteristics or cognitive styles postulated by most cognitive theorists is difficult. However, researchers in artificial intelligence are taking the next step beyond the creative cognition approach and looking for algorithms that at least simulate creativity mechanically. If such a model can be found, it may provide insight into the processes of human creativity.

Schank (1988), for example, viewed creativity as comprising two subprocesses. The first is a search process, looking among previously experienced explanation patterns. The second is an alteration process, modifying an explanation derived from one situation to be used in another. In this case, creativity is using a rule or idea in a circumstance wherein it is not expected. In theory at least, a computer could be provided with an extensive array of explanation patterns (which might look a great deal like a list of proverbs) to use in solving problems. Although not providing evidence of computer creativity as yet, Schank did demonstrate that a human being can use a parallel process to generate original solutions to problems.

Boden (1991, 1992, 1994, 1999) described a computational model of psychology in which the semantic nets and systems of artificial intelligence can be used to represent possible models of human thought. Semantic nets are computer systems constructed to parallel the connections that cognitive psychologists hypothesize exist in the human brain. Connections among the nets offer possible explanations for apparent leaps of creative insight, much like the chance permutations in Simonton's (1988) associative networks. She described computers using similar processes to write poems, draw pictures, and discover mathematical rules. Although none of these operates at the level of Langston Hughes, Georgia O'Keeffe, or Ada Lovelace, "this does not destroy the main point: that poetic [and other] creativity requires a rich variety of mental processes, intelligible in ... computational terms" (Boden, 1991, p. 133).

Computer models simulate scientific creativity by using heuristics, or specific procedures, to guide searches through problem spaces. A problem space can be envisioned as the network of information and associations available regarding a particular issue, topic, or idea. Heuristics are rules that can be used to guide a search through the problem space looking for important combinations or insights. For example, a computer model called BACON was provided with planetary data, including distance from the sun and period of revolution. It also was provided with three heuristics:

1. If the values of a term are constant, then infer that the term always has that value.
2. If the values of two numeric terms increase together, then consider their ratio.
3. If the values of one term increase as those of another decrease, consider their product.

Given these guidelines, the computer "explored" the available data and "discovered" Kepler's third law of planetary motion. More complex programs have derived scientific laws in a variety of areas. Johnson-Laird (1988) developed a jazz improvisation program that creates novel varia-

Computers may help us understand the creative process.

tions on the basic chord based on principles of jazz and random choice. Other programs have created architectural drawings, line drawings, and poems (Boden, 1999).

Although no writer, at least thus far, claims that computers are creative to the same degree and through the same processes as human beings, the use of computer modeling is a logical extension of theories that represent creativity as a function of ordinary cognitive processes. Just as artificial intelligence can simulate many aspects of human thought, perhaps someday artificial creativity will simulate human ingenuity. In the meantime, computers offer another way to learn about the intricacies of the creative process. Boden (1999) stated, "The prime question for psychologists is not, 'Are these computer models *really* creative?' ... but rather, 'What light do they throw on how human creativity is possible?'" (p. 353) Whether any of these computer processes actually functions in the same way as the human mind will be a problem for human intelligence and creativity to tackle!

SYSTEMS APPROACHES

The final and most complex set of theories approaches creativity as an interaction between the individual and the outside world. In these theories, the mechanisms of the mind are not sufficient to explain the creative process. They must be placed in the context of an external environment. Simonton (1988) stated, "Creativity cannot be properly understood in isolation from the social context, for creativity is a special form of personal influence: The effective creator profoundly alters the thinking habits of other human beings" (p. 421). Of course, just as creative individuals affect those around them, systems theories propose that creativity is influenced by the environment in which it takes place. Systems theorists generally study extraordinary creativity—creativity that changes our world, or some discipline in our world, in profound and irreversible ways. However, the idea that creativity is part of complex systems of individuals and cultural contexts can be applied in varied circumstances.

Feldman: Defender of Insight and the Unconscious

Feldman (1988, 1994, 1999) can best be described as a systems theorist with a developmental perspective. As a systems theorist, he recognized the complex interactions that come into play to allow high-level creativity to function. He listed seven dimensions that may influence creative processes:

(a) cognitive processes, (b) social and emotional processes, (c) family aspects—growing up and current processes, (d) education and preparation—formal and informal, (e) characteristics of the domain and field, (f) sociocultural contextual aspects, and (g) historical forces, events, and trends (Feldman, 1999, pp. 171–172).

As a developmentalist, Feldman (1994) believed that creativity develops along these multiple dimensions. In contrast to Rogers, who believed creativity was part of the natural developmental process for all human beings, Feldman's focus on extraordinary creativity led him to focus on extraordinary or nonuniversal development. Nonuniversal development encompasses developmental changes that are unique to highly creative individuals. All human beings, according to developmental theory, experience internal transformations as their cognitive systems respond to interactions with the world. Feldman (1994) stated, "Creativity is a particularly strong and powerful instance of development, in which a personal, internal reorganization also leads to a significant change in the external form of a domain" (p. 87).

This may be most easily understood by examining the relationship of Feldman's ideas to Piaget's theories. Piaget postulated two processes to account for all changes in thought structures: assimilation and accommodation. *Assimilation* is to the tendency to fit information into past experiences, allowing for a constant reality. *Accommodation* is the process of adjusting one's perception of reality to fit new information (Boden, 1980). Neither process deals well with novelty, the really new restructurings of experience. Feldman postulated a third process: transformation. In the *transformation* process, the mind constructs ideas and images that are not based on experience. Transformation can lead to cognitive reorganization that is so profound it allows the individual to view the world in new and unique ways.

Feldman contradicted, to some degree, the basic premise of some contemporary theories that creativity represents the use of ordinary cognitive processes in unique ways rather than being an unusual or distinct process. He defended the importance of insight and the unconscious in the creative process. Citing the importance of dreams and the sudden crystallizing of ideas in the development of his own psychological theories, Feldman presented a model of creativity comprising three elements.

The first element is the mind's natural tendency to "take liberties with what is real, mostly in nonconscious [preconscious or unconscious] ways" (Feldman, 1988, p. 288). This tendency forms the basis of his transformation processes. These nonconscious transformations may be directed by conscious purposes and may be accessed by the conscious mind through dreams or moments of insight. The conscious mind's need for a stable reality necessitates that transformation be a largely nonconscious process.

If, as Feldman hypothesized, transformation is a nonconscious process, mechanisms outside rational thought are necessary to explain creativity. Whether these differ from the mechanisms necessary to explain other kinds of thought remains an open question. It could be argued that other thought processes also may occur outside consciousness. How many individuals can explain exactly how they chose a golf club for a particular shot or understood a friend's need for a good joke? They may be able to construct a relevant explanation after the fact, but they probably are not sure that was the actual process they used. It may be possible to reconcile Feldman's emphasis on insight and nonconscious processes with other theories focusing on ordinary cognitive processes if, in fact, ordinary processes are not always conscious.

The second aspect of Feldman's (1988) theory is "the conscious desire to make a positive change in something real" (p. 288). As did Perkins (1981), Feldman believed creativity is rooted in the desire for creative change. Feldman's third aspect would probably ring true for several other theorists: He believed that new creative efforts are inspired by the results of previous creative efforts. Although Perkins or Weisberg might attribute this influence to the effects of knowledge, Feldman emphasized that seeing the results of others' creativity illustrates that it is possible to make a difference. He believed that interaction with the creative efforts and products of others may allow the fruits of nonconscious transformations to enter one's consciousness. This emphasis on essential interaction with the crafted world is one of the key attributes that place Feldman among the systems theorists.

Thinking About the Classroom

Feldman believed that creative efforts are inspired by the creativity of others. Consider how this idea may affect your students. How might you share the creative efforts of other young people in a manner that encourages rather than overwhelms?

An Investment Model and Thoughts About Wisdom

Sternberg and Lubart (1991, 1993) and Sternberg and O'Hara (1999) proposed an investment theory of creativity: Individuals must buy low and sell high to achieve creativity. Instead of investing in stocks or diamonds, these individuals invest in ideas. Creative individuals pursue ideas that are novel or out of favor (buying low), then convince the field of the value of those ideas. Once the ideas gain favor, they allow others to pursue them (selling high) while they go on to other endeavors. Individuals who pursue already popular trends or solutions are less likely to achieve valuable original results. The investment theory suggests that six types of interacting resources contribute to creative performance: intellectual processes, knowledge, intellectual style, personality, motivation, and environmental context.

As did Perkins and Weisberg, Sternberg and Lubart (1991, 1993) explained the intellectual processes of creativity with the same model they used to understand other intelligent activities. However, unlike these two theorists, Sternberg (1985) devised a triarchic model of intelligence that includes components specifically tied to creative insight. For example, although selective encoding (sifting relevant from irrelevant information) is important to understanding any type of input, it may be particularly important in creative insights. Sternberg gave the example of Sir Alexander Fleming's discovery of penicillin. When Fleming's bacteria culture was spoiled by mold, he was able to recognize the important information at his fingertips and, rather than despair at his unsuccessful experiment, make an important discovery. Other components of intelligence seen as important to creativity are problem definition, strategic use of divergent thinking, selective combination, and selective comparison of information. Sternberg's (1988b) theory of creativity originates in this model.

The investment theory also examines the role of knowledge in creative performance, hypothesizing that it is an upside-down U. A low amount of knowledge is associated with limited creativity. An extremely high amount of knowledge may limit creativity because the individual becomes so immersed in the current state of the art that he or she is unable to find a truly new perspective. It is possible that a moderate amount of knowledge may be the most supportive of creativity. What exactly constitutes a moderate amount of knowledge and how it might vary by age or discipline remain questions for further investigation.

In addition to linking creativity with knowledge and specific aspects of intelligence, Sternberg and Lubart (1991, 1993) believed that creativity is characterized by a mental style that prefers to create its own rules, to attack unstructured (rather than rigid or prefabricated) problems, and to be involved in legislative tasks such as writing, designing projects, and creating business or educational systems. They also noted ties to specific personality characteristics such as tolerance of ambiguity, intrinsic motivation, and moderate risk taking. Finally, as did several other theorists, Sternberg and Lubart (1991, 1993) noted the importance of task-focused motivation and environmental variables in supporting creative activities. In this view, the complex interactions among the six types of resources necessary for high-level creativity account for the relative rarity of such accomplishments.

Sternberg (2000) has been clear that just as he believes intelligence can be developed, so he believes creativity can be increased through specific choices (e.g., the choice to redefine problems or take sensible risks). He also has examined the relationships among creativity, intelligence, and wisdom (Sternberg, 2001). He has described intelligent people as whose who "somehow acquire the skills that lead to their fitting into existing environments" (p. 360). Although what is considered intelligent behavior in one place may differ from behavior considered intelligent in another, behaviors considered intelligent generally are rewarded as appropriate to the society. The rewards are reaped as a result of adapting to an environment or environments.

In contrast, most definitions of creativity focus on ideas that are novel in a particular environment. Whereas intelligence may cause individuals to adapt to and succeed within cultural norms, creativity can cause them to reject such norms. The more novel the work, the more the individuals question existing paradigms, standards, and conventions—and the higher the level of personal and professional risk. Sternberg (2001) described wisdom as the synthesis of intelligence and creativity, balancing the need for change with the need for stability and continuity in human affairs. Wise individuals, according to this theory, would be sought after as leaders because of their ability to seek both balance and progress.

The role of wisdom in balancing continuity and change may be manifested differently within varied contexts. This could account, in part, for differences in the types of creativity considered appropriate across cultures. In societies threatened with the extinction of cultural traditions, wisdom may lead to an emphasis on creativity within those traditions. Rejection of cultural paradigms is less risky to society at large when practiced in dominant cultures.

Gruber's Evolving Systems

Gruber and his associates (Gruber & Davis, 1988; Gruber & Wallace, 1999, 2001; Wallace & Gruber, 1989) began with a basic assumption of the uniqueness of each highly creative individual. Believing that creative people develop along such ideosyncratic paths that generalizations about them are likely to be minimally useful, they used case studies to investigate in depth the distinctive processes of highly creative individuals. Gruber's (1991) most famous work, *Darwin on Man: A Psychological Study of Scientific Creativity*, examined the evolution of Darwin's ideas through a painstaking analysis of his notebooks and other writings.

In describing the evolving-systems model of creativity, Wallace and Gruber (1989) described several alternative paths for searching to find a model of creativity. One, designated the Holy Cow! path, searches for some special unexplained trait or ability that underlies creativity. The second, the path of Nothing But, describes creative processes as nothing out of the ordinary. Certainly, we have seen examples of both paths in the models described thus far. The third path "is to focus attention on the way the creative person is organized as a unique system for recognizing, embracing and doing the new job at hand. To see and understand this system requires neither fragmentary measurement nor ineffectual mystification, but patient attention to each unique creative person at work" (Wallace & Gruber, 1989, p. 3). Detailed case studies of eminent individuals provide the lenses through which these systems are examined.

The evolving-systems approach entails a set of complex attitudes and approaches for studying the efforts of creative people. First, the approach is developmental and systematic. It views creativity as developing over time and being affected by purpose, play, and chance. Second, it is complex, seeking to identify multiple insights, projects, metaphors, and so on in the work of a creative individual. An evolving-systems approach does not seek to identify a single "Aha!" in the work of a creative individual, but rather to track the many insights that occurred across time. The phrase "network of enterprise" (Gruber & Wallace, 2001, p. 347) is used to underscore the complex and branching nature of the creative endeavors studied. Third, it recognizes creative activity as interactive, affected by historical context, interpersonal relationships, and professional collaborations. The evolving-systems approach recognizes the creative individual both as a constructor of tasks and a human being interacting with the world with emotions, aesthetics, and needs. The degree of detail possible in individual case studies allows the researchers to consider multiple, complex factors interacting over time to influence a body of creative work.

Gruber and Davis (1988) noted major aspects of evolving systems that have been observed across case studies. First, and most clear-cut, is that creative activity takes a long time. As noted by Weisberg (1993), major creative insights do not come out of the blue, but are the result of years of learning, thought, and preparation. Because of the length and potential frustration of this process, creative individuals must of necessity invent and pursue subgoals. Early sketches and metaphors also were seen as helpful in shaping and maintaining continuing efforts over time. Darwin's (1859) branching-tree image was part of his writing years before its use in *On the Origin of Species*.

The second aspect noted is a "loose coupling of knowledge, purpose, affect, and milieu" (Gruber & Davis, 1988, p. 266). The evolution of creative ideas is influenced by an individual's expertise, motivation, emotions, and environment. "Loose coupling" represents the limited effects of one on the other. As an illustration, although depression and discouragement may affect an individual's thought processes, they do not eliminate that person's knowledge and expertise.

The third aspect observed in the evolving-systems theory is non-homeostatic processes, or processes designed to seek not closure but additional achievement and challenge. The creative individual seeks not just answers, but additional questions.

Despite these patterns, Gruber's focus remained on the idiosyncratic nature of creative processes: "Every creative person is unique in ways that are relevant to his or her creative achievements" (Gruber & Wallace, 2001, p. 348). Only by in-depth study of individuals, Gruber believed, can we recognize the multiple complexities of significant creative contributions.

Creativity, Culture, and Csikszentmihalyi

Csikszentmihalyi (pronounced, approximately, "chicks sent me high"; 1988, 1990, 1996, 1999) presented a three-pronged systems model of creativity, including aspects of the person, the domain, and the field (Fig. 2.4). The model has been embraced by other prominent theorists (e.g., Feldman, Csikszentmihalyi, & Gardner, 1994). The model changes one of the basic questions in the study of creativity from "What is creativity?" to "Where is creativity?" It examines creativity profound enough to be described as "the transformation of a cultural system (e.g., chemistry, medicine, poetry)—the incorporation of novelty into the culture." (Nakamura & Csikszentmihalyi, 2001, p. 337).

Csikszentmihalyi saw creativity not as a characteristic of particular people or products, but as an interaction among person, product, and environment. The person produces some variation in the information gained from the culture in which he or she lives. This variation may result from cognitive flexibility, motivation, or an unusual and inspiring life experience. However, according to Csikszentmihalyi, examining the mechanisms of novelty in the individual is only part of the picture.

Individuals are not creative in a vacuum (except perhaps on creativity tests). They create in a domain. A playwright creates in a symbol system and tradition of a culture. Without knowledge concerning the conventions of theater and script writing, it would be impossible to be a successful creative playwright. Creativity demands a knowledge base in some

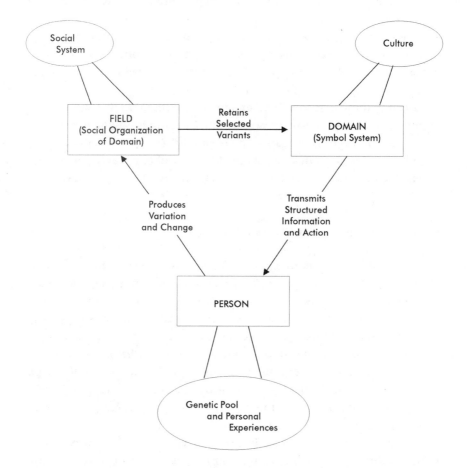

FIG. 2.4.   The locus of creativity. From *The Nature of Creativity,* p. 329, by R. J. Sternberg (Ed.), 1988, New York: Cambridge University Press. Copyright © 1988 by Cambridge University Press. Reprinted with permission.

domain. A creative mathematician must know mathematics. A biologist must know biology.

However, the domain is not the only entity that influences creative production. Variations also come into existence in the context of a field, or the social structure of a domain. The field comprises those people who can affect the structure of a domain. The field of theater, for example, is made up of theater teachers, drama critics, audience members (especially season ticket holders), producers, actors, directors, and any other individuals who help shape the definition of good theater at a particular time in a particular society. To be perceived as creative, the playwright must strike a balance with the order of the field. If the play is too similar to past standards, it will be considered mundane; if it is too different, it will not be considered art. If the variation is accepted, it becomes part of the domain to be transmitted by the field to novices. In some domains, notably the arts, it is possible for individuals to create works that are not accepted by the field at the time they are created. This rejection may mean poverty for the creator, but in time (possibly posthumously), acceptance may come.

Even in objective domains such as the sciences, there is a structure to the field that influences the possibilities for high-level creative accomplishments. It is difficult to become influential without the ability to publish in the right journals or to be accepted by the right conferences. A creative individual's work must be valued by some portion of the current field if it is to be given a professional hearing. In some cases, such as Mendel's work in genetics, the importance of creative ideas can be seen only later, as the field and domain change. It is interesting to speculate whether Einstein would have been viewed as a genius or a crackpot (and what his theories might have been) had he been born 100 years earlier when his field was very different.

Individuals are not only judged by the field: they are formed by it as well. In the course of preparation and in their environments of practice, individuals are shaped by those who practice around them, particularly those in mentoring relationships. The potential interactions among individual, domain, and field are complex, and may change considerably in different times, different environments, and different domains and fields. For example, the personal characteristics that might lead one to be a highly creative physicist in the 21st century in the United States might be very different from those that would have been necessary for one to be a 19th-century Parisian painter because the personalities necessary to find acceptance in those domains and fields vary so enormously.

It is interesting to consider whether the linkages among individual, field, and domain described by Csikszentmihalyi are relevant in creativity on a smaller scale than the transformation of a cultural system. Although individuals may be creative in ways that do not influence a field or domain in significant ways (at least according to many definitions), all creativity does occur within a domain that exists within a context.

Consider, for example, the anonymous storyteller cited at the beginning of chapter 1. A fine storyteller will bring to that effort a host of personal characteristics and processes. He or she works within the domain of storytelling, using the tools and conventions of that form. The storyteller also works within a context. The society provides the cultural context in which the storyteller's art is developed and practiced. It includes conventions within which the storyteller must work: traditional tales and frameworks within which variations are accepted, structures for learning to tell stories, and relationships with mentors, possibly even politics regarding who tells which tales under which circumstances. Although they look somewhat different from the factors influencing innovation in Western science or theater, the interactions of individual, content discipline (domain), and context (field, surrounding culture) appear important in many types of creativity.

Thinking About the Classroom

Creative efforts are not always accepted by the field at the time they are initiated. Make a bulletin board of Great Failures to help students understand that new ideas are not always immediately appreciated.

Building on Csikszentmihalyi's model, Gardner (1993a, 1993b) described an interactive perspective on creativity that recognized the importance of the interactions among individuals, domains, and fields. Drawing on his own theory of multiple intelligences, Gardner (1983) came to believe that individuals are creative in particular, domain-specific ways. Although an individual may certainly be creative in more than one domain (consider the poetry and artwork of William Blake), Gardner's definition of creativity reflects creative functioning, not as a general personal characteristic ("He or she is a creative person"), but in a particular area. He stated, "The creative individual is a person who regularly solves problems, fashions products, or defines new questions *in a domain* in a way that is initially considered novel but that ultimately becomes accepted in a particular cultural setting" (Gardner, 1993a, p. 35, italics added). The domain(s) in which a person becomes creative are affected by the individual's kinds of intelligences, personality, social support, and domain and field opportunities.

Like Gruber, Gardner based his theories on in-depth studies of highly creative individuals. In his studies of eminent creators, Gardner found wide variations in the types of intellectual strengths demonstrated by creators in different domains. In addition, he found that the symbol systems to be mastered and the activities in which individuals must be engaged vary enormously across disciplines. He described five types of activities in which creative individuals may be involved.

1. Solving a particular problem. This includes primarily scientific or mathematical research questions, but also covers tightly constrained artistic tasks such as musical arrangements.
2. Putting forth a general conceptual scheme. This includes the development of artistic or scientific theories—for example, the theory of relativity or the characteristics of cubism.
3. Creating a product. Creative products include works of visual art, literature, or choreography.
4. Giving a stylized performance. Stylized performances are defined generally by a script or score, but include opportunities for interpretation, improvisation, or innovation. Examples are dance, drama, or musical performances.
5. Performing for high stakes. Gardner described this as a type of creative endeavor in which one's words and actions are the substance of creativity, and in which one may risk security, health, or life in the service of a mission. This type of creativity is exemplified by public figures such as Gandhi.

It is possible that the intelligences, personality traits, and cognitive processes necessary for creativity may vary depending on which type of creative product is necessary or desired. As additional components are considered—the language of the domain, the characteristics of the field at a particular time, or the type of product necessary for the desired contribution—the potential elements of the system defining or controlling creativity become increasingly complex.

Thinking About the Classroom

One of the key questions in theories of creativity is whether there are general creative processes that span the disciplines or whether creativity is discipline specific. Baer (1993) found evidence of discipline-specific strengths in students in grades 2, 4, 5, 8, and college. Try giving your students creative tasks in several disciplines. Do the same students demonstrate exceptional creativity in every subject? You may want to ask a colleague to help assess the products to increase the reliability of your findings.

Creativity, Individuality, and Collaboration

Systems theories invariably entail human interaction. Creative individuals exist within cultures and fields made up of other human beings. Vygotsky (1960) described the origins of creative thinking itself as occurring in social interactions. One of the more interesting questions raised by such theories is whether creativity is—or need to be—an individual process. John-Steiner (2000), after studying creative collaborations wrote:

> The study of collaboration supports the following claim; productive interdependence is a critical resource for expanding the self throughout the life span. It calls for reconsidering theories that limit development to a progression of stages and to biologically preprogrammed capabilities. The study of partnered endeavors contribute to cultural–historical and feminist theories with their emphases upon the social sources of development.

John-Steiner proposed that the development and functioning of creative processes can be enhanced through collaborative thinking—thought communities—more powerful than that of a single individual. She cited mathematician Phil David, who described collaboration as "almost as though I have two brains" (p. 190). Playwright Tony Kushner (1997) wrote,

> The fiction that artistic labor happens in isolation, and that artistic accomplishment is exclusively the provenance of individual talents, is politically charged, and, in my case at least, repudiated by the facts. While the primary labor on Angels [in America] has been mine, more than two dozen people have contributed words, ideas and structure to these plays .... Had I written these

plays without the participation of my collaborators, they would be entirely different—would, in fact, never have come to be. (pp. 145–146)

The concept of creativity as a collaborative rather than an individual process flies in the face of stereotypical images of lone creators in garrets or laboratories. Yet history is full of creative collaborators, and the labs of the 21st century are inhabited by research teams.

John-Steiner (2000) described four different types of collaborative patterns that have characterized creative partnerships. In *distributive collaboration*, relationships are widespread and relatively informal, An individual draws on multiple relationships to enhance creative endeavors. Sometimes partnerships result. *Complementarity collaboration*, such as that of Marie and Pierre Curie, entails a division of labor based on complementary expertise. These relationships entail "mutual appropriation ... the stretching of human possibilities through the collaborative partner's shared experience that sustains their endeavors" (p. 199). In *family collaborations*, relationships within the creative collaboration are more integrated across areas of expertise and may change significantly across time. They may involve collaborations of literal families or groups of individuals working together in intense relationships. The final type of collaboration, *integrative collaboration*, requires a long period of shared activity. John-Steiner hypothesized that the difficulty in transforming a discipline means that a new mode of thought or art form is more likely to be successful when it is the result of collaborations. It is particularly interesting to think about what factors contribute to the widespread creative relationships that characterize particularly fertile venues of artistic or scientific development such as the Harlem Renaissance. Similarly, as teachers we must be challenged to think about ways to develop shared creativity in our classrooms in ways perceived as collaborative and not cheating.

A joy of writing books such as this one is that I sometimes hear from the people who read them. One of my most interesting correspondences thus far has been with Welsh storyteller Michael Harvey. Michael sent me some extraordinary poetry created by elementary-age children (see chapter 6). When I asked him to describe the strategies he used to help children write so beautifully, he explained that whereas older children might have individual responses, with children 7 to 11 years of age, he facilitates collaborative processes toward group products. It is interesting to consider that the collaborative creativity demonstrated by these elementary students may be similar to that used by some highly creative adults. As we consider ways to structure school experiences to support creativity, it is important to remember that the approach need not always be targeted at individual responses. Facilitated group activities may be particularly appropriate for younger students as well as for those whose cultural norms are more cooperative than competitive.

PATTERNS, QUESTIONS, AND ISSUES

Having examined numerous complicated and conflicting theories, we are left to consider this: Are there any patterns here? Do the theories of creativity give us any firm ground on which to base classroom practice, or are they all so much ivory tower speculation? Table 2.1 provides an overview of the available psychological theories, demonstrating clearly that definitive answers as to the origins and mechanisms of creativity are simply not available today. As in most fields, I suspect, the more we understand about creativity, the more questions rather than answers we probably have. If nothing else, a review of this chapter should show that anyone who claims to have the theory of creativity or boasts that he or she can teach you all you need to know about creativity in four easy steps should be taken with a generous pinch of salt. On the other hand, it is possible to find commonalities among the theories that may provide a basis for both research and practice.

Several theories note that creativity demands time, persistence, and motivation. Classroom activities that always are completed in 15 minutes or are so simple that they offer no opportunities for struggle do little to develop commitment to task. Creativity also demands a knowledge base. Most theorists concur that individuals are creative in some subject area and need a base of knowledge and skills to succeed. Certainly, a student who is to be a creative physicist will need a solid background in physics. However, if we teach only the facts about classroom subjects, we have presented only half the picture. Students also will need to be taught the skills of questioning, investigation, and creativity in a variety of disciplines. Our budding physicist needs to learn how to frame a question, how to plan research, and how to represent ideas in a variety of forms. Students of writing need to learn about generating story ideas, using metaphors, and writing dialogue. Whether the processes and attributes of creativity are subject specific or cut across disciplines remains to be investigated. Either way, a knowledge base in a particular domain is necessary for high-level creativity in that area.

Some theorists postulate insight as a key element in the creative process. For some (such as Sternberg), insight represents a specific cluster of cognitive processes that can be enhanced through training. For others

TABLE 2.1 Theories of Creativity—Some Possible Clusters

	Theorists	Explanation
Psychoanalytic theories	Freud Kubie Kris Jung Rothenberg Miller	Creativity can be explained largely by unconscious or preconscious processes.
Humanist and developmental theories	Malow Rogers Vygotsky	Creativity is a natural part of healthy development and/or develops in predictable stages.
Behaviorist or associationist theories	Skinner Mednick	Creativity is the result of responses to specific stimuli
Creativity as cognition	Guilford Perkins Weisberg	Creativity can be explained using the same processes as other aspects of cognition. It is possible that these processes may be modeled by computers (Boden, Schank).
Systems theories	Simonton Feldman Sternberg & Lubart Gruber Csikszentmihali Gardner	Creativity entails complex interactions of elements that may include cogntitive processes, personality traits, and interactions with the environment, domain, and field.

(such as Feldman), it is the result of nonconcious processes that are difficult to evaluate. Other theorists deny any role for insight. However, most theorists do postulate strategies, processes, or habits of mind that make creative ideas more likely. These may include generating analogies, defining problems, or looking for multiple solutions. It is possible that such strategies can be taught and improved. Several theorists stress the importance of purpose, attitude, and the desire to be creative as well as the effects of the outside environment.

Of course, there remains the question of whether any single theory, or even any conception of creativity, can encompass the multiple creative activities of human beings across many cultures.

In the succeeding chapters, I consider classroom ideas and techniques designed to provide the knowledge base, motivation, attitudes, and strategies conducive to creativity in a classroom environment. Although your implementation will vary depending on your preferred theory or theories, there are enough commonalities, especially among the most current theories, to provide a reasonable place to start.

JOURNEYING AND JOURNALING

1. Which theory or theories of creativity seem most consistent with your creative experiences? As you continue your creative project, do any of the ideas ring true? Do any seem far removed from your experiences?

2. Read about creative activities in a culture very different from your own. You may find information in books about art, literature, or anthropology—or even in *National Geographic* magazine. As you read, try to determine the implicit definitions and/or theories of creativity that are operating.

3. Sometimes it can be difficult to keep the various theories of creativity straight. Try making a picture or other graphic organizer to help yourself. You might make one picture for each set of theories (one for psychoanalytic theories, one for humanistic, and so on) or try to incorporate all of them into one complex graphic. Try not simply to list theorists in categories, but use images and shapes that will help you remember them.

4. Read descriptions of creative activities written by creative people. Two good sources are *The Creative Process* (Ghiselin, 1985) and *A World of Ideas* series (Moyers, 1990). Think about how those descriptions fit with various theories or models of creativity. Describe your reactions to them. Do any of the writers describe processes similar to your own?

5. Try thinking as B. F. Skinner did. Construct a series of events and reinforcements that could have led Shakespeare to write *Hamlet* or a favorite author to write another work.

6. Write an imaginary debate between theorists. Think about which points they might argue about and which they might agree on. If you were to score the debate, who would win?

REFERENCES

Baer, J. (1993). *Creativity and divergent thinking.* Hillsdale, NJ: Lawrence Erlbaum Associates.

Boden, M. A. (1980). *Jean Piaget.* New York: Penguin.

Boden, M. A. (1991). *The creative mind: Myths and mechanisms.* New York: Basic Books.

Boden, M. A. (1992). Understanding creativity. *Journal of Creative Behavior, 26,* 213–217.

Boden, M. A. (Ed.) (1994). *Dimensions of creativity.* New York: Cambridge University Press.

Boden, M. A. (1999). Computer models of creativity. In R. J. Sternberg (Ed.), *Handbook of creativity* (pp. 351–372). New York: Cambridge University Press.

Boykin, A. W. (1994). Harvesting talent and culture: African American children and educational reform. In R. Rossi (Ed.), *Schools and students at risk* (pp. 116–138). New York: Teachers College Press.

Boykin, A. W., & Bailey, C. T. (2000). *The role of cultural factors in school relevant cognitive functioning: Synthesis of findings on cultural contexts, cultural orientations, and individual differences.* Report No. 42. Washington, DC: Office of Educational Research and Improvement.

Boykin, A. W., & Cunningham, R. T. (2001). The effects of movement expressiveness in story content and learning context on the analogical reasoning performance of African American children. *Journal of Negro Education, 70*(1–2), 72–83.

Caduto, M. J., & Bruchac, J. (1988). *Keepers of the earth.* Golden, CO: Fulcrum.

Campbell, J. (1996*). The eastern way: Creativity in oriental mythology.* Joseph Campbell audio collection, Volume 3, Tape 5. San Anselmo, CA: Joseph Campbell Foundation.

Catjete, G. (2000). *Native science: Natural laws of interdependence.* Santa Fe, NM: Clear Light Publishers.

Courlander, H. (1996). *A treasury of Afro-American folklore.* New York: Marlowe and Company.

Csikszentmihalyi, M. (1988). Society, culture, and person: A systems view of creativity. In R. J. Sternberg (Ed.), *The nature of creativity* (pp. 325–339). New York: Cambridge University Press.

Csikszentmihalyi, M. (1990). The domain of creativity. In M. A. Runco & R. S. Albert (Eds.), *Theories of creativity* (pp. 190–212). Newbury Park, CA: Sage.

Csikszentmihalyi, M. (1996). *Creavity: Flow and the psychology of discovery and invention.* New York: HarperCollins.

Csikszentmihalyi, M. (1999). Implications of a systems perspective for the study of creativity. In R. J. Sternberg (Ed.), *Handbook of creativity* (pp. 313–335). New York: Cambridge University Press.

Darwin, C. (1859). *On the origin of species.* London: John Murray.

Dewey, J. (1920). *How we think.* Boston: Heath.

Eisenberger, R., Armeli, S., & Pretz, J. (1998). Can the promise of reward increase creativity? *Journal of Personality and Social Psychology, 74,* 704–714.

Eisenberger, R., & Cameron, J. (1996). Detrimental effects of reward: Reality or myth? *American Psychologist, 51,* 1153–1166.

Fauconnier, G., & Turner, M. (2002). *The way we think: Conceptual blending and the mind's hidden complexities.* New York: Basic Books.

Feldman, D. H. (1988). Creativity: Dreams, insights, and transformations. In R. J. Sternberg (Ed.), *The nature of creativity* (pp. 271–297). New York: Cambridge University Press.

Feldman, D. H. (1994). Child prodigies: A distinctive form of giftedness. *Gifted Child Quarterly, 37,* 188–193.

Feldman, D. H. (1999). The development of creativity. In R. J. Sternberg (Ed.), *Handbook of creativity* (pp. 169–186). New York: Cambridge University Press.

Feldman, D. H., Csikszentmihalyi, M., & Gardner, H. (1994). *Changing the world: A framework for the study of creativity.* Westport, CT: Praeger.

Fine, E. C. (2003, Summer). Stepping. *American Legacy, 9*(2), 19–22.

Gardner, H. (1983). *Frames of mind.* New York: Basic Books.

Gardner, H. (1993a). *Creating minds.* New York: Basic Books.

Gardner, H. (1993b, May). *From youthful talent to creative achievement.* Paper presented at the Henry B. and Jocelyn Wallace National Research Symposium on Talent Development, Iowa City, IA.

Ghiselin, B. (Ed.). (1985). *The creative process.* Berkeley, CA: University of California Press.

Glover, J., & Gary, A.L. (1976). Procedures to increase some aspects of creativity. *Journal of Creative Behavior, 9,* 12–18.

Gruber, H. E. (1981). *Darwin on man: A psychological study of scientific creativity* (2nd ed.). Chicago: University of Chicago Press.

Gruber, H. E., & Davis, S. N. (1988). Inching our way up Mount Olympus: The evolving- systems approach to creative thinking. In R. J. Sternberg (Ed.), *The nature of creativity* (pp. 243–270). New York: Cambridge University Press.

Gruber, H. E., & Wallace, D. B. (1999). The case study method and evolving systems approach for understanding unique creative people at work. In R. J. Sternberg (Ed.), *Handbook of creativity* (pp. 93–115). New York: Cambridge University Press.

Gruber, H. E., & Wallace, D. B. (2001). Creative work: The case of Charles Darwin. *American Psychologist, 56*(4), 346–349.

Guilford, J. P. (1959). Three faces of intellect. *American Psychologist, 14,* 469–479.

Guilford, J. P. (1986). *Creative talents: Their nature, use, and development.* Buffalo, NY: Bearly.

Guilford, J. P. (1988). Some changes in the Structure-of-Intellect model. *Educational and Psychological Measurement, 48,* 1–6.

Harmon, D. (2002). They won't teach me: The voices of gifted African American inner-city students. *Roeper Review, 24*(2), 68–75.

Hershman, D. J., & Lieb, J. (1998*). Manic depression and creativity.* Amherst, NY: Prometheus Books.

Holman, J., Goetz, E. M., & Baer, D. M. (1977). The training of creativity as an operant and an examination of its generalization characteristics. In B. C. Etzel, J. M. LeBlanc, & D. M. Baer (Eds.), *New developments in behavioral research: Theory, method, and application* (pp. 441–447). New York: Wiley.

Hughes, L. (Ed.). (1968). *Poems from black Africa.* Bloomington, IN: Indiana University Press.

Isaksen, S. G., Dorval, K. B., & Treffinger, D. J. (2000). *Creative approaches to problem solving* (2nd ed.). Dubuque, IA: Kendall/Hunt.

Isaksen, S. G., & Treffinger, D. J. (1985). *Creative problem solving: The basic course.* New York: Bearly.

Johnson-Laird, P. N. (1988) Freedom and constraint in creativity. In R. J. Sternberg (Ed.), *The nature of creativity* (pp. 202–219). New York: Cambridge University Press.

John-Steiner, V. (2000). *Creative collaboration.* New York: Oxford University Press.

Jung, C. G. (1972). *The spirit in man, art, and literature.* Princeton, NJ: Princeton University Press.

Khaleefa, O. H., Erdos, G, & Ashria, I, H. (1997). Traditional education and creativity in an Afro-Arab Islanic Culture: The case of Sudan. *Journal of Creative Behavior, 31*(3), 201–211.

Kris, E. (1976). On preconcious mental processes. In A. Rothenberg & C. R. Hausman (Eds.), *The creativity question* (pp. 135–143). Durham, NC: Duke University Press. Reprinted from *Psychoanalytic explorations in art* (pp. 303, 310–318). New York: International Universities Press.

Kubie, L. S. (1958). *Neurotic distortion of the creative process.* Lawrence, KS: University of Kansas Press.

Kushner, T. (1997). Is it a fiction that playwrights create alone? In F. Barron, A. Montuori, & B. Barron (Eds.), *Creators on creating* (pp. 145–149). New York: Putnam Books.

Liep, J. (2001). *Locating cultural creativity.* Sterling, VA: Pluto Press.

Lubart, T. I. (1990). Creativity and cross-cultural variation. *International Journal of Psychology, 25,* 39–59.

Lubart, T. I. (1999). Creativity across cultures. In R. J. Sternberg (Ed.), *Handbook of creativity* (pp. 339–350). New York: Cambridge University Press.

Ludwig, A. M. (1992). Culture and creativity. *American Journal of Psychotherapy, 46,* 454–469.

Martin, C. L. (1999). *The way of the human being.* New Haven, CT: Yale University Press.

Maslow, A. H. (1954). *Motivation and personality.* New York: Harper & Row.

Maslow, A. H. (1968). *Toward a psychology of being* (2nd ed.). Princeton, NJ: Van Nostrand.

Mednick, S. A. (1962). The associative basis of the creative process. *Psychological Review, 69,* 220–232.

Miller, A. (1990). *The untouched key: Tracing childhood trauma in creativity and destructiveness.* New York: Doubleday.

Morrisseau, N. (1997). *Norval Morrisseau: Travels to the house of invention.* Toronto, ON: Key Porter Books.

Moyers, B. (1990). *A world of ideas II.* New York: Doubleday.

Nakamura, J., & Csikszentmihalyi, M. (2001). Catalytic creativity: The case of Linus Pauling. *American Psychologist, 56*(4), 337–341..

Osborn, A. F. (1963). *Applied imagination* (3rd ed.). New York: Scribner's.

Parnes, S. J. (1981). *Magic of your mind.* Buffalo, NY: Bearly.

Perkins, D. N. (1981). *The mind's best work.* Cambridge, MA: Harvard University Press.

Perkins, D. N. (1988). The possibility of invention. In R. J. Sternberg (Ed.), *The nature of creativity* (pp. 362–385). New York: Cambridge University Press.

Perkins, D. N. (1994). Creativity: Beyond the Darwinian paradigm. In M. A. Boden (Ed.), *Dimensions of creativity* (pp. 119–142). Cambridge, MA: MIT Press.

Rogers, C. (1961). Toward a theory of creativity. In C. Rogers *On becoming a person: A therapist's view of psychotherapy* (pp. 347–362). Boston: Houghton Mifflin.

Rothenberg, A. (1990). *Creativity and madness.* Baltimore: Johns Hopkins University Press.

Rothenberg, A., & Hausman, C. R. (1976) *The creativity question.* Durham, NC: Duke University Press.

Rudowicz, E., & Yuer, X. (2000). Concepts of creativity: Similarities and differences among Mainland, Hong Kong, and Taiwanese children. *Journal of Creative Behavior, 43*(3), 175–192.

Schank, R. C. (1988). Creativity as a mechanical process. In R. J. Sternberg (Ed.), *The nature of creativity* (pp. 220–238). New York: Cambridge University Press.

Simonton, D. K. (1988). Creativity, leadership, and chance. In R. J. Sternberg (Ed.), *The nature of creativity* (pp. 386–426). New York: Cambridge University Press.

Skinner, B. F. (1972). *Cumulative record: A selection of papers* (3rd ed.). Englewood Cliffs, NJ: Prentice-Hall.

Smolucha, F. (1992). A reconstruction of Vygotsky's theory of creativity. *Creativity Research Journal, 5,* 49–68.

Sternberg, R. J. (1985). *Beyond IQ: A triarchic theory of human intelligence.* New York: Cambridge University Press.

Sternberg, R. J. (1988a). *The nature of creativity.* New York: Cambridge University Press.

Sternberg, R. J. (1988b). A three-facet model of creativity. In R. J. Sternberg (Ed.), *The nature of creativity* (pp. 125–147). New York: Cambridge University Press.

Sternberg, R. J. (Ed.). (1999). *Handbook of creativity.* New York: Cambridge University Press.

Sternberg, R. J. (2000). Identifying and developing creative giftedness. *Roeper Review, 23*(2), 60–64.

Sternberg, R. J. (2001). What is the common thread of creativity? Its dialectical relation to intelligence and wisdom. *American Psychologist, 56*(4), 360–362.

Sternberg, R. J., & Lubart, T. I. (1991). An investment theory of creativity and its development. *Human Development, 34,* 1–31.

Sternberg, R. J., & Lubart, T. I. (1993). Creative giftedness: A multivariate investment approach. *Gifted Child Quarterly, 37,* 7–15.

Sternberg, R. J, & O'Hara, L. A. (1999). Creativity and intelligence. In R. J. Sternberg (Ed.), *Handbook of creativity* (pp. 251–272). New York: Cambridge University Press.

Torrance, E. P. (1988). The nature of creativity as manifest in its testing. In R. J. Sternberg (Ed.), *The nature of creativity* (pp. 43–75). New York: Cambridge University Press.

Treffinger, D. J., & Isaksen, S. G. (1992). *Creative problem solving: An introduction.* Sarasota, FL: Center for Creative Learning.

Treffinger, D. J., Isaksen, S. G., & Dorval, K. B. (1994). Creative Problem Solving: An overview. In M. A. Runco (Ed.), *Problem finding, problem solving, and creativity* (pp. 223–236). Norwood, NJ: Ablex.

Treffinger, D. J., Isaksen, S. G., & Dorval, K. B. (2000). *Creative problem solving: An introduction* (3rd ed.). Waco, TX: Prufrock Press.

Treffinger, D. J., Isaksen, S. G., & Dorval, K. B. (2003). *Creative problem solving (CPS Version 6.1 TM): A contemporary framework for managing change.* Available from the Center for Creative Learning, Inc.: www.creativelearning.com

Vernon, P. E. (Ed.). (1975). *Creativity.* Baltimore: Penguin.

Vygotsky, L. S. (1960). Imagination and its development in childhood. In L.S. Vygotsky (Ed.), *The development of higher mental functions* (pp. 327–362). Moscow: Izdatel'stvo Academii Pedagogicheskikh Nauk RSFSR. (Originally a lecture presented in 1930).

Wallace, D. B., & Gruber, H. E. (1989). *Creative people at work.* New York: Oxford University Press.

Wallas, G. (1926). *The art of thought.* New York: Harcourt Brace.

Wang, P. W. (1990). How to appreciate a Chinese painting. *Vision, 2,* 1.

Ward, T. B. (2001). Creative cognition, conceptual combination, and the creative writing of Stephen R. Donaldson. *American Psychologist, 56*(4), 350–354.

Ward, T. B., Smith, S. M., & Finke, R. A. (1999). Creative cognition. In R. J. Sternberg (Ed.), *Handbook of creativity* (pp. 189–212). New York: Cambridge University Press.

Ward, T. B., Smith, S. M., & Vaid, J. (1997). *Creative thought: An investigation of conceptual structures and processes.* Washington, DC: American Psychological Association.

Weiner, R. P. (2000*). Creativity and beyond: Cultures, values, and change.* Albany, NY: State University of New York Press.

Weisberg, R. W. (1986). *Creativity: Genius and other myths.* New York: Freeman.

Weisberg, R. W. (1988). Problem solving and creativity. In R. J. Sternberg (Ed.), *The nature of creativity* (pp. 148–176). New York: Cambridge University Press.

Weisberg, R. W. (1993). *Creativity: Beyond the myth of genius.* New York: Freeman.

Weisberg, R. W. (1999). Creativity and knowledge: A challenge to theories. In R. J. Sternberg (Ed.), *Handbook of creativity* (pp. 226–250). New York: Cambridge University Press.

Wheeler, J. A. (1982). Bohr, Einstein, and the strange lesson of the quantum. In R. Q. Elvee (Ed.), *Mind in nature: Nobel Conference XVII* (pp. 1–30). San Francisco: Harper and Row.

Xu Bing. (2001). *Words without meaning, meaning without words: The art of Xu Bing.* Washington, DC: Smithsonian Institute.

chapter 3

Creative People

I hated school. From age 12 or 13 I knew I wanted to be a movie director, and I didn't think that science or math or foreign languages were going to help me turn out the little 8-mm sagas I was making to avoid homework. During class I'd draw a little image on the margin of each page of the history or lit book and flip the pages to make animated cartoons. I did just enough homework to get promoted every year with my friends and not fall to the wrath of my academically minded father. I give my dad credit for single-handedly keeping my math grades high enough so I wouldn't be held back. My other worst subject was phys ed; I failed that three years in a row in high school. I couldn't do a chin-up or a fraction. I can do a chin-up now, but I still can't do a fraction. (Steven Spielberg, 1985)

Sarah's mother calls her Sarah Bernhardt for the dramatic emphases she puts on all her expressions. Sarah is never just happy; she is exuberant, dancing from one corner to the next, leaping over furniture, and singing. Sarah is never tired; she is exhausted, panting, and at risk of immediate collapse. When Sarah is angry, the family moves back. Sarah's teacher finds her a constant challenge. When Sarah is bored (which happens often), everyone knows it. And yet she can always be counted on to put a new spin on a class discussion or come up with a new amusement on a rainy day. Having Sarah in class makes life interesting.

José makes his teacher's life easy. She always knows where to find
him—in the library or science room, usually buried in a book. Al-
ways interested in the latest discoveries, he reads several science
magazines cover to cover each month. He doesn't say much in
class; in fact, he doesn't say much at all. The rest of the students
think Jose is a little odd, but they generally accept him. They joke
about the "mad scientist" and speculate as to what he might be
building in the basement. Occasionally his teachers wonder, too.

Words such as "artist," "inventor," and "musician" bring to mind images that
often are larger than life. We may picture a starving painter shivering in rags
in a windy garret, a wild-eyed Dr. Jekyll amid bubbling beakers, a rock star
surrounded by screaming fans, or a violinist playing for coins on a street
corner. It is difficult to tell which of these images are grounded in reality,
which are products of Hollywood, and which may be helpful in identifying
and nurturing students' creative potential. Students as diverse as Steven
Spielberg, Sarah, and José can lead us to question what a creative student
really looks like. In this chapter, I examine characteristics that have been associated with highly creative persons, imagine how they might be manifested in children, and discuss how they might be supported in classrooms.

Many kinds of personal characteristics may be important in the development of creative potential. These can be divided into three general categories: cognitive characteristics, personality traits, and biographical
events. Creative individuals may be distinguished by the ways they think;
by their values, temperament, and motivation; and by the things that happen during their lives. It is important to note that these patterns and the
relationships among them are enormously complex. Just as there is no
single theory of creativity, there is no generic creative person. The characteristics of creative individuals vary among people and among disciplines.
A creative composer has strengths, needs, and values different from those
of a creative physicist, and no two creative physicists are exactly alike. Despite these variations, there are enough patterns to suggest some commonalities worth exploring.

In examining these commonalities, one more caveat is in order. Identifying traits in highly creative adults does not guarantee that similar traits
are present in creative children or children who may grow into creative
adults. At the end of the chapter, I look at some research on young people
who have been identified as creative and show how it dovetails with research on creative adults. It does present some promising beginnings. We
must, however, admit that our knowledge of creativity as manifested in

children is limited. Having done so, we use the research available as well as we can. Because we lack definitive answers, our most practical course of action is to consider identifying and supporting positive characteristics associated with creativity wherever we find them. Identifying them is our goal for this chapter.

CREATIVITY AND INTELLIGENCE

In chapter 2, the most accurate description of the relationship between creativity and intelligence was designated "it depends." If, like Guilford (1986), you define creativity as part of intelligence, the relationship is quite simple: Creativity is intelligence, or at least part of it. Most theorists, however, distinguish between the two, even if they do so somewhat muddily. In most cases, those who hypothesize that creativity is the product of the same basic cognitive processes as other thoughts recognize that the production of novel, appropriate ideas is distinct from the production of accurate, analytical but unoriginal ideas. Yet experience and common sense seem to indicate a relationship between the two. We probably would be surprised to see an outstanding creative contribution coming from a person of severely limited intelligence. Notwithstanding the extraordinary accomplishments of some individuals with savant syndrome, the vast majority of inventions, scientific breakthroughs, great works of literature, and artistic innovations appear to be made by intelligent people. How intelligence facilitates creativity is the subject of debate and ongoing study.

In the 1950s, MacKinnon (1978) identified a minimal relationship between creativity and intelligence in creative architects, writers, and scientists. He found a low, positive relationship between intelligence and creativity in mathematicians. These findings do not mean that the architects and writers were not intelligent, but that the most intelligent subjects were not necessarily the most creative. It was difficult or impossible to predict creativity on the basis of their IQ scores.

Barron (1969) examined the relationship between creativity and intelligence in a variety of disciplines. He identified a moderate relationship over the total range of scores, but for an IQ higher than 120 the relationship was small. He, among others, postulated a *threshold effect*, a minimum IQ necessary for major creative contributions. Beyond that level (perhaps IQ 120), other factors may be more important than intelligence in predicting creativity. If, as seems likely, the majority of MacKinnon's architects had IQs at or above the threshold level, little relationship would be expected.

Roe (1952) studied creative scientists with similar results. She found that although the IQs of creative scientists were generally high and the patterns of intelligence (verbal, quantitative, and so on) varied by field of science, the relationship between creativity and intelligence in her subjects was not strong. She postulated that a minimum level of intelligence was necessary for a person to make inventive or elaborative contributions in science, but above that level, other factors came into play.

The idea of a threshold relationship between creativity and intelligence probably is still the most widely accepted theory today. Sternberg and O'Hara (1999) listed three findings regarding conventional conceptions of intelligence as measured by IQ and creativity: (a) creative people tend to show above-average IQ; (b) when the IQ is above 120, IQ does not seem to matter as much to creativity as it does when IQ is lower than 120; and (c) the correlation of creativity to IQ is variable, ranging from weak to moderate. This is determined, at least in part, by the measures chosen. Therefore, more than 40 years later, the threshold effect still has support. Yet the variety of theories makes it clear that many other personality, cognitive, and environmental variables also affect an individual's ability to be creative in a particular discipline. These variables are examined later in this chapter.

There have been some efforts to distinguish highly creative from highly intelligent individuals. Probably the best known of these is Getzels and Jackson's (1962) research, which they described in *Creativity and Intelligence*. In this study, the researchers assessed high school students' intelligence and creativity through IQ tests and tests of divergent thinking. (This is an important difference from the studies of MacKinnon [1978], Barron [1969], and Roe [1952], in which creativity was assessed by adult creative accomplishment. In reading research about creativity, it is very important to ask how creativity was identified and measured.) Getzels and Jackson identified two groups for concentrated study: those who had high IQ scores (in the top 20%) but lower creativity scores (below the top 20%) and those who had high creativity scores but lower IQ scores. Those who scored in the top 20% on both measures were eliminated from the analysis. Although personality characteristics varied (and the high-IQ group clearly fit a traditional school mold more neatly), both groups did equally well on achievement measures, leading some to conclude that creativity without intelligence can lead to success in school or that high-level creativity and intelligence are somehow incompatible.

This is an oversimplification. Certainly there were students who were both highly creative and highly intelligent. They simply were not part of the groups studied. The study took place in an upper-middle-class school in which the range of scores was restricted. None of the IQ scores in the identified groups were actually low. (The mean IQ in the high creativity–low IQ group was 127!) Even with these restrictions, the study identified a positive correlation between creativity and intelligence if the entire subject pool was considered.

> Let us be clear. We are not saying there is no relationship between IQ and creative thinking. Obviously the feeble-minded by IQ standards are not going to be creative. But at the high average level and above, the two are sufficiently independent to warrant differentiation. (Getzels & Jackson, 1962, p. 26)

The study does provide evidence that the top scorers on IQ tests are not necessarily the top scorers on creativity tests, and that both groups have the potential for high school achievement. This finding, of course, provides additional support for the threshold effect. It also provides food for thought. One interesting finding of the study was that teachers preferred the high-IQ students to average students. Despite equal levels of achievement, they did not similarly prefer highly creative (divergent) students. If the characteristics that distinguish highly creative students cause them to be less preferred, perhaps even disliked by teachers, they are certainly at risk for educational disadvantage, despite their potential for high achievement.

It is important to note, however, that even a concept as firmly entrenched in creativity literature as the threshold theory is far from certain. Although the majority of today's theorists tie intelligence to high-level creativity, it is not clear whether the threshold of intelligence is necessary or consistent. Sternberg and O'Hara (1999) listed five possible relationships between creativity and intelligence, with at least some research evidence to support each one: creativity is a part of intelligence; intelligence is part of creativity; intelligence and creativity overlap to some degree; creativity is intelligence; or creativity has nothing to do with intelligence. Although the overlapping theories currently prevail, each approach has proponents.

Runco (1991) pointed out that few researchers have empirically examined the threshold theory and that those who have done so have produced mixed results. The findings are further complicated by populations and measures that vary widely among studies. It is very difficult to draw conclusions from studies all purporting to examine creativity and intelligence, but using completely different measures to do so. We know that the relationships between intelligence, as measured by any number of tests, and creativity, as measured by tests of divergent thinking or the number of remote word associations or the number of patents listed, are likely to differ. Runco's own research compared scores on IQ tests, a composite score from California Achievement Tests, and tests of divergent thinking in middle school students. He did not find support for the threshold theory and found little evidence of a relationship between creativity and IQ scores. He did find significant correlations between the achievement test composite scores and creativity, but still no evidence of a threshold.

Because there are no universally agreed-on measures for either creativity or intelligence, the relationship between the two constructs cannot be cleanly defined, at least for now. There does seem to be a relationship, however. A high level of adult creative accomplishment seems to be accompanied by at least high-average intelligence. It is possible that there is a minimum threshold of intelligence that makes this level of creativity possible. It also appears that factors outside those measured by most IQ tests (e.g., divergent thinking and motivation) affect both school achievement and creativity. Being alert to those factors may help us identify and nurture students whose abilities may not be fully assessed by traditional IQ testing.

THE IPAR STUDIES: IN SEARCH OF HUMAN EFFECTIVENESS

The most extensive studies investigating the characteristics of creative individuals were conducted at the University of California at Berkeley from the 1950s to the 1970s. At the Institute of Personality Assessment and Research (IPAR), under the direction of Donald MacKinnon, psychologists examined effective functioning in a variety of fields including architecture, creative writing, mathematics, industrial research, physical science, and engineering. Although MacKinnon's work with creative architects probably is the most well known, other investigations followed similar patterns.

The researchers began by asking experts in the field, in this case architects, to nominate and rank the most creative architects in the United States. The experts included professors of architecture, editors of architectural journals, and architects. The editors' rankings were highly correlated with the rankings of the architects themselves, providing substantial agreement as to some of the most creative architects in the field at that time. These individuals, along with two other samples of architects who had not been identified as highly creative, were invited to Berkeley for 3 days of intensive assessment. The assessment included intellectual and personality tests, self-assessments, and observations in a variety of situations. These and parallel studies of other fields provided the low correlations between creativity and intelligence cited previously.

The results of the IPAR studies are much too complex to be summarized adequately in this discussion. However, they have provided the basis for much of the writing on characteristics of creative people. Although groups varied by field (e.g., architects differed from writers or mathematicians), there were commonalities. MacKinnon (1978) listed seven of the "most salient characteristics of all the creative groups we have studied" (p. 123).

According to MacKinnon, creative people are intelligent. Although the relationship between creativity and intelligence in their subjects was essentially zero, the subjects were certainly intelligent. He did note that some creative subjects scored lower on tests of intelligence if they were penalized for guessing. Even in test-taking situations, they displayed a willingness to try, take a risk, and see what might work. Such subjects might

> make up for what they lack in verbal intellectual giftedness with a high level of energy, with a kind of cognitive flexibility which enables them to keep coming at a problem using a variety of techniques from a variety of angles; and, being confident of their ultimate success, these people persevere until they arrive at a creative solution. (MacKinnon, 1978, p. 124)

MacKinnon also found that creative people are original. In his study, originality was often, but not always, associated with fluency of thought. That is, those who came up with original ideas often generated many ideas. However, some people tended to have many ideas that were not very good, whereas others had a few high-quality ideas. MacKinnon (1978) noted:

> These findings point to individual differences in creativity, some persons being strong in just those aspects of the creative process in which others are weak. The implications are obvious: There is no single method for nurturing creativity; procedures and programs must be tailor-made, if not for individual students, at least for different types of students. (p. 125)

This concept will be important when the techniques for facilitating creative thinking are considered in chapter 5.

MacKinnon found that creative subjects are independent. They were highly motivated in his study to achieve in situations that allowed or demanded independence, and much less so in situations that called for conformity. They were not necessarily well-rounded, nor did they always fit smoothly into group situations. They also were open to experience, both of the inner self and the outer world. The subjects were curious, receptive, and willing to learn. They were accepting of multiple aspects of their own character and apt to express traditional female characteristics if they were men and traditional male characteristics if they were women. They could tolerate the confusion and anxiety that often accompany openness to experiences not immediately understood.

Creative individuals were found to be intuitive. They were not tied to the immediate perceptions of their senses (sometimes known as being stimulus or object bound), but were "alert to the as-yet-not- realized" (MacKinnon, 1978, p. 130). They often looked for hidden meanings, potential, metaphors, implications, or alternate uses in the things they saw, heard, and learned. They also had strong theoretical and aesthetic interests. On a test of values that compared the relative strength of theoretical, economic, aesthetic, social, political, and religious values, all groups of creative subjects valued the theoretical and aesthetic most highly.

Finally, MacKinnon found that creative subjects had a strong sense of destiny. Despite periods of difficulty or depression, the successful creative individuals had an ongoing belief in the worth and validity of their creative efforts. Perhaps this conviction, together with openness to experience, allows the type of courage MacKinnon described as essential. It is not physical courage, but courage to experience the opposites of one's nature and be receptive to elements of the unconscious. He described it as

> the courage to question what is generally accepted; the courage to be destructive in order that something better can be constructed; the courage to think thoughts unlike anyone else's; the courage to be open to experience both from within and from without; the courage to follow one's intuition rather than logic; the courage to imagine the impossible and try to achieve it; the courage to stand aside from the collectivity and in conflict with it if necessary; the courage to become and to be oneself. (MacKinnon, 1978, p. 135)

The challenge we face as teachers to develop this type of courage in ourselves and in our students is awesome indeed.

Thinking About the Classroom

Begin collecting books and stories about individuals who display the characteristics associated with creativity in positive ways. Share them with your students. Consider the kinds of models presented in your literature, science, or social studies curricula. Would students be able to tell from them that you value flexibility, originality, or persistence? Will they see examples of collaborative creativity as well as independence?

BIOGRAPHICAL TRAITS: LEARNING FROM LIFE STORIES

Some studies of creative individuals have not examined their intellectual or personality characteristics, but rather the kinds of things that have happened during their lives. Highly creative individuals are more likely to be firstborn and to have lost one or both parents early in life. Despite this loss, they often have been reared in stimulating, diversified, and enriching home environments, exposed to a wide range of ideas. Creative adults report that as children they liked school, enjoyed books, had many hobbies, and learned outside of school. Whereas some report warm, supportive peer groups, others report some marginality in social situations. In their careers, they benefit from role models and mentors, exert sustained effort, and often enjoy early successes (Tardif & Sternberg, 1988). Other studies have reported that creative adolescents come from homes with clear expectations but few rules, that their parents have well-established interests, and that the adolescents have more childhood traumas than less-creative students, more collections, and more unconventionally furnished homes (Dacey, 1989).

Of course, the difficulty with lists such as these is that they reflect particular bodies of research on specific populations during given times. You can no doubt think of a creative exception to virtually every item listed. Certainly, there are creative individuals who have grown up with both parents, who had minimally stimulating childhood environments, and who did not collect anything. Moreover, the experiences in creators' lives, as do their other characteristics, vary by field. The family environments of creative scientists and mathematicians may be happier than those of artists and writers. They often have had more formal education and different hobbies (Piirto, 1998a).

Examining biographies of eminent 19th-century creators across domains, Gardner (1993, 1994) found some themes and characteristics that seemed to transcend disciplines. Eminent creators lived somewhat removed from the center of society, came from families of moderate means who valued learning and hard work, and often were somewhat estranged from their immediate families. They were more likely to have warm relationships with a nanny or a more distant relative. Early in their careers it was necessary for these creators to move to a larger city to develop their growing expertise. These attributes and activities are similar to those identified by other researchers. Gardner also noted two additional themes and a possible 10-year rule.

The first new theme that emerged from Gardner's (1993) case studies was the matrix of support that surrounded the creators at the times of their creative activities. During periods of intense creative activity, these eminent creators needed both cognitive support in the form of someone with whom they could share newly formed ideas and affective support from someone whose friendship was unfailing. These roles could be met either by the same person or by different individuals. In either case, this type of support appeared necessary to major creative contributions. Albert (1990, 1993) also noted the importance of focal relationships in the developing careers of highly creative individuals.

Gardner's (1993) second emerging theme he called the "Faustian bargain." As did Faust, eminent creators made enormous sacrifices to their work. In many cases they sacrificed interpersonal relationships. Some undertook lives of extreme asceticism. In making the preeminent force in their lives work, these highly creative individuals left little room for other pasttimes, pleasures, or people.

Finally, Gardner (1993) identified a pattern of achievements he called the 10-year rule. Individuals in a variety of domains tended to produce major ideas, breakthroughs, or other creative products at approximately 10-year intervals. It would be interesting to examine biographies of 20th-century creators to learn whether the 10-year rule continued to hold true during the contemporary knowledge explosion.

Key to Gardner's view of the lives of creative individuals is his concept of fruitful asynchrony. Gardner believed creative individuals are characterized by a tension, or lack of fit, between the elements involved in creative work. Highly creative individuals are unlikely to fit smoothly into the conventions of a field or to have a conventional set of talents developed in conventional ways. Tensions may emerge between areas of strength and weakness, political forces in a field, or new conceptions and traditions of the past. Creative individuals, according to Gardner, do not chafe at these stressors; they thrive on them. The marginality experienced at various points in their lives seems tied in important ways to their creative strengths.

Csikszentmihalyi (1996) and his associates conducted interviews with 91 exceptionally creative individuals between 1991 and 1995. Individuals were selected according to three criteria: the person must have made a difference to a major domain of culture; he or she still had to be actively involved in that domain; and he or she had to be at least 60 years old. Csikszentmihalyi identified personality and biographical characteristics sometimes similar to and at other times divergent from those found by Gardner and other researchers. For example, whereas Gardner's creators struck Faustian bargains that often sacrificed personal relationships, most of Csikszentmihalyi's participants had stable and satisfying marital relationships. The most marked of Csikszentmihalyi's findings was the existence of contrast or paradox. Creative individuals experienced early years that were both nurturing and precarious, supportive and marginal. The patterns of the dualities varied from individual to individual, but the contrasts remained. For example, one individual may have grown up in a warm supportive home, but experienced racial discrimination. Another may have grown up in an economically struggling or dysfunctional family, but experienced support from extended family or other mentors. This type of bimodal early experience, providing both support and challenge, appeared tied to later creativity. The idea of paradox may provide one explanation for the sometimes conflicting lists of characteristics and experiences attributed to creative individuals, particularly if researchers are not aware of all the dimensions of the person being studied.

In the end, however, perhaps the most relevant characteristic of biographical traits is that we cannot change most of them. We can, perhaps, help to provide role models, encourage parents to provide a stimulating environment, and support hobbies and interests. We can be part of the matrix of cognitive and affective support that may be necessary for creative activity. However, although there is evidence that the number and spacing of children in a family are associated with differences in divergent thinking (Gaynor & Runco, 1992; Runco, 1991), we do not have the power to affect the order or number of our students' siblings. In considering classroom practice, it may be most productive for us to examine the cognitive and affective characteristics associated with creativity, hypothesize how they may appear in children, and consider how we may support some of them.

Thinking About the Classroom

Read two biographies of the same creative person—one written for adults and the other for children. Keep track of the emphases and information that are different. Do both books accurately describe the successes and failures in the person's life, the triumphs and setbacks? How might the differences affect your students?

CHARACTERISTICS ASSOCIATED WITH CREATIVITY

Researchers have compiled a great many lists of characteristics associated with creative individuals, each slightly different (Barron, 1969; Dacey, 1989; Isaksen, 1987; MacKinnon, 1978; Torrance, 1962). The characteristics described here are adapted from Tardif and Sternberg (1988), who synthesized collections of characteristics from the writings of theorists in *The Nature of Creativity* (Sternberg, 1988). The traits are divided into lists of cognitive and personality characteristics, but the distinction between the two is not always ironclad. For example, the ability to deal with novelty most likely has both a cognitive and an affective aspect. Individuals must be not only intellectually capable of dealing with new ideas and situations, but emotionally able to do so. Note also that the characteristics listed were almost always determined through research on creative adults. Comments on how these might be manifested in children are, unless noted, not research based, but are the results of my experience, intuition, and logic.

Cognitive Characteristics

In this section I consider cognitive abilities that have been identified with creative individuals. You might think of these as the mental mechanisms that allow people to use their imaginations or generate original ideas.

Metaphorical Thinking.   Creative people often are able to find parallels between unlike ideas. They take ideas from one context and use them in another context to create a new synthesis, transformation, or perspective. Metaphorical thinking makes it possible to use one idea to express another, as in Carl Sandburg's famous poem that compares the silent grayness of incoming fog to the movement of "little cat feet," or as in a sculptor's use of a cracked stone to convey ideas about war, pain, or broken romance. The ability to think in metaphors also allows individuals to use parallels to solve problems or generate new ideas. I have heard that the inventor of Velcro first thought of it while he was walking through a field of cockleburs. Metaphorical thinking allowed DeMestral to think beyond the annoyance of the moment to imagine how a synthetic material might fasten as tenaciously as the burs did.

Several theories of creativity refer implicitly or explicitly to metaphorical thinking. For example, Mednick's (1962) remote combinations imply a new synthesis of the remote ideas, and Rothenberg's (1990) homospatial process brings ideas together in the same physical or psychological space to construct metaphors. The strategies of synectics (see chap. 5) are grounded in an implied theory of creativity based on the power of metaphor.

Gardner and Winner (1982) researched the development of metaphorical thinking in children and found the beginnings of metaphorical thinking and language in preschool children. Children adapted objects to new uses in play (e.g., pretending a pencil was an ear of corn) on the basis of similarities between the actual and imagined objects. Students from preschool to adulthood were able to generate pretend names for objects based on some attribute of the object. One interesting finding was that among the study subjects, the spontaneous use of metaphors declined during the elementary school years, but the ability to produce metaphors in a cued situation did not.

Not surprisingly, the types of metaphors the children generated and understood appeared to change developmentally. Young children can effectively use metaphors based on some physical property or function. They might describe a hose as a snake or a daisy as an umbrella for an elf. They are much less likely to use or comprehend metaphors based on abstract or psychological comparisons. Gardner and Winner (1982) told about a group of young children at a Passover Seder who, during the story of the plagues before the Exodus, heard that Pharaoh's heart turned to stone. The youngest child, age 5 years, understood this to mean that God literally had turned Pharaoh's heart into a stone. Two slightly older children (ages 6 and 8 years), although understanding that hearts could not really turn into stones, still based their explanations on physical comparisons, one claiming Pharaoh lived in a stone house, the other that Pharaoh's muscles must have been hard like a stone. Only after adult explanation did the oldest children understand that it was not Pharaoh's physical heart but his emotions that changed.

Understanding these developmental changes can help teachers more effectively assist students in using and understanding metaphorical thought. Metaphorical thinking starts with making connections. Young children begin this process as they are encouraged to find alternate play uses for objects. (Remember Vygotsky?) They have a much wider range for creative thinking if they are given a refrigerator box to use as a house, a rocket, or a truck than if they are given elaborate plastic houses or vehicles. Teachers can join in this process by modeling—for example, waving a piece of blue fabric under a block bridge to make a river. It is easy to make a game out of "What else could I do with this?" or "What else could I use for an umbrella?" or "What else looks like a snail?"

As children progress through school, teachers can model metaphorical thinking in their everyday speech. Comments such as "That tree looks like an arrow pointing at the sky" or "Your sweater feels as soft as a new little chick" can help and encourage students to make physical connections. In later elementary grades, these comments could be expanded to include more abstract concepts: "The colonists' hearts were full of fire" or "I'm feeling like a balloon today." These could sometimes be the basis for discussion (How does a balloon feel?) or assignments (What do you feel like today?). In middle and high schools, metaphors can increase in abstraction and distance from the learner to include metaphors about content: "Iago was a serpent"; "Erosion is a thief." More detailed suggestions for lessons focused on metaphors are found in chapter 5.

The development of metaphorical thinking may be affected by gender as well as age. Lutzer (1991) noted that 5- and 6-year-olds were more successful at interpreting common metaphors than 3- and 4-year-olds, and that boys were more successful than girls. Lutzer hypothesized that the results may be explained by boys' willingness to take risks. If that is true, it underscores the importance of the teacher's role in making metaphorical thinking and other forms of creative expression safe in the classroom to encourage greater participation by more timid students, both boys and girls.

Teachers should be alert to evidence of students' metaphorical thinking. Piirto (1998a) found the use of metaphor to be a characteristic of the work of young, gifted writers. A child who at 6 years is describing rain as "ripples of liquid caterpillars" (p. 175) that roll down the window is ready for exposure to more sophisticated language than the average first-grade student. The student who suggests that chemicals bond like puzzle pieces or that now you could write about a Marine Romeo and a Iraqi Juliet is demonstrating one of the kinds of thinking that underlie creativity. As a teacher, it is important for you to listen for these connections. The child who compares flying to the moon with going to summer camp may not be making a flippant remark, but may be expressing the feelings of loneliness and fear that accompany a venture into any unknown place. The student who dumps his snack-time milk on his bean plant may not be avoiding calcium, but drawing comparisons between his needs and the needs of the plant.

Flexibility and Skill in Decision Making. Flexibility in thinking generally denotes the ability to look at a situation from many points of view or to generate many categories of responses. Flexible thinking may not always be perceived as an asset in school. It can lead students to overanalyze standardized test questions ("Well, it could mean this. But they might mean that. And if you look at it this way, any of the answers could be true …"). It can spur students to make comments that take class discussions in a direction not anticipated in the teacher's carefully constructed plan. Students thinking flexibly may ask, "Why didn't the three bears have Goldilocks arrested?" or "Isn't it racist to write a book about keeping an Indian in a cupboard?" It is important to recognize the difference between comments that are irrelevant to the discussion ("So, how did the Celtics do last night?") and those that represent a different focus.

Flexibility in decision making requires a person to consider a variety of options and perspectives before selecting one. You can use a number of strategies to teach decision making to students. Decision making is an integral part of the Talents Unlimited model (Schlichter, Palmer, & Palmer, 1993) in which students are taught several steps: (a) think of many varied things you could do; (b) think more carefully about each alternative; (c) choose one alternative that you think is best; and (d) give many varied reasons for your choice. In Talents Unlimited, students learn to consider many alternatives and to use specific criteria for evaluating possible choices. Older students can learn to prioritize criteria and to deal with circumstances in which the alternatives are, or appear to be, limited.

Decision making can be used to make judgments in many content areas. Kindergarten students can practice making decisions about when it is appropriate to tell on a classmate or what kind of costume to wear for a class party. Middle-school students can decide on the best format for a school recycling program or high school students can determine what alternative automotive fuel holds the most promise. In each case, the dilemma to be solved is open-ended. There is no one correct solution, so consideration of varied possibilities and criteria is likely to lead to a better decision. Although there may be times in school to practice decision making on more closed problems, they are less likely to foster the flexible decision making that appears important in creativity.

Independence in Judgment. Individuals exhibiting independence in judgment are able to assess situations and products by their own standards. They do not feel compelled to seek approval from others or follow the latest trends. The actor described in chapter 2 exhibits considerable independence in judgment. He uses his own standards of quality to assess his performances instead of relying on someone else's opinions. Sarah, described at the beginning of this chapter, may be exhibiting similar independence. Her dramatic responses seem to be unaffected by others' judgments.

It is perhaps easiest to visualize independence in judgment by considering its opposite. Young children who lack such independence are constantly seeking approval, usually from the teacher. They want the teacher to praise their artwork, notice their new clothes, and acknowledge each correct answer. It is easy to encourage this type of behavior unwittingly because dependent students seem so needy. They can make their teachers feel important, needed, and loved. Unfortunately, dependence on others' approval is not only emotionally unhealthy, but also stands in the way of creative thought. New ideas are seldom accepted immediately and frequently cannot be judged by existing standards. Unless people are able to set their own standards for evaluation, they can make little progress in independent thinking.

Older students can be just as dependent as younger ones, but the standards on which they depend frequently are set not by adults but by peers. From the middle grades on, students lacking independence in judgment may feel they must wear the approved style of clothing, express themselves in the correct slang, and create school projects that do not stand out from those of their peers in any way. Being different can be perceived as a social disaster.

Independent students of any age may not always be easy to teach. They may be stubborn, argumentative, or resistant to authority. Sarah, when angry or frustrated, probably was not pleasant to have in the classroom. Students with independent judgment may resist correction or doubt the teacher's ability to assess their creative work. Our challenge is to help students develop independence in ways that support their creativity in school. To develop this type of independence in judgment, students of all ages must be encouraged to evaluate their ideas, writing, and other projects. Self-evaluation is discussed in more detail in chapters 7 and 8. For now, it is important to note that independence in judgment demands some standards with which to judge. Such standards do not imply arrogance, but rather knowledgeable assessment. Students must be taught about the criteria that might be used to assess various types of work. Kindergarten art students could be taught to be sure that they have used the whole paper. High school art students might examine their use of light and shadow. In creative writing, elementary students might look for a beginning, middle, and end to their stories, whereas older students might check the realism of their dialogue. Understanding that judgment is based on criteria, not whim, can help students move from "But do you like it?" to their own assessments. It is also possible that, as Gardner (1982) hypothesized, children who practice judging their work in childhood may not fall prey to the harsh self-judgments of many adolescents that squelch their creative endeavors in the teen years. Runco (1992, 1993; Runco, Johnson, & Gaynor, 1999) noted the importance not only of independence in judgment, but also of good judgment or evaluative skills in creativity. He stated that the creative process begins with identifying a problem or task, and then requires generating multiple ideas. However, generating numerous ideas is not enough. Creative individuals must assess which of the many ideas produced are good ones. Runco noted differences in elementary students' ability to identify original ideas and suggested that the ability to evaluate creative ideas may be as essential as the ability to generate them. This theory would lend more support to activities that assist students in evaluating their own work, particularly in assessing which of their ideas are particularly original.

Finally, independence in judgment does not mean that the judgment of creative individuals is self-centered or without concern for consequences. Helping students make independent judgments entails helping them develop means for evaluation along many dimensions including the potential impact on self, community, and environment.

Coping Well With Novelty.   Students who cope well with novelty enjoy and work well with new ideas. They thrive on the question "What if?" These students will not argue "But I couldn't breathe under water," but will cheerfully imagine their life as a fish. Older students enjoy the challenge of contemplating changes on earth that might result from global warming or of imagining what happened next to Holden Caulfield in *The Catcher in the Rye*. Sarah's original contributions to class discussions and invented rainy-day games indicate her ability to deal with novel ideas.

Creative people deal well with novelty.

Encouraging the type of thinking that helps students deal well with novelty necessitates exposing them to novel situations. These may range from the imaginary to the realistic. The teacher might announce, "For the next half hour we will pretend that my crew and I have just arrived with from a distant planet that has always been ruled by a governing life form. Please explain to me what it means to have a democracy and why we think it is a good idea. To be successful, you must convince both the governing and the governed populations to experiment with your ideas." Or students might be challenged by experiencing an authentically novel event: watching an excerpt of Chinese opera, visiting a restored village, or listening to African chants or Indian sitar music. Each experience that forces students to break out of their comfortable frame of reference can be an asset in helping them deal with novel situations.

Another strategy is to create questions and assignments for which there can be no correct or incorrect answers. In my experience, many children who do not deal easily with new ideas are overly concerned with being right. For some students, it is enough to explain that for this assignment there can be no wrong answers. For others, it is necessary to help them understand the criteria by which the assignment will be judged. Although there may be no correct or incorrect answers, almost always in an assignment, as in any creative endeavor, there are standards of quality. For example, if Massachusetts students are being asked to speculate on how their lives might be different if the Spanish had settled New England, responses based on the characteristics of Spanish explorers (we probably would speak Spanish; there might be more Catholic churches) would be more appropriate than random guesses (there might be more football teams). If students are given cues for dealing with the context of a novel situation, they will find it less threatening.

Thinking About the Classroom

Next week, plan one class activity that you believe is truly novel, something no one in your class has experienced before. Observe how your students respond.

Logical Thinking Skills.   At first glance, logical thinking skills as a creative characteristic may seem to present a paradox. We sometimes think about creativity as the opposite of logic, or logic as a barrier to creativity. In fact, highly creative people have excellent logical thinking skills. If students are to be effective in gathering information about a situation, to focus on important issues, or to evaluate potential ideas, logical thinking is indispensable. Students who display logical thinking can use evidence to draw conclusions, give reasons for their responses, and make use of logical sequences such as if–then or cause–effect.

Borland (1988) argued that logical thinking is a characteristic associated with divergent thinking in gifted elementary school children. He found that a cognitive style described as strict precept–strict concept was associated with two of three divergent thinking measures. The strict precept–strict concept style emphasizes attention to detail, analytic thinking, order, and control. Any time we ask students to support an opinion with facts, find evidence in a story to support a statement, or explain their thought processes, we encourage logical thinking.

Logical thinking can even be a tool for dealing with novelty. In a new or different situation, starting with what is known or familiar often is an effective strategy. For example, if a student is challenged to create an animal that might live on Venus and a home for the creature to live in, that probably is a novel task. Yet one of the most powerful ways to begin is with the information he or she currently knows about Venus. What is the temperature? The atmosphere? The terrain? What types of adaptations would be most effective under these circumstances? Why? What resources are available for building? Such questions can lead to truly creative responses—those that are both novel and appropriate—rather than fanciful drawings of four-eyed green creatures. Also, this assignment provides the opportunity for students to synthesize information on the solar system with information on animal life, reinforcing and integrating two science units. Helping students to practice this type of assignment, in which logic is used to support originality, can impact both their creative thinking and content learning.

Visualization.   Creative individuals can visualize things they cannot see. Kekulé (regardless of whether he was actually asleep) visualized snakelike benzene rings (Weisberg, 1986). Some say that Einstein derived parts of his theories by visualizing movement within a moving train. Countless artists across cultures have visualized images they attempted to transfer to canvas, stone, paper, or sand. Children who are adept at visualization can imagine things they have not seen and enjoy playing with mental images. They might enjoy picturing C. S. Lewis's land of Narnia or the Hanging Gardens of Babylon, or playing games of visual What If? These students may whisper to one another, "What if all the teachers had to wear pajamas to school?" and then collapse in helpless giggles. Older students may be transported by picturing the details of their imagined meeting with the latest heartthrob.

Helping children practice visualization can be interesting and sometimes politically challenging. In some parts of the country, efforts to encourage students' imaginations have been interpreted as efforts at mind control, with the predictable political fallout. You will need to match the types of activities you choose to the climate and flexibility of your community. Activities designed specifically to encourage visual imagery are included in chapter 5. You also may want to consider more traditional sources of visual images, such as reading aloud to students from preschool through high school and having them listen to radio dramas. Visual imagery can be promoted by having students plan and create images. Students who study filmmaking or video production must learn to visualize the effects of varied camera angles, length of shot, and movements of the camera or subject before committing images to film. Similarly, students who plan and generate computer graphics usually visualize the desired effects and then plan strategies to achieve them.

Escaping Entrenchment.   Individuals who can escape entrenched thinking are able to get out of the ruts of their everyday ideas and consider things in new ways. This type of thinking might be viewed as a combination of flexible thinking and dealing well with novelty. If creative individuals find themselves repeating predictable thought patterns, they look for a new angle, a new perspective, or a break in the pattern.

Children who are adept at this type of thinking will exhibit many of the characteristics already described. They also may become bored or impatient with routines, repetitious assignments, or practice activities. Finding a balance between a secure and efficient classroom routine and the creative individual's preference for novelty can be difficult. Although the need for reinforcement is sometimes important, as teachers we certainly must be alert for assignments that are repetitious simply because we cannot think of anything else to do. A change from the daily journal entry or weekly vocabulary definitions not only will relieve boredom, but also will allow students to understand that patterns can be broken. Doing an oral presentation in the persona of the book's main character or cutting out magazine pictures that represent vocabulary words are student activities that can reinforce both language arts content and the strategy of escaping entrenchment. Students, too, can help to break the mold of entrenchment. If they are asked, "What is a new way we could practice vocabulary, share information about Iowa, or line up for lunch?" they may just find one!

Finding Order in Chaos.   One of the more interesting characteristics associated with creative people has its roots in Barron's research as part of the Institute of Personality Assessment and Research (IPAR) project at Berkeley. In his early work on that project, Barron (1968, 1969) investigated subjects' preferences among visual displays, concentrating on symmetry versus asymmetry and complexity versus simplicity. More creative individuals preferred visual images that were complex over those that were simple, and asymmetrical images over symmetrical ones. These patterns of preference form the basis for the Barron–Welsh Figural Preference Test (Barron & Welsh, 1952).

According to Barron, the underlying variable in these preferences is disorder. He believed that disorder is preferable for creative people because it gives them the opportunity to bring order to the chaos in their own unique ways. MacKinnon (1978) found a similar preference for complexity among all creative groups studied. He noted:

> It is clear that creative persons are especially disposed to admit complexity and even disorder into their perceptions without being made anxious by the resulting chaos. It is not so much that they like disorder per se, but that they prefer the richness of the disordered to the stark barrenness of the simple. They appear to be challenged by disordered multiplicity, which arouses in them a strong need … to achieve the most difficult and far-reaching ordering of the richness that they are willing to experience. (p. 62)

Should we then expect creative students to look like cartoonist Charles Schulz's character Pigpen, swirling in a cloud of dust to attack the chaos of their desks? Well, maybe. Perhaps a better indication would be seen in the complexity of their written or artistic projects. Writing that contains elaboration, intricate plots, or unexpected endings may provide a clue. Artwork that is not symmetrical and uses multiple colors and complicated designs, even if messy, is a better indication of creativity than the most carefully colored house, tree, and smiling-face sun.

Students who enjoy finding order in chaos must have chaos to begin with. Although we certainly cannot have classrooms in constant disarray, it may be worthwhile to hold our tongues regarding the condition of the art table part way through the project, even if the project must continue over several days. It also is important to recognize that students with this strength will chafe if asked to create a neat hand-traced turkey or symmetrical tile mosaic that mimics the teacher's model. The joy in finding order is in finding one's own order, not that imposed from outside.

Personality Characteristics

Personality characteristics, as opposed to cognitive traits, are less focused on the intellectual patterns or mechanisms with which a person thinks than on affective traits: the emotional patterns and personal values that shape thinking and action. These characteristics determine not so much how people are able to think, but how they choose to use their thinking, in what ways and to what ends. There are multiple lists of characteristics from which to choose. In the following discussion, they are synthesized to nine clusters of traits.

Willingness to Take Risks.   One of the affective characteristics most commonly associated with creativity is the willingness to take risks. This is not necessarily the type of risk taking that spurs a person to bungee jumping or mountain climbing. Rather, it is a willingness to accept intellectual risks. It is the courage described by MacKinnon (1978) as necessary to think thoughts others are unwilling to think or express ideas that are off the beaten path. Creative risk taking opens an individual to criticism, ridicule, or feelings of foolishness. On any given night, a jazz musician standing up to improvise could perform poorly. Dustin Hoffman, speaking on the *Tonight Show* (Leno, 1992), compared his feelings about acting with Greg Louganis's 1990 Olympic diving. Louganis was the greatest diver in the world, yet on one dive he hit his head on the diving board. Hoffman noted that the goal of the dive is to come as close to the board as possible, so the difference between a score of 10 and a humiliating knock on the head is measured in a fraction of an inch. "I looked at that," said Hoffman, "and thought—there it is." Even an actor of Hoffman's quality recognized that in every creative endeavor there is the risk of failure, sometimes by a fraction of an inch. Continuing to create means accepting that risk.

Students willing to take creative risks are not always at the top of the jungle gym or the bottom of the pile of football players. They may be the ones willing to express an opinion that differs from the teacher's, admit that they like classical music, or submit an assignment in a form different from that of their friends. They may be willing to sing their original song, suggest a new due date for an assignment, or organize a schoolwide protest against cafeteria food or national politics.

Supporting students in risk taking requires something of a balancing act because we must help them not only to take intellectual risks, but also to assess which risks are worth taking and understand that with risk taking comes responsibility for consequences. Creating a classroom climate in which students are safe in expressing differences of opinion is an essential component in this type of support, as are iron-clad rules against sarcasm and put downs. Even when students' efforts at originality are unacceptable (e.g., the new format they devised for an assignment omits critical elements of the task), it is important to help them see exactly what caused the problem. If a

Creative people take risks.

student's assignment was to give a persuasive speech and, he instead, did an imitation of the principal's morning announcements, the assignment was not fulfilled. Here you need to help the student understand that taking on a new character was not the problem, and that an original element could have added interest to the speech. To be successful, however, he needed to portray the principal in a persuasive mode as the assignment required. (It also may have been appropriate to reiterate that class rules against sarcasm and unkindness toward other students also apply to adults. Young people sometimes need help finding the line between humor and cruelty.)

Perseverance, Drive, and Commitment to Task.   It is not, of course, enough simply to take a risk. Many risks involve failure or less-than-complete success that requires continuing, persistent efforts. Willingness to continue in the face of obstacles, to maintain motivation without immediate reward, and to stay focused on a task for long periods are essential to successful creative efforts. José, described at the beginning of the chapter, showed enormous drive and commitment to his interest in science. Numerous theories of creativity talk about time as a key element. For high-level creativity to occur, individuals must stick at a task long enough to develop creative ideas. If our students are to be successfully creative, they must be able to maintain motivation and concentration long enough for it to happen.

We have a special obligation to dispel the common notion that really creative or really smart people do not have to work hard, or that if you are good enough, ideas will come quickly and easily. In my own research on problem finding in creative writing (Starko, 1989), I found that even among high school students, the most able writers consciously manipulated ideas and experiences to generate writing projects. Less able writers thought that if they just waited, ideas would pop out, that nothing popped, they had no ideas. They did not understand that they could improve their ideas through their own efforts.

It is important to provide models of risk taking, failure, and continued efforts. If students equate a single failure with total failure, they are unlikely to continue creative or other efforts. Stories of creative individuals can be helpful models. If students learn about the number of filaments Edison tried before finding a successful material for the light bulb, or the scorn heaped on Amelia Bloomer for wearing split skirts, or "bloomers," they may find courage for their own struggles. (In fact, it is likely you may be familiar with Ms. Bloomer only in conjunction with her infamous split skirts. She also was a journalist, whose paper *The Lily* was said to be the first owned and operated solely by women [Hanaford, 1882].) Be alert to this need when exposing young children to biographies. Sometimes biographies written for children seem more concerned with modeling good behavior than portraying truth. They may omit realistic struggles and substitute simplistic stories of bright, kind children who grew up to be successful adults. Such stories not only are trivial, but also can be damaging. If young children believe that achievement is supposed to come easily, the buffetings of real life will be an unwelcome surprise.

Telling stories of your own efforts, struggles, and successes also can project a powerful model. One of my colleagues brought all the drafts of her master's thesis to school so her students could see how many times it was written and rewritten before it was completed. I have occasionally shared with young people my beginning efforts to learn a new instrument. I believe those struggling, flawed performances, although not providing a great model of musicianship, showed both the willingness to take risks and the necessary continuation of less-than-perfect efforts on the way to success.

Finally, it is important to recognize that creative individuals almost always persist and struggle over self-selected tasks, not over those assigned by others. When we look for evidence of persistence and drive in our students, we may not always find it in the areas we select. The fact that a student does not always complete math assignments or struggle to understand French grammar is not necessarily an indication of potential creative failure. Although we certainly want to assist students in developing the self-discipline to complete less-preferred tasks, we may look for evidence of their perseverance elsewhere. We may find it in the kindergarten student who does not want to stop building an imaginary village just because free time is over or in a high school student who wants to spend all his or her time in the technology lab, but frequently skips history. Recognizing such behaviors as inappropriate or inconvenient in school should not keep us from recognizing them as clues to positive, task-focused motivation.

Thinking About the Classroom

Make a bulletin board entitled Problems, Problems, Problems or Famous Flops. Challenge your class to fill it with examples of problems that were overcome by successful creative people or ideas they tried that did not work.

Curiosity.   Creative people are curious. They want to know how things work, how people think, what is out there, and how it got there. They maintain the childlike persistence that asks "Why?" at every turn and struggles constantly to understand the world around them. I have a vivid memory of a musician friend coming to visit one summer day and sitting in our shady backyard. Suddenly he noticed something unusual in one of the large maple trees. Quick as a flash, he had walked up the side of the tree (I still don't know how; there are no branches lower than 10 feet up) and sat above us grinning and examining the tree limbs. That incident typified his approach to life. To the creative individual, every new sight and sound brings questions that must be investigated. Every new idea has nuances that must be explored.

Intense curiosity is necessary to allow many creative people to address difficult problems. A prize-winning research mathematician said:

> You have to have the question that you want to know. You have to have that. You have to just get a charge out of knowing this thing. You want to know why it works. You do it because you want to be recognized .... That's one of the reasons .... But you cannot make yourself work hard enough to do a really hard problem unless you want to know why it works. You just have to be fascinated by it. You just want to know. (Gustin, 1985, p. 321)

It usually is easy to see curiosity in young children. Preschool and kindergarten teachers are constantly bombarded with questions and must be alert that overly enthusiastic, exploring students do not put themselves in danger. Yet when these same students are older, such behavior is much more rare. I have had numerous interviews with elementary and middle-school students who, when asked what they would learn about if they had a choice, could think of no interests, questions, or problems that intrigued them.

I suspect that to some degree this lack of interest is a result of their school experiences. In early childhood, exploring and questioning are children's main tools for learning about the world. In school, they are taught to learn about the things the teacher chooses, in the way the teacher chooses, at the time the teacher chooses. In time, the idea of choosing to learn or asking a question just because it is interesting becomes far removed from students' daily experiences. Sometimes when I have asked students what they would like to learn, they have looked at me as if I were speaking a foreign language. I believe that at least occasionally giving students choices about the things they learn can help maintain the curiosity that underlies creativity. Helping students learn to identify interests and ask as well as answer questions is discussed in chapter 6. For now, one example will suffice. I once met a teacher who had a permanent classroom bulletin board entitled Great Questions. If a student asked a question that could not be immediately answered, would take a discussion too far off course, or just seemed interesting, it would be recorded and placed on the bulletin board. When the class (or individuals) had a few extra minutes, questions were taken from the board for exploration. This strategy not only provided a forum for interesting questions, but also sent a message that the questions themselves, not just the answers, were valuable.

Openness to Experience. To be curious, a person must have something to be curious about. Creative individuals provide themselves with constant sources of questions, ideas, and problems through their receptiveness to experience. One aspect of openness to experience is receptiveness to the complex input of all the senses. I once visited a beautiful formal garden on an island in Maine. As I walked amid the profusion of colored flowers, I noticed a woman painting at one end of the garden. Not wishing to disturb her, I avoided that area until I noticed her taking a break from her work. As I walked toward her, she exclaimed, "Can you believe all the greens here?" I looked at her canvas and realized that she was not painting the gardens but the woods surrounding them, all in various shades of green. Up to this point I had not noticed the greens at all. As I looked through her perspective, they were breathtaking. The subtle differences in tone and hue that had escaped me were the inspiration for her creative work. I have always been grateful to that woman. Greens have never been the same to me. However, without her observation of that diversity, neither I nor any of those who subsequently viewed her painting could have had that experience.

Openness to experience also is characterized by the willingness to try something new and different: octopus at an Italian restaurant, an exhibit of Japanese paper folding, a concert of Elizabethan (or contemporary) music, or lessons in tap dancing. Children who become entranced looking at the rocks in the driveway, middle school students who are willing to listen to opera with open ears and open minds, and high school students who, as one of my friends did, take their dates to a medical school film festival of exotic operations all are exhibiting a willingness to be open to the experiences around them.

Adults can help develop this capacity in young people. Pianist Jeannette Haien describes her father's influence on her openness and expectation in experiencing the world.

> One of my first memories is of my father calling excitedly to say, "Look." He was looking up at the sky. I couldn't see what I had to look at. Then he said, "Listen," and I heard this peculiar sort of sound, very distant. He kept saying, "Look higher, look higher," and I did. Then I saw my first skein of geese and heard their call. He took my hand and said to me, "Those are the whales of the sky." [Note the metaphoric language!] I have never forgotten it. And I

never look up at a sky without the expectation of some extraordinary thing coming—airplane, owls at night. I'm a great looker up to the sky. (Moyers, 1990, p. 53)

I believe we must cultivate this openness to experience in ourselves before we can share it with young people. Unless we are able to experience the wonder, we cannot convey it. I know of no way to do this except by committing ourselves to look more closely and listen more deeply to the things that surround us. As I have learned to distinguish the songs of birds, the clamor in my yard is transformed from interesting noise to a series of conversations. As I have watched theatrical lighting more closely, I have come to appreciate and notice subtle changes I once ignored. If you are able to point out to students the marvels of the patterns on the snake's back, the subtle differences in descriptive language between authors, or the fantastic patterns of crystals, these experiences may allow them to open their own eyes. If we do not see the beauty in the things we teach, how will our students see it?

Openness to experience also means openness to inner emotional experiences. Children who weep at the death of Charlotte the spider in *Charlotte's Web* or become irate at the treatment of homeless people are willing to experience emotions even when they are difficult. Dramatic Sarah, described earlier, experienced and expressed a wide range of emotions. It is possible that this type of openness ties to the emotional overexcitability described by Dabrowksi as a characteristic of highly creative individuals (Piechowski & Cunningham, 1985). Openness to experience can sometimes be painful and confusing. In describing the process of writing a poem, Stephen Spender said:

A poem is a terrible journey, a painful effort of concentrating the imagination; words are an extremely difficult medium to use .... Above all, the writing of a poem brings one face to face with one's own personality with all its familiar and clumsy limitations. In every other phase of existence, one can exercise the orthodoxy of a conventional routine; one can be polite to one's friends, one can get through the day at the office, one can pose, one can draw attention to one's position in society; one is—in a word—dealing with men. In poetry, one is wrestling with a god. (Ghiselin, 1985, p. 125)

Yet, without wrestling with the god, and with himself, Spender could not have been a poet. Opening one's mind to experiences also necessitates opening it to confusion and disorder, frequently causes of anxiety for young people. Especially in adolescence, creative individuals may be troubled by uncertainty as to life's goals or purpose, crises in religious beliefs, conflicts in personal or social roles, and so on. Although all young people experience such difficulties to some degree, the turmoil can be particularly painful to those who acknowledge and examine it rather than ignore it or wait for it to go away. Creative adolescents have enormous need for empathetic understanding that conveys confidence in their ability to overcome the anxiety while not belittling the intensity of its effects or the reality of its causes. MacKinnon (1978) suggested:

> When counsel of this sort can be given inconspicuously or casually in the directing of the teenager to more and more sources of knowledge out of which he himself can find the answer which he needs, such counsel will be most conducive to his creative development. Such nondirective counseling, of course, is not suited to all students, but it is, I believe, the type of guidance indicated for those with creative potential. (p. 130)

Of course, the need for such counsel and understanding is not limited to adolescents. Young children, too, can exhibit unusual openness to experience. A friend's daughter returned from a typical first-grade field trip to a farm determined to become a vegetarian. Whereas the other children had enjoyed seeing and feeding the animals, she was absorbed in thinking about why the animals were being raised. Her parents' respect for her values and assistance in planning her meals (she was permitted to omit meat as long as she consumed sufficient protein) allowed her to deal with the experience in a positive way. It should also be noted that she wrote a note of protest to one of the fast-food companies complaining that there were no children's meals for vegetarian children. She could order a salad, but she could never get a toy!

Thinking About the Classroom

Pick an experience you usually take for granted—eating an apple, looking at a tree, listening to the sound of the rain—and try to be more open to the experience. Use all the senses you can. Plan an activity for your students that allows them to do the same.

Tolerance for Ambiguity.   Sternberg (1988) called tolerance for ambiguity "almost a sine qua non of creative performance" (p. 143). Clearly one cannot be open to experience without being tolerant of ambiguity, for life is practically always confusing, contradictory, and ambiguous. If an individual cannot tolerate loose ends, unanswered questions, or gray areas where black and white would be easier, that person is left to a diet of TV situation comedies or rigid judgments.

The creative process itself also demands tolerance for ambiguity. Despite Mozart's claims (see chap. 2), creative solutions rarely spring forth full blown. More often, they emerge over a period that includes moments of insight and times of struggle, persistence, and confusion. To survive this process, the creative individual must be able to live with half-formed ideas, possible solutions, and images that might be good, but could be better.

Children who are able to tolerate ambiguity have much in common with those who are independent in their judgments or who deal well with novelty. They are willing to keep trying and experimenting although they are not sure if they are right. My experience in schools is that we do little to tolerate, much less encourage, ambiguity. Generally, school tasks deal with correct answers and incorrect answers, but nothing in between. Unfortunately, school probably is the only place on earth where answers are so clear-cut. I cannot think of any other aspect of my life that has an answer key!

If we are to help students tolerate ambiguity, there must be questions, assignments, and problems in school that do not have one best answer. There must be discussions in which there is room for genuine difference of opinion. Dillon (1988) said that the best discussion questions are the ones the teacher would like to discuss because he or she genuinely does not know the answer. Although sometimes such discussions may lead to consensus, it is important to understand that sometimes the real answer is "We don't know." Our best ideas today may not be good enough or may not be our best ideas next week. As teachers, we should not feel compelled to tie everything up in a neat package. Neat packages are easy to carry, but they do not make us think about the contents.

Tolerance for ambiguity also can be encouraged when discussions, projects, or problems extend over time. Of course, the periods that may be appropriate vary developmentally. For kindergarten students, a project conceived and carried out over several weeks may seem to last an eternity. High school students can develop projects that take a semester or even a school year. In some classes, it may be interesting to repeat key projects or discussions over the course of a school year. A fifth-grade class might want to discuss and record their ideas on what constitutes a hero two or three times over a school year. It would be interesting to see how and whether their ideas are affected by the literature and history they study that year. A science class might want to repeat a challenge (lifting a 10-pound bag of flour to the ceiling, trapping a mouse, or packaging an egg) after several units have been studied to see how solutions change with additional knowledge. In addition to the content taught, these long-term activities reinforce the notion that a good idea may not be the only idea, or that opinions and ideas grow and change.

Broad Interests. Many creative people have broad interests, particularly in creative endeavors. This characteristic seems strongly tied to openness to experience. If you are open to many experiences, many things become interesting! In students, a wide number of interests may lead to many interesting endeavors or to overscheduling and exhaustion. It is important to support and encourage students in their creative interests, but it may occasionally be necessary to counsel them that it is not essential to pursue all of them simultaneously.

Note also that some creative individuals pursue interests that are not broad, but very focused. José, the young scientist, may be one such case. Individuals who become highly skilled musicians spend many hours each day on their art, even in early childhood. Midori, the violinist, gave her first public concert at age 6. When asked if her mother, also a violinist, made her practice the long hours necessary for such accomplishment, she replied, "She didn't force me to play the violin. She only taught me because I wanted to learn" ("Interview with Midori," 1992, p. 5).

A prize-winning research mathematician described the narrowness of his adult interests, "I did absolutely nothing else [but mathematics] for many, many, many years. It's impossible. I don't know anyone who does first-class mathematics who doesn't work all of the time. Your world becomes very small" (Gustin, 1985, p. 321).

Young people may not spend all their time solving mathematical problems, but those who are to become outstanding researchers—perhaps like José—may devote their days to reading, experimenting, and model building. Although we may not always have musical prodigies or future Nobel prize winners in our classes, if students are happily involved in creative pursuits, we need not be overly concerned that their interests are not broad or their lives sufficiently well rounded. All creative individuals are unique, and it is a no-win proposition to try to fit them into a one-size mold.

Value Originality. Creative people want to be creative. They value original ideas and would rather generate a new, better idea than repeat an old one. It is hard to imagine anyone who would be willing to endure the rigors of the creative process if he or she did not believe it to be valuable.

Van Gogh described drawing the same subject repeatedly until there was one drawing "different from the rest, which does not look like an ordinary study" (Ghiselin, 1985, p. 46).

Children who value originality can have a difficult time in school. I recall observing an art lesson in an elementary school in which students were to use patterns to cut out the appropriate green doughnut shape, red bow, and three red berries to construct a holiday wreath. Students who dared to glue more than the prescribed number of berries on their project were chastised for not following directions. I can only imagine what further deviation from the norm might have brought.

It certainly is important, particularly in earlier grades, to have exercises in which students practice following directions. It may even be valuable to have young children practice cutting on designated lines to practice fine muscle control. But if the hands-on projects experienced in school—be they making advertising posters, clay hogans, or model Egyptian villages—are designed for students to recreate a specified model, there is little room for originality. If this type of activity is pursued year after year, students not only do not practice originality, but they also have no reason to think that we value it. If the art teacher, for whatever reason, felt it was important to make wreaths, surely the directions could have been altered to allow students to plan their own decorations. The instructions "Try to make your project different from everyone else's; see if you can think of an idea no one else will think of" can be added to almost any class project.

We can help students value originality by valuing it ourselves. We can point out to students the originality in their own work and in things we see day to day. We can share our own original solutions to home or school problems. Newspaper accounts of unique problem solving or even unusual items we see in a catalogue can spark a brief discussion on the importance of new and unusual ideas.

Intuition and Deep Emotions.   Many creative people are intuitive. MacKinnon (1978) found that on the Myers–Briggs Type Indicator (Myers, 1962), most creative subjects preferred intuitive perception (indirect perception of deeper meanings and hidden possibilities in situations) to sense perception (becoming aware of things via the senses). This was exactly the opposite the findings for the general population. Whereas only 25% of the general population preferred intuitive perception, it was preferred by 90% of the creative writers, 92% of the mathematicians, 93% of the research scientists, and 100% of the architects. Contrary to popular stereotypes that portray artists and writers as intuitive and scientists as sticking to hard facts, intuition was associated with creativity across disciplines.

Innovative director Peter Sellers described artists as "extremely sensitive, not usually consciously, to the deep vibrations that are moving through a society" (Moyers, 1990, p. 22). He believed this sensitivity allowed him and others to anticipate political developments in their work. (Sellers, in fact, portrayed Reagan invading Panama in an opera 6 months before the event.) Intuitive understandings in both children or adults are clear without being explicable. We know, but we cannot explain how.

It is difficult to envision encouraging intuition in school systems designed to facilitate clarity, accountability, and justification of actions. MacKinnon (1978) suggested that teachers could search for common principles across domains; stress analogies, similes, and metaphors; plan exercises in imaginative play; and look toward a broader context. Clark (1986) called intuitive and creative processes "expressions of the highest level of human intelligence" (p. 161). She described three levels of intuition: (a) rational intuition (putting together known facts so as to see them in a new light), (b) predictive intuition (enlarging on the known by including new information, as might be seen in forecasting or the "Aha!" experience), and (c) transformational intuition (defying scientific explanation—the type of intuition seen in the enlightenment or illumination sought by many of the world's religions). Clark believed that the second level of intuition may be the same as creativity. She lists seven conditions that foster intuition: (a) a relaxed state, (b) silence, (c) focused attention, (d) a receptive nonjudgmental attitude, (e) an ability to synthesize all brain functions, (f) novelty and variety in the environment, and (g) a teacher who values and encourages intuitive processes; provides opportunities for educated guessing, hypothesis setting, probability testing; is comfortable with mistakes, both the students' and personal errors; emphasizes personal discovery over memorization of facts; and models intuitive behavior (Clark, 1986, p. 164).

Logically enough, conditions contrary to this list are seen to inhibit intuition: avoiding change, focusing on mistakes, seeking control and predictability, adhering rigidly to rules, and so on. Clark did not advocate throwing out the rule book, but did suggest that we adopt as flexible an attitude as possible. She also advocated the use of imagery, fantasy, and visualization as tools to assist students in developing their intuitive capabilities (see chap. 5).

Perhaps our most important role as teachers in developing intuitive thought is to treat it with respect. Even if students must show all the steps by which a problem is be solved mathematically, we can acknowledge that sometimes they might just know the answer (and it might not be because they copied someone else!). They can then go back and figure out how they might have done it mathematically. Giving students the opportunity to express opinions and feelings that are not always be explained may also provide support for intuitive thought. Challenges such as "Write a story that makes you feel the same way this music makes you feel" allow emotional expression without demanding a logical analysis of the connections.

The use of intuition, combined with openness to emotional experience, can lead to very intense emotions. Some creative children and adults are moody or sensitive. Recognizing that the feelings are real and helping students find appropriate means of expressing them can be a valuable service. Steering students to paint an angry picture rather than hit someone or to collect blankets for the homeless rather than rail against the system can help them channel emotions into positive creative action.

Being Internally Occupied or Withdrawn.   Although some creative children may have an active social life, others may be quiet loners. José may fit into that pattern. The pursuit of creative activities, for many, demands a great deal of alone time. I believe it is important to distinguish between students who are alone because they are unhappy or rejected and students who are alone by choice. Although we certainly want all students to be able to communicate with others and get along socially, it truly is not necessary that every child or adult be a social butterfly. A quiet student who spends his or her time with one or two friends and a paintbrush (or a cello or a computer) may be perfectly happy and well adjusted. Well-meaning attempts to force students to participate in activities they do not enjoy so they will become one of the group may be counterproductive. At times, helping a student find another painter (or musician or computer programmer) with whom he or she can share the passion may be more appropriate. At other times, the best course of action may be to let the student paint.

Thinking About the Classroom

Divide a large piece of paper into squares and list one characteristic associated with creativity in each square. Leave the paper on your desk for 2 weeks. Each time a student does something to demonstrate a characteristic, put his or her name in that square (after the first time, just use tally marks). Be sure to mark the characteristic even if it is displayed in a negative way. At the end of 2 weeks, see which students are listed most often. Are they the students you expected?

Creativity and Complexity.   You may have noticed that some characteristics of creative individuals seem potentially contradictory: flexible yet logical, risk taking yet committed to task, escaping entrenchment yet finding order in chaos. Csikszentmihalyi (1996) believed the complex personalities exemplified by these dichotomies are a hallmark of creativity. After interviewing nearly 100 extraordinary creators, he listed 10 dimensions of complexity on which creative individuals appear to develop both dimensions of a continuum simultaneously:

Creative individuals have a great deal of energy, but also are often quiet and at rest. They may work long hours with great intensity, yet value time for rest, reflection, and rejuvenation.

Creative individuals tend to be smart, yet naïve and able to look with new eyes on the world around them.

Creative individuals are playful yet disciplined.

Creative individuals alternate between imagination and fantasy and a rooted sense of reality. It is this balance that allows their responses to be both original and appropriate.

Creative individuals seem able to express both introversion and extroversion as needed.

Highly creative individuals can be humble while simultaneously being proud of their accomplishments.

Creative individuals seem to be minimally affected by gender stereotyping, able to express both masculine and feminine dimensions of their personalities.

Creative individuals typically are seen as rebellious and independent, yet it is impossible to be an eminent creator without having internalized an existing domain. Therefore, creative people can be at once traditional and rebellious.

Creative individuals can be passionate about their work while maintaining objectivity in their judgments.

Creative individuals, because they are open, experience both suffering and enjoyment in connection with their creative activities.

It is clear from this list that any shallow, stereotyped, or simple characterization of a creative person does a disservice to complexity that appears to be associated with highly creative individuals—those whose creativity affects us on a daily basis. It also is important to recognize that characteris-

tics of creative individuals are not always positive. After reviewing literature on characteristics of creative individuals in the arts and sciences, Feist
(1999) concluded that personality commonalities across disciplines are
"distinguished by relatively high levels of asocial characteristics, namely
introversion, independence, hostility, and arrogance .... A second cluster
of distinguishing traits revolve around the need for power and for diversity of experience: drive, ambition, self-confidence, openness to experience, flexibility of thought, and active imagination" (p. 284). According to
Csikzsentimihalyi (1994), the characteristic that most consistently differ-
entiates successful artists from those who give up an artistic career is a
cold and aloof disposition. Although we may not wish to encourage aloof-
ness, arrogance, or hostility in our students, it is important to recognize
that the characteristics that allow individuals to be creative—independence, courage, and persistence—may not always be expressed in ways that
are easy on classroom routines. Helping students channel their drive in
ways that can be positive for both them and their community is one of our
responsibilities as adults and mentors. Perhaps we can be facilitators of
creativity that is confident without being arrogant, and self-confident
without being self-centered.

Discipline, Gender, and Cultural Differences.   Biographical experiences and personal characteristics of creative individuals vary across
disciplines. For example, whereas creative individuals in both art and science tend to be open to experience, artists may tend to be less emotionally
stable and less conforming than scientists (Feist, 1999). Researchers have
studied characteristics specific to scientific creativity, artistic creativity, creative writing, and a host of other disciplines (Innamorato, 1998; Neihart,
1998; Piirto, 1998b). It seems likely that the patterns of intelligence and the
personality characteristics necessary to be creative in the domain and field
of physics are different from those necessary to make a contribution of
equal stature in the domain and field of choreography. The more we come
to understand the complexities underlying the creative process, the more
difficult it is to give a one-size-fits-all description of a creative individual.

There also may be gender differences in the life patterns and characteristics of creative men and women. It is difficult to determine whether
this is so because there have been few studies of creative women or because studies of creative individuals seldom include enough women to
allow valid comparisons. The types of differences that might be uncovered was illustrated in Helson's (1983) study of creative women mathematicians. As part of the IPAR project, the researcher examined female
mathematicians who had completed their degrees between 1950 and

1960. Although differing in generally predictable ways from less-creative women mathematicians (higher in flexible thinking, more independent, and less tolerant of rigid routines), they also differed from creative male mathematicians. Helson found that creative female mathematicians were more likely to describe themselves as nonadventurous and inner focused. Male mathematicians were more likely to emphasize ambition. Certainly, the fact that the women subjects had entered the work force during a time when women's professional roles were more constrained than they are today must have had an impact on their perceptions of their careers and personnel development.

It is possible also that differences resulted, not from innate differences in creative individuals, but from how that creativity was met in homes, schools, and other environments. Fabricant, Svitak, and Kenschaft (1990) reviewed research showing that boys in math classes were allowed more freedom to deviate from rules and discover alternative solutions to problems, whereas girls were required to follow the rules more closely and were criticized more often. Such experiences, especially over a period of years, might certainly have had an impact on women's confidence, initiative, and ambition. Other research suggests that girls in general receive less teacher attention and are required to be less assertive than boys. For example, teachers are much more likely to respond to boys who call out in class. Girls are more likely to be told to raise their hands (Sadker & Sadker, 1986, 1995, Sadker, 2002). If we treat creative boys and girls differently, we should not be surprised if the end results are different.

Despite the changes of the last century, the differences in gender expectations make it likely that men and women may have different experiences exercising their creativity. bell hooks (1995) wrote:

> Long after the contemporary feminist movement stirred up questions about great art and female genius ... we still must confront the issues of gender and work with respect to the politics of making space and finding time to do what we women artists do. Most artistic women I know feel utterly overextended .... We spend much time trying to figure out how to use our time wisely. We worry about not giving enough of our care and personhood to loved ones. Despite feminist thinking and practice, women continue to feel conflicted about the allocation of time, energy, engagement, and passion. (pp. 126–127)

The focus and devotion to task that can be viewed as necessary concentration in creative men may be viewed as selfishness when practiced by women—particularly women with families. Even if the individual "mechanics" of creativity are similar in men and women, it is possible that some women may need different characteristics and strategies to be successfully creative in their fields. For example, highly creative women may be freer to express that creativity within some disciplines during periods when they are not raising young children (Reis, 1987, 1998). Of course, childrearing offers many opportunities for creativity, but not in most traditional disciplines.

Some have suggested that women's natural means of knowing and working are more collaborative than those of men (Belenky, Clinchy, Goldberger, & Tarule, 1997; Gilligan. Lyons, & Hanmer, 1990). If so, women may have an advantage when developing creative collaborations. John-Steiner (2000) argued that interdependence is a human rather than a gender-linked characteristic, but still believed that women's life experiences mean they "face fewer barriers than men when attempting collaboration" (p. 122). This may shape differences in the ways women pursue creative endeavors and the characteristics they bring to bear on the process.

It is possible that, as Reis (1987, 1998) hypothesized, women and men often have different paths and time lines for creative accomplishment. They may bring different personal characteristics to their creative endeavors or encounter gender-defined responses from the fields in which they create. Until more research gives us a better understanding of these possibilities, we should recall that the vast majority of research underlying our understanding of creative individuals (and their processes) describes creative men. It simply is not clear whether the same characteristics are found with the same frequency in equally talented women. It also is important to monitor our own responses to characteristics associated with creativity in male and female students. Do we respond in the same way to boys and girls who are insistent in their questioning, persistent in their arguments, and independent in their manner? Do we expect female students to "act like ladies" while acknowledging that "boys will be boys"? Do we encourage both individual creative efforts and the more collaborative processes for creative endeavors? Do we accept sensitivity and displays of emotion from female students while rejecting it in male students? If so, we may be at risk of encouraging creativity in some students while discouraging it in others. How do we respond to a powerful high school senior who wants to quit football to devote more time to theater? In at least one case I know, that decision resulted in an immediate conference between the senior and the horrified principal. The school's honor was at stake and clearly could not be upheld by outstanding theatrical productions! It is important that the full range of characteristics and processes associated with creativity be accepted and supported in all students, regardless of gender.

It also is possible that factors influencing the development of creativity differ for men and women, boys and girls. For example, Baer (1998) suggested that the effects of extrinsic motivation on creativity may vary by gender in middle school students. As this type of research continues, we may come to understand how creativity may be differently manifested in boys and girls.

Just as our knowledge of possible gender differences in the characteristics or processes of creativity is limited by lack of research on creative women, little is known about how such characteristics or processes may vary across cultural groups. Virtually all research on characteristics of creative individuals reports the characteristics of European or European American men. It is possible that Samoans creating original dances, Native Americans weaving, African Americans improvising gospel music, or Japanese composing highly unusual flower arrangements may have different cognitive and personality traits from those traditionally studied. We simply do not know. It seems likely that because the very nature and definition of creativity varies across cultures, the characteristics associated with creativity vary as well. In addition, the challenges presented by differing levels of support provided to individuals on the basis of gender or culture seem likely to affect the characteristics necessary for success. For example, if the time line for women's creativity is extended, it is possible that motivation or persistence may play particular roles in their creative development. Csikzsentimihalyi (1994) described the political pressure on a talented African American painter in the 1960s that led to that individual leaving an artistic career. It is interesting to contemplate whether Spike Lee may have needed a different constellation of characteristics than John Sayles to be a creative director in the 1990s. Perhaps your observations of the creative characteristics of children from varied cultures will add to our understanding of this important question.

Finally, we do not know the personal characteristics necessary for success in collaborative creative endeavors, or how they may vary from those identified in the preceding discussion. Although it seems likely that some characteristics will be similar among individuals whose creativity is individually versus collaboratively focused, there may be important differences. Differences also may occur across different types of group efforts. It is interesting to consider whether the characteristics that might be necessary (or sufficient) for one type of collaboration (e.g., an informal distributed collaboration) may be different from those required for a more intense integrative partnership. Only more investigation into collaborative creative processes will provide the answers. In the meantime, it seems wise to be cautious about identifying only one type of individual as having the potential for creativity, while all the while supporting characteristics that may help students develop creative strengths.

Thinking About the Classroom

Keep track of your responses to boys and girls who ask questions in class. See if you respond the same way to their calling out or probe to understand their thoughts equally. You may want to ask a colleague to observe you. When you look at student papers, notice how much emphasis you put on original content and how much on form or neatness. Do you weight them equally for boys and girls? You may want to make similar observations regarding your responses to students from different cultural, ethnic, or socioeconomic groups.

What Were They Like as Children?

Perhaps even more difficult than the questions of whether the characteristics listed apply equally to men and women or to varying cultural groups is the question whether it is appropriate to try applying research on adults to young people. There are few studies on creative children, largely because such studies pose enormous logistical difficulties. Researchers who define creativity as adult creative accomplishment must either identify creative adults and work backward to determine what those individuals were like as children or identify a group of children, analyze their characteristics, wait for them to become adults, and hope some turn out to be creative! Neither course of action is simple. An alternative path is to identify students who seem to have creative potential, usually through a test of divergent thinking, and identify their characteristics. Of course, we then are left wondering whether the students who scored high on the tests are the same students who will be creatively productive as adults. The best answer to that question is "maybe" (see chap. 8). Despite these challenges, some research suggests that the characteristics identified in creative adults also may be found in young people.

MacKinnon (1978) cited a 1968 study by Parloff, Datta, Kleman, and Handlon in which characteristics of creative adolescents paralleled those of adults. These researchers compared the performances of Annual Science Talent Search applicants who had been classified as "more creative" and "less creative" with samples of more and less creative adult mathematicians, architects, research scientists, and writers from the IPAR project. The groups were compared using the California Pychological Inventory. In both the adult and adolescent samples, the creative groups scored higher than the noncreative groups on factors that involved assertive self-assurance and adaptive autonomy. The groups were not differentiated by humanitarian conscience. It is interesting that on a factor associated with disciplined effectiveness (e.g., self-control, socialization, tolerance, achievement through conformity), the creative adolescents scored higher than less-creative adolescents, whereas creative adults scored lower than less- creative peers. In this sample at least, although creative adults and adolescents seemed to have many personality similarities, creative adolescents had to learn to work the system in order to have opportunities to exercise their creativity. Well-established creative adults were more able to function as free, nonconforming spirits. It is possible that assisting students in maneuvering this balance may be valuable. More recently, Feist (1999) also found that personality characteristics associated with creativity tend to be stable, at least from adolescence on. The characteristics that distinguish creative from less creative adolescents parallel those that distinguish comparable groups of adults, and these characteristics appear to remain consistent across time.

In his research on creative adolescents Walberg (1988) examined a national sample of 771 high school students from which he identified three groups: those winning competitive awards in science, those winning awards in the arts, and those not winning awards. The three groups were compared using a self-report biographical questionnaire. Members of both creative groups were more likely to describe themselves as friendly, outgoing, and self-confident, although they were also more likely than the third group to find books more interesting than people. They were more interested in detail, were more persistent, and had less time to relax.

Creative individuals were more likely to describe themselves as imaginative, curious, and expressive, and to value creativity. They did not see themselves as more likely to generate wild ideas, but did find satisfaction in expressing their ideas in new and original ways. They attached a greater importance to money than the less creative students, but when choosing the best characteristics to develop in life, they chose creativity more often and wealth and power less often. Their self-descriptions parallel in many ways the research that suggesting that creative adults are curious, flexible, imaginative, persistent, and likely to value creativity.

Differences were noted in the characteristics of those who had received awards for creativity in the arts and in the sciences. The scientists, as compared with the artists, were less social and less involved in organized school activities. They had more detailed plans for the future and expressed more confidence in their own intelligence. Artists tended to have more diversified interests and confidence in their creativity. In a follow-up study of 3,000 students, Walberg found no relationship between IQ score and membership in one of the prize-winning groups. The mean IQ for the sample was between 117 and 119, and he suggested that this IQ level provided additional support for the threshold theory among people of this age group.

Runco (1991) studied the relationships between independence and divergent thinking with three groups of preadolescent boys: exceptionally gifted boys as identified by IQ, exceptionally gifted boys selected for math and science abilities, and a control group of gifted boys. Even with a very restricted range of scores, independence and divergent thinking were moderately correlated. Keating (1983) reported that, as with adult creative mathematicians, junior high school boys who were highly able in math (and who thus, perhaps, had the potential for creative contribution in that field) had a high regard for theoretical values and a low interest in religious values. Unlike adult creative mathematicians, the junior high school students were low in aesthetic values.

Piirto (1998a) examined the writings of highly able and creative child writers. She defined 16 qualities that characterized their work, including playfulness with words, a sense of humor, an ear for the sounds of language, and the use of visual imagery and figures of speech. Many of these characteristics require cognitive or personality traits associated with creativity, such as metaphorical thought, visualization, openness to experience, and willingness to play with ideas. Watson and Schwartz (2000) found that the development of individual styles in children's drawings, some with higher aesthetic and creativity ratings, could begin as early as age 3. Leibermann (1977) associated playfulness and make-believe with higher divergent thinking in preschool children.

Johnson and Hatch (1990) examined the behavior of four highly original young children. All four children were independent, persistent, fluent, and expressively elaborate. However, each had a specialty area that was the focus of his or her creativity, and thus each expressed that creativity in a different way. This study lends support to the idea that creativity may be specific to a given discipline or area beginning at a very early age. Similarly, Han and Marvin (2002) found that the 109 second-grade students in their study demonstrated a range of creative abilities across different domains of performance tasks rather than a single uniform strength or weakness. On the other hand, Plucker (1999) reported that a strong content-general ability could explain much of the variance in creativity checklists reporting various creative activities for high school students. Clearly, some of the key issues regarding both the nature and measurement of creativity in adults are puzzling for young people as well.

Still, there are helpful trends. Although none of these studies assures that characteristics of creative children and creative adults are the same, or that creative adults necessarily had the same traits when they were children, the patterns are consistent enough to suggest that the characteristics discussed may well emerge in childhood. There certainly is no body of research suggesting that they do not. With that being the current state of the art, the most reasonable course of action is to support and encourage characteristics associated with creativity whenever possible. At the very least, our classrooms should be more flexible, responsive, and attuned to the wonders around us. At best, we may make a difference in the creativity of a young person who may one day bring greater knowledge or beauty into the world—sounds like a good risk.

JOURNEYING AND JOURNALING

1. Reflect on your own characteristics. Do you see evidence of traits associated with creativity in your own life? Have you seen them as you pursue your creative project?
2. Read a biography of a creative individual. Compare the individual's traits and experiences with those associated with creativity. You may want to compare an individual's autobiography with a biography written by someone else. Do the same characteristics emerge? Are some emphasized more in one work than the other?
3. Invite a panel of creative people to visit your college or university class. (I have sometimes called university department chairs and asked them to nominate the most creative person in the department.) Ask them about their creative process and activities. Find out how they are alike and different and if you can identify traits listed in the chapter. How did you respond to the speakers? Were all the characteristics associated with creativity manifested in ways that were comfortable for you? Reflect on what these individuals might have been like as children.
4. Think about the dichotomies Csikszentimihalyi described as characteristic of creative individuals. Examine the characteristics of a

media character who might be considered creative. Is the person portrayed simplistically or with depth of character?

5. Pick one or two characteristics associated with creativity that you would like to increase in your own life. For example, you might want to become more open to experience or more persistent. For a month, try to exercise that characteristic whenever you can. Record your efforts and see if you find the characteristics can be changed.

6. This book considers the challenge of identifying and supporting characteristics associated with creativity in students. Reflect on how similar characteristics are supported or not supported in teachers. In your school, how are teachers who take risks, espouse novel ideas, or persist in their own tasks received? How might the acceptance of teachers by others affect the development of creativity in the classroom?

REFERENCES

Albert, R. S. (1990). Identity, experiences, and career choice among the exceptionally gifted and eminent. In M. A. Runco & R. S. Albert (Eds.), *Theories of creativity* (pp. 13–34). Newbury Park, CA: Sage.

Albert, R. S. (1993, May). *The contribution of early family history to the achievement of eminence.* Paper presented at the Henry B. and Jocelyn Wallace National Research Symposium on Talent Development, Iowa City, IA.

Baer, J. (1998). Gender differences in the effects of extrinsic motivation on creativity. *Journal of Creative Behavior, 32,* 18–37.

Barron, F. (1968). *Creativity and personal freedom.* Princeton, NJ: Van Nostrand.

Barron, F. (1969). *Creative person and creative process.* New York: Holt, Rinehart & Winston.

Barron, F., & Welsh, G. S. (1952). Artistic perception as a possible factor in personality style: Its measurement by a figure preference test. *Journal of Psychology, 33,* 199–203.

Belenky, M. F., Clinchy, B. M., Goldberger, N. R., & Tarule, J. M. (1997). *Women's ways of knowing: The development of self, voice, and mind* (19th anniversary ed.). New York: Basic Books.

Borland, J. H. (1988). Cognitive controls, cognitive styles and divergent production in gifted preadolescents. *Journal for the Education of the Gifted, 11*(4), 57–82.

Clark, B. (1986). *Optimizing learning.* Columbus, OH: Merrill.

Csikzsentimihalyi, M. (1994). The domain of creativity. In D. H. Feldman, M. Csikszentimihalyi, & H. Gardner (Eds.), *Changing the world: A framework for the study of creativity* (pp. 135–158). Westport, CT: Praeger.

Csikszentmihalyi, M. (1996). *Creativity: Flow and the psychology of discovery and invention.* New York: HarperCollins.

Dacey, J. S. (1989). *Fundamentals of creative thinking.* Lexington, MA: Lexington Books.

Dansky, J., & Silverman, I. (1980). Make-believe: A mediator of the relationship between play and associative fluency. *Child Development, 51,* 576–579.

Dillon, J. T. (1988). *Questioning and teaching.* New York: Teachers College Press.

Fabricant, M., Svitak, S., & Kenschaft, P. C. (1990). Why women succeed in mathematics. *Mathematics Teacher, 83,* 150–154.

Feist, G. J, (1999). The influence of personality on artistic and scientific creativity. In R. J. Sternberg (Ed.), *Handbook of creativity* (pp. 273–296). New York: Cambridge University Press.

Gardner, H. (1982). *Art, mind, and brain.* New York: Basic Books.

Gardner, H. (1993). *Creating minds.* New York: Basic Books.

Gardner, H. (1994). The creators' patterns, In D. H. Feldman, M. Csikszentmihalyi, & H. Gardner (Eds.), *Changing the world: A framework for the study of creativity* (pp. 69–84). Westport, CT: Praeger.

Gardner, H., & Winner, E. (1982). The child is father to the metaphor. In H. Gardner (Ed.), *Art, mind and brain* (pp. 158–167). New York: Basic Books.

Gaynor, J. L., & Runco, M. A. (1992). Family size, birth order, age interval and the creativity of children. *Journal of Creative Behavior, 26,* 108–118.

Getzels, J. W., & Jackson, P. W. (1962). *Creativity and intelligence.* New York: Wiley.

Ghiselin, B. (1985). *The creative process.* Berkeley, CA: University of California Press.

Gilligan, C., Lyons, N., & Hammar, T. (Eds.). (1990*). Making connections.* Cambridge, MA: Harvard University Press.

Guilford, J. P. (1986). *Creative talents: Their nature, use and development.* Buffalo, NY: Bearly.

Gustin, W. C. (1985). The development of exceptional research mathematicians. In B. Bloom (Ed.), *Developing talent in young people* (pp. 270–331). New York: Ballantine.

Han, K., & Marvin, C. (2002). Multiple creativities? Investigating domain specificity of creativity in young children. *Gifted Child Quarterly, 46*(2), 98–109.

Hanaford, P. A. (1882). *Daughters of America.* Jersey Heights, NJ: True and Company.

Helson, R. (1983). Creative mathematicians. In R. Albert (Ed.), *Genius and eminence: The social psychology of creativity and exceptional achievement* (pp. 211–230). London: Pergamon.

hooks, b. (1995). *Art on my mind: Visual politics.* New York: The New Press.

Innamorato, G. (1998). Creativity in the development of scientific giftedness: Educational implications. *Roeper Review, 21,* 54–59.

Interview with Midori. (1992, October 1). Entertainment Weekly, *Ann Arbor News,* p. 5.

Isaksen, S. G. (Ed.). (1987). *Frontiers of creativity research: Beyond the basics.* Buffalo, NY: Bearly.

Johnson, L. G., & Hatch, J. A. (1990). A descriptive study of the creative and social behavior of four highly original young children. *Journal of Creative Behavior, 24,* 205–224.

John-Steiner, V. (2000). *Creative collaboration.* New York: Oxford University Press.

Keating, D. P. (1983). The creative potential of mathematically gifted boys. In R. Albert (Ed.), *Genius and eminence: The social psychology of creativity and exceptional achievement* (pp. 128–137). London: Pergamon.

Leibermann, J. (1977). *Playfulness: Its relationship to imagination and creativity.* New York: Academic Press.

Leno, J. (1992, September 30). [Interview with D. Hoffman]. In (H. Kushinick), *Tonight Show.* New York: NBC.

Lutzer, V. D. (1991). Gender differences in preschoolers' ability to interpret common metaphors. *Journal of Creative Behavior, 25,* 69–74.

MacKinnon, D. W. (1978). *In search of human effectiveness.* Buffalo, NY: Creative Education Foundation.

Mednick, S. A. (1962). The associative basis of the creative process. *Psychological Review, 69,* 220–232.

Moyers, B. (1990). *A world of ideas II.* New York: Doubleday.

Myers, I. B. (1962). *Myers-Briggs type indicator manual.* Princeton, NJ: Educational Testing Service.

Neihart, M. (1998). Creativity, the arts, and madness. *Roeper Review, 21,* 47–50.

Piechowski, M. M., & Cunningham, K. (1985). Patterns of overexcitability in a group of artists. *Journal of Creative Behavior, 19,* 153–174.

Piirto, J. (1998a). *Understanding those who create* (2nd ed.). Dayton, OH: Psychology Press.

Piirto, J. (1998b). Themes in the lives of successful contemporary U.S. women creative writers. *Roeper Review, 21,* 60–70.

Plucker, J. (1999). Reanalysis of student responses to creativity checklists: Evidence of content generality. *Journal of Creative Behavior, 33*(2), 126–137.

Reis, S. M. (1987). We can't change what we don't recognize: Understanding the special needs of gifted females. *Gifted Child Quarterly, 31,* 83–89.

Reis, S. M. (1998). *Work left undone.* Mansfield Center, CT: Creative Learning Press.

Roe, A. (1952). *The making of a scientist.* New York: Dodd Mead.

Rothenberg, A. (1990). *Creativity and madness.* Baltimore: Johns Hopkins University Press.

Runco, M. A. (1991). *Divergent thinking.* Norwood, NJ: Ablex.

Runco, M. A. (1992). The evaluative, valuative, and divergent thinking of children. *Journal of Creative Behavior, 25,* 311–319.

Runco, M. A. (1993, May). *Giftedness as critical and creative thinking.* Paper presented at the Henry B. and Jocelyn Wallace National Research Symposium, Iowa City, IA.

Runco, M. A., Johnson, J., & Gaynor, J. R. (1999). The judgmental bases of creativity and implications for the study of gifted youth. In A. S. Fishkin, B. Cramond, & P. Olszewski-Kubilius (Eds.), *Investigating creativity in youth: research and methods* (pp. 115–143). Cresskill, NY: Hampton Press.

Sadker, D. (2002). An educator's primer on the gender war. *Phi Delta Kappan, 84*(3), 235–240, 244.

Sadker, D., & Sadker, M. (1986). Sexism in the classroom: From grade school to graduate school. *Phi Delta Kappan, 67,* 512–515.

Sadker, D., & Sadker, M. (1995). *Failing at fairness: How American schools cheat girls.* New York: Simon & Schuster.

Schlichter, C., Palmer, W. R., & Palmer, R. (1993*). Thinking Smart: A primer of the Talents Unlimited model.* Mansfield Center, CT: Creative Learning Press.

Spielberg, S. (1985, July 15). The autobiography of Peter Pan. *Time, 126*(2), 62–63.

Starko, A. J. (1989). Problem finding in creative writing: An exploratory study. *Journal for the Education of the Gifted, 12,* 172–186.

Sternberg, R. J. (Ed.). (1988). *The nature of creativity.* New York: Cambridge University Press.

Sternberg, R. J., & O'Hara, L. A. (1999). Creativity and intelligence. In R. J. Sternberg (Ed.), *Handbook of creativity* (pp. 261–272). New York: Cambridge University Press.

Tardif, T. Z., & Sternberg, R. J. (1988). What do we know about creativity? In R. J. Sternberg (Ed.), *The nature of creativity* (pp. 429–440). New York: Cambridge University Press.

Torrance, E. P. (1962). *Guiding creative talent.* Englewood Cliffs, NJ: Prentice-Hall.

Walberg, H. J. (1988). Creativity and talent as learning. In R. J. Sternberg (Ed.), *The nature of creativity* (pp. 340–361). New York: Cambridge University Press

Watson, J. W., & Schwartz, S. N. (2000). The development of individual styles in children's drawings. *New Directions for Child and Adolescent Development, 90,* 49–63.

Weisberg, R. W. (1986). *Creativity: Genius and other myths.* New York: Freeman.

chapter 4

Creativity and Talent Development

After school on Wednesday afternoon, Ms. Moran sat at her desk, alternately gazing at the fall landscape and the pile of papers on her desk. She had started the year full of anticipation. This was going to be the year her writing program really worked. She was not going to begin the year by asking what students had done over their summer vacation. She would free their imaginations for new, original stories. They would solve problems by writing about them, invent new characters, and experiment with different types of literature. It had all sounded like such a good idea, but now she was beginning to wonder. The first set of stories all sounded about the same—and a whole lot like the example she had given during the prewriting activity. Didn't these kids have any ideas of their own? Now what?

If we as teachers hope to help students increase their creativity, we need to determine which aspects of creativity can be influenced and what our role is in that process. As the preceding chapters make clear, there are diverse points of view as to the origin of creativity comes, how it is exhibited, and what types of activities might encourage it. Our role as teachers will vary depending on the theories and models of creativity we follow. If, as did Plato, we believe that creativity stems from the intervention of the muses, there is not much we can do (unless we can determine what attracts the muses!). If we believe Skinner, we will reward each endeavor that approximates a creative response in an effort to increase such responses. If we favor a humanist position, we will emphasize an atmosphere that supports mental health. Any attempts to enhance creativity must be grounded in a perspective or set of perspectives. This chapter outlines some of the key research that has influenced the recommendations to follow, and the strategies for creating a classroom in which creativity can flourish.

Imagine a classroom in which creativity is welcomed. If you are like many teachers, you may picture a wildly colorful room, busy students, and an enthusiastic—and perhaps eccentric—teacher. Our stereotypes of teaching for creativity sometimes lean toward Robin Williams' costumed character leaping across desks in the movie *Dead Poets Society* (or perhaps, more currently, something out of Hogwarts). To be truthful, I probably would love to be a student in a either place. Still, neither my temperament nor my agility make it likely that I will be levitating feathers, dressing up or clambering across the furniture in most of my classes. Does that mean my ability to create a classroom full of creativity is limited? I hope not. I believe there are at least three things we can do as teachers to help create a classroom in which creativity can flourish: teach the skills and attitudes of creativity, teach the creative methods of the disciplines, and develop a problem-friendly classroom.

Teaching the skills and attitudes of creativity entails teaching students explicitly about creativity. It includes teaching about the lives of creative individuals, the nature of the creative process, and strategies that can be used to generate creative ideas. Chapter 5 focuses on teaching the skills and attitudes of creativity.

Teaching the creative methods of the disciplines requires teaching students how individuals are creative in the disciplines they study. In science, for example, this type of teaching entails learning the processes of scientific investigation, in addition to the concepts and generalizations resulting from such investigations in the past. This is more complex than teaching the five steps of the scientific method, although that is a place to start. Real science rarely progresses in such neat and predictable steps. Learning how creative scientists operate entails learning the kinds of questions scientists ask and the methods they use to investigate them. It examines the obstacles that can impede progress, the circuitous paths that can lead to success, and the skills necessary to conduct investigations. Parallel kinds of knowledge can be examined for any field in which creativity emerges. Chapter 6 examines teaching content areas in ways that are compatible with this type of creativity.

Developing a problem-friendly classroom entails creating a classroom atmosphere in which seeking and solving problems is welcomed. The concept of a problem-friendly classroom is based on three major knowledge bases: research on problem-finding and creativity, research on creativity and motivation, and research on talent development. These bodies of knowledge are the subjects of this chapter. Additional information on classroom procedures and structures that are supportive of creativity are addressed in chapter 7. In brief, a problem-friendly classroom provides experiences with choice, provides informational feedback in assessment, encourages self-assessment, uses rewards thoughtfully, teaches both cooperation and independence, encourages questioning and experimentation, and addresses appropriate stage(s) of talent development.

These suggestions for a problem-friendly, or creativity-friendly, approach to teaching are based largely on three bodies of research: studies of talent development by Bloom (1985) and his associates as well as Csikszentmihalyi (1996), investigations of problem finding, and research on motivation and creativity, particularly by Amabile (1989, 1996) and Collins and Amabile (1999). This chapter offers a brief overview of each of these areas and how they may influence our classroom choices. Throughout the remainder of the book, you should see the influence of these theories in both the organization of information and the content presented The theories may provide an organizing framework for our own reflections on creativity, classrooms, and children.

STUDIES OF TALENT DEVELOPMENT

The studies of talent development conducted by Bloom (1985) and his associates did not deal with creativity per se. The research was designed to examine "the processes by which individuals who have reached the highest levels of accomplishment in selected fields have been helped to develop their capabilities so fully" (Bloom, 1985, p. 1). It examined young adults of extraordinary accomplishment in a variety of areas including athletic, aesthetic, and cognitive or intellectual fields. In each field, the researchers contacted experts who could help specify criteria that could be used to identify outstanding individuals. In the area of athletics, subjects included swimmers who had earned a place on an Olympic swimming team in a sprint event and tennis players whose top rankings had been determined by major tennis organizations and publications. In the aesthetic areas, subjects included pianists who had been finalists in one or more of six major international competitions and sculptors who had won both a Guggenheim Fellowship and a National Endowment for the Arts award. Subjects in the cognitive areas were selected from research mathematicians who were winners of Sloan prizes in mathematics and research neurologists who had been awarded a 5-year special grant for research from the National Institutes of Health. Both the mathematicians and the neurologists also were identified through frequent citations in the Science Citation Index and expert nominations. Most subjects were younger than 35 years at the time they were identified. Extensive interviews were conducted with the subjects, the subjects' parents, and major teachers who had influenced the subjects' development. Approximately 25 subjects in each talent area were studied.

Although the talent development studies were not designed to center on creativity, it is clear that they chronicle the development of many creative individuals. Although it is possible to question the degree of creativity necessary in swimming sprints, or perhaps even in tennis, it would be hard to argue that the nation's most recognized young pianists, sculptors, research mathematicians, and research neurologists did not represent creativity of the highest level. As such, the generalizations on the development of talent hold promise as keys to the development of creativity as manifested in a variety of disciplines.

Phases of Learning

All the subjects, regardless of area, spent an enormous amount of time developing their talent. For example, the pianists had, on the average, spent 17 years studying, practicing, and performing before being identified for the talent development studies. This finding rings true with theorists such as Gruber (Gruber & Davis, 1988, Gruber & Wallace, 1999) and Perkins (1981), who emphasized the importance of time and persistence in developing creative ideas. However, time alone is not sufficient. I, too, have played the piano for over 17 years, yet I am hardly a candidate for such a study. What the learner does with the time, how he or she does the activity, and how the activity changes over the years are critical to the development of talent and creativity.

The lengthy process of talent development was divided into three phases, first identified in interviews with concert pianists. Three phases emerged as researchers examined changes in "(a) the learners' relationship with the piano and the world of music; (b) the parents' and teachers' roles in the process of development; and (c) the motivators, rewards, and symbols of success" (Sosniak, 1985, p. 409). Although the phases overlap, the timing varies, and the edges may be fuzzy, the three general areas were consistent across talent areas and may provide important clues to the processes underlying the development of creativity.

Phase 1: The Early Years. In the early years of talent development, learning was playful. Learners explored their fields: they ran their hands across keyboards, played with numbers, and experimented with paint, clay, and paper. Instruction was personal, informal, and enjoyable. Teachers were warm and affectionate, child-centered, and nurturing. The emphasis was on exploring and curiosity, and early efforts were met with enthusiasm and approval. As the learners developed skills, they identified principles and patterns that made their learning more systematic. These discoveries helped them become aware that music, art, math, or science were not just areas for fun, but that they could be studied seriously.

The timing of the early years as well as the other phases varied from discipline to discipline. The pianists, for example, began studying formally about the age of 6 years. The mathematicians did not begin formal study of mathematics until high school. Thus the early years in one field may occur 10 years after it occurs in another. The key is not chronological age, but experience in the field studied. Whenever the first phase occurs, it provides the inviting atmosphere and early hook of the field that sustain talented individuals through the intensity of the second phase.

Phase 2: The Middle Years. At some point during the early period of exploration, it became clear that tinkering around was not enough. To develop effectively, the student needed to master the techniques, principles, and vocabulary of the chosen field. If the key word in the early years is exploration, the dominant theme in the middle years is precision. Pianists played the same thing over and over, consciously making slight variations. Mathematicians worked and reworked the same complex problems. The emphasis in all fields was technical mastery.

The subjects' teachers during this period were very different from teachers of the early years. Entering the middle years virtually always meant a change in instructor. Effective instructors in the middle years were knowledgeable, thorough, disciplined, and systematic. "The personal bond between teachers and students shifted from one of love to one of respect" (Sosniak, 1985, pp. 416–417). Teachers were not just demanding taskmasters, but advocates and encouragers as well. They assisted learners in finding and attending special camps, entering competitions, and locating opportunities for involvement in the chosen field. These efforts allowed students both to improve technically and to enter into the communication and culture of their field. Eventually, middle-year teachers became instrumental in guiding students to new instructors for the third stage.

Phase 3: The Later Years. In the third phase, learners make the transition from technical precision to art, regardless of discipline. During this time students find their voice—their own interpretations, styles, problems, and research areas. Although during the mastery of technical skills much time may be spent in imitation, students who are to progress must go beyond that. Sosniak (1985) quoted one teacher: "That's fine, if it's a stimulant [to creativity], but not if it remains as a product .... We all learn by imitation of a sort. But we have [to have] a way of making it our own" (p. 420).

In the talent development studies, the relationship between teacher and student during this period was full of contradictions. Teachers were accomplished professionals at the top of their fields. They demanded a tremendous amount of time and dedication and had little patience for anything less than perfection. Students reported being terrified before lessons or in tears afterward until they adjusted to a new level of commitment. They found that the technical precision that served so well in previous experiences sometimes had to be adjusted or sacrificed for the artistry demanded by beginning professionalism. The pianists had to find their own interpretations, not mimic their masters. Researchers could no longer focus on the tried and true. Important research demanded that they view problems in new ways and generate new ideas, techniques, and questions.

In one sense, it is this stage at which creativity appears. After all, it is here that we find the truly new discoveries, proofs, and sculptures. Yet those accomplishments had their roots in each of the stages that went before. A teacher's role in developing creativity must vary according to the students' experience with the subject matter and stage of learning. If Ms. Moran, at the beginning of the chapter, is teaching primary grades, her students will have little experience with writing and almost certainly will be in phase 1. They will need a playful approach to writing, exploring words in a warm, supportive atmosphere. She will need to get them hooked on writing if they are to progress further.

If Ms. Moran is teaching older students, some of them may already be enthusiastic writers, but lacking the technical skills to produce high-quality work. In that case, careful analysis of the work of expert writers, study of the techniques of plot and character development, and exercises to build vocabulary may be the most effective means to improve their work. The students may practice writing in the style of various authors, creating passages that convey a particular mood, or they may rewrite a particular piece numerous times until it is as tight and precise as possible. If students do not move from exploration and fun to mastery of technique, they can never improve. On the other hand, attempts to impose the precision of techniques before there has been sufficient exploration and enjoyment to foster commitment to the discipline are likely to fail.

If Ms. Moran is teaching advanced students or working at a professional writers' retreat, her dilemma is somewhat different. She needs to help her students go beyond her examples, to see multiple ways to approach a task and find their own, unique voices. This can be a painful and difficult transition. Students who have always been successful imitating others may find it frightening to be themselves without a correct way of working. They will need to develop their own point of view and assessment of success. Their previous mastery of the standard techniques of the discipline can help them develop both the confidence and the judgment necessary to succeed at this level. At this point, Ms. Moran's students probably will spend little time in class and long hours writing. They may meet for individual critiques or peer editing groups. Emphasis will be on identifying the messages and techniques that characterize each individual and how that writer works most effectively.

Thinking About the Classroom

Think about the content area(s) you teach. Do you consider yourself primarily a phase 1, 2, or 3 teacher? Is your most important role introducing a subject area and developing interest, honing technical skill, or eliciting artistry? Do you teach in a manner that is effective for that stage? What would you do if one or more students were ready for the next stage? Compare your responses with someone who teaches the same level and subject you do.

Home Influences in Talent Development

Of course, teachers were not the only important influences on the development of individual talent. Learners also were influenced by ideas, values, and practices in the home. Sloane (1985) discussed home influences on the development of athletes, pianists, and sculptors. She described the parents in these homes as "hardworking, active people ... [who] wanted to be involved in something, learning about something, working on something, as often as possible" (p. 440). The families valued achievement and looked down on wasting time, shirking responsibilities, or doing a sloppy job. The parents provided models of high standards and hard work.

In addition, many parents demonstrated interest in the general area of talent developed by the child. Whether as participants or spectators, they valued athletics, music, or the arts. Frequently the parents were the source of the students' first exposure to the talent field. Some homes were continually filled with music. Other families visited art museums or played sports together. As children expressed interest in these activities, informal instruction began. Parents also initiated formal instruction, deciding, for example, when students began tennis or piano lessons. They monitored practice periods and provided an enthusiastic audience for beginning efforts.

The one variation in this pattern was observed with the sculptors. Few sculptors were involved in formal instruction during elementary years, nor did they practice regularly, as did the athletes and pianists. There was, however, an emphasis on independent learning and working alone, with parents as resources for needed skills in beginning projects such as artwork or model building.

As all the learners progressed, parents' roles changed. Increasingly expert teachers, demanding practice schedules, and distant competitions consumed an enormous amount of the family resources. Parents worked to manage logistics, smooth obstacles, and provide encouragement in times of difficulty. Family routines and activities frequently were rearranged to accommodate lessons, competitions, and other events. Parents' continued interest and support, both financial and emotional, were essential elements in the learners' talent development in athletic and aesthetic areas. Although parents of research mathematicians and neurologists often were not as involved in supervising practice periods or transporting students to special lessons in early childhood, they too provided support and valued the talent areas. Parents of these learners valued learning, independence, curiosity, and questioning. They were willing to provide information, chemistry sets, models, and books, and they encouraged their children to pursue independent interests (Bloom, 1985).

Teachers certainly cannot take on the important role of parents in developing talent. We can, however, sometimes influence parents and supplement the support and encouragement they provide.

Csikszentmihalyi's Biographies

Biographical studies by Csikszentmihalyi (1996) provide examples not identical to, but often supportive of, Bloom's stages. Csikszentmihalyi's subjects reported childhoods that varied widely, but were consistently characterized by a prodigious curiosity. As phase 1 individuals explored the world playfully, the individuals interviewed in Csikszentmihalyi's studies described a drive to explore the world in a variety of domains. Csikszentmihalyi (1996) cited a story told about Charles Darwin's youth:

One day as he was walking in the woods near his home he noticed a large beetle scurry to hide under the bark of a tree. Young Charles collected beetles, and this was one he didn't have in his collection. So he ran to the tree, peeled off the bark, and grabbed the insect. But as he did so he saw that there were two more specimens hiding there. The bugs were so large that he couldn't hold more than one in each hand, so he popped the third in his mouth and ran all the way home with the three beetles, one of which was trying to escape down his throat. (pp. 156–157)

Certainly, not all early explorations Csikszentmihalyi described were quite as challenging to life and limb as young Darwin's, but most individuals did recall joy in early exploration. Future astronomers spent fascinated hours stargazing; writers and artists experimented with forms. In many cases, parents' efforts to provide intellectual stimulation and support were important factors in the discovery and development of talent. In other cases, parents were absent or unsupportive. School per se was rarely mentioned as a source of talent development, but individual teachers were credited. Two main factors were noted about the teachers singled out as important influences. First, the teachers noticed the students, believed in their abilities, and cared. Second, the teachers showed that care by providing greater challenges and opportunities to develop talent than those received by the rest of the class. For example, Rosalyn Yalow, a Nobel prize winner in medicine (although trained as a physicist), recalled her interest in mathematics being awakened when she was 12 years old.

I was a good student, and they always gave me lots of extra work to do. I took geometry from Mr. Lippy. He soon brought me into his office. He'd give me math puzzles and math beyond what was formally given in the class, and the same thing happened in chemistry. (Csikszentmihalyi, 1996, p. 174)

Some students found the recognition and support of their talents in extracurricular activities. Still others, particularly in the arts, found little or no support for their talent in their K–12 experiences. For many of Csikszentmihalyi's (1996) subjects, college or graduate school represented a high point of life. It was the place where they found their voice, identified their vocation, and were exposed to teachers who appreciated their unique strengths.

Although these biographical studies do not break down into neat phases, they do provide examples of a progression from playful exploration to the identification of adult voice and direction. Along the way, these individuals required exposure to advanced skills and challenges commensurate with their emerging talents

Related Research on the Development of Creativity and Talent

Other researchers and theorists also have investigated the development of talent and creativity over time. Gardner (1982) proposed an informal model of artistic development based on his studies of artwork in young children. During the first years of life, he believed, children are involved in developing basic sensory and motor capacities and in constructing knowledge about the world around them. These activities are not art, but are a prerequisite for artistic activity. One cannot use symbol systems (color, lines, shapes, and language) to express some aspect of the world until the world becomes understandable, at least to some degree.

The second stage, from approximately age 2 to 7 years, is a time during which children's abilities to use, manipulate, and transform symbols increase at a rapid pace. This type of development occurs across cultures with very different symbol systems. By the age of 7 or 8 years, children have a broad idea of how the major symbol systems of the culture work. In our culture, they can use language, understand what makes a story, have a sense of what makes a piece of music, read pictures, and produce works of art that approach standards of balance, composition, and so forth. Gardner (1982) dubbed the child at this stage an incipient artist because he possesses the raw materials or mental processes necessary to become involved in artistic processes.

During ages 7 to 13 years, children are ready to develop as artists. Although they may have a great deal to learn about techniques in various media, composition, perspective, and so on, they improve quickly when given instruction. Students of this age who show little sensitivity to differences in painting style or little tendency to produce metaphorical language can be trained in these skills in a few weeks. This amenability to instruction is in marked contrast to that of students just a few years older.

In the fourth stage, beginning in later adolescence, students show much less enthusiasm for developing artistic skills and less capacity to "immerse [themselves] fully in an expressive medium" (Gardner, 1982, p. 215). They are not less intelligent nor necessarily less motivated than younger children. It is possible that the key may be found in Piaget's developmental theories. During adolescence, children develop their critical analysis skills at a new level. If these newfound reasoning skills find adolescent artistic efforts less than satisfactory, students may no longer be motivated to pursue artistic endeavors. Gardner suggested two measures that may ease this transition. First, students should be provided with instruction in preadolescence that allows them to develop sufficient skills to produce work that has merit. They should then be less likely to reject it. Second, students should be gradually encouraged to look critically at their own work during early adolescence, trying different approaches to a problem and seeing how they might improve. In that way, students can become accustomed to the process of criticism and experience its benefits before developing advanced levels of critical analysis. Both suggestions fit neatly into the middle years of Bloom's (1985) talent development model, providing techniques that will allow high-quality performance.

Runco (1991) cited research supporting two broad personality and cognitive transformations in the development of eminence in persons with high cognitive ability. The first is the development of outstanding creative ability during, but not entirely through, the first two decades of life. The second begins in adolescence and entails the transformation of creative abilities into "a well-integrated set of cognitive skills, career-focused interests and values, specific creative personality dispositions, and moderately high ambitions" (p. 4). The earlier this transformation occurs, the more likely the person is to attain eminence. This stage, too, is reminiscent of Bloom's talent development phases, with the exploratory, creative phase preceding a more focused development of discipline-related attitudes and skills. Neither Gardner nor Runco dealt with the issues of Bloom's third phase, in which high-level individual artistry comes into play. The omission is understandable, because only the most accomplished few in any field attain this stage. Those of us dealing with kindergarten through 12th-grade (K–12) education are likely to have little influence at that level except in directing students to master teachers, unless we ourselves are world-class masters of a particular body of content. We may begin to help students find their individual voices, but probably not at the level attained by Bloom's subjects. However, all of us—master and beginner, student and teacher—may be involved in some aspect of problem finding.

PROBLEM FINDING

Problem finding, or the identification and framing of problems, is the second key concept and body of literature that underlies this book. In chapter 1, I note that individuals undertake creative activities to communicate ideas or solve problems. Problem finding provides the why for much creativity.

The most quoted passage in problem finding literature is probably from Einstein and Infeld:

> The formulation of a problem is often more important than its solution, which may be merely a matter of mathematical or experimental skill. To raise new questions, new possibilities, to regard old problems from a new angle, requires imagination and marks real advance in science. (Dillon, 1982, p. 98)

In a similar vein, Mackworth (1965) noted:

> Most people are quite clear by now that there are real differences between scientists who are largely solving problems and those who are mainly raising questions .... Problem finding is more important than problem solving. Indeed the greatest contribution that can be made nowadays is to formulate new and testable ideas; the scientist who does not speculate is no scientist at all. (pp. 51–52)

A similar argument could be made in virtually any discipline. A painter who merely duplicates work created by others or an author who replicates others' writing probably will not be called creative or make an important contribution to his or her field. Seeking the piece worth painting or the story worth telling is at the crux of the creative process and key to the progress of the disciplines. If we are to encourage students to be creative, we must learn how to help them find problems.

Some theorists have examined the nature of problem finding and compared it to problem solving. Mackworth (1965) discussed the nature of problem finding in basic research. He envisioned basic researchers "grubbing around the roots of knowledge ... looking for the problems ... not just to hit the targets but to find them" (p. 54). He pointed out the difficult paradox that characterizes problem finding in science. Successful scientists must be knowledgeable. The scientific process frequently involves comparisons between a framework of knowledge and experimental data. However, the key to discovery is identifying the times when this faithful framework must be discarded and a new framework identified. In such a case, not just the solution but the very nature of the problem has changed.

This challenge points up the key role of knowledge in the creative process. It is necessary for the creator to have enough knowledge to take him or her to the edge of the field, but still to be flexible enough to go over the border!

The Nature of Problems

To help students become successful problem finders, we must understand problems. Problems come in various shapes, sizes, and forms, some with more potential than others. A "problem" is not necessarily a difficulty; it may be a shift in perspective or a perceived opportunity. Blues musician Moby said:

> I think that creativity can create a lot of problems. I think that creativty can solve a lot of problems .... I don't see the world as a big mess of problems that need to be solved; I see the world as a really interesting miasma of things going on. And something that looks like a problem to us right now might end up looking like a wonderful thing from a future perspective. (Vaske, 2002, p. 122)

There are several ways to categorize problems.

Getzels (1964) distinguished between presented and discovered problem situations. These differ according to the degree to which the problem, method, and solution are already known. More recently, Getzels (1987) identified three problem types. In a type 1 problem, there is a known formulation, a known method of solution, and a solution known to others but not to the problem solver. Students who have been taught the formula for computing the area of a square use this formula to calculate the area of a particular square. Most classroom problems are of this type. The teacher presents students with a problem and expects that they will arrive at a specific answer through a particular means.

Type 2 problems also take the form of a presented problem, but the method of solution is not known to the problem solver. In this case, students might be asked to calculate the area of a rectangle before they have been introduced to that particular formula. They must discover a satisfactory method before they can solve the problem.

With type 3 problems, there is no presented problem. The problem itself must be discovered, and neither the problem nor its solution may be known to anyone. In Getzels' series of examples, a type 3 problem might entail drawing a rectangle on the board and asking, "How many questions might be posed about this rectangle?" or "Pose an important question about this rectangle and solve it." Type 1 problems primarily involve memory and retrieval processes. Type 2 problems demand analysis and reasoning. Only type 3 problems, in which the problem itself becomes a goal, necessitate problem finding.

Thinking About the Classroom

Examine your lesson plans for the week. Tally how many opportunities you have planned for presenting type 1 (presented),
type 2 (emergent), and type 3 (discovered) problems. Try to plan
at least one problem of each type.

Csikszentmihalyi and Sawyer (1993) proposed that the creative process varies in presented and discovered problems. On the basis of interviews with eminent contemporary creators in a variety of fields, they
noted a common structure in descriptions of creative insight. Their subjects described four stages closely paralleling Wallas' stages described in
chapter 2: (a) hard work and research preceding the moment of insight,
(b) a period of idle time alone, (c) a moment of insight, and (d) elaboration needed to bring the idea to fruition. However, although the stages remained relatively constant, subjects described them as occurring in time
frames from a few hours to several years. Csikszentmihalyi and Sawyer
suggested that these widely varying time frames may represent the ends of
a continuum of creative insights ranging from short-term presented problems to long-term discovered problems. Figure 4.1 illustrates their proposed models of presented and discovered problem solving. Although
both types of problems demand input from a domain and field, as would
fit Csikszentmihalyi's system model, the information necessary to identify
and solve discovered problems is likely to span several domains and
fields, whereas presented problems are already part of existing structures.
In this framework, presented problems may be thought of as part of the
normal work in a particular field, whereas discovered problems require
the creator to think outside the usual boundaries, question existing paradigms, and ask questions no one else is asking.

Another model for categorizing problems comes from Dillon (1982),
who distinguished the levels of problems as existent, emergent, or potential. An existent problem is evident. A problematic situation exists, and the
appropriate activity is to recognize it and solve it. This is the type of situation usually referred to in the commonplace of the word problem. Something is troublesome or standing in the way of a desired state. For the
situation to be resolved, the obstacle must be recognized and a solution
found. School problems are almost always existent. The teacher has the
problems and presents them to the students to solve.

An emergent problem is implicit rather than evident. It must be discovered before it can be solved. In this case, the appropriate activity is to

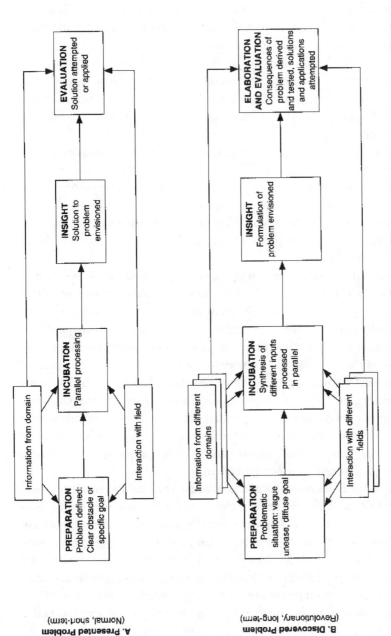

FIG. 4.1. Csikszentmihalyi and Sawyer's (1993) proposed models of presented and discovered problem solving. From *The Nature of Insight* (p. 338), by R. J. Sternberg and J. Davidson, Cambridge, MA: MIT Press. Copyright © 1995 by MIT Press. Reprinted with permission.

probe the data for an unclear, hidden, or incipient problem and elements of a possible solution. Emergent problems are important to people in management dealing with complex situations and data sets. A good manager is able to discover what the problem is before setting out to solve it. The Framing Problems stage of the creative problem-solving process (Treffinger, Isaksen, & Dorval, 2000, 2003) refers to emergent problems. Problem solvers are instructed to examine all the data in a given situation in order to identify problems to address. Chapter 5 discusses using Creative Problem Solving in schools.

Students also may have the opportunity to discover emergent problems in school content. This is probably most common in math, in which students may be asked to find the errors in a problem or solution, but such discoveries could also be appropriate in other disciplines. For example, students could identify art forgeries or false historical artifacts using their knowledge of appropriate content as clues to problems with the objects presented.

A potential problem does not yet exist as a problem. Its elements exist and may strike the discoverer as an unformed problem, interesting situation, or idea worth elaborating. By combining the elements in some way, the observer creates or invents a problem where none previously existed. Perhaps potential problems are most clearly seen in the invention process. No one was assigned the problem of inventing stick-on pull-off notes. However, some astute observer was able to combine the elements of temporary glue with office logistics and identify a problem that had previously gone unrecognized. In a parallel manner, an author finds a story that must be told where none existed before. If students devise original story lines or plan scientific investigations to test a question of interest, they have discovered their own problems.

In examining the means teachers may use to enhance creativity in students, one of the issues we must address is how we may vary the types of problems students solve in schools. Certainly, the vast majority of problems assigned to students would be categorized by Getzels as type 1 problems. The problem is clearly defined by the teacher or text, and the students are expected to derive the correct answer using the correct methods. Only rarely are students required to identify emergent problems or even to identify multiple ways to solve a problem. Still more rarely are students asked to create problems to solve. Yet if we consider the processes necessary for problem solving in real life, it is clear that real-world challenges do not come in neat packages with an answer key in the back. The kinds of problems that matter must be discovered and focused before they are solved. Although there is little research on problem finding by young people, it seems logical that practice in the processes of problem finding may be an important component in our quest for creativity.

Firsthand Accounts

One promising means for examining the processes of problem finding is to discuss them with someone who has successfully found one or more problems. Artists, scientists, writers, and others have discussed their methods in letters, essays, and interviews. Some reports describe an almost mystical process in which the creative individual may not have been aware of the problem until the idea was nearly formed. Among the most famous of these is Mozart's controversial letter cited at the beginning of chapter 2. In a more contemporary example, Albee described the process of writing a play:

> I have to use a pregnancy analogy .... I discover from time to time that I am "with" play. Somewhere along the line, without my being aware of it, I've gotten creatively "knocked up" and there's a play growing in the womb of my head .... By the time I become aware of a play, I've obviously been thinking about it for quite a while because the characters and situation are forming and eventually crowd into my conscious mind. (Queijo, 1987, p. 28)

Others are able to describe specific moments that triggered their ideas. In the afterword to *Unaccompanied Sonata and Other Stories*, Owen Scott Card (1981) described the origin of each short story in the collection. One story originated in a childhood question: "What kind of war games would prepare soldiers for three-dimensional warfare in space?" (p. 269), and one had its source a friend's dreams. Another story had its roots in an editorial challenge. "[An editor] wrote an editorial one month in which he complained that science fiction authors were still writing the same old stuff, not touching such new ideas as recombinant DNA research. I took the challenge personally" (p. 270). Still another story came from a moment of insight that could have happened to many parents: "I was walking [my son] to sleep and realized that his breath on my shoulder was exactly in rhythm with my wife's breath as she slept in the other room" (p. 270). The striking thing about the descriptions is not that the author had unusual experiences, but that he was able to find new ideas in situations that would leave many others untouched.

Toni Morrison is also able to explain many of the sources of her ideas and the power they have in the writing. She wrote "not because I can, but only when there's some overwhelming idea that I feel I can't not write." She explained the origin of her novel *Beloved*:

> I was haunted by a story I read from an 1855 newspaper article about a woman who had escaped from slavery with her children but tried to kill them to avoid their being returned to their owner .... I became curious about that kind of love and its self-sabotage, the curious self-murder that a certain sequence of events can lead to. (Queijo, 1987, pp. 28–29)

As in Card's descriptions, this explanation leaves the most important question unanswered: How did Morrison find the story in that article? Although the stimulus may be clear, the process is far from defined. Many others have read that paper. It is likely that many were touched by the tragedy of the slave's story, yet only one reader found *Beloved* there.

Other creative individuals not only can pinpoint the events that triggered their work, but also can describe their strategies in consciously seeking ideas or problems. Van Gogh's letter to van Rappard described drawing a model repeatedly until he attained an original result. "The first attempts are absolutely unbearable. I say this because I want you to know that if you see something worth while in what I am doing, it is not by accident but because of real intention and purpose" (Ghiselin, 1985, p. 47).

Surrealist Max Ernst (1948) treads the path between mystical, unexplained inspiration, and conscious seeking. He stated: "Since the becoming of no work which can be called ... surrealist is to be directed consciously by the mind, ... the active share of him hitherto described as the work's 'author' is disclosed as being a mere spectator of the birth of the work" (p. 20).

Yet this "mere spectator" is able to describe the "essentially poetic processes" that allow the surrealist to be "freed from the sway of ... conscious faculties" (Ernst, 1948, p. 20). These include a "systematic putting out of place, ... the pairing of two realities which apparently cannot be paired on a plane apparently not suited to them [such as an umbrella and a sewing machine on a dissection table]" (p. 21). Ernst's description brings to mind Mednick's paired associates, Rothenberg's homospatial process, and the combinations of Boden's computer networks discussed in chapter 2. In all these cases, bringing together remote ideas is essential in generating new ones. Ernst described his own efforts to intensify his mind's irritability and find a problem through a series of rubbings of cracks in the floor. As he created repeated rubbings, he believed each became less tied to the character of the floor and more closely associated with the unconscious powers of his mind. Like van Gogh, he did not find a worthwhile image instantaneously, but only after creating many images.

In fact, Ernst (1948) stated, "Surrealist painting is within the reach of everybody who is attracted by real revelations and is therefore ready to assist inspiration or make it work to order" (p. 25). Although he believed the creation of surrealist art is dependent on unconscious processes or inspiration, the artist, in his view, was not left to the whims of the muse. Conscious manipulation of materials or activities allowed him to find or at least watch the birth of original ideas. The idea that conscious strategies can be used to generate, focus, and enhance problems is the key to problem finding.

After interviewing eminent creators, Csikszentimihalyi (1996) described three main sources from which problems typically arise: personal experiences, requirements of the domain, and social pressures. The creators cited here attributed their problem identification to events in their personal lives. However, many eminent creators recognize the influence of knowledge in the domain. Not only is sufficient knowledge necessary to recognition of a puzzling situation in a particular discipline, but the direction of the field and the pressures of the surrounding environment can combine to make certain problems substantially easier to find. The popularity of a particular style of painting presents artists with a challenge: either find new avenues within that style or find a new style. Scientists in wartime often live in an environment that shapes problems in powerful ways. Just as systems theories envision creativity as a whole existing in the center of multiple complex variables, so this view of problem finding sees the very topics addressed by creative endeavors as a complex interaction of the person, the discipline, and the environment.

Research Describing Problem Finding

The processes that creators use to discover or create problems have been studied in a variety of disciplines. The studies of problem finding may be divided into two general groups using categories devised by Dillon (1982): those dealing with the creation of new problems and those concerning the discovery of emergent problems.

Key to the development of this body of research is Getzels and Csikszentmihalyi's (1976) study of problem finding in art. College art students were presented with two tables, a drawing board, paper, and a variety of dry media. On one table were placed 27 objects used to create still-life problems. The students were asked to use one or more of the objects to create a still life on the empty table and to produce a drawing based on the still life.

Researchers observed the strategies used in creating the problem: the number of objects examined, the amount of exploration of each object, and

Creative people find problems worth exploring.

the uniqueness of the objects used. These variables were used to rank students according to the breadth, depth, and uniqueness of their problem finding. The drawings produced were evaluated by artist-critics of graphic skill or craftsmanship, originality, and overall aesthetic value. These scores were correlated with the problem-finding rankings.

The correlation between craftsmanship and problem finding was positive, but not statistically significant. However, correlations between problem finding and both originality and overall aesthetic value were statistically significant, and in the case of originality, highly significant. Seven years later, the original problem-finding rankings were compared with the success of the former students as artists. Although the relationship was not as strong, it was nevertheless statistically significant. In a later follow-up evaluation, 20 years after the original study, the correlation between problem finding in art school and success of artists at midlife still was positive and significant (Getzels, 1982). The identification of problem finding, not just as a significant predictor of creative achievement, but as one that endures for decades, provided the foundation for a variety of other research.

Two studies of creative writing parallel the investigations with art students. Starko (1989) examined the problem-finding strategies of four groups: professional writers, high school students identified as having specific interest and ability in creative writing, students in above-average-ability language arts classes, and students in average-ability language arts classes. In the problem-finding task, subjects were presented with a collection of 18 objects and asked to generate ideas for writing that could relate to one or more of them. After this experience, the subjects were asked to complete a questionnaire about the processes they used to generate ideas and to select their best idea. Interviews with the subjects elaborated on these explanations.

As related in chapter 3, more able writers (professional writers and students identified as having specific ability in creative writing) were more likely than other groups to manipulate ideas deliberately to generate themes for writing, and they were more fluent in the number of ideas generated. Less able writers were more likely to wait for ideas to pop out without any strategies to enhance that possibility. They not only used no problem-finding strategies, but they seemed to have no idea such things were possible. For them, getting ideas was a passive activity.

Moore (1985) followed procedures that paralleled those of Getzels and Csikszentmihalyi (1976) even more closely. Moore presented middle school students with a collection of objects on one table and asked them to arrange some of the pieces on a second table and then to produce a writing based on the objects. Problem-finding scores were generated by analyzing the number of objects manipulated, the uniqueness of the objects chosen, the type of exploratory behavior the writers exhibited, the prewriting time, and the total time spent on the activity. The writing project was assessed using varied measures of creativity. Again, the relationship between problem-finding strategies and originality of solution was significant and positive.

Other studies of problem finding or problem posing might be more accurately described as studies of problem discovery. In these cases, the problems were not new, as are original works of art or writing, but were, at least in part, embedded in a data set to be found by subjects. In some cases the data sets were created by researchers; in other cases they were part of the subjects' natural environment. Problem areas ranged from teacher education to mazes, interpersonal problems, administration, scientific research, and collections of objects.

A review of the research to date (Starko, 1999) suggested several hypotheses about problem finding that may have implications for education. Firsthand accounts of the process vary from the mystical to the methodical, but at least some creators are able to describe the conscious manipulation of ideas that underlies their processes. Studies investigating these behaviors have made tentative ties between exploratory behavior and the successful finding of problems and solutions in a variety of fields. Problem finders were not assigned a problem, nor did they wait for an idea to appear from the blue. They explored, manipulated, and combined ideas until they found a problem worth solving.

A key variable in several studies is time: Subjects who are more successful in problem finding spent more time than others in deliberate exploration. In some cases, they explored more stimuli or more unique stimuli. Possibly we may be able to enhance students' problem-finding abilities by providing experiences that help them practice spending time in exploratory behavior before attempting to find or solve a problem. We also may be able to provide exercises that help them identify situations in which they will want to examine many unique ideas or variables before proceeding, and also to find those in which it is most important to focus on a few key ideas. Much about problem finding remains to be uncovered. Although some researchers (Porath & Arlin, 1992; Rostan, 1992) have found correlations among various areas of problem finding, the relationships among the many processes and tasks currently designated problem finding remain largely unknown. Additional study is needed to correlate or standardize measures of problem finding, and to develop qualitative means for its assessment.

Also unclear is how problem finding differs in children and adults. A key question in such investigations must be the relationship of problem finding to the development of other cognitive processes. Arlin (1975, 1990) postulated that problem finding can develop only after a person is capable of formal operational reasoning, which typically emerges in early adolescence. Smilansky (1984) asserted that one can become a problem finder only after one is able to solve similar problems. If problem finding emerges as postoperational thought and not before, efforts to identify it as a variable in young children may be futile. However, we still do not know whether problem finding is a single variable or whether it is multidimensional or domain specific. It is possible that various types of problem finding may develop along different time lines or that individuals may have profiles of problem finding, perhaps paralleling Gardner's (1983) multiple intelligences. Certainly, a number of studies have identified problem-finding behavior in middle school and high school (Allender, 1969; Hoover, 1994; Moore, 1985; Wakefield, 1985, 1992).

Londner (1991) studied the connection-making patterns of sixth-grade students, using the Picture Completion test in the Torrance Test of creative thinking. The study identified four strategies used by students to develop ideas for picture completion: content-bound thinking (looking at the evident characteristics of the shape), association shifting or developing multiple visual images, story weaving (moving from basic descriptions to complex characters and emotions), and vantage (physically changing the position of the shape to get a new perspective). The highest originality scores were associated with the story-weaving strategy. These strategies may provide a glimpse into simple problem finding with middle grade students.

One study (Starko, 1992) examined problem-finding behaviors among elementary school students in a task adapted from Getzels and Csikszentmihalyi (1976). Students in kindergarten, grade 2, and grade 4 were presented with an assortment of materials and asked to make something. These students showed little outward evidence of the types of exploratory behaviors found in other studies. Most students plunged immediately into the task (occasionally before the researcher had completed the directions). However, discussions after the task gave clues to emergent problem-finding processes. Some children described beginning the task and discovering midway what the creation was going to be ("I started sticking things together and then it turned into a dog, so I made a dog"). In other cases, it was clear that students had found a problem (because they successfully completed the task), but were unable to articulate how they did it. This result is consistent with other discussions of primary students' metacognition. In many cases, young children seem able to succeed at complex tasks without being able to explain how they did so. In related studies (Starko 1993, 1995), students in grades 2, 4, and 6 were presented with a similar task and asked to tell the researcher when they thought they had an idea of what they would make, any time they changed their mind about what to make, and when they finished. This was an effort to discover whether, indeed, some students find the problem they wish to address while manipulating materials. The results were inconclusive. Some students whose products were judged highly creative did spend considerable exploratory time before deciding on a project, whereas others did not. The difference in exploratory time may be a reflection of differences in problem-finding strategies or difficulties in assessing which students' products are exceptionally creative. For example, one child whose product was deemed by judges to be exceptionally original said he copied the idea from something his brother had made. His borrowing may account for the limited amount of time he spent in exploration and may not truly reflect the exploratory time children spend in finding original ideas.

Other seeming contradictions of Getzels and Csikszentmihalyi's (1976) original study may reflect young children's difficulties in selecting their best idea. Some students explored several ideas, but did not select the one most likely to be judged original. Such choices may reflect the importance of evaluative thinking in problem finding. To be a creative problem finder, one must not only generate potential problems, but must also select problems that lend themselves to effective, original solutions (Runco & Chand, 1994).

One of the most interesting questions regarding the development of problem finding in young people is whether it can be influenced through intervention. Delcourt (1993) noted problem-finding activity in adolescents identified as creative producers in secondary school. These students were described as "continuously explor[ing] their many interests as they actively sought project ideas through a variety of techniques including reading, sharing information with others, and taking courses both in and out of school" (p. 28). In this study, the opportunities and encouragement for students to identify and pursue individual problems occurred during specialized services for gifted students. Information on the problem-finding processes of students not participating in such services is not available. Without a comparison group, it is impossible to tell whether Delcourt's students' problem-finding processes were affected by their participation in a program designed to facilitate individual investigations. Burns (1990) examined a similar program for elementary students. Although not writing specifically about problem finding, she investigated the effects of training activities on students' initiation of creative investigations. Students who engaged in a series of lessons on identifying interests and problem focusing initiated significantly more investigations than students not receiving such training. Her results were echoed by Kay (1994), who described the use of a discovery unit in assisting elementary students to conduct original investigations.

In essence, it is clear that problem finding is an important component in adult creativity. We can identify some of the variables that make it more effective, but have a great deal yet to learn. Even less is known about problem finding in children. From the middle grades up, evidence seems to point to the same processes seen in adults. In young children, we are not sure. It is possible that activities designed to teach students strategies for identifying interesting problems may enhance the possibility that they will choose to investigate some. But the evidence is not clear-cut.

In the meantime, however, children are going to school and facing an array of rigidly constructed, presented problems. We are left to choose whether we will continue business as usual until the research base is firmer or attempt to incorporate problem finding into our educational endeavors today. I opt for the latter. It seems only logical that encouraging the types of behaviors that make children explorers and questioners rather than passive accepters cannot help but enhance creativity, thinking, and learning. To help you begin, I discuss in chapters 5 and 6 some examples of how you can teach problem-finding strategies and incorporate problem finding in the major curriculum areas. It remains for you to experiment, innovate, and observe how these principles translate into classroom activities in a variety of disciplines. This kind of innovation may not only enhance creativity and learning, but also add to our knowledge of problem finding in young people. I am very eager to hear about your efforts!

Thinking About the Classroom

Try a miniresearch project on problem finding. Gather a collection of objects that students may use as inspiration for an art or writing project. Observe whether some students spend more time than average examining the objects before beginning their projects. Do you notice any difference in their products?

AMABILE, MOTIVATION, AND A MODEL OF CREATIVITY

The last model and body of literature that play a major role in framing the remainder of this book involve Amabile's (1989, 1996, 2001) componential model of creativity. Amabile was interested not just in characteristics of creative individuals, but in "creative situations" (Amabile, 1996, p.5)—what are the circumstances conducive to creativity?. She found that the social environment can have a large effect on creativity, primarily through the mechanism of motivation. This insight led to the development of her componential model of creativity. The model brings together in a clear, concise way major components found in many models of creativity. The model has three components: domain relevant skills, creativity-related processes, and task motivation (Fig. 4.2).

Domain-relevant skills define the area in which the individual can be creative: factual knowledge about the domain, technical skills, or particular do-

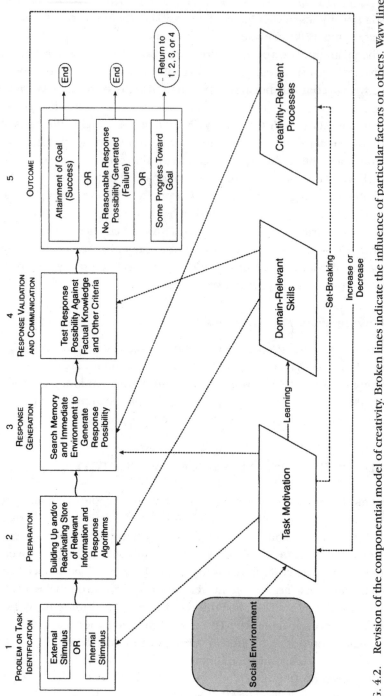

FIG. 4.2. Revision of the componential model of creativity. Broken lines indicate the influence of particular factors on others. Wavy lines indicate the steps in the process (where large variations in the sequence are possible). Only direct and primary influences are depicted. From T. M. Amabile, *Creativity in Context*. Boulder, CO: Westview Press. Copyright © 1996 by Westview Press.

main-related talents . If a person is to be creative in music, he or she must be knowledgeable about music, probably playing an instrument, and in most cases reading musical notation. Particular talent in music would also be considered a domain-relevant skill. A scientist who is to make a creative contribution in astronomy or oceanography will need extensive education in that field before he or she is prepared to do original work. Creative contributions do not spring forth in a vacuum. They are built on the knowledge and efforts of those who have gone before. It is not enough for children to have fun with creative puzzles, activities, and games. They must know enough about something to change it, elaborate on it, derive implications from it, or use it in a new way. Bloom's (1985) subjects had to spend years learning the structure, content, and techniques of their disciplines, yet traditional content teaching, with its emphasis on learning facts and producing single correct answers, seldom encourages flexible or original thought. If we are to facilitate creative thinking, we must teach content in such a way that it supports rather than threatens the attitudes and habits of mind that allow creative ideas. Any of the content we teach can form the basis for creative activities if we provide students with the opportunity to learn information, techniques, and strategies and then encourage them to use these in new ways. Chapter 6 concentrates on teaching domain skills in a manner that is consistent with creative activity.

The second component in the model is creativity-relevant processes, originally called creative thinking and working skills. It includes cognitive style, implicit or explicit knowledge of means for generating novel ideas, and a conducive work style—generally including the orientation toward hard work (Amabile, 1996, 2001). In this area are found the habits of mind as well as the specific strategies and abilities typically thought of as creative thinking. These might include looking at situations from many points of view, using metaphors, or exploring and problem finding. When we teach students brainstorming, use creative dramatics, or teach techniques for developing story ideas, we are developing creative thinking skills or general heuristics for approaching problem tasks. In the process, we also support habits of mind that are conducive to creative thinking such as suspending judgment or looking for a novel response. This component also includes the creative working skills that allow an individual to persevere at a task over time: concentration, focus, organization, and tolerance of ambiguity. The ability to maintain attention to a task over time has been identified as important in several aspects of creativity. It takes time in exploration to identify a problem. As noted in chapter 2, Gruber and Davis (1988) and Weisberg (1999) both noted that high-level creativity activities demanded a commitment to task that spanned years. Creative thinking and working skills are the focus of chapters 5 and 7.

The final component of Amabile's (1989, 1996, 2001) componential model is her most important contribution to the literature on creativity: task motivation, particularly intrinsic motivation, or motivation that comes from within a person and not from some outside source. A child who plays the piano for the joy of playing is intrinsically motivated. The child who plays to earn TV-watching privileges or to avoid a scolding is not. All the skills, habits, and abilities in the world will not ensure that an individual will persist with a task unless he or she wants to do so. In 1989, Amabile wrote: "People will be most creative when they feel motivated primarily by the interest, enjoyment, challenge, and satisfaction of the work itself ... and not by external pressures" (p. 54). Her later work indicates that although intrinsic motivation is important, the interactions of motivation and creativity are complex.

Thinking About the Classroom

Have students make a list of things they like to do. Discuss why they like the activities. Try to determine whether they are intrinsically motivated or compelled by an outside reward.

No activity, by itself, is intrinsically motivating. It can be so only to a particular person at a particular time. Amabile (1989) identified three hallmarks of intrinsic motivation. The first and most obvious is interest. Anyone is more likely to be motivated by something that has captured his or her interest than something that is boring or of no perceived value. A second aspect of intrinsic motivation is competence. Individuals will seek out activities and persist in them longer if they feel they are mastering something on their own. I once took a community education class on playing the mountain dulcimer. It was an interesting and highly motivating experience. The instrument is simple enough that I was able to play simple melodies the first time I picked it up. This early success and feeling of competence made practicing enjoyable and left me eager to learn more. Later, as I struggled with more difficult techniques, I still enjoyed my growing feeling of accomplishment. Later, I decided to try to teach myself to play the folk harp. I found that my motivation to play has followed a similar pattern. As my efforts sound more and more like music, it is more and more fun. Although it is unlikely that I will ever become a professional-caliber musician, the satisfaction I receive from my gradual improvement has been enough to keep me playing amid a schedule that allows very little free time. I am intrinsically motivated to do it. As I continue to improve, I am able to explore new ideas and techniques and hope to become increasingly creative in my efforts.

This idea ties closely to Bandura's (1977) construct of self-efficacy. *Self-efficacy* is a person's assessment of confidence in his or her ability to perform a specific task. The more confident (efficacious) people feel, the more likely they are to begin the task and persist in the face of obstacles. As an illustration, I feel confident in my ability to bake bread. I have been successful in baking bread in the past and am willing to experiment with new techniques, ingredients, and recipes. Perhaps some day my exploration will lead to a wonderful new recipe or bread-making invention.

I feel much less sure of my mechanical abilities. I do not willingly take on mechanical projects. If I am forced to tackle a broken toilet, a flopping windshield wiper, or some other small disaster, I deal with it in the quickest, most efficient manner I can. I have no desire to explore, experiment, or be elegant; I just want to get through it. Amabile (1989) compared these feelings with those of a rat in a maze. If the rat is motivated by an extrinsic reward (cheese, or a functioning windshield wiper), it takes the straightest line to the reward and gets out of the maze as quickly as possible. If the rat is intrinsically motivated, it enjoys being in the maze. It wants to explore it, take time in it, and find all the interesting nooks and crannies there. Of course, the intrinsically motivated rat is more likely to find an interesting or creative way through the maze. Until I feel more competent in tackling mechanical projects, I am unwilling to spend time in the maze and am unlikely to exhibit any creative activity in that area.

Thinking About the Classroom

For 1 week, keep track of the things you say and do to try to motivate students. Think about the kind of motivation you are promoting. Save the list for consideration when you read chapter 7.

Amabile's (1989) third hallmark of intrinsic motivation is *self-determination*: the sense that we are working on something for our own reasons, not someone else's. To be intrinsically motivated, I not only need to feel successful, but I also need to feel that I am pursuing the activity because I have chosen to do so. Amabile describes a research study in which college students worked on three-dimensional wooden block puzzles. All the students worked individually. Half the students were allowed to choose which of three puzzles they would do and how to use the allotted 30 minutes. The other half were told which of the puzzles to do and given time allocations. Clearly, the first group had much more self-determination.

After the 30-minute period was over, the subjects were left alone in the laboratory and told to do whatever they wished. The students in the self-de-

An intrinsically motivated rat likes to explore the maze.

termining group spent significantly more time playing with the puzzles during this period than the other group. They also were more likely to say "yes" when asked if they would be willing to return to the lab to work on additional puzzles. The group that had the opportunity to choose how they would pursue the activity was more intrinsically motivated to continue it than the group that had been given specific directions.

Thinking About the Classroom

Try a miniresearch project on self-determination. Try to identify two activities that should be equally interesting to your students (perhaps two art activities, if you teach elementary school). One week, do the activity with maximum control and direction. Put out extra materials and note how many students choose to use them. The next week, do the second activity. This time, give students more choice about how they pursue the activity (what to do first, which materials to use, and so on). Again put out extra materials and note who uses them. See if you find any differences.

Already it should be clear that developing intrinsic motivation in schools is a challenge. In traditional classrooms, students are assigned material in which they may or may not have any interest, given tasks at which they may or may not succeed (or which may or may not provide any challenge), and given specific instructions on how to proceed. A situation less conducive to intrinsic motivation can hardly be imagined! Chapter 7 focuses on motivation in the classroom and outlines strategies to maximize the possibility of intrinsic motivation for students.

The three components of Amabile's model parallel several of the creativity models discussed in chapter 2. Where Amabile emphasizes domain-relevant skills, Sternberg focuses on aspects of intelligence that allow individuals to gain information and use it in novel ways, and Gruber and Weisberg discuss expertise in content areas. Amabile outlines creativity-relevant processes. Numerous theorists talk about the use of combinations, metaphors, divergent thinking, and problem finding as important strategies supporting creativity. Amabile's focus on task motivation ties to the persistence across time noted by Gruber, Weisberg, Csikszentmihalyi, and others. You can undoubtedly identify similarities to other models. Those familiar with literature on education of the gifted and talented will also see strong parallels with Renzulli's (1978) three-ring conception of giftedness. It is even possible to see ties to Bloom's (1985) phases of talent development. Individuals must develop a love of the discipline, skills in the discipline, and the ability to use them artistically.

Whichever theory or outline we choose, there are at least three fronts that must be addressed in the development of creativity. We must deal with the necessity that the creative person acquire knowledge and expertise in some content area. It is also important that we be familiar with strategies for manipulating content, finding problems, and looking at content in new ways. Finally, it is essential for us to foster the motivation and positive attitudes that keep individuals committed to a task long enough for exploration, problem finding, and creative thinking to take place. These are the challenges of the next three chapters.

JOURNEYING AND JOURNALING

1. Think about your own development in your greatest talent area. What kinds of instruction have helped you? What kind of teacher would you need to help you develop further?
2. Read Bloom's (1985) *Developing Talent in Young People*. Discuss it with friends.

What do you think of the sacrifices the families made for the talented individual's development? Do you think the sequence of instruction described holds for other talent areas?

3. Problem finding appears to demand that one spend time in exploratory activity before finalizing a creative endeavor. Experiment with developing more exploratory behavior in your own creative activities. Reflect on both the process and the product of your effort. How did it feel? Did it affect other aspects of your creative process? Did it affect your product?

4. Make a list of activities that you find intrinsically motivating, things you like to do for their own sake. See if they match the characteristics of interest, competence, and self-determination.

REFERENCES

Allender, J. S. (1969). A study of inquiry activity in elementary school children. *American Education Research Journal, 6,* 543–558.

Amabile, T. M. (1989). *Growing up creative.* New York: Crown.

Amabile, T. M. (1996). *Creativity in context: Update to the social psychology of creativity.* Boulder, CO: Westview Press.

Amabile, T. M. (2001). Beyond talent: John Irving and the passionate craft of creativity. *American Psychologist, 56*(4), 333–336.

Arlin, P. K. (1975). A cognitive process model of problem finding. *Educational Horizons, 54*(1), 99–106.

Arlin, P. K. (1990). Wisdom: The art of problem finding. In R. J. Sternberg (Ed.), *Wisdom: Its nature, origins, and development* (pp. 230–243). New York: Cambridge University Press.

Bandura, A. (1977). Self-efficacy: Toward a unifying theory of behavioral change. *Psychological Review, 84,* 191–215.

Bloom, B. (Ed.). (1985). *Developing talent in young people.* New York: Ballantine.

Card, O. S. (1981). *Unaccompanied sonata and other stories.* New York: Dial Press.

Burns, D. E. (1990). The effects of group training activities on students' initiation of creative investigations. *Gifted Child Quarterly, 34,* 31–36.

Collins, M. A., & Amabile, T. M. (1999). Motivation and creativity. In R. J. Sternberg (Ed.), *Handbook of creativity* (pp. 297–312). New York: Cambridge University Press.

Csikszentmihalyi, M. (1996). *Creativity: Flow and the psychology of discovery and invention.* New York: HarperCollins.

Csikszentmihalyi, M., & Sawyer, K. (1993, May). *Creative insight: The social dimension of a solitary moment.* Paper presented at the Henry B. and Jocelyn Wallace National Research Symposium on Talent Development, Iowa City, IA.

Delcourt, M. A. B. (1993). Creative productivity among secondary school students: Combining energy, interest, and imagination. *Gifted Child Quarterly, 37,* 23–31.

Dillon, J. T. (1982). Problem finding and solving. *Journal of Creative Behavior, 16,* 97–111.

Ernst, M. (1948). *Max Ernst: Beyond painting.* New York: Wittenborn Schultz.

Gardner, H. (1982). *Art, mind, and brain.* New York: Basic Books.

Gardner, H. (1983). *Frames of mind.* New York: Basic Books.

Getzels, J. W. (1964). Creative thinking, problem solving and instruction. In E. Hilgard (Ed.), *Sixty-third National Society for the Study of Education yearbook: Part 1, Theories of learning and instruction* (pp. 240–267). Chicago: University of Chicago Press.

Getzels, J. W. (1982). The problem of the problem. In R. Hogath (Ed.), *New directions for methodology of social and behavioral science: Question framing and response consistency* (pp. 37–49). San Francisco: Jossey-Bass.

Getzels, J. W. (1987). Problem finding and creative achievement. *Gifted Students Institute Quarterly, 12*(4), B1–B4.

Getzels, J. W., & Csikszentmihalyi, M. (1976). *The creative vision: A longitudinal study of problem finding in art.* New York: Wiley.

Ghiselin, B. (1985). *The creative process.* Berkeley, CA: University of California Press.

Gruber, H. E., & Davis, S. N. (1988). Inching our way up Mount Olympus: The evolving-systems approach to creative thinking. In R. J. Sternberg (Ed.), *The nature of creativity* (pp. 243–270). New York: Cambridge University Press.

Gruber, H. E., & Wallace, D. B. (1999). The case study method and evolving systems approach for understanding unique creative people at work. In R. J. Sternberg (Ed.), *Handbook of creativity* (pp. 93–115). New York: Cambridge University Press.

Hoover, S. M. (1994). Scientific problem-finding in gifted fifth grade students. *Roeper Review, 16,* 156–159.

Kay, S. (1994). From theory to practice: Promoting problem finding behavior in children. *Roeper Review, 16,* 195–197.

Londner, L. (1991). Connection-making processes during creative task activity. *Journal of Creative Behavior, 25,* 20–26.

Mackworth, N. H. (1965). Originality. *American Psychologist, 20,* 51–66.

Moore, M. (1985). The relationship between the originality of essays and variables in the problem-discovery process: A study of creative and noncreative middle school students. *Research in the Teaching of English, 19,* 84–95.

Perkins, D. N. (1981). *The mind's best work.* Cambridge, MA: Harvard University Press.

Porath, M., & Arlin, P. (1992, February). *Developmental approaches to artistic giftedness.* Paper presented at the Esther Katz Rosen Symposium on the Psychological Development of Gifted Children, Lawrence, KS.

Queijo, J. (1987). Inside the creative mind. *Bostonia, 61*(6), 26–33.

Renzulli, J. S. (1978). What makes giftedness? Re-examining a definition. *Phi Delta Kappan, 60,* 180–184.

Rostan, S. M. (1992, February). *The relationship among problem finding, problem solving, cognitive controls, professional productivity and domain of profes-*

sional training in adult males. Paper presented at the Esther Katz Rosen Symposium on the Psychological Development of Gifted Children, Lawrence, KS.

Runco, M. A. (1991). *Divergent thinking.* Norwood, NJ: Ablex.

Runco, M. A., & Chand, I. (1994). Problem finding, evaluative thinking and creativity. In M. A. Runco (Ed.), *Problem finding, problem solving, and creativity* (pp. 40–76). Norwood, NJ: Hampton.

Sloane, K. (1985). Home influences on talent development. In B. Bloom (Ed.), *Developing talent in young people* (pp. 439–476). New York: Ballantine.

Smilansky, J. (1984). Problem solving and the quality of invention: An empirical investigation. *Journal of Educational Psychology, 76,* 377–386.

Sosniak, L. A. (1985). Phases of learning. In B. Bloom (Ed.), *Developing talent in young people* (pp. 409–438). New York: Ballantine.

Starko, A. J. (1989). Problem finding in creative writing: An exploratory study. *Journal for the Education of the Gifted, 12,* 172–186.

Starko, A. J. (1992, November). *Problem finding in elementary students: An exploratory study.* Paper presented at the conference of the National Association for Gifted Children, Los Angeles, CA.

Starko, A. J. (1993, May). *Problem finding in elementary students: Two explorations.* Paper presented at the Henry B. and Jocelyn Wallace National Research Symposium on Talent Development, Iowa City, IA.

Starko, A. J. (1995, May). *Problem finding in elementary students: Continuing explorations.* Paper presented at the Henry B. and Jocelyn Wallace National Research Symposium on Talent Development, Iowa City, IA.

Starko, A. J. (1999). Problem finding: A key to creative productivity. In A. S. Fishkin, B. Cramond, & P. Olszewski-Kubilius (Eds.), *Investigating creativity in youth* (pp. 75–96). Cresskill, NJ: Hampton.

Sternberg, R. J., & Davidson, J. (1995). *The nature of insight.* Cambridge, MA: MIT Press.

Treffinger, D. J., Isaksen, S. G., & Dorval, K. B. (2003). *Creative problem solving (CPS Version 6.1 TM): A contemporary framework for managing change.* Available from Center for Creative Learning, Inc. www.creativelearning.com.

Treffinger, D. J., Isaksen, S. G., & Dorval, K. B. (2000). *Creative problem solving: An introduction* (3rd ed.). Waco, TX: Prufrock Press.

Vaske, H. (2002). *Why are they creative?* Maplewood, NY: fivedegreesbelowzero Press.

Wakefield, J. F. (1985). Towards creativity: Problem finding in a divergent thinking exercise. *Child Study Journal, 15,* 265–270.

Wakefield, J. F. (1992, February). *Creativity tests and artistic talent.* Paper presented at the Esther Katz Rosen Symposium on the Psychological Development of Gifted Children, Lawrence, KS.

Weisberg, R. W. (1999). Creativity and knowledge: A challenge to theories. In R. J. Sternberg (Ed.), *Handbook of creativity* (pp. 226–250). New York: Cambridge University Press.

part II

Creativity and Classroom Life

$\mathbf{P}$art I examines research and theory concerning the creative process, characteristics of creative individuals, and the development of creativity. Part II discusses classroom activities, practices, and organizational strategies that are supportive of creativity. Chapter 5 reviews a variety of general strategies and techniques for developing creative thinking. Chapter 6 overviews each major subject area—language arts, social studies, science, and mathematics—as it might be taught through the goals and principles of creative thinking. The chapter examines the question, "How might teaching look if we approached each area as an opportunity to find and solve problems and communicate ideas?" Chapter 7 examines the research on motivation and creativity and investigates the implications of this research for classroom management, grading, and questioning. Finally, chapter 8 discusses assessment and creativity, including an examination of standardized creativity tests and a variety of techniques that can be used to assess creative efforts in the classroom. These include performance-based assessment and other forms of alternative assessment.

chapter **5**

Teaching Creative Thinking Skills and Habits

A group of workers were charged with solving the difficulties of potato-chip packaging. The standard bag packaging was inexpensive but fragile, allowing a large number of chips to be broken in transit. The workers tried using the synectics approach in which analogies are used to solve problems. They tried to imagine things in nature that are like potato chips, and one worker thought of dry leaves. These are brittle and break easily, as do chips. One worker recalled that after a rain, a large number of leaves are easily bagged without breaking, many more than can normally fit into a standard bag. The group convened outside, wet down some leaves, and noted that, indeed, wet leaves could be compressed easily into a compact space without breaking them. This analogy formed the basis of the Pringles potato-chip line, which features chips that are formed while wet into a shape that is easily and compactly packaged (Gordon & Poze, 1981).

In Sweden, a group of high school students received training in lateral thinking, a series of techniques for generating ideas by looking at situations from fresh perspectives. Corporate and industrial leaders provided problems for the young people to address. One of the problems involved the difficulty of motivating workers in a plant that needed to be kept running over the week-

*end. The students suggested that, rather than motivating the exist-
ing workers to take weekend hours, a fresh workforce be
employed that only worked on weekends. The idea was tried, and
applicants for the weekend jobs far exceeded the number needed
(de Bono, 1992).*

*Ms. Cochran was concerned that her class's science project ideas
were unoriginal and often represented displays or demonstrations rather than research. After teaching the differences among
the three types of projects, she demonstrated how to use the
SCAMPER acronym to generate ideas for improving projects. Beginning with the idea of a display on beekeeping, students suggested research projects that included assessing the effects of color
on bees' attraction to flowers and comparing honey production in
differently shaped hives. Although some students' efforts still were
deficient in originality, Ms. Cochran was pleased to see the variety
of projects her students produced for that year's fair.*

*Mr. Brown was concerned about the lack of creativity his students
displayed in both their art and creative writing. He purchased a
book of creative activities and, using suggestions from the book,
began engaging his students in activities for 30 minutes each Friday afternoon. One week the class brainstormed to name as
many types of birds as possible. Another week they thought of
ways to communicate with an alien, and another Friday they
made all the pictures they could think of from a square. After several weeks Mr. Brown began to question whether these activities
were a good use of class time. He had seen little evidence of improvement in students' art or writing.*

Many techniques sometimes called tools for creative thinking, have been
designed to assist individuals in generating original ideas. A number of
these strategies originated in business, where new ideas are essential for
developing products and maintaining a competitive edge. Some techniques have been used in schools in an effort to help students become more
creative. There is evidence that many of the strategies described can be effective in assisting both children and adults in producing novel, appropriate ideas. Exactly why or under what circumstances they work is not always
clear. Possibly some of the techniques mimic or stimulate the cognitive processes that underlie creativity. Possibly use of the techniques develops attitudes or habits of mind that facilitate creativity: independence in judgment,

willingness to explore multiple options, and persistence beyond the first idea. In any case, familiarity with techniques designed to enhance creative thinking gives individuals a set of tools to use in their exploratory behavior. Instead of sitting and waiting for the muse to strike, students can use deliberate strategies to channel their thoughts in new directions.

Having tools, however, is not always sufficient. As Mr. Brown discovered, practice with creative thinking skills does not automatically result in the transfer of such skills to other circumstances. Students must be taught how to use them, when to use them, and under what circumstances they might be useful. Using techniques in diverse circumstances and discussing their application elsewhere can enhance the possibility that they will be seen not as Friday afternoon diversions, but as valuable approaches to life's dilemmas. In addition, time spent in activities that specifically teach creative thinking skills and attitudes sends a valuable message to students: "Creativity is valued here. It is so important that we will spend precious time and energy to help you be more creative." Such messages are an important aspect of the problem-friendly classroom. Students who have spent class time learning to question and explore seem much more likely to believe that these activities will be accepted and appreciated if they initiate them later.

This chapter examines a variety of techniques designed to help generate new ideas. It describes how they work and how they might be used with students. It also offers suggestions for helping children transfer the techniques from classroom exercises to real-life habits of mind. First, I consider the Incubation Model, Torrance and Safter's (1990, 1999) design for organizing the teaching of creative thinking skills. Next, I explore possible strategies for teaching the concept of problem finding. The rest of the chapter is divided into four major sections: divergent-thinking strategies, use of metaphors and analogies, imagery and creative dramatics, and commercial and competitive programs.

As you read, consider which strategies fit most smoothly with the content you teach and the developmental level of your students. Although many techniques, such as brainstorming, can be used at almost any level, others, such as some of the more sophisticated uses of metaphor, are best for students with more highly developed abstract thinking abilities. Only you can determine which ideas are best for your students, how they can be adapted, and which areas of the students' lives may provide the best opportunities for transfer.

THE INCUBATION MODEL OF TEACHING

Torrance and Safter's (1990, 1999) Incubation Model is a general design for teaching creative thinking that takes into account both the rational cognitive processes that can enhance creative thinking and the "suprarational" processes that may underlie moments of "insight, intuition, revelation" (p. vii). The model can be used to organize activities based on any of the creative- thinking strategies described in this chapter. In many ways, the Incubation Model parallels the principles of inductive teaching described in chapter 6. Students use information and creative thinking skills to draw conclusions, solve problems, or consider alternatives. Torrance and Safter (1990) described the creative process as a method of searching for information or solutions.

> To learn creatively, a person must first become aware of gaps in knowledge, disharmonies, or problems calling for new solutions. She must then search for information concerning the missing elements or difficulties, trying to identify the difficulty or gap in knowledge. Next she must search for solutions, making guesses or approximations, formulating hypotheses, thinking of possibilities, and predicting. Then comes the testing, modifying, retesting, and perfecting of the hypotheses or other creative products. Then there is the important process of puzzling out, mulling it over, fitting the pieces together–incubation. Finally there is the communication of results. (p. 13)

The goal of their model is to provide students with experiences that will encourage them to identify problems or gaps in knowledge, think about them in new ways, and take time for incubation.

The Incubation Model has three parts. It considers the types of activities that will enhance a person's creative thinking before, during, and after a lesson. The model is designed for use in conjunction with content. Sample lessons include both a content objective and a creative thinking skill objective. Torrance and Safter (1990, 1999) listed numerous creative thinking skills that may be addressed, such as being original, producing alternatives, visualizing inside, and letting humor flow. The model could also be used to organize lessons designed to teach or use any of the creative thinking techniques described in this chapter.

The first stage of the Incubation Model is heightening anticipation. The purpose of this stage is to "heighten anticipation and expectations and to prepare the learners to make clear connections between what they are expected to learn and something meaningful in their lives" (Torrance & Safter, 1990, p. 7). This stage may be thought of as a warm-up process, piquing students' interest and tying to prior knowledge. It might include activities that ask students to look at the same information from different viewpoints, respond to a provocative question, become aware of a future problem, or make predictions. In each case, the aim of the activity is to arouse students' curiosity, focus their attention, and give them purpose and motivation for the activities to follow.

The second stage is called deepening expectations. This stage, which might be considered the body of the lesson, requires learners to process new information and address the puzzling situations raised in stage 1. Students may be asked to gather information, reevaluate results, process familiar information in new ways, or identify important data.

Finally, in the third stage, going beyond, students are asked to do something with the information and skills they have encountered. They may give personal meaning to the situation, make predictions for the future, use information in fantasy, or solve real problems. Activities may extend over a period of days, allowing time for incubation. Torrance and Safter (1990) gave numerous examples of strategies that may be appropriate for each stage. A full discussion of each strategy is impossible here, but two examples will demonstrate how the model can be used from primary grades to high school.

One sample lesson, designed for primary grades, is planned to teach the creative writing goal of imagining conversations and the creativity goal of enhancing fantasy. In stage 1, the teacher displays a large picture of a bumblebee in a flower and asks, "What do bees say to flowers? What do flowers say back? Suppose that, in addition to coming to this flower to get nectar with which to make honey, this bee is also a friend of the flower. He's stopped by for a friendly chat" (Torrance & Safter, 1990, p. 84). Students are asked to offer suggestions about what the bee and the flower might discuss. In stage 2, students are asked to think of things that may be having conversations we have never noticed: the butter and the knife or two foods on the kitchen shelves. Each student chooses one pair and writes the imaginary conversation. In stage 3, some of the students' ideas may be enacted through role play. It is likely that the role-play activity would be conducted a day or two after the original conversations were written, leaving students time for incubation and elaboration.

Another lesson teaches high school students about the Kwakiutl people. The creativity goal is elaboration. In stage 1, students are presented with information on the Kwakiutl practice of presenting their rivals with so much wealth the rival can never repay it. They are asked the following questions (Torrance & Safter, 1990, p. 59):

1. What motives might prompt these actions?

2. What explanations would the Kwakiutl offer for this practice?

3. What pictures of these people emerge from knowledge of this practice?

4. What else do you need to know before you can get a clear picture?

In stage 2, students read information about the Kwakiutl culture. After reading, they may role play conflict situations, write a dramatization of Kwakiutl life, or list questions they would like to investigate to understand the Kwakiutl better. In stage 3, students' questions, comments, and understandings are discussed, and then compared with the writings of anthropologists who have lived with the Kwakiutl. Students may reorganize their information to accommodate the new insights.

Many lesson models contain stages similar to those described in the Incubation Model: a readiness phase, a processing-information phase, and an application phase. Unique to the Incubation Model is its use of each phase of the lesson to enhance students' content knowledge as well as their creative thinking skills. You may find the Incubation Model useful in at least two ways. First, it may provide a framework for the content activities discussed in chapter 6. Second, it may be used to structure lessons that use the creative thinking strategies described in this chapter, whether the lesson centers on the skill itself, on traditional school content, or on applying the skill in a real-world context. You may find that thinking about a careful sequence of building student interest, processing new information, and applying information and skills over time that allows ideas to develop can be a useful planning strategy for teaching content and skills.

Thinking About the Classroom

Examine your lesson plans for the week. Can you identify lessons in which you planned to heighten students' interest, help them process information, and apply it to new situations? Did any of the lessons incorporate aspects of creative thinking? Choose one lesson and adapt it using the Incubation Model.

FINDING PROBLEM FINDING

I am frankly fascinated with problem finding. Thinking about the strategies used by creative individuals to identify the very challenges they address raises both my curiosity and my awe. Still, I have been a teacher long enough that my questions always come back to "Could we help people learn to do this—or learn to do it better? If I helped students think about their own problem finding, would they find better problems?" It seems a potentially important question. Carson & Runco (1999) found that problem finding and problem solving skills were associated with more adaptive personal coping strategies in college students—and less linked with confrontation, avoidance, and the like as means of dealing with stress. Could we help students gain this advantage? As in much there is to learn about creativity, the answer to that question is not clear. There is no established research base suggesting that training in problem finding will improve students' creativity. Likewise, there is no ready-made lesson manual to help us do it. However, I have found enough hints in the writings of creative individuals to help me get started, and my experiences sharing these ideas with children have been positive enough to encourage me. I believe that watching students find problems—in addition to watching them solve them—can be an important clue to understand their thinking (Starko, 2000). I hope to continue gathering data on my efforts—and I would be very interested to hear about yours.

Reading the writings of creative individuals about their search for new creative endeavors has led me to identify several themes: exploring with interest, playing and wondering, and capturing questions. Exploring with interest entails approaching the world with wonder. A strange new insect is an opportunity for curiosity, not disgust. Paint that drips in places we did not expect may be a discovery, not a mess. Ray Bradbury (1996) wrote, "[I]deas lie everywhere, like apples fallen and melting in the grass for lack of wayfaring strangers with an eye and a tongue for beauty, whether absurd, horrific, or genteel" (p. 8). Each new day, each new place, brings something to think about. Naturalist Cathy Johnson (1997) exemplified exploring with interest when she described the value of wandering.

> Wandering is the best way I know to feed that flame [curiosity], to answer those questions. Wandering—but with a conscious step, an openness to experience. "Wandering" may *sound* aimless, ... but it is as purposeful in its way as the migration of monarchs each fall. Like their erratic, drifting flight, it only looks aimless taken a step at a time. In the larger picture a good wander is a search for questions, for the answers that lead inevitably—and happily—to more questions .... How will I know what lies over the next ridge, beyond the next trail's turning along a creek, in the corners of my mind, if I don't give myself permission to wander? (pp. 59–60)

Students can be taught the value of wandering and wondering. Wanders may by physical or mental. Students can explore the paths of a nature trail or practice asking questions about a fish tank. In either case they must observe, think, and wonder. Creative individuals are great observers. Composer Igor Stravinsky (1997) said,

> The faculty of creating is never given to us all by itself. It always goes hand in hand with the gift of observation. And the true creator may be recognized by his ability always to find about him, in the commonest and humblest thing, items worthy of note. He does not have to concern himself with a beautiful landscape; he does not need to surround himself with rare and precious objects. He does not have to put forth in search of discoveries: They are always within his reach. (p. 192)

Science lessons that help students observe, not just for accuracy, but also for curiosity, are part of wandering. So are writing lessons that help young people find interest in the characters they create or history lessons that inspire them to notice the words spoken by people long ago and wonder at their thoughts. Therefore, instead of always asking, "What do you see?" we might sometimes ask, "Is there something here that puzzles you? What questions might we ask about this character, this soap bubble, this math puzzle?" Part of teaching students to explore with interest is helping them understand school as a place where students ask questions rather than just answer them. More strategies for helping students ask questions are found in chapter 6.

5.1. Stories in Quilts: Problem Finding in the Visual Arts (5–12)

Share *Stitching Stars: The Story Quilts of Harriet Powers* (Lyons, 1997), or another book that explores the art forms of early story quilt makers. Harriet Powers' story is particularly important because she was both a slave and an artist. Her work can be compared with that of Faith Ringgold, whose quilts can be seen in the illustrations of her children's books. Talk about how the women found their ideas. Challenge students to find a story that could be expressed either in a quilt or collage.

A second theme in the writings of creative individuals is playing and wondering. Creative individuals do not just explore; they play. They enjoy the chance to think about things just for the joy of it, the "Oh, wow!" of all human endeavors. My favorite description of this process is from Richard Feynman (1997), a Nobel Prize–winning physicist. He described a time when, after having success in his field, he found himself without ideas. After a period of considerable stress, he had an important insight.

> I used to *enjoy* doing physics. Why did I enjoy it? I used to play with it … So I got this new attitude. Now that I am burned out and I'll never accomplish anything, … I'm going to play with physics, whenever I want to, without worrying about any importance whatsoever. Within a week I was in the cafeteria and some guy, fooling around, throws a plate in the air. As the plate went up in the air I saw it wobble and I noticed the red medallion of Cornell on the plate going around. It was pretty obvious to me that the medallion went around faster than the wobbling. I had nothing to do, so I started to figure out the motion of the rotating plate …. I went on to work out equations of wobbles …. The diagrams and the whole business that I got the Nobel Prize for came from that piddling around with the wobbling plate. (p. 67)

I am not sure that we can teach playfulness, but we can model it. Teachers who approach their subject with the attitude "This is so interesting. I just can't wait to show you" have the beginnings of playfulness. Playfulness entails thinking about things just for fun and sharing those thoughts with students. It is not the same as silliness. It is approaching a subject not as content to be covered, but as a part of the world worthy of curiosity. Playing with ideas gives us the energy and impetus to ask new and interesting questions.

Finally, creative individuals pay attention to their wonderings. They capture their ideas and build on them. This is essense of the theme-capturing questions. In the example just discussed, Richard Feynman certainly explored his world with interest. He was open to curiosity about the plate wobbling above his head, whereas many of the rest of us may have concentrated on ducking. He was willing to play with his observations, thinking about the wobbling plate just for fun and curiosity. But he did not stop there. Although some individuals may have noticed the wobble, and still others may have been curious about the spinning, for most people these would have been fleeting thoughts, immediately lost to the clamor of the demands of everyday life. Feynman continued to ponder and play with the ideas, to calculate and reexamine until his series of questions and answers led him to truly new territory. The persistence so often noted as a characteristic of exemplary creators is required not just for solving problems, but also for sticking with an area of curiosity long enough to find the really interesting questions. Teaching students to nurture their ideas requires lessons that do not demand a problem be identified and solved in one 43-minute class period. Good problem finding is a serial drama, not a situation comedy.

It can be valuable to teach lessons the sole purpose of which is to ask questions or find problems. You may have students practice generating story topics, possibilities for plant experiments, or ways to get ideas for a painting. Later lessons may or may not actually entail writing the stories, conducting the experiments, or painting the paintings. At times, it may be useful to practice asking questions the way basketball players practice jump shot—understanding the way they fit into the game, even if we are not going to play four quarters today. For example, the book *A Rainbow at Night* (Hucko, 1996) contains paintings by Navajo children along with the artists' descriptions of how they chose their subjects. Many of the paintings can lead naturally to a discussion of how a similar strategy could help students find subjects for their own paintings. If one girl's painting reflects a traditional story important to her family, students might discuss the types of stories their families tell. Perhaps the story of Aunt Suzy's childhood mischief or Great Grandpa's courage in a difficult situation could inspire a new artwork. Figures 5.1 and 5.2 are taken from lessons designed to raise students' awareness of the ways people in various careers need to ask research questions (Schack & Starko, 1998; Starko & Schack, 1992). It may also be interesting to discuss the ways authors find the ideas to explore in a story. Sometimes this might be investigated through the authors' own explanations. Other times it can be interesting to hypothesize the kinds of experiences that may have led an author to a particular story. Tom Stoppard translated that type of speculation into an Oscar-winning movie, *Shakespeare in Love*.

5.2. Artist in Overalls: More Problem Finding in the Visual Arts (5–12)

It is interesting to share the problem finding of quilt makers with that of other artists. One interesting comparison is the life and art of Grant Wood, presented in the short book *Artist in Overalls* (Duggleby, 1994). The book explores the roots of Wood's art and also makes clear the many setbacks and disappointments that came before his success. This story could form the basis for lessons either on finding problems in one's surroundings or on the need for persistence and drive in creativity. Students might be challenged to find other examples of individuals who persisted in their creative endeavors despite hardship and rejection.

We also may teach lessons focusing on the third aspect of problem finding: capturing question. A great question or idea is unlikely to bear fruit if it flits across our mind and is gone. Lessons that practice problem finding can help students begin to attend to their own curiosity or flexible thinking. It

Who Does Research?

Who does research? Did you think of scientists wearing white coats boiling things in glass tubes? There are many other people who do research. Think about the kind of questions the people below might investigate. What questions might they ask?

Person	Questions
Newspaper reporter who writes about schools	
Doctor	
Football coach	
Toy store owner	
Cancer researcher	
School principal	
Restaurant manager	
Author	

Think of someone you know. What questions might they ask as part of their job?

FIG. 5.1.   Who does research? From Starko, A. J., & Schack, G. D., 1992. *Looking for Data in All the Right Places,* p. 9. Creative Learning Press, Mansfield Center, CT. Reproduced with permission (by CLP).

All Kinds of Questions

Just like newspaper reporters, researchers make use of key question words such as Who, What, When, Where, Why, and How. Using these key words, it is possible to think of interesting questions about just about anything. For example, take a look at these questions about ordinary classroom pencils.

Who uses pencils?
What kind of pencil is easier for young children to use?
When did pencils become common household items?
Where are most pencils used?
Why do people choose to use a pencil instead of a pen?
How does the way you hold a pencil affect your handwriting?
How does a #2 pencil compare to a #3 pencil? How could you gather samples that would demonstrate the differences?
How many pencils are sold by the school store?
What if they advertised the pencils? Would sales go up?
What if someone didn't have a #2 pencil? Would anything else work in marking a standardized test?

Pick a common item that seems interesting to you. Using the question stems, write the most interesting questions you can think of.

Who _____ ?

What _____ ?

When _____ ?

Where _____ ?

Why _____ ?

How _____ ?

How does _____ compare to _____ ?

How many _____ ?

What if _____ ?

What if someone didn't _____ ?

FIG. 5.2. All kinds of questions. From Schack, G. D., & Starko, A. S., 1998. *Research Comes Alive*, p. 25. Creative Learning Press. Mansfield Center, CT. Reproduced with permission.

also can be useful to teach students the value of recording ideas. Creative individuals in almost every domain keep notebooks in which they record sketches, snatches of dialogue, intriguing story ideas, or puzzling questions. Students can do the same. The appendix contains a series of lessons designed to teach problem finding in several domains. The lessons were designed originally for students in fourth grade, but can easily be adapted for a variety of grade levels. They include lessons on problem finding in inventing, writing, and science, as well as discussions on creating an idea notebook and developing habits of mind that are conducive to problem finding.

DIVERGENT THINKING STRATEGIES

Many techniques of creative thinking are designed to increase students' divergent thinking or their ability to think of many different responses to a given situation. The most common definition of divergent thinking includes those types of thought discussed in chapter 2 as part of Guilford's Structure of Intellect (SOI) model: fluency (thinking of many ideas), flexibility (thinking of different categories or points of view), originality (thinking of unusual ideas), and elaboration (adding detail to improve ideas). Fluency often is the basis of activities designed to improve divergent thinking. The more ideas you have, the more likely it is that at least one of them will be a good idea.

There is some research to support this premise (MacKinnon, 1978; Parnes, 1967). Baer (1993) examined the effects of training in divergent thinking on students' creative performance in a number of domains. Divergent thinking activities were associated with higher quality creative products in storytelling, collage making, and poetry writing for second-grade students. Basadur, Runco, and Vega (2000) worked with managers who learned a process similar to Creative Problem Solving and applied it to real-world problems. They identified the most important skill in generating high-quality solutions as the ability to generate a large number of solutions. However, the link between fluency and originality is not airtight. MacKinnon (1978) noted that some individuals have many ideas, including high-quality ones; some have many ideas with little originality; and others have only a few ideas, but all of high quality. He suggested that no one approach will increase creative thinking for such diverse individuals. Individuals in the first group might be encouraged to develop their fluency, those in the second to consider criteria for evaluating their ideas, and those in the third to increase their output. He noted that people who produce only a few, high-quality ideas often have many more ideas that they do not make public. These ideas could provide useful input for building more original ideas. Runco and Sakamoto (1999) cited a variety of research indicating that explicit directions asking for more fluent or more original ideas increase the likelihood of such ideas occurring. Logically, it would seem that instruction that makes such instructions clearer should have a similarly positive effect.

All researchers are not in agreement, however. Perkins (1981) described fluency as a "red herring" (p. 141). He suggested that unmediated or unevaluated fluency leads to many mediocre ideas in a quality–quantity trade-off. He described a study in which poets who scored high on a fluency task—listing properties of an apple—also were rated higher on their poetry. This would lead us to suspect that the better poets were more fluent in the way they wrote poetry, that they considered more alternatives before settling on the best idea. This is not what Perkins observed when the poets actually wrote. No poet, regardless of rating, spent time searching through many alternatives before finding a satisfactory phrase. It is possible that more fluent poets might go through more revisions, but that could not be determined from the research design. It seemed that, at least in poetry writing, creative individuals internally screened ideas, preferring to generate a few good ideas rather than many poor ones. Thus, fluency for its own sake may be questionable.

Yet it appears that at least some individuals increase their production of good ideas by considering many. It would seem that to be most effective, activities involving divergent thinking must make the purpose of the strategy clear. The goal is good ideas. Divergent thinking is one path to get there.

One approach, recommended in the Talents Unlimited model (Schlichter, 1986; Schlichter, Palmer, & Palmer, 1993), is direct teaching about divergent thinking. In the Talents model, this type of thought, called productive thinking, is taught as one of several types that are important for success in a variety of tasks. (You may recall that another one of the talents, decision making, was described in chapter 3.) Students are taught that when the task calls for productive thinking they should do four things (Schlichter, 1986, p. 364):

1. Think of many ideas (fluency).
2. Think of varied ideas (flexibility).
3. Think of unusual ideas (originality).
4. Add to their ideas to make them better (elaboration).

In addition to teaching the model, teachers can encourage fluent, flexible, original, and elaborative thinking through their comments and questions. For example, asking "How many ways can you think of to ...?" encourages fluency. "What are some different kinds of ideas?" or "So far, all our ideas involve food. Try to think of ideas that solve the problem in a different way" encourages flexibility. Comments such as "Try to think of something no one else will think of" are designed to elicit originality, whereas "How can we build on this idea?" encourages elaboration.

I have taught students the four aspects of divergent thinking, along with the aphorism, "Your first idea is practically never your best idea." I believe that teaching students this principle, along with a variety of strategies for increasing divergent thinking, can provide valuable tools as long as students understand the situations in which the tools are useful. There is no point in understanding how to use a lathe unless you are able to tell when you need it and when you might be better off with a saber saw, circular saw, or handsaw. Without such knowledge, you waste time, energy, and wood. In the same way, teaching students to think divergently without teaching them when such thinking is useful can lead to inefficiency and wasted time that our classes can ill afford.

5.3. Flexible Thinking in Social Studies

Read a biography of George Washington Carver. Listen for examples of fluency, flexibility, originality, and elaboration. Brainstorm uses for the peanut in the school or community.

Consider the first three examples at the beginning of this chapter. In each case, individuals were trying to solve a problem or generate a new and better idea. These are the types of situations in which divergent thinking can be most useful. If we are trying to plan an original party menu, build an emergency shelter in the woods, or find a plastic that will suit a manufacturer's needs, it is unlikely that the first idea we consider will be the best possible idea. In such circumstances, there probably is value in considering multiple possibilities before choosing one.

On the other hand, Mr. Brown's students, who are brainstorming as many types of birds as possible, are not trying to solve a problem or come up with a new type of bird. They are simply listing all the birds in their collective memory. They may even attack the task flexibly and generate responses such as a badminton birdie or a bird-of-paradise flower. Such tasks may provide a pleasant diversion for a Friday afternoon, but they do not provide clues into the nature or purpose of divergent thinking. Coming up with many ideas simply for the sake of making a long list does not teach students divergent thinking. It is essential for them to understand that divergent thinking is used when we need to solve problems or come up with new and better ideas.

The same caveat applies to the other strategies in this chapter. If students are to use strategies to increase their creative thinking, the strategies must be taught in meaningful ways. Students must understand how these techniques can be used—not just to talk to aliens, but to communicate their ideas to friends and neighbors, come up with a better idea for their science project, or figure out how to get their baby brother out of the locked bathroom. The only possible value I can see in generating long lists of birds, things that are red, or uses for a brick is its value as a practice activity for students who already know about fluency and how it should be used. They could discuss how this task is different from the types of tasks in which they would really need to have many ideas, or look to see whether their most unusual ideas were early or late in the list. Young children, in particular, may sometimes benefit from practice activities that are easier than most real-world problems.

Even so, the same goals could be accomplished while you are using divergent thinking in a meaningful situation. When I was teaching in Connecticut, the state was hit with its first hurricane since 1938. Because the same trees that create the scenic tree-covered roads of New England also hang over the power lines, the hurricane caused millions of downed tree limbs and massive power losses. In the weeks after the storm, the branches were transformed into mountains of mulch along every roadside, far beyond the immediate demand for garden use. Rather than list the classic "uses for a red brick," which is fairly meaningless except to brick companies, my class used divergent thinking to come up with uses for the state's overabundance of mulch. This was a time when original ideas were needed and could be suggested to the proper authorities. Students could examine their list, realize that only after some effort had they come up with their best ideas, and begin to understand that this strategy might be useful in solving other problems. Similarly, the techniques described in this chapter can be used in the context of students' lives, community issues, and course content, allowing students to experience the strategies' usefulness.

Finally, it is important to help students see how divergent thinking fits into the whole of creative thinking. Divergent thinking alone is not creativity. Creativity entails finding a problem or issue worth addressing, generating ideas for addressing it, and evaluating the ideas generated. It may not be necessary for you to evaluate ideas in every activity involving divergent thinking, but it is important to do so often enough for students to understand that just having a lot of ideas is not sufficient. They must also be able to choose from the ideas those that are most original, most interesting, or most promising.

Brainstorming

Of all the strategies for generating ideas, brainstorming is probably the most familiar. It is based on Osborn's (1953) principle of *deferred judgment*: not evaluating any ideas until a number of them have been produced. Osborn compared the process to driving, noting that it is inefficient to drive while pushing on the gas and brake pedals simultaneously. In a parallel fashion, he believed that braking to evaluate ideas may hinder their production. According to this principle, generating many ideas and then applying evaluation criteria is more productive than judging each idea as it is produced. The intent is not to eliminate evaluation, but simply to delay it.

The process of brainstorming strives for a nonjudgmental supportive atmosphere in which idea production can flourish. One of the four cardinal rules of brainstorming even prohibits judgment. The four rules are:

1. Criticism is ruled out. No person is to evaluate any idea until all ideas have been produced. When you work with students, make sure they understand that this rule precludes both verbal and nonverbal criticism: no eye rolling, face making, or other signals.
2. Freewheeling is welcomed. In brainstorming, way out notions are seen as stepping stones to creative ideas. Suggestions that appear to be farfetched can open a new point of view that may lead to a workable idea. For example, while brainstorming ways to make a gloomy basement classroom more attractive, one student suggested replacing the glass block windows with stained glass. This suggestion was clearly not within the class's budget, but it led students to begin thinking about the windows and provided the inspiration for cellophane designs applied to the windows that were reminiscent of stained glass.
3. Quantity is wanted. Quantity is not desired for its own sake, but because a large number of ideas seems more likely than a small number to yield a good idea.
4. Combination and improvement are sought. This rule is sometimes described as hitchhiking. It suggests that many good ideas can be found by building on or combining previous ideas. Such elaboration is to be encouraged. Sometimes extra effort is required to

convey the notion of shared ideas to students accustomed to competition and individual ownership. One friend displayed a poster with the four rules of brainstorming. Underneath the fourth rule she wrote, "This is called teamwork, not 'stealing ideas!'" That phrase and the discussion about it helped her sports-minded students to understand that the successes of group processes are group successes, not individually owned triumphs or failures.

These four rules can be used in their original form or adapted for younger grade levels. One preschool teacher called brainstorming "popcorn thinking." Her students were taught that when they did popcorn thinking, they should try to have lots of ideas pop out, just like popcorn in the popper. They were also taught that no one is allowed to criticize ideas during popcorn thinking, and that it is all right to use someone else's popcorn idea if you change it a little. The teacher did not find that her 3- and 4-year-olds needed any special encouragement to generate freewheeling ideas!

Whatever form the rules take, the focus during the first brainstorming sessions—as for the remaining strategies in this chapter—should be on learning the process rather than on analyzing complex content. If the first few experiences are fairly simple, such as planning a Halloween costume or selecting an animal as the class mascot, students will have the chance to learn the skill, see when it is useful, and be ready to apply it to many new situations.

Brainstorming can be an appropriate strategy any time you want a large number of ideas. This occurs most often when you need to solve a problem or come up with a new, original idea. Students could brainstorm new endings for a story, options for making a graph, strategies that might have aided a historical figure, variables for a possible science experiment, synonyms for an overused word, features for the school newspaper, or strategies for reducing cafeteria noise. They could brainstorm art materials for printing, resources in the school that could be recycled, or ways to encourage adults to use metric measurement. In each case, the strategy has a meaningful use. The list of ideas is generated so that one or more particularly good ideas can be selected, a much more purposeful reason than merely making a list.

In traditional brainstorming, participants work in groups with a leader or recorder to keep track of ideas and monitor the rules. Although Davis (1998) suggested groups of 10 or 12 adults, such groups are probably too large for most students to manage independently. You may find group sizes of three to five more appropriate, except with highly motivated older students. Usually in a heterogeneous class, the brainstorming groups should also be heterogeneous in knowledge, experience, race, and gender. There may be times when brainstorming is used with specifically targeted groups. A group of students with above-average interest, ability, or knowledge in a particular content area working together can provide an appropriate challenge that may not be possible in heterogeneous groups. Conversely, a group with less background or skill in a particular area may provide more opportunities for each student to contribute than might be found in a more diverse, fast-moving group. Flexible grouping patterns (whole-class groups, heterogeneous groups, or homogeneous groups) will allow you to use brainstorming in varied ways for different circumstances and content areas.

Whatever the group composition, groups typically brainstorm for a set period of time, perhaps 3 to 10 minutes, depending on the age of the participants, recording all suggestions without comment. At the end of that time, the group members review and evaluate the ideas using appropriate criteria. A group brainstorming alternative strategies that Lincoln might have used in dealing with Southern secession might consider the economic impact of the suggestions, their political viability given the climate of the time, and how the suggestions relate to Lincoln's expressed personal beliefs. Although the students themselves certainly could not implement any chosen suggestions, they may gain insight into the thought processes that go into such decisions. A discussion like this could be valuable in understanding the Civil War as well as the role of the presidency. A group brainstorming solutions to the cafeteria-noise problem might consider factors such as cost, whether the idea has the support of the principal or teachers, and the amount of noise likely to be affected.

There are numerous variations on brainstorming that can be effective under varied circumstances. Periods of brainstorming can be alternated with periods of evaluation. For example, groups can brainstorm for 5 minutes, select their best ideas, and then continue brainstorming, presumably in a productive direction. This process can be continued as long as necessary or desired. Students can brainstorm silently by writing rather than verbalizing their ideas. Obviously, this technique is appropriate only for students who are old enough and sufficiently skilled that the writing itself does not get in the way of producing ideas. One way to organize this type of exercise is to group students as you would for a standard brainstorming session. Each person writes an idea on a piece of paper and passes it to the person on his or her right. That person may modify the idea or add a new idea before passing the paper on. Depending on the size of the group, the papers may circulate one or more times before the ideas are discussed.

In reverse brainstorming, the group thinks up opposites of the desired ideas. Students might brainstorm ways to waste resources in school or increase arguments in the school yard. Reverse brainstorming is intended to open fresh perspectives and allow participants to attack the original problem from a new point of view. For this to be effective, students must be able to understand the purpose of the activity, to abstract principles from reversed data, and to use them in a new situation. It is probably most effective with secondary students and adults, who are more likely to have the abstract reasoning skills to manage these transitions. Younger students may enjoy reverse brainstorming, but are likely to become silly without making the transition back to the original issue—or even to implement some of the negative ideas suggested!

In other variations, individuals record their own ideas in an individual brainstorming session before joining a group. In one version, individuals list their suggestions and then read their ideas to the group in round-robin style, crossing out any duplicate ideas until all have been recorded. Ideas are then evaluated as usual.

There is no one correct way to brainstorm, nor is there a single technique that guarantees positive results. Osborn himself did not propose brainstorming as a cure-all for any situation demanding creative ideas. Individuals vary in their approaches to and strengths in creative thinking, so no technique will work equally well for all. Some research suggests that the fluency associated with brainstorming increases the likelihood of participants' producing original ideas, but there is also research that calls into question the effectiveness of traditional brainstorming. Dunnette, Campbell, and Jastaad (1963) compared brainstorming groups of 12 adult scientists and workers in advertising with the combined results of 12 similar individuals working alone. They found that the combined efforts of individuals working alone produced more ideas and higher quality ideas than the same number of individuals working together in a group. These authors noted that the groups tended to fall into a rut and pursue the same direction longer than individuals did, leading to less diversity of ideas. This study was used as evidence showing that it is better for people to work alone when they are generating ideas (Weisberg, 1986). It is important to note that the research did not say specific individuals generated more ideas than the brainstorming groups, but that the combined efforts of individuals produced the largest number of ideas.

In a similar fashion, Paulus, Dzindolet, Poletes, and Camacho (1993) found that individuals brainstorming alone produced more ideas than individuals brainstorming in a group, although individuals in groups rated their performances higher than did those working alone. Paulus et al. (1993) referred to this phenomenon as "the illusion of group productivity" (p. 78).

Brilhart and Jochem (1964) compared three types of groups: standard brainstorming groups, brainstorming groups that discussed evaluation criteria before beginning, and groups that discussed evaluation criteria but did not operate by the rules of brainstorming. They found that standard brainstorming groups and groups that considered the evaluation criteria before brainstorming produced the same total number of ideas, although the standard brainstorming group produced more good ideas. Both groups generated more ideas and more good ideas than the group that considered only the evaluation criteria with no mention of brainstorming. Weisberg (1986) noted that despite these differences, the percentage of good ideas was highest in the evaluation-criteria group, the one with the lowest number of ideas and good ideas overall. In trying to assess these results, we are left with a value judgment. Which do we want, the highest percentage of good ideas or the highest total number of good ideas? Unless there were some risk associated with poor ideas, I would usually opt for the latter.

The productivity of group members did not appear to be affected by their considering the evaluation criteria at the beginning of the brainstorming session, suggesting that in some circumstances considering such criteria before the generation of ideas may be productive. We are reminded of Perkins' (1981) poets, who appeared to evaluate ideas as they wrote, coming up with a few high-quality ideas. It is possible that knowing they were writing for an audience of researchers made the poets more self-conscious and concerned about the percentage of high-quality ideas they produced than when they were working at home. The higher the percentage of good ideas desired, the more important it seems to use the evaluation criteria while working. For a higher number of total good ideas, brainstorming appears to be most appropriate. It is also possible that the poets' competence at generating a small number of good ideas may be part of a developmental process. Perhaps less-experienced writers would benefit more from fluency than those who already have a substantial degree of skill.

Finally, some research suggests that elementary school students faced with a divergent thinking task are affected by the instructions given. Runco (1991) reported a study in which students, some of whom had been identified as gifted and talented, were given five tests of divergent thinking. Some groups were given the standard directions asking for many responses, whereas others were instructed to give only original responses. Runco found that in all groups, those who were cued to be original were more likely to be original. They also were less fluent. An interesting observation in Runco's study is that the instruction to be original improved the scores of students not identified as gifted more than it improved the originality of students identified as gifted.

It appears that divergent thinking in general and brainstorming in particular can be helpful in generating new and appropriate ideas, but these strategies offer no guarantees. The quality of ideas is likely to improve when students understand the purpose of fluency—we are trying to be fluent, not because the teacher likes long lists but because we are trying to come up with new and better ideas. Deferred judgment is an important component of brainstorming, but in some situations, considering the criteria for good ideas may not always hurt, and may sometimes help. It is important for researchers and teachers to continue investigating the type and timing of evaluation that is best for varied circumstances, subject areas, and levels of expertise.

The remaining strategies in this section can be considered aids to divergent thinking. Divergent thinking or the technique of brainstorming suggests that it is good to think of many varied ideas, but it does not provide strategies for generating ideas when none are forthcoming. Although it is true that many brainstorming groups come up with original ideas after a period of dead time, it is also useful to know some cues for thinking of new ideas, changing direction, or getting started when you are feeling stuck.

Thinking About the Classroom

If your students have not had previous experience with brainstorming, try some action research. Plan a lesson that requires them to generate many varied answers to a question or problem, such as planning new endings for a story or deciding how a character might solve a problem. Before the next lesson, teach students the rules and purpose of brainstorming. Then do a lesson that closely parallels the first lesson. With the students, examine the results. Under which conditions did students generate more ideas? Under which conditions were there more good ideas? If you want to avoid the effect of practice, randomly divide the class in half and give each half the same task, one with brainstorming instruction and one without.

SCAMPER

One of Osborn's original suggestions for improving divergent thinking was to use idea-spurring queries. His work included checklists of questions such as "How can we simplify? What combinations can be utilized? What adaptations can be made?" (Parnes, 1967, p. 35). When individuals or groups are generating ideas, and suggestions begin to slow, such questions can point to a new direction or point of view.

Eberle (1977, 1996) took some of Osborn's key questions and arranged them into an easy-to-remember acronym, SCAMPER. Eberle used the acronym to write a book using visual imagery and titled, naturally enough, *SCAMPER*. It is described later in the chapter. The acronym SCAMPER can be a useful tool for many creative endeavors other than visual imagery. Because it is easy to remember, it can assist children as well as adults in using the idea-spurring questions that can help them generate diverse ideas. In this section, I examine the questions and strategies that underlie SCAMPER and how they may be used to facilitate divergent thinking.

The S in SCAMPER stands for *substitute*. It suggests asking questions such as "What could I use instead?" or "What other ingredients, materials, or components could I use?" Many new products and solutions to problems large and small are the result of substitution. The individual who first considered substituting artificial sweetener for sugar in soft drinks changed the country's habits forever. The person who realized napkins could be made of paper rather than fabric used substitution, as did the child who used a paper clip to repair a bicycle chain and the driver who held a car together with duct tape. In each case, a solution or innovation was found by substituting a new material or part for the original one.

The C stands for *combine*. It asks, "How can I combine parts or ideas? Are there two things I could blend rather than come up with something new?" Many common products are the result of combinations. Think of the things that have been combined with watches: watch-timers, watch-radios, watch-alarms, watch-video games, and even TV-watches. Similar innovations are occurring as telephones, personal digital assistants, and aspects of personal computers merge in ever-new combinations. Food products also frequently result from combinations. I once saw an innovation in a local grocery store that combined a serving of dry cereal with an individual-size carton of milk. This combination may be particularly useful for children who would like to serve themselves cereal, but cannot manage a heavy milk jug without disaster. Any of the SCAMPER verbs also can be used to stimulate works of art or literature. Lukman Glasgow's sculpture *Watergun* consists of a faucet at the end of the barrel of a pistol. Other combinations could be used to create interesting visual puns from compound words or figures of speech. Imagine how a carpool, a fan belt, or a handspring might be portrayed. Picasso used this technique to recombine elements of figures or objects that had been taken apart. A parallel process could be used to recombine parts of a familiar object in new ways to create a work of art. Similarly, characters from diverse literary forms could be combined for new story ideas. Imagine what kind of story might emerge if Curious George met the seven dwarfs, or the personality of Lady MacBeth were one of the characters in *The Grapes of Wrath*.

Thinking About the Classroom

Look through magazines or gift catalogues. On your own or with students' help, collect pictures that illustrate the use of each of the SCAMPER verb in developing new products. You may want to use the pictures to create a bulletin board. Or pick a common household item and have students use the SCAMPER verbs to plan ways to improve it.

The A stands for *adapt*. It suggests questions such as "What else is like this?" or "Could we change or imitate something else?" In adapting, we change something known to solve the problem. Many computerized communication programs for individuals without speech began as adaptations of boards that allowed the user to point (or blink) at the desired word. Countless fashion trends have started as adaptations of earlier styles. The first person to hook a trailer behind an automobile probably adapted the idea from wagons hooked behind horses.

Many times, creative solutions to problems come from adaptations of old ideas. In my graduate creativity class, the most daunting assignment probably is the requirement to identify a personal or social problem and invent something to solve it. Students are always relieved to realize that many inventions are adaptations of earlier ideas and products. Their adaptations have included a perforated pizza box that divides into individual plates, eliminating dishes and fitting more easily into the trash or recyling bin, and a cutting board adapted for use by individuals with limited use of one arm. The board was equipped with prongs to hold food securely in place so that only one hand was needed for cutting. In these two cases the adaptations must have been good ones, for we have since seen commercial versions of both.

The M can have several meanings. It can stand for *modify*. In modifying we ask, "Could we change a current idea, practice, or product slightly and be successful?" Modifications might include changing the flavor or color of toothpaste to be more appealing to children or adding nuts and raisins to a popular cookie recipe. Slight changes in the styling of automobiles also could be characterized as modifications. The M can also stand for *magnify* or *minify*. Magnifying allows us to ask, "How could I make it bigger, stronger, more exaggerated, or more frequent?" It could lead to big-screen television sets, giant Goldfish crackers and supersized meal portions, double-length garden hoses, or a weekly (rather than monthly) collection of recyclables. One of my students magnified the idea of a dentist's mirror by attaching an angled mirror to the end of a broomstick. He used it to check the gutters of his house without dragging out the ladder and climbing to the roof. Magnifying common objects to many times their size also can spur original works of art. Andre Peterson's *Staple Remover* is a 30-inch magnification of a familiar object. Viewed at that size, form becomes more important than function, allowing us to see the object in a new way. To minify is, of course, just the opposite. To go in this direction, we ask, "How can I make it smaller, more compact, lighter, or less frequent?" Minifying has led to RitzBitz (bite-size crackers), 3-inch television sets, concentrated fabric softener, and 10-second commercials. (Actually, the shortened commercials combine both magnifying and minifying: They take less time, so we get more of them. I am not at all sure I am grateful for that innovation.)

The P stands for *put* to other uses. It suggests that we ask, "How can I use this in a new way?" The switch from advertising Kleenex as a makeup re-

"M" can stand for magnify or minify.

mover to billing it as a pocket handkerchief was a brilliant and profitable use of this strategy. Using resealable food storage bags to organize a suitcase, planting flowers in an old wheelbarrow, and recycling plastic milk jugs as part of a stage set all are examples of putting materials to uses other than those for which they were intended. When my elementary students considered alternate uses for the hurricane-generated mulch, they were using this part of the SCAMPER acronym.

5.4. Put to Other Uses: Using Part of SCAMPER (K–12)

Joan Steiner's book *Look Alikes** is a fabulous example of putting objects to other uses, in this case, using common objects to create extraordinary landscapes. It can provide a challenge for anyone from child to adult to find new ways to use the things around us.

Steiner, J. (1998). *Look alikes.* New York: Little, Brown and Company.

*Many of the suggested activities in this text make use of picture books. Do not make the mistake of assuming picture books are appropriate only for young children. Many of the works of art and literature contained in such books speak powerfully to individuals of all ages. Moreover, they have the added advantage of being short enough to share easily in a brief period.

The E is for *eliminate*. It leads us to ask, "What can be omitted or eliminated? Are all the parts necessary? Is it necessary to solve this problem at all?" Grocery stores are full of products from which fat or sugar have been eliminated. Poets constantly strive to eliminate unnecessary words. Concentrated laundry detergents are the result of omitting or reducing fillers. Sometimes the problem itself can be eliminated if it is found to be unimportant or not worth the effort required to solve it. In some schools, efforts to reduce cafeteria noise were eliminated when would-be problem solvers determined that as long as students can hear emergency signals over the cafeteria noise, it may be good for students to talk in the cafeteria, or that the energy spent trying to keep them from doing so could more profitably be spent elsewhere.

Finally, the R stands for *rearrange* or *reverse*. It suggests questions such as "Could I use a different sequence? Could I interchange parts? Could I do the opposite? What would happen if I turned it upside down, backward, or inside out?" Left-handed scissors, knives, and garden tools are examples of rearranging or reversing. I had a reversible winter coat that cut my dry-cleaning bills in half. One of my students used the principle of reversing to reduce the frustration she experienced in trying to get catsup and salad dressings out of the bottles. She built a rack for her refrigerator door that holds all the bottles upside down. When she removes them from the refrigerator, they are ready to pour.

The questions generated by the SCAMPER acronym can be used to address many types of problems. Because the acronym itself is quite complex, teachers of young children many want to teach one or two letters at a time. Students of all ages can benefit by looking for examples of how others have used these strategies before using them independently. Students can look through magazines for examples of cartoons, advertisements, or products that illustrate the use of one or more SCAMPER verbs. These can be collected and displayed in the classroom. A commercial jingle may substitute new words in a popular song. A paper towel advertisement may use magnification as it portrays its product absorbing a small lake. Many new products can be identified as the result of idea-spurring questions.

You may find it easiest to have students begin to use the SCAMPER acronym in ways similar to those they see around them. They could use the questions to suggest ways to improve a familiar product or suggest new items for the school menu. Older students could try using idea-spurring questions to draw political or humorous cartoons or advertisements. However, the most important understanding is that all or parts of the SCAMPER acronym can be used any time students need to generate many ideas or solve a problem. They do not have to sit and wait for ideas to pop into their heads, but can use the SCAMPER questions to help the ideas come.

In the example at the beginning of the chapter, Ms. Cochran used the SCAMPER questions to help students improve their science projects. Suppose second-grade students wanted to duplicate a demonstration in the science book that used colored water traveling up a celery stalk to illustrate the structure of the celery stalk. The SCAMPER questions could be used to generate ideas for modifying the project. Students could ask a number of questions: "Could another plant be substituted for celery? Would it still work? Would other liquids work? Would they travel the same distance or at the same speed? Would big stems and little stems work the same way? What if you used a root instead of a stem? Would it work upside down? Do all colors travel the same way? At the same speed? If you cut a notch in the celery, what would happen?"

Older students could use a similar strategy for more sophisticated projects. If a seventh-grade student was interested in teaching mice to go through a maze, he or she might ask: "Does the shape or material of the maze affect the speed of learning? Could I combine this study with another variable, such as nutrition, noise level, or social interactions? Is there a famous experiment I could adapt? Does the height or width of the maze affect learning? If I reverse the maze in the room, will it matter? Could the idea of a maze be used in other types of experiments? How do human beings find their way through mazes? Are people who are good at paper-and-pencil mazes also good in three-dimensional mazes?"

In either case, a variety of novel projects could be devised through responses to the SCAMPER questions. In a similar manner, SCAMPER can be used to modify and elaborate story plots, create ideas for three-dimensional art projects, or address school or community problems. It gives students a set of tools they can use when they are struggling to find an idea or to improve the ideas they have.

Thinking About the Classroom

Take your class to visit an art museum. Try to find pieces of art that may have been generated using SCAMPER verbs. You may find contemporary galleries the most fruitful.

Attribute Listing

Another strategy for generating creative ideas is attribute listing (Crawford, 1954). With this technique, the problem or product is divided into key attributes that are addressed separately. For example, an individual charged with creating a new candy bar might determine first what the key attributes of a candy bar are, and then consider how each one might be altered or combined to form a new product. The attributes to be considered could include the shape, coating, basic filling, additions to the filling, size, packaging, and possible ties to famous characters. Instead of trying to plan a new product all at once, the candy designer might first think about variations in shape (What about a round candy bar or animal shapes?) and then consider each attribute in turn, using a list like the one in Fig. 5.3. This process could result in a rocket-shaped bar filled with peanut butter and jelly or tiny orange-filled candies in a package tied to a Saturday-morning cartoon show. A similar process might be followed by those designing cars, playgrounds, or any other complex product. By identifying the key attributes of the product, the design task can be broken into manageable components that can spur new combinations of ideas.

A similar process can be used to address problems that do not result in a physical product. Imagine a town council trying to develop an advertising scheme to lure shoppers downtown. Attribute listing could be used to iden-

Shape	Coating	Basic Filling	Additions	Size	Package	Tie-In
rectangle	milk chocolate	peanut butter	nuts	regular	singles	sports
circle	white chocolate	chocolate	caramel	double	buddy-pack	sports figure
sphere	peanut creme	vanilla	cookie pieces	mini	family-pack	cartoons
triangle	fruit coating	mint	coconut	varied	clear package	movie
prism	coconut	cashew butter	raisins	family	toys inside	TV show
animals	nuts	white chocolate	dates		package is a toy	news hero
rocket	cookie crumbs	orange	jelly		musical	story figure
truck	pretzel crumbs	cherry	sprinkles		personal	superhero
donut		other fruit	chopped candy			
			marshmallow			

FIG. 5.3. Attribute listing for a new candy bar.

tify key features of the downtown area and how each could be used to attract consumers. A school library media specialist trying to ease congestion at the checkout desk might look at each step of the process separately. He or she might examine the path and direction of the line, the responsibilities of the student with the book, the position and responsibilities of the worker(s), and the physical arrangement of the desk. If he or she determines that young children cause delays because they have trouble placing their books on a high counter, and the counter cannot be adjusted, perhaps a different area can be used when primary classes come to the center. If one person is responsible for checking books in and out at the same time, perhaps these responsibilities could be separated. The strength of this process is that it forces the problem solver to examine the situation from several angles. If, for example, the problem solver had not used attribute listing, but had simply viewed the desk traffic jam as a whole, he or she might not have noticed multiple causes for the difficulties.

5.5. Attribute Listing in Spanish IV: "If" Clauses and The Mexican Revolution

This lesson should be taught simultaneously with lessons on contrary-to-fact "if" clauses. List key events of the Mexican Revolution on the board. For each event, use contrary-to-fact clauses to imagine what might have happened if each event had been altered in some way. For example, how would the revolution have been different if Carranza had not ordered the assassination of Emiliano Zapata? As an assignment, students can be asked to select an event not discussed in class and write a brief essay (in Spanish) describing what might have changed if the event had been altered.

Adapted from a lesson by Lynn Massucci.

Students can be taught to use attribute listing in planning their school or personal projects. To be successful at it, most students will need assistance in learning to identify the important attributes of a product or situation. As they become adept at identifying key components, they can begin to consider the effects of changing each one, first by examining changes planned by others and later by instigating change themselves.

In an art class, students may use observation skills to identify attributes of a particular style of painting. They might then observe what changes resulted when one or more attributes were changed. After determining the key attributes of impressionist paintings (e.g., departure from realistic representation, a subject that is usually outdoors, varied colors to represent the effects of light and shadow), they might determine which attributes were altered by postimpressionists such as Seurat or Cezanne. Later, they might experiment with first mimicking a particular style, then choosing some aspect of the style to change.

In science, students can identify the key attributes or variables in an experiment or demonstration and hypothesize what might happen if specific changes were made. One first-grade class listed the key needs for growing bean plants (sun, soil, and water), then hypothesized what would happen if each were changed. The result was a series of experiments that added considerably to students' understanding of plant growth.

A classic use of attribute listing is to represent story structure. After students learn about key attributes of stories (character, setting, conflict, and others), not only can they analyze the stories they read, but they also can use the knowledge to generate new stories. One possible exercise asks students to list 10 possible characters, 10 settings, 10 problems the character might have, and 10 sources of help. These can be combined to suggest many varied story lines. One variation is to require students to create a story based on the last four digits of their phone numbers. If my phone number ends in 0263, I would have to write a story using the tenth character, the second setting, the sixth problem, and the third source of help.

Davis (1998) described how Fran Striker used a similar technique to generate plots for the *Lone Ranger* series. Striker combined lists of characters, goals, obstacles, and outcomes to plan each episode. Older students may enjoy hypothesizing how such techniques may be used in planning contemporary television shows, perhaps using lists of attributes to develop a new episode for a favorite show.

Attribute listing also can be used to create fantasy characters, inventions, or products that can form the basis of creative writing. Very young children can combine lists of heads, bodies, and tails to invent new animals. Older students can use a similar process to invent new superheroes or other fantasy characters. They might list superpowers, animals, or other sources of unusual characteristics, secret identities, or weaknesses. These attributes may be combined to design new comic book characters. The idea of fantasy characters could be combined with science content to create characters that might live in a particular environment. Students might identify key attributes of the environment on Venus and then list possible features that could allow a living thing to exist in that situation. Characteristics could be used to develop characters for science fiction writing. Students might also examine commercial science fiction and speculate on how the characters were developed, how attribute listing might have been used, or whether the characters could actually exist in the situations described. Attribute listing also can be used to modify existing products and to develop real or imagined inventions that could be the basis of persuasive speeches, advertisements, or stories.

In social studies, attribute listing can be used to identify key issues or components in current events or historical stories. Hypothesizing about the possible results if one attribute were altered can allow students to process content in an interesting way while becoming aware of the complex relationships in historical events.

5.6. Attribute Listing in Spanish II: Restaurant Dialogue

List basic categories (or events) to be considered in creating a dialogue that might take place in a restaurant, for example, asking for a table, ordering a meal, engaging in conversation while waiting for the meal, and making requests of the wait staff. Under each category, list several possible scenarios, expressions that might be used, and useful vocabulary. Individuals or groups of students write a dialogue using something from each category. Additional content requirements regarding the usage of various verb forms may be included in the assessment rubric.

Adapted from a lesson by Lynn Massucci.

As you can see, virtually any subject area can be analyzed through attribute listing. Examining real or hypothetical changes and combinations of changes can allow students to examine content from new points of view as well as develop new and creative ideas.

Morphological Synthesis

A variation of attribute listing, morphological synthesis, combines two attributes in the form of a grid. Young students wishing to invent a new animal could list animal heads on one axis and animal bodies on the other axis (Fig. 5.4). Each square on the grid would represent a particular combination of head and body. Students could design an animal by choosing a particularly appealing combination or by random selection, such as pointing to the paper with their eyes shut or dropping a small object on the paper.

One of my favorite uses of morphological synthesis was created by a graduate student who lived in a house with several other international students. In addition to the usual stresses of graduate school, these students had to deal with language difficulties, limited budgets, and unfamiliar American food. One discovery that generated great enthusiasm in the group was prepared biscuit mix. It was inexpensive and flexible and could be mixed with a variety of foods to create new dishes. One student created a

Animal Bodies

	Frog	Pig	Squirrel	Robin	Cat	Ant	Lion	Whale	Mouse
Cow									
Bear									
Snake									
Tiger									
Elephant									
Ostrich									
Alligator									
Goldfish									

(Left vertical label: Animal Heads)

FIG. 5.4. Create an animal through morphological synthesis.

morphological synthesis grid to generate new recipes. Along one axis she listed ways the biscuit mix could be cooked, such as baked, deep-fried, boiled for dumplings, steamed, or pan-fried. On the other axis she listed things that could be combined with biscuit mix, with items ranging from chopped ham and onions to chocolate chips and raisins. Each square represented a possible dish. Although not all the combinations were delicious, the group was very pleased with some of the new dishes and planned to use the same technique to invent other new foods.

One advantage of using morphological synthesis with young students is that it teaches techniques that parallel those necessary to read and create graphs. When students identify the square that represents a giraffe head on a pig's body, they are reading x and y axes just as surely as they might in any math activity. Combining materials and strategies to invent a new game, mixing pop-up forms and holidays to devise new cards, and adding seeds to

---

5.7. Morphological Synthesis in Kindergarten

After listening to *Color Zoo* (Ehlert, 1989), use morphological synthesis to choose three color/shape combinations to be used in creating a picture in the style of Lois Ehlert. Use students holding cards to create a human grid. Practice having designated students walk forward to create their combination. Read the book and discuss the shapes used by the illustrator. Have students use the morphological synthesis grid to create three shapes to be used in constructing an animal.

Adapted from a lesson by Melinda Spicer.

growing media for a science experiment all provide opportunities for creative thinking that parallel those of many real-world creators while also giving students practice in several types of content and skills.

Random Input and Other Techniques of Lateral Thinking

In a book titled *Serious Creativity*, de Bono (1992) described strategies designed to promote lateral thinking and the creation of new ideas. De Bono, a prolific writer in the field of creativity for decades, has provided training in strategies designed to increase creative ideas for numerous companies and organizations around the world. The basis of de Bono's work is the systematic promotion of lateral thinking, defined as "seeking to solve problems by unorthodox or apparently illogical methods" (p. 52). He contrasted vertical thinking, in which the thinker delves more deeply into familiar or typical paths of thought—often compared with digging the same hole deeper—and lateral thinking, which tries a different perspective or vantage point—digging a new hole. De Bono believed that it is possible to increase lateral thinking through the systematic use of strategies that stimulate alternate paths of thought. His serious creativity does not rely on inspiration, intuition, or natural creative talent, but teaches specific tools that anyone can use to increase the production of original ideas. Although the tools of lateral thinking are too numerous and complex to be fully explained here, we can examine a few examples.

The Creative Pause.   One strategy an individual can learn for spurring creative effort is the creative pause. In using a creative pause, an individual stops midstream in a line of thinking, not because there is a problem but because the thinker has chosen to stop. The pause allows the thinker to pay deliberate attention to some point, opening the possibility that there could be a new idea. A teacher might stop, purposefully, at a random point in lesson planning and consider whether there might be another way to approach the task about which he or she is thinking. Students could be taught to pause periodically in the midst of any potentially creative endeavor. Midway through a writing assignment, problem-solving task, social studies project, or art piece, they might pause and consider whether what they are doing might be approached in another way.

The creative pause is not used to focus on problems or force thinkers to wrack their brains for a novel response. It is an opportunity for focus and change. It is not the result of inspiration, but a deliberate strategy that is undertaken purposefully, with the recognition that in any train of thought there may be alternative, perhaps better, ideas to be considered. If, after a brief period, no new ideas are forthcoming, the original line of thought can be continued. It is interesting to consider what ideas might result if every classroom held a sign reading, "PAUSE—and think." Students might occasionally look up, pause, consider their thinking, and move to new, more original ideas.

Provocations and the Use of Po.   One way to cue lateral thinking is to set up provocations. In using provocations, statements are put forward to provoke new patterns of thought rather than to describe realistic situations. De Bono (1970) suggested the word "po" to instigate provocations. When po precedes a statement, it indicates understanding by the writer or speaker that the statement is not true and may even be impossible, yet the speaker would like to consider it anyway in the hope that it might open new avenues of thought.

In many ways, "po" is parallel to children's use of "what if" or "just suppose." Young children often have little difficulty imagining what would happen if dogs could fly, if schools had no doors, or if pencils had to be kept in the refrigerator. Older students and adults sometimes have trouble maintaining focus on obviously ridiculous propositions long enough to see whether new, helpful ideas might be derived from them. The word "po" may be of particular value to middle-grade and older students who sometimes consider themselves much too mature to play silly games like Just Suppose. If they understand that po is a tool used by top business executives to spur creative ideas, they may be more willing to suspend judgment long enough to try it.

There are four common provocations that may be preceded by the word "po." The first is a reversal, similar to the R in SCAMPER. In a reversal provocation, you invert the situation being considered. Elements are not eliminated; they are reversed. For example, po, the Native American Indians landed in Portugal in 1492. This provocation might form the basis of a class discussion on the impact of Columbus's voyage.

A second type of provocation is an exaggeration. This type of provocation takes one variable being considered and expands or diminishes it to unreasonable proportions. In developing a school recycling plan, the provocation might be po, each classroom produces 100 boxes of waste paper a week. This may suggest processes that might not otherwise be considered. An alternate provocation might be po, each class uses only one piece of paper per year. Such an exaggeration might help students focus on how we might treat paper if it were a rare and valuable commodity.

The third provocation is distortion. Here, relationships between elements or time sequences are altered. An interesting provocation for a teacher education class might be po, the students give tests to the teachers. A high school class studying the development of language might consider po, written language developed before oral communication. Distortion provocations can be very challenging, yet powerful. The distortion po, you die before you die sounds bizarre, and yet it is the type of provocation that led to the development of living benefits life insurance, a successful form of insurance that brought profits to the insurance companies and financial relief to the terminally ill (de Bono, 1992). Of course, any of the provocations or other tools of lateral thinking also can be interpreted through visual or literary arts. Many art classes learn to enlarge or reduce images through the use of grids. When the grids are distorted, creating curves or angles not present in the original, students can find new perspectives.

As provocations become more unrealistic, the students will need increasing cognitive and emotional maturity to deal with them profitably. Young children can enjoy fantasy Just Suppose situations, but may have trouble abstracting principles from the provocations to real life. You will need to use your professional judgment to gauge the types of provocations that are most powerful for your class. As students gain in sophistication and experience, they can recognize seemingly silly statements as serious invitations to new, innovative ideas.

Random Input.   Another way to cue lateral thinking is to use random input. With this strategy, the problem or subject for creative thought is juxtaposed with a randomly selected word. By attempting to make connections between the subject and the unrelated word, individuals may see the problem from a new vantage point or generate new ideas. If I were trying to think of a new approach to an upcoming social studies unit on pioneers, I might try the random-input approach. I could open the dictionary to a randomly selected page (say, 68) and choose a random word position (perhaps the seventh word). If the seventh word is not a noun, I would continue down the page until I came to a noun because nouns seem to be the easiest sources of random input. In my dictionary, the seventh word on page 68 is bangalore torpedo. (You can tell this activity is authentic because I'd never make that up!) A bangalore torpedo is a metal tube that contains explosives and a firing mechanism and is used to cut barbed wire and detonate buried mines.

My task now is to make some kind of connection between a bangalore torpedo and pioneers. Pioneers did not have to detonate buried mines, at least to my knowledge, so I have to consider other uses for explosives. Perhaps some students might be interested in the mechanics of the weapons used by pioneers. We might examine how explosives were used in creating pathways through the mountains or how pioneers managed to get through the mountains without artificial pathways. Miners sometimes used explosives. Perhaps I could incorporate information on prospecting and mineral rights into my unit. We could examine the varying motives that led people westward. How were the solitary prospectors different from the mining companies or the homesteaders? The idea of focusing the unit on why people went west has potential for making ties to other aspects of the social studies curriculum.

I might take a totally different approach. How might the bangalore torpedo relate to my processes in planning the unit? Should I blow up all my previous plans and start over? Perhaps I need to review my ideas thus far for hidden mines or sources of difficulty. Whatever idea(s) I pursue, in approximately 5 minutes an unusual and unrelated word has provided me with numerous avenues for potentially creative changes in my planning.

The same approach can be taught to students. High school students trying to develop a theme for a yearbook or dance, middle school students trying to develop a character for historical fiction, or elementary students brainstorming new ideas for the playground all may benefit from randomly selected input. Students can use random input when they have no ideas—for example, when they cannot think of a subject for an art project or cannot decide what area of independent study to pursue. Random input also can be useful when they have run out of ideas or when all their ideas are starting to sound the same. Perhaps they have already done three reports on various states and want to make the fourth project unique. Practice activities with random input can work well during the last 5 minutes before lunch or at the end of the day. Pick a problem or issue from course content, school problems, or current events and match it with a random word. For example, "The problem is trash in front of the school. The word is lumberyard. What ideas does this bring us?"

In addition to choosing a page and place number in the dictionary, de Bono (1992) suggested alternate sources of random words. Students might compile a list of 60 words, perhaps randomly selected from a dictionary. They then would select the word to be used by glancing at a watch and noting the reading of the second hand. If the hand is at the 14th second, they would select the 14th word. The list could be changed every month or every 2 months for variety. Words could be placed in a bin or box and drawn out, or a designated student could, without looking, randomly point to a word in a book or magazine. If the books and dictionaries used are appropriate for the grade level, the possibility is increased that students will be able to make enough connections for the process to be effective.

Thinking About the Classroom

Try using random input in planning a lesson (or unit) where you are feeling stuck and looking for a new approach. Or working with others who teach on your grade level, agree on a common topic. Ask each teacher to pull a word randomly from the dictionary and spend 5 minutes individually using it to generate ideas. Compare your results. See what varied directions the lesson might take from these random ideas. Try the same thing with a different type of problem—perhaps when you are trying to plan an interesting and novel party for your friends.

Six Thinking Hats. One of de Bono's best-known strategies is the use of the six thinking hats. Here six different roles or ways of approaching a situation are defined as different-colored hats. A person taking on the white-hat role, for example, focuses on information. White-hat thinking asks questions such as "What information do we have? What information is missing? How are we going to get needed information?" The green hat requests creative effort, whereas the red hat looks for feelings, intuition, or emotion. Black-hat thinking requires critical judgment; yellow-hat thinking looks for benefits and possibilities; and blue-hat thinking monitors the kinds of thinking being used. By switching the type of thinking requested about a given problem, problem solvers can find new perspectives and avoid becoming trapped in familiar patterns of thought.

In using this strategy, teachers evaluating a textbook series might start with blue-hat thinking to define the goals of the group. Next, white-hat thinking might be used to gather information, and green-hat thinking could help in the development of possible selection criteria. Yellow-hat thinking could be used to look for good points about the list of criteria, followed by black-hat thinking to help in spotting weaknesses and flaws. Finally, red-hat thinking could be used to assess how the group feels about the criteria as they now stand (de Bono, 1991a, 1991b, 1999).

With young people or less complex tasks, a more limited sequence could be used. For example, students could use the thinking hats to respond to a poem. Students could begin with red-hat responses, explaining how they feel about the work: "I really like that poem" or "It gives me a feeling of loneliness." Next, the white hat could be used to identify interesting or missing information: "I can't tell why the writer went into the woods" or "I wonder what made him think the woods was like a cave." The yellow hat could be used to point out things students like about the poem: "I like the picture it makes in my mind of the bright stars near the dark woods" and "The last line has a lot of 's' sounds." If desired, this discussion could be continued using the black and green hats.

The key to each of these activities is that various hats, or frames of mind, are used and changed purposefully. The six thinking hats strategy is designed to break apart different types of thinking, allowing the thinkers to concentrate more efficiently on each type of thought and ultimately provide a more rounded view of the task or situation. Effective use of the six-hats strategy demands more information than is possible in a brief overview. Information on resources supporting deBono's teaching strategies is best obtained through his authorized Web site, currently at http://www.edwdebono.com.

Another skills program that includes lateral thinking is CoRT (de Bono, 1986), an acronym for Cognitive Research Trust, the site of the program's origin. In using CoRT, students are taught strategies, each with an accompanying acronym, that provide cues for effective thinking. The first tool taught is called PMI (plus, minus, and interesting). The PMI tool is designed to overcome our natural tendency to continue thinking about a situation in the same direction as our original impression. Take a minute and think about what might happen if, starting tomorrow, all public schools were open 24 hours a day. Jot down a few of your ideas before continuing.

Chances are, if you look at your list, you will see that most of your ideas were generally positive or generally negative. If your first impression was that 24-hour schools were a good idea, you probably thought of several points to support that position. If your first impression was negative, it is likely that you listed several problems that might accompany 24-hour schools. Few people, unless cued, automatically look with equal care at multiple sides of an issue or situation. If you were to use PMI to think about 24-hour schools, you would list all the positive things and all the negative things you could. You would also list interesting things, those that are neither positive nor negative. Interesting things often are questions that might be raised, such as "What does 'open' mean? Would schools conduct traditional classes all day or would they take on different roles?" or "How would vacations be scheduled?" Other tools in the CoRT program provide similar cues for examining issues. Some, but not all, of the tools are designed to foster lateral thinking. The assumption underlying the program is that if students' perceptions of a situation can be broadened, their thinking about the situation can be more effective. Like the six thinking hats, CoRT demands more information and training than can be provided in a brief overview. Resource information is available through the same Web site.

Using Divergent Thinking in Creative Problem Solving

As discussed in chapter 2, Creative Problem Solving (CPS) is a model designed to facilitate as well as describe the creative process. Each of the components of CPS has both divergent and convergent aspects (called generative and focusing phases), so it is a natural context in which to use divergent thinking. Many of the tools described so far can be used effectively in the CPS process to enhance the number and diversity of ideas. Because CPS is complex, teachers of young children may wish to teach and use single parts of the process separately or to use them in a simplified fashion. Students of any age will need many varied experiences with CPS to master the stages and be able to apply them to varied situations. However, I believe the time and trouble required to teach CPS are worth the effort.

With CPS, students have a powerful process for attacking school, social, and personal problems from elementary grades into adulthood. Although early practice activities may focus on fantasy situations or fairy tales, CPS is most potent when used to interact with the real world. A book that will inspire you and your students to use your new problem-solving skills to benefit your community is *The Kid's Guide to Social Action* (Lewis, 1991). This book provides examples, skill instruction, and tips for problem solving that can be applied to a host of community issues. The basic components of CPS were discussed in chapter 2. This section reviews each component and follows two classes through early problem-solving activities. As you review these two examples, it is important to remember that they are provided merely as examples of possible steps, not as an illustration of stages to be undertaken in every problem-solving activity. The effective use of CPS entails making good decisions about which components and stages to undertake in a given situation (Isaksen, Dorval, & Treffinger, 2000; Treffinger, 1995; Treffinger, Isaksen, & Dorval, 2000, Treffinger, Isaksen, & Dorval, 2003).

Understanding the Challenge

Constructing Opportunities.   Recall from chapter 2 that the first stage of Understanding the Challenge is Constructing Opportunities. It is necessary to identify a general area on which to focus problem-solving efforts. Sometimes opportunities are obvious or come up in day-to-day classroom conversation. In one class, a sixth-grade girl returned from a vacation outraged over the limitations in restaurant children's menus. Because the girl had a small appetite, her mother insisted that she order children's meals. Although her mother ate a variety of interesting food on her vaca-

The first step in Creative Problem Solving is finding a mess.

tion, the sixth grader spent the entire week eating hamburgers, hot dogs, fried chicken, and spaghetti. For her, this was the beginning of a project that spanned nutrition, restaurant regulations, age discrimination, and many other issues. In another school, frequent injuries on the blacktop playground provided an obvious focus for concern.

If a challenge does not present itself immediately, students can be taught to look for problem areas. Newspapers or news magazines can be used to generate lists of concerns. Local or school officials can be interviewed to identify issues affecting the community. For young children, teachers may wish to identify real or fictional challenges. I have selected two opportunities for following the CPS process through. The first is an imaginary primary teacher's fictional problem-solving exercise revolving around Horton and the Who-ville situation (Seuss, 1954). In a second real-world example from my own teaching, the mess was not a trouble spot, but an opportunity. Two students became curious about the historical marker near the school and went out to read it after the school day ended. The marker described the town's beginnings, and, with a few calculations, the students realized that the town was approaching its 250th birthday. This was not a problem, but an opportunity for creative problem solving.

In each case, students should be able to identify the general goal of the problem-solving activity and whether the goal was self-selected or presented by the teacher. Students who have some experience with Creative Problem Solving could begin by Appraising the Task to determine whether CPS is an appropriate tool for this opportunity or not. They might also Design the Process by selecting which stages of CPS are most appropriate for the situation at hand. In this case, I will describe each possible component as if the decision had been made to pursue each available stage.

Exploring Data.   In Exploring Data, students learn as much about the situation as possible. The young students investigating Who-ville could write down everything they know about Horton's situation. The list should include facts, feelings, and impressions obtained by reading the book. Students could determine which ideas are facts, which are opinions, and which cannot be fully determined. They also could record information they would like to have if they could visit Horton at the site of his dilemma. This exercise would provide practice in Exploring Data, and in supporting ideas with information from text.

For the 250th anniversary group, Exploring Data had a wider range. The curious students read town history, talked to local officials about planned celebrations (there were none), and spoke to community members about town activities during the 1976 national bicentennial. One of the interesting facts they uncovered related directly to the school. Several people believed that near the bicentennial (no one knew exactly when), some elementary school students had buried a time capsule in front of the school. No one knew exactly where!

Framing Problems. Framing Problems is a stage in which problem solvers identify potential subproblems in their challenge. Problems usually start with IWWMW ("In what ways might we?"). In the *Horton Hears a Who* exercise, problem statements might start with "In what ways might Horton …." Students should list as many problem statements as possible before choosing the one (or a combination) that best expresses the dilemma they choose to address. The primary school group might ultimately settle for a problem statement such as "In what ways might Horton keep the people of Who-ville safe without having to sit still all the time?" The anniversary group's problem was something like "In what ways might we celebrate the town's 250th anniversary so that it will be remembered?"

Generating Ideas

In the Generating Ideas stage, problem solvers generate as many varied and unusual ideas as possible for solving the problem. At this stage of the CPS process, many other tools for divergent thinking can be useful. Attribute listing, SCAMPER, morphological synthesis, metaphorical thinking, and others all can be used to increase the number and diversity of solutions put forth. After the group has produced as many ideas as needed, a smaller number of ideas usually is selected to continue the CPS process. At this stage, no formal criteria are used for selecting the ideas. The group simply chooses the ideas that seem best. The Horton group might choose such ideas as building a stand to hold Who-ville, getting someone else to hold it for a while, getting the people in Who-ville to get off the dust ball for a vacation, and building a new Who-ville. The 250th anniversary group suggested numerous ideas for a community celebration: a town festival, articles in the paper, commemorative souvenirs, a new time capsule, and a variety of school projects.

Preparing for Action

Developing Solutions. In Developing Solutions, the short list of ideas is evaluated using criteria determined by the group. The number of criteria and the sophistication of the evaluation will vary with grade level. Young children should begin with a small number of criteria, simply evalu-

---

5.8. Using CPS in American History

Review the immigrant groups who settled in the colonies and the varying types of technological knowledge they brought with them. Discuss why people moved to the frontier or backcountry. Brainstorm the types of messes likely to be found on the frontier. Small groups of students choose a problem situation to study, researching facts relevant to the situation. For example, a group studying the problem "limited food" might study climate, soil conditions, vegetation, wildlife, and the like. They also would investigate the technology related to food production available in the 18th century. Frame a problem statement in the form "In what ways might we ..."

Generating Ideas

Using a period tool as a basis, groups use SCAMPER to modify the tool to improve it. Select criteria for evaluating the tool. (Evaluation criteria may be generated as a whole-class activity.)

Planning for Action

Plan the materials and steps necessary to create either the new tool or a model of the tool.

Adapted from a lesson by Linda Gayer.

---

ated. For example, in judging Horton's options, students might be asked how Horton could decide which was the best idea. They might ask, "Could he do it without dropping Who-ville? Would the Who people be safe? Would the Who people be happy? Would Horton be happy?" These criteria might be evaluated with the simple grid shown in Fig. 5.5. Each suggestion

	Could Horton do it?	Would the Who people be safe?	Would the Who people be happy?	Would Horton be happy?
Build a stand for Who-ville	☺			
Get someone else to hold it	😐			
Get the people of Who-ville off the dust ball	😐			
Build a new Who-ville	☹			

FIG. 5.5. Solution-finding for Horton.

could be judged on each criterion and given a happy face, sad face, or neutral (can't tell or maybe) face. The solution with the greatest number of happy faces is likely to be the best solution. As students mature and gain experience with CPS, they can use more sophisticated focusing tools. Rather than smiling faces, students can use numerical rankings for each criterion, adding totals to determine the highest-ranked solution. If students use CPS in real-world contexts, they probably will soon determine that the point totals may not always identify the best idea. Sometimes an idea may rank high but be impossible to carry out. For example, if the 250th anniversary group had an idea that was ranked high on every criterion except "Will the principal let us do it?" the high rankings probably will not be sufficient to make it a viable idea.

In other cases, students may realize that they omitted an important criterion (e.g., money or time available), or that some criteria simply are more important than others. In the actual 250th anniversary group, building a time capsule did not outrank all other ideas, especially those concerning community involvement, but the group really wanted to build a time capsule. The enthusiasm of many class members was much greater for that project idea than for any other. They determined that for this project, class interest was particularly important, so they gave it additional weight.

Students also need to understand that ideas do not have to be mutually exclusive, that sometimes they can be combined, or that many can be pursued simultaneously. The 250th anniversary group demonstrated this diversity. They divided in half, with one half planning to build and bury the time capsule while attempting to locate the previous mystery capsule on the school grounds. The other half, who had been investigating the stock market, decided to create a business to produce and market commemorative souvenirs. They planned to market company stock to finance their venture and, rather than plan a town celebration, to incorporate sale of their souvenirs into the town's annual spring festival.

Building Acceptance. The final stage of the CPS process asks problem solvers to create a plan of action. They are to determine what needs to be done, who will be responsible for each task, and what a reasonable time frame is. In addition, those involved in planning attempt to identify in advance what the major stumbling blocks might be. These barriers could be difficult parts of the plan or they could be individuals or groups who oppose the plan. If planners can identify the problem areas in advance and develop strategies for avoiding or minimizing them, their chances of success are increased.

The primary school children trying to solve Horton's problem might decide on a simple three-stage plan for building a stand for Who-ville: (a) gather materials; (b) build a sturdy stand with a soft top; and (c) gently put the dust ball on the stand. If Horton cannot put Who-ville down to gather materials and build the stand, those responsibilities will need to be assigned to someone else. Maybe a friend would do it. Students also should identify any possible problems that might arise: What if the friend refuses to help? What if the Whos at the bottom of Who-ville are crushed? Planning for these eventualities—Horton could call another friend or he could ask the Whos to travel to the top of the dust ball while he puts it down—allows students to begin to envision how difficulties can be anticipated and avoided in other situations.

In real-world applications of CPS, Building Acceptance becomes particularly important. The 250th anniversary group needed detailed plans to realize their ideas. This stage of the process, in which they thought about the details of cost, timing, and responsibilities for each project, allowed them to plan ahead, thus avoiding many difficulties later on. From their difficulty in locating the bicentennial time capsule, they learned that if they wanted to be sure their capsule was eventually located, it would have to be clearly marked. In addition to leaving a map in the school office safe, the students topped the capsule with a large piece of scrap metal that could be located easily with a metal detector!

Even detailed planning will not eliminate all difficulties. At one point, the 250th anniversary souvenirs were not selling well and the students' dreams of profits were rapidly evaporating. Divergent thinking tools and strategies were never so welcome as when they were needed to salvage this important project. The group quickly devised new sales strategies and were able to sell the souvenirs. This example is perhaps CPS at its best. The skills the students had learned in one context they suddenly needed, used, and found successful in another. The wider the variety of contexts in which students practice these skills, the more likely they are to be able to transfer the skills to other situations. It is important for you to teach explicitly about transfer. As students learn the skills of CPS, you can ask them, "When else might we use this process? When have you had a problem that needed a creative solution?" It is also important that students understand that it is not necessary or desirable to use all the CPS components or stages in a given situation. The key (and a key purpose of the Planning Your Approach component) is to determine which processes are needed and to use them appropriately.

You also can use individual steps of the process as appropriate in many classroom contexts. Sometimes only one or two stages of the process are necessary or appropriate. Students may use Framing Problems to clarify conflicts in the classroom, Building Acceptance to plan class activities or projects, and Developing Solutions to select the site for a class field trip or to choose the class pet. The metacognitive skills required for deciding which steps to apply in a given situation provide powerful opportunities for analysis. If students think CPS must always be used in its entirety, they will miss valuable opportunities for transfer and critical thinking. In fact, at the beginning, you may choose to teach three broad components of CPS (Understanding the Challenge, Generating Ideas, and Preparing for Action) rather than all the individual steps. Once students have seen the importance of understanding a problem before trying to address it, they will be better prepared to learn specific strategies for doing so. Whether students are dealing with fictional or actual problems, CPS can allow them to develop valuable problem-solving skills, foster habits of mind that are supportive of creativity, and process important content all at the same time. The depth and breadth of possible benefits make it clear that the time and effort expended in teaching this complex process can be well spent. A host of materials on using the Creative Problem Solving model with students is available from the Center for Creative Learning, Inc. at www.creativelearning.com.

Thinking About the Classroom

Find a friend who teaches at the same grade level as you and list curriculum areas in which you might use CPS. Choose one example to try with your class.

USING METAPHORS AND ANALOGIES

Several theories of creativity emphasize the importance of bringing together remote ideas to stimulate a new point of view or to forge a new synthesis (Boden, 1990; Mednick, 1962; Rothenberg, 1990). Among the most powerful tools in this process are metaphors and analogies. Their use can also be considered a mechanism for divergent thinking because it can produce many varied ideas, but it generally is focused more on the types of ideas produced than on the number. In analogical thinking, ideas from one context are transferred to another in a search for parallels, insights, fresh perspectives, or new syntheses.

Creative individuals have transformed, have been inspired by, and occasionally have plagiarized the ideas of others throughout history. Composers have based works on familiar folk melodies, other composers' themes, and their own earlier compositions. In the best cases, these original sources have been transfigured into unique wholes by being merged with new themes or set with interesting instrumentation. The new wholes may not only be valuable in themselves, but may also add to our understanding of the works from which they originated.

The same processes operate in art, literature, and other disciplines. Fashion designers pull key ideas from one era and merge them with the materials and sensibilities of another. Writers use imagery that evokes earlier stories, heroes, and times. We understand Frodo Baggins more fully when we place him in the context of mythic heroes such as Gilgamesh or Odysseus. We understand *West Side Story* because of *Romeo and Juliet*. Langston Hughes (1951) invited his readers to understand the consequences of a dream deferred by comparing it to a raisin in the sun, a festering sore, a sagging load, and an explosion. Each comparison brings a fresh perspective and raises new questions and understandings. Because we know raisins and sores, we may begin to know dreams. The power of metaphor and analogy to communicate and bring new insight is one reason for teaching children to use these techniques.

Metaphors also can play an important role in problem solving and scientific discovery. Numerous inventors and scholars have attributed their ideas to parallels with objects or events around them. Gutenberg developed the idea of movable type by looking at the way coins were stamped. Samuel Morse found the idea for the relays used to transmit telegraph signals over long distances while he was traveling by stagecoach and noticing the stations where horses were replaced as they began to tire. Eli Whitney said he developed the idea for the cotton gin while watching a cat trying to catch a chicken through a fence. (Others claim he usurped the idea from a Mrs. Greene, who could not obtain a patent in her own name because she was a woman! [Gordon & Poze, 1979; Hanaford, 1882].)

A variety of scientific insights originated in metaphor. Pasteur began to understand the mechanisms of infection by seeing similarities between infected wounds and fermenting grapes. Darwin's evolutionary tree was a powerful image that was unchallenged through years of research. Einstein used moving trains to gain insight into relationships in time and space. The process of seeing or imagining how one thing might be like something else can allow new parallels to unfold, spurring hypotheses, syntheses, and perspectives.

Synectics

Synectics is an original word coined to mean "the joining together of different and apparently irrelevant elements" (Gordon, 1981, p. 5). Synectic

---

5.9. Use of Metaphor in Spanish IV: The Conquest of Mexico

Describe the process by which a germ enters the body and causes an infection. Discuss how this process is similar to the conquest of Mexico. As an assignment, students create their own analogy and create a visual image that illustrates the comparison between their analogy and the conquest of Mexico.

Adapted from a lesson by Lynn Massucci.

---

methods are metaphor- or analogy-based techniques for bringing elements together in a search for new ideas or solutions. They have been used by businesses, think tanks, and research organizations and have been the impetus behind the ideas for Pringles potato chips, magnesium-impregnated bandages, disposable diapers, dial-your-own-octane gas pumps, the space-saver Kleenex box, and a host of other innovations. Synectic ideas also have been adapted for teachers and students in a series of workbooks and curriculum development guides (Gordon & Poze, 1972, 1975, 1979, 1981, 1984).

The basic processes of synectics are "making the strange familiar" and "making the familiar strange" (Prince, 1968, p. 4). To make the strange familiar, you combine something familiar with a new problem or situation to solve the problem or come to an understanding. To make the familiar strange, you also combine something new or strange with something familiar, this time to gain new insights into or perspectives on the already familiar idea. These two processes are facilitated through the creation of various types of analogies.

Direct Analogies.   Direct analogies are the simplest type of comparison. In a direct analogy, individuals look for parallels between one idea, object, or situation and another. Students first learning to make direct analogies start with simple comparisons between similar objects and progress to more abstract processes. Early comparisons might examine how a bird is like an airplane or how a kite is like a balloon. Beginning comparisons are most likely to be successful if they are based on clear similarities in either form or function. Even young students likely can see physical similarities between a tree and a hat rack or functional similarities between a campfire and a stove. Students will be most successful if they first practice describing the connections in an analogy selected by someone else before they begin to create their own. They should have opportunities to identify the connections and similarities in such activities as how a comb and a rake are alike before being asked, "What things are like a comb?"

The power of the technique comes as students begin to generate their own analogies and see similarities between more remote objects. They might examine how a rock is like a tree or a dog, or how a feather is like grass. As students mature and develop abstract thinking, direct analogies can encompass abstract ideas. Students might discuss how happiness is like fire, how freedom is like chains, or how erosion is like a thief. They can make these comparisons as exercises to practice metaphorical thinking or to process important curricular ideas. Students studying immigration might discuss how immigration is like banking, migrating, or cooking a meal. Students studying imperialism might be asked, "What animal is like imperialism?" By discussing student-generated analogies about content, students can process content at complex levels of thinking and teachers can gain insight into students' understanding of key ideas.

Direct analogies also are powerful tools for creating visual images. Roukes' (1982) *Art Synectics*, although not directly paralleling all the synectic processes, uses various types of analogies to stimulate art activities. Direct analogies can be made between emotions and a variety of objects: a twisted ribbon to signify laziness or a broken mirror glued over a photograph to signify anxiety. For one activity, Roukes (1982) suggested that such items be collected and displayed in a small box with many compartments to create an emotion box (p. 68). Other projects use strategies ranging from personal analogies to magnification, combination, and distortion to stimulate new points of view in the visual arts.

Personal Analogies.   For personal analogies, students are asked to be the thing. They do not physically act out the object or situation, as they might in creative dramatics. In fact, many of the objects and situations that might be investigated through personal analogy do not easily lend themselves to dramatic interpretation. Doing a dramatic interpretation of a plant cell or a sedimentary rock would be difficult, but if students could imagine they were those things in specific situations (the cell splits, or the rock is

---

5.10. Analogy in Religion: 1 Corinthians 13

Have students restate 1 Corinthians 13 in light of one of their roles. For example, "If I speak in the tones of men and of angels but have not love, I am only a resounding gong or a clanging cymbal" can be restated as it might be lived by someone who works at a fast food chain: "If I could take orders at the speed of light, but did not have love for each of my customers, I would be just as well sweeping the floor."

Adapted from a lesson by Tanya Hart.

subjected to increasing heat and pressure), they could gain greater under-standing and new perspectives.

The amount of experience students have had with personal analogies, as well as their developmental level, will affect their depth of connection and empathetic involvement in the analogies they create. The greater the conceptual distance between the person and the analogy, the more difficult it is for him or her to attain empathetic involvement, but the greater the like-lihood that the analogy will lead the person to new ideas.

There are four levels of involvement for a personal analogy (Joyce, Weil, & Calhoun, 2000):

1. First-person description of facts. At this level, the person describes what is known about the object or animal, but shows no empa-thetic involvement. In describing a porcupine, the student might say, "I feel prickly," or "I feel my tail bump on the ground."
2. First-person identification with emotion. At the second level, the per-son recites common emotions, but does not present new insights. In describing the porcupine, the student might say, "I feel happy walk-ing through the woods," or "I feel protected by my quills."
3. Empathetic identification with a living thing. At this level, the stu-dent shows more insight into the life, feelings, and dilemmas of a porcupine. For example, "It's confusing. Sometimes I like my quills; sometimes I don't. I feel safe with quills around me, but no one can come near. Even other porcupines don't come close be-cause we might hurt each other. I wish I could take them off."
4. Empathetic identification with a nonliving object. At the high-est level of personal analogy, students are able to make the same type of empathetic connection with nonliving things. They might express a plane's feeling of exhilaration on reach-ing the speed for takeoff or the sadness of skis being put away for the summer.

Personal analogies can provide the bases for class discussions, writing projects, or art activities. Primary school students might be asked to be a let-ter going through the postal service and to write in their journals about their adventures. Intermediate school students studying simple machines could be asked to discuss what it might be like to be a lever or a pulley. How would they feel as they were used? What might change their feelings? High school students might be asked to create a work of art or a written descrip-tion of life from the perspective of an electron or a sound wave.

Personal analogies can also form the basis for problem solving or design projects. If you were the kickball, what would you do about the fights on the playground? If you were the stop sign in front of the school, how would you get more people to come to a complete stop? If you were a seatbelt, how would you get people to wear you? If you were a school desk, how would you feel? How would you like to feel? How could the desk be redesigned so that it could feel that way? In each case, taking on the identity of the object may allow the designer or problem solver to view the situation in new ways.

Compressed Conflicts.   Compressed conflicts, or symbolic analogies, bring together words that express diametrically opposed ideas. In a technique reminiscent of Rothenberg's (1990) janusian process, they force the user to consider two opposite ideas at the same time. Sometimes these juxtapositions may be literal antonyms, such as happy sadness or cold heat. Other times they may express more complex or oblique yet conflicting relationships, such as shameful hero or independent follower. Compressed conflicts frequently have broad, abstract applications and can be applied to many varied situations. The level of abstraction they require makes compressed conflicts most appropriate for students in later elementary grades and above.

Using Synectics.   Among the many ways synectics can be used in classrooms, three applications are basic: stretching or practice activities, activities designed to help students investigate previously learned content from a new perspective (making the familiar strange or creating something new), and activities designed to help students understand new content by tying it to something known (making the strange familiar). In stretching activities, students are taught the concepts of direct analogy or connections, personal analogy, and compressed conflict. These strategies are used in practice exercises, much as ball-handling exercises are used to practice the skills necessary for many sports. Practice exercises usually are not tied to new content, but rather use familiar ideas or fantasy content to help students become comfortable with making connections. They may be tied to creative writing exercises or class discussions, or they may be used simply as a sponge for the 10 extra minutes left before lunch. Students might be asked questions such as the following:

Direct analogies

How is snow like a merry-go-round?

What animal is like a clock?

How is fear like a grapefruit?

Which is harder, a rock or a scream?

Personal analogies

Be a pencil. How do you feel during the school day?

How do you feel at night?

Pretend you are your favorite animal. What are you?

How do you feel? What do you want most?

Compressed conflicts

What in nature is like a sad happiness?

What animal is like submissive independence?

How is a clock like a stopped stream?

What actions are like living death?

Stretches also can be used to process content in a manner that invites open-endedness, humor, and playfulness as well as critical analysis. If the topic is *Hamlet*, students might be asked, "What animal is most like Ophelia?" Students studying food chains might be asked, "Which is stronger, a food chain or an iron chain?" In a unit on the Revolutionary War, students might be asked to create a compressed conflict representing Benedict Arnold or to express the feelings of the bullets at Lexington and Concord. These activities often are designed to help students think in new ways about previously presented content.

Joyce, Weil, and Calhoun (2000) presented two outlines (called syntax) for teaching with synectics: one for creating something new and one for making the familiar strange. The outlines are adapted from *Teaching Is Listening* (Gordon & Poze, 1972), a self-instructional text on designing curriculum using synectics. The first outline is designed to create something new by making the familiar strange. Although more complex than a simple stretching exercise, it can allow students to examine previously learned content from a new point of view. The steps of the outline are as follows:

1. Students describe the situation as they see it now.
2. Students suggest direct analogies, select one, and explore it.
3. Students become the analogy they selected, creating a personal analogy.
4. Students use descriptions from steps 2 and 3 to create a compressed conflict.
5. Students generate another analogy based on the compressed conflict.
6. Students use the last analogy (or the rest of the synectics experience) to examine the original task or problem.

Imagine that Mr. Lopez's class has been studying Martin Luther King's march in Selma, Alabama.

Mr. Lopez: Today we are going to talk again about Dr. King's march in Selma, but we are going to think about it in a new way. What do you remember about the march?

[He records students' responses on the board.]

Yes, those are the facts. Next, we are going to use synectics to help us understand the facts in new and different ways. I'd like you to think for a moment about an animal that reminds you of the march on Selma.

Sam: It reminds me of mosquitoes. There are a lot of mosquitoes in Alabama—huge ones. I bet the marchers got bit a lot.

Mr. Lopez: That could be true, but we are not trying to think about animals that actually were on the march, but animals that are like the march in some way. One way to do that is to think about one of the characteristics of the march and see if there is an animal that also has that characteristic.

Gina: Well, it could be like coral. Coral has lots of little parts, and the march had lots of people.

Jared: Yeah, but coral's dead. The marchers weren't!

Mr. Lopez: When we make analogies there often are some characteristics that fit and some that don't. We'll think of several alternatives until we find one we can agree on.

Deb: It probably marched like a giant snake down the road.

Diane: I think it was more like an army of fire ants. Each ant alone isn't very strong, but an army of ants can be strong and dangerous. The march was strong because there were so many people.

Ben: Yes, but the people weren't violent like fire ants. They were more like a bunch of sheep, or …

Maria: Wolves! I read that wolves are really gentle animals; they only kill for food when they need it. They work together in packs to kill much bigger animals.

[The class decides to work with the idea of wolves.]

Mr. Lopez: All right. Wolves. What does it feel like to be a wolf?

Bob: Furry!

Mr. Lopez: Bob, what kind of feeling might a wolf have? How does it feel to be a wolf?

Bob: Confident. I know I have my wolf brothers around me.

Katie: Nervous. I don't like killing, but sometimes I have to. I wish I could eat grass and be a peaceful animal.

Bruce: I'd rather be a lone wolf if I could.

Wendy: It's weird. There could be a lot of fear. A wolf would feel strong, but it would be scary to try to kill a moose or some big thing.

[The class continues to talk about the feelings a wolf might have. Mr. Lopez continues to record their responses.]

Mr. Lopez: Looking at the things you've said about wolves, do you see any words that conflict, words that are opposite or don't seem to go together?

[The class makes several suggestions, including confident–nervous, peaceful–killing, lone–brothers, strong–scared. They choose strong–fear as the most interesting conflict.]

Mr. Lopez: Okay, can you think of another analogy for strong–fear? You may think of another animal or some type of machine.

Diane: A burglar alarm. It is strong, but you wouldn't have it if you didn't have fear.

Bob: A bird. Birds are really strong for their size, but they fly away at the slightest disturbance.

Wendy: A soldier. It's not exactly an animal, but a soldier is strong even though he might be afraid.

Deb: Salmon swimming upstream. They have to be really strong, but they don't know where they're going. They must be afraid.

Ben: How about a building being bombed? It's strong, but afraid it won't be strong enough.

At this point Mr. Lopez may either help the class select one of these analogies or let individual students select their own. They go back to the original topic, the march on Selma, and write about how the march is like the analogy selected. Deb might write about salmon willing to battle the stream for the sake of the next generation, and Bob might write about how flocks of birds stick together in times of danger. Each analogy has the potential to bring insight into the strength, motivation, and courage of the marchers.

In addition to processing content that has already been introduced, synectics can be used to present new content. The second outline is designed to make the strange familiar by using familiar analogies for new material. The steps for this synectics format are (Joyce, Weil, & Calhoun, 2000):

1. The teacher provides information on a new topic.
2. The teacher suggests a direct analogy and asks students to describe the analogy.
3. The teacher has the students "become" the direct analogy.
4. Students identify and explain points of similarity between the new material and the direct analogy.
5. Students explain where the analogy does not fit.
6. Students reexplore the original topic on its own terms.
7. Students provide their own direct analogy and explore the similarities and differences.

Imagine that a teacher wanted to teach a lesson on animal communities. She might provide the students with some basic information on food chains and how changes in one part of the chain affect all the other parts. Next, she could ask the students to look at a mobile hanging in the classroom and describe it: how it is made up of individual pieces, how they are connected by strings, how it is balanced, and so on. Next, students should be asked to become the mobile. (Gordon & Poze, 1972, do not always include this step.) They should describe what it feels like to be the mobile. How do they feel blowing in the breeze? How do they feel if a string breaks?

Individually or as a class, they could identify elements of the mobile that are in some way like the animal communities. For instance, each piece of the mobile is like a separate animal. The strings holding them together are like the connections between one animal and its food. If one piece is taken away, the whole mobile gets off balance. The students also may describe things about the mobile that are different from an animal community. For example, the mobile does not really demonstrate that there are many animals of the same type.

At this point, students may return to a discussion of the animal communities and try to develop their own analogies. The student-generated analogies allow students to process information in a creative way, and their explanations can provide valuable information for teachers on how well they understand the concept being taught.

As you can see, synectics processes can have a wide variety of applications across curriculum areas and real-world problems. They may be used in simple, mind-stretching exercises or to provide a framework for presenting or processing key concepts. (If you are interested in learning more about synectics, a variety of instructional materials are available from SES Associates, 121 Brattle St., Cambridge, MA 02138). Teachers of secondary students may be particularly interested in a revised version of synectics called the Box Step Method (Gordon, 1981). The Box Step Method method uses analogical thinking in a four-step process particularly appropriate for problem solving. Although it is slightly more difficult than earlier strategies, it can provide older students with an interesting and potentially powerful problem-solving technique.

Other Uses for Metaphorical Thinking

The synectics processes provide powerful tools for generating and using analogies, but there are certainly times when you may wish to help students use analogical thinking in other ways. In particular, experiences in metaphorical or analogical thinking can help students generate ideas and forms for creative expression.

Thinking About the Classroom

Plan a lesson using one of the synectics outlines. Have a friend give you feedback on your plan. Teach the lesson and then discuss the results.

We probably associate metaphors and analogies most commonly with literature. Most students, at some point, must memorize the differences between the two. Less often, students actually may use such literary devices as tools for their own expression. To use metaphors and analogies in their own writing, students must become familiar with the use of analogies elsewhere, as in Langston Hughes's question about the dream deferred. Students might discuss why Hughes chose those particular images and what the images communicated. They may brainstorm other analogies Hughes might have used and another dream poem or a work about some other thought and its effects on an individual.

The history of film is full of analogical thinking. Students studying mythic heroes might examine *Star Wars*, *Lord of the Rings* or *Superman* to find parallels that may have been inspired by ancient mythology. *On the Waterfront* is a potent source of religious imagery. *The King of Hearts* examines war and peace, sanity and insanity. *A River Runs Through It* is, on the surface, a movie about fly fishing, but it is also a movie about struggling, conquering, and growing up. One chief value of using films to explore analogical thinking, especially with secondary school students, is the insight that this type of thinking surrounds us and affects our understanding on a day-to-day basis.

Studying how these techniques are used commercially can provide the impetus for students to use them. The same strategies can be used to create a new mythic hero in a different time or place. What might a mythic hero have done during the American Revolution? (Do we have some?) What might a mythic hero in today's high school be like? Students might brainstorm other vehicles that could have been used to carry the message in *A River Runs Through It*. If the family had not gone fly fishing, where might they have gone? Would the imagery work in the same way for a group of young women? What alternatives could be used? This type of exercise can move analogical thinking from an example on a multiple-choice test to a tool for personal expression.

Analogical thinking also can provide insights and creative stimuli in the arts. Students can examine paintings and sculpture for images that use one form to portray another idea before they try generating new images for the same idea. This type of exercise can be considered as part of the technical skills instruction necessary for talent development. Sometimes a more constrained activity, demanding the use of a specific technique to portray a given idea, can be more valuable in developing creative expression than unstructured projects. Certainly, there are times when students should express their own ideas in their own ways, but training in analogical expression or other specific techniques make their own efforts richer.

Analogical thinking can provide exercises in fashion design or architecture. Students might be challenged to create clothing or buildings inspired by but not duplicating those of a specific period. Analogies also can be used to create political or other cartoons. I have a cartoon in my office from the years I lived in New England. Entitled "Moses in Connecticut," it pictures Moses raising his arms to part the snow drifts in front of a New England home. Although Moses probably would not be an appropriate theme for public school class activities, it is easy to imagine how a similar image could be used in a variety of settings. Picture Moses on the football field, Moses at rush hour, or Moses finding a parking place on campus! Other cartoon analogies could be expanded in a similar manner.

Political cartoons are frequently based on familiar literature, children's stories, or fables. Cartoons have portrayed George W. Bush and Sadaam Hussein as cowboys in a face off at sundown, or "Humpty Hussein" falling off the wall never to be assembled again. Crusaders attempting to go against established interests can be portrayed as tilting at windmills or "huffing and puffing and blowing the house down." Those with a new political view can be pictured as leading the country to Camelot or Never Never Land, all depending on the cartoonist's point of view.

Students from upper elementary grades on can use these techniques with varying degrees of sophistication. Younger students can learn how to use familiar stories or images to create more original posters or advertisements. Certainly, many fire prevention or substance abuse poster contests I have seen would have benefited from entries making original use of analogies. Middle school students can study the use of metaphors and analogies in political cartoons, perhaps graphing the number of times cartoons are based on children's stories, seasonal events, or other sources. As students learn to recognize metaphorical images, they can use them to create their own humorous and political statements.

Frequently, various techniques of creative thinking can be used together for even more powerful results. Analogical thinking can be triggered through the use of morphological synthesis. For example, current events or issues could be listed on one side of the grid and children's stories or current movies on the other side. The grid could be used to generate ideas for political cartoons. Examine the grid in Fig. 5.6. Consider how a cartoonist might create a cartoon about pollution using "Cinderella" or "The Three Bears." Similarly, a grid could be created with important ideas about friendship or common teenage dilemmas on one side and possible settings on the other side. These could be used as the basis for short stories. In either case, students have a tool for generating creative analogies while becoming aware that the same statement can be made in many different ways.

Thinking About the Classroom

Start collecting cartoons that use metaphors or analogies to make a point. Use them as the basis for a lesson or bulletin board.

Try creating a political cartoon by matching a political issue with a children's story and creating an analogy.	
Issues	**Stories**
Pollution	Cinderella
Homelessness	The Three Bears
Recycling	Snow White
Endangered Species	Peter Pan
Drugs	Jack and the Beanstalk
Gun Control	The Three Pigs
TV Violence	Aladdin

FIG. 5.6.   Using analogies to create political cartoons.

A songwriter friend of mine makes frequent use of analogies in helping students learn to write songs. Young children can begin with activities as simple as changing the words to "Row, Row, Row Your Boat." If the beginning were changed to "Drive, drive, drive your car" or "Slide, slide, slide your skates" or even "Stretch, stretch, stretch your smile," the parallels could be continued through the song. Older children can learn how music portrays ideas and emotions without lyrics by listening to a variety of music. Students can draw the images the music brings to mind and discuss the feelings it elicits. This idea can be extended by writing lyrics that fit the mood of the music. (I'd love to hear student lyrics to the beginning of Beethoven's *Fifth Symphony*!) Eventually, students can begin writing original songs that express their own ideas.

As in all creative activities, we must recognize the stages in the processes of analogical thinking. Students must recognize analogies before they can create them. They must be able to generate ideas in a structured situation before they can do so alone. I suspect that when students' creative efforts in schools fall short, it often is because they have been given freedom but no tools. Simply saying, "Write a song about something that interests you" presents an overwhelming task for most students—and adults. Beginning gradually by recognizing the images in familiar songs and adapting them or by writing lyrics to familiar tunes is much less intimidating. Learning how other composers used and reused melodies can give students the freedom to do the same. Students also should have experience in understanding how others have used analogies in design or cartooning before attempting to use these devices in original ways. Perhaps this is what Feldman (1988) had in mind when he emphasized the importance of seeing others' original works as part of the creative process. No real-world creative works come forth in a vacuum. It is unrealistic to expect such efforts from children.

VISUALIZATION AND CREATIVE DRAMATICS

Two additional strategies for enhancing the production of creative ideas are visualization and creative dramatics. Both techniques involve bringing ideas to life, one in the imagination and the other in physical activity.

Visualization

Visualization involves creating mental images of something that cannot be seen or does not exist. If I were to say, "Picture your bedroom," you probably could easily conjure up an appropriate mental image, even if you are not in your bedroom right now. If I were to ask you to picture your bedroom in the home in which you grew up, it is likely that it, too, would be a clear image. In fact, for many of you, that image probably is laden with emotion. For the fortunate among us, picturing home brings feelings of love and security. For others, the emotions are much more painful. In either case, a mental image of home demonstrates one characteristic of visualization: Clear visual images are frequently accompanied by powerful corresponding emotions. This combination can make visualization a potent learning tool, but one that must be used with caution and sensitivity. Perhaps it is the power of visualization to carry strong emotions that has made it a target of some political groups.

Parents concerned about mind control or nontraditional religions have attacked the use of visualization in schools as inappropriate and potentially dangerous. As mentioned in chapter 3, it is important that you take local sensibilities and concerns into account when planning the content and format of visualization activities. Although some individuals may be uncomfortable with fantasy images involving witches, dragons, or water sprites, few parents object to picturing a journey through the digestive system, imagining a new invention, or visualizing spelling words if such activities are approached sensitively.

Visualization can be used to reinforce course content. Elementary school students may be asked to visualize the roaring seas, crowded conditions, and bad food aboard the Mayflower. Secondary school students may gain insight into Shakespeare's theater by visualizing the experiences of the groundlings in the Globe Theatre.

Inaccurate pictures (visualizing the Globe as a movie theater, for instance) can be counterproductive. Students will need prior knowledge and careful guidance if their images are to increase their content knowledge effectively. Visualization assisted in this way is sometimes called guided imagery.

To be most effective in stimulating this type of visualization, the teacher should have a script, written or mental, of the images to be portrayed. Students can be encouraged to sit in a comfortable position, usually with their eyes covered or closed, while the teacher guides them through the content. The descriptions and suggestions should be presented slowly and clearly, with time allowed for students' images to develop. For example, a teacher guiding students through the circulatory system could start with oxygen entering the system:

> Picture yourself in a tiny submarine, just big enough for you. Everything you need is there. You have a comfortable chair and plenty of air for the journey. You even have food in case you get hungry. Picture yourself in your comfortable capsule .... Today you and your capsule are going on a wonderful journey all through your body. First you will have to shrink until you are very, very small—small enough to fit into the tiniest blood vessel. You are so small that you can see all the molecules in the air around you. In front of you is a person breathing. He looks so big you can't even see the whole person; all you can see is the giant nose. Oh! You are being inhaled. Into the nose you go, along with all the air molecules and dust around you .... Now you are in the nose. It is hard to maneuver around the hairs in there; dust particles are trapped on all sides of you ...

Clearly, students would need prior experience with guided imagery before they could be expected to focus on such an extended image. Early exercises can be as simple as picturing spelling words in the shape of the object (e.g., picture the C in cat turning into a cat) or visualizing the characters in math story problems. Students also can be encouraged to draw illustrations for books without pictures or books for which the illustrations have not been shown.

Guided imagery focused on content can enhance students' memory and stimulate their writing or other creative expression. Students who experience the difficulties on the Mayflower through imagery are more likely to begin to understand the emotions of the people there than students who merely read a section in the social studies text. If they write about the experiences of a child on the ship, their writing is likely to be more vivid. A high school student who has experienced life as a groundling is less likely to associate Shakespeare only with highbrow intellectual elitists.

I once did a guided imagery experience about traveling under the sea with a group of second graders. The images portrayed in their writing were far superior to those usually demonstrated by the group. In one of my favorite pieces, a student described what it felt like to "feel the sand under my stomach ... see the sun shining down through the water and not feel the wind." I believe it is unlikely that this degree of insight would have occurred without the imagined experience of being under water.

5.11. Using Multiple Strategies: Hansel and Gretel

This series of lessons is designed to prepare students for a theatrical production of Hansel and Gretel.

1. Read the story, preferably from a version without illustrations so students must visualize the story themselves.

2. Brainstorm new endings for the story under a variety of circumstances:

What if the witch was a fairy godmother?

What if the father refused to leave them in the forest?

What if the birds did not eat the bread crumbs?

What if the candy house could talk?

What if the children had a magic charm?

3. Create a grid containing the characters, the settings, and the main events of the story. Scramble the attributes so different characters do different things in different settings. Create a new story. For example, what might happen if the father found the candy house?

4. Play a selection from Humperdink's opera *Hansel and Gretel*. Have the children close their eyes and describe and open-ended visualization. For example: "You are walking in the woods. Listen to the sounds around you. What do you hear? Walk down the path until you see a very unusual house? Look at it carefully ...." Have the students open their eyes and describe what they visualized.

5. Use creative dramatics to allow children to experience being Hansel, Gretel, and the talking Candy House. Imagine what they could say to each other.

Adapted from a lesson by Patricia Barnes.

Bagley and Hess' (1987) *200 Ways of Using Imagery in the Classroom* gives some idea of the diverse ways in which imagery can be used to reinforce content. It contains activities ranging from flying in an imaginary plane as a source for written expression to visualizing the Constitutional Convention and picturing multiplication with decimals.

Of course, guided imagery and visualization also can be used to imagine things that do not exist. Eberle (1977) provided a series of visual images that were created using the SCAMPER acronym. In one piece, students picture doughnuts filled with various substances stretching into different shapes and enlarging to the size of a house. A potent image has them jumping into a swimming pool filled with applesauce in the middle of a giant doughnut. That portion of the experience is invariably met by giggles and squirms. Students can be guided to picture an imaginary trip in a hot-air balloon, a tour through an enormous strawberry (echoing *James and the Giant Peach* [Dahl, 1961]), or a voyage to a distant planet. These types of images can spur artwork, creative writing, or discussions of literary forms such as science fiction.

Bagley (1987) suggested that imagery also can be used in creative problem solving. It might spur random associations, metaphors, or new perspectives on the problem. One exercise involves visualizing the problem in a past era. Another asks participants to visualize aspects of the situation enacted by an animal. In each case, the visualization is used to trigger new ideas and points of view.

Finke (1990) discussed the use of imagery in the invention process. Finke conducted numerous research studies in which individuals used selected images to generate new ideas for inventions. In such exercises, subjects might be asked to visualize combinations of a cone, half a sphere, and a hook. They could change the size and position of the images as desired until they found an image that gave them an idea for an invention. Finke was particularly interested in the function of preinventive forms—that is, combinations of simple images that may be interpreted in various ways to solve diverse problems (Ward, Smith, & Finke, 1999).

One of the more interesting results of Finke's (1990) research was that subjects, generally college undergraduates, were more successful at devising creative inventions when the task was somewhat restricted. Subjects given a large range of shapes from which to devise any invention were less creative in their responses than those given a limited number of images from which to work and a particular category of object to create. Surprisingly, subjects also had more original ideas when they generated a preinventive form combining images into an interesting and potentially useful shape before identifying the category of object to be devised instead of trying to plan a form to suit a particular category.

Perhaps the common thread in these results is exploratory behavior. If an individual has a limited number of images to consider, it is possible for him or her to explore each one more fully. If it is necessary to select a form for an unknown purpose, multiple possibilities for that form must be considered. It would be interesting to experiment with variations on Finke's (1990) techniques with younger students. They could be given specific geometric forms to visualize, manipulate mentally, and use to create new ideas for inventions. It also may be worthwhile to consider whether the concept of restricted tasks could be valuable in teaching other creative thinking techniques.

Creative Dramatics

In creative dramatics, students are asked to explore ideas with their bodies as well as their minds. These exercises can be valuable for developing concentration, sensory awareness, self-control, empathetic understanding, and a sense of humor. In creative dramatics, students have the opportunity to be someone or something else in a safe and accepting context (Heinig, 1992; McCaslin, 1999).

It is important to distinguish creative dramatics and role play from children's theater. As discussed in chapter 6, students involved in role-play activities address problem situations by taking on a variety of roles and portraying their decisions. Children's theater is theater produced for children to watch, often by adults and sometimes by talented student actors. It is derived from a script, rehearsed, and presented to an audience. Creative dramatics, like role play, is not scripted and seldom intended for an audience. Although creative dramatics or role-play activities may be repeated, they are not rehearsed for consistency, but reexplored for new ideas and interpretations. For Wilder (1977), creative drama implied

learning through using all the senses, including the kinesthetic

experiencing as well as talking about, reading about

making selective and imaginative choices

collaboration among individuals rather than teacher-direction thinking/experiencing/evaluating/communicating

group interaction rather than "I for myself." (p. 2)

Students involved in creative dramatics explore a situation physically in an effort to find and express creative ideas. At times, this may involve the types of problem-solving activities and exploration of issues described in the discussion of role playing. Creative dramatics can be seen to encompass such activities. However, it also includes explorations of less realistic situations and investigations of animals or objects. In role play, students typically take on fairly realistic roles to solve a problem. Creative dramatics often moves also into fantasy; students can become melting snow, stalking animals, or the walls of a building.

Like role playing, creative dramatics activities can be divided into three stages: warm-up, dramatic activities, and debriefing. Warm-up exercises are used to warm up both brain and body. Physical and mental stretching activities provide a transition from other class activities and allow muscles to loosen. Warm-ups can sometimes be used to focus students on the issue or topic of the day. At other times they may be unrelated to the activities that follow. My experience has shown that older students need warm-up activities more than younger ones. Most young children readily throw themselves into any kind of dramatic activity. At the drop of a hat, they are ready to be a lion, a rubber band, or a lost child. Students from the middle grades on are much more self-conscious and need more warm-up and focus activities before proceeding. It is helpful to point out that many of these same activities are used by professional actors preparing for the stage or screen. Warm-ups can include the following:

Stretching. Students stretch all their muscles from the head down. Students should be cued to stretch as many muscles separately as possible.

Relaxing. Students lie on the floor and relax one group of muscles at a time.

Mirrors. Each student needs a partner. One person becomes a mirror, reflecting each movement the partner makes. Mirrors work most easily with slow, smooth movements. Occasionally students may be directed to switch roles without disrupting the flow of the movement.

Catch. Students play catch with a variety of imaginary balls. They should try switching from a softball to a beach ball to a bowling ball.

Walking. Students walk in place under a variety of circumstances: through the jungle, on hot sand, or going to school when their homework is not done.

Rubber bands, ice cubes, and other objects. Students become an object whose form changes. They might portray melting ice, frying bacon, or a stretching rubber band. Older students may imagine stretching rubber bands around various parts of their bodies.

Dramatic activities may include movement exercises, sensory-awareness exercises, pantomime, and other forms of storytelling. Movement exercises are designed primarily to help students gain control of their bodies and become aware of how their bodies move. Most of the warm-up activities described in this discussion could also be used as movement exercises. Other movement activities could include the following:

Puppets. Students pretend to be pulled by strings attached to various parts of their bodies.

Tug-of-war. Students are divided into teams pulling an imaginary rope over an imaginary line.

Animals. Students imitate animals' movements and mannerisms. Secondary students may develop human characters based on some aspect of the chosen animal.

Human machine. Students in small groups form machines, or they can create one giant machine as a whole-class build-on activity. There are many variations to this exercise. One of my favorites entails having each participant identify one sound and one movement. One student may choose to raise and lower one leg while whistling with each downward movement. The goal is to build the parts into a machine in which each piece is attached to the next in a logical fashion, with moving parts interacting. If your class can assemble the entire machine before dissolving in hysterics, they have demonstrated enormous self-control!

Sensory-awareness exercises are exactly what the name implies: exercises to increase students' awareness of their five senses. You may ask your students to eat imaginary food, listen to imaginary sounds, or feel imaginary textures. You may find that limiting one of the senses can enhance the others. The opportunity for students to feel a variety of textures while they are wearing blindfolds may sharpen their ability to imagine other textures.

Perhaps the most familiar dramatic activities involve pantomime and other forms of story making activities. Students are asked to use their bodies to portray situations with or without the use of dialogue. These may range from simple activities, such as pantomiming someone using a common household tool, to complex problem-solving scenarios. More complex dramatic activities may require a planning phase as well as an acting phase. Students who are asked to portray an interviewer with a panel of guests, portray Phillis Wheatley discussing her poetry, or present the story of *Peter and the Wolf* will need discussion time before the activities can be presented successfully. Also, most creative dramatics activities are enhanced by a debriefing discussion. Students may discuss what they did, how it felt, what worked, what did not, and what they might try another time. These discussions make it clear that creative dramatics activities, although enjoyable, are not part of recess. They are kinesthetic activities that can bring insight into a variety of situations.

Creative dramatics also can provide impetus for content discussions, art activities, and writing projects. As did visualization, they can bring an enhanced understanding, especially of the emotions underlying problems or events. If students are given sufficient background knowledge, a creative dramatics activity about a young woman wanting to go to battle during the Civil War can increase their understanding of women's roles during that period. A representation of key individuals in the French Revolution can help students focus on the characteristics that motivated important participants and more fully understand their interactions.

Fantasy activities such as creating the human machine can be used as the basis for discussion and journal writing. One second-grade class, after doing the human machine activity, talked about what things could be done by an amazing machine such as the one they had built. Students then wrote their ideas and created illustrations of their own amazing machines. The stories included machines that ate foods the owner did not like, one that turned bad people good, and one that made scrambled eggs. In the scrambled egg story, the author's mother became jealous of the machine because everyone preferred the machine's scrambled eggs to her breakfasts. However, this was not because Mom's cooking was inferior, but because the machine served breakfast in bed. One day the machine made breakfast for Mom, too. After that, she loved it "like a pet."

Like the stories that students wrote after their underwater visualization activity, these efforts were much better than everyday journal entries. Similar results can be attained when older students write about their experiences surviving in a hostile environment, dealing with a shoplifter, or asking someone out on his or her first date after living these events through creative dramatics. Creative thinking techniques, with the new perspectives, emotional insights, and enthusiasm they can generate, can be a valuable asset to any language arts program.

Thinking About the Classroom

Invite some children and adults to participate in creative dramatics together. See if you notice any differences in the ways they approach the activities. Adults all should have the chance to participate! You also might try this activity with students of different ages. See what you observe about their approaches.

COMMERCIAL AND COMPETITIVE PROGRAMS

A number of commercial programs and interscholastic competitions designed to enhance creative thinking are available. The CoRT program and six-thinking-hats materials have already been described. Because the number of commercial materials is increasing so fast, it is impossible to discuss all of them. This section samples the menu and describes some of the better-known offerings.

Future Problem Solving

Future Problem Solving (FPS), originated by Torrance and Torrance (1978), involves students in using Creative Problem Solving (CPS) to address problems of the future. It offers both competitive and noncompetitive programs. In the original program, students in three divisions (grades 4 to 6, 7 to 9, and 10 to 12) work in four-person teams to complete problem booklets on assigned topics. Each year FPS topics are selected from three strands: business and economics, science and technology, and social and political issues. Information on ties between FPS topics and content curriculum standards is available at the Web site listed at the end of this section.

The goals of the FPS program are to develop creative and higher level thinking skills via a multistep problem-solving method, to help students develop capabilities to deal with the unknown of the future, to encourage students to make knowledgeable decisions after investigating a variety of resources, to help students develop skills needed for teamwork and group process, to help students develop skills of organization and coherence in both written and oral communication, to help students become more self-directed, and to help students contend with ambiguity (Michigan Future Problem Solving Program, n.d.). Students address these goals by researching and attempting to solve problems in three major areas each year. The topics for the problems are the same nationwide for any given academic year. The first two topics are considered to be practice problems through which students learn and practice the steps of CPS. Practice problems typically are submitted to a state FPS organization for evaluation and feedback. The third problem, which must be completed by the teams without assistance, is the basis for statewide competition. Teams earning the highest number of points on the third problem may be invited to a state and possibly the international FPS competition.

The actual problem-solving process used in FPS begins with a fuzzy situation. A fuzzy situation extrapolates current issues into the future and describes possible results. The one given for prisons described Maxintern, an overcrowded orbiting space prison. Students begin by researching topics related to the fuzzy part. In this case, they would investigate prison costs, conditions, effects of overcrowding on prisoners, and similar issues. With this background information, they would be ready to begin the problem-solving process.

Although competitive conditions require that the problem solving be completed in 2 hours, practice problem activities may be spread out over days or weeks. The first step in the process is to brainstorm problems, paralleling the problem-finding stage of CPS. One underlying problem is selected and written using IWWMW ("In what ways might we?") or a similar form. A problem statement for the Maxintern might be "In what ways might we provide prisoners in the year 2040 with a secure environment that will help them become more productive citizens?" Next, students generate possible solutions to the problem. After these have been listed, team members generate five criteria for evaluating solutions and use them to rank solutions on an evaluation grid. The one with the most points is considered the best solution and is described in more detail. All the stages of the process (listing possible problems, solutions, and so forth) are recorded in problem booklets. Points are allotted for each section of the booklet, not just the final solution. For a team to be successful, at least some team members must have the skills to record the group's ideas coherently.

Several variations on the FPS process are offered by some state organizations. The primary division is a similar noncompetitive program designed to teach problem solving to students in grades K–3. Scenario writing is a competition in which individual students write scenarios of life as they see it at least 20 years in the future. Scenarios usually are focused on one of the

FPS topics for that year. Community problem solving is an opportunity for students to use their problem-solving skills to address issues in their own community. At least one state also offers a Governor's Problem Solving Institute, a summer experience in which students attempt cooperatively to solve a problem posed to them by the governor. Future Problem Solving also is associated with the Mars Millennium Project, a joint project with NASA, the National Endowment for the Arts, and the U.S. Department of Education that focuses on problem solving for the environment on Mars. (For additional information, contact your state FPS program or write to the Future Problem Solving International office, 2500 Packard, Suite 110, Ann Arbor, MI 4810-6827. As can most of the other organizations listed later, Future Problem Solving can also be located on the World Wide Web. Its current address is http://www.fpsp.org.)

Destination ImaginNation

Destination ImaginNation also is a team-based program with a state and national structure similar to that of FPS. However, the problems addressed and the types of products produced in the two programs are very different.

Students participate in Destination ImagiNation in teams of up to seven members who work to solve two different types of challenges: team challenges and instant challenges. There are five possible team levels: primary, elementary, middle, secondary, and university. Teams have the opportunity to present their solutions in tournaments, and all but the primary level are evaluated by appraisers.

In a team challenge, teams work over a period of several months to solve a problem and prepare a presentation of their solution. Each year, Destination ImagiNation presents approximately six challenges and teams select one to solve. In contrast to FPS, in which students generate and record ideas for solving problems, many Destination ImagiNation team challenges require students to create some type of vehicle, structure, machine, or other physical object that must function to solve the problem. Each challenge also includes a performance element. For example, in 2002–2003, the viDIo Adventure challenge required participants to create an 8-minute presentation of a three-dimensional video game. The game's theme had to tell a story of a modern day quest. The team was required to design and build a seeker who would travel through three nations. In each nation, it had to overcome an obstacle and collect a reward used to solve the quest.

Team challenges are focused around a central challenge, as in the Quest game, but they also include additional creative opportunities. The first is called "side trips" (Destination ImagiNation, 2002, p. 10). Side trips provide opportunities for the team to earn points by showcasing the special talents and interests of team members within their solution. Based on the theory of multiple intelligences (Gardner, 1983), side trips provide the opportunity for team members to showcase their collective talents. Teams also have the opportunity to earn points through "improv elements" (Destination ImagiNation, 2002, p. 12), specific props or ideas presented immediately before their presentation to be incorporated in the solution. Instant Challenges are presented at the tournaments and must be solved in a very short time. These typically involve improvisation and Creative Problem Solving.

Although Destination ImagiNation and FPS both require divergent thinking and have similar competitive structures, the nature of the problems often makes the competitions appealing to different students. Students most successful in FPS are comfortable with library research and written and verbal communication. In some schools, FPS is incorporated into the social studies curriculum. Students who most enjoy Destination ImagiNation often are tinkerers or performers. They like to solve three-dimensional problems or use their creativity in artistic or dramatic ways. (For additional information on Destination ImagiNation write to Destination ImagiNation, P.O. Box 547, Glassboro NJ 08028 or at http://www.dini.org.)

Odyssey of the Mind

Odyssey of the Mind (Micklus & Micklus, 1986) is a competitive program in which teams solve problems very similar to those in Destination ImagiNation. In fact, the two groups represent a split in the original Odyssey of the Mind (then abbreviated OM), in which Destination ImagiNation continued as a nonprofit organization and Odyssey of the Mind affiliated with Creative Competitions, a for-profit organization. Both groups involve both short- and long-term problem solving. Both include problems with both building and performance elements. You will need to check your local schools to see which organization is most active in your area. (For additional information on Odyssey of the Mind write to Odyssey of the Mind, c/o Creative Competitions, 1325 Route 130 South, Gloucester City, NJ 08030 or at http://www.odysseyofthemind.com.)

Inventing and Invention Conventions

One of the most interesting and enjoyable ways to learn about creativity is through the invention process. Learning about inventors' experiences and walking in their footsteps bring students unique insights into the generation and implementation of new ideas. Numerous companies, foundations, and organizations sponsor activities designed to teach students about inventing and provide audiences for young inventors. I have also found that identifying a problem and inventing something to solve the problem is a powerful assignment for adults. The task seems initially intimidating, but I have watched scores of graduate students find success, pride, and renewed faith in their own creativity by tackling this challenge (and never once has a student been unable to find something that needed inventing).

Regardless whether you and your students become involved in a formally organized invention program, the basic steps of inventing are essentially the same. At the beginning, it is important to become aware of inventors and stories of inventions. It is easy to go through life assuming that Scotch tape or facial tissues or drinking straws always existed. If questioned, most of us probably would realize that these ideas must have come from somewhere, but it is easy to forget that all the objects that fill our lives, from paper clips to computer chips, are the product of someone's new idea. Someone had to ask, "What is needed here?" "What is the problem here?" or "How could this be better?" There is an ever-growing collection of books available to help students learn about inventors and inventing. The following are possible places to start: *Steven Caney's Invention Book* (Caney, 1985), The Kid's Invention Book (Erlbach, 1999), *African American Inventors* (Sullivan, 1998), *African American Women Scientists and Inventors* (Sullivan, 2001), and *Women Who Invent* (Casey, 1997). It is very important to share invention stories of men and women from a variety of races and cultural groups. If you limit yourself to the stories that are easiest to find, you are likely to leave the impression that all major inventions were created by a very limited group. In fact, the characteristics of great inventors are widespread.

New inventors need to become sensitive to problems and opportunities around them. One way to do this is to brainstorm "things that bug me." In small groups, students generate lists of everyday annoyances. These vary enormously—from second-grade students, who may be bugged by too-small lunch boxes or demands to clean their room, to adults who hate walking to the mailbox on a rainy day, cleaning up after their children in restaurants, and finding unidentified fluids leaking from their cars.

It also is sometimes helpful to look through catalogues, especially the unusual gift catalogues that arrive in November and December. Many of the products in them are the result of someone's effort to alleviate one of life's annoyances. On several occasions, students have appeared in my office with catalogues offering solutions to problems that appeared on their bug lists the year before. Frequently, they accompany their discovery with wails of "Why didn't I think of that?" or "They're selling my invention!" Young students may enjoy seeing children's inventions in *The Kid's Invention Book* (Erlbach, 1999). My personal favorite is an edible pet food server designed by a first-grade student who was disgusted by the dirty spoons used to scoop pet food. Her server could be crumbled into the pet's dish, and the pet food never touched human hands! Becoming aware of inventions and the need for inventions can change the way individuals look at the world. During this process, it is not uncommon to hear people say, "This is driving me crazy. Everywhere I look I see inventions. Everything I do, I think, 'How could this be easier or better?' Everywhere I go I look for something to improve. It's driving my spouse (or parent) up the wall." With due sympathy to the beleaguered families, this sensitivity to opportunities is an essential part of problem finding and a valuable asset to any inventor.

Once the problem has been identified, the exploration begins. Many of the divergent thinking strategies discussed earlier can be helpful in generating beginning solutions. In many cases, numerous designs and materials must be tried before a workable solution is found. Sometimes it is necessary to find technical assistance for engineering questions or physical assistance for molding new materials. All of these are difficulties encountered by real inventors as a normal part of the invention process. An invention log can help students record the process, keeping track of their successes, failures, and untested ideas. It is a place for them to draw and revise plans, jot down ideas, and record dreams. If carefully kept and dated, the log can also serve as a record in case the invention should be patented.

After the planning, the building can begin. In some cases, students construct their initial efforts using alternate materials or a miniature scale until they can fine-tune the idea. It is important, however, that they be encouraged to plan inventions they actually can create. It is enjoyable to imagine fantasy inventions beyond available levels of technology, but for a student to decorate a box and say, "This would be a machine you could touch to the fluids leaking out of your car and it would instantly analyze them" does not expose him to the same problem-solving processes that he could learn by creating a simpler but manageable invention. Even so, such far-fetched ideas sometimes lead to practical applications. The student with the leaking car but few technological skills created a large pad on which he sketched a full-scale drawing of the underside of his car. By driving the car in the tire prints drawn on the pad, he could position the vehicle so that its underside was exactly over the corresponding parts in his drawing. Then, when the car leaked, the drip fell from the real car part onto the analogous part of the drawing, allowing him to locate the origin of the leak. A color key to identify brake fluid, oil, or other liquids completed the product. It worked!

If you would like students to work on inventions, but are not part of a formal invention program, you may want to organize an invention convention yourself. The steps for organizing such a conference parallel those for any science fair. There is one caution you may want to consider. Be sure participants understand that inventions must be self-contained. That is, they must not require running water, outside electricity, or other such externalities. Without the self-containment rule, you could easily find yourself with 30 projects needing electricity and 5 needing running water, all in a gym with two electric outlets and no faucets! Additional information on inventions and invention conventions can be obtained from Invent America, an organization whose goal is to encourage students to become inventors (P.O. Box 26065, Alexandria, VA 22313 or www.inventamerica.com).

Science Olympiad

Science Olympiad is a national nonprofit organization devoted to improving the quality of science instruction, increasing interest in science, and providing recognition for outstanding accomplishments in science. Although it is not targeted specifically at increasing students' creative thinking skills, Science Olympiad does provide the opportunity for them to use creativity in a content area.

Science Olympiad provides a menu of activities at various levels. These represent a balance among life science, physical science, and earth science, and also among events requiring knowledge of science facts, concepts, processes, skills, and applications. Some of the activities, particularly those that are fact based, have single correct answers and offer minimal opportunities for creative thinking. In other activities, the application of scientific principles leads to the possibility of many correct solutions. For example, in Division B (grades 6–9), one event asked students to identify various rock samples by using standard testing procedures. Although this is a fine activity for developing the domain skills that students will need eventually to be creative in earth science, it probably is not an activity for which original answers are appropriate. Another activity at the same level asked teams to construct, in advance, an insulated houselike structure, 20 to 40 cm on each side, that will retain the heat of 100 ml of water in a 250-ml beaker for 20 to 30 minutes. In this case, many varied solutions are possible. Using flexible thinking within the parameters of the discipline is likely to increase students' success (Science Olympiad, 1990).

Science Olympiad (1989, 1990) has four divisions. The elementary division A1 (grades K–3) is noncompetitive. Events are organized in a Science Fun Day for groups ranging from a single class to all the students in a particular school from kindergarten through third grade. There are three other divisions: Elementary A2 (grades 3–6), Middle School (grades 6–9), and Secondary (grades 9–12). In the three upper divisions, events typically are used to organize school or regional tournaments. (For additional information, contact Science Olympiad, 5955 Little Pine Lane, Rochester, MI 48306 or http://www.soinc.org.)

There are numerous other interscholastic programs that can facilitate creativity in particular disciplines. Young Authors' programs encourage and support young writers. History days, organized to parallel a science fair, provide outlets for creative research and presentations in history. In all cases, teachers will need to assess the impact of such programs on several dimensions. Does the program help students use important content and processes? Do the products required allow flexible responses? What is the impact of the competitive aspect of the program? Chapter 7 offers evidence that competition in creative endeavors may inhibit students' intrinsic motivation. Others may argue that rewarding creative products parallels processes in the real world and may encourage students to greater progress. Only you can judge what is best for your students as you balance the benefits with the risks for any given group of students.

Thinking About the Classroom

Find out when the local Destination ImagiNation tournament is taking place and visit it. Or contact local coaches or participants in FPS, Science Olympiad, or other competitions. Find out what is going on in your area.

Commercial Products, Transfer, and the Real World

There are many commercial products and programs designed to enhance creativity: books, kits, software, and more. Some are single activities or books focusing on a targeted idea or skill. Others are comprehensive programs. Most recently, there has been a proliferation of software programs designed to spur divergent thinking and help record and organize ideas. The assessed effectiveness of materials and programs varies from study to study (Mansfield, Busse, & Krepelka, 1978; Torrance, 1987). How you define success will affect your assessment of these activities. It is one thing to review research and discover that students using a particular program become better at exercises very much like those used in the program. It is quite another to discover that students can develop skills in commercial or other activities and transfer them into new, real-world situations. The ways materials and strategies are introduced and taught can affect how or whether students use them outside a teacher-directed situation. If teachers cue students that the skills might transfer, the students are more likely to try using them in other situations (Bransford, Sherwood, Vye, & Rieser, 1986; Crammond, Martin, & Shaw, 1990).

As you select activities, whether commercially produced or teacher designed, consider first how they mesh with the research and theory available and also how they might be adapted to enhance the possibility of transfer. If any of these activities and the processes they teach are to be of long-term value, they must develop skills and attitudes in students that help them think creatively both inside and outside the classroom. They also must support students' increasing independence in their use. Although imaginative activities can be valuable and important in themselves (e.g., using CPS to solve Horton's dilemma or planning a new space creature), I believe their value is enhanced when students understand how they can use similar processes to improve their ideas at school, at home, or in other locations.

I have frequently used my experience with my first Thanksgiving turkey as an introduction to lessons on fluency or brainstorming. I learned all my cooking skills in a family of seven. This practice provided me with unique advantages and disadvantages. I learned to cut a pie into seven pieces equal enough to pass the most discriminating judgment. I also learned to cook turkeys averaging 20 to 25 pounds. The first Thanksgiving I was married I prepared the turkey as I had done before, only to realize once it was placed on the table that there was no longer room even for our two plates. Needless to say, we ate turkey for some time after the holiday. I needed many ideas about what to do with leftover turkey.

This story and students' stories about times they needed many ideas have helped children make the transition from seeing brainstorming sessions as an enjoyable diversion to viewing them as useful exercises. Using brainstorming to solve class dilemmas is an even more powerful tool for transfer. Whatever creative thinking techniques you choose to teach, students eventually should be able to answer the questions "What are you do-ing?" "Why?" and "When might this be helpful?" Without such cueing, we may end up like Mr. Brown, described at the beginning of the chapter, whose students enjoy creative exercises on Friday afternoon, but demonstrate little creativity in other aspects of their lives.

The transfer process might be viewed as paralleling any other tool we might give students. Few adults could imagine giving a young person a box full of saws, wrenches, and hammers and hoping he or she would figure out when to use them. If we are to provide students with mental hammers and creative nails, we must also help them see how many things in the world could benefit from a little hammering and a few nails. In some places, we could use the whole box.

JOURNEYING AND JOURNALING

1. Reflect on the processes you have used thus far in developing your own creative product. Do any of them resemble strategies described in this chapter?
2. Choose at least two strategies and use them in an area of your life that would benefit from increased creativity. You may use them to work on your creative product or in any other aspect of your life. Record your feelings while using them and the results of your efforts.
3. Read a biography or an autobiography of an inventor or other creative individual. Look for evidence of the use of metaphor or other strategies in his or her thought processes. Discuss the strategies that individual seemed to use most successfully.
4. The idea of divergent thinking is an important component of Guilford's Structure of Intellect (SOI) model. Activities designed to enhance divergent thinking would seem consistent with this model of creativity. Consider the models of creativity in chapter 2 and the activities described in this chapter. Try to make connections between models of creativity and activities that are consistent with those models. Which activities are most consistent with the model(s) that appealed to you?

REFERENCES

Baer, J. (1993). *Creativity and divergent thinking*. Hillsdale, NJ: Lawrence Erlbaum Associates.

Bagley, M. T. (1987). *Using imagery in creative problem solving.* New York: Trillium Press.

Bagley, M. T., & Hess, K. K. (1987). *200 Ways of using imagery in the classroom.* New York: Trillium Press.

Basadur, M., Runco, M. A., & Vega, L. A. (2000). Understanding how creative thinking skills, attitudes and behaviors work together: A causal process model. *Journal of Creative Behavior, 34*(2), 77–100.

Boden, M. A. (1990). *The creative mind: Myths and mechanisms.* New York: Basic Books.

Bradbury, R. (1996). *Zen in the art of writing.* Santa Barbara: Joshua Odell Editions.

Bransford, J. D., Sherwood, R., Vye, N., & Rieser, J. (1986). Teaching thinking and problem solving. *American Psychologist, 41,* 1078–1089.

Brilhart, J. K., & Jochem, L. M. (1964). Effects of different patterns on outcomes of problem- solving discussions. *Journal of Applied Psychology, 48,* 175–179.

Caney S. (1985). *Steven Caney's invention book.* New York: Workman.

Carson, D. K. & Runco, M. A. (1999). Creative problem solving and problem finding in young adults: Interconnections with stress, hassles, and coping abilities. *Journal of Creative Behavior, 33*(3), 167–190.

Casey, S. (1997). *Women who invent: Two centuries of discoveries that have shaped our world.* Chicago: Chicago Review Press.

Crammond, B., Martin, C. E., & Shaw, E. L. (1990). Generalizability of creative problem solving procedures to real life problems. *Journal for the Education of the Gifted, 13,* 141–155.

Crawford, R. P. (1954). *The techniques of creative thinking.* New York: Hawthorn Books.

Dahl, R. (1961). *James and the giant peach.* New York: Puffin Books.

Davis, G. A. (1998). *Creativity is forever* (4th ed.). Dubuque, IA: Kendall Hunt.

de Bono, E. (1970). *Lateral thinking.* New York: Harper & Row.

de Bono, E. (1986). CoRT thinking: *Teacher's notes* (2nd ed., Vols. 1–6). New York: Pergamon.

de Bono, E. (1991a). *Six thinking hats for schools: Adult educators' resource book.* Logan, IA: Perfection Learning.

de Bono, E. (1991b). *Six thinking hats for schools: 3–5 resource book.* Logan, IA: Perfection Learning.

de Bono, E. (1999). *The new six thinking hats.* New York: Little, Brown & Company.

de Bono, E. (1992). *Serious creativity.* New York: HarperCollins.

Destination ImagiNation. (2002). *Rules of the road.* Glassboro, NJ: Author.

Duggleby, J. (1994). *Artist in overalls: The life of Grant Wood.* San Francisco: Chronicle Books.

Dunnette, M. D., Campbell, J., & Jastaad, K. (1963). The effects of group participation on brainstorming effectiveness for two industrial samples. *Journal of Applied Psychology, 47,* 10–37.

Eberle, R. F. (1977). *SCAMPER.* Buffalo, NY: DOK.

Eberle, R. F. (1996). *SCAMPER* [Reissue]. Waco, TX: Prufrock Press.

Ehlert, L. (1989). *Color zoo.* New York: J. B. Lippincott Pub.

Erlbach, A. (1999). *The kids' invention book.* Minneapolis: Lerner Publications.

Feldman, D. H. (1988). Creativity: Dreams, insights, and transformations. In R. J. Sternberg (Ed.), *The nature of creativity* (pp. 271–297). New York: Cambridge University Press.

Feynman, R. (1997). The dignified professor. In F. Barron, A. Montuori, & A. Barron (Eds.), *Creators on creating* (pp. 63–67). New York: Putnam.

Finke, R. (1990). *Creative imagery: Discoveries and inventions in visualization.* Hillsdale, NJ: Lawrence Erlbaum Associates.

Gardner, H. (1983). *Frames of mind: The theory of multiple intelligences.* New York: Basic Books.

Gordon, W. J. J. (1981). *The new art of the possible: The basic course in synectics.* Cambridge, MA: Porpoise Books.

Gordon, W. J. J., & Poze, T. (1972). *Teaching is listening.* Cambridge, MA: SES Associates.

Gordon, W. J. J., & Poze, T. (1975). *Strange and familiar.* Cambridge, MA: SES Associates.

Gordon, W. J. J., & Poze, T. (1979). *The metaphorical way of learning and knowing.* Cambridge, MA: SES Associates.

Gordon, W. J. J., & Poze, T. (1981). *The new art of the possible.* Cambridge, MA: SES Associates.

Gordon, W. J. J., & Poze, T. (1984). *Presentor's manual for the SES seminar for teachers.* Cambridge, MA: SES Associates.

Hanaford, P. A. (1882). *Daughters of America or women of the century.* Augusta, ME: True.

Heinig, R. B. (1992). *Creative drama for the classroom teacher* (4th ed.). Upper Saddle River, NJ: Prentice-Hall.

Hucko, B. (1996). *A rainbow at night: The world in words and pictures by Navajo children.* San Francisco: Chronicle Books.

Hughes, L. (1951). Dream deferred. In *The panther and the lash: Poems of our times* (p. 14). New York: Knopf.

Isaksen, S.G., Dorval, K. B., & Treffinger, D. J. (2000). *Creative approaches to problem solving* (2nd ed.). Dubuque, IA: Kendall/Hunt.

Johnson, C. (1997). Lost in the woods. In F. Barron, A Montuori, & A. Barron (Eds.), *Creators on creating* (pp. 59–62.). New York: Putnam.

Joyce, B., Weil, M., & Calhoun, E. (2000). *Models of teaching* (6th ed.). Boston: Allyn & Bacon.

Joyce, B., Weil, M., & Showers, B. (1992). *Models of teaching.* Boston: Allyn & Bacon.

Lewis, B. A. (1991). *The kid's guide to social action.* Minneapolis, MN: Free Spirit Press.

Lyons, M. E. (1997). *Stitching stars: The story quilts of Harriet Powers.* New York: Alladin Paperbacks.

MacKinnon, D. W. (1978). *In search of human effectiveness.* Buffalo, NY: Creative Education Foundation.

MacNelly, J. (1992, November 2). Shoe, cartoon. *Detroit Free Press,* p. 12D.

Mansfield, R. S., Busse, T. V., & Krepelka, E. J. (1978). The effectiveness of creativity training. *Review of Educational Research, 48,* 517–536.

McCaslin, N. (1999). *Creative drama in the classroom and beyond* (7th ed.). White Plains, NY: Longman.

Mednick, S. A. (1962). The associative basis of the creative process. *Psychological Review, 69,* 220–232.

Michigan Future Problem Solving Program. (n.d.). *The Michigan Future Problem Solving program.* Ann Arbor, MI: Author.

Micklus, C. S., & Micklus, C. (1986). *Program handbook: Instructional Manual for OM teams and coaches.* Glassboro, NJ: OM.

Osborn, A. F. (1953). *Applied imagination.* New York: Scribner's.

Parnes, S. J. (1967). Education and creativity. In J. C. Gowen, G. D. Demos, & E. P. Torrance (Eds.), *Creativity: Its educational implications.* New York: Wiley.

Paulus, P. B., Dzindolet, M. T., Poletes, G., & Camacho, L. M. (1993). Perception of performance in group brainstorming: The illusion of group productivity. *Personality and Social Psychology Bulletin, 19*(1), 78–89.

Perkins, D. N. (1981). *The mind's best work.* Cambridge, MA: Harvard University Press.

Prince, G. (1968). The operational mechanism of synectics. *Journal of Creative Behavior, 2,* 1–13.

Rothenberg, A. (1990). *Creativity and madness.* Baltimore: Johns Hopkins University Press.

Roukes, N. (1982). *Art synectics.* Worcester, MA: Davis Publications.

Runco, M. A. (1991). *Divergent thinking.* Norwood, NJ: Ablex.

Runco, M. A., & Sakamoto, S. O. (1999). Experimental studies of creativity. In R. J. Sternberg (Ed.), *Handbook of creativity* (pp. 62–92). New York: Cambridge University Press.

Schack, G. D., & Starko, A. J. (1998). *Research comes alive.* Mansfield Center, CT: Creative Learning Press.

Schlichter, C. (1986). Talents unlimited: Applying the Multiple Talents approach in mainstream and gifted programs. In J. S. Renzulli (Ed.), *Systems and models for developing programs for the gifted and talented* (pp. 352–389). Mansfield Center, CT: Creative Learning Press.

Schlichter, C., Palmer, W. R., & Palmer, R. (1993). *Thinking smart: A primer of the Talents Unlimited model.* Mansfield Center, CT: Creative Learning Press.

Science Olympiad. (1989). *Coaches' manual and rules.* Rochester, MI: Author.

Science Olympiad. (1990). *Student manual division B.* Rochester, MI: Author.

Seuss, Dr. (1954). *Horton hears a who.* New York: Random House.

Starko, A. J.(2000). Finding the problem finders: Problem finding and the identification and development of talent. In R.C. Freidman and B.M. Shore (Eds.) *Talents unfolding: Cognition and development.* Washington, D.C.: American Psychological Association.

Starko, A. J., & Schack, G. D. (1992). *Looking for data in all the right places.* Manfield Center, CT: Creative Learning Press.

Steiner, J. (1998). *Look alikes.* New York: Little, Brown and Company.

Stravinsky, I. (1997). Poetics of music. In F. Barron, A Montuori, & A. Barron (Eds.), *Creators on creating* (pp. 189–194.). New York: Putnam.

Sullivan, O. R. (1998). *African American inventors.* New York: John Wiley.

Sullivan, O. R. (2001). *African American women scientists and inventors.* New York: John Wiley.

Taylor, B. A. (1987). *Be an inventor.* New York: Harcourt Brace.

Torrance, E. P. (1987). Can we teach children to think creatively? In S. G. Isaksen (Ed.), *Frontiers of creativity research: Beyond the basics* (pp. 189–204). Buffalo, NY: Bearly.

Torrance, E. P., & Safter, H. T. (1990). *The incubation model of teaching: Getting beyond the aha!.* Buffalo, NY: Bearly.

Torrance, E. P., & Safter, H. T. (1999).*Making the creative leap beyond.* Buffalo, NY: Creative Education Foundation.

Torrance, E. P., & Torrance, J. P. (1978). The 1977–1978 Future Problem-Solving Program: Interscholastic competition and curriculum project. *Journal of Creative Behavior, 12,* 87–89.

Treffinger, D. J. (1995). Creative problem solving: Overview and educational implications. *Educational Psychology review, 7,* 301–312.

Treffinger, D. J., Isaksen, S. G., & Dorval, K. B. (2000). *Creative problem solving: An introduction* (3rd ed.). Waco, TX: Prufrock Press.

Treffinger, D. J., Isaksen, S. G., & Dorval, K. B. (2003).*Creative problem solving (CPS Version 6.1 TM): A contemporary framework for managing change.* Available from Center for Creative Learning, Inc. www.creativelearning.com.

Ward, T. B., Smith, S. M., & Finke, R. A. (1999). Creative cognition. In Sternber, R. J. (Ed.), *Handbook of creativity* (pp. 189–212). New York: Cambridge University Press.

Weisberg, R. W. (1986). *Creativity and other myths.* New York: Freeman.

Wilder, R. (1977). *A space where anything can happen.* Rowayton, CT: New Plays Books.

chapter 6

Creativity in the Content Areas

Dave sat at his desk with his student teacher, Nancy. Nancy's les- son plans for the next 2 weeks were on the desk between them. The plans were outstanding, organized around important concepts, and full of opportunities for student involvement and creative thinking. The problem was that they covered only 2 of the 10 objec- tives and a small fraction of the content Dave expected to teach during that period. The conversation between Dave and Nancy centered on a problem common to many teachers: how to select and organize the content we teach.

Dave: Nancy, I love a lot of the ideas you have presented. Your plans provide students with the experiences they need to build new concepts and really think about them. The problem is that the lessons take so long. If we take 2 weeks on these two outcomes, the year will be over before we are halfway through the district's cur- riculum guide. The guide is ridiculously long, but we have to do better than this.

Nancy: I know my plans are lengthy, but I've tried to work with concepts and skills that are important—things that are worth teaching. I don't think I can do a good job teaching anything if I have to try to teach all 10 outcomes in 2 weeks.

Dave: That may be true. Many of the articles I've been reading lately stress that we need to teach students more about less, teach-

259

ing for depth rather than breadth. But that's hard. Even after years of teaching experience, it is hard to know what to emphasize and what to leave out. What content and skills are essential?

Teaching content is at the heart of most school activities. We know the explosion of information ensures that much of the knowledge our students will need in the future is not available today—and most of us acknowledge that many students may not remember the details of the Taft-Hartley Act or the importance of equivalent angles for the rest of their lives. Still, teachers spend most of the school day teaching content in four basic areas: language arts, mathematics, social studies, and the sciences. Content can help students understand the world around them, gain an appreciation for cultures, live healthier lives, express themselves more clearly, and make more knowledgeable decisions in many areas of their lives. It also can be a vehicle for learning the types of problem solving and critical and creative thinking that may be considered the basic skills of the next century.

The overwhelming amount of content information available and frequently covered in texts, combined with tomorrow's pressing need for skills such as cooperation, creative thinking, and problem solving, can pose dilemmas for teachers such as Dave and Nancy. Faced with recommendations to teach for greater depth of understanding, with an emphasis on concept building and real-world problem solving (Dempster, 1993; Holt & Willard-Holt, 2000; Newmann, 1996; Schack, 1993), teachers must make decisions about the content and skills they will emphasize, teach, and omit. It simply is impossible to teach everything in depth. One approach to such decisions is to examine how the content being considered might relate to creativity. Because the processes involved in thinking creatively and solving problems also are associated with learning, content used in the creative process is likely to be learned. Considering the types of content and skills most likely to support students' creativity may assist teachers in making some of the difficult decisions regarding content selection, organization, and emphasis. Planning experiences that allow students to use important content in creative ways may serve double duty: supporting the development of creativity and allowing students the involvement in complex processes associated with the development of expertise.

This chapter examines the teaching of content and how it relates to the basic goals and processes of creativity. I suggest that creative acts entail finding and solving problems and expressing individual ideas in unique ways. Neither the problems solved nor the ideas expressed exist in a vacuum. People are creative in one or more disciplines, functioning as creative scientists, creative musicians, and creative writers. Recall that Amabile (see chap. 4) identified domain-relevant skills, or knowledge and skills of the content base, as an essential component of the creative process. Individuals need knowledge in order to be creative; finding problems of increasing sophistication demands increased understanding of the domains in which the problems are found. It is possible to become so entrenched in established knowledge that it is difficult to view a field with a fresh perspective (Sternberg & Lubart, 1991; Sternberg & O'Hara, 1999). However, too much knowledge is seldom the major concern of elementary or secondary school teachers. A more immediate issue is determining how the major disciplines might be taught so that they are supportive of students' creativity.

If content knowledge is essential to creativity, teachers should be able to teach each discipline in such a way that students have the opportunity to work in the same manner as those who are creative in that area. They might, at least at times, view language arts as would a creative writer, see science from the perspective of a creative scientist, and approach social studies as would a creative investigator in those domains. They must learn not just the content of the disciplines, but also how the disciplines work. Content teaching must include strategies for finding problems, gathering information, focusing on important ideas, and expressing discoveries in the forms and language of the domain.

Recommendations for strategies that enhance understanding of content have, in fact, described activities that involve students in creative thinking. Perrone (1994) described the common elements of learning activities in which students were most engaged intellectually:

Students helped define the content.

Students had time to wonder and to find a particular direction that interested them.

Topics had a strange quality—something common seen in a new way, evoking a lingering question.

Teachers permitted—even encouraged—different forms of expression and respected students' views.

Teachers were passionate about their work. The richest activities were invented by teachers.

Students created original and public products; they gained some form of expertise.

Students did something—participated in a political action, wrote a letter to the editor, or worked with the homeless.

Students sensed that the results of their work were not predetermined or fully predictable. (Pp. 11–12)

Virtually every element listed echoes a key attribute of creativity: finding interests and problems, looking in new ways, communicating personal ideas, and creating new products and solutions to problems. Yet the list was not developed to focus on creativity, but to describe activities that best assist students in understanding content.

This kind of teaching does not minimize the importance of factual information. An individual seldom finds a powerful and interesting problem without having substantial background knowledge. It does suggest that this content can be put to work. It also forces us to look on both the content and the students with new eyes. When we teach students to find and solve problems, we can never know exactly where the problems may lead. We must look at students not as empty vessels or blank slates, but as fellow investigators who come to us with ideas, experiences, and thoughts worth pursuing.

This chapter examines content teaching from several angles. First, it discusses an example of content teaching in art and how it may provide a model for other disciplines. Next, it surveys four major areas of curriculum (language arts, social studies, science, and mathematics) and gives examples of content teaching that may support creativity. Finally, it examines additional strategies that cut across disciplines, including inductive teaching, role play, and simulation strategies and investigates questioning patterns and discussion techniques.

Thinking About the Classroom

Think about the strategies your school district has used to determine the content that is most important to teach. Compare your experiences with those of teachers in other schools. How do you feel about the results? What kinds of decisions are being made? Are the decisions actually being implemented?

TEACHING FOR CREATIVITY: A MODEL

Artist George Szekely fell in love with children's art. He was captivated by the honesty and the excitement of their work. He also was struck by the ways in which the work of young artists paralleled the activities of adult artists. When absorbed in their paints, clay, or dances, they were engaged in authentic ways in the processes of art. Unfortunately, as an art teacher he also was struck with the contrast between the ways student artists made art on their own and the ways they were expected to make art in schools. School art usually involved tasks selected and planned by the teacher. Any deviation from the plan was considered to be misbehavior or failure. He describes one young art teacher who burst into tears because one of her students refused to complete her carefully planned projects—all he wanted to do was paint!

Szekely's (1988) efforts to design school art activities that allowed students to act as artists resulted in his book *Encouraging Creativity in Art Lessons*. In it he described his interaction with students as fellow artists, discoverers, and seekers. This section reviews some of Szekely's strategies as an artist–teacher and considers how they may model the processes of finding and solving problems and communicating ideas. The following sections explore ways to apply these principles to other domains, discussing students as creative producers rather than reproducers of knowledge in various disciplines, seeking problems and communicating ideas. These sections point out content areas in which some of the strategies designed to enhance creative thinking are particularly appropriate. In these efforts, we must continually examine the role of the teacher. Just as Szekely views himself as an artist–teacher, making and living art while he shares it with students, so the processes of creativity across disciplines may lead us to recreate ourselves in new roles. As we, too, seek problems worthy of attention and ideas that are exciting to share, we may need to become scientist-teachers, writer-teachers, and so forth. Perhaps by immersing ourselves in the questions, problems, and mysteries of our content, we may find new adventures for ourselves as well as our students. To begin, let us examine the journey in art.

Finding Art

Art teachers are perpetually short of time. Whatever tasks are planned for a particular day must be explained, accomplished, and cleaned up within an allotted time. To meet such demands, some art classes take on the air of an assembly line. The teacher explains the task with as much clarity as possible and provides needed materials. Students are responsible for listening carefully and following directions. If all goes well, the period ends with a collection of products that all approximate the teacher's plan, ready to hang on bulletin boards or home refrigerators.

Although such strategies are efficient, they bring to mind one of the basic questions addressed in chapter 1: Who is being creative here? If the teacher selects the problem and decides how it should be solved, the end products (although potentially providing the opportunity for students to practice artistic techniques) are more a reflection of the teacher's creativity than the students'. It is the teacher's idea, the teacher's selection of materials, and the teacher's clear set of instructions; the students merely provide the labor. In such a class, students do not experience art. When teachers present preplanned problems and designated solutions, they short-cut one of the keys to creativity: finding important and interesting problems to solve.

> When teachers assume that students can make artworks simply by following instructions, they are forgetting how important *thinking about art ideas and preparing for the artwork* are in the art process. Artists prepare for art making by thinking about their ideas, visualizing the works they might make, recording ideas in notes and sketches, planning for the works, searching for materials, and playfully experimenting with various possibilities for carrying out the ideas. Lessons that place the major emphasis on following instructions and learning set techniques of art making do not come to terms with the basic problem of introducing students to the art process. Time has to be found *within* the lessons to help students prepare for art making by responding to experience of the environment, thinking about art ideas, and making the other essential preparations. Also, since there can never be enough time within the period for adequate preparations for art making, lessons must be designed to motivate students to use their own time *outside* of art class—not only at home but during all sorts of daily experiences—to prepare for art making by seeing, thinking, and responding as an artist does. (Szekely, 1988, pp. 4–5, italics in the original)

Instead of shielding students from the frustration of seeking ideas, teacher-structured problems rob students of the art-making process: looking for ideas; choosing materials, tools, and forms; and visualizing a variety of possibilities. Art lessons, at their best, are not designed solely to impart the knowledge of the teacher or techniques of the field, but to allow students to experience the life of an artist. They should explore the kinds of questions that intrigue contemporary artists and, as artists do, use art to explore and express the world around them.

> The aim of building an art lesson, then, is to create a situation in which children can invent, and as Piaget has said, discover struc-

tures and principles. We want to ensure that students will continue to generate their own ideas and act on them after their schooling is over. In this way we show that art is not just a body of special techniques used to produce school projects but something relevant—indeed central—to our lives .... Art teaching is helping individuals to develop their own unique ideas. Promoting individual investigation must therefore be the center of importance in all of our teaching. Students need to be taught to take their own ideas and observations seriously and to turn to themselves first and foremost for solutions and answers. Art teaching needs to exemplify the process of independent research, the willingness to be different, and the ability to try new things. Students need to view art as a process of questioning and experimenting rather than one of looking for answers from the teacher or others. Art lessons, therefore, need to be stated in the form of questions, posing problems and presenting challenges, so that students can learn to seek their own solutions and become aware that new possibilities exist. (Szekely, 1988, pp. 7, 9)

Parallel concerns, challenges, and potential solutions can be found in any discipline. Because art instruction should exemplify the processes of art, instruction in other content areas, at least part of the time, should share the processes of creative individuals in those areas. Students learning science need to learn information about the world around them. If they are to develop as creative scientists, they also need to begin learning how scientists view the world—how they question and explore. Students learning mathematics need to begin seeing the wonder with which mathematicians view the patterns around them and the types of questions they ask.

Thinking About the Classroom

Think about the subject or subjects you teach. Consider the types of questions that professionals in that field, or those fields, pursue. Jot down a list of skills necessary to identify and explore problems in at least one area you teach. How many of them are taught in your curriculum?

Although each discipline has investigative techniques to be learned and particular types of questions that may be explored, there also are ideas, values, and attitudes that support creativity across domains. I recall a summer conference at which, as a graduate student, I was serving in several capacities. In the morning, I was teaching investigative techniques in science to a group of elementary teachers. In the afternoon, I was serving as an assistant to a well-known expert on visual arts, a subject about which I knew very little. I hoped that by assisting I might gain enough knowledge and confidence to do a better job teaching in that area. After a few days, I was startled to realize that my morning and afternoon activities were parallel. In each class we taught students to observe carefully, to look for patterns, to decide what was interesting, and to investigate further. In art, as in science, we encouraged students to value their observations and ideas and to approach the world as a source of inspiration and amazement. The tools we used to explore were different, but the processes of questioning were often the same. Looking back now, I can see that the shared experiences follow the patterns of problem finding described in chapter 5.

The experiences of observing, investigating, and dreaming do not occur unplanned or emerge from an atmosphere of chaos. Creativity requires new ways of seeing, new excitement and explorations across content areas. Helping children see in new ways entails understanding the ways children see now: observing the images, experiences, and languages of children's lives. From there, students can be invited to play, to question, and to bring what is best of their outside ideas, observations, and trials to bear on the task. The lesson becomes an invitation to create, not a demand to reproduce.

If the invitation is key, we must allot time in which to do the inviting. If it is impossible to help students both discover and address the problem in one 43-minute period, then some periods may be given over exclusively to the exploration. Spending time helping students find their ideas, whatever the discipline, is an essential piece of the creative process. If there is nothing to hang on the refrigerator this time, so be it.

Planning for Problems

If students are to gain the independence necessary to be artists (or scientists or writers), they must have the opportunity to work on individual projects, as do adults. Twenty-five versions of a trace-the-hand turkey, essays on "What I Did on My Summer Vacation," or identical graphs of the month's rainfall do not provide students with the vision or skills necessary to ask their own questions or explore their own ideas. Rather, during some of their school experiences, students must be presented with broad areas of concern in which to identify and frame individual problems. The process may be divided into at least four parts: exploring the environment, investigating ideas and materials, recording ideas, and experimenting with production.

Exploring the Environment.   Ideas for problems come from students' internal or external environments. The first stage in problem finding is helping students begin to look. This is the exploring-with-interest part of problem finding discussed in chapter 5. In art, environmental searches could include looking for possible art materials, tools, or ideas. Writers look for scenes, moods, characters, conflicts, and struggles that might be interesting to explore. Scientists look for patterns, variables that might be related, and unexplained or unexpected occurrences. In each case, the environment is approached purposefully, with an eye to identifying individual interests and concerns.

One way to help students begin environmental searches is to structure their explorations of the world outside the school. Szekely (1985) suggested that students may be challenged to look for art materials in a fast-food restaurant or for ideas about color in a fabric store. Young writers may be instructed to spend several days finding something interesting that fits in their pocket, a character from their neighborhood who might have had an adventure, or a magazine picture that makes them curious. Beginning scientists could look for the types of plants growing naturally at different places in the neighborhood, or young historians could investigate the dates on local buildings or grave markers. The key in each case is that students undertake the search in an effort to find questions or ideas that intrigue them. Why did so many people die in 1817? Why are some lawns full of moss? Why is the woman in this picture smiling?

Teachers can model the processes of exploration by sharing their own efforts. Writer-teachers might describe the walk through the woods that inspired their latest poem or the interesting character they observed in the laundromat. Mathematician-teachers might describe their search for natural spirals and their delight at finding a new, interesting shell. Historian-teachers could share their efforts to learn about the history of their house or their curiosity about the town's defunct trolley system: Where did those tracks once lead? Whatever the discipline, teachers will be better models if, in at least one area, they are involved themselves in the processes of exploration.

Initially, such involvement may prove a challenge. Teachers' lives are very busy, and the pursuit of outside interests may feel like a luxury we can ill afford. Or worse, we, ourselves, may have spent so many years pursuing teacher-designed, teacher-assigned projects that we may have difficulty imagining ourselves pursuing an academic task without an assignment. It may be easier to look for opportunities to be creative in cooking, woodworking, or making Halloween costumes than in language arts, history, science, or math. Yet, although creativity is valuable in any area from costumes to casseroles, if we expect creative questioning in academic domains from our students, we must be willing to experience it ourselves. Think about how you might use at least one of the disciplines you teach to explore the world in ways that interest you, and share your experiences with your students. A teacher who is also an artist or mathematician or scientist or writer can better share the adventures of these domains with the people around him or her.

In addition to sharing your own explorations outside school, you can also assist students in finding problems by structuring the school environment. In an art class, creating an environment for exploration may entail putting out buckets of different brushes, shining lights on different surfaces, or displaying collections of sea life, boots, wrapping papers, or packaging. In a math class, an environment may be a poster of Fibonacci numbers, a collection of Escher posters, or a roulette wheel. Whatever the environment, it invites students to explore an area of general concern, to raise questions, and to investigate and experiment.

Thinking About the Classroom

Plan an activity designed specifically to encourage students to look for questions or projects in your subject area. Discuss the questions raised with your students. Consider which might be pursued by individuals or groups.

Investigating Ideas and Materials.   The next stage in assisting students in finding problems is providing the opportunity to experiment with ideas—the playing and wondering of problem finding. Once an idea in the environment catches their attention, students must be free to play with it, generate multiple hypotheses, make several sketches, or try out half a dozen brushes before deciding on a product or investigation. In art class, many of these explorations may be concrete and visible. We can see the student try out several painting tools, shine the light in different directions, or experiment with combinations of materials for a sculpture. In other areas, explorations may be less visible but equally important. A student interested in the paths fish swim in an aquarium needs to spend time watching fish, thinking about fish, and reading about fish before deciding exactly what aspect of fish paths she wants to investigate. A student intrigued by the town's population statistics from 1860 may consider questions about age, occupation, gender, marital status, and ethnicity before deciding to concentrate on changes in educational level. Preliminary consideration of diverse variables not only allows for multiple ideas, but also can provide suggestions of how variables might be connected. Perhaps changes in educational level are linked with gender, ethnicity, or age.

Although the creative process sometimes demands that explorations be conducted and problems framed by individuals, it also is important to experience shared creative experiences. A class may explore a given stimulus or environment and generate many possible paths for exploration. A trip to an old cemetery, a collection of rodents, or an interesting story all can provide inspiration for class discussions and investigations. Questions such as "What did you observe that was interesting?" "What do you wonder about this?" "What made you curious?" or "What would you like to investigate?" can cue students that they might make choices about the things they learn and the questions they investigate.

Exploration time can also include sharing ideas, questions, or possibilities. A class period spent discussing things we might do with these brushes or questions we might ask about gerbils provides many more possibilities for rich, creative activities than art projects or research plans compressed into a 40-minute time slot. Students may also conduct artists' seminars, writers' workshops, or research think tanks in which they discuss ideas in process. Such discussions center on what students might create, write about, or investigate. They provide the opportunity to support and encourage good ideas, even if not all of them can be pursued immediately.

Recording Ideas. Virtually every kind of creative endeavor entails some format for recording ideas, inspirations, and thoughts in progress, the capturing-questions part of my problem-finding sequence. (It is fascinating to me that my reading of creative individuals' writings and Szekely's study of art yield virtually identical initial stages of the creative process.) Inventors' notebooks, writers' journals, and artists' sketch pads provide a space for trapping the idea that appears just before you sleep, while you are in the shower, or at other unbidden moments. They provide a record of ideas as they develop, as well as a safe keeping for ideas that may not be developed now but may prove fruitful at another time. A third-grader's sketch pad might contain six drawings of his dog, each in increasing detail; a sticker of a robot figure (some day it would be fun to make a robot); a rough sketch of several types of balls; a sample of silver paper; and rubbings of five leaves. The dog drawings represent a work in progress. The robot, balls, and silver paper are representations of ideas for future projects, and the leaves are a response to a teacher's request to look for interesting textures. Similarly, a writer's journal may contain phrases, pictures, and works in progress, whereas a scientist's notebook might hold sketches of observations, articles from the newspaper, and interesting questions.

Students should have at least one journal for recording their creative ideas. This should not be a notebook in which required daily entries are assessed by the teacher, but an idea book that is convenient to carry and fun to use. Idea books may occasionally be shared during class discussions or teacher conferences to demonstrate the value of good questions or the progress of an idea. However, their chief value is as a record of good ideas and not-so-good ones, problems that were solved, and problems that remain. The expectation that some ideas will work and some will not, that learning takes place in all experimentation, and that every idea need not become a final product is both basic to the creative process and essential to the attitude of risk taking associated with creativity.

Experimenting with Production. Once a problem is selected and explored, production can begin. The artist begins drawing or sculpting; the scientist designs the experiment; and the writer begins to write. Even at this stage, problem finding may continue. The sculptor may find that a new angle changes the play of light; the scientist may make new hypotheses; and the writer may change direction. Such is the nature of the process. It is helpful to understand that although each idea may continue to develop, creative products or projects may come to closure. Learning when to stop revising and begin a new piece is an art in itself. As creator-teachers, we may model this process by sharing our own efforts, discussing how the project progressed and where we will go next. Similar lessons can be gained through studying the lives and particularly the notebooks of creative individuals. Class sharing, displays, and publication opportunities also can help students experience the transition between problems and look toward the future.

Planning Lessons

The types of lessons that allow students to see the processes of finding and solving problems have characteristics that cut across disciplines. First, lessons focus on broad, important ideas rather than specific facts or techniques. An art lesson might center on texture rather than screen printing, a social studies lesson on the relationships between geography and economic development rather than land forms in the western United States. Facts and skills become part of the lesson rather than its focus; they are

Students can capture many types of ideas in a notebook.

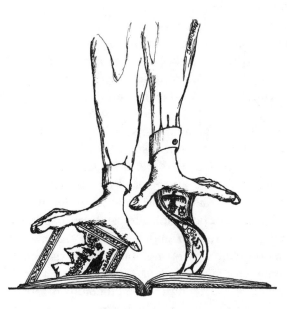

tools for exploring broader issues. The concepts and generalizations that structure the unit must have room for a variety of individual or small group questions.

Second, the lessons must tie in some way to the world of the students. On one hand, such a statement seems painfully obvious. Cognitive psychology makes it clear that learning requires tying new experiences to prior knowledge. If we wish students to learn, they must be able to make sense of school activities in terms of their previous experiences. However, if we want students to find meaningful problems, they must not only be able to understand them, but they also must care about them.

The creative process is an extraordinarily personal thing. Individuals create because they must—because the problems they must solve and the things they must say matter enormously to them. The literature abounds with stories of scientists who stay in their labs, artists in their studios, or writers at their desks for days and nights without ceasing, so absorbed are they in the work at hand. Although the intensity of adult creative behavior probably is not reasonable or desirable for school, the process of finding problems is inseparably bound to individual (or shared) interests. Creators choose problems because they care about them; the problem is somehow important, intriguing, or puzzling and must be addressed. For students to approximate this process, they must be able to choose problems of interest and importance to them.

To tie lessons to the world of the student, we must find a balance between traditional academic content and aspects of contemporary culture that can illuminate general principles. Texture may be explored in paintings by Seurat, in wooden masks, in stuffed toys, or in the costumes of contemporary musicians. Economic development can be studied through the activities of prospectors as well as pioneers, through the fate of the local mill as well as the growth of economic centers, or even through the potential economy of Tolkien's fantasy world. If students are to choose investigations, there must be room for real choice. If student selections are limited to "Which Greek god will you study?" or "Which system of the body will you choose for your report," students are unlikely to view the process of selecting and investigating as a powerful, interest-driven experience. I once interviewed eighth-grade students about the school projects on which they worked the hardest, the most memorable in their experiences. Outside special programming for gifted students, I did not find a single student who could remember ever selecting a subject for study because of personal interest. It is not surprising that many of those students displayed little enthusiasm for school projects and saw the efforts as having limited value and influence in their lives. Although we may not always be able to give students a broad range of choices, some choice should be an important part of content teaching whenever possible.

Finally, lessons should be structured to nurture and support student independence. Students may approach problems as individuals or as small groups, but they should do so under their own power as much as possible. Students who work independently are able to use time and materials well without constant teacher direction, making decisions about the scope, scheduling, and results of their efforts. Chapter 7 discusses classroom structures that support student independence in more detail. For now, it may be sufficient to say that the success of these lessons is best measured not only by students' appropriate classroom behavior, attention to the teacher, or even scores on content tests, but also by the ways they are able to take information, learn from it, and apply it in new ways.

What Is a Problem?

If we are to assist students in finding and solving problems in content areas, it is important to consider first, what is a problem? What characteristics define real or authentic problems and how are they distinct from the kinds of problems typically addressed in schools? Theorists espousing authentic outcomes, real-world tasks, and multidimensional problem solving fill the pages of educational journals (Newmann & Wehlage, 1993; Renzulli & Reis, 1997; Sternberg, 1985). However, in many cases, the meanings of such terms are unclear. The authors assume, perhaps, that we will know real tasks when we see them.

One helpful key to defining real problems is in the work of Renzulli (1977) and Renzulli and Reis (1997), whose Enrichment Triad Model centers on individual and small-group investigations of real problems. This model was originally developed for the education of gifted and talented students, but many of its components are appropriate for all students, and the strategies for the pursuit of real problems can hold the key to problem finding and solving in many arenas.

First, a real problem springs from the interest of a student or group of students. A real problem has personal interest and value to the student who pursues it. If everyone is assigned to do it, it is less likely to be a real problem. Second, a real problem does not have a predetermined correct response. It involves processes for which there cannot be an answer key. As I consider the real problems with which my students have become involved, they seem to fall into three general categories.

1. Some real problems are research questions. They involve gathering and analyzing data and drawing conclusions. True research questions entail collecting information from primary sources through observation, surveys, interviews, or document analysis. The students who surveyed food preferences in the school cafeteria, those who interviewed local citizens on life in the community during World War II, and the first graders who observed the effects of milk on plant growth all investigated research questions.

2. Other real problems fall into the category of activism. In these activities, students attempt to improve some aspect of the world around them. Students who set up school recycling programs, teach peers what to do if they suspect a friend is being abused, create community nature trails, or lobby for bike paths are pursuing this type of real problem.

3. Finally, real problems in the arts entail the expression of some theme, aesthetic, or idea. Adult creators use words, movement, paint, or clay as tools for expression. Students whose artwork explores the changing light, whose stories reflect their ideas about

friendship, or whose dance reflects their rage all address real problems in meaningful ways.

In pursuing real problems, students should use authentic methodology as much as possible. That is, they should address the problem the way a professional would address it. The student who wants to survey cafeteria preferences must learn something about survey design. The first-grade student with the bean plants should make a hypothesis and have a control group. Although some types of authentic methodology are easier to implement than others, each aspect of a project provides opportunities to stretch students toward professionalism. It will be much easier for students to use authentic historical research techniques in a local history project than in a project about a distant place. However, even when primary sources are limited, students can use professional techniques for sharing information in a manner that is appropriate to the discipline.

Finally, when they are pursuing real problems, students eventually share information with a real audience. What constitutes a real audience will vary enormously with the age of the students and the sophistication of their problems. The key is that the audience should have a genuine interest in the product instead of viewing it as a source for a grade or other evaluation. Some real audiences are part of the natural school environment. A group of first-grade students may write an original play and produce it for the class next door. Other audiences may be created by school events to provide a vehicle for student efforts: art exhibits, invention conventions, and science fairs (Schack & Starko, 1998; Starko & Schack, 1992). Still other audiences may be part of the local community. Our local chamber of commerce was pleased to display a student-produced brochure on the history of local buildings along with other pamphlets the chamber made available to the public. The radio station often aired student-generated public service announcements. Local-access cable television, historical societies, and other community organizations can provide enthusiastic audiences for appropriate student products.

Certainly, the types of problems pursued, the methodology employed, and the audiences approached will vary enormously from the first kindergarten puppet show or garden experiment to the high school seniors' computer program for displaying the location of archeological artifacts. However, at each stage, students may be nudged just one notch closer to professionalism: the kindergarten student to plan a puppet before building it, the high school senior to present his or her work to the state archeological association. Each represents a legitimate step toward pursuing real problems.

Thinking About the Classroom

Examine a local newspaper looking for real-world problems that might be investigated by students. You may want to look daily for a week or two. See if you discover any that might tie to your curriculum.

TEACHING FOR CREATIVITY IN THE CONTENT AREAS

At least superficially, what constitutes creativity in one discipline is considerably different from what comprises creativity in another. To most of us, what a physicist does appears quite different from what a novelist or painter does. Although theorists debate whether there are underlying creative processes that cut across disciplines, teachers must make decisions about content teaching. Many teachers, I suspect, would like to make decisions that allow them to teach content in a way that is supportive of students' developing creativity in the discipline being taught. Teachers would like to support mathematical creativity in math class, scientific creativity in science class, and so forth. If indeed there are true differences in the processes used for creativity in varying disciplines, it will be important for teachers to teach for creativity in many different subject areas. If creative strategies, even in part, transfer from one discipline to the next, teaching for creativity in multiple disciplines provides important reinforcement and opportunities for transfer. In either case, when teachers teach for creativity in the content areas, the resulting experience helps students understand that creative individuals are creative about something. Content-free exercises may be enjoyable. They may allow students to practice needed skills. However, until students use their creativity on substantive content and real-world problems, they will not experience creative thinking as it is used and valued in society.

Teachers must address two major considerations when they make decisions about teaching in the content areas. First, they must decide what to teach: which concepts, generalizations, skills, or strategies to emphasize. Second, they must decide how the content will be taught: what teaching approaches or organizational strategies can best approach their goals. This section briefly reviews some major curriculum trends and what they suggest about the what and how of content teaching. Next, it presents some general recommendations for the what and how of teaching for creativity, and finally, it gives specific examples of how the recommendations may be implemented in language arts, social studies, science, and mathematics.

Before beginning, I must explain briefly my decision not to discuss arts instruction in this chapter. I recognize that there are many opportunities for creativity in the visual and performing arts. Viewing and participating in such activities has brought me much joy. However, I have decided to concentrate on basic academic content areas for three reasons. First, I believe that creativity is already more readily recognized and nurtured during arts instruction. Second, arts instruction is generally (but not always) carried out by specialists in arts education who already may be familiar with the ideas discussed here. Finally, the basic content areas take up by far the largest amount of time during most students' school day. If we are to support creativity in school, we must do this during the large blocks of traditional content, not just during specialized instruction. Having said this, I must affirm my commitment to the importance of arts education for all students. I hope its supporters will understand my reasoning and find something of use in the discussion of other content areas.

Curriculum Trends and Issues

The 1990s was a time of curriculum reform across content areas. In a review of curriculum reforms emerging from professional organizations dealing with content teaching, VanTassel-Baska (1993) identified 10 attributes that were shared across disciplines, and these have continued into the 21st century. Many of the trends also can be linked to research and theory in creativity. The 10 identified characteristics are as follows:

1. *Learner outcomes of significance.* Content learning is focused toward activities that allow learners to use content in significant ways. Significant outcomes have many of the same characteristics as authentic learning or real problems.
2. *Authentic assessment.* Logically, complex significant applications of learning demand equally complex assessment procedures. Authentic assessment is discussed in more detail in chapter 7.
3. *Inquiry-based learning.* Inquiry learning is organized around students' explorations of data in order to draw conclusions. Instead of the teacher presenting information, students generate information from experiences organized by the teacher. Inquiry learning strategies are discussed later in this chapter.
4. *Active learning.* Students are to be active participants rather than passive receptors in the learning process.

5. *Thinking skills.* Across disciplines, there is an emphasis on skills that have been designated higher level thinking. Recommended areas of emphasis often include both critical and creative thinking strategies.

6. *Metacognition.* Students are taught to think about their own thinking processes.

7. *Technology relevance.* Students should be taught to use technology to gather, analyze, and express content across disciplines.

8. *Habits of mind.* Students are taught habits of mind that are important to practitioners in the field.

9. *Conceptual orientation.* Content is organized around key concepts and principles of the discipline in contrast to a emphasis on isolated facts.

10. *Interdisciplinary orientation.* Students should be taught to use and understand content as it spans disciplines.

Many of these recommendations tie directly to the ideas and processes that underlie creativity. Students should be actively involved in lessons in ways that allow them to learn important content while using critical and creative thinking. They should be taught to understand their own thinking and the habits of mind that are necessary for professionals in various disciplines. They should have the opportunity to use information in significant ways that include solving problems. Each of these recommendations parallels research on creativity. Teaching that supports creativity also supports good content teaching, and vice versa!

Thinking about the Classroom

Examine your curriculum materials. Do you see evidence of any of the trends listed? You also may wish to talk to curriculum specialists in your district to see how curriculum trends have affected district level planning.

What to Teach, How to Teach

If individuals are to be creative in an effort to find and solve problems and to find and express ideas, teaching that supports creativity must allow them to do these things in school. If they are to be creative in the content areas, they must also have content knowledge.

In considering what to teach, at least two major categories of information seem important. First, students must gain enough understanding of the major concepts, generalizations, and big ideas of the discipline to be able to ask reasonable questions. Second, they must learn the techniques and methodologies (as well as habits of mind) of creative individuals in the field. Students of science must learn not just facts and rules, but how science works. Whatever the content area, students must learn what kinds of problems are explored in that area, how they are addressed, and how information is shared. Students of social studies must learn how social scientists view their fields, what they explore, and how they proceed. Young writers must learn the kinds of questions and problems writers face and how they address them. Of course, the level and sophistication of techniques used must vary enormously with grade level, but the general principle remains: If students are to work creatively in content areas they must learn both the content and the methods of the subjects they study.

It is also important to consider how the content and methodologies will be taught. One way to think about the how of content teaching is to consider three general phases in the learning of new content: preparation, building understanding (or presentation), and application. It is possible to incorporate strategies that support creative thinking into any or all of these phases. Certainly, it would not be appropriate (or possible) to use such strategies for every part of every lesson. However, it is valuable to consider how creative thinking might play a part in each of the three phases.

The first part of a lesson sequence prepares students for learning. In this phase, teachers find out what students know, make ties to prior knowledge, provide advanced organizers, and spur interest and curiosity. Any preparation activities that allow students to express questions of interest, use analogies or diverse points of view to tie to prior knowledge, ask students to make hypotheses, or challenge them with unexplained events will support the curiosity, exploration, and wonder that are essential for creativity.

It is also possible to structure the presentation of content—building understanding—in ways that support questioning, hypothesis testing, and independent thinking. Many inductive teaching strategies, discussed later in the chapter, are appropriate for this purpose. The presentation phase does not imply that the teacher is directly presenting information, only that content is being introduced. If we want to present content and reinforce creative thinking strategies at the same time, at least some of the content can be introduced in a way that allows students to question, explore, and draw conclusions.

Once content has been introduced, it must be applied and extended. This is the stage at which most problem-solving activities are appropriate. Students can apply known content to explore new areas and raise original questions. Teachers can design application activities that may not solve problems, but will allow students to practice the attitudes or strategies that are important in creativity. For example, a role-play activity that allows students to see multiple points of view, a writing activity in which students practice content by generating original analogies, or a simulation in which students must use information in a situation very different from that in which it was learned all reinforce creative thinking skills and attitudes.

The next four sections examine finding and solving problems, learning the methodologies of disciplines, and structuring teaching to enhance creativity in various disciplines. In no case are the suggestions intended to be a comprehensive program in the discipline discussed. Rather, they reflect activities, points of view, and organizational strategies that can form an important part of many programs.

Finding and Solving Problems in the Language Arts

Helping students find and solve problems in the language arts requires a major shift in perspective. Students must—at least at times—shift from thinking "I write because I have an assignment" to "I write because I have an idea." Understanding that good writing and good language are based in the communication of ideas is at the heart of creativity in the language arts.

Finding Purpose and Technique for Communication.   Authors write for a variety of purposes. Some writing is designed to convey factual information, some to persuade, some to share emotions or ideas, and some to raise questions. Other important communication uses oral language or other media or symbolic forms for similar purposes. If students are to use writing or other forms of language to share their own ideas, they must recognize the efforts at communication in the works they read or hear.

In considering the role of language and language arts in creativity, teachers must be aware of at least two perspectives. The first is that language, oral or written, is an essential vehicle for communicating creative ideas, strategies, and solutions across disciplines. Students may write about problems and ideas in math, science, social studies, or any other area. A second perspective is that schools may play a role in supporting the kind of creativity inherent in the language arts themselves: poetry, storytelling or story writing, play writing, and so on. In either case, the heart of the process is identifying an idea worthy of communication. This section deals primarily with the second perspective: creativity in the more traditional language arts. Keep in mind, however, that writing and language activities can and should be organized around the problem identification and solving experiences in the other disciplines discussed later.

The links among thought, speaking, and writing are at the heart of current balanced literacy approaches. Students learn that if they can think it, they can say it. If they can say it, they can write it and read it. Writing is, above all, communication. As students develop as readers and writers, they can approach the processes of finding and expressing ideas with increasing sophistication. Process writing, an approach to writing popularized by Graves (1983, 1994), can support many of the attitudes and ideas associated with creativity at a wide range of grade levels (Atwell, 1998; Calkins, 1994). Done well, process writing places communication squarely at the center of all writing. The focus is on writing techniques and strategies as tools for conveying ideas. Although the terminology may vary with authors, most advocates of the writing process identify at least five stages: prewriting, writing, revising, editing, and presenting.

Process writing often is associated with approaches to reading instruction that link the reading, speaking, and writing processes. In the early 21st century, the teaching of reading is (again) a matter of considerable controversy. As districts make decisions about reading and writing instruction, it is important to read research and recommendations carefully. For example, evidence that systematic phonics instruction is helpful in learning to read (Ehri, Nunes, Stahl, & Willows, 2001) sometimes is interpreted to mean that phonics should be at the center of all reading instruction (something the aforementioned authors never suggested). Some educators are concerned that National Reading Panel evidence suggests that programs linking reading and writing are ineffective, when according to Yatvin (2002), investigation of the relationships between reading and writing simply were not part of the study. As research continues to emerge, it will be vital to adapt and evolve programs carefully, holding on to those aspects of literacy instruction that are important in helping students become independent and creative writers.

Although a complete description of the writing process is beyond the scope of this chapter, we consider here how some stages may tie to research and theory in creativity. In the prewriting stage, students can engage in problem finding and focusing if they are given the flexibility to choose an idea, topic, or question of personal concern. The prewriting stage may include at least three components: caring, observing, and focusing. Writers first must care about something; they must be moved to say something. Caring can spring from previous experiences and interests or from experiences structured by the teacher. This component also includes time to let ideas brew or incubate.

After caring comes observing. The author observes his or her experiences and attitudes regarding the idea or topic, past or present. This can be followed by focusing: determining point of view, identifying audience, selecting relevant observations, and narrowing goals. In one class, sixth-grade students were challenged to think about an interesting character they had come across during summer recess. The prewriting process included thinking about people who were interesting, people who related to topics of interest, or people who made a difference in their summer. A student might consider the camp counselor with the purple hair, the coach of a well-loved sport, or the woman next door who hired him or her to do yard work.

One student chose to write about an older woman whose stories of days gone by had made summer evenings interesting. The student cared about the woman and wanted others to care about her as well. Next, the student considered all the sensory and emotional details she could recall about the woman. Webbing, or clustering, is often used to organize such ideas and information on a topic. Even emergent readers with limited writing skills can use clustering by drawing in items, locations, or activities associated with an idea. Finally, it was necessary for the student to sort the information and decide what she wanted to convey about her friend. Her decision to use descriptive language to portray the dignity and grace with which the woman spoke gave focus to the project. The activities of caring, observing, and focusing allowed the student to find and focus on a specific problem in a general assignment.

Later stages of the writing process, particularly revision, in which students often work together to examine a draft from the reader's point of view, also support creativity by helping students develop the necessary internal locus of evaluation and standards for judgment (see chap. 7). Skills instruction can include not just lessons on punctuation or grammatical form, but also activities that help students focus on the techniques or strategies used by proficient writers in many disciplines.

Young beginning authors can examine the ideas and emotions underlying stories they hear. They might discuss the feelings the author tried to convey in *The Snowy Day* (Keats, 1962) or what ideas the author tried to share in *Ira Sleeps Over* (Waber, 1972). They can experiment with listing words that might make the reader feel happy or frightened, or try to write a brief story that evokes a particular feeling. They could discuss why authors might write happy stories or sad stories. Later, students might write a piece designed to evoke a particular feeling, share the piece with peers, and discuss whether readers understood the intended mood.

Students also can explore the language play fundamental to some works of literature. Children, young and old, reading *Ding Dong Ding Dong* (Palatini, 1999) can enjoy the many plays on words in the story of the giant gorilla (Ding Dong) who climbs the Empire State Building attempting to sell Ape-On cosmetics. More sophisticated readers can examine the word play in the dialogue of Tom Stoppard's plays. Understanding the authors' enjoyment of the clever use of language can inspire students to new types of writing while reinforcing flexible thinking about the words they choose. Other writing tasks might encompass broad areas, allowing students to write about topics they identify as important: their favorite after-school activity, the thing about school they would most like to change, or a person they think is important. Although such tasks are still relatively constrained, they do begin to convey the idea that writing is designed to communicate ideas and feelings that matter to the author.

Students in intermediate and higher grades can begin to discuss how authors get ideas for their writing. Reading biographies and interviewing local authors can give students clues to the writers' processes. Older students can analyze the writings of creative adults describing their work. They can begin to practice the careful observations and sense of wonder that characterize many authors. When students view the world through writers' eyes, every experience becomes a potential story source. Recall from chapter 3 that Orson Scott Card found ideas for short stories in everyday moments by noticing and focusing in extraordinary ways. Many authors look at the world and think "Isn't that strange—or interesting—or sad—or confusing," and want others to notice as well. From those desires, perhaps, springs their drive to write.

One of my favorite examples of an author describing his process is Ray Bradbury's (1996) *Zen and the Art of Writing: Essays on Creativity*. In it, Bradbury describes the process of finding stories within oneself and nurturing the Muse that stores them there. "Ideas," he writes, "lie everywhere, like apples fallen and melting in the grass for lack of wayfaring strangers with an eye and a tongue for beauty, whether absurd, horrific, or genteel" (p. 8). His suggestions for finding the ideas range from reading poetry every day and reading to improve color sense to long walks in the country to long walks through bookstores. "By living well, by observing as you live, by reading well and observing as you read, you have fed Your Most Original Self" (p. 43). Bradbury writes of masterful problem finding.

6.1. Mama, Do You Love Me? Using Flexible Thinking in Language Arts (K–12)

Read the picture book *Mama, Do You Love Me?* (Joosse, 1991). The book uses images and examples from Inuit culture to describe a mother's love for her child. Students could write a similar book using images from their own culture or a culture they research.

Joosse, B.M. (1991). *Mama, do you love me?* San Francisco: Chronicle Books.

Students can begin to observe the world around them as writers through the vehicle of a writer's notebook. Separate pages might be set aside for jottings of a particular type. Students might create sections for "Things I wonder about," "Strange things people do," "Peaceful things," "Nice-sounding words or phrases," "Ideas about the future," "City things," or any other categories that suit their interests and needs. Some categories might be required as a basis of class discussions. For example, a class that read *Gilgamesh* or the *Autobiography of Malcolm X* (X, 1965) might spend several days looking for ideas or examples regarding heroics. These might be shared in a class discussion on how such ideas may form the basis for a new piece of literature. The pieces may or may not be actually written.

At other times, students may engage in activities that parallel those described by particular authors. Students who have read how Toni Morrison (1987) found the idea for the novel *Beloved* by reading a 19th-century newspaper might be assigned to examine a paper (past or present) for possible story ideas. Younger students might be challenged to imagine the story behind the story in familiar tales. Why did Goldilocks go into the woods that day? Why weren't the three pigs sharing a house? Books such as *The True Story of the Three Little Pigs* (Scieszka, 1989) can help students view familiar stories from another perspective and provide an example of an author finding ideas in seemingly common sources.

Students who have heard E. L. Doctorow describe his struggle with writer's block might follow his example. According to a television interview I heard years ago, after the success of *The Book of Daniel* (1971), Doctorow found himself struggling for a new idea. As an exercise in self-discipline, he forced himself to write for a portion of each day, hoping to find an idea among the unsatisfactory efforts. One day, lacking any inspiration, he sat staring at a spot on the wall. Because he had no immediate ideas, he began thinking about the wall. The wall made him think of the house, and he let his imagination wander to the time the house was built. He imagined the people who might have been walking by, what they might have been doing, and where they might have been going. The result, in the end, was the novel *Ragtime* (Doctorow, 1975). Students, too, might pick a familiar place or object and imagine connections that might lead to a story idea. Again, the stories may be written, or the ideas may be simply discussed and set aside for another day.

Apol (2002) described an exercise in which secondary students were challenged to write poetry about ordinary things. First, they read poetry that centered on common objects, discussing the way big ideas can be attached to small objects, Next, their instructor presented a table full of familiar objects that could suggest poetry. In this case Apol modeled the way problem finding might have occurred in others before presenting the opportunity for students to have a similar experience. In addition to stories and poems, students should examine authors' purposes in a variety of fiction and nonfiction formats. Think about the diversity of purposes that may be represented in the following forms, each involving writing: poems, novels, short stories, essays, reports, plays, screen plays, documentaries, technical reports, pamphlets, grant applications, research, reports, project proposals, legislative bills, advertising copy, and song lyrics.

Perry (1999) interviewed more than 75 best-selling authors about their experiences and strategies in writing. She was particularly interested in their accounts of writing in the flow state, described in chapter 7. The resulting book, *Writing in Flow*, can be helpful in working with secondary school students who want to experiment with strategies that have been helpful to professional writers. Her five keys to writing in flow offer suggestions very similar to those discussed previously: (a) have a reason to write, (b) think like a writer (deferring judgment, taking risks, and being open to experience), (c) loosen up (play with ideas), (d) focus in, and (e) balance among opposites (work with both thought or craft and inspiration). You also may find her suggestions useful as you experiment with your own writing processes.

As we consider the possibility of creativity as a collaborative process, it is important to envision how we can support that collaboration in our classrooms. An extraordinary example of collaborative creativity was shared with me by Michael Harvey, a Welsh storyteller. Michael (personal communication, 2002) sent me some poetry written by groups of elementary and middle level students based on his telling of Bible stories. I was so touched by the poems I had to learn how they were created. How did primary grade children come up with ideas like "I can feel a winged woman inside me with thunder and lightning in her heart"? Michael generously shared some of his process with me. As you read, think about the aspects of problem finding exemplified in this class.

[After telling the story] What I start on is their experience of listening to and being in the story .... We talk about what it was like for them. I try [to] keep this part of the conversation based in the senses so as to avoid anxiety about how much they remember .... In the early establishing stage I try [to] maintain the group dynamic by avoiding competition between the kids and giving approval to whatever is said .... Before long they're giving me vivid sense impressions of the story. This age range (7–11's) have incredible group consciousness and this gives focus and momentum to this part of the process.

It really does feel like an archaeological dig to me. The thing, whatever it is, is out there and we need to use such skill as we have to find it. Sometimes I talk about metal detectors—when the thing goes "bleep" you know you've found something but you don't know what. It's like that going through a story. When we go through it after the proper telling—they're looking out for an internal imaginative prompting that says "there's something there." They all know what I mean ...

In an older group you would expect a lot of individual responses but with the 7–11's they negotiate a group response. What is great is that they always choose—I never have to prompt them or hurry them along or play referee. [Once] we've decided which bit we're going to look at in more detail, usually I retell this bit of the story to take them back to the images and feelings and then I just ask what they experienced .... If, say, we're inside the Temple where Samuel is asleep and someone says they can see the walls in the lamplight, I'll ask what they're like. "Smooth."

"OK, what kind of smooth?"

"Very smooth."

"Uh, huh, can you think of anything that might be as smooth as the walls?"

They get stuck.

"Is there anything in the temple that smooth—or outside the temple?"

"A sand dune!"

Great! I can see a high level of consensus behavior not to mention smiles of creation and no doubt relief, so I write it down ...

When I run these sessions, although I am in charge and have done it before, I play the game of doing it with them. In that respect I am as delighted as they are when things go well and as frustrated when we get stuck. This means that it is easier to move onto a more demanding and subtle level by asking "Is that right, or nearly right?" If they say "Yep, that's exactly right," then I leave it even if I've got a brilliant idea just bursting to come out. I've seen so many teachers destroy rapport by saying something along the lines of "Don't you think it would be better if ..." You can see the light going out in the kids' eyes when they do that!

Michael went on to describe identifying the form that fits the ideas emerging. Notice the opportunities for exploring the story, identifying something that speaks to the group, and shaping the words to fit their images. Think about the type of classroom atmosphere created in this type of collaborative effort. The poem about Samuel is as follows:

Samuel Asleep in the Temple

The temple walls were as smooth as a sand dune's shadow

The lamp's flame shone like a sword glistening in the sun

On the battered ark's ancient patterns.

They swirled like a sand storm in the desert—as wild as freedom.

God's voice whispered like the wind on the waves

rumbled like the deep Red Sea

murmured like a baby in a cradle

sighed like the Angel of Death ... Samuel!

Bryn Deri CP School, Year 6 (age 10)

Students as Critics. Sloan (1991) suggested that students can learn the strategies and conventions of literature, not just as authors, but as critics. She emphasized the importance of developing a sense of story and the centrality of narrative in students' lives. She quoted Barbara Hardy:

My argument is that narrative, like lyric and dance, is not to be regarded as an aesthetic invention used by artists to control, manipulate, and order experience, but as a primary act of mind transferred to art from life …. For we dream in narrative, remember, anticipate, hope, despair, believe, doubt, plan, revise, criticize, construct, gossip, learn, hate, and love by narrative. In order really to live, we make up stories about ourselves and others, about the personal as well as the social past and future. (Hardy, in Sloan, 1991, pp. 105–106)

A sense of story is one of the key methodologies needed by any writer. Sloan (1991) suggested that students who understand the structure and function of stories may be able to identify and use literary conventions and to identify the stories of value in their own lives. Students develop a sense of story by examining the stories of others, often in guided reading experiences. They may discuss the type of story (What signs and signals indicate whether a story will have a realistic or fantasy setting?), setting and plot (Suppose you thought of a new ending—how would the rest of the story have to be changed to fit the new ending?), characters (Are there any characters that could be eliminated? How would that affect the rest of the story?), point of view, mood, tone, style, theme, or illustrations. Basic story types can be discussed with varying degrees of sophistication. Whereas older students may examine quest patterns in literature, young children can address similar issues by looking at circle stories in which the main character leaves home, has an adventure, and returns home again. Imagery can be introduced to young children by discussing which animals are usually the good and bad characters in stories, whereas older students can think about stories that might be categorized as spring or winter stories, not because of the season in which the story takes place, but because events in the story portray life and rebirth or darkness and death. When students are aware of these conventions, they become part of the methodology of the discipline for the students as their own stories portray crafty foxes (or, defying convention, heroic foxes) or use seasonal imagery to support themes.

Students should also be exposed to the conventions and purposes of culturally specific forms. These could include anything from Irish Fin McCool stories to rap poetry, from Faith Ringgold's story quilts (Ringgold, 1991) to storytelling forms from diverse cultures. If the first part of problem finding is caring, at least some of the literature students read, and the writing or oral expression they create must center on ideas and forms they care about. The communication usually fostered in language arts programs also may be expressed in nonlinguistic forms instead of or in addition to language assignments—as Ringgold's story quilts led to the written telling of her stories. Students can express ideas and values of importance through creating Hmong needlework, designing African kente cloth, planning Chinese scroll paintings, or creating masks or dances from many traditions. These expressions can be explained orally or in writing, providing variety in problem finding and new opportunities for expression.

6.2. Family Treasures: Historical Research and Creative Expression (K–12)

Read *The Lotus Seed* (Garland, 1993), the story of a Vietnamese family's immigration to the United States, and the way a lotus seed became an important symbol of their strength and heritage. Have students talk to family members about important stories from their past. These may form the basis for many types of creative expression: stories or essays, dance or theater, or a variety of visual arts.

Garland, D. (1993). *The lotus seed.* New York: Harcourt Brace Jovanovich.

Language Arts: Creative Strengths.   Many aspects of creativity can be supported in any discipline, but each discipline has aspects of the traditional curriculum that lend themselves particularly well to creativity. In language arts, the most obvious vehicle is creative writing. Imaginative writing activities can provide natural opportunities for the use of creative thinking skills and strategies. Most of the strategies designed specifically to enhance creative thinking (see chap. 5) lend themselves to language arts activities. Students can write stories based on metaphorical thinking, visual imagery, or creative dramatics experiences. They can use metaphors and synectics techniques to enhance descriptions, plan advertisements, or improve poetry. However, it is important for teachers not to lose track of the possibilities for enhancing students' creative thinking through content writing.

Writing in content areas can give students the opportunity to express their questions, concerns, and interests in addition to their understanding of content. Worsley and Mayer (1989) described a variety of writing assignments as part of secondary school science instruction. Suggestions include not just giving the typical lab reports, but also relating histories of specific places (a river bed or a phone booth), describing of sensory experiences, rewriting textbooks, describing inventions of the future, recounting a history of one's personal ideas, and "positing wild theories" (p. 72). One of my favorite examples was a student essay about television written by a high school junior. Almost the entire essay is a series of questions, for example:

What type of people watch exercise programs? Are they uncontrollably fat? Are they exercise fanatics? Do they watch Channel 7 exercise at 5:20 a.m. or Channel 4 where the girls always jump around in those tight-fitted leotards? Maybe it depends on if they are male or female, or maybe it depends on how hard they want to work out .... Why do people become addicted? How do people decide the amount of time they have to watch TV? (Worsley & Mayer, 1989, pp.116–117)

That essay sounds like an exercise in problem finding!

6.3. Flexible Thinking in the Language Arts

Talk about stories in which the size of characters is an important aspect of the story—Jack and the Beanstalk, Tom Thumb, Alice and Wonderland. Discuss what life would be like if you were 1 inch tall. Read *Inch Boy* by Junko Morimoto (1988). Discuss his creative adjustments to his size. Create a morphological synthesis chart of characters and sizes. Use the grid to imagine how stories might have changed if the characters had been different sizes.

Adapted from a lesson by Cindy Pinter.

Finally, language arts activities provide multiple opportunities for modeling creative behaviors. Students can examine the problem solving and flexible thinking of characters from Pippi Longstocking to Harry Potter to Oliver Twist. Selecting literature for young people that models the characteristics we seek is one more way to demonstrate that our classrooms are safe for creative thinking.

Thinking About the Classroom

Plan a class activity in which you discuss writers' purposes and problem finding with students. Send the students out in search of interesting problems to write about and see what happens.

STANDARDS-BASED INSTRUCTION EXAMPLES FROM MI CLiMB

Sometimes teachers can be concerned that effectively teaching to content standards means limiting or eliminating teaching for creativity. In these standards-based examples I share lessons from my home state of Michigan that can meet both sets of goals. You will find similar selections on social studies, science, and mathematics. These materials were developed specifically to address content standards—but since they were also designed to exemplify good teaching, they often enhance creativity as well. Michigan's content standards include content strands, broad standards, and specific benchmarks for elementary, middle level, and high school students. Examples are taken from the Michigan (MI) CLiMB (Clarifying Language in Michigan Benchmarks) project. For each standard and benchmark, explanatory material, instructional examples, and appropriate assessments are provided. I have chosen a few of the many appropriate examples for each subject area as a chance to demonstrate that teaching to high standards does not require limiting creative activities. Additional information can be found at the Michigan Department of Education website www.michigan.gov/mde/ by following the links for instructional materials to MI CLiMB.

Standards Based Examples—Language Arts
Language Arts Example 1
Standard 1
All students will read and comprehend general and technical material.
Elementary Benchmark 3
Employ multiple strategies to construct meaning, including word recognition skills, context clues, retelling, predicting, and generating questions.
Instructional Example
During Guided Reading the teacher uses retelling to model comprehension strategies. The teacher previews the book while students make predictions, then reads the text. S/he models the retelling process in order to facilitate student understanding. In pairs, students retell a portion of the text through illustrations. Then, using this information, students summarize the whole text by writing, illustrating, or conferencing with the teacher.
This lesson has the possibility for flexible thinking as originally presented, since students have the opportunity to present the information in a new way, retelling the story with illustrations. If a teacher wanted even more opportunities for creativity, it could be extended by asking students to retell the story as if some key event had changed.
Language Arts Example 2
Standard 1, Middle School Benchmark 5
Respond to a variety of oral, visual, written, and electronic texts by making connections to their personal lives and the lives of others.
Instructional Example
Using Literature Circles and focusing on specific themes, the teacher aids students in making connections between various multi-media texts and their personal lives.
The teacher models Reader's Response Log by writing a summary and/or a personal reflection. The teacher assigns a study selection for literature circles. Students read, reflect, and write summaries and/or respond to focus questions in reader's logs. . .
The teacher who wishes to enhance creativity during this lesson can easily do so by careful selection of focus questions. At least one question for each

selection can ask students to look from another perspective, use a metaphor, etc. while still making ties to their personal lives.
Language Arts Example 3
Standard 8
All students will explore and use the characteristics of different types of texts, aesthetic elements, and mechanics—including text structure, figurative and descriptive language, spelling, punctuation, and grammar - to construct and convey meaning.
High School Benchmark 2
Describe and use characteristics of various narrative genres and complex elements of narrative technique to convey ideas and perspectives. Examples include use of symbol, motifs, and function of minor characters in epics, satire, and drama.
Instructional Example
The teacher displays five pieces of colored construction paper. Students take five post-it notes to write what each of the colors mean to them and place their interpretation on the corresponding colored sheets. Students divide into five groups. Each group writes a summary of what the color represents and shares with the whole class. Students select a title of a book or poem to read. After reading, students write a reflection on how color is used as a symbol in their selection. Students with the same reading form groups and share the reflections on color as a symbol.
As-is this lesson provides fine opportunities for students to look at colors in multiple ways while also developing the narrative technique of symbolism—a useful skill for their own creative efforts.

Finding and Solving Problems in Social Studies

The National Council for Social Studies has defined Social Studies as follows.

Social studies is the integrated study of the social sciences and humanities to promote civic competence. Within the school program, social studies provides coordinated, systematic study drawing upon such disciplines as anthropology, archaeology, economics, geography, history, law, philosophy, political science, psychology, religion, and sociology, as well as appropriate content from the humanities, mathematics, and natural sciences. The primary purpose of social studies is to help young people develop the ability to make informed and reasoned decisions for the public good as citizens of a culturally diverse, democratic society in an interdependent world. (www.ncss.org)

Although other definitions may differ slightly, most discussions of social studies seem to center on two general types of student goals: to gain important understandings from the social sciences and to prepare to be knowledgeable participants in a democratic society. If students are to find and solve problems in social studies, the problems would logically fall into a similar division. We must consider the types of content and teaching methods that may allow students to find and solve problems in the social science disciplines and to identify and address problems as citizens of a community, state, or nation.

Students as Historical Researchers.   If students are to identify and investigate problems in the social science disciplines, they must have two types of knowledge. First, they must have knowledge of the discipline itself. Historians must know something about history, and geographers must know geography and maps. Second, they must know how the discipline works. Historians must understand the sources of historical information, what kinds of questions it answers, and how to investigate them, and geographers must know what geographers do, what kinds of information they value, and how geographical information is gathered, assessed, and used.

Unlike language arts, in which both the content of literature and the strategies for creating it have traditionally been included in school curricula, many students go through school experiencing social studies only as a body—or perhaps more accurately, a disembodied mass—of content. Some of you probably recall reading social studies texts and answering countless Chapter Checkup questions, many of which entailed copying the appropriate sentence from the text onto your paper. In such cases, social studies facts can be emphasized in ways that limit students' understanding of more important concepts and exclude any consideration of the origin of the facts in question. How do we know what the Pilgrims ate, or wore, or played? How do we know which kings were loved or hated, how medieval communities were organized, or how the public viewed the United States' involvement in World War II, as compared with the Vietnam War? Without a consideration of the methods or the content of the disciplines, students are left with little choice but to believe it is true if it is in print, particularly in a textbook—hardly a healthy assumption for a discipline that purports to prepare students for citizenship!

If students are to be prepared for creative thinking in the social science disciplines, they need to understand not only the facts, but also the broad trends and concepts that organize the disciplines. These include ideas such as interdependence and systems; cause, effect, and change; and conflict, power, rights, and justice. They also will need skills for gathering, organizing, and analyzing information, as well as a knowledge concerning social scientists' habits of mind. For example, Parker (1991) cited examples of "History's Habits of Mind," including "Appreciate the often tentative nature of judgments about the past, and thereby avoid the temptation to seize upon particular 'Lessons' of history as cures for present ills" (p. 74). How could one better learn the values and habits of history than when acting like a historian?

Although students certainly can be taught the methodologies of many social science disciplines, I discuss here only strategies for historical research. Space precludes a full discussion of all areas, and the emphasis on history in social studies curricula makes it a logical place to begin. Involving students in historical research allows them to identify and investigate problems in the same manner as creative historians.

Historical research answers the question, "How did things used to be?" Its purpose is to reconstruct the past as accurately and objectively as possible. A magazine interview with a former politician discussing key events of his or her term, a book on changes in 19th-century fashion, or a newspaper article on the memories of local residents older than 100 years are reporting historical research. Students who interview their parents about the parents' school experiences, investigate the past occupants of stores on Main Street, or learn about the Civil War by examining the lyrics of popular music of the period also are doing historical research.

Much historical research is interesting and appropriate for elementary school students. There is, however, one important caution: the younger the students, the closer to home the research must stay. Young children have a difficult time distinguishing history and fantasy. After all, George Washington and Snow White both lived "long ago and far away." However, even primary school students can investigate information about their immediate family or

---

6.4. Children's Books: Historical Research and Language Arts (7–12)

Children's books from other regions or eras can provide students with the opportunity to view the world through another's perspective and attempt to make hypotheses about another time. Both the stories and the illustrations can provide clues to lifestyle and values. Many times, children's books can be found in local used bookstores or flea markets. One of my favorites is a reproduction of *General Lee and Santa Claus* (Bedwell & Clark, 1997), originally published in 1867. The story of children wondering if Santa still loves little rebel children gives a unique perspective on a child's view of wartime. It could spur students to additional research on children's literature of the period or on children's perspectives of other wars.

6.5. Anonymous Women Creators: Problem Finding and Historical Research (7–12)

Watch the PBS video *Anonymous Was a Woman* (Adata, 1977) or share the book of the same title (Bank, 1995). Discuss the forces that affected the ways women expressed their creativity in the 18th or 19th centuries. This book could inspire a number of historical research projects. Students could investigate attics or local antique shops for further examples of women's creative activities. With permission, these could be photographed for a display. Or students could interview women currently active in creative arts, framing their questions around issues raised by the film or book.

Bank, M. (1995). *Anonymous was a woman.* New York: St. Martin's Griffin.

---

possibly their school. Community history as a concept may seem very abstract, but "How is second grade today different from when our parents were in school?" is a very real question about real people. From the intermediate grades up, of course, students are more likely to be able to deal with issues of local, state, or possibly even world history in a professional manner.

In describing to students the task of a historian, one effective analogy is to compare him or her with a detective. As does a detective, a historian looks for clues about things that have already happened, and, as with a detective, the best source for a historian is an eyewitness. Even young children seem to be familiar enough with TV mysteries that the concept of an eyewitness usually is familiar and useful for explaining to them primary and secondary sources. Primary sources are original documents or artifacts, preferably those in which the author or creator was a direct observer of the recorded event. Secondary sources are those in which the author is reporting and analyzing information from primary documents. He or she may be one time or many times removed from the actual event.

One of the key differences between historical research and typical library research is the reliance of historical research on primary sources. In a typical research report on the response of U.S. citizens to World War II, a student would go to an encyclopedia, reference book, or other secondary source, take notes, and summarize the information. A student doing historical research on the same topic would look for primary sources of information. He or she might look at magazines or newspapers of the period, listen to music of the time, and interview local citizens regarding their experiences. The student would look for similarities and variations, drawing conclusions from the data.

Most historical research is structured with a research question. Without it, research can be an unorganized, often confusing fishing expedition. The more sophisticated the student-researcher, the more fine-tuned the questioning and conclusions. Although many students might be able to draw conclusions about how women's clothing from 1860 to 1865 is different from clothing today, a more able or knowledgeable student might investigate the differences in women's clothing in the Northern and Southern states from 1860 to 1865, or the differences in women's clothing as portrayed in *Harper's Bazaar* and the Montgomery Ward catalogue from 1860 to 1865. Similar investigations using the same tools of historical research could investigate trends in much more current sources, for example, questioning how the advertising or allocation of story space in *Time* magazine has changed in the past 10 years. In either case, the key is in the transformation. Students conducting historical research do not simply summarize information. They make inferences, look for patterns, and draw conclusions from data. As historical researchers, they should become aware of the difference between fact and inference, and the tentative nature of their conclusions. Key to drawing reasonable conclusions in historical research is careful consideration of the motives, limitations, and biases presented in primary sources. Although primary sources are always preferable to secondary sources, it is important for students to be aware that eyewitness accounts are not necessarily accurate, complete, or even truthful. Each historical source presents a particular point of view, shaped through the lives and experiences of particular individuals. Understanding historical sources as reflections of individuals allows students to develop the flexibility in point of view that supports creative thinking. They might consider what could have caused someone to write or act in a particular way and how that perspective might differ in another individual.

6.6. Perspectives on History: Using Historical Research (5–12)

The Perspectives on History series provides short collections of primary sources on a variety of periods and events selected to be accessible to young people. These are particularly valuable when multiple perspectives are available. For example, two books provide sources from the American Civil War: *Echoes of the Civil War: The Blue* (Forman, 1997a) and *Echoes of the Civil War: The Gray* (Forman, 1997b). Comparing the letters and diaries of individuals from both sides of the conflict can allow students insight into multiple points of view, as well as the universal horrors of the war.

Forman, S. M. (Ed.). (1997a). *Echoes of the Civil War: The blue.* Carlisle, MA: Discovery Enterprises.

Forman, S. M. (Ed.). (1997b). *Echoes of the Civil War: The gray.* Carlisle, MA: Discovery Enterprises.

Difficulties with primary sources become clear when students deal with multiple interviews. Personal accounts of the same event often differ widely. Four citizens recounting local events on VE (Victory in Europe) Day are likely to present remarkably different stories. Even student recollections of the recent past are likely to vary and can help students understand the subjectivity and variation inherent in historical sources. Such understanding and resulting habits of mind can lead students to question historical sources and raise questions that a historian would ask. Is the clothing portrayed in magazines the same as that worn by most women? (Does your closet include clothes from *Vogue* or *GQ*?) If clothing in some publications looks different from clothes in the other sources, what might be the explanation? The analysis in historical research is an outstanding opportunity to practice flexible and analytical thinking.

Access to a variety of primary sources is essential for historical research. Some may be available in local libraries or museums, or through interlibrary loan. In many cases, reproductions of paintings, books, magazines, or catalogues are available and more durable than the originals. You may want to consider the following:

1. *Works of art.* Look for reproductions, art books, or secondary sources that may reproduce original artworks as illustrations. Much of what historians have learned about fashion, pets, architecture, household items, and even the lifestyles of particular societies has been learned through art. Consider how much of our knowledge of life in ancient Egypt has come through paintings, or what could be learned by studying portraits from the 18th century.

2. *Magazines.* Many public libraries have periodicals dating to the 19th century, either in a back room or on microfilm. Do not hesitate to ask the library media specialist for assistance. I have particularly enjoyed reading magazines written for teachers around the turn of the 20th century. It is fascinating to see how some concerns are dramatically different and others virtually unchanged.

3. *Newspapers.* Microfilmed newspapers are even more common than other types of periodicals. Do not forget that newspapers can be used in historical research not just research on the headline stories, but also research on advertising, sports, weather, fashion, editorial cartoons, or even the history of journalism.

4. *Books and magazines.* Again, do not hesitate to ask your library media specialist for assistance in locating originals or repro-

ductions of books from the period to be studied. For a student reading about education in the 19th century, reading about the changes in textbooks or school procedures is just not the same as reading the textbooks themselves. Museum stores, library sales, and used book stores can also serve as sources, frequently at minimal expense. Books for teachers such as *Teaching With Documents* (National Archives and Records Administration, 1989) sometimes contain reproduced historical documents. *Teaching With Documents* includes material from the National Archives ranging from the Navigation Act Broadside of 1785 to Nixon's letter of resignation. The process of working with these reproductions is virtually identical to the experience of using the actual materials—without the expense of a trip to Washington, DC. One of my favorite sources for teaching American History to elementary and middle level students is *Cobblestone* magazine (www.cobblestonepub.com). It includes a combination of secondary sources and primary sources selected to be accessible to young people. The same company publishes a similar publication on African American history called *Footsteps*.

5. *Music.* Song lyrics from a particular period of history can provide valuable insights into the attitudes, activities, and concerns of the time. Music stores often carry recordings of music from a particular period. I gained new insights into the attitudes and values of the 1940s by listening to an album of contemporary songs about the war—very different from the songs about war I recalled from the 1960s and 1970s! Music stores also can be sources for recordings of speeches and broadcasts of important moments in modern history.

6. *Interviews and surveys.* Few things students do in school can have as much long-lasting value as preserving the written and oral history of their community. Older community members can provide information and insights unavailable through any other means. Other citizens can recount their experiences relating to local, community, or world issues. Imagine the importance of a class project interviewing service personnel returning from Iraq or Somalia, factory workers affected by a local plant closing, or even a city mayor leaving office.

7. *Diaries and journals.* Either family journals or reproductions of journals available in many libraries provide information on everyday life seldom found in history texts. It is helpful to share your quest for primary sources with your school library media specialist.

If the library media specialist knows the types of resources you are seeking for your class, he or she may be more likely to spend limited library funds on this type of reference material.

8. *Household items and other artifacts.* Family collections, grandparents' attics, and local museums can provide artifacts from which young historians can draw conclusions. In one area in which I taught, a local intermediate school district circulated collections of artifacts that could be examined and handled by students.

9. *Computer databases and other technology.* Increasingly, students can have access to historical material through technology. This material can include statistical databases and a variety of documents available in electronic formats (Murphy-Judy & Conruejols, 1993) or from distant sources through the Internet. Many of the items listed here can be found on the World Wide Web more easily than in traditional forms. Many government and museum sites contain links to primary sources that can form the basis of original research for students as well as adults. For example, the National Museum of American History site includes You Be the Historian activities and a variety of virtual exhibits. A large number of links to historical and other sources can be found at the Federal Resources for Educational Excellence (FREE) site linked to the U.S. Department of Education (at this writing, www.ed.gov/FREE). As new technology becomes available, it will be increasingly important to stay up to date on the capabilities of your school and community libraries. Again, be sure the library media specialist is aware of your interests so that you are notified as relevant new technology is acquired.

Thinking About the Classroom

Visit used book stores, antique stores, or flea markets in your area. See what you can find to enhance one of your teaching units. Next, go to www.ed.gov/FREE (or the current site of FREE) and see what else you can find to add to your collection.

Locating primary source materials, either for an individual or a class project, may seem daunting—especially with the encyclopedia so readily available—but historical research provides benefits to students that are unavailable by any other means. Aside from the obvious development of research and thinking skills it fosters, this type of investigation makes history come alive. Students who have been touched by the words and sounds and

---

6.7. Scout Museum Shops: Sources for Historical Research (7–12)

One of my favorite sources for reproductions of historical artifacts is museum shops. A visit to the National Historic Site at Seneca Falls, New York led me to copies of the *Report of the Woman's Rights Convention*, *The Lily* (August 1852), a newspaper published by Amelia Bloomer, and *The Revolution* (January 1868), a paper published by Susan B. Anthony and edited by Elizabeth Cady Stanton and Parker Pillsbury. The issue of *The Revolution* I purchased contained quotations from other newspapers' responses to the creation of the new paper. These artifacts could easily provide the beginnings of historical research examining questions such as these: How did the statements in *The Lily* differ from those in *The Revolution*? Did they reflect changes in the women's movement or differences in editors? How did other papers vary in their responses to *The Revolution*? Were these responses typical of other publicity of the time? It also might be interesting to compare these papers with current publications of the National Organization for Women or other groups lobbying for change. In what ways are their styles, strategies, and the like similar or different? Your trips to other historic sites may lead to equally valuable finds!

---

images of real people from long ago, who have considered these peoples' lives and points of view and have drawn conclusions from those lives form links with the story of history that are not forged in other ways. This power to touch the reality of history makes historical research a vital tool to consider, both to expand students' understanding of historical information and to help them ask the kinds of questions historians might ask.

Although you may find many local resources electronically, I have also found it worthwhile to haunt flea markets and used book stores looking for items that tie to major units in the curriculum. Often for minimal expense it is possible to locate items that can benefit students for many years. For example, a fourth-grade teacher who commonly teaches the history of the community may scout library sales or flea markets for reproductions of early maps, old postcards depicting the community, or histories of local families. Such materials could allow students to investigate questions as diverse as "How have the boundaries of our town changed since 1800?" and "What were the most common architectural styles in our community in 1920? How closely does the current restoration resemble the original buildings?" A teacher who deals with American history may want to consider old magazines, sheet music, advertising brochures, or reproductions of catalogues or news photos. Such additions might result in a class investigation into point of view in news coverage of a particular period or an individual study comparing 19th-century yellow journalism with modern tabloids. Even a second-grade teacher whose class studies Our School may want to search the district archives for old photos, records, or yearbooks that might be duplicated for class use in examining changes in school dress, studies, or personnel. In each case, students are able to experience the thrill of touching the world of the past and working as bona fide historians. They also experience history, not as something one learns, but as something one questions, wonders about, and investigates—certainly key activities for those who are to be creative in that field.

Jorgensen (1993) described an approach to teaching history the she called "history workshop," which parallels approaches used in writing workshops and process writing. She used the reading and writing of historical fiction and the examination of artifacts to help elementary school students build historical understanding. Unlike more directive experiences in historical research, the history workshop places students' questions, ideas, and investigations at the center of the curriculum.

> Learning history is an ongoing process in which children construct historical meaning as they talk, read, write, draw, and reflect. Through language they propose and test historical ideas by predicting, confirming, and negotiating with others. They weigh new ideas against what they already know about the world, their own purposes, their understanding of relevant historical source materials, and the responses of fellow learners. The historical meaning they create—theories about how long ago events occurred, how events are sequenced in time, how events influence each other, and what makes an event historically significant—helps them to define their personal identity and construct social meaning in everyday life. (Jorgensen, 1993, pp. 1–2)

A history workshop centers around prediction and confirmation, organized through the use of primary sources, stories, drawings, and interactions with others. Students have the opportunity to explore primary sources and listen to historical stories. They use this raw material to make hypotheses about history, expressed through their own historical stories, drawings, and conversations with the teacher and fellow students. This approach to history provides multiple opportunities for identifying and investigating questions and problems of interest. One third-grade class had the opportunity to explore a number of centers containing artifacts relating to the Ohlones, a Native American tribe. After spending time exploring and role-playing with animal skins, one girl wrote:

I had on a fox fur. I pretended that I was a fierce fox. I practically scared everyone. I noticed some interesting fur. Some of it was soft and some of it was rough. Did they cut off the head? I hope so. I think if I cut the head it would be pretty disgusting. What did they use the fur for? Clothing? I don't know. I hope to find out the answer. (Jorgensen, 1993, p. 82)

This student has identified a problem of interest for investigation.

Students as Participants in Democracy.   In addition to helping students gain important understanding from the social sciences, social studies also has the challenge of preparing students to be active participants in our democratic society. Helping students become involved citizens entails not just assisting them in understanding the branches of government, but also giving them the vision of empowered individuals affecting the community around them and the tools to achieve empowerment. Among the best ways to achieve this is to allow students to become involved in problem solving in their communities. Needless to say, this type of activity reinforces not just social studies content, but also problem solving and creative thinking. The Creative Problem Solving (CPS) process (see chap. 5) can be a particularly valuable tool in facilitating this type of activity.

One sixth-grade class created a group called the Amesville Thinkers that set out to identify and address a community problem (Elasky, 1989). They conducted interviews with local community members in an effort to identify major problems. Whereas the most commonly cited problem, unem-

---

6.8. Looking at Cookbooks: Another Source for Historical Research (5–12)

Cookbooks can provide interesting sources for historical research into the lives of ordinary families. Many used bookstores contain cookbooks and various guides to homemaking from the 19th century. Other books can be found in reproduction, often in museum shops. Dover Publications, a source for many interesting reproductions, publishes *The First American Cookbook, a Facsimile of "American Cookery," 1796* (Simmons, 1984). This book, which includes many types of advice "for the improvement of the rising generation of Females in America" (p. 3), can allow students to draw conclusions about lifestyle and values as well as nutrition. Another of my favorites, purchased at a museum store, is a reproduction of *Directions for Cooking by Troops in Camp and Hospital* prepared for the Army of Virginia. It includes essays by Florence Nightingale on the types of food most suitable for sick or injured soldiers. Recipes like "Fresh Beef Soup for 100 Men" give a new perspective on camp life.

ployment, seemed too daunting to be tackled by a group of elementary school students, the second most commonly mentioned, uncertainty about the responsibilities of elected officials, seemed more manageable. The students wrote and produced a series of public service announcements designed to educate the community on the functions of local government. The following year, the same sixth-grade teacher worked with students who chose to analyze contamination in local waterways. This group called themselves the Amesville Sixth-Grade Water Chemists.

Involving students in such projects—whether they are first-grader students planting seeds to lure butterflies to a local park or high school students making a proposal for bicycle paths to the town council—helps the young people develop both the skills and attitudes necessary for creative involvement with content. Students have the opportunity to care about the content, take risks, try strategies, make mistakes, and try again until they reach some kind of conclusion. This attitude was described by the Amesville teacher in his response to a student who said testing water made him feel "like a real scientist."

> I told him he was, because he was doing what real scientists do. The real world of scientists, writers, and teachers had invaded our room and given students reasons to begin changing the theory of content importance into the practice of meaningful content use. This didn't happen because the Amesville Sixth-Grade Water Chemists or the Amesville Thinkers were uniquely talented or gifted, or because their teacher is extraordinary, or because we handled what we did in a superior way—or even exploited it to its fullest. None of these things are true. It is because we used a process that works. One that creates intellectually challenged, enthused people who are in control of more of what they are doing. (Elasky, 1989, p. 13)

This example shows that community problem solving can and should involve multiple disciplines. Although community problem solving is included in this section because of the importance of involved citizenship in social studies, it is virtually impossible to address any meaningful community problem without involving language arts, math, and science. The complexity of the problems and the skills needed to address them is one more support for the complex, multidimensional thinking associated with creativity. If you are interested in assisting your students in community action, an outstanding resource is *The Kid's Guide to Social Action* (Lewis, 1991). In it, Lewis describes students' involvement in attacking problems from toxic waste to endangered species and provides information on numerous skills essential for social action, such as preparing a press release, taking a survey, or writing a letter to the editor. Although the examples generally involve elementary school students, the skills are appropriate for any grade level or for an adult activist!

Social Studies: Creative Strengths. As a content area, social studies has numerous aspects that support especially strong ties to creativity. It provides outstanding opportunities for problem solving and data gathering, particularly in the local community. Studies of history and diverse cultures are natural vehicles for exploring multiple points of view, attempting to view events and ideas from more than one perspective. Diverse points of view may be identified in the persons or cultures studied or in the materials themselves. The Michigan Educational Extension Service (1992) described the efforts of two teachers who wanted students to question the point of view from which their social studies text was written. After months of teaching students about the need for multiple perspectives, they found students asking questions such as "How come whenever they mention a woman it is on a gray page? And it's only a little" (p. 7) or "Why are there two pages in the book on the Boston Tea Party ... when there's only a paragraph on the Trail of Tears? Four thousand people died on the Trail of Tears and no one died in the Boston Tea Party?" (p. 4). Some of the teaching strategies that are particularly effective in helping students take on new viewpoints and explore the world from another's perspective are particularly well suited to social studies. These include simulation and role-play activities discussed later in the chapter.

Social studies is also concerned with values. Although the idea of promoting values in school is fraught with controversy, social studies has traditionally included an emphasis on democratic and social values. The kinds of discussions that allow students to develop and focus ideas and values also are important in helping them develop an appreciation for multiple viewpoints and flexibility in thinking.

Finally, social studies that focuses on key concepts can provide opportunities for interdisciplinary transfer that can be both flexible and original. Concepts of interdependence, power, change, or revolution can be explored, not just in history but in science, literature, or art. Helping students examine how a literary work may be powerful, how cause and effect operate in music or science, or how a painting may express the idea of revolution provides fuel for new perspectives and flexible thinking.

Standards Based Examples—Social Studies
Social Studies Example 1
Strand I Historical Perspective
Content Standard 3 Analyzing and Interpreting the Past
All students will reconstruct the past by comparing interpretations written by others from a variety of perspectives and creating narratives from evidence.
Early Elementary Benchmark 1
Use primary sources to reconstruct past events in their local area.
Define primary sources for students (e.g. the actual records that have survived form the past) and list examples such as diaries, letters and photographs. Ask students to brainstorm a list of objects that could be useful as primary sources in the future to help people reconstruct the history of your school. (E.g. newsletters, a school year book, photographs, a lunch ticket). Expand students' thinking by exploring primary sources relating to the history of their local community obtained from local historical societies, museums, etc. Useful resources include copies of photos, diaries, business records, etc.
This is an excellent opportunity for students to become historical researchers even in the primary grades. Students could not only identify primary sources but begin to discuss what might be learned from available sources. One of my most enjoyable expeditions into historical research was with a group of second graders investigating how second grade was different than it was when their parents were second graders. We used photographs, report cards (generously offered by parents) and interviews with eye-witnesses to draw our conclusions.
Social Studies Example 2
Content Standard 3 Analyzing and Interpreting the Past
All students will reconstruct the past by comparing interpretations written by others from a variety of perspectives and creating narratives from evidence.
Middle School Benchmark 2
Analyze interpretations of major events selected from African, Asian, Canadian, European and Latin American history to reveal the perspectives of the authors.
Instructional Example
Using primary documents, have the students read at least three articles or documents about the conquest of the Aztecs in Mexico. These documents can be found in a packet available from Jackdaws 2000 or from a variety of books. . . .Once the students have read and discussed the documents, have them write a paragraph for each. They should write about the feelings of the person who authored the document. Encourage the students to use statements from their readings to back up their information. They need to tell why each person felt as they did and how this influenced their actions. Have

the students form small groups to discuss their writing, adding to their paragraphs as they share their writing and ideas.

This lesson combines two strategies supportive of creative thinking, using primary sources to draw conclusions and examining events from multiple perspectives.

Social Studies Example 3

Strand III Civic Perspective

Content Standard 1 Purposes of Government

All students will identify the purposes of national, state, and local governments in the United States, describe how citizens organize government to accomplish their purposes, and assess their effectiveness.

High School Benchmark 1

Explain the advantages and disadvantages of a federal system of government.

Instructional Example

Have students read the following opinion on federalism for emerging democracies. Use students' answers to the questions to understand of the advantages and disadvantages of federalism.

> **Federalism for All**
>
> If the Peoples' Republic of China and North Korea are to become fully democratic, they should adopt the type of federalism used in the United States. It is the only way to govern populous nations and to maintain an ever-lasting democracy. What has worked for the United States is certainly good enough for other nations, no matter how far away or how different.

Why might both China and North Korea both want/not want federalism?

As a citizen of China would you be likely to support federalism? Explain.

As a citizen of North Korea would you be inclined to support federalism? Explain.

This lesson also provides the opportunity to view the world from another's perspective. An additional opportunity for flexible thinking could be to ask that if they (from the perspective of a particular nation) would not support federalism, what alternate form of government that would be more acceptable. Sample lessons from MI CLIMB. Additional examples can be found at www.michigan.gov/mde/ by following links for MI CLIMB.

Finding and Solving Problems in Science

Of all the curriculum areas, perhaps science is the one in which the importance of finding and solving problems is most obvious. Science, and particularly the scientific method, is about posing hypotheses and solving problems. In the introduction to her book, *Science is Golden*, Finkelstein (2002) said, "I was struck by how much children are like scientists. They seem to have an insatiable curiosity, they love to investigate unfamiliar concepts and object, and they analyze what they observe" (p. xiii).

Physicist David Bohm (1998) described the motivation in science as enmeshed in creativity.

> Scientists are seeking something that is much more significant to them than pleasure. One aspect of what this something might be can be indicated by noting that the search is ultimately aimed at the discovery of something *new* that had previously been *unknown*. But, of course, it is not merely the novel experience of working on something different and out of the ordinary that the scientist wants—this would indeed be little more than another kind of "kick." Rather, what he is really seeking is to learn something new that has a certain fundamental kind of significance ... a kind of harmony that is felt to be beautiful. In this respect, the scientist is perhaps not basically different from the artist, the architect, the musical composer, etc. who all want to *create* this sort of thing in their work (p. 2, italics original).

Unfortunately, the processes and understandings that are integral parts of real-world science have not always been translated into science teaching. Some approaches have treated the sciences as a collection of facts, rules, and definitions to be memorized. Others have emphasized process skills or hands-on instruction, which generated more involvement, but did not guarantee meaningful understanding of content. The National Science Education Standards state:

> Learning science is something students do, not something that is done to them. In learning science, students describe objects and events, ask questions, acquire knowledge, construct explanations of natural phenomena, test those explanations in many different ways, and communicate their ideas to others.

> In the *National Science Education Standards*, the term "active process" implies physical and mental activity. Hands-on activities are not enough—students also must have "minds-on" experiences. (Center for Science, Mathematics, and Engineering, 1995, p. 20).

Teaching for conceptual change implies that students come to class with prior notions of scientific phenomena. If those notions are inaccurate, it is necessary for students to have experiences that allow them to address their prior knowledge, question its validity, and build new concepts. Merely telling students what is true or what is our best understanding of truth at this time does not suffice. In building concepts, students should be involved in the processes of science: observing, making hypotheses, manipulating variables, and so on. Both of these recommendations emphasize the sciences as explanatory in nature. "Science is our best attempt to explain how and why events happen as they do in the natural world. How does light help us to see, for example? How do we see colors? Why do plants need light to grow? Why is the sky blue?" (Anderson, 1987, p. 77).

These emphases in science teaching also are supportive of the attitudes and processes of creativity. They center around student experiences and student questions, predictions, and experiences. Assisting students in building a small number of key concepts through experience instead of exposing them to myriad ideas also allows students to live the persistence, confusion, and muddiness that are essential elements of creativity in science.

Watson and Konicek (1990) set forth three key elements in assisting students with conceptual change. First, the teacher must connect new concepts to the students' everyday lives. Unless students see connections between the things they do in science class and their assumptions about the way the world operates, it is easy for them to dismiss science activities as a series of strange things that happen only in class. Second, students should be asked to make predictions. Hypothesis making creates essential ties between prior knowledge and new experiences and also practices a critical element of any scientific investigation. Third, the teacher should stress consistency. Students should be helped to see contradictions or inconsistencies in their thinking and be encouraged to address them. Science is about making sense of the world. Students should be encouraged to seek understanding that makes logical sense, not to memorize rote information. With these emphases, teachers can structure lessons so students observe phenomena that challenge their current ideas and then provide appropriate, testable alternatives.

Watson and Konicek (1990) described several days of experiments in which fourth-grade students tested their belief that sweaters generate heat. Years of experience dressing for winter weather had taught the students that heat comes from fire, from the sun—and from sweaters, hats, and coats. When the initial experiment (placing thermometers inside sweaters and hats for 15 minutes) did not provide evidence of heat production, the students designed new efforts using longer times and sealing the sweaters in enclosed spaces. Still, no heat was produced. The students were confused and probably frustrated because their predictions were not supported. Only then, when the students seemed at an impasse, did the teacher offer an alternative hypothesis that might be tested. The article ends with the students heading to recess, thermometers under their hats! Their experience brings to mind the words of a Nobel prize winner, quoted by Brandwein (1986):

> Method, in Greek, means essentially "after a way." But the scientific method is not a straight way, but a jungle, a bog, a melee, and with the help of all you've read, called literature, of those who came before you and with the help of the friendly colleagues you have, and with luck you will wade through the gauntlet of opposites, of contradictions—of wrong and right leads, and come out with something you're willing to talk about. It may even turn out to be a fleck of truth. And remember we call all this "scientific inquiry." (p. 241)

With equal candor Brandwein (1962) wrote, "The way of the scientist … is not to be interpreted as a calisthenics of discovery but as an art of investigation. In the long run the scientist knows a kind of success, but daily it comes from intelligent failure" (p. 8).

Thinking About the Classroom

Interview a student about what he or she has learned in science recently. Probe to see whether the student can apply the information to a new situation. Do you see evidence of conceptual change or misconceptions?

Involving students in the successes and failures of science begins with questions. Because most class time in science classes is likely to be framed around content determined by the teacher, district, or state, one of the teacher's key responsibilities is to provide experiences that will spur students to ask questions about the content. Sometimes questions can be triggered by familiar tried-and-true demonstrations such as air pressure crushing the gas can. However, instead of explaining the phenomenon and expecting the demonstration to prove it, the teacher can use the activity in a different way. After the students watch the can deflate, the teacher might ask questions such as "What happened?" "What questions does it raise in your mind?" "Have you seen anything like this before?" "What other experiences have you had with things collapsing like this?" "Why did it happen?" "Why do you think this happened?" and "What could we do to test your ideas?"

One second-grade teacher described her first attempt at adapting a standard science lesson for student investigation. The prepared lesson called for the teacher to blow soap bubbles, ask the students to observe and respond to questions, and present the necessary content. Instead, the teacher gave the bubble liquid and straws to the children. Afterward she reflected:

> In no time at all everyone was blowing bubbles, big ones, little ones, stacks of bubbles and huge bubbles. Students were talking about what they did, what they saw, comparing, and analyzing. After 15–20 minutes we put the cups down and started to list questions .... Students listed about 40 questions. Some were very simple. "How are bubbles made?" "Why are they so messy?" Some were quite astounding. "Why do they spin? Why do they have colors? Why does your finger pop it but the straw doesn't?" ... I was truly amazed when my students were able to answer all of the questions except one .... I was so excited that I shared my experience with the other second-grade teachers and was met with skepticism. I guess one has to try it to believe it! (Bingham, 1991, p. 6)

Similarly, traditional lab activities often can be revised to allow for student questioning. Many prepared labs look a great deal like recipes. Students are given a list of ingredients and materials and step-by-step directions for the procedure. In such situations, students do not participate in the questioning or design phases of the activity. They can easily fail to grasp the purpose of such labs and their relation to the scientific process. Certainly, few scientists begin their days or their research with a set of illustrated directions! Consider whether some of your traditional science labs might be adapted to allow students to participate in the design process. The Center for Gifted Education Staff (1996) described a process of adapting labs, Uncanning the Experiment, that is appropriate for students of many ability levels. Instead of handing students the prepared lab worksheet, the authors suggested that students be engaged in a prelab class session in which they develop or are given the key question and figure out how to investigate it. The procedures are likely to be very similar to those in the prepared directions, but in this case they are the students' own, prepared purposefully.

The Center for Gifted Education Staff (1996) gave the example of a lab in which students are to grow seeds in pots covered with varied colors of cellophane. Uncanning this experiment requires starting with an introduction of the topic. This could include a discussion of what students know about light

Even young children can carry out experiments.

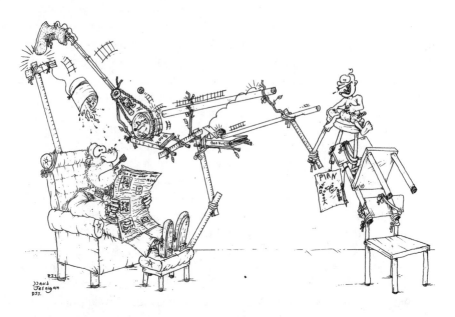

and plants. Although raising the research question directly would be possible, approaching it indirectly is preferable so students have the opportunity to figure it out on their own. Students might be given prisms and asked what they can learn about the nature of sunlight from the rainbow created by the prism and what implications this knowledge suggests for growing plants. The research question could be developed by students or posed directly by the teacher: "Do you think plants need all the colors of light or only some of them?" Once the basic question has been established, lab groups can be challenged to develop a protocol for investigation. All lab groups need not follow identical protocols as long as their plans are reasonable and address the question. After experimentation and data collection, students can discuss information gained, questions remaining, and additional experimentation that might address remaining questions. Although not all labs can be opened to student design (particularly in chemistry when safety considerations may limit flexibility), many can be adapted to allow students more participation in authentic scientific processes, granting them the freedom to act more like scientists than preparers of boxed macaroni and cheese. Finkelstein (2002) also provided guidance in helping students develop and answer their own questions. Additional information on students and research can be found in Cothron, Giese, and Rezba (1989), Moorman (2002), Starko and Schack (1992), and Schack and Starko (1998).

This process of raising questions and testing hypotheses in an effort to understand observations brings students in touch with both the techniques and the habits of mind of scientists. Neither textbooks nor hands-on experiences are sufficient for either student learning or creativity. Students also must be involved in discussing, hypothesizing, defending ideas, questioning, and testing, both verbally and in writing. The Michigan Educational Extension Service (1991) quoted Roth on her experiences working with fifth-grade students:

6.9. Uncanning Study of the Heart

A study of the heart provides several opportunities to adapt "canned" activities to support creative thinking.

1. Once students have learned to take their pulse, they can be encouraged to imagine the types of activities that could make their pulse faster or slower, then test their hypotheses.

2. When discussing circulation, students can devise a model for testing how blood flows through clear and impeded arteries. They might test the speed at which liquid can flow or how hard the heart has to work.

Adapted from a lesson by Jill M. Finney.

Involving students as scientists has enabled them to develop richer understandings of both the concepts we explored and of the nature of scientific inquiry. I'm pleased with the meshing of scientific learning with active reflection on the ways in which our understandings and explanations are developed through experimentation, discussion and questioning. *Doing science is not enough. Reflecting on the doing of science has added an important dimension to my students' understanding of science.* (p. 5, italics added)

Providing students with experiences and allowing them to ask questions, test hypotheses, and reflect on results is time-consuming. However, regardless whether our goal is to understand science concepts or to develop creativity in science, such time is essential. It is simply necessary to trade coverage for understanding.

Thinking About the Classroom

Take a science lesson you typically plan as a demonstration or recipe lab and uncan it so that students derive the questions and plan the investigations. Note any differences you see in student involvement and understanding.

Building Blocks of Science Curriculum.   If it is necessary to spend more time on less content, it becomes increasingly important to consider the kinds of content and outcomes that should be emphasized in planning and implementing science curricula. As in other disciplines, it is necessary to identify fundamental concepts and generalizations that tie together important ideas and allow those ideas to shape the curriculum, instead of accumulating unstructured, disconnected facts. We also must consider the processes and attitudes of science we want to share with students.

Sher, VanTassel-Baska, Gallagher, and Bailey (1993) described an outline of the scientific process and parallel science outcomes that may be suitable for many situations. They described the fundamental steps of the scientific process as follows (Sher et al., 1993, p. 8):

1. Learn a great deal about your field.
2. Think of a good (interesting, important, and tractable) problem.
3. Decide which experiments, observations, and calculations would contribute to a solution of the problem.
4. Perform the experiments, observations, and calculations.
5. Decide whether the results really do contribute to a better understanding of the problem.
6. Communicate your results to as many people as possible. (p. 8)

6.10. Uncanning Biology in High School: Testing Food Samples

Present students with a variety of food samples, Benedict's solution, iodine, oil, Fehling's a and b, a heat source, and test tubes. Tell the students that they are to determine what chemicals are used to test for starch, sugar, fats, and proteins. Suggest that they choose foods that they are certain have one of the four elements and test. Before students heat any chemicals, their plan must be approved by the teacher. Once students have identified testing procedures, they are to test unknown substances.

Adapted from a lesson by Dana Nichols.

From this given set of steps, general student outcomes were generated. These described behaviors to be developed in all students, with obvious differences in sophistication according to age and grade level, are as follows: explore a new scientific area, **identify** meaningful questions within that scientific area, and address scientific questions in the subject area directly in one of several ways—demonstrate good data-handling skills, analyze any experimental data as appropriate, evaluate their results in the light of the original problem, use their enhanced understanding of the area under study to make predictions about similar problems whose answers are not yet known to the student, and communicate their enhanced understanding of the scientific area to others (Sher et al., 1993, p. 8). Many states have similar required science process outcomes.

6.11. Uncanning Biology in Kindergarten: What Gets Moldy?

Have students observe two pieces of bread, one moldy and one not. Discuss the ways scientists ask questions about things they see. Have students generate ideas about things they think might make bread get moldy faster and ways to test their hypotheses. Carry out the investigations.

Adapted from a lesson by Melinda Spicer.

First-grade students evaluating the growth of plants in sun, shade, and darkness, sixth-grade students measuring pollution in local streams, and high school students analyzing the location of cases of an unknown disease all are asking and attempting to answer meaningful scientific questions at appropriate levels. Planning for such questioning, by both groups and individuals, is an essential part of planning science curricula. Although it is important to help students address questions within required content outcomes, there also is a place for student-generated questions. Anderson and Lee (1997) demonstrated that unless students found enough connections between science instruction and their personal agendas, even the best-planned science instruction failed. Good science requires significant student focus and effort, which are ultimately controlled only by the students. It may be that time invested in allowing students to investigate questions they care about is essential to effective science teaching as well as creativity.

It is also essential that students be supported in developing habits of mind similar to those necessary for scientists. These might include attributes such as curiosity, seeking logic and consistency, looking at a problem from multiple perspectives, and persistence in the face of confusion. We need to consider the affective components of both the content and methods of our teaching. If we want to support curiosity, we must not only respond to evidence of curiosity positively, even when it is not part of our lesson plan, but also structure activities designed to pique curiosity and model curiosity ourselves. If we want to model curiosity, persistence, and seeking, we cannot present ourselves as, nor can we be, the ones with all the answers. At least part of the time, we need to address, and encourage students to address, questions that truly puzzle us as well.

Problem-Based Learning. One strategy for organizing science content that supports both creativity and science processes is problem-based learning (Center for Gifted Education Staff, 1996; Coleman & Gallagher, 1997; Finkelstein, 2002; Lambros, 2002; Ngeow & Kong, 2001; Stepien & Gallagher, 1993) This strategy is, of course, appropriate in other disciplines as well.

In problem-based learning, students begin with an ill-structured problem. Typically, an ill-structured problem describes a real-world event for which students must formulate a solution, reaction, or explanation. As in most real problems, students often do not have most of the information needed to solve the problem at the onset, nor do they know the processes or actions necessary for solutions. They are forced to observe, seek connections, gain additional information, learn techniques, and use knowledge in particular situations. Often the nature of the perceived problem may change during the course of the task. What seemed at first to be the important issues may become secondary as new information is gained. The teacher's role is to act as a model of problem solving, help students become aware of their own thinking, and allow them to take control of the problem-solving process. This role can be facilitated through the use of questions such as "What do we know?" "Do we have enough information?" "Is the information reliable?" or "What's the problem as we see it now?"

One problem-based unit developed for high-ability students in grades 4 to 6 was based on the problem of an overturned truck spilling an unknown chemical into a local creek (Center for Gifted Education Staff, 1996). Initially, students are asked to take on the role of supervisor of the State Highway Patrol. They must decide what they know about the situation, what they need to know, and how to find out. Content emphases for the unit include the concept of systems (ecosystems and transportation systems), acid–base chemistry, and scientific processes. However, during the course of the investigation, students will, of necessity, gain and consider information on weather patterns, laboratory techniques, government responsibilities, and other content. Although this particular unit is planned for use by high-ability students over an extended time, the processes of problem-based curricula can be used at a variety of ability levels and in differing time schedules.

Stepien and Gallagher (1993) described the use of short "posthole" problems (inquiries that delve deeply into a relatively narrow problem) when teachers want to introduce problem-based learning, but do not wish to use it to structure an entire unit or course. In one example, a third-year German class arrived in class one day to find a letter in German from the Nazi Ministry of Propaganda. The letter, dated 1938, addressed the students as Gallery Directors and informed them that they must review their collection and discard any work that was degenerate, because degenerate art would no longer be tolerated in Germany. Failure to comply would result in severe penalties. Similar to the students facing the truck-spilled chemical, these students started with, "What do we know?" and "What do we need to know?"—except that they did so in German. Younger students might be faced with posthole problems such as a dying patch in the teacher's vegetable garden, a kite that will not fly, or an unusual number of dead woodchucks by the side of the road. I have found the following guidelines helpful for teachers who are beginning to write posthole problems.

6.12. Uncanning the Great Gum Dilemma

Provide students with the following scenario: Your group has just been hired as gum experts for Acme Food Company because they want to produce a new chewing gum. Because the company has identified sixth graders as the target group, you must decide which type of gum to produce. Acme already makes the gum base. You are to provide information on the flavor, type of sweetener, and ratio of flavor/sweetener to base you recommend, as well as data to support your recommendations. The company is most interested in determining how its new product will compare with current products on the market.

It may be necessary to provide students with cues and/or modeling for them to understand that information regarding the relative amounts of sweetener and flavoring in gum can be found by weighing gum before and after chewing. This will allow them to provide data, other than survey data, to back up their recommendations.

Adapted from a lesson by Deborah Melde.

- Is the problem realistic, clearly tied to the real world? Problems based on demonstrations or events not naturally occurring in the world are less desirable. Students should be able to see clear connections between their efforts and real-life phenomena. If you want to focus on a problem using a prepared demonstration or activity, think about circumstances that might realistically (or close to realistically) cause the phenomenon or situation to occur.
- Is the problem situation intriguing for students of this age?
- Are both the solution and the method for the solution unknown? An ill-structured problem should not have an immediately evident solution or method of solution. Multiple methods (and usually multiple solutions) should be possible.
- Is the students' role as stakeholder intrinsic to the problem? Does it provide a logical and useful focus? Giving students a role they

perceive as powerful usually is more motivating than any role asking them to be students. The role selected should logically direct students to the content on which you want to focus.

- Does the problem situation elicit the need for substantive content? Do the materials and information provided focus the students in the desired direction? In a well-structured ill-structured problem, the situation itself points students in the direction of key content.

Even with shorter post-hole problems, it is important to provide scaffolding for the types of thinking required in this type of learning. It is not as simple as posing a question and then waiting for students to figure it out. Learning through problems is complex. It requires careful modeling, dividing of the task into manageable portions, and assistance in focusing on key elements of the task. Of course, problem-based learning need not be based on teacher-structured problems. Although planned problems can ensure a more structured consideration of major curriculum concepts, important learning can take place in the investigation of authentic real-world problems. The Amesville Sixth-Grade Water Chemists, described earlier, addressed this type of problem.

Sometimes technology can provide astonishing opportunities for real-world learning. Bollman, Rodgers, and Mauller (2001) described the Goldstone Apple Valley Radio Telescope (GAVRT) project, in which middle and high school students have the opportunity to collect and process telescope data as part of a larger scientific community. In Serbia, the Petnica Science Center for high school students was originally funded partially by businesses who paid the school to have students address and solve their real-world problems. In the same center, students were challenged to analyze outdated, ideology-ridden textbooks and write new ones—certainly, an ill- structured, real-world problem. For some time I was concerned that the center succumbed to the political turmoil around it. Happily, it continues to operate in Serbia, providing real-world opportunities for science students and teachers (Petnica Science Center, 1992, 2003).

Thinking About the Classroom

Plan a posthole experience that introduces students to problem-based learning through a short-term, ill-structured problem. Keep a journal of your experiences.

Science: Creative Strengths.   Certainly, the sciences provide clear and important avenues for students to develop and pursue questions. Inquiry teaching, described later in the chapter, should be a mainstay of science instruction. Beyond the obvious ties to problem finding and problem solving, science activities can be particularly valuable in developing attitudes and values that underlie creativity. Good science demands persistence, patience, and commitment to task. It requires flexible thinking and the examination of new avenues when old ones prove fruitless. Studies of scientific discoveries can help students see the value of analogies, reframed questions, and risk taking. Experiences with puzzling situations can help develop curiosity. Perhaps most important, good science teaching shows clearly that scientific knowledge is tentative, often temporary. Science helps us understand the world and also should help us question it. Students who understand that the answers are not all in the books, that the questions change from day to day, and that the road to understanding is muddy but exciting may see the beginning of scientific creativity.

6.13. Posthole Problems for Elementary and Secondary Students

You own a large eagle statue that sits in front of your house. It is 10 feet tall with a wingspan of 10 feet. It weighs 1,000 pounds. One day Mr. Big arrives at your house and loves your statue. If you can deliver it to his house unbroken, he will pay you 1 million dollars. How will you do it?—Kevin Learned

I just bought a farm although I do not know very much about farming. My farm has 600 acres. Some is in a valley, some on a hill, and some right next to my house. I would like to grow my crops without pesticides. I have come to you, experts in my county extension agency, for assistance. Can you help me figure out what crops would be best?—Pat Furnner

A recent newspaper article states that an iceberg the size of Rhode Island has sheared off the edge of Antarctica and could drift for 10 years before it melts. It rises 100 to 600 feet above the water and reaches about 1,000 feet below. It is important to predict the path of the iceberg to avoid difficulties. The National Oceanic and Atmospheric Administration has asked for your assistance in this matter. You will be hired as temporary consultants until the iceberg's path for the next 2 years has been determined.—John Watson

Standards Based Examples—Science
Science Example 1
Content Standard 1
All students will ask questions that help them learn about the world; design and conduct investigations using appropriate methodology and technology; learn from books and other sources of information; communicate findings of investigations using appropriate technology.

Elementary Benchmark 1:
Generate reasonable questions about the world based on observation.

Instructional Example
Using pictures of scientists and the *book Oobleck: What Do Scientists Do?* (Sneider, 1999), discuss and list scientists' activities. Explain that children do many of the things scientists do. Discuss the importance of sharing discoveries with others and have students make science logbooks. The first assignment is to draw a picture of themselves doing something a scientist might do and complete the sentence, "I am a scientist when. . ."

This is the only instructional example not taken from the MI CliMB project. It is a summary of a lesson from the SCoPE project, a curriculum project also sponsored by the Michigan Department of Education. It is an excellent opportunity for students to begin thinking of themselves as scientists who ask questions worthy of recording. It would be important to make the sure the notebooks were used to record genuine student questions and observations and not simply teacher dictation.

Science Example 2
Strand 3 Using Scientific Knowledge from the Life Sciences in Real-World Contexts
Standard 2
All students will use classification systems to describe groups of living things; compare and contrast differences in the life cycles of living things; investigate and explain how living things obtain and use energy; and analyze how parts of living things are adapted to carry out specific functions.

Elementary Benchmark 2
Compare and contrast (K-2) or classify (3-5) familiar organisms on the basis of observable physical characteristics.

Instructional Example
[After reading and discussing a biography of Gregor Mendel] Divide students into groups of four. Provide each group with a container filled with approximately twenty different items. Ask each group to find a small, inconspicuous item in the container. Appoint one student in each group to be the "timer" and record how long it takes the group to find the item. Challenge each group to divide the items in their container into three groups or categories. Groups then will explain the criteria they used to group the items.

The lesson continues until the groups have created five subdivisions and they investigate how long it takes to find the item once the items are categorized. An assessment example associated with the same benchmark asks students to create their own classification system for a group of animals. Both activities allow students to examine many attributes of the items and view them in multiple ways. There should be many types of classification that emerge from the lesson. A logical extension might use attribute listing or morphological synthesis to create a new animal to fit a particular category.

Science Example 3

Strand 3 Using Scientific Knowledge from the Life Sciences in Real-World Contexts

Content Standard 5

All student will explain how parts of an ecosystem are related and how they interact; explain how energy is distributed to living things in an ecosystem; investigate and explain how communities of living things change over a period of time, describe how materials cycle through an ecosystem and get reused in the environment, and analyze how humans and the environment interact.

High School Benchmark 5

Describe how carbon and soil nutrients cycle through selected ecosystems.

Instructional Example

Students will work in small groups and write a story explaining how the carbon in carbon dioxide passes from plants to animals from animals to decomposes, and from decomposers back to plants. Students will include explanations of photosynthesis and cellular respiration n their stories. The teacher will tell them their target audience is a class of upper elementary students. Diagrams or visual aids may be added.

This lesson is an excellent opportunity for taking on a new point of view, explaining the carbon cycle from the perspective of a carbon atom. It would be particularly effective with students who were experienced in using personal analogies through Synectics. Sample lessons from MI CLIMB. Additional examples can be found at www.michigan.gov/mde/ by following links for MI CLIMB.

Finding and Solving Problems in Mathematics

If you were to ask a group of people what subject they thought of first when you said the word "problems," chances are good the answer would be math. Yet if you asked the same people for the subject first associated with the word "creativity," I suspect the responses would be different. When we envision math problems, we can easily picture rows of multiplication tables and stories about Johnny giving six apples to Suzy or two trains leaving from point A and point B. Such problems, presented by the teacher, solved by a method prescribed by the teacher, and evaluated by the teacher from a prepared answer key, have little to do with creativity. They present a mathematics with very neat edges; every important question is in the book, and every question has one correct answer. This type of instruction eliminates important aspects of mathematics. As in science, true math is muddy. Halmos (1968) stated:

> Mathematics ... is never deductive in its creation. The mathematician at work makes vague guesses, visualizes broad generalizations, and jumps to unwarranted conclusions. He arranges and rearranges his ideas, and he becomes convinced of their truth long before he can write down a logical proof. (pp. 380–381)

Math is about raising questions as well as answering them, finding new relationships and generalizing old ones. In fact, the ability to shape and solve mathematical problems in ways that allow students to construct mathematical meaning is at the core of modern research on mathematical thinking (Battista, 1999). This type of thinking about mathematics instruction is at the heart of the National Council of Teachers of Mathematics (2000) "vision" of instruction.

> Imagine a classroom, a school, or a school district where all students have access to high-quality, engaging mathematics instruction .... The curriculum is mathematically rich, offering students opportunities to learn important mathematical concepts and procedures with understanding. Technology is an essential component of the environment. Students confidently engage in complex mathematical tasks chosen carefully by teachers. They draw on knowledge from a wide variety of mathematical topics, sometimes approaching the same problem from different mathematical perspectives or representing the mathematics in different ways until they find methods that enable them to make progress. Teachers help students make, refine, and explore conjectures on the basis of evidence and use a variety of reasoning and proof techniques to confirm or disprove those conjectures. Students are flexible and resourceful problem solvers. (p. 2)

Notice the emphases on activities we associate with creativity: looking at problems in more than one way, asking questions, making hypotheses, and thinking flexibly.

In considering the types of thinking that may allow students to use creative thinking in the area of mathematics, we should distinguish two types of questions. First, we may help students explore questions in which math is used to do creative things. Students may consider how to plan a class budget, design an aluminum foil boat with maximum cargo area, build a catapult to launch a ping-pong ball, or calculate the total volume of air in the school. In some ways we may consider these engineering questions because, as do engineers, students use mathematics to solve relatively practical problems. This type of math parallels the real-world problem-solving and problem-based instruction discussed in the preceding two sections. Students learn mathematics because they need it to accomplish a task. They may learn percentages to calculate acidity, volume to build boats, or geometric constructions to create a work of art. In addition to demonstrating the utility of mathematical principles, this type of problem allows for the flexibility of multiple approaches and varied solutions. It also helps students to make the problems their own, finding their own angles and following their own instincts.

Thinking as a Mathematician. The second type of question we may want to help students formulate (find) is mathematical questions. Unlike engineering questions, which are raised to accomplish a task, mathematical questions are raised to gain understanding. Here students ask the kinds of questions mathematicians ask and think the way mathematicians think. Mathematical questions are not a matter of calculation; certainly, mathematicians do not routinely contemplate the sum of 2 + 2, or even 2,837,495 + 483,882. Mathematicians—as do scientists and artists—look for patterns and try to understand them. They look at the current understanding of numerical relationships and wonder, "What logically might follow next?" "Could this be true in all cases?" and "What would happen if I changed one aspect of the problem?" A mathematician friend described the process as trying to forge new paths into the body of mathematical knowledge.

6.14. Flexible Thinking in Math: Circumference and Diameter

About a week before the lesson, have students begin bringing in spherical objects of various sizes (e.g., marbles, beachballs, oranges). Without cutting the objects, students are to use tape measures and rulers to compare the diameters and the circumferences of a variety of spheres. Teams of students work together to determine how to measure these dimensions. When it is determined that the ratio is a little more than 3 to 1, the concept of pi can be introduced.

Adapted from a lesson by Kandi Baran.

For many of us, thinking like a mathematician presents a new challenge, particularly if we are accustomed to equating mathematics with computation. Schoenfeld (1992) described a spectrum of understanding regarding mathematics. At one end, math is seen as a body of facts, procedures, and formulas. If one has learned the procedures, one knows math. At the other end, math is seen as the science of patterns, closely akin to the sciences. Schoenfeld believed "a curriculum based on mastering a corpus of mathematical facts and procedures is severely impoverished—in much the same way that an English curriculum would be considered impoverished if it focused largely, if not exclusively, on issues of grammar" (p. 335). This perspective was echoed by the National Research Council (Kilpatrick, Swafford, & Findell, 2001):

> Mathematical proficiency ... has five strands:
>
> 1. *Conceptual understanding*: comprehension of mathematical concepts, operations, and relation
> 2. *Procedural fluency*: skill in carrying out procedures flexibly, accurately, efficiently, and appropriately
> 3. *Strategic competence*: ability to formulate, represent, and solve mathematical problems,
> 4. *Adaptive reasoning*: capacity for logical thought, reflection, explanation, and justification
> 5. *Productive disposition*: habitual inclination to see mathematics as sensible, useful, and worthwhile, coupled with a belief in diligence and one's own efficacy. (p.5, italics original)

Finding ways to help students ask and answer mathematical questions can be the basis of sound mathematical and creative thinking and an in-depth understanding of mathematics. One of the long-standing dilemmas of teachers of mathematics is that students do not always "get it." One of the key principles emerging from multiple sources is that mathematics must be taught for understanding. The National Council of Teacher of Mathematics (NCTM) (2000) states:

> Being proficient in a complex domain such as mathematics entails the ability to use knowledge flexibly, applying what is learned in one setting appropriately in another. One of the most robust findings of research is that conceptual understanding is an important component of proficiency, along with factual knowledge and procedural facility .... Students who memorize facts or procedures without understanding often are not sure when or how to use what they know, and such learning is often quite fragile. (Bransford, Brown, & Cocking, 1999, p. 19)

The importance of teaching mathematics for understanding is echoed in neuropsychologist Brian Butterworth's (D'Arcangelo, 2001) writing on brain research regarding mathematical reasoning. He suggests that strategies for enhancing understanding include solving problems in more than one way, using a wide range of examples, and actively engaging students with numbers in different ways. Each of these suggestions entails both fluent and flexible thinking around mathematical questions.

There are at least three ways in which new mathematical questions can be generated, each beginning with something known. First, a question may ask if a specific known case might generalize to other cases. Imagine, for example, the long-ago mathematician who first recognized that the area of a particular triangle could be calculated by multiplying the length of its base by its height and dividing by two. He or she might have wondered, "Could I do this with all triangles? Does it matter if the triangle is acute or obtuse? Can I prove that this will always work?" Second, some mathematical questions attempt to tie one body of knowledge or area of mathematics to another. A mathematician might examine an interesting algebraic relationship and wonder, "What geometric shape might this describe?" Third, some mathematical questions ask the question, "What if?" They begin with a theorem or relationship known to be true and explore what would happen if one of the assumptions were changed. For example, if the area of a triangle on a flat surface is $\frac{1}{2}(b \times h)$, what would happen if the triangle were drawn on the surface of a sphere? Would the same equation still work?

Finally, sometimes mathematicians look at a problem that has already been solved and try to solve it in a new way. In this type of problem, the aesthetics of math becomes most obvious. Mathematicians not only try to solve problems, but also try to solve them beautifully. To a nonmathematician, the idea of a beautiful solution may seem curious: Either a solution works or it does not. However, some solutions may contain loose ends, unnecessary pieces, or awkward constructions, such as fixing the drooping muffler on your car using half a belt, two scraps of tin foil, several pieces of chewing gum, and three banana peels. The muffler may not drag on the ground, but it will not be beautiful, either. An expert who can weld the pieces together so that the joints barely show has also solved the problem, but has done so elegantly. Soderborg (1985) argued:

> Let me explain why I feel math can be beautiful. First, mathematical statements can contain significant meaning succinctly and elegantly expressed. They can simultaneously compress the expression and generalize the meaning of significant ideas, much like well-written poems. Second, mathematical statements can produce aesthetic pleasure in the person who studies them. A well-constructed solu-

tion or proof can evoke wonder from a student aware of its fluid logic and broad implications .... Studying beautiful mathematics can be like listening to a symphony or studying an inspiring painting. One feels intrigue and admiration for something so well put together that produces such marvelous results. (p. 10)

To help students find and solve problems like mathematicians, we must help them see both the effectiveness and the elegance of their efforts.

When mathematicians address problems, they do not use neat, prescribed algorithms. They must have a battery of problem-solving strategies and select the methods that produce the most effective, most aesthetic solution. Deciding which strategies to use is an enormously important task and one that is eliminated in assignments in which every problem on a page demands the same kind of manipulations.

Although students in grades K–12 are not likely to generate new mathematical knowledge, they can address problems that demand mathematical thought and personal creativity. Tasks that allow students to experience the ambiguities of math may not be real-world problems, but they can be attacked in multiple ways to help students discover the relationships that constitute the field of mathematics. Mathematical tasks may help students discover patterns, series, or relationships. The teacher might demonstrate that a paper folded in half once forms two sections. Students might be challenged to figure out how many sections would be formed if the paper could be folded eight times. Some students might try folding a paper eight times; others might make a chart and see a pattern. Students who are familiar with exponents may have other insights.

6.15. Flexible Thinking in Math: The Playscape Problem

Using the playscape as an example, develop a problem that uses one of the listed formulas, an explanation as to how to solve the problem, and a reason why someone might need the information. For example, if a student fell off the playscape bridge, the Health Department might require warning tape along the edges of the bridge. How many rolls of tape would you need to buy? Possible formulas include area of a rectangle, perimeter of a rectangle, circumference of a circle, and so forth.

Adapted from a lesson by Tamara Dodge.

Sometimes problems may help students see new systems or change previous assumptions. Our number system is based on units of 10. If that assumption is changed, many new systems can be created: base 5, base 2, and so on. Problems and activities that challenge students to think about numbers in new ways foster mathematical problem finding and problem solving. (Think about what the pattern of sections created by various folds of paper would look like in base 2 and base 8.)

Problems that allow students to discover a new idea or find a new, possibly more elegant method of solution also foster mathematical thinking. The aforementioned paper-folding example fits this category. So do number bracelets (Burns, 1992). These are created by choosing two numbers from 0 to 9 and following this rule: Add the two numbers and record next the digit that appears in the ones place in the sum. For example, if I started with 5 and 4, I would record the number 9. Next, I would add 9 and 4 and record 3, because that was the digit in the ones place. I would continue until I got back to 5—5 4 9 3 2 5. Students are challenged to find the longest and shortest possible bracelets and to look for odd and even patterns in the bracelets. Students who look carefully for patterns may be able to find elegant solutions without recording every possible combination. Identifying and using such patterns is an "Aha!" of mathematical creativity.

Planning Math Activities. A number of specific recommendations for teaching strategies are appropriate for both the NCTM goals for understanding and the creativity goals set forth in this book. Three of the strategies are discussed briefly here: students inventing arithmetic, focus on elementary problem solving, and problem posing with secondary school students.

Kamii (1985, 1989) questioned the assumption that carefully structured instruction beginning with concrete examples and moving toward abstract levels necessarily leads to mathematical understanding in young children. Instead, she based her recommendations on a constructivist approach rooted in the work of Piaget. Constructivism says that children acquire mathematical and other concepts "by construction from the inside and not by internalization from the environment" (Kamii, 1989, p. 3). In this view, mathematical ideas are created by each child internally based on two basic types of relationships: order and hierarchical inclusion. For example, "three" and "more" and "longer" are abstract ideas constructed by children as they interact with the world around them. Teaching students the labels before they have internalized the abstractions will not lead to understanding. On the other hand, children who have constructed the abstraction "three" are able to create their own symbols to represent it. According to this view, students will develop abstract generalizations such as time and volume only when they are developmentally ready to understand them, not when the ideas are presented in the curriculum (Long & Kamii, 2001; Reece & Kamii, 2001).

Kamii's approach to beginning math instruction centers on providing situations in which students can discover mathematical relationships and invent ways to use and represent them rather than on teaching students the standard techniques for computing correct answers. Her basic principles of teaching include the following (Kamii, 1989):

1. Encourage children to invent their own procedures rather than showing them how to solve problems.
2. Encourage children to invent many different ways of solving the same problem.
3. Refrain from reinforcing correct answers and correcting wrong ones, and instead encourage the exchange of points of view among children.
4. Encourage children to think rather than to write, and write on the chalkboard for them to facilitate the exchange of viewpoints. (p. 77)

This approach uses three basic types of activities: situations in daily living, games, and discussions of problems. Situations in daily living might include voting for various class activities, counting soup labels, or deciding how many pizzas are necessary for a class party. However, instead of using daily situations as an opportunity to teach standard algorithms (i.e., now that we need to order pizza I can teach them to divide), teachers encourage students to invent ways to solve the problems. They can calculate pizza orders by drawing, using paper pizzas, or working mental arithmetic.

Games include both unique games and those that are adaptations of traditional pastimes. These might include the game of concentration played so that each pair must add up to 10, or dominos adapted so that connections adding up to an even number win points. Later (second grade), students are introduced to discussions of computational and story problems. For example, students who have not been taught regrouping might be asked to solve the problem 27 + 16. The class might discuss the many ways the problem was solved and resolve any differences as to the sum. This type of activity over an extended period can allow students to use mathematical relationships in a variety of ways, experiment with flexible approaches to problem solving, and develop the concept of regrouping, not as a teacher-imposed strategy, but as a logical result of their own efforts. According to Kamii's research, students taught in this way are more likely to be able to explain and use mathematical ideas when presented with nonroutine problems than students who receive more traditional math instruction. Certainly, the processes of inventing strategies, trying multiple paths, and discovering relationships are supportive of creative thinking in mathematics.

Like many ideas, the idea of student constructions of mathematical ideas has been questioned and sometimes misused. Pinker (1997), working from the perspective of evolutionary psychology, pointed out that children are likely to spontaneously create intuitive notions of small numbers and simple arithmetic that are based in their experiences. They are not likely to generate more complex mathematical principles without considerable guidance. Helping students construct mathematics should not entail "giv[ing] them a bunch of blocks and tell[ing] them to do something" (Pinker, 1997, p. 342), but should involve presenting carefully structured lessons focused on mathematical ideas.

Burns (1992) echoed many of the recommendations in Kamii's work for teaching basic arithmetic. In addition, she presented examples of problem-based mathematics instruction in six strands: measurement, probability and statistics, geometry, logic, patterns and functions, and number. She puts forth four criteria for a mathematical problem (Burns, 1992):

1. There is a perplexing situation that the student understands.
2. The student is interested in finding a solution.
3. The student is unable to proceed directly toward a solution.
4. The solution requires use of mathematical ideas. (p. 17)

Students are taught to address problems using a variety of problem-solving strategies such as looking for a pattern, constructing a table, working backward, or solving a simpler or similar problem. Burns presented strategies for using both cooperative and individual problem-solving experiences.

In cooperative experiences, the lesson starts with an introduction that includes any necessary presentation of concepts and introduction of the problem to be solved. Next, students work in cooperative groups toward solving the problem. Finally, groups share their strategies and results. Discussion questions might include "How did you organize the work in your group?" "What strategies did your group use?" "Did any group use a different strategy?" "Are there patterns or relationships you can see from your solution?" and "Does this remind you of any other problems you have solved?" Problem-solving lessons may be completed in one class period or extended over several days.

6.16. Graphing and Flexible Thinking

Make a model of a bungee jumper using rubber bands and fishing weights. Collect data using at least seven different weights and graph your data. Write a short summary explaining any correlations you find between the jumpers' weight and the amount of stretch in the rubber bands.

Adapted from a lesson by Tamara Dodge.

One sample activity is designed to introduce pentominoes. First, the teacher demonstrates the rule for making pentominoes and shows how to determine, by flipping or rotating, whether two pentominoes are congruent. Next, the class is presented with a problem similar to that planned for the cooperative groups: "Imagine you were trying to find all the possible arrangements of three squares. How many would there be?" The students could then try the same for four squares. Next, cooperative groups investigate possible ways to arrange five squares. They cut them out of graph paper and test for congruence. Finally, the groups come back together to compare strategies and results. Individual problem-solving opportunities are organized using a menu or collection of problem-solving tasks. Similar to the group problem-solving experiences, menu tasks are designed to have multiple solutions and to provide students with the opportunity to develop mathematical reasoning. They also build independent thinking and working skills that are important in creative activities (see chap. 7).

Some teachers post directions for menu tasks on a bulletin board. Others make copies that students can take to their desks when needed. Systems for recording the tasks that have been completed also may vary. A menu can be prepared for several days or longer. Menu problems are generally not hierarchical, but pose problems, set up situations, and ask questions that may be addressed in any order by an individual or small group. Menus can be used from primary grades up to high school. Very young children may do menu tasks at centers, often without written directions. High school students can carry menu tasks over from one day to the next, allowing productive time to begin when the bell rings. In most classes, instructional time is likely to be divided among group problem solving, class discussions, direct instruction, and menu time.

Some mathematical problems can foster flexible thinking by requiring students to look at situations from multiple points of view. Sobel and Maletsky (1999) cite a problem in which a customer buys a pair of slippers for $5, paying with a $20 bill. Unable to make change, the merchant asks the grocer next door to change the bill and sells the customer the slippers giving $15 change. Later, the grocer discovers the $20 bill is counterfeit and demands that the merchant make good for it. The merchant does so, then must turn the counterfeit bill in to the FBI. The problem asks how much the merchant lost. It can be more easily solved by viewing the situation from a different point of view—that of the customer-counterfeiter.

Problems can be especially appealing when they spring from the environment in which students live. In materials developed for the Detroit Historical Museum, Caniglia (2003) presented a series of questions and problems to be investigated during a cemetery visit. Students use pictographs to depict the birth months of the deceased, bar graphs to compare the number of deaths by decade, box and whisker plots to analyze data regarding gender, age at death, and so forth. They use plotting to create maps to the five most interesting headstones. Such activities are challenging in their own right, but also provide opportunities for students to generate and investigate their own additional questions.

Thinking About the Classroom

Create a menu of math problem-solving activities that is appropriate for your students. Incorporate menu activities in your class for at least 2 weeks. Observe students' responses.

Brown and Walter (1990) described activities for secondary school students that focus specifically on finding or posing mathematical problems. They suggested that, like mathematicians, students should be encouraged to ask questions about mathematical propositions. For example, they described activities derived from the equation

$$x^2 + y^2 = z^2$$

When faced with this equation, most of us (if our memories of high school math are clear enough) are likely to assume that our task is to come up with values of x, y, and z that make the equation true—for example, 3, 4, and 5. However, the equation did not actually ask us to do that. The equation did not ask anything at all; it is a statement. In fact, "What are some values for which $x^2 + y^2 = z^2$ is true?" is only one of the many possible questions one could ask about the equation. Other questions could include "Are the solutions always integers?" "What is the geometric significance of this?" "How could you find solutions without trying out every possible number?" Each of these is an example of what Brown and Walter called the first phase of problem posing. They accept the given statement as true. Problem posing can be initiated by stimuli other than mathematical statements: definitions, theorems, questions, or objects. In the first phase of problem posing, students might ask questions about a right triangle ("Why is it called right?"), about the definition of a line, or about a geoboard. In each case, the questions relate to the stimulus as it is presented.

Brown and Walter (1990) coined the phrase What-if-Not for the second phase of problem posing. In that case, some aspect or assumption of the stimulus is changed to create a question or problem. Remember that this is one of the key strategies used by mathematicians in developing new ideas. For example, changing assumptions for the equation $x^2 + y^2 = z^2$ might lead us to wonder, "For what values is it true that $x^2 + y^2 > z^2$?" or "What happens to the values for a triangle that is not a right triangle?" Using the What-if-Not strategy begins with listing the attributes of the stimulus to be investigated. For example, a right triangle has three sides and three angles, one of which is a right angle. It is helpful to break up the attributes so that each is listed separately and can be considered individually.

1. It has three sides.
2. It has three angles.
3. One angle is a right angle.
4. The longest side is opposite the right angle.
5. $x^2 + y^2 = z^2$.   (And so on.)

Next comes What-if-Not. Students select some attribute to change. Suppose the shape had more than three sides. The next stage is to raise questions based on the new assumption. If the shape had more than three sides, we could ask, "Is it possible to draw such a shape so that the rest of the statements are still true?" "What would be the area of a shape like that in the figure on the board?" "Would $x^2 + y^2 = z^2 + a^2 + b^2$?" or "Would another equation better describe the relationship?" Finally, one or more of these questions could be chosen for analysis. This example illustrates the four levels of the What-if-Not strategy:

Level 1   Attribute Listing

Level 2   What-if-Not (change some attribute)

Level 3   Question Asking

Level 4   Analyzing a Problem

Another interesting strategy described by Brown and Walter (1990) is the writing of mathematical journals with students serving as authors and members of the editorial boards. Papers may include problem solutions or nonsolutions, discussions of attempted strategies, insights, and misconceptions. The journals also include abstracts of each article, letters of acceptance sent to the author—including the reflections of the editorial board on the piece, lists of interesting problem ideas, and suggested readings. The journals provide a fine outlet for the results of creative mathematical thinking. Equally important, they publish unsuccessful attempts with as much validation of the insights provided as that accorded to successful solutions. This balanced attention encourages risk taking and persistence in the face of difficulty. Students are much more likely to attempt challenging tasks when they understand that their success depends more on their thinking and learning than on their finding the correct answer to the problem.

Mathematics: Creative Strengths

Mathematics has natural ties to creativity: seeking patterns and beauty, looking in many directions, solving problems, and seeking new ideas. Unfortunately, some math instruction—always focusing on one correct way to find one correct answer—can rob from math much of its beauty and make it difficult for students to see links between creativity and mathematics. Perhaps the greatest service we could give to the development of creative thinking in math is to help students understand that math does not equal computation, and that the math problems are not all in the book. Helping students to raise math questions, discover mathematical relationships, and challenge math assumptions can bring them closer to the creative thinking that brings joy to the lives of creative engineers and mathematicians.

Thinking About the Classroom

Plan a math activity that is designed to help students discover a mathematical idea or principle independently. Try to include a problem that can be solved in more than one way and see what happens.

Standards Based Examples—Math
Math Example 1
Content Standard 1:_ (Patterns) Students recognize similarities and generalize patterns, use patterns to create models and make predictions, describe the nature of patterns and relationships, and construct representations of mathematical relationships.
Elementary Benchmark 2:_ Represent and record patterns and relationships in a variety of ways including tables, charts and pictures.
Instructional Example
Students should engage in activities such as these.
Use sounds, motions, shapes, objects, pictures, and symbols as different ways to represent patterns, repetitions of events, and designs._
Explore and compare multiple ways of representing patterns and relationships such as using tables versus graphs. . . .
Exploring patterns in multiple ways is a good opportunity to foster flexible thinking. For example, the same pattern might be expressed as sound, motion, shapes, etc. Students who use multiple ways to express information (for example, original shapes for graphing) also have the opportunity to develop habits-of-mind that are supportive of creativity. It is essential that when teachers ask for additional ways of expressing information that they be open to all relevant options and not silently seeking a hidden answer (i.e, "Yes, we could use a bar graph!")
Math Example 2
High School Benchmark 5: Use patterns and reasoning to solve problems and explore new content.
Instructional Example
Students should engage in activities such as these.
Expand existing mathematical patterns that lead to new mathematical insights. . .
Solve problems stressing the use of patterns. . .
Collect 5 years of data on the best times for various running events for the school track team and analyze them to determine possible patterns.
In particular, the data analysis activity has multiple opportunities for creative thinking. First, there are multiple ways to address the problem and multiple conclusions that could be drawn depending on the aspects of data students choose to examine. It is a real world problem that will be relevant to many students. Best of all, it gives students skills so that a logical follow-up activity might be, "Now you think about another aspect of our school that might entail data—a different type of sports data, the number of snow days per year, the gender of student council officers, the number of tickets sold for various types of theatrical events, etc. In teams, select a question that interests you, identify a data source, and draw conclusions based on the identification of patterns.

Math Example 3
Strand 2 Geometry and Measurement
Content Standard 1
Students develop spatial sense, use shape as an analytic and descriptive tool, identify characteristics and define shapes, identify properties and describe relationships among shapes. **Middle School Benchmark 2** Generalize the characteristics of shapes and apply their generalizations to classes of shapes.
Instructional Example
Students should engage in activities such as these.
Identify from a group of real-world pictures the one that does not belong to the set. . . .
Use paper folding, geoboards, and other models to discover shape characteristics
Draw or construct and name shapes that satisfy given criteria such as "a 4-sided figure with 1 pair of parallel sides.
These activities provide several opportunities to support creative thinking. In the first example, there could be multiple answers to a "which does not belong" question depending on the characteristics chosen for analysis. Demonstrating more than one way to solve the problem is a good exercise in flexible thinking. Open-ended problems such as the next two suggestions provide for multiple processes and multiple solutions. Additional examples can be found at www.michigan.gov/mde/ by following links for MI CLIMB.

Thinking About the Content Areas

Pondering the kinds of teaching that support creativity in the content areas, I thought of several themes. I have said that such teaching requires us to help students learn both the key concepts and the methods of the disciplines. If students are to develop new ideas, they must know the ideas of others and how ideas are developed. In many disciplines, problem-based instruction can provide an avenue for both strong content teaching and creative thinking. At times, real-world problems are most appropriate; at other times teacher-structured problems are more manageable. I would hope that there also is a place for student-generated problems, questions, and ideas as the basis for instruction. I have thought recently that if I had a classroom of my own—my current teaching is done in many rooms—I would hang a giant sign that says, "Ask a good question." Perhaps under that I would list the questions that keep appearing whatever the discipline:

What is?

What was?

How do you know?

Why?

Why not?

What if?

What if not?

ADDITIONAL STRATEGIES FOR CONTENT TEACHING

This section examines lesson designs and teaching strategies that support creative thinking while presenting or using content information. Instead of addressing what should be taught, most of these strategies concern the how of teaching. The strategies discussed are by no means a comprehensive list, nor is the section meant to suggest that all teaching should be done in the ways described. It does provide alternatives to more direct presentation and practice strategies that may be used to increase variety, interest, and flexibility in teaching. The strategies are divided into three sections: inductive strategies, simulation and role play, and questioning and discussion techniques.

Inductive Approaches

When an argument or process of logic is said to be inductive, it proceeds from the specific to the general. That is, individuals draw general conclusions based on particular examples. If I notice that the four small dogs in my neighborhood all bark more than the larger dogs and draw the conclusion that small dogs bark more than large dogs, that is inductive reasoning. If I read the biographies of five famous scientists and conclude that they have characteristics in common, that is also inductive. Detectives, particularly the television variety, use inductive reasoning when they draw conclusions about what happened at the crime scene from isolated bits of evidence. Although in direct lessons a teacher is likely to present an idea or skill and then cite specific examples of how it may be applied, in inductive lessons the students are given the examples and challenged to figure out the concept or generalization that ties the examples together. It is only an inductive lesson if the students engage in inductive thinking. Inductive lessons provide opportunities for thinking independently, taking risks, and generating original ideas. Although some inductive lessons lend themselves to a relatively limited number of conclusions, others provide for multiple conclusions, strategies, or points of view.

Taba (1967, also described in Joyce, Weil & Calhoun, 2000) identified three basic inductive thinking tasks: concept formation, interpretation of data, and application of principles. Concept formation involves identifying and enumerating data, grouping items into categories, and then developing labels. For example, students might list all the things they would buy if they were in charge of the family's budget for a month and group the items by common attributes. Through this process, they may eventually, with some teacher guidance, develop the concepts of wants and needs.

Interpretation of data, Taba's (1967) second inductive task, entails examining data, making hypotheses about relationships, inferring causes, and building generalizations. For example, one group of students had examined magazine advertisements and developed a number of categories to describe the sales techniques the ads used. The teacher then asked them to examine the ads and look for relationships between the types of products being advertised and the technique used. Students noticed that certain techniques, such as snob appeal, were more commonly used for nonessential products than for basic needs. They hypothesized that advertising techniques varied depending on whether the product was a want or a need. Drawing this conclusion required them to interpret data. (It is interesting to note that in this particular lesson, the conclusion reached by the students went beyond the teacher's expectations. She was anticipating that students would notice that some strategies were used more often with particular products—for example, sports figures selling athletic shoes—but she had not previously recognized a pattern around wants and needs. The teacher and students together became investigators testing this hypothesis.)

Application of principles may logically follow the interpretation of data. In this task, individuals try to predict new situations or consequences based on identified patterns. Students might predict the type of advertising most likely to be used for promoting a particular product or hypothesize as to whether their observations of print advertisements would likely hold true for television ads. The three tasks of concept formation, interpretation of data, and application of principles may be used separately or in combination in inductive lessons.

In the next sections I discuss two basic types of inductive experiences: experiences designed to build concepts and inquiry experiences requiring the interpretation and application of data. Many of the research and problem-solving activities previously discussed also incorporate inductive thinking. Any time students draw conclusions from data, they are thinking inductively.

Experiences Designed to Build Concepts. Taba's (1967) concept formation lessons have three basic components. First, students are asked to list or enumerate data regarding a particular question or problem. In the previous example, students were asked to list all the items they would buy if they were in charge of the family budget. Next, students are asked to group items with similar characteristics. For example, they may be asked to divide into groups the items that are alike in some way. This process may be assisted by such questions as "You said that the new TV and the new bikes go together because they both help you have fun. Would any other items on your list do that?" or "Try to divide the items into the smallest number of groups that still make sense together." The final step of a concept formation lesson is labeling the concepts. In this lesson, the teacher hopes to develop the concepts of wants and needs.

In planning a concept-formation lesson, there are two major considerations. First, it is important to plan a question or problem that allows students to generate a list of data rich enough to include the concept you wish to develop. If I had started the lesson on wants and needs with the statement "Imagine that you had $500. Let's list all the things you might buy," it is possible that all the items listed might be wants. In that case, it would be impossible to develop the desired concepts without asking additional questions. By having students imagine they are in charge of all family purchases for an extended time, it is more likely that some students will mention food, electricity, rent, and other essentials.

The second key to a successful concept development lesson is recognizing when students need additional direction to assist them in generating items or focusing the categories. It is always wise to try predicting in advance what types of categories may be formed initially and to think how students can be guided to the desired concepts. Sometimes very general questions or directions may be helpful. Suggesting that students generate the smallest possible number of categories is an example of a general guide. Other times you may need to be more specific: "Let's remember that you are in charge of everything your family will buy for the month. Are there any important ideas missing from your list?" Concept formation lessons may stand alone or be part of a sequence leading to interpretation and use of data.

A related type of lesson, the concept attainment lesson, is also designed to help students develop new concepts. Whereas concept formation lessons require students to determine criteria and develop categories, concept attainment lessons require them to identify the attributes that differentiate categories already formed by someone else. They do this by analyzing examples and nonexamples of the concept to be attained (Bruner, Goodnow, & Austin, 1977). The examples and nonexamples are called exemplars.

A concept attainment lesson begins with the teacher's presenting exemplars and categorizing them as "yes" (an example of the concept to be developed) or "no" (a nonexample). By comparing the yes and no exemplars, students begin to form ideas about the critical attributes of the concept. After a number of exemplars have been presented, students are asked to describe the characteristics or attributes held in common by the yes examples presented thus far. As additional examples are presented, students may be asked to categorize them as yes or no and determine whether the criteria originally developed continue to hold. After additional examples are examined, students refine the criteria and develop concept labels. Next, the teacher gives the label, and students are asked to produce examples of their own. Finally, students describe their thinking and how their ideas changed as they moved through the activity. Imagine, for example, that a teacher wanted the students to attain the concept of natural resources. He or she would begin by presenting examples and nonexamples of natural resources and placing them in the correct categories. The example of the ocean would be categorized as a yes, whereas a table would be a no. As the pattern emerged, students would be challenged to determine the category of new examples, describe what the examples have in common, and generate examples and nonexamples of their own. Finally, the teacher would present the concept label—natural resources.

There are three major steps in developing a concept attainment lesson. First, you must carefully define your concept, decide on its key attributes, and think about which attributes are critical (essential for this concept) and noncritical (common but not essential). For example, if the concept is mammal, critical attributes are that mammals are warm-blooded, are covered with hair or fur, give birth to live young, and nurse them. Noncritical attributes are that many mammals have four legs and live on land. It is important to develop your concept attainment lesson to clarify as many of the critical attributes of the concept as possible.

Next, you need to select your exemplars. Exemplars may be provided in the form of words, pictures, or even concrete items. You need to select examples and nonexamples that highlight critical attributes. It would be extremely difficult to provide sufficient examples to enable young students to extrapolate the characteristic of warm-blooded. You could, however, provide examples that would highlight other relevant characteristics. For example, in choosing the examples and nonexamples of the concept mammals, you might anticipate that students would initially think of the concept as animals in the zoo or animals in the woods. You could help clarify these misconceptions by including a snake or an ostrich as nonexamples. If you used pictures of these animals, including their eggs, you could focus attention on important attributes. Using a whale as an example may be confusing if students do not know whales have hair or give birth to live young. A picture of a nursing whale may be an important clue.

Finally, it is important to consider the order in which you will present the examples and nonexamples. In most cases, broadly differing examples are given first, with finer and finer distinctions presented as the concept is developed. For example, you might decide to present pictures of a bear and a fish early in the lesson and save the whale photo for later fine-tuning of the concept. In determining the order of the exemplars, it is important to consider the purpose of the activity. If, as in a concept attainment lesson, the intent is to provide students with information from which they can build a new concept, it is most appropriate to start with clear examples and save those that demand careful analysis for later in the lesson. Occasionally, activities resembling concept attainment lessons are used to review or reintroduce concepts that have already been learned. In this case, teachers sometimes use trickier examples first and allow clues to become more and more obvious until students arrive at the concept. This activity can be a highly motivating and appropriate introduction to a lesson, but it is not a concept attainment lesson because students are attempting to identify a concept they have already internalized.

Both concept development and concept attainment lessons provide opportunities for thinking logically, exercising flexibility, and drawing conclusions from data. Although the lessons generally are structured to lead students to predetermined conclusions, they still can reinforce attitudes that are important to creativity. Direct teaching of concepts sends the implicit message, "The teacher will tell me what is important or true." Concept development and concept attainment lessons, on the other hand, imply that "I can figure this out myself."

Inquiry Lessons: Interpreting and Applying Data.   Experiences that require students to interpret and apply data are frequently called inquiry lessons. Inquiry lessons naturally, require students to inquire, examine information, make hypotheses, gather data, and draw conclusions. They involve students actively in discovering a generalization that explains a puzzling event or set of data. Inquiry lessons are particularly valuable because they involve students in many processes of authentic investigation used by adults in a variety of fields.

One variety of inquiry lesson was developed by Suchman (1962). In this model, the teacher begins the activity by explaining the inquiry process and the ground rules. Students are not given any response from the teacher except "yes" or "no" during the questioning period. Next, the teacher presents a puzzling event—something that conflicts with our typical notions of reality. Then the students ask questions to get more information and learn the conditions under which different results would occur. The students, through their questions, begin to isolate relevant variables and to form hunches about causal relationships (hypotheses). Through questions or experiments that test their hypotheses, they formulate an explanation for the puzzling event. Finally, the teacher leads the students to analyze their own thinking processes. The teacher may present a science demonstration, such as the can crushed by air pressure mentioned earlier, and challenge students to determine what happened in a method that resembles 20 Questions. Students strive to identify relevant variables and plan additional experiences that can verify their hypotheses.

Other inquiry lessons involve students in drawing conclusions, not about a particular puzzling event, but about a set of data. The lesson described earlier in which students made and investigated hypotheses about the relationship between advertising strategies and product type could be described as an inquiry lesson. Students examined the data set (magazine ads), made hypotheses about variables (product and strategy), and tested their conclusions (looking at additional print or TV ads). The key attributes of inquiry lessons are examining data, making hypotheses, and drawing conclusions. This cycle may be repeated as many times as it seems productive.

One of my students developed an inquiry lesson based on occupations during the Revolutionary War period. Elementary students were shown photographs of artifacts of the period and asked to hypothesize what occupations must have existed in that society. The activity demanded careful observation and willingness to stand up for one's point of view. Later, during a trip to a local museum, students looked for additional information to support or refute their hypotheses. They had the opportunity to consider multiple possibilities, think independently, and support their ideas, all while learning fairly traditional social studies content. For additional detail on strategies for concept development, concept attainment, and inquiry lessons, see Joyce, Weil, and Calhoun's (2000) *Models of Teaching*, 6th edition.

Simulation and Role Play Activities

One key characteristic of creative thinking is that it is flexible, considering more than one category or point of view. Role-play and simulation activities are particularly effective strategies for developing this type of thinking because they involve looking at the world through someone else's eyes (Taylor, 1998).

Role Play.   Role play can be an effective tool for enhancing understanding of content as well as social understandings. In role-play activities, students take on a role—pretend they are a particular person—to solve a problem or act out a situation. Joyce, Weil, and Calhoun (2000) stated: "In role playing students explore human relations problems by enacting problem situations and then discussing the enactments. Together, students can explore feelings, attitudes, values and problem-solving strategies" (p. 59).

Role play may be done in small groups or in front of the whole class. It usually is a brief activity, often completed in less than 1 hour. Torrance (1975) has used the term "sociodrama" to describe a related process in which students solve present and future problems through a variety of dramatic techniques. The activities described as role play in this section are most closely related to the direct presentation technique of sociodrama. For other, more complex forms of sociodrama, see Torrance (1975).

Role play can be used to enhance content in a variety of areas. Students could role play Emmy Noether convincing her father that she wanted to become the only woman studying math at the university, a pioneer family making the decision to stay in Missouri or travel farther west, or characters in a work of literature trying to work out a new solution to their dilemma. It also can be used to solve real-world social problems, such as a friend offering drugs or an argument over playground equipment. Joyce, Weil, and Calhoun (2000) stated: "The essence of role playing is the involvement of participants and observers in a real problem situation and the desire for resolution and understanding that this involvement engenders" (p. 60). Any area of content in which it is important to understand a variety of points of view can provide opportunities for role playing.

There are four main steps in planning a role play.

1. Decide on the general problem area to be addressed. In choosing a topic you will want to consider your students' needs, interests, and background. In addition to selecting a problem area that is relevant and interesting, it is important for you to choose a topic about which students have sufficient prior knowledge to take on

roles knowledgeably (or to provide them with such background before attempting the role play). If you are role playing in content areas, background knowledge can make the difference between an amusing skit and a powerful learning experience.

2. Once you have decided on a general problem area, define the specific situation to be portrayed. A good role play puts the characters in a specific situation that requires action. If the topic is the causes of the Civil War, the situation might be two siblings in a Virginia family arguing over whether the sons should go to war.

3. Plan a role for the audience. It is important that students not playing particular roles have an active part in the role-play experience. They may be listening for particularly effective arguments, deciding which of several solutions they think is best, or deciding what they might do in a particular character's place.

4. Decide how you will introduce the role play. Some role-play situations might be introduced by a story, others by a discussion of the issue or small-group sharing.

When you actually present the role-play experience, you will first conduct the introductory activities, and then explain clearly and explicitly the situation to be enacted. Select students for each role and assign the observation task to the audience. Conduct the role play one or more times. If you repeat a scenario, you can give more students the opportunity to participate as well as obtain varied points of view. For some role plays, you may wish to discuss each version as it occurs. For others, you may prefer to delay discussion until after several versions have been portrayed. In either case, be sure to allow ample time for discussion of role-play experiences. Helping students understand why individuals made particular choices, what those individuals were thinking and feeling, and what alternative choices might be made is at the heart of role-playing activities. Some writers have used role play to foster in-depth understanding of particular times or topics. For example, Manley and O'Neill (1997) used role play to explore African American heritage ranging from portrayals of the Underground Railroad to activities based on Jacob Lawrence's artwork depicting the Northern migration after World War I. Insights into decision making and alternate points of view also can be found through the use of simulations.

Simulation. In role-play activities, the goal is to allow students to understand people, perspectives, and events by taking on the roles of particular individuals in specific situations. The goal of simulations is similar, but more complex. Whereas role-play activities generally encompass short, tightly defined problem-solving situations, simulations allow students to experience a simplified version of reality over a more extended period. Role play usually involves a small number of students at a time and generally is completed in a class period whereas simulations are likely to involve many students over a period of days, weeks, or even months.

A role-play activity regarding international relations might involve a student portraying the president of Russia discussing with the president of the United States the nuclear capabilities of developing nations or terrorist groups. If several pairs of students portrayed the same situation, the activity might span approximately 45 minutes. A simulation on international relations would probably involve the entire class. Each student would have a role as a representative of a particular country. Representatives might be organized into delegations as part of a simulated United Nations. Students portraying developing nations could argue their right to nuclear protection at a meeting of the U.N. Security Council or other appropriate venue. Preparing for and conducting such activities could easily span several weeks.

Good simulations have a variety of roles that demand differing strengths and interests. Students address complex situations from points of view that vary with the needs and interests of their respective roles. It is important that the results of a simulation not be predetermined. Events should take place as a natural consequence of student actions. One common form of simulation is courtroom reenactments. These may range from very realistic portrayals to trials involving storybook characters (Is Goldilocks guilty of breaking and entering?). The guilt or innocence of the character should be assessed by the jury based on the evidence presented. If one attorney does a better job arguing and preparing than the other, he or she is likely to win the case. Teachers may provide information on procedures or other necessary input, but they should not direct students' actions. Students should act as they believe their roles demand.

Naturally, the depth and complexity of simulation that is appropriate for a group of students will vary with the age of the students and their familiarity with simulations and role play. Primary-grade students may set up a simulated postal system that functions for several weeks, or create a pioneer household that lasts only for a day. Older students may set up businesses, a banking system, or a simulated stock market. Some classes or even whole schools have created minisocieties, complete with currency, daily expenses, and employment for all students. In such minisocieties, students may spend a portion of each day earning the currency necessary to rent their desks or pay their portion of the lighting bill in classroom currency. Some may earn their hypothetical living as part of the government, others by operating banks or businesses, and still others as publishers. Minisocieties may operate for a few weeks or for most of the school year. It also is possible to simulate historical events. Students might take on roles of individuals organizing a party traveling westward or spend a day simulating life in an early schoolhouse.

Several interesting and challenging simulations are available commercially. However, not all materials labeled simulation actually involve students in important aspects of real life. Materials purporting to be simulations that involve students with dragons or talking space creatures probably have other goals. A number of simulations also are available on computers. Although computer simulations are less likely to involve an entire class simultaneously, they allow students to experience the results of decisions that would be impossible or dangerous in real life. Computer simulations can allow students to affect their environment, travel to dangerous places, and conduct elaborate experiments that could not be managed in a school. With computers, students can build cities, manipulate gene pools, mix chemicals, or attempt to control environmental disasters without danger or enormous expense. Computers also can allow students to participate in simulations with students in other schools or countries. Interactive Communications and Simulations at the University of Michigan links students around the globe in simulations that have included the Mideast conflicts, an environmental decisions simulation, and the creation of literary journals. The guidelines for assessing computer simulations are similar to those for other simulation materials. The simulation should present a version of reality that is simplified for students' use, but is as complex and authentic as appropriate for the grade level. The results should be determined by students' participation and should be a natural consequence of students' actions and real-world forces, not primarily luck or chance.

If you would like to create a simulation activity for your class, four key questions may prove helpful (Jones, 1985). The questions may be considered in any order you wish, but all will need to be answered before the simulation is complete.

1. What is the problem? In this question you will consider the general topic, area, or problem to be addressed. Imagine, for example, that you decided to develop a simulation around local government.

2. Who are the participants? Participants in a local government simulation might include the mayor, members of the city council, and concerned citizens.

3. What do they have to do? In this question you determine the goal of the simulation. It usually is helpful to set up a situation in which some sort of problem needs to be addressed in a particular format. In the government simulation, you might set up a situation in which a group of citizens wants the city to create bike lanes in the downtown area to allow bikers safer access to stores. Some business owners welcome the idea of bikers downtown, whereas others are concerned about bike lanes interfering with available parking.

4. What do they have to do it with? This question concerns the physical materials that will be available for participants. You may consider creating role cards for some roles. For example, "You are T. S. Wheels, owner of Wheels' Bike Shop. Your shop is located in the downtown area." You also may consider providing documents such as a downtown map, statistics on road width, or procedures for conducting hearings. Materials for a simulation may be simple or elaborate, depending on your needs, desires, and creativity. You may want to start with a fairly simple simulation and add complexity and materials over several years.

Thinking About the Classroom

Plan a series of inductive, simulation, or role-play lessons for your class. Remember that it will probably take six or eight experiences with a new technique for you and the students to become comfortable with it. Do not give up if your first attempts are shaky.

Questioning and Discussion Strategies

Students as Questioners. One key goal of a problem-friendly classroom is to encourage student questions. It is, after all, impossible for students to investigate, challenge, or dream without raising questions. Although it is important that students feel comfortable expressing confusion or lack of understanding about content being taught, it also is essential that they feel free to ask questions that go beyond the immediate issues. The essence of this type of question is not, "I do not understand," but "I wonder." Wondering is an important key to learning and creativity. Productive people wonder all the time—about the things they see, the things they hear, the things that trouble them, and the things that bring them joy. Unfortunately, students seldom experience this type of questioning in school. School questions generally have one correct answer, and it can be found in the back of the book. The real world is not like that. Teaching students to question, to wonder, is to provide them with a skill for lifelong learning—as well as creativity.

There are at least five strategies you may consider to encourage student questions. First, teach students the difference between checking for understanding and genuine questions. Help them understand that you will ask them many questions to which you already know the answers. You do this because you need to check to see if they understand important content. Sometimes they too may want to ask clarifying questions to make sure they understand something you are teaching. Make sure students understand that you will be pleased to respond to such questions. Help students understand the difference between these activities and your real questions—questions that make you curious because you do not have an answer.

Second, model questioning behaviors. Share your puzzlement and curiosity with your students. Sometimes this may be as simple as a casual comment, "Isn't it interesting how some fashion trends return and some don't? I wonder what determines which fashions recycle and which don't? Will I ever get to wear my [insert your favorite fossil-fashion here] again?" Other times your questions maybe more serious and related to the content, "I wonder sometimes why some conflicts between nations result in wars and some do not. When you think about the modern wars we've studied, do you see any patterns that could help us figure this out?"

Third, teach students to ask questions. You may want to do a lesson on what constitutes a question, why people ask questions, and why questions are important. Consider lessons focusing on questions one could ask about a given event, experiment, story, or idea. Teach students about the different types of questions that could be valuable for a restaurant manager, a crossing guard, or a farmer to ask. Figure 6.1 shows an example of an activity used with elementary students to demonstrate the types of questions that may be important in various situations. Figure 6.2 is an example of a similar questioning activity that could be used with middle-level students.

Fourth, respond to student questions with respect. A friend's young daughter came stomping home from school one day, disgusted with her teacher's use of the K-W-L reading strategy. In the K-W-L technique, students are asked what they Know about a topic, what they Want to know, and, later, what they have Learned. Her response was, "I don't know why they bother with the W anyway. She asks us what we want to learn, and then we just do what the teacher wants to do anyway." Although we know it is impossible to investigate every question posed by an enthusiastic group of learners, students should have confidence that at least some of their questions will be addressed and others will be met with enthusiasm and suggestions for follow-through. One teacher even created a bulletin board on which to hang interesting questions. Not all the questions were investigated, but they all were acknowledged as important and valuable.

Finally, teach students the investigative skill of your discipline(s). This type of teaching is discussed in each of the content areas in this chapter.

When You Ask the Questions.   It is also important to think about the ways we use questions as part of our professional repertoire. Few skills are more important to any teacher than good questioning. Both the content

I Wonder...

Good researchers are always asking questions about the world around them. They notice things that are interesting and wonder about the things they do not know. This exercise will help you practice being a good questioner. For each topic, think of as many interesting questions as you can. Try to think of some unusual questions—questions no one else will think of.

For example, if the topic were baseball you might wonder

How did the greatest baseball hitters learn to swing?

What team won the most pennants? Why?

You could also wonder

What type of food makes the most profit at the baseball stadium?

How has Little League changed since girls started playing?

Does the color or style of the uniform affect playing?

Now, you wonder about these topics:

Your school building

Cookies

Birds

Cars

What other topics (things) do you wonder about?

FIG. 6.1.   I wonder. From Starko, A. J. & Schack, G. D. (1992). *Looking for Data in all the Right Places*, p. 8. Mansfield Center, CT: Creative Learning Press. Reproduced with permission.

Question, Question, Who's Got the Question?

Albert Einstein once said that finding a good problem or asking a new question was the most important part of real advances in science. Good researchers are always asking questions about the world around them. They notice things that are interesting and wonder about the things they don't know. This exercise will help you practice being a good questioner. For each topic, think of as many interesting questions as you can. Try to think of some unusual questions, ones no one else will think of. For example, if the topic was athletic shoes, you might wonder

Do athletic shoes really improve sports performance?

Do you really need different kinds of shoes for different sports?

When did athletic shoes become popular with people who weren't professional athletes? Why? How?

You could also wonder

Which brands are most popular with athletes? Students at our school?

What is involved in celebrity endorsements of athletic shoes?

How many crimes involve the stealing of athletic shoes?

Now, what questions might you have about these topics?

Customs in your school:

Teenagers' eating habits:

Friendships:

Cars:

What other things do you wonder about?

FIG. 6.2. Question, question, who's got the question? From Schack, G. D. & Starko, A. J. (1998). *Research Comes Alive,* p. 23. Mansfield Center, CT: Creative Learning Press. Reproduced with permission.

strategies described in this chapter and the strategies for developing creative thinking described in chapter 5 rely heavily on the use of questions. In particular, divergent questions, those with many possible appropriate responses, are at the heart of many activities that encourage creative thinking. After all, if the questions asked in school always have one and only one correct response, students are unlikely to believe that original ideas are valued or accepted. A complete discussion of questioning strategies is much too complex to be included here, but four key points may serve as reminders when you consider questioning strategies.

First, plan the purposes of your questioning. Many times you may ask questions to determine whether students understand the content being discussed. However, questioning that focuses primarily on checking for understanding can lead students to believe every question is a quiz with the purpose of producing a single correct answer. In such an atmosphere, it is difficult to induce students to risk offering original ideas or opinions when they are desired. A balance of question types including comprehension checks, questions in which students apply information, opinion questions, and "what if" questions is more supportive of flexible student responses. If students have been taught the varied purposes of questioning, you can give students cues as to the purpose of a given activity: "I'd like to check to make sure this information is clear," "Let's talk for a minute about our own personal views on this subject," or "This time, let's really let our imaginations run wild." Such cues can help students anticipate the types of responses that are appropriate.

One purpose that can be damaging to student creativity and learning is the use of questioning as a weapon. Regardless of the provocation, it is important not to use questions to point up student inattention or put students in their place. Although questions can appropriately be used to draw an inattentive student back into the conversation, it is important to do so in a way that maximizes the chances that the student can respond appropriately. Students who have been humiliated by pointed questioning are not likely to have a positive learning experience, nor are those who witnessed the humiliation. Such strategies are extremely detrimental to the atmosphere of acceptance and risk taking that supports creativity.

Second, consider the pacing of your questions. Rowe (1974) discovered that, on the average, less than a second passed between the time teachers asked a question and the time they asked another question, called on another student, or answered the question themselves. The use of wait time, a brief pause between the question and the response—typically 3 to 5 seconds—has been associated with increased student responses, more complex responses, and greater willingness to respond. If we hope to

Students must be taught to ask questions as well as answer them.

prompt diverse or original responses, it is only reasonable to give students some time to think of them. Few people do their best thinking under a barrage of rapid-fire questions.

Third, consider the distribution of your questions. Creative thinking is important for all students. Neither our society nor the global community can afford citizens who do not think flexibly and solve problems. Consequently, it is important that the questions prompting creative thinking are distributed equitably to all students. This is not as easy as it sounds. Many teachers distribute questions unequally, calling on boys more than girls, high achievers more than low achievers, majority students more than minority students, or students on one side of the room more than those on the other. Without some cues to assist you, such patterns are difficult to break. Some teachers pull students' names randomly from a collection of Popsicle sticks or index cards. Others record the names of students who respond in order to ensure more equitable distribution.

One additional advantage of random questioning—that is, asking a question and then randomly selecting a student to respond rather than choosing volunteers—is the message it sends about high expectations for all students. If teachers usually call on volunteers, students reasonably assume that if they do not volunteer, they are free of the responsibility to respond and need not necessarily concentrate on the lesson. The same message is conveyed when a teacher names the student to respond before asking the question. The question, "Bob, why do you think Castro continued to believe communism would succeed after the fall of communism in Europe?" allows everyone except Bob to breathe a sigh of relief without listening to the question. If, on the other hand, the teacher phrased the question, "Let's think for a moment, why do you think Castro continued to believe communism would succeed" ... (wait time), and then randomly chose a student to respond, all students would understand that they were expected to be prepared to answer.

Some teachers are concerned about calling on nonvolunteers for fear of embarrassing students who do not know the answer. Such concerns should be minimal with divergent questions, because there is no one correct response. Even so, some teachers are more comfortable allowing students a given number of pass responses per day. If a student is called on and genuinely has no response, he or she is allowed to say, "Pass," and the question goes to someone else. Limiting the number of these options per day makes it more likely that students will attend to the issue at hand and expect to think with creativity and care.

In addition to distributing questions equitably, make sure that you use probing and prompting responses equally for all students. Sometimes a student's initial response is unclear or incomplete. If only highly able or highly creative students are prompted for further responses, other students may come to believe they need not be concerned with questions that demand creative thought.

Thinking About the Classroom

Ask a colleague to observe your questioning technique. You might ask the observer to keep track of the number of boys and girls you question, or the percentage of convergent and divergent questions you use. If the observer knows your class well, you might want him or her to note the number of high and low achievers you question. See what patterns of questioning you are using.

Fourth, remember that there is a difference between questioning and discussion. Both questioning and discussion are important classroom strategies. In questioning, most of the interaction is between the students and the teacher. The teacher asks a question, a student or students respond, and then another question is asked. In a discussion, students talk both to the teacher and to each other. The teacher may ask a stimulus question, but the bulk of the responses and additional questions come from the students. The goal is to examine points of view or to reach consensus rather than identify a correct response. Discussions are an important classroom strategy that have particular value in communicating to students that diverse opinions and ideas are valued.

The teacher's role in a discussion is to provide the stimulus question; paraphrase, summarize, or clarify student positions as needed; help to maintain focus; and draw the discussion to a close. True whole-class discussions are difficult to initiate and maintain. You may find that smaller discussions with partners or small groups may pave the way for larger efforts. Some teachers find that a no-hands rule helps students learn to listen to each other during discussion periods. If a teacher controls the discussion by calling on students with raised hands, a student with something to say may become more concerned with gaining the teacher's attention than following the course of the discussion. The no-hands rule simply states that no raised hands and no interruptions are allowed. Students must listen carefully to know when the speaker has completed a thought and another person may reasonably enter the discussion.

Finally, if you are interested in planning a discussion, a good discussion question is of prime importance. One good gauge for such a question is whether you, yourself, have an answer. If a question has a right answer, it may be more suited for a question-and-answer session. A good discussion question is one for which the discussion leader is truly seeking an answer, one that invites multiple perspectives.

Content Teaching and Creativity. Content teaching provides many rich opportunities for encouraging creativity in students. The type of content we teach and the methods we use for doing so send messages to students about the types of learners and thinkers we expect them to be. Content and lessons that expect students to question as well as answer, investigate as well as comprehend, and identify problems as well as solve them allow students to learn important content while exercising their creativity—surely an unbeatable combination.

JOURNEYING AND JOURNALING

1. Szekely stated that he is an artist-teacher. If you had to define yourself in terms of the discipline in which you exhibit most of your creativity, what would you call yourself? A writer-teacher? A

scientist-teacher? Pick an area in which you would like to develop your own creativity and begin keeping an idea book. After a month, read over your ideas and see whether there are any you would like to pursue further.

2. Explore your own environment. Pick a nearby location—a mall, a park, or any area you enjoy exploring. Visit that location as an artist, writer, scientist, historian, or mathematician. Look carefully and jot down as many interesting ideas, problems, and questions as you can. Reflect on how your point of view affected your experience.

3. Try some historical research yourself. Go to the library and locate a newspaper from the day you were born. Examine the headlines. Look at the advertising, the sports, and the classified ads. Ask any available relatives what they remember about that day. Listen to music or watch a movie that was popular then. Try to be aware of what you are learning and how you feel as the project progresses. Did history come alive for you? Record your feelings and think about what your experience as an authentic historian might imply for your teaching.

4. Try some of the activities suggested in this chapter. Record your experiences as you vary your teaching techniques. Discuss them with colleagues. Think about the risk taking, perseverance, and response to novelty that are necessary for the endeavor.

REFERENCES

Adata, P. M. (Executive producer), & Bank. M. (Director). (1977). *Anonymous was a woman* (video). Chicago: Homevision Cinema.

Anderson, C. W. (1987). Strategic teaching in science. In B. F. Jones, A. S. Palincsar, D. S. Ogle, & E. G. Carr (Eds.), *Strategic teaching and learning* (pp. 73–91). Alexandria, VA: Association for Supervision and Curriculum Development.

Anderson, C. W., & Lee, O. (1997). Will students take advantage of opportunities for meaningful science learning? *Phi Delta Kappan, 78,* 720–724.

Apol, L. (2002). What do we do if we don't do Haiku? Seven suggestions for writers and teachers. *English Journal, 91*(3), 89–97.

Atwell, N. (1998). *In the middle: Writing, reading, and learning with adolescents* (2nd ed.). Portsmouth, NH: Boynton/Cook.

Bank, M. (1995). *Anonymous was a woman.* New York: St. Martin's Griffin.

Battista, M. T. (1999). The mathematical miseducation of American's youth. *Phi Delta Kappan, 80,* 424–433.

Bedwell, R., & Clark, L. (1997). *General Lee and Santa Claus.* Nashville, TN: Spiridon Press.

Bingham, C. (1991). *Journal of creative activities.* Unpublished manuscript, Ypsilanti, MI.

Bohm, D. (1998). *On creativity.* New York: Routledge.

Bollman, K. A,, Rodgers, M. H., & Mauller, R. L. (2001). Jupiter Quest: A path to scientific discovery. *Phi Delta Kappan, 82*(9), 683–686.

Bradbury, R. (1996). *Zen and the art of writing: Essays on creativity.* Santa Barbara, CA: Joshua Odell Editions.

Brandwein, P. F. (1962). *Elements in a strategy for teaching science in the elementary school.* New York: Harcourt Brace.

Brandwein, P. F. (1986). A portrait of gifted young with science talent. *Roeper Review, 8,* 235–242.

Bransford, J. D., Brown, A. L., &. Cocking R. R. (Eds.) (1999). *How people learn: Brain, mind, experience, and school.* Washington, D.C.: National Academy Press.

Brown, S. I., & Walter, M. I. (1990). *The art of problem posing* (2nd ed.). Hillsdale, NJ: Lawrence Erlbaum Associates.

Bruner, J., Goodnow, J., & Austin, G. (1977). *A study of thinking.* New York: Wiley.

Burns, M. (1992). *About teaching mathematics.* White Plains, NY: Math Solutions Publications.

Calkins, L. M. (1994). *The art of teaching writing* (2nd ed.). Portsmouth, NH: Heinemann.

Caniglia, J. (2003). *Math and the great fire of 1805.* Detroit, MI: Detroit Historical Museum.

Center for Gifted Education Staff. (1996). *Acid, acid everywhere: A unit designed for grades 4–6.* New York: Kendall/Hunt.

Center for Science, Mathematics, and Engineering (CSMEE). (1995). *National science education standards.* Washington, DC: Author.

Coleman, L., & Gallagher, S. A. (Eds.). (1997). [Theme issue]. *Journal for the Education of the Gifted, 20*(4).

Cothron J. H., Giese, R. N., & Rezba, R. J. (1989). *Students and research: Practical strategies for science classrooms and competitions.* Dubuque, IA: Kendall/Hunt.

D'Arcangelo, M. (2001). Wired for mathematics: A conversation with Brian Butterworth. *Educational Leadership, 59*(3), 14–19.

Dempster, F. N. (1993). Exposing our students to less should help them learn more. *Phi Delta Kappan, 74,* 432–437.

Directions for cooking by troops in camp and hospital (1861). Reproduction Laramie, WY: Sue's Frou Frou Publications.

Doctorow, E. L. (1971). *The book of Daniel.* New York: Random House.

Doctorow, E. L. (1975). *Ragtime.* New York: Random House.

Ehri, L. C., Nunes, S., Stahl, S., & Willows, D. (2001). Systematic phonics instruction helps student learn to read: Evidence form the National Reading Panel's Meta-Analysis. *Review of Educational Research, 71*(3), 393–447.

Elasky, B. (1989). Becoming. *Democracy and Education* (Occasional Paper No. 3), 6–13.

Finkelstein, A. (2002). *Science is golden: A problem-solving approach to doing science with children.* East Lansing, MI: Michigan State University Press.

Forman, S. M. (Ed.). (1997a). *Echoes of the Civil War: The blue.* Carlisle, MA: Discovery Enterprises.

Forman, S. M. (Ed.). (1997b). *Echoes of the Civil War: The gray.* Carlisle, MA: Discovery Enterprises.

Fort, D. C. (1990). From gifts to talents in science. *Phi Delta Kappan, 71,* 664–671.

Gardner, H. (1993). *Creating minds.* New York: Basic Books.

Garland, D. (1993). *The lotus seed.* New York: Harcourt Brace Jovanovich.

Graves, D. (1983). *Writing: Teachers and children at work.* Portsmouth, NY: Heinemann.

Graves, D. (1994). *A fresh look at writing.* Portsmouth, NY: Heinemann.

Halmos, P. R. (1968). Mathematics as creative art. *American Scientist, 4,* 380–381.

Holt, D. G., & Willard-Holt, C. (2000). Let's get real: Students solving authentic corporate problems. *Phi Delta Kappan, 82*(3), 243–246.

Jones, K. (1985). *Designing your own simulations.* New York: Metheun.

Joosse, B. M. (1991). *Mama, do you love me?* San Francisco: Chronicle Books.

Jorgensen, K. L. (1993). *History workshop.* Portsmouth, NH: Heinemann.

Joyce, B., Weil, M., & Calhoun, E. (2000). *Models of teaching* (6th ed.). Boston: Allyn & Bacon.

Kamii, C. (1985). *Young children reinvent arithmetic.* New York: Teachers College Press.

Kamii, C. (1989). *Young children continue to reinvent arithmetic.* New York: Teachers College Press.

Keats, E. J. (1962). *The snowy day.* New York: Scholastic.

Lewis, B. (1991). *The kid's guide to social action.* Minneapolis, MN: Free Spirit Press.

Kilpatrick, J., Swafford, J., & Findell, B. (Eds.). (2001). *Adding it up: Helping children learn mathematics.* Washington, DC: National Academic Press.

Lambros, A. (2002). *Problem-based learning in K–8 classrooms: A guide to implementation.* Thousand Oaks, CA: Corwin Press.

Long, K., & Kamii, C. (2001). The measurement of time: Children's construction of transitivity, unit iteration, and conservation of speed. *School Science and Mathematics, 101*(3), 125–132.

Manley, A., & O'Neill, C. (1997). *Dreamseekers: Creative approaches to the African American heritage.* Portsmouth, NH: Heinemann.

Michigan Educational Extension Service. (1991). *Changing minds: A bulletin of the Michigan Educational Extension Service* (Spring).

Michigan Educational Extension Service. (1992). *Changing minds: A bulletin of the Michigan Educational Extension Service* (Winter/Spring).

Moorman, T. (2002). *How to make your science project scientific.* New York: John Wiley & Sons.

Morimoto, J. (1988). *Inch boy.* New York: Penguin Putnam.

Morrison, T. (1987). *Beloved.* New York: Penguin.

Murphy-Judy, K. A., & Conruejols, C. F. (1993). Multicultural multimedia across the curriculum: A pilot project. *T.H.E. Journal, 20*(7), 77–79.

National Archives and Records Administration. (1989). *Teaching with documents.* Washington, D.C.: National Archives and Records Administration.

National Council of Teachers of Mathematics. (1989). *Curriculum and evaluation standards for school mathematics.* Reston, VA:

National Council of Teachers of Mathematics. (2000). *Principles and standards for school mathematics.* Reston, VA: Author.

Newmann, F. K (1996). Authentic pedagogy and student performance. *American Journal of Education, 104*(4), 280–312.

Newmann, F. K., & Wehlage, G. G. (1993). Five standards of authentic instruction. *Educational Leadership, 50,* 8–12.

Ngeow, K., & Kong, Y. (2001). Learning to learn: Preparing teachers and students for problem- based learning. *ERIC Digest.* ED457524.

Palatini, M. (1999). *Ding dong ding dong.* New York: Hyperion Books.

Parker, W. C. (1991). *Renewing the social studies curriculum.* Alexandria, VA: Association for Supervision and Curriculum Development.

Perrone, V. (1994). How to engage students in learning. *Educational Leadership, 51*(5), 11–13.

Perry, S. K. (1999). *Writing in flow.* Cincinnati, OH: Writers Digest Books.

Petnica Science Center. (1992). *Bilten, 12.*

Petnica Science Center. (2003). *Petnica Science Center almanac.* Author: Petnica, Serbia.

Pinker, S. (1997). *How the mind works.* New York: W. W. Norton.

Reece, C. S., Strange, & Kamii, C. (2001). The measurement of volume: Why do young children measure inaccurately? *School Science and Mathematics, 101*(7), 356–361.

Renzulli, J. S. (1977). *The enrichment triad model.* Mansfield Center, CT: Creative Learning Press.

Renzulli, J. S., & Reis, S. M. (1997). *The schoolwide enrichment model: A how-to guide for educational excellence* (2nd ed.). Mansfield Center, CT: Creative Learning Press.

Ringgold, F. (1991). *Tar beach.* New York: Crown.

Rowe, M. (1974). Wait time and rewards as instructional variables: Their influence on language, logic, and fate control. *Journal of Research in Science Teaching, 11,* 81–94.

Schack, G. D. (1993). Involving students in authentic research. *Educational Leadership, 50,* 29–31.

Schack, G. D, & Starko, A. J. (1998). *Research comes alive.* Mansfield Center, CT: Creative Learning Press.

Schoenfeld, A. H. (1992). Learning to think mathematically: Problem solving, matacognition, and sense making in mathematics. In D. Grouws (Ed.), *Handbook of research on mathematics teaching and learning* (pp. 334–370). Reston, VA: National Council of Teachers of Mathematics.

Scieszka, J. (1989). *The true story of the three little pigs.* New York: Viking Kestral.

Sher, B. T., VanTassel-Baska, J., Gallagher, S. A., & Bailey, J. M. (1993). *Developing a curriculum framework in science for high ability learners K–8.* Williamsburg, VA: William and Mary Center for Gifted Education.

Simmons, A. (1984). *The first American cookbook: A facsimile of "American Cookery," 1796.* New York: Dover Publications.

Sloan, G. D. (1991). *The child as critic* (3rd ed.). New York: Teachers College Press.

Sneider, C. (1999). *Oobleck: What do scientists do?* Berkley, CA: Great Explorations in Math and Science (GEMS).

Sobel, M. A., & Maletsky, E. M. (1999). *Teaching mathematics.* Boston: Allyn and Bacon.

Soderborg, N. (1985). Å{%&*^\(=)–Å}. *Insight, 2*(1), 9–10, 13.

Starko, A. J., & Schack, G. D. (1992). *Looking for data in all the right places.* Mansfield Center, CT: Creative Learning Press.

Stepien, W., & Gallagher, S. (1993). Problem-based learning: As authentic as it gets. *Educational Leadership, 50,* 25–28.

Sternberg, R. J. (1985). Critical thinking: Part 1. Are we making critical mistakes? *Phi Delta Kappan, 67*(3), 194–198.

Sternberg, R. J., & Lubart, T. I. (1991). An investment theory of creativity and its development. *Human Development, 34,* 1–34.

Sternberg, R. J., & O'Hara, L. A. (1999). Creativity and intelligence. In Sternberg, R. J. (Ed.), *Handbook of creativity* (pp. 251–272). New York: Cambridge University Press.

Suchman, J. R. (1962). *The elementary school training program in scientific inquiry* (Report to the U.S. Office of Education). Urbana, IL: University of Illinois.

Sunal, C. S., & Haas, M. E. (1993). *Social studies and the elementary/middle school student.* New York: Harcourt Brace.

Szekely, G. (1988). *Encouraging creativity in art lessons.* New York: Teachers College Press.

Taba, H. (1967). *Teacher's handbook for elementary school social studies.* Reading, MA: Addison-Wesley.

Taylor, P. (1998). *Redcoats and patriots: Reflective practice in drama and social studies.* Portsmouth, NH: Heinemann.

Torrance, E. P. (1975). Sociodrama as a creative problem-solving approach to studying the future. *Journal of Creative Behavior, 9,* 182–195.

VanTassel-Baska, J. (1993, May). *National curriculum development projects for high-ability learners.* Paper presented at the Henry B. and Jocelyn Wallace National Research Symposium on Talent Development, Iowa City, IA.

Waber, B. (1972). *Ira sleeps over.* New York: Scholastic.

Watson, B., & Konicek, R. (1990). Teaching for conceptual change: Confronting children's experience. *Phi Delta Kappan, 71,* 680–685.

Worsley, D., & Mayer, B. (1989). *The art of science writing.* New York: Teacher and Writers Collaborative.

X, M. (1965). *Autobiography of Malcolm X.* New York: Grove Press.

Yatvin, J. (2002). Babes in the woods: The wanderings of the National Reading Panel. *Phi Delta Kappan, 83*(5), 364–369.

chapter 7

Motivation, Creativity, and Classroom Organization

The art table in Joan's preschool was one of the most popular areas in the room. It was full of materials for a variety of projects. There was an adult nearby to supervise, and student efforts were always met with enthusiastic praise. Joan thought it strange that two of her students never went near the art table. For the first 3 months of school, neither David nor Diane touched the paints, crayons, scissors, or other available materials.

It was time for the yearly substance abuse essay contest sponsored by a local radio station and Jim couldn't decide whether he wanted his class to be involved. He knew drug abuse was an important topic, and the contest did offer the opportunity for students to win gift certificates to local stores, but the contest never seemed to bring out the best in his students. In past years, the essays didn't seem particularly creative, and students seemed angry that no one from their class won a prize. Jim felt confused.

Mr. Monk's third-grade class was examining bean seeds. The students were to study the seeds and record their findings in their lab notebooks, including an illustration. Nancy had drawn her seed carefully and labeled each part: "baby," "blanket," "crib," and "bottle." When Mr. Monk came to her desk he exclaimed, "Nancy, what are you doing? We don't have time for this kind of silliness in

357

third grade—baby dolls belong in the kindergarten. I want the sci-entific names. Do this again, and this time use your science book."

It is not enough for students to know the content and skills that provide the grist and the mill for creativity. Students also must have the motivation to be creative: the will, you might say, to turn the millstone. There are, of course, many sources of motivation. Some sources are extrinsic; they come from outside the individual. Students may be motivated by grades, praise, privileges, or other rewards. Other sources of motivation are intrinsic, coming from within the individual or from an interaction between an individual and a particular task. Students who love to write, paint, or work with computers are motivated to do those things by the interest and enjoyment they gain from the tasks, not by a promised grade or smiley face.

Amabile (1987, 1989, 1996) identified intrinsic motivation as one of the three key elements in creative behavior. As described in chapter 4, she demonstrated that this type of motivation underlies individuals' willingness to experiment, try new ideas, and explore new paths rather than seek the quickest route to any kind of closure. If this is true, developing classroom structures that support intrinsic motivation is an essential element in the development of creativity in schools. We have seen that independence in judgment, willingness to take risks, and perseverance in self-chosen tasks are characteristics associated with creativity. If we are to enhance these traits in students, we must create classrooms that increase their autonomy. If students are to be creative, they must begin to develop their own ideas, judgments, and interests instead of always pursuing paths forged by their teachers.

This chapter considers ways to support and develop students' autonomy and intrinsic motivation in the classroom—to create the problem-friendly classrooms described in chapter 4. It examines theories associated with intrinsic and extrinsic motivation, classroom organization and independent learning, grouping patterns, and evaluation and grading, each as they affect student motivation, autonomy, and creativity. It discusses how common classroom practices may undermine these goals and how such practices might be changed to support student independence, risk taking, and exploration.

PSYCHOLOGICAL SAFETY, INTRINSIC MOTIVATION, AND FLOW

Psychological Safety

Rogers' (1962) concept of psychological safety, although not directly addressed to the topic of motivation, expressed his understanding of the conditions necessary for an individual to develop creativity freely. Rogers, you recall from chapter 2, believed that creativity is a natural product of healthy development, but that it may be blocked by a person's need for psychological defenses. Whether an individual moves toward creativity and self-actualization can be affected by internal and external factors. In addition to the personal characteristics that enhance creative growth (such as openness to experience), Rogers believed that circumstances surrounding the individual affect his or her opportunities for creativity. His description of psychological safety parallels recommendations made by those using brain research to design supportive classroom environments (Wolfe & Brandt, 1998). Although some of the educational recommendations based on brain research seem overgeneralized at this time (Bruer, 1999), there are many logical reasons for establishing a warm and supportive classroom environment.

Rogers (1962) used the analogy of a farmer and a seed. Although the farmer cannot force a seed to grow, he can provide the nurturing conditions that will permit the seed to develop its own potential. In the same way, teachers, therapists, and others hoping to promote human growth can establish the conditions of pyschological safety that allow individuals to develop. Psychological safety is associated with three processes: acceptance of the individual, lack of external evaluation, and empathetic understanding.

Acceptance of the individual as having unconditional worth is at the core of psychological safety. This type of acceptance means that whatever his or her current condition, the person is seen as having value and potential. Some individuals are fortunate enough to find this type of acceptance in a warm, loving family. In such situations, the individuals know that no matter what they do, they are loved. The love and acceptance are not tied to passing tests, winning ball games, or playing concerts; they are unconditional.

It is impossible for any teacher to provide all the advantages of a loving home in a few hours each day. It is possible, however, to have a classroom in which students are valued just because they are there, a room in which all students, no matter what their current situation or behavior, are seen as having potential. Unconditional acceptance does not mean all student behavior is acceptable. The most loving families have rules and clear consequences when the rules are broken. However, even when the behavior is not acceptable, the child can feel accepted if he or she is treated with respect and dignity.

Unconditional acceptance can be manifested in many ways. Any act sending the message that students are important, valuable, and full of potential builds a foundation of psychological safety. Perhaps the most obvious type of acceptance is the teacher's willingness to examine student ideas, even when they initially appear strange or inappropriate. If Mr. Monk had asked Nancy to tell him about her illustration before he exploded, he could have determined whether her unusual labels came from a lack of understanding, inattention, or an attempt to use analogy to express the relationships among the seed parts. Nancy's use of this type of analogy could be a cue to both her understanding of content and her ability to express it in novel ways. Unfortunately, her teacher's rejection of her ideas make it less likely that Nancy will feel welcome to make similar connections in the future. Worse yet, Mr. Monk rejected not just the ideas, but Nancy herself. By implying that such ideas were suitable only for a kindergarten student, he left Nancy feeling small, inadequate, and unhappy.

Most teachers would recognize Mr. Monk's behavior as unsupportive. However, other acts that undermine psychological safety may be less easily recognized. In a safe class, all students feel that they are important and that the teacher has high expectations for them. These expectations are manifested in equitable patterns of questioning, in literature that recognizes and honors the cultures represented in the class, and in classroom posters and illustrations that portray many kinds of students in positive ways. If students are to feel safe enough for exploration, risk taking, and challenge, they must feel that their teacher and the school accept students just like them. This type of classroom sends a message that says, "Of course you are important. Of course you'll work hard. I expect you'll make mistakes and some of your ideas will not work, but that's okay. I expect that you'll keep trying and eventually we'll all make it." If this message is sent to all students, regardless of achievement, gender, race, family background, or any other factor, students have a chance to feel psychologically safe in school, whatever the rest of their lives may bring.

The second aspect of psychological safety is lack of external evaluation. Rogers (1962) believed that evaluation by external sources hinders psychological safety. It forces individuals to put up defenses and keeps them from being open to their own self-evaluation. Rogers believed that an internal locus of evaluation—the use of one's own judgment to determine the ultimate worth of a creative product—is a key to creative behavior. He made it clear that lack of evaluation does not mean lack of feedback or that outside evaluators cannot express opinions about creative efforts. Such opinions can be helpful. It does mean that the final determination about the value of a creative effort is most powerfully and safely determined by the creator.

This aspect of psychological safety poses real difficulties in schools. Few areas of life have more continuous outside evaluation than the classroom. Students are evaluated many times each day on numerous academic and behavioral variables. The teacher's challenge is to provide feedback and information on behaviors and ideas without leading students to believe that the only valid sources of evaluation are outside themselves. This idea is further discussed later in the chapter, in the section dealing with evaluation and grading.

The final aspect and pinnacle of psychological safety is empathetic understanding. Empathetic understanding goes one step beyond acceptance. It accepts not only who the person appears to be, but also who he or she is inside. In empathetic understanding, we see the world from another's point of view, enter that person's private world, and still accept him or her. Empathetic understanding of all our students is a lofty goal, particularly for secondary teachers with enormous class loads, but it can allow students to feel safe and accepted in many difficult circumstances. For some students, a teacher's willingness to learn enough about them to see the world through their eyes may provide the key to both content learning and creative thinking.

Thinking About the Classroom

Psychological safety requires that every child in your room feel accepted, important, and valued. Examine the images of children and adults found in your room. Consider those in textbooks, posters, calendars, and any other available materials. Think about the mixture of genders and races portrayed. Will it support psychological safety for all your students?

Intrinsic Motivation

Some of Rogers' (1962) ideas about psychological safety and the circumstances that enhance it ring true in the context of more recent research on intrinsic motivation. Intrinsic motivation comes from within, as a positive response to the task itself. It spurs a person to explore, to persist, and to achieve based on the satisfaction of the task itself. I note in chapter 4 that interest, choice, and a growing feeling of competence all contribute to an individual's intrinsic motivation regarding a particular activity. Extrinsic motivation arises from sources outside the task: evaluation, contracted for reward, external directives, and the like.

Researchers have examined factors affecting motivation in a variety of activities—some creative, others not. Several types of studies have reported the effects of external constraints on work that was originally motivated internally. Such constraints might include rewards, deadlines, and overt supervision. In a variety of circumstances, the imposition of external controls actually can decrease intrinsic motivation for the targeted task. Lepper, Greene, and Nisbet (1973) observed preschool students playing with magic markers. After identifying students who displayed a high level of interest in the markers, the researchers asked the students to draw some pictures with the markers. Some of the students were promised a reward if they drew the pictures; others were not. Afterward, the students who had been promised a reward demonstrated less interest in the markers than those who had drawn pictures without the promised reward. It was as if the students could conceive of no other reason to draw once they had drawn for a reward. Drawing for the sake of drawing no longer seemed worthwhile. Similar findings have been observed for varying constraints and target behaviors (Amabile, DeJong, & Lepper, 1976; Deci, 1971; Deci, Koestner, & Ryan 2001a, 2001b; Lepper & Greene, 1975, 1978).

Taking cues from this body of research, Amabile (1987, 1989, 1996) and Collins and Amabile (1999) investigated the effects of factors affecting intrinsic motivation for creative tasks. If, as hypothesized, intrinsic motivation is an essential element of creativity, variables that decrease intrinsic motivation should also decrease the level of creativity displayed in a given task. Amabile's research has used varied types of information: retrospective reports of creative people gleaned from their writings, experimental studies of children and adults involved in creative tasks, and interviews and surveys in which individuals reflect on the factors affecting their creativity. In her studies, the creativity assessed was not a test score, but the subject's response to an open-ended task or other real-world problem situation. A consensus of judges expert in the particular domain (consensual assessment) was used to evaluate the level of creativity in the responses. The experimental studies of children and adults generally involved the researchers' manipulating the circumstances under which individuals performed a creative task and assessing the responses. In one study, children were asked to tell stories from a picture book. One group was told they would be rewarded for this activity by having the opportunity to take a picture with a Polaroid camera. If they agreed to tell the story, they were allowed to take the pictures first and then complete the story task. Other children also took pictures and told stories, but were simply presented with the activities as two unrelated things to do. Students who worked in the no-reward condition produced stories judged to be significantly more creative than those who told their stories for a reward (Amabile, Hennessey, & Grossman, 1986). These findings are similar to those from the Lepper et al. (1973) magic marker study, but they take the theory one step further. Whereas Lepper et al. documented the negative effects of reward on motivation toward a potentially creative activity, Amabile et al. (1986) found that the reward affected creativity itself. Numerous other studies had similar results (Amabile, 1996; Collins & Amabile, 1999).

Like virtually every other idea about creativity, Amabile's position on the importance of intrinsic motivation can be called into question. Weisberg (1992) cited adult creators who were highly motivated by external rewards. Watson and Crick wanted the Nobel prize for their modeling of DNA. Da Vinci, Michelangelo, Mozart, Dickens, and others frequently worked for commissions or contracts. Their creativity did not seem to be blunted by the promise of financial reward. Many of Bloom's (1985) subjects prepared and practiced for competitions. Eisenberger and his colleagues, arguing from a behaviorist perspective, cited research in support of rewards increasing divergent thinking (Eisenberger, Armeli, & Pretz, 1998; Eisenberger & Cameron, 1996). Cameron (2001) argued that negative effects of reward are very limited, and that most rewards are not problematic. It is possible that the importance of internal motivation changes developmentally or varies by task or by discipline.

As her research continued, Amabile, herself, (1993b, 1996, 2001) revised her original hypothesis. The original Intrinsic Motivation Hypothesis argued that any extrinsic motivation is detrimental to creativity. In 1996, Amabile set forth a revised Intrinsic Motivation Principle: "Intrinsic motivation is conducive to creativity; controlling extrinsic motivation is detrimental to creativity, but informational or enabling extrinsic motivation can be conducive particularly if initial levels of intrinsic motivation are high" (p. 119). That is, intrinsic motivation is supportive of creativity. Some types of extrinsic motivation are harmful to creativity, some are not. Of course, our task is to determine which is which and how best to use them in classrooms.

The key distinction between good and bad extrinsic motivation, at least in so far as it affects creativity, may be the degree to which the extrinsic factors are controlling or informational. Controlling extrinsic motivation is the driving force behind an activity, perhaps the only reason it is undertaken. Classrooms that operate under a constant threat of tests and grades are centering on controlling extrinsic motivation. So are those that focus students' attention primarily on prizes, stars, or accolades rather than on learning. Praise that is doled out to good students without a clear indication of what they did well can have a similar effect. Students may expend so much energy figuring out how to get the praise that they have less left for creative thinking. Praise that gives students information about what they did well and enhances their sense of competence is less detrimental. The more obvious the external motivation, the more problematic it is. A 3- foot trophy in the front of the classroom for the most creative story is likely to shift students' focus from their stories to the trophy. This is unlikely to enhance creative thinking. The prize has become the controlling factor in this situation.

Using a series of studies varying the circumstances under which subjects pursued diverse creative tasks, Amabile (1989, 1996) and Collins and Amabile (1999) identified five factors that affected creativity, particularly in children. These factors have two key attributes: (a) they have been associated with reduced student creativity and (b) they are a major part of many classroom cultures. The factors are evaluation, surveillance, reward, competition, and lack of choice. In this discussion, I examine how they may affect motivation in complex ways and how that may impact students.

I must admit, the first time I read Amabile's (1989) research, I felt discouraged. Developing creativity in classrooms is important to me, yet some of the factors she designated creativity killers are so much a part of the ebb and flow of classroom life that I began to wonder if I were working for an impossible dream. As research continued and it became evident that motivation and creativity interact in more complex ways than originally thought, I felt less discouraged—but possibly more confused! The key when considering this research is to refrain from trying to determine how to eliminate these factors from our classrooms. Few teachers will be able to eliminate all evaluation or rewards, and probably few would want to. What we can do is think carefully about the ways these factors operate in our classes and do what we can to minimize their detrimental effects on students' intrinsic motivation and creativity.

The first two factors to be considered are evaluation and surveillance. There is evidence that students whose creative efforts are evaluated express less creativity in their next efforts even if the evaluations are positive. This observation immediately brings to mind Rogers' (1962) ideas about evaluation and psychological safety. According to this theory, external evaluation forces individuals to put up defenses and makes them less open to creative ideas. Rogers' theory suggests that evaluation makes individuals less motivated to explore multiple ideas and possibilities. Regardless of the mechanism, the results are the same: Evaluation can have an inhibiting effect on creativity.

The story of Joan's preschool art table at the beginning of the chapter illustrates this effect. After reading research on intrinsic motivation, Joan decided to see what would happen if she eliminated evaluative comments on the children's artwork. She met with the preschool staff and volunteers and decided to make two changes. First, there would no longer be an adult seated at the art table. Adults would be available for assistance if it was needed, and they would continue to ensure that materials were used safely, but they would do so from a distance. Some studies have shown that close surveillance of individuals inhibits their creativity, possibly because it makes them feel as though they are being evaluated even if they are not. The second change was in the types of comments made to students. Rather than comments that implied evaluation such as "Good job!" or "What a nice picture," adults would limit themselves to descriptive comments such as "I see you used a lot of blue today." If they were asked directly whether they liked a picture, the adults were to turn the question around and ask the student how he or she liked it.

The results of these simple changes were remarkable. Within a week, the two students who had avoided art activities for months were both active at the art table. One student, Diane, was obviously nervous at her first attempt. She kept glancing over her shoulder to see if any adults were watching; the adults all studiously averted their eyes. When she completed her first painting she brought it to the teacher for assessment. When it became clear her teacher was not going to pass judgment on her work, Diane heaved a sigh and returned to work. There were no further difficulties with students avoiding art activities.

Certainly, we cannot expect students to improve in their creative efforts, in visual arts or any other area, with no feedback. Our goal can be to provide the type and timing of feedback that are most helpful. One consideration is the student's maturity and level of expertise. Bloom's (1985) first-level students' greatest need was to fall in love with the subjects. Second-level students needed to develop discipline and technique appropriate to the content area. Certainly, the types of feedback appropriate at these two stages differ. However, even when evaluative feedback is necessary, there is a difference between feedback that is basically informational and feedback that is controlling (Amabile, 1989, 1996). Controlling feedback lets students know how the teacher assesses their progress. It answers the students' frequent question, "How did I do?" In controlling feedback, the teacher is the primary and usually the sole judge of students' success or failure. Students are told "A," or "Good work!" or "You can do better than this," or even "I'm disappointed in you." Such comments clearly let students know where they stand in the teacher's eyes and probably how they stand in relation to others in the class. They do not, however, give students any information that will help them learn much except "I'm a success," or "I'm not." This type of feedback can be called controlling because the teacher is the arbiter of good and bad, successful and not successful, valuable and not valuable.

Informational feedback assumes that students are in charge of organizing and evaluating their own learning. It provides useful information for their guidance. It addresses the questions "What did you learn?" and "Which parts of this can help you learn more?" For example, "Good work!" is controlling. It tells students that their work was good, but not what made it good or how to make it better. Students are no better informed or able to learn after reading the comment than they were before. Compare that comment to the following: "The character of Danny was really believable. His dialogue was realistic and sounded just like a real 12-year-old." "The description of the forest on page 2 became a bit wordy. Try to paint a clear picture with fewer, well-chosen words." "Good work multiplying fractions. You seem to be having some trouble with division. Read page 67 again; then see me." A note asking students to "Look at this one" or "Try this part again" provokes a very different response from the response to a giant red X or an F at the top of the page. In each case, the feedback provided students with specific information about what made them successful or how they might succeed in the future. Value judgments clearly are not being made about students as individuals, but about the strengths and weaknesses of various aspects of their work. Informational feedback also provides gauges against which students can assess their own work. If Alex knows that his last description was wordy, he can try next time to be more precise and economical with his writing. In a classroom atmosphere of acceptance, such comments can be considered valuable help rather than personal judgments or threats to self-esteem.

As more information is gathered about the interactions of evaluation, motivation, and creativity, increased complexity emerges (Amabile, 1996). The prospect of evaluation may depress creativity in shy students more than in less shy students, in less-skilled students more than in more-skilled students. Effects may vary with the activities that precede the creative effort. As the research continues to emerge, it seems sensible to work toward informational rather than controlling feedback in our classroom interactions. It seems likely that it will enhance creativity—and it is certain to be more helpful to our students in their efforts to improve.

Thinking About the Classroom

Look through a stack of papers you corrected recently, preferably those that required some creativity on the part of students. Check to see how often you used controlling versus informational feedback. Try to add informational feedback where necessary.

The second, frequently related, threat to creativity is reward. In many ways this idea runs counter to our intuition, and the role of reward has been subject of considerable debate (Cameron, 2001; Deci, Koestner, & Ryan, 2001a, 2001b). Students like rewards and frequently work hard to receive them. Elementary school teachers have kept sticker companies in business for many years, and secondary school students frequently have been enticed with class parties, honor rolls, and a variety of special privileges. Unfortunately, research tells us that rewards, when promised before a creative effort, can diminish both the motivation to continue similar activities later and the creativity of the activity itself. This can be called contracted-for reward—a reward that becomes the purpose of the activity. Jim, whose dilemma about the substance abuse essay contest was described at the beginning of the chapter, may well have cause for concern. Students who are writing with the possibility of a prize uppermost in their minds may not only produce less-creative essays now, but also may be even less inclined to write later when there is no possibility of reward.

There is a place for rewards in school. There is some evidence that individuals pursuing simple, straightforward tasks or practicing tasks already learned perform better and faster for promised rewards. I suspect I would do a much better job at housecleaning if someone were to pay me for doing it. It also is likely that students practicing math computation, handwriting, verb conjugations, or grammar drills may benefit from some system of rewards. Rewards also may be effective for some students with learning difficulties or a history of school failure. There is even evidence to suggest that reward may be helpful in straightforward divergent thinking tasks such as coming up with multiple uses for an object or multiple ways to use a shape (Eisenberger & Cameron, 1996). However, for complex tasks involving problem solving or creativity, rewards often can be counterproductive, and there is some evidence that the negative effect is more pronounced in children (Deci, Koestner, & Ryan 2001a). Such tasks generally should be interesting and motivating in themselves.

To reward students is to imply that the tasks are dull, to suggest that without an external stimulus, there is no reason students would want to think, experiment, or explore these ideas.

There are times when you may want to reward an especially creative effort. Runco (1993) suggested that such rewards may be particularly important with disadvantaged students. If a reward is occasionally presented after the fact as a pleasant surprise rather than regularly as an expected payoff, it should not negatively affect student motivation. There is some evidence that unexpected rewards may even have a positive influence on creativity (Amabile, 1996). You also may want to devise rewards that point out the inherent value and interest of the task itself. Students who write an excellent story may be rewarded with the opportunity (not the assignment) to spend extra time in writing. Those who devise a particularly original experiment may be allowed to earn more time in the science room. Outstanding art projects may be rewarded with the opportunity to create a personal gallery or compile a special portfolio. These strategies send the message that creative activities are interesting and valuable, and that participating in them is reward in itself.

Fortunately, studies have shown that just as we can use inoculations to protect children from disease, we can apply immunizing strategies to minimize the detrimental effects of reward or other extrinsic motivators (Amabile, 1993a, 1996). In one study, students viewed a videotape in which children and an adult discussed the things the children enjoyed about school. The children served as models of intrinsic motivation, explaining which subjects they enjoyed and the pleasure they obtained from learning. When they were questioned about grades, they stated that good grades were nice, but the really important thing was learning. Exposure to this modeling appeared to protect students from the negative effects of reward, perhaps by limiting its effect as a controller. Presented with a creative task, the students who had received the training did not decline in creativity when they were offered a reward, unlike the students who had not seen the videotape. In fact, students who had seen the videotape were more creative in their products when promised a reward. In this circumstance, intrinsic and extrinsic motivations seemed to work together. If we have similar conversations with students, emphasizing the interesting aspects of a task and minimizing the importance of extrinsic motivators, we may have similar results. Repeated references to tests, grades, prizes, or other external rewards, particularly with students engaged in creative tasks, are likely to have the opposite effect.

Thinking About the Classroom

In chapter 4 you may have made a list of the strategies you used to motivate students in your classroom during the course of a week. If not, try it now. See what proportions of intrinsic and extrinsic motivations you used. Examine the types of motivation you used for different types of tasks. Are you using the same motivation strategies for both creative and mundane tasks? Do you notice any differences in the ways boys and girls respond to your motivators?

Matson (1991) suggested that some students may benefit from having their failed creative efforts rewarded. Matson described a college-level entrepreneurship class (Failure 101) in which students were rewarded for intelligent, fast failure rather than cautious success. Such rewards may be appropriate for students who are afraid to take the risk of trying an original idea for fear of jeopardizing their course grade. Odyssey of the Mind competitions (see chap. 5) give the Ranatra Fusca Creativity Award to a team whose entry demonstrates exceptional creativity, regardless whether it is successful in solving the competition problem. The prize is named after a classification of water spider. It commemorates a vehicle built by students at Glassboro State College in a flotation device competition. The flotation devices were supposed to cross a body of water. Instead of being powered by the usual paddle wheels or sails, the Glassboro entry was designed to walk across the water like a water spider. It capsized before completing the crossing, but did so spectacularly and with considerable originality (Micklus & Micklus, 1986). Prizes such as the Ranatra Fusca may give students a very different idea about rewards!

The fourth problematic factor frequently found in classrooms also is a part of Jim's essay contest dilemma: competition. However, as should be clear by now, the relationships are not straightforward. In two studies, one with children and one with adults, individuals produced less creative products in a competitive situation than in a noncompetitive situation (Amabile, 1982, 1987). Two subsequent studies indicated that girls may be more negatively affected by competition than boys, and that boys may even show higher levels of creativity in some competitive situations (Conti, Collins, & Picariello, 1995, cited in Amabile, 1996). In the world of work, there is some evidence that within-group competition is associated with lower levels of creativity, whereas between-group competition is associated with greater creativity (Amabile, 1988, Amabile & Gryskiewsicz, 1987). Competitions in creative problem solving such as Future Problem Solving or Destination ImagiNation count on between-group competition to enhance teams' creative efforts. Competition also may be less problematic for individuals who have already developed strong intrinsic motivation. For example, the talented pianists studied by Bloom (1985) encountered many competitions in their career paths. Although not focusing on creativity, literature on cooperative learning has provided information on the potentially negative consequences of competition in the classroom. Like most educational dilemmas, however, the answer to competition in the classroom is not simple. It is not enough to tell students, "Use cooperative learning." Some forms of cooperative learning entail considerable competition between groups. Others forms can force students to work together on tasks that do not lend themselves to cooperation. The use of cooperative strategies in the classroom is discussed in greater detail later in this chapter.

Finally, the last common classroom factor that can inhibit creativity is lack of choice. Collins and Amabile (1999) put it bluntly, "The best way to help people maximize their creative potential is to allow them to do something they love" (p. 305). Unfortunately, it is easy for students to go through years of schooling without ever having the opportunity to make meaningful choices about their learning. I have talked to many students about independent study opportunities, asking them what they would like to learn about if they could study anything they liked. As I noted in chapter 3, on far too many occasions when I have asked this, students have gazed at me as if I were from another planet. They simply could not conceive of learning anything voluntarily. Learning was something you did when it was assigned. In school, one learned what the teacher said to learn when the teacher said to learn it. Period.

Students can experience choice in school in a wide range of areas. They can have input into the class rules. They can plan games for the class parties or the destination for the yearly field trip. They can help determine the curriculum focus for particular units and pursue short- and long-term projects around individual interests. Kohn (1993) suggested that increasing student choice affects both students' attitudes and their achievement. Although much research remains to be done, the suggestion is eminently logical. If students are allowed choice in learning tasks, they may work harder and learn more than when tasks are consistently imposed from outside. Once again, a strategy that enhances students' creative thinking may increase their learning as well.

Older students may be more adept at individual research, but even young children can plan and pursue individual goals. One of my graduate students decided to let each of her kindergarten students pick one thing they would most like to investigate. They collected all the ideas, and she promised that before the school year was over, she would help each student learn more about his or her choice. Because she had two half-day kindergartens and more than 50 students, this effort took most of the school year. Projects ranged from learning how to bake a cake (they did, and the class enjoyed it) to investigating which animals run fast. Each project was photographed and recorded in a class album. Her students certainly learned much interesting content that year, but I believe the most valuable lessons were these: You may choose to learn about something you like and learn about it. Learning things you want to learn is fun!

Thinking About the Classroom

In your next unit, think about how you could incorporate more choice into student activities. Plan at least one set of activities that allows students to select topics for further study.

At this point, the research regarding intrinsic motivation and creativity is complex. There is a considerable body of research suggesting that intrinsic motivation enhances creativity and that many sources of extrinsic motivation depress it. But it is not quite that simple. Where intrinsic motivation is well established, for example, in adult professional artists, a promised reward may not be detrimental (for which any institution commissioning an art work can be grateful). It is possible that different types of motivation may be necessary at different stages of the creative process. Where the flexibility demanded in the initial stages of problem finding and idea generation might be best instigated by intrinsic motivation, the persistence necessary to continue a long-term creative project may benefit from the judicious use of external motivators. Certainly, many writers may get through difficult periods thinking about deadlines and promised royalties, even though those factors are not likely to be the ones supporting good problem finding.

Similarly, students engaged in a lengthy science project will be best served by a focus on interest and choice when engaged in selecting a project, but may be encouraged 3 weeks into data gathering by the impending science fair. Some research suggests that the impact of intrinsic versus extrinsic motivators may vary by personality characteristic or gender, with girls more likely to be negatively affected by extrinsic motivators than boys (Amabile, 1996; Baer, 1998).

The types of conversation we have about the intrinsic and extrinsic motivators in school life influence the impact of the motivators on all students. Our daily talk about joy-in-learning or learning-for-reward has far reaching consequences.

The concept of motivational synergy suggests that there are times when intrinsic and extrinsic factors can come together in beneficial ways. If rewards and recognition are used in ways that confirm competence and provide information without undermining a sense of self-determination, they may contribute to later intrinsic motivation. I observed such an incident when a friend's teenage son won special recognition for his writing at an end-of-school-year ceremony. This bright creative young man has learning difficulties that have caused him to struggle in school. To his family's astonishment, he spent the entire summer after that award working on his writing. When questioned by a friend he replied, "Well, I'm a writer, you know." This incident illustrates the paradox of rewards and other extrinsic motivators. In many circumstances, they diminish both motivation and creative responses. Certainly, if this young man had been encouraged to write in order to enter a writing contest he likely would have responded with characteristic reluctance and minimal creative energy. However, in this case, a wise teacher understood that public recognition of his blossoming talent—as a joyous surprise rather than a contracted-for reward—would help forge his identity as a creative writer. Finding the balance of intrinsic and extrinsic factors that best enhances your students' creativity will take similar wisdom, balance, and careful observation.

Flow

Pursuing tasks because they are fun may seem to be a frivolous objective. Yet if we think for more than a moment, we will realize that helping students learn ways to find happiness, and to lead lives that are more meaningful, satisfying, or growth promoting may not just be a goal, but rather the goal, of school. Csikszentmihalyi (1990) summarized decades of research examining happiness, focusing on the concept of optimal experience. Optimal experience is hard to describe, yet easy to imagine. It encompasses those moments when one feels life is in focus, exhilarating, and satisfying. For some, it may be the moment they attain the summit of a mountain. For others, it may be understanding how the melodies of a symphony come together in a unified whole, feeling the colors on a canvas become something new, or experiencing the birth of a child. Each of these experiences adds to our richness and complexity as human beings. In a sense, it helps us create ourselves. In describing these moments, Csikszentmihalyi (1990) wrote:

> Happiness is not something that happens. It is not the result of good fortune or random chance. It is not something that money can buy or power can command. It does not depend on outside events, but rather on how we interpret them. Happiness, in fact, is a condition that must be prepared for, cultivated, and defended privately by each person. People who learn to control inner experience will be able to determine the quality of their lives, which is as close as any of us can come to being happy. (p. 2)

Csikszentmihalyi's (1990) research on optimal experiences began with interviews of thousands of people in all walks of life: adults in Thailand, teenagers in Tokyo, farmers in the Italian Alps, assembly-line workers in Chicago, and others. Later, his research team developed the Experience Sampling Method, which involved having subjects wear electronic pagers for a week and writing down what they were doing and how they felt when the pager signaled. From this enormous collection of data emerged the concept of flow, "the state in which people are so involved in an activity that nothing else seems to matter; the experience itself is so enjoyable that people will do it even at great cost, for the sheer sake of doing it" (Csikszentmihalyi, 1990, p. 4).

The search for flow may be at the heart of much human discontent. For that reason alone, it seems worthy of further consideration. It certainly is related to intrinsic motivation. In fact, flow may be seen as the ultimate example of intrinsic motivation. It also seems to have ties to creativity. Many of the activities that traditionally elicit flow entail creative behavior. Artists painting, musicians practicing, and scientists absorbed in their work are classic examples of individuals in flow. In this discussion, I briefly examine the nature of flow and the conditions that allow it to occur, and then consider how these variables operate in classrooms.

Csikszentmihalyi (1990) described the researchers' surprise at the uniformity of the flow experience in widely varying cultures and activities. The subjects may have been doing very different things—sailing, meditating, painting, or working on an assembly line—but the feelings they described when the activities were at their best had remarkable similarity. Moreover, the reasons they enjoyed the activities also showed many similarities. When these key components were present, the activities caused such a deep sense of enjoyment in people that they were willing to expend enormous amounts of energy just to have the experience.

One cluster of elements found in most flow experiences was that the activities were not random but goal-directed activities that demanded some type of energy and skill. This type of focus is easy to see in physical activities. The mountain climber has a goal, expends considerable energy to attain it, and needs prerequisite skills. However, similar demands can be made of intellectual or psychic energy. The listener who suddenly hears the unity of a symphony is not listening casually. Such an experience demands concentration. It is enhanced by knowledge and skills. The more the listener knows about symphonic structure, the more attuned he or she is to nuances of instrumentation and performance, and the more meaningful and powerful will be the experience.

One key condition of flow is the optimal match it brings between challenge and skill. Too much challenge or too little skill leads to frustration. Too little challenge leads to boredom. To maintain flow, the level of challenge must constantly be raised to match the person's increasing skills.

> In our studies, we found that every flow activity … had this in common: It provided a sense of discovery, a creative feeling transporting the person into a new reality. It pushed the person to higher levels of performance, and led to previously undreamed-of states of consciousness. In short, it transformed the self by making it more complex. In this growth of the self lies the key to flow activities. (Csikszentmihalyi, 1990, p. 74)

These observations have implications for schools. If insufficient skill development precedes a challenging, potentially creative activity, it is likely to be met with frustration and resistance. It is highly unlikely that a student will be intrinsically motivated to pursue a task he or she perceives as impossible. Conversely, too little challenge also impedes motivation. A task that previously may have been motivating becomes less so as one's skills increase and the challenge diminishes. I found this to be true with my fledgling efforts at dulcimer playing and now in my new challenges with my Celtic harp. Although I periodically enjoy reviewing beginning pieces, I do not want to play them for long. I have enjoyed attending dulcimer classes offered by our city's community education program. They have offered me a chance to learn new techniques and play harmonies I cannot manage alone. However, because of the range of experience in the class, pieces that are appropriate challenges for some students are mastered in 10 minutes by others. As long as all of us worked on the same piece, we could not all be challenged. Now, as I attempt to teach myself to play the harp, I have different problems. Because I am alone (and motivated), the level of challenge usually is appropriate, but I must work to find the strategies that are most effective for learning and practicing on my own. These dilemmas seem to provide one link among motivation, autonomy, and flow. Because students will always have varied levels of skills, if we want them to develop intrinsic motivation, perhaps leading to flow, some of the activities they pursue in school must vary from student to student. For students to manage these varied challenges, they must learn to become more autonomous learners.

Flow activities have meaningful goals and some type of feedback that allows participants to know whether they are approaching the goal. Some types of feedback are obvious. The dancer knows when she is leaping higher, and the pianist knows when he is playing faster trills. Other types of feedback are less obvious, but still essential. The painter must be able to look at a piece and tell whether it is working, and an actor must know whether the performance reads or not. These demands seem to tie again to the need for an internal locus of evaluation, standards by which one can judge his or her own product. The demands of flow activities provide one more bit of evidence to support informational assessment and self-evaluation as keys to students' understanding the dimensions and quality of their work, not just its quantitative value.

A second cluster of elements present in most flow experiences are concentration, loss of self-consciousness, and a diminished sense of time. People involved in activities from dance to reading to chess to rock climbing have described a level of concentration that essentially shut out the rest of the world. All of us have had occasions in which we simply could not believe time had flown by so quickly.

In considering how this variable might operate in schools, I was struck by how difficult it is to find time in schools to concentrate long on any task without interruption. It would be interesting to see how motivation and creative efforts might be affected simply by longer uninterrupted blocks of time to work. If a fifth-grade teacher usually scheduled 1 hour each for reading, math, science, and social studies every day, consider how the possible activities might change in one 2-hour block that was used for math or reading (or perhaps science and social studies) on alternate days. Or imagine social studies and reading combined in one interdisciplinary block. The block scheduling used in some middle and secondary schools can facilitate this type of involvement. Instead of scheduling individual classes and teachers, larger groups of students can be scheduled to a group of teachers for a

In flow, a person is so involved in an activity that nothing else seems to matter.

block of time. The time and the students can be regrouped in various ways as needed. Any of these alternatives can provide increased opportunities for intense involvement in creative projects or problem solving without the interruption of the 43-minute bell.

There are many variables that affect student engagement in the learning process. Speaking to Sherer (2002), Csikszentmihalyi suggested that student engagement and flow are more likely when students understand the goal of each lesson and the relevance of the material; receive clear consistent feedback, including that from computer-aided instruction; have the opportunity to solve a problem or work together; and have the opportunity to study content of interest.

Finally, note that the constellations of factors associated with flow do not happen in passive activities. Individuals seldom find flow watching television or lying for hours in a hammock. Although enjoyment often is found in recreation, it also is found in work—and in recreation that requires work. Helping students to find this truth—that the motivation, involvement, energy, and creativity we seek from them can bring them happiness—also can bring focus and energy to our own efforts.

Thinking About the Classroom

Individuals in flow have reported a balance between the challenge of the task and their skill level. Achieving that balance for a diverse student population can be difficult. Examine your plans for the next week. How many times during the week have you planned activities that challenge each child at his or her own level? Talk about that challenge with some colleagues and share ideas.

CLASSROOM ORGANIZATION, MOTIVATION, AND AUTONOMY: TEACHING FOR INDEPENDENCE

Organizing a classroom to facilitate motivation and autonomy implies many things. Certainly it demands a classroom climate that accepts diversity, welcomes new ideas, respects questions, and promotes exploration. There also are logistic elements that can support student creativity and independence. Among these are strategies that allow students to spend part of each school day working without specific teacher direction. Neither smooth classroom organization nor students' skills of independent work happen automatically. If most of your teaching has been teacher-directed whole-group instruction, your transition to a less directive mode will be smoothest if you make it gradually. This section examines strategies for moving students toward more autonomy and choice in classroom activities. It discusses teaching students the skills of independent learning and the use of centers and contracts. It also deals with the physical arrangement of the classroom. These strategies work best in a classroom context wherein differentiated instruction—instruction varied to meet the needs of different students—is the norm. In a classroom based on differentiated instruction, students sometimes work together, sometimes individually, and sometimes in groups, depending on the need of the moment. Students of varying skill levels can be challenged by varying activities. A full discussion of differentiated instruction is beyond this book. An excellent overview can be found in *The Differentiated Classroom* (Tomlinson, 1999).

Teachers' experience with independent learning strategies varies enormously, affected greatly by the time and place the teachers began their careers. As the educational pendulum has swung back and forth, individually guided instruction, individualized instruction, centers, management plans, and a host of other educational buzz words have come and gone. As with many innovations, when one aspect of a practice falls out of favor, the rest of it often follows. As a result, some teachers have had experiences with a variety of independent learning techniques. Others, whose training encompassed a different swing of the pendulum, have had none. If you have a great deal of experience teaching with a variety of grouping patterns, you may want to skim the next section. You probably will find the ideas there familiar. If you are accustomed to whole-group teaching and would like to vary the pattern occasionally, but are not sure how to make the transition, read on!

Teaching Skills of Independent Learning

If students are to have opportunities to identify and pursue questions and interests and to develop creative products, all students in the class must be taught the skills of independent working. Not only is independent work a logistical necessity if students are to work at varied levels of challenge, but as chapter 3 explained, many creative people need time alone to pursue their creative endeavors effectively. The skills of independent learning are not just for the most able, the most creative, or the most motivated. It may be that such students ultimately have more opportunities to work independently. But if you are to interact with all your students in various groupings, at some point, each student must be able to work without your direct guidance.

The first key to making the transition to independent student work is realizing that you need to teach students how to work independently. It is not sufficient to tell them to be independent; you must teach them how to do it. In most cases, you may start this process by planning a series of lessons on independent work time. These lessons should be planned and executed with as much care, planning, and practice as any other teaching unit. Major topics should include the following:

- Becoming independent
- Uses of independent work time (sometimes for the whole class, sometimes for a small group, and sometimes for an individual)
- Planning your time (e.g., complete assigned tasks before going on to independent projects or choice activities)
- What to do if you are stuck or do not understand a task

- How to signal the teacher for assistance or a conference (the teacher may not be available immediately, and students should know what to do in the meantime)
- Expectations about noise, conversation, and other disruptions
- Rules about materials (what may be used and how to return materials)
- Choice activities and what to do when tasks are completed.

No set procedures are better than all others. There is no single best strategy for students to follow if they are stuck or do not understand a task. The key is that there must be a strategy. A friend teaching first grade had students place small balls of clay at the corners of their desks. They made signs on popsicle sticks that read, "Help me!" or "I'm stuck." In that class, students were instructed to use the following procedure if they were stuck during independent work time: (a) put up your sign; (b) go on to something you know how to do; (c) if there is nothing left that you know how to do, read your library book until Mrs. K. can help you.

Other classes have very different procedures for the same dilemma. Some students are told to ask three people before asking the teacher. Some classes are divided into teams. The teacher may not be consulted unless no one on the team can answer the question. Other classes have sign-up sheets for requesting assistance. The key in each case is that the procedure must be carefully taught. Mrs. K's first-grade students spent 20 minutes learning, modeling, and practicing using the signs before their first independent work period. The need for specific instruction, modeling, and practice, however, is not limited to young children. Even secondary students who have had limited experience with independent work benefit from careful instruction in the procedures and expectations for this time. Once the procedures are established, independent work time can be initiated. The goal is to move students from seat work—during which they may be quiet, but for which all activities are chosen, directed, and monitored by the teacher—to a period during which many activities are planned, organized, and implemented by students.

The first time you have independent work time, do not try to introduce any new content. The important lesson is independence. Give the students an assignment (preferably one with enough challenge that some students may practice getting assistance) and two or three choices of activities. During the work time, do not try to give other instruction. You may wish to circulate and give students feedback on their independent work skills, but do not assist with content except through the procedures established for inde-

Students must be taught to work independently.

pendent work time. After the independent work time, discuss the results with the class. Identify areas of difficulty and devise strategies to reduce them. Students should be aware of independence as a goal and monitor their progress toward that end.

The next stage in establishing independent work time involves having students work independently while you give your attention to individuals or small groups. This is a good opportunity to pull together groups needing practice in a particular skill or to spend time with individuals needing assessment or help with projects. Be sure you are situated so you can easily monitor the class while you are working with small groups. It is important that students know you are aware of all the activities in the room. Try not to interrupt the group to answer individual questions, but refer students to the procedures for independent work time. You may wish to circulate among instructional groups and answer questions.

Remember that independent work skills are complex and will be built over time. Early in the year, most whole-class-choice activities should be fairly simple, building in complexity as the year progresses. You may wish to progress from activities not tied directly to academic content (art activities, free reading, or brain teasers) to activities reinforcing class content (games centering on a current unit) to activities that explore new content (interest development centers, or independent projects). Of course, some students probably will be ready for individual independent projects before the rest of the class. Providing the varied levels of challenge necessary to build intrinsic motivation in students is one purpose of independent work.

As the year progresses, you may wish to introduce other independent work skills. These might include directions for working at centers (when they may be used, how many students may use them at a time, and other rules) and instruction on planning an individual project (choosing a topic, creating a time line, making daily plans, and other steps).

Students also may become responsible for planning and working independently for longer periods. Most students from intermediate grades and up and some younger students can learn to plan independent work responsibilities that span several days. This, too, necessitates instruction. If students have daily math assignments, a social studies assignment spanning 5 days, and an individual research project, they will need teaching, modeling, and practice in dividing the tasks into manageable chunks and deciding what to do each day. You might consider modeling several alternative plans. For example, given a 90-minute work time, Student A might decide to do one page of math each day. He might start each work period with math, work 20 minutes on social studies, and reserve the remaining time for his independent project. On Thursday, he could evaluate his progress in social studies and decide whether he needs to allot extra time to complete the project by Friday. Student B might prefer working in longer blocks of time. Perhaps, too, she has an appointment to interview the principal for her independent project on Wednesday. She might decide to try to complete three pages of math on Monday. Tuesday might be devoted entirely to her social studies project. Wednesday could be spent doing the interview and recording her notes. On Thursday, she could try to complete two pages of math and evaluate her progress in order to plan for Friday.

Either of these schedules could result in assignments completed on schedule in a style that suits a particular student. When you teach students to schedule their time, help them understand that many routes are possible as long as the goal is attained. Resist the temptation to point out the best schedule. Although some schedules are clearly inappropriate (such as "Do it all on Friday"), many are acceptable. The one that seems obviously superior to you probably suits your learning style, but may not be right for every student. One fifth-grade teacher discussed planning daily work time with her students. A student with a diagnosed attention disorder found that for him, the best plan was to do five or six math problems, a little English, and some science or social studies, then a few more math problems, beginning the cycle again. In this manner he was able to complete all his assignments successfully, something he had never been able to do when the teacher insisted that he finish one task before beginning another.

Thinking About the Classroom

Visit a teacher who uses centers in his or her classroom or invite such a teacher to visit your college class. Talk about getting started, rules for independent learning, and how the centers are used.

Centers, Contracts, and Independent Learning

Two of the most common vehicles for implementing independent learning activities are centers and contracts. Each of these strategies has many possible variations and implementations in diverse subjects and grade levels. In this section, I describe general definitions, uses, and patterns. It will be up to you to adapt this general framework to the needs of your students.

Centers.   Initially, I make a distinction between three kinds of centers: learning centers, interest development centers, and exploratory centers.

Physically, learning centers and interest development centers look much the same. Each has a designated area of the classroom designed to facilitate independent work on a particular topic or discipline. Centers may be constructed in study carrels on table tops, on a pair of desks in the corner, or on an easel, a cutting board, a refrigerator box, or virtually any structure that can store materials and provide directions. The difference between learning centers and interest development centers is the intent. A learning center is designed to introduce and reinforce a specific part of the regular curriculum. An interest development center is designed to spur students' curiosity and interest in areas outside the regular curriculum. Exploratory centers are designed for more flexible use, typically in primary classrooms. In these centers are variety of materials are available for exploration but without specific directions or preplanned. activities.

Because a learning center is designed to reinforce core curriculum, activities at a learning center are frequently required of students. However, the nature of a center makes it easy to provide choice within the requirements and to vary the difficulty of assignments for individual students. In constructing a center, the first decision you must make is the topic. Some centers are focused on particular skills such as reading maps or solving story problems. Some may be focused on specific materials such as Cuisenaire rods or geoboards. Still others are directed toward areas of content such as birds, weather, or mobiles.

Once you have determined the topic, your next step is to gather available materials. If the topic is weather, you would start by gathering books, web sites, computer programs, and any other available materials on weather. Next, you would brainstorm a list of possible activities that could be pursued independently by individuals or small groups. Typically, activities focus on or branch off from key concepts and generalizations planned for the unit. Activities should include opportunities for data gathering, problem solving, individual research, and creative expression, in addition to more traditional vocabulary practice and fact-gathering exercises.

Your unit on weather might be planned around three general content clusters: basic causes of weather and weather forecasting, safety during extreme weather, and changes in weather trends. The list of possible activities could include a crossword puzzle of weather vocabulary and a worksheet on building a barometer from the science text. You might bookmark web sites that allow students access to up-to-date radar and worldwide weather information. In addition, you might decide that students could gather and graph local temperature and pressure data for a week, research and report on global warming, design a brochure to teach young children about tornado safety, create a series of paintings of cloud types, examine state trends in temperature and precipitation over the past 10 years, and so on. Each of these activities could be carried out independently and would reinforce one of the content emphases for this unit. You would need to decide which activities might be done during class time with teacher supervision, which will be required center activities, and which will be electives. You also must decide if and how assignments will be varied to meet students' needs.

You could organize the center activities in many ways. You might decide to glue the directions for each kind of activity on a different-colored card. Red cards could be for core activities, blue for enrichment activities, and green for more challenging activities. You could give a blanket assignment, such as requiring each student to complete three red cards and at least two blue or green cards. This requirement still would allow choice within a well-defined structure. Alternatively, you could vary assignments for individual students. Some students might be required to complete only the red cards, with additional activities optional. Others, who had demonstrated prior knowledge or ability in this area, might be required to choose at least one green card. It also would be necessary to provide a title and some kind of backdrop for the center using a poster, bulletin board, large box, or other type of display. This part of the construction can be regarded as advertising for the center. It helps define the area encompassed by the center and serves to provoke student interest and curiosity. The same activities will be received differently if they are presented in a different setting. If your weather activities are written in pencil on white index cards and placed in a file box, they are not apt to generate a lot of excitement. The same activities on multicolored cards displayed with a collection of books and weather instruments, a colorful poster of pictures of storms, and the title "Weird Weather Wonders" may be received quite differently.

Regardless how activities are assigned or organized, several factors can allow students to use centers more smoothly. Each activity should be accompanied by clear directions. You probably should demonstrate the complex activities when a center is introduced, but do not depend on students' remembering the directions for a variety of center activities. Even young children should be given directions. For nonreaders, rebus directions or directions on audiotape not only allow students to pursue activities without teacher assistance, but also accustom them to looking to the materials rather than the teacher for direction.

If some activities have correct answers, set up as many of these as possible to be self-correcting. If activities are not self-correcting or you want to see students' work, be sure to designate a location where products can be placed for your later attention. For the center to function smoothly, students must be able to pursue and complete the center activities and check their products without immediate teacher intervention. It is important to decide in advance how many students may use a learning center at one time and whether center materials must be used in place or may be taken to other parts of the room. For older students, a sign may be used to designate the number of students permitted at a given center. Younger students may retrieve colored chips or clothespins from a central location and bring them to the center. For example, green chips might be used for the weather center. When no green chips are available, students would know they must work elsewhere until someone has finished in the center and returned a green chip. The chip system works particularly well if you plan to change the activities at a center periodically. If a new center activity is particularly messy or demands a large amount of space, the number of chips can be reduced.

If the learning center activities are required, you need to consider how to keep records of completed activities. Certainly, if some activities must be checked, you can record them as you would any other student work. If graphs of the week's temperatures are required, students could deposit these in a basket, and you could evaluate them at your convenience. However, other activities might not produce a physical product (e.g., a role-playing or discussion activity) or may produce a product that is not easily saved (e.g., a completed jigsaw puzzle or a demonstration). In these cases, it may be more important for you to record the activities that have been pursued than to evaluate the end products. One possible way to organize such records is to provide students with a list of center activities. Students could check off activities as they are completed. If you are concerned about honesty in reporting, a second student's initials could also be required. Younger children can color in numbered shapes to indicate completed activities. For example, if a student completed the activity labeled "2" at the fish center, he or she would color the spot numbered 2 on a picture of a fish. Alternatively, a sign-up sheet near specific activities could be used to record students' participation.

Finally, you will need to decide when the center is to be used. Some teachers plan for students to use centers when other assignments are complete. The problem with this arrangement is that some students may never complete required assignments in time to work on center activities. If center activities are considered important, other arrangements should be considered. One option is to have students rotate in and out of center time. One middle level math teacher divided his class into three groups, which were changed for each unit, and divided the class period into two sections.

At any given time, one group was working with the teacher, one was at a learning center on problem solving, and one was using computers. The teacher rotated instruction among the groups, meeting with groups 2 out of every 3 days. The same type of organization is possible in an elementary school classroom during skills instruction. The teacher could meet with a group needing a particular skill while part of the class works on seat work and part works at the centers. The groups could rotate until all the students have worked at the centers. Still other teachers, who have multiple centers, schedule specific times when everyone pursues center activities.

Some teachers use centers as a key organizing feature of their curriculum. Such classrooms typically feature multiple centers that are less elaborate than the weather center described earlier, often changed on a weekly basis. One traditional way is to organize centers around subject areas. The result is a math center, a language arts center, an art center, a science center, and so on, with each center providing support materials for studies in these areas. Another way to use subject-focused centers is to organize all activities around a thematic unit or shared book. For example, a first-grade class reading about the three bears may do math activities adding bears, science studies on bear habitats, writing activities on adjectives describing bears, and so on. A third approach to organizing multiple centers is to create centers around multiple intelligences rather than subject areas—in this case perhaps writing about bears, creating a dance in the style of a bear's walk, measuring out the size of a father, mother, and baby bear, and so forth. In classrooms with multiple centers, the general principles of organization are similar to those of single learning centers. Students who have the chance to organize their time using multiple centers have an exceptional opportunity to develop as independent workers.

In most ways, the construction and use of interest development centers parallel those of learning centers. They, too, start with a topic. However, the topic generally is not part of the regular curriculum. It may be selected because of student interest, as an offshoot of a unit, or as an extension of some local or national event. Next, activities are listed, but because the intent is to spur student interests rather than reinforce content, the activities are likely to be more wide-ranging and less tied to specific generalizations. If I were to plan an interest development center on photography, I could include activities on constructing cameras, taking and developing pictures, the lives and art of great photographers, the development of photography, historical research based on photographs, the use of photography in motion research, stop-action photography, the development of moving pictures, and on and on. My goal would not be to have everyone in the class understand the basic processes of photography, but to have as many students as possible find some question, idea, or activity that looks interesting enough to investigate. I would want to reinforce the idea that " we sometimes we choose to learn more about something because it is interesting."

Because the goal of the center is to pique interest, the activities in an interest development center generally are optional. Some teachers require students to try at least one activity. This approach parallels Mom's insistence that her children try at least one spoonful of a new vegetable—they might like it! You will need to decide whether requiring some activities will lessen or enhance your students' interest.

You also need to decide how much record keeping and assessment is necessary to meet the goals of this type of center. Some teachers prefer to keep track of the number and variety of activities explored by various students. Others feel they can gauge the general success of the center by observation and do not need more detailed records. If interest development centers are used as an occasional source of enrichment, you probably need only minimal record keeping. If they are used as part of a concerted effort to help students identify and pursue interests, you may want to track patterns of student involvement. When you know which students are making and following through on independent learning choices at a variety of centers, you can more easily gauge whether uninvolved students lack independent learning skills and motivation or simply are not interested in a particular topic. Noting the types of activities that are most successful can give you clues to areas of student interests and needed skills.

As with learning centers, if you value the message the interest development center sends, it is important to schedule some time for all students to explore it. Because the content of interest development centers is not part of the required curriculum, it is tempting to view it as superfluous and appropriate only when the real work is completed. From my perspective, beginning to make choices about learning is part of students' real work and it is important for all students to have that opportunity. Interest development centers offer very appropriate activities for students who have completed other assignments or have previously mastered the day's topic for instruction. However, I hope you will not limit their use to able students or those who work quickly. The lessons of choice and independence are important for everyone. Work in interest development centers can also be scheduled as part of a planned rotation of activities or as a specifically designated time for exploration, allowing all students to benefit from such activities.

In early grades, particularly in prekindergarten through first grade, classrooms may be organized using *exploratory centers*, or free play areas. These areas typically are designed not to organize specific tasks, but to allow students to interact with materials in ways that provide background or reinforcement for concept development. Planned well, they set the stage for many teachable moments and interaction with materials from a variety of perspectives. For example, young students studying their community might have a costume area that encourages them to role play community workers, a block area with various vehicles, or a play store complete with goods to sell.

With careful planning and teacher interaction, exploratory areas help students develop and practice key concepts through play. Teachers observing children interacting with materials in these areas have the opportunity to help students label concepts appropriately and develop verbal skills. Many preschool teachers use interactions at the block area to help students learn concepts such as "over," "under," and "through." Conversations within exploratory centers also give teachers the opportunity to model flexible thinking. A teacher who uses a plastic bowl as a hat, a steering wheel, and a bed for a stuffed dog—in addition to its typical use in the kitchen—engages in the social interactions Vygotsky (1960, also Smolucha, 1992) described as developing creativity through interactive play.

Contracts. Learning contracts provide a structure for a student and teacher to agree on a series of tasks to be completed in a given time frame. Many contracts allow students to work independently through a body of required content, and then carry out an individual project during times when part of the class is involved in other activities. The appropriate complexity and duration of contracts vary enormously with the students' maturity and experience with independent work. The first independent contracts completed by primary school students should entail no more than one or two work periods. Short time periods also are appropriate for many older students who have never worked outside of whole-group teacher-directed lessons before. As with other aspects of independent learning, students must develop facility with contracts gradually, starting with simple short-term forms and advancing to more complex tasks.

Most contracts entail specific assignments from the regular curriculum and optional activities that may be drawn from the curriculum or planned around student interests. Regular curriculum assignments may be specific pages to be completed or concepts that must be mastered in preparation for some type of evaluation. When basic skills are part of the agreement, many contracts can be tailored to individual students' needs through the use of preassessment. Figure 7.1 shows a contract that might

LEARNING CONTRACT

CHAPTER: _____

NAME: _____

✓	Page/Concept	✓	Page/Concept	✓	Page/Concept
___	___	___	___	___	___
___	___	___	___	___	___
___	___	___	___	___	___
___	___	___	___	___	___

● ●

ENRICHMENT OPTIONS: _____

Special instructions

YOUR IDEA:

● ●

WORKING CONDITIONS

Teacher's signature _____

Student's signature _____

FIG. 7.1.   Learning contract. From *Teaching Gifted Kids in the Regular Classroom* (p. 24), by S. Winebrenner, 1992, Minneapolis, MN: Free Spirit. Copyright © 1992 by Free Spirit Publishing Inc. Reprinted with permission.

be used as part of many units, particularly those emphasizing specific skills. After preassessment, the teacher can check the content an individual student needs.

Optional activities might be planned by the teacher or student. Older students more experienced in independent learning should have considerable input in planning the optional activities. Open-ended activities based on student interests and those emphasizing problem finding, problem solving, and expression of creative ideas should be an important part of this section of the contract. Figure 7.2 is a simple, short-term contract. It might be used as the first independent study opportunity for both student and teacher. Although it represents a short period, it still includes clearly designated activities and opportunities for individual questioning and investigation.

Contract activities can be pursued during any independent work time: while other students are involved in skills instruction, when other assignments have been completed, or any other time designated by the teacher as

---

Independent Learning Contract

I will learn about _____ rockets _____

The questions I will answer are   What makes rockets go so fast?

How high has the highest rocket gone?

How can they control a rocket that is already in space?

I will investigate by   reading books about rockets
talking to Mr. Connett about his model rockets

I will share what I learn by   making a poster with a rocket
diagram and information

If I need help I will   sign up on Ms. Toronto's list

I will complete my investigation by   next Friday

_____
Student Signature

_____
Teacher Signature

FIG. 7.2.   Independent learning contract.

appropriate for independent work. It is not necessary for all students to be working on individual contracts in any given subject. You may want to begin with a small group of students who have demonstrated independent working skills. As the year progresses, the opportunity to work on independent contracts can be expanded or rotated to other students. Other examples of contracts can be found in *Teaching Gifted Kids in the Regular Classroom* (Winebrenner, 1992) and in numerous teacher education texts published in the early to mid-1970s.

Thinking About the Classroom

Contracts are one way to give students diverse levels of challenge and to promote autonomy. Plan a contract for one or more students. You may want to have several of your friends try this strategy with their classes and compile the contracts into a booklet of samples to share.

Helping students become autonomous, confident, and self-motivated is an important part of structuring a classroom to support and enhance creativity. Amid all the emphasis on independence, however, it is important that you not lose sight of the value to students of sharing creative activities and insights. The classroom must be an interactive community of autonomous learners, an environment Pace-Marshall (1993) called a "learning community."

Csikszentmihalyi and Sawyer (1993) described the social aspects of creativity in an interview study of eminent creative adults. Often students and adults envision creative individuals as solitary geniuses secluded in a studio or lab. In fact, Csikszentmihalyi and Sawyer found that every stage of the creative process is heavily dependent on social interaction. One scientist used the metaphor of a door.

> Science is a very gregarious business; it's essentially the difference between having this door open and having it shut. If I'm doing science I have the door open. That's kind of symbolic, but it's true. You want to be all the time talking with people .... It's only by interacting with other people in the building that you get anything interesting done, it's essentially a communal enterprise. (p. 9)

Although not every creative person or product requires the same amount of social interaction, students should understand that sharing thoughts, experimenting with ideas, and asking questions of peers are important parts of both individual and collaborative creativity. The interactive teaching strategies described in chapters 5 and 6, group-learning activities, and discussions of individual creative efforts all can help to build the sense of a creative community. You also may want to structure discussions around independent work time or class think tanks to which students bring ill-structured problems, research dilemmas, or creative ideas. Achieving a balance between autonomy and community is a delicate business, but an essential part of the creative process.

Classroom Arrangement, Autonomy, and Creativity

The physical arrangement of the classroom can send messages to students about the role of independence, choice, and creativity in the class. Desks that all face the teacher make large-group instruction simpler. They also send a message to students that the source of information is found in one place.

If students are sometimes to work independently or in teams, these practices can be facilitated through classroom arrangements that make them convenient. If students are to pursue independent research, they should have easy access to reference books. If they are to work on long-term projects, they must have safe places to store their projects and materials between work periods. If they are to develop openness to sensory experiences, they need to be exposed to a variety of materials. Isenberg and Jalongo (1993) suggested that we examine the sensory experiences of the classroom from the students' eye level. Items that are interesting from an adult perspective may be much less interesting seen from below or from an awkward angle. (Think of most crib mobiles!) If students are to create a variety of products, they need materials, models, and clear directions for product options.

Even in a small classroom, you may want to consider a variety of work areas for various purposes. Both elementary and secondary classrooms might have an area for small-group skills instruction that still allows other students space to work undisturbed. If the classroom is too small to provide this type of space while still allowing for whole-group instruction, it is possible to have two or three basic classroom arrangements. You might have one arrangement for whole-class lessons, one for team work, and another for independent work time. The basic pattern might vary from day to day. If patterns are designed to demand minimal moving of furniture, students can be taught to make the transition. You might say, "Today we'll need to be working in teams. Please turn your desks into team formation. We will begin work in 1 minute." Such transitions cause momentary chaos, but the end result allows you to conduct class activities in a room arrangement that supports the activities.

Some students with an intense need for concentration benefit from personal study areas in which they can pursue individual projects. Even a cardboard box on a table can be made into a study carrel. Ongoing projects also necessitate places for storing work in progress. Milk crates or food storage containers can be used to keep young students' projects. Older students may need access to locked cabinets for the safekeeping of long-term efforts. These precautions are particularly important when incomplete projects are messy, nontraditional, or difficult to understand at first glance. One of my most haunting teaching memories is the look on the faces of a group of elementary school students who came in one morning and found their project, representing several weeks of effort, missing from the back counter. They had been planning and building artifacts for a simulated ancient civilization. A custodian had seen the pile of undistinguished art materials on a counter near a waste basket, assumed it was junk, and thrown it away. After that experience, I have been much more systematic and careful about classroom storage.

You also may want to consider mailboxes or other communication vehicles that allow you to provide individual contracts, assignments, or other comments without using a large amount of time passing out paper. Some teachers have created a system of mail slots for each student. Others use individual pocket folders to disseminate assignments. If the folders are filled before class, the materials in each one can differ slightly. You can easily distribute the right folder to each student so students do not feel conspicuous and you do not spend time juggling piles of assignments while students are waiting.

It also is helpful to have a clear system for both students and teachers to indicate the need for an individual conference. You may want to consider a place where students can sign up to report progress or ask for assistance on a project. It is equally important for students to know when you want to see them. One teacher, fortunate enough to have a paraprofessional in her classroom, made a list of all her students' names. She clipped a clothespin of one color next to the names of students with whom she wanted the paraprofessional to check, with relevant folders stacked nearby. A clothespin of different color reminded her of students she wished to see herself. A similar system could certainly be used by a teacher alone.

Many other communication systems and classroom arrangements can facilitate flexibility in class activities as well as autonomy and motivation in students. A system that works well for one teacher may seem burdensome and unwieldy to another. The particular strategies themselves are not as important as the messages they send. Schools are full of unspoken curricula: values, ideas, and assumptions that shape students' lives within those walls. It is important to examine the simple things that build classroom life—the arrangement of the furniture, the possibilities for communication, the materials that surround students during their hours in school—and to make sure that the unspoken messages tell them of their importance, potential, and ability to grow and take on responsibility as independent learners.

Classroom Groups and Cooperative Learning

Classroom grouping patterns have been the subject of vigorous debate in the educational community. Negative reactions to rigid ability grouping and ineffective educational practices in lower tracked classes have resulted in calls to limit or eliminate ability grouping in schools. This trend has raised concerns about the potential of heterogeneous classes to challenge high-ability students (Allan, 1991; Kulik, 1991; Slavin, 1991). Reactions to the debate have caused confusion and in some cases extreme positions that appear unwarranted by either research or reason. It is hard to imagine any experienced teacher who believes that all students in any class need identical experiences in all subjects. It is equally hard to believe any educator would think that high-ability students or students with other special needs should never mix in heterogeneous groups. Yet the application of grouping research sometimes seems to take this dichotomous approach: either grouping is good or bad; either we group students or we do not.

Confusing the issue even further is the practice of cooperative learning. Cooperative learning, an effective educational practice in many situations, has sometimes been proposed as the magic bullet to solve the educational debate. "If we would just put students in cooperative groups," goes the argument, "all these grouping problems would disappear." I believe even the most ardent supporter of cooperative learning would view this position as simplistic. Cooperative learning, as any other educational practice, can be used well or poorly. It can be used in ways that support the development of autonomy and creativity, or it can be used in ways that undermine them, as can grouping. Either practice can be used in many different ways that are appropriate for varying situations. Sometimes the strategies overlap; sometimes they do not. A full-blown discussion of the issues of grouping, cooperative learning, and the needs of students with varying abilities is beyond the scope of this book. This section examines how grouping and cooperative learning may be used in ways consistent with theories underlying the development of creativity.

Groups in Schools.   The most reasonable approach to grouping in schools is to avoid debating whether we should group and to decide what grouping arrangements best meet the needs of a given student group for a particular activity. The effectiveness of rigid, long-term grouping based on ability can be questioned, but flexible, within- or between-class groupings based on particular academic needs is associated with increased achievement (Slavin, 1987).

In deciding how various groupings may impact motivation for creativity, we should consider at least four points. First, if students are to view themselves as increasingly autonomous learners and problem solvers, they must spend some of their time in school working outside teacher-directed whole-group lessons. Second, if students are to develop intrinsic motivation leading to flow, there must be a match between their skills and the level of challenge. Students have widely differing skill levels necessitating a variety of challenges. Third, we know that choice increases both motivation and quality in creative products. If students have choices, they clearly cannot always be working on identical tasks. Finally, competition can inhibit motivation and quality in creative efforts. Creating a classroom atmosphere that minimizes competition necessitates some type of cooperation. Cooperation demands someone with whom to cooperate.

Each of these factors provides support for diverse patterns of grouping in classrooms. If students are to have choice, challenge, and autonomy, they must spend at least part of the school day outside whole-group instruction, either as individuals or small groups. If they are to learn cooperation, they must spend time in cooperative groupings. No one pattern precludes the others or meets all students' needs. Most students probably should spend parts of the school day working in larger, heterogeneous groups. They also should spend some time on individual tasks, projects, and interests and some time in small groups. The small groups may be heterogeneous or homogeneous, skills-based or interest-based, depending on the needs of the students and the demands of the task. At times, you may want students to work in groups based on the need for a particular skill. This type of grouping is particularly appropriate for basic skills instruction or instruction in areas that have been introduced previously but not mastered by all students.

Few things will kill motivation more quickly than repeated practice in a long-mastered skill or instruction in a task that is well beyond a student's current skill level. More targeted groupings can provide an appropriate level of challenge (see Tomlinson, 1999, for additional detail.)

In addition to specific skills needs, some complex tasks are best suited to homogeneous groups. Particularly challenging problem-solving activities or projects demanding research in advanced resources may provide an appropriate challenge for students with demonstrated abilities or interests in a particular area, but they could be unsuitable for a whole-class task. At times, groups of students with more limited skills can benefit from tackling a research task that presents a challenge to them, but would be less challenging to others. Managing the task alone can give them chances for problem solving and persistence that they might not have in a more heterogeneous group.

At other times, groups may be based on students' expressed interests. Sharan and Sharan's (1992) group investigation procedures suggest allowing students to generate questions they would like to investigate about a particular topic. Students then can be divided into groups according to the questions they would most like to investigate. A class studying the Renaissance may be divided into groups examining Renaissance art, music, and dance; weaponry and warfare; or other areas of interest. Some students may want to learn about culture and events in Asia or Africa during the time of the Renaissance in Western Europe. The groups may be heterogeneous in skills, but homogeneous in interests. There also are tasks appropriate for groups that are heterogeneous in many dimensions. Much of the literature on cooperative learning stresses the importance of heterogeneous groups. Students in such groups can learn to help one another, to get along with those who are different from themselves, and to understand the value of diversity. Unfortunately, improperly used heterogeneous groups also can cause a host of problems. Less able students can rely on more able students to carry out the tasks for them. More able students can become resentful or bored at having to explain information repeatedly to team members that they mastered easily themselves. If heterogeneous groups are to provide motivation, challenge, and interdependence for all students, cooperative tasks must be carefully planned. Fortunately, many of the factors that characterize effective tasks for heterogeneous groups also are associated with creativity.

Slavin (1990) stated that appropriate cooperative learning activities have group goals and individual accountability. The group as a whole must complete some task together, but the information to be learned or the skills to be acquired must be mastered by each individual in the group. Individual assessment ensures that no group member can slide by, assuming that others will carry the load. These certainly are important factors. However, the teacher must look carefully at the tasks and make sure that the interdependence assumed in group goals is real. Sometimes an effort toward group tasks produces group efforts that are more illusion than substance.

This type of difficulty is particularly likely in tasks that are closed. Such tasks have a single correct answer or procedure that the group is to discern. In tasks of this kind, it is likely that some students will already know the correct answer or deduce it in very little time. Other students will not. Here there is no true interdependence. Students who do not know the answer are dependent on those who do. Those who already know the answer receive little academic benefit from their participation in the group.

Imagine a spelling team whose group goal is to have the highest possible total score on Friday's test. Jan received a score of 100% on Monday's pretest of the spelling words. Ben received a 50%. During the week, Jan and her teammates work hard to help Ben improve his score. In this case, Jan may be dependent on Ben for her team to reach a goal or receive a reward, but not to improve her spelling. Similarly, if Jan and Ben are together in a social studies group, each may be assigned to look up specific information on Sitting Bull. Jan may be a fluent reader and able to manage the research easily. Ben may work much more slowly or need help from team members to make his contribution. If the task is simple fact gathering, Jan could have carried it out more efficiently on her own. She then could have gone on to a more appropriately challenging task. In neither of these tasks did all the students really need each other. Some of the students could have completed the assignments more easily alone. Any student in the group could tell you who helped whom, who were the teachers, and who were the students. This type of dependent (rather than interdependent) relationship can undermine both the desirable level challenge and the understanding of all individuals as important contributors that is the heart of cooperative learning.

Cohen (1986) suggested guidelines for cooperative learning tasks that avoid these pitfalls. The key is that cooperative learning tasks, particularly those for heterogeneous groups, should be tasks for which group participation is a genuine asset for everyone in the group. This emphasis reflects the way groups function in business and society. Automobile manufacturers do not typically use groups to fill out reports or gather facts. Those tasks are more efficiently done by individuals acting alone. Groups are important in design teams, in think tanks, and in many other problem-solving situations.

A good group task is one that benefits from many strengths and points of view. Cohen's guidelines may be grouped in the following clusters.

1. Cooperative learning tasks should have more than one answer or more than one path toward a solution. No student should be able to come to the task with the solution in hand. Imagine that instead of gathering facts about Sitting Bull as a cooperative learning exercise, the class had the opportunity to learn from a movie or class discussion the basic facts surrounding Sitting Bull, Geronimo, and the events at the Little Big Horn. Cooperative groups then might be charged with designing a suitable monument for the battle site at Little Big Horn. There is no simple solution to this task. Each student's opinion could be valuable in helping the group decide on a focus and perspective for their monument.

2. Cooperative learning tasks should be intrinsically motivating and offer challenge to all students. They should work together to create a worthwhile product, not simply to earn team points. Intrinsically motivating tasks, such as the monument assignment, require students to make choices about interesting topics at a level of challenge suitable for their knowledge and skills.

3. Group tasks should allow students to make different kinds of contributions by demanding a variety of abilities and skills. Jan may be able to read and analyze reference materials easily. Ben may be able to see issues from more than one point of view. Sally may be able to draw and Chris to organize materials and keep the group on the task. Each contribution is needed and valuable.

4. Cooperative learning tasks should involve multiple media and multisensory experiences in addition to traditional text. Complex experiences are good education under any circumstances. In a heterogeneous group, they increase the probability that each student will have the opportunity to take in information and express ideas in the form that best matches his or her learning style.

Complex, open-ended tasks such as these benefit from diverse student interests, ideas, and skills. Although some students still may prefer learning independently, as do many creative individuals, group efforts of this type are much more likely to help students see the value of diverse contributions than activities that purport to be group efforts, but in fact merely demand that some students tutor others. By happy coincidence, complex open-ended tasks also are supportive of the skills and attitudes associated with creativity. Involving students in a balance of individual and group activities that can support such skills and attitudes will help them develop motivation and autonomy while learning the skills necessary for cooperation.

Thinking About the Classroom

Talk to other teachers about how they use cooperative learning. Examine your own use. See what kinds of tasks are most commonly used and how they promote interdependence. Plan a cooperative learning task that meets Cohen's (1986) criteria.

EVALUATION, GRADING, AND CREATIVITY

Few factors are as consistent in school settings as evaluation. Whatever the grade level, school organization, educational philosophy, or subject matter, students are evaluated. Evaluation information is used to diagnose students' needs, plan curriculum, communicate with parents, and make decisions about teacher advancement and credentialing. When you consider evaluation in conjunction with creativity, you should address at least two major questions: "How can we evaluate creativity?" and "How can we use evaluation of the regular curriculum in a manner that supports creativity?" The first question, assessment of creativity, is addressed in chapter 8. This section considers the second question: What types of evaluation might best support and encourage creativity in schools?

Traditional Evaluation and Curriculum Development

Traditionally, evaluation in schools has been represented by grades. Students' progress was summarized in a single letter. An A in math meant all was well in the mathematical world. An F represented mathematical failure. In recent years, nationally normed, standardized tests have become even more powerful arbiters of success or failure. A 95th percentile could mean college admission, a high school diploma, or a positive parent–teacher conference. In some places, students' achievement on standardized tests has been tied to student rewards, teacher salaries, and even school closings. The influence of such forces should not be underestimated.

Traditional evaluation conflicts with creativity research and theory on at least two fronts. First, traditional testing and grading epitomize the factors of evaluation, reward, and competition that have been found to undermine both the intrinsic motivation for creative activities and the quality of creative products. Second, the kinds of products associated with creativity—solving problems and expressing original ideas—do not lend themselves to single-letter grades or multiple-choice testing. In fact, creative thinking can be risky business on a multiple-choice test. The ability to say, "Well, A could be the answer, but if you think about it this way, it could be B" is not an asset if the goal is to choose one correct response.

This type of dilemma is not limited to those concerned with the development of creativity. It also is part of a larger concern about the role of assessment in schools (Marzano, 2000; Resnick & Resnick 1991; Rothman, 1997; Shepard, 1989). There is ample evidence that in schools, we get what we assess (Darling-Hammond & Wise, 1985; McNeil, 1988). As the stakes for test performance become higher and higher, test preparation takes on a larger role in shaping instruction. At times, the influence is obvious. Teachers may spend time teaching the test format and emphasizing topics known to be on standardized tests.

At other times, the influence is less obvious. Standardized tests are designed to evaluate a large number of students economically. To do this, they must rely on questions that can be answered quickly and scored mechanically. Questions that readily fit in a bubble-sheet format can do so only by relying on two basic assumptions: decomposability and decontextualization (Resnick & Resnick, 1991). Decomposability assumes that complex tasks and thoughts can be broken down into component parts. If each part is assessed and found satisfactory, the greater whole is assumed to be satisfactory as well. The classic example of decomposability is a skills-based approach to language arts. In this approach, if a student can demonstrate skill in the component parts of composition—writing a complete sentence, identifying the main idea of a paragraph, understanding metaphors—the assumption is that the student also can compose.

Decontextualization assumes that each component of a complex task is fixed and will take the same form no matter where it is used. If a student can tell a fact from an opinion in one context, it is assumed the student can distinguish the two under any other circumstances.

In fact, both of these assumptions have come into question. Complex processes appear to be more than the sum of their parts, and skills do not seem to transfer automatically from one domain to another. Learning seems to take place best in the context of complex experiences and problem solving. The transfer of skills requires specific instruction and focus on students' metacognitive processes (Perkins, 1992). However, the assumptions of decomposability and decontextualization have profoundly influenced the ways curriculum has been presented. Texts and workbooks are filled with items for practicing individual skills in formats very similar to those found on standardized tests, a practice that makes workbooks easy to correct. Unfortunately, this practice also allows students to learn the skills of composing paragraphs, stories, or essays without learning the greater task of composing itself. It allows them to compute the answers to math examples without actually being able to solve any problems using math. As teachers, we have sometimes found ourselves in the position of teaching what was easy to grade and score rather than what was important or what helped students to learn.

Authentic Assessment and Creativity

Fortunately, assessment is changing. Dissatisfaction with existing standardized testing combined with the need to evaluate students' progress has led to a host of assessment alternatives. Alternative assessments have been proposed for populations ranging from those in individual classrooms to those who participate in national testing. These new options represent a trend away from isolated skills assessment and toward the performance of complex tasks in specific contexts. Authentic or performance assessment means that students are evaluated on their performance of realistic, exemplary tasks.

The distinction between traditional and performance assessments is illustrated well in the procedures for obtaining a driver's license. In the traditional testing part of the assessment, potential drivers are given a paper-and-pencil test on the rules of the road. In the performance assessment, they must actually drive the car. In performance assessment, students being tested on composition must write. Students being assessed in math or science must solve problems in those areas.

In one assessment, ninth-grade students were required to complete an oral history project based on interviews and written sources. The subject of the project was determined by the students. Samples of possible topics included their families, the operation of a small business, substance abuse, a labor union, teenage parents, or recent immigrants. Students were required to make three working hypotheses based on preliminary research and develop four questions to test each hypothesis. The criteria for evaluating the oral history project were presented to the students in advance. They included such standards as these: prepare at least four questions for each hypothesis; ask questions that are not leading or biased; and use evidence to support your choice of the best hypothesis (Wiggins, 1989, p. 707).

An example of performance assessment in elementary school comes from Mark Twain Elementary School in Littleton, Colorado (Lockwood, 1991). Fifth-grade students are asked to write two questions they would like to investigate for 1 week. The questions are submitted to the teacher, who helps to refine them. On the day the evaluation begins, the teacher selects one of the two questions. Students are allotted a half day for four consecutive days to work on the assignment. The final products include a written paper and an oral report with accompanying visual presentation. Designated criteria allow teachers to rate the projects on a 5-point scale. A 5-point response meets the following criteria:

> The student clearly describes the question studied and provides strong reasons for its importance. Conclusions are clearly stated in a thoughtful manner. A variety of facts, details, and examples are given to answer the question and provide support for the answer. The writing is engaging, organized, fluid, and very readable. Sentence structure is varied, and grammar, mechanics, and spelling are consistently correct. Sources of information are noted and cited in an appropriate way. (Lockwood, 1991, p. 5)

A 3-point response includes the following:

> The student briefly describes the question and has written conclusions. An answer is stated with a small amount of supporting information. The writing has a basic organization, although it is not always clear and sometimes difficult to follow. Sentence mechanics are generally correct with some weaknesses and errors. References are mentioned, but without adequate detail. (Lockwood, 1991, p. 5)

Tasks evaluated on performance assessments should reflect real-world concerns and problems, using information in ways that are meaningful to students (Wiggins, 1996). Because real-world contexts rarely entail clear-cut multiple-choice alternatives to problems, alternative assessment techniques frequently offer open-ended problems with multiple paths to solution. The oral- history project offered numerous topics and avenues for exploration while still assessing students' abilities to make and test hypotheses, analyze historical sources, and express valid conclusions. The fifth-grade assignment allowed students to design and investigate questions of interest to them. Their product demonstrated their use of resources, organization, writing, and presentation skills. In each of these cases, students were assessed on content relevant to particular disciplines. They also were evaluated on their abilities to find and solve problems and to express ideas in coherent, thoughtful, and original ways (Herman, Aschbacher, & Winters, 1992; Maeroff, 1991; Wiggins, 1989).

What does all this have to do with creativity in schools? It means that teachers no longer need to hesitate about assigning creative projects, wondering, "How will I grade this?" The techniques of performance assessment are designed to evaluate complex, open-ended tasks. Moreover, the research literature that supports performance assessment makes it clear that the types of tasks requiring creative thinking—solving problems, expressing ideas, and looking at information in multiple contexts and from varied perspectives—are essential tasks for effective content mastery and for success in the types of assessment students will face in the future. Authentic assessment is an ally to those promoting creativity in schools, both in providing technology that allows assessment of creative products and in supporting the need for such products to be developed.

Performance Tasks

A comprehensive review of performance assessment techniques is beyond the scope of this book. This section briefly examines the characteristics of alternative assessment tasks and beginning strategies for developing assessment activities.

Herman et al. (1992) identified common characteristics in alternative assessments. These characteristics are listed with examples of each, taken from Mitchell (1989).

1. Alternative assessments ask students to perform, create, produce, or do something. This type of assessment does not rely on isolated skills to measure student competence; it demands a complex performance. For example, the 1986–1987 Connecticut Assessment of Educational Progress (CAEP) in foreign language included an assignment requiring students to write a letter in the designated language to a foreign student coming to live with them.

The letter was to include information on the host student's family, school, daily activities, interests and hobbies, and a recent local event. Such a task is far different from conjugating lists of verbs in the designated language.

2. Alternative assessments tap higher level thinking and problem-solving skills. The New York State grade 4 manipulative science test presented students with a mystery box. Students were to manipulate the box to determine the number, characteristics, and shapes of the objects in the box.

3. Alternative assessments use tasks that represent meaningful instructional activities. Pennsylvania teachers developed a unit final for a music appreciation class that required students to write a letter to a record company persuading the company to audition their new jazz group. The letter had to compare their group's music with that of great jazz players and explain how it fit into the jazz tradition.

4. Alternative assessments invoke real-world applications. A mathematics exercise from Holland presented students with information on the country's defense budget. It posed two problems: lecturing a pacifist society on how the defense budget is decreasing and lecturing a military academy on how the defense budget is increasing. Both used the same set of data.

5. Alternative assessments are scored by people, not machines. Human judgment is an important part of alternative assessments. Although specific criteria make evaluation clearer and provide both students and teachers with guidelines, there is no substitute for judgment and expertise. Such assessment fits with long-standing traditions in the evaluation of creative products. Paintings, novels, dances, and plays rarely earn a score of 87% or 93%. Their merits cannot be evaluated through multiple-choice items. Rather, individuals with understanding and experience in the domain apply general standards with taste and artistry. The effective use of alternative assessment will demand the development of (and respect for) this type of expertise in educational personnel.

6. Alternative assessments require new instructional and assessment roles for teachers. Each of the examples given demonstrates that teaching and evaluating using alternative assessment cannot be business as usual. Teachers cannot use these techniques and teach as they were taught or test as they have been tested. They will need a variety of alternative assessment techniques to develop

tasks appropriate to the diverse subject areas and grade levels of their students.

Assessment alternatives can be divided into two general categories: those assessing processes and those assessing products. Assessment designed to assess process examines how a student approaches and pursues a task. The task itself may vary from designing a science experiment to writing a poem. Information on how the student pursued the task may be gathered through interviews, observations, student self-evaluations, or think-alouds in which students attempt to explain their thought processes as they complete the task.

Assessment designed to evaluate products looks at the end results of students' efforts. Unlike traditional testing situations, product assessment generally examines complex products produced over a certain period. These may include single products such as essays, projects, works of art, demonstrations, or performances. They also may include portfolios that contain a variety of products. In either case, product assessment involves comparing products with a designated set of criteria. The students' work in the oral history project described earlier was assessed on the number of hypotheses, appropriateness of questions, evidence supporting conclusions, and other measures.

The distinctions between process and product assessment are not hard and fast. The same task may produce evaluation data on both process and product. For example, if the evaluators wanted information on how students approached a task in historical research, data could have been gathered on the same oral history project. Students could have kept logs of their progress or completed self-report questionnaires. Teachers or other evaluators could have questioned students on their methodology and completed a checklist or anecdotal record. The techniques for gathering information in alternative assessment are not always new. In many cases, strategies that have been used for years in some educational settings are being elaborated or expanded to other domains.

Creating Performance Assessment Tasks. Creating an authentic or performance assessment task for a particular body of content begins with the question "What do you want the students to do?" In considering that question, imagine how the students might use the knowledge or skills being studied in a real-world context or apply them in a new way. Imagine, for example, that you are planning a unit on simple machines. You probably want students to be able to combine the machines to solve a problem. You might decide to challenge students to design a series of steps that would allow them to move a 50-pound weight from one side of the classroom to the other. The path the weight must travel is blocked by your desk, so the weight must go over your desk without touching it. Students must be able to explain why they chose the procedures and how each step minimizes the amount of work to be done. If you hope that students will move the weight in an original or unique way, that also can be part of the task.

Once you have a general idea of the task to be accomplished, you must develop specific guidelines for the assessment. For this task, questions such as the following need to be considered: (a) Will students be required actually to construct the machines and move the weight or merely design the procedure on paper? (b) Will this be an individual or group task? (c) What materials will students be permitted to use? (d) What sources of help will be allowed? and (e) What amount of time will be allotted?

After considering these questions, you can develop student directions for the task. It is important that student directions be as clear as possible. Students should be told what they are to accomplish, what resources are available to them, and how the product will be assessed. Do not be discouraged if your first attempts at designing performance tasks are unclear or confusing. As with any new skill, developing these tasks demands time and practice. If you find you have omitted essential information, explain it as well as you can and revise the task next time. A first draft of the directions for the machine assignment reads as follows:

Now that you have learned about how simple machines can be used to make work easier, you are ready for the 50-Pound Challenge. Your task is to move a 50-pound bag of potting soil from the door of the classroom to the plants on the windowsill. The bag must travel in a straight line. Because the path from the door to the window is blocked by my desk, your plan must include a way to get the bag over my desk without touching the desk or damaging anything on the desk. Try to design a plan that not only is effective, but also uses simple machines in an original way. You must complete your plan for the 50-Pound Challenge alone. You may use any of the reference books in the classroom, but you may not work in teams. Your plan should have two parts. The first part should describe, step by step, how you will move the bag. Be sure to include what equipment you will use and how you will use it. You may include a diagram if you wish. The second part of your plan should tell me why your plan is a good one. Explain how you have minimized the work involved in moving the bag.

You will be evaluated on four questions:

1. How clearly is the plan described?

2. How practical is the plan?

3. How well did the plan use simple machines to reduce work?

4. Did the plan use original or unusual strategies?

When all of you have completed your plans, we will choose three plans to try in the classroom.

Once the task has been defined, a scoring rubric must be designed. After the scoring is determined, you may find that the student directions need to be changed to make the goals of the activity clear. Creating a scoring rubric has three general stages: identifying the dimensions or variables to be assessed, determining the scale of values to be used, and setting standards or descriptors for each value. For example, the California Assessment Program for 1990 History–Social Science task for grade 11 involves groups of students in analyzing and using primary source materials to solve problems. It is scored along four dimensions: group and collaborative learning, critical thinking, communication of ideas, and knowledge and use of history. The dimensions are not equally weighted: Critical thinking and the use of history each contribute 30 possible points, and the other two dimensions are worth 20 points. The scoring guide designates five possible levels of achievement for each dimension—from minimal achievement to exceptional achievement. The criteria for level IV (superior achievement) for the knowledge and use of history dimension require that a student does the following: offers accurate analysis of the documents, provides facts to relate to the major issues involved, and uses previous general historical knowledge to examine issues involved (Herman et al., 1992, p. 47).

Sometimes products are scored along only one dimension. This is a holistic scoring approach. Holistic scoring might be used to rate the overall quality of a performance or product. Your scoring rubric for the 50-pound challenge probably will be simpler than the one used in the California model, but it may include more than one variable. You could decide to score the plans along three dimensions: communicating ideas, creating a feasible plan, and knowing and using simple machines. If it is important to you to assess originality or some other aspect of creativity, you could either create a separate scale for that dimension of assessment or incorporate it into the three other scales. In this case, you may have decided to incorporate originality into the scoring of your three basic scales. Because this is a first effort, you may decide to keep things simple and give each scale equal weight: Each scale could earn up to 10 points.

The last step in creating a scoring rubric is the most complicated, but it is essential in creating authentic assessments that are reliable and fair. You must decide what constitutes a 2 or a 9 on the 10-point scale for each dimension. It is not necessary to give a description for every possible point value. For a 10-point scale, you might create five levels: minimal achievement (1–2 points), basic achievement (3–4 points), satisfactory achievement (5–6 points), superior achievement (7–8 points), and exceptional achievement (9–10) points. For each level, you need to determine criteria or descriptions of a typical performance. Your completed scale might resemble that in Fig. 7.3. Descriptions of the criteria at each level allow evaluations to be consistent from product to product and keep the evaluator focused on important dimensions instead of assessing one project on its plan and the next on the quality of its artwork.

Thinking About the Classroom

Choose an open-ended task as part of your assessment for an upcoming unit. Create a scoring rubric with criteria for varying levels. If this is your first effort at authentic assessment, you may wish to work with a partner or small group.

	Minimal 1–2	Basic 3–4	Satisfactory 5–6	Superior 7–8	Exceptional 9–10
Clear Communication	Plan and/or diagram is missing or not clear.	Plan and diagram are present but unclear.	Communicates main ideas clearly; diagram is basic but clear.	Plan is detailed and complete with step-by-step directions; diagram is detailed. Either may be somewhat unclear.	Both plan and diagram are extremely clear, detailed, easy to follow.
Feasible Plan	Plan is not workable.	Plan partially solves problem.	Plan uses content in a practical way. It is theoretically feasible even if not truly workable.	Plan solves problem in a realistic manner.	Plan solves problem in an original, realistic manner.
Knowledge and Use of Simple Machines	Does not use machines correctly.	Uses 1 or 2 machines to solve problem or uses 3 machines with some errors.	Uses at least 3 machines to solve the problem in a manner similar to examples done in class.	Uses more than 3 machines in a straightforward manner.	Uses more than 3 machines in unusual combinations or original manner.

FIG. 7.3.   Scoring rubric for the 50-pound challenge.

Fostering Self-Evaluation

The techniques of authentic assessment allow teachers to use complex tasks in evaluating students' understanding of content. Many of the skills associated with creativity can be vital parts of authentic assessment tasks. Activities can require students to solve open-ended problems, create multiple solutions to the same problem, examine a situation from multiple dimensions, discover or create problems, and express individual ideas. They also help students to understand that complex and creative tasks are not assessed at the whim of the evaluator, but have qualities that add to or subtract from their value. These qualities can be learned and used to improve future efforts.

If used well, this type of assessment becomes an integral part of instruction. Because complex tasks are used to assess instruction, they become part of it. Authentic assessment also can become a vehicle for informational feedback. If a product is not simply labeled A or B, but is assessed along clear dimensions, the information from the evaluation can be used by students to understand the strengths and weaknesses of their products and to improve future projects.

Understanding the criteria by which their work is evaluated brings students one step closer to effective self-evaluation. Developing the ability to assess one's own work and learning the importance of an internal locus of evaluation are important factors in creativity. It also is important that students learn to assess the creativity of their own ideas because creative individuals must not only generate original ideas but also recognize which ideas are original (Runco, 1993). Allowing students to correct their own spelling tests is not self-evaluation. An outside source (the dictionary) is the absolute determiner of the quality of the work. Effective self-evaluation requires students to measure their efforts against some scale or criterion and make judgments about how they measure up.

Beginning in primary school, students can be taught to evaluate their own products. They can assess their stories for complete sentences (a clear beginning, middle, and end) or the use of interesting descriptions. They can judge the use of color in their paintings or the precise definitions of variables in science projects. Initially, teachers should provide guide sheets or checklists to help students focus their evaluations. Later, students can add their own variables or develop their own forms of assessment. The goal is to help students internalize the evaluation process, both to improve the quality of their products and to build confidence in their own judgment.

Szekely (1988) emphasized the importance of allowing students to discuss creative products and the teacher's role in encouraging students

7.1. Rubric for Algebra 1

Task: Create a problem that exhibits a minimum of three of the objectives learned in the study of chapter 4.

Rubric:Scoring

Criterion	1 point	2 points	3 points	4 points
Creativity	The problem was not appropriate or was not clear	The problem was appropriate but not original	The problem exhibits a degree of originality and a high degree of appropriateness	The problem exhibits a high degree of originality and appropriateness
Objectives	Less than two objectives have been explained in an adequate or below-adequate manner; objectives were not stated; objectives were very closely related	Minimum of two objectives were stated and explained in an adequate manner; objectives closely related	Minimum of three objectives were explained in an adequate manner; objectives are not closely related	More than three objectives were explained in a complete manner; thought was given regarding ways to relate objectives that are not closely related
Work	Work is not shown	Work was shown and explained; some thought involved	Work was shown fairly well and explained at least two objectives; an average amount of thought involved	Work was completely and extensively explained; a great deal of thought was demonstrated
Solution	Solutions attempted, but fewer than 2/3 were correct; problem does not match stated objectives	2/3 of solutions are correct; at least two objectives compatible with problem	Vast majority of problem and solution correct; stated objective and problem match	Solutions correct and well explained; objectives and problem match
Writing	Five or more technical errors (spelling, grammar, punctuation, readability)	3–4 technical errors; paper written in pencil	1–2 errors; paper written in ink	No technical errors; paper neatly written in ink or typed

Adapted from a lesson by Tamara Dodge.

to explore works, not just critically, but also playfully and creatively. Carefully structured conversations with both the teacher and other students can help creators recognize that audience members each bring something different to a work and hence respond differently. Discussion allows students to clarify their intentions, explain their works, and better understand audience responses.

By definition, creative products are different from those that came before. Individuals who produce creative products often are faced with skepticism and doubt about the quality or validity of their efforts. Helping students to develop standards for self-assessment can help them view evaluation as a tool for improvement rather than an arbitrary or capricious judgment, by either the creator or an outside evaluator. Products are not good or bad because "I say so" or "I like it," but because the product meets some standard or accomplishes some objective.

Developing self-evaluation also can help students understand that, at times, the standards or objectives by which something is evaluated may differ from standards that came before. That is how fields and domains change. Picasso's art could not be judged by the standards of his predecessors. Although some traditional ideas could be applied (e.g., the use of color or balance), Picasso changed many of the rules for evaluation. His art was not random or without standards. It simply tried to solve problems of different kinds from those that had been addressed before. Similarly, although the standards of the discipline must be taken into account, students may sometimes evaluate their products along different dimensions or focus on goals different from those of other evaluators. They should recognize that although setting new standards carries risks, such evaluations also can have value and promise. Figures 7.4, 7.5, and 7.6 are examples of forms that may help guide students in their efforts at self-assessment.

Finally, as you consider evaluation that supports and enhances creativity, it can be helpful to consider your own self-analysis. In-depth study of individual students' work can help you determine how your efforts to encourage creativity are faring (Goff, Langer, & Colton, 2000; Langer, Colton, & Goff, 2003). Working with colleagues to analyze students' efforts can provide important insights on student progress in any content and process goals. Examining students' work with an eye to analyzing your effectiveness in encouraging diverse and flexible responses can help you gauge the impact of your instructional strategies.

Student _____   Date _____

Title _____

I am working on: My evaluation:

	Not yet	Improving	Well done
Correct spelling			
Punctuation			
Capital letters			
Comments			

FIG. 7.4.   Self-evaluation, writing.

Thinking about Your Thinking

Think about how you solved today's problem. Which did you do?

_____ I didn't try any of the strategies from the list.

_____ I tried one strategy from the list.
        _____ The strategy helped me solve the problem successfully.
        _____ The strategy did not help me.

_____ I tried more than one strategy from the list.
        _____ The strategies helped me solve the problem successfully.
        _____ The strategies did not help me.

_____ I tried a strategy that was not on the list. It was _____
        _____ My strategy helped me solve the problem.
        _____ My strategy did not help me.

I used these strategies:
_____ Guess and check   _____ Make a table
_____ Look for a pattern   _____ Make a list
_____ Draw a picture   _____ Work backward
_____ Try a simpler problem   _____ Write an equation

Next time you have a similar problem, what will you do?

FIG. 7.5.   Self-evaluation, mathematical problem solving.

412

What Am I Learning?

This sheet will help you think about what you are learning now and what you will learn during the school year. Thinking about the things you are learning in school now, answer the following questions.

What things are you doing well?

What things are you working on and improving on?

What things are causing difficulties for you?

What do you plan to do to help with your learning?

What things are you not studying in school that would be interesting to learn?

FIG. 7.6.   Self-evaluation, general.

Thinking About the Classroom

Plan a checklist that will allow students to evaluate a project according to several criteria. Discuss students' feelings about self-evaluation.

Whatever the form of evaluation chosen, classroom assessment that supports creativity will have at least three characteristics. First, it will be based on complex tasks that allow students to practice the skills and attitudes associated with creative thinking. Second, it will provide informational feedback to students, allowing them to see evaluation as a source of growth rather than merely a label. Finally, evaluation activities should be designed to move students in the direction of self-evaluation, helping them learn and practice the processes by which complex products are judged.

This type of assessment provides one more strand in the net of class-room activities that can support creative thinking. One challenge of using authentic assessment and self-assessment is that they demand new ways of teaching and learning that can be at once complex, reliable, equitable, and worthwhile (McDonald, 1993). Thinking about classroom practices in terms of creativity may be one way to begin approaching the new assessment. The knowledge, skills, and attitudes associated with creativity are affected by every aspect of classroom life—from the content and method of our lessons to the arrangement of chairs and the day-to-day assessment of students' efforts. Looking at each factor with an eye to creativity can be a complicated business, but one that may lead to schools transformed from within, places of both learning and wonder.

JOURNEYING AND JOURNALING

1. Think about your own intrinsic motivation. Are the things that motivate you consistent with Amabile's ideas?
2. How did your own experiences as a student affect your motivation? Was school an intrinsically motivating place for you? Why or why not?
3. Reflect on how your school environment now affects the intrinsic motivation of the teachers. If necessary, how might it be changed to enhance their motivation?
4. Examine how evaluation, reward, competition, and choice are operating in your classroom. Consider the degree to which your feedback to students is controlling or informative. Create a plan that may enhance some aspect of student motivation.
5. When are you in flow? Think about your own optimal experiences. Discuss how they do or do not match the characteristics found in Csikszentmihalyi's (1990) research.

REFERENCES

Allan, S. D. (1991). Ability grouping research reviews: What do they say about grouping and the gifted? *Educational Leadership, 48,* 60–65.

Amabile, T. M. (1982). Children's artistic creativity: Detrimental effects of competition in a field setting. *Personality and Social Psychology Bulletin, 8,* 573–578.

Amabile, T. M. (1987). The motivation to be creative. In S. G. Isaksen (Ed.), *Frontiers of creativity research* (pp. 223–254). Buffalo, NY: Bearly.

Amabile, T. M. (1988). A model of creativity and innovation in organization. In B. M. Shaw & L. L. Cummings (Eds.), *Research in organizational behavior* (Vol. 10, pp. 123–167). Greenwich, CT: JAI Press.

Amabile, T. M. (1989). *Growing up creative.* New York: Crown.

Amabile, T. M. (1993a, May). *Future issues.* Panel discussion at the Henry B. and Jocelyn Wallace National Research Symposium on Talent Development, Iowa City, IA.

Amabile, T. M. (1993b, May). *Person and environment in talent development: The case of creativity.* Paper presented at the Henry B. and Jocelyn Wallace National Research Symposium on Talent Development, Iowa City, IA.

Amabile, T. M. (1996). *Creativity in context: Update to the social psychology of creativity.* Boulder, CO: Westview.

Amabile, T. M. (2001). Beyond talent: John Irving and the passionate craft of creativity. *American Psychologist, 56*(4), 333–336.

Amabile, T. M., DeJong, W., & Lepper, M. (1976). Effects of external imposed deadlines on subsequent intrinsic motivation. *Journal of Personality and Social Psychology, 34,* 92–98.

Amabile, T. M., & Gryskiewicz, S. S. (1987*). Creativity in the R&D laboratory.* Technical report No. 30. Greensboro, NC: Center for Creative Leadership.

Amabile, T. M., Hennessey, B. A., & Grossman, B. S. (1986). Social influences on creativity: Effects of contracted-for reward. *Journal of Personality and Social Psychology, 50,* 14–23.

Baer, J. (1998). Gender differences in the effects of extrinsic motivation on creativity. *Journal of Creative Behavior, 32,* 18–37.

Bloom, B. (Ed.). (1985). *Developing talent in young people.* New York: Ballantine.

Bruer, J. T. (1999). In search of … brain-based education. *Phi Delta Kappan, 80,* 648–657.

Cameron, J. (2001). Negative effects of reward on intrinsic motivation—a limited phenomenon: comment on Deci, Koestner, and Ryan. *Review of Educational Research, 71*(1), 29–42.

Cohen, E. G. (1986). *Designing group work.* New York: Teachers College Press.

Collins, M. A., & Amabile, T. M. (1999). Motivation and creativity. In R. J. Sternberg (Ed.), *Handbook of creativity* (pp. 297–312). New York: Cambridge University Press.

Csikszentmihalyi, M. (1990). *Flow: The psychology of optimal experience.* New York: Harper & Row.

Csikszentmihalyi, M., & Sawyer, K. (1993, May). *Creative insight: The social dimension of a solitary moment.* Paper presented at the Henry B. and Jocelyn Wallace National Research Symposium on Talent Development, Iowa City, IA.

Darling-Hammond, L., & Wise, A. E. (1985). Beyond standardization: State standards and school improvement. *The Elementary School Journal, 85,* 315–336.

Deci, E. (1971). Effects of externally mediated rewards on intrinsic motivation. *Journal of Personality and Social Psychology, 28,* 105–115.

Deci, E. L., Koestner, R, Ryan, R. M. (2001a). Extrinsic rewards and intrinsic motivation in education: reconsidered once again. *Review of Educational Research, 71*(1), 1–27.

Deci, E. L., Koestner, R, Ryan, R. M. (2001b). The pervasive negative effects of rewards on intrinsic motivation: response to Cameron (2001). *Review of Educational Research, 71*(1), 43–51.

Eisenberger, R., Armeli, K. S., & Pretz, J. (1998). Can the promise of reward increase creativity? *Journal of Personality and Social Psychology, 74,* 704–714.

Eisenberger, R., & Cameron, J. (1996). Detrimental effects of reward: Reality of myth? *American Psychologist, 51,* 1153–1166.

Goff, L., Langer, G., & Colton, A. (2000, Fall). The collaborative analysis of student learning. *Journal of Staff Development, 21*(4), 44–47.

Herman, J. L., Aschbacher, P. R., & Winters, L. (1992). *A practical guide to alternative assessment.* Alexandria, VA: Association for Supervision and Curriculum Development.

Isenberg, J. P., & Jalongo, M. R. (1993). *Creative expression and play in the early childhood curriculum.* New York: Merrill.

Kohn, A. (1993). Choices for children: Why and how to let students decide. *Phi Delta Kappan, 75*(1), 8–20.

Kulik, J. (1991). Findings on grouping are often distorted. *Educational Leadership, 48,* 67.

Langer, G. M., Colton, A. B., & Goff, L. S. (2003). *Collaborative analysis of student work: Improving teaching and learning.* Alexandria, VA: Association for Supervision and Curriculum Development.

Lepper, M., & Greene, D. (1975). Turning play into work: Effects of adult surveillance and extrinsic rewards on children's intrinsic motivation. *Journal of Personality and Social Psychology, 31,* 479–486.

Lepper, M., & Greene, D. (1978). *The hidden costs of reward.* Hillsdale, NJ: Lawrence Erlbaum Associates.

Lepper, M., Greene, D., & Nisbet, R. (1973). Undermining children's intrinsic interest with extrinsic rewards: A test of the "overjustification" hypothesis. *Journal of Personality and Social Psychology, 28,* 129–137.

Lockwood, A. T. (1991). From telling to coaching. *Focus in Change, 3*(1), 3–7.

Maeroff, G. I. (1991). Assessing alternative assessment. *Phi Delta Kappan, 73,* 272–281.

McDonald, J. P. (1993). Three pictures of an exhibition: Warm, cool and hard. *Phi Delta Kappan, 74,* 480–485.

McNeil, L. M. (1988). Contradictions of control, Part 3: Contradictions of reform. *Phi Delta Kappan, 69,* 478–485.

Marzano, R. (2000). *Transforming classroom grading.* Alexandria, VA: Association for Supervision and Curriculum Development.

Matson, J. V. (1991). Failure 101: Rewarding failure in the classroom to stimulate creative behavior. *Journal of Creative Behavior 25,* 82–85.

Micklus, C. S., & Micklus, C. (1986). *OM program handbook.* Glassboro, NJ: Odyssey of the Mind.

Mitchell, R. (1989, October). *A sampler of authentic assessment: What it is and what it looks like.* Paper presented at the meeting of the Curriculum/Assessment Alignment Conferences, California Association of County Superintendents of Schools and the California Assessment Program, Sacramento and Long Beach, CA.

Pace-Marshall, S. (1993, May). *Our gifted children: Are they asking too much?* Keynote address presented at the meeting of the Michigan Alliance for Gifted Education, Dearborn, MI.

Perkins, D. (1992). *Smart schools.* New York: Free Press.

Resnick, L. B., & Resnick, D. P. (1991). Assessing the thinking curriculum: New tools for educational reform. In B. R. Gifford & M. C. O'Connor (Eds.), *Changing assessment: Alternative views of aptitude, achievement, and instruction* (pp. 37–75). Boston: Kluwer Academic.

Rogers, C. R. (1962). Toward a theory of creativity. In S. J. Parnes & H. F. Harding (Eds.), *A source book for creative thinking.* New York: Scribner's.

Rothman, R. (1997). *Measuring up: Standards, assessment, and school reform.* San Francisco: Jossey-Bass.

Runco, M. (1993). *Creativity as an educational objective for disadvantaged students.* Storrs, CT: National Research Center on the Gifted and Talented.

Sharan, Y., & Sharan, S. (1992). *Expanding cooperative learning through group investigation.* New York: Teachers College Press.

Shepard, L. A. (1989). Why we need better assessments. *Educational Leadership, 46*(7), 4–9.

Sherer, M. (2002). Do students care about learning? A conversation with Mihaly Csikszentmihalyi. *Educational Leadership, 60*(1), 12–17.

Slavin, R. (1987). Ability grouping and student achievement in elementary schools: A best- evidence synthesis. *Review of Educational Research, 57,* 293–336.

Slavin, R. (1990). *Cooperative learning: Theory, research, and practice.* Englewood Cliffs, NJ: Prentice-Hall.

Slavin, R. (1991). Are cooperative learning and "untracking" harmful to the gifted? *Educational Leadership, 48,* 68–69.

Smolucha, F. (1992). A reconstruction of Vygotsky's theory of creativity. *Creativity Research Journal, 5,* 49–68.

Szekely, G. (1988). *Encouraging creativity in art lessons.* New York: Teachers College Press.

Tomlinson, C. A. (1999). *The differentiated classroom: Responding to the needs of all learners.* Alexandria, VA: Association for Supervision and Curriculum Development.

Vygotsky, L. S. (1960). Imagination and its development in childhood. In L. S. Vygotsky, *The development of higher mental functions* (pp. 327–362). Moscow: Izdatel'stvo Academii Pedagogicheskikh Nauk RSFSR. (Originally a lecture presented in 1930).

Weisberg, R. W. (1992). *Creativity: Beyond the myth of genius.* New York: Freeman.

Wiggins, G. (1989). A true test: Toward more authentic and equitable assessment. *Phi Delta Kappan, 70,* 703–713.

Wiggins, G. (1996). Designing authentic assessments. *Educational Leadership, 153*(5), 18–25.

Winebrenner, S. (1992). *Teaching gifted kids in the regular classroom.* Minneapolis, MN: Free Spirit Press.

Wolfe, P., & Brandt, R. (1998). What do we know from brain research? *Educational Leadership, 56*(3), 8–13.

chapter 8

Assessing Creativity

Barbara looked across the table at Kenneth's mother, Mrs. Greene. The conference was not going as well as Barbara had hoped. Mrs. Greene was concerned about the difficulties Kenneth was having in some areas, particularly spelling, but did not seem to see the strengths Barbara thought so important. Barbara considered Kenneth one of the most creative students she had ever taught. His comments in class frequently reflected a unique point of view, and his projects, although not always the neatest in the class, almost always included elements Barbara had never considered. Mrs. Greene was unimpressed. "Creative," she exclaimed. "I'm not even sure I know what that means. How can you tell he's creative, anyway? In math, 100% means he did a good job. Can you be 100% creative? It looks to me as if he's pulling a fast one on you. Kenneth can be pretty tricky." Barbara didn't know what to say. How did she know Kenneth was creative? Could she prove it? Should she try?

Barbara's dilemma is not unique. Efforts to assess creativity have been as challenging as the quest to define it. The complex and elusive nature of the construct, combined with limitations in the technology of our measurements, make precise assessment of creativity a daunting task. Yet efforts to enhance creativity in children seem doomed to failure unless we can recognize creativity when it occurs. Allowing these judgments to

419

move from the individual instincts of "I know it when I see it" to greater consistency and agreement among professionals is the goal of assessment. This chapter reviews efforts to assess creativity. It discusses why we might want to assess creativity, difficulties in assessment, creativity tests, observations, and product assessments. Finally, it describes how some schools have combined techniques in an effort to identify students with outstanding creative potential.

WHY ASSESS CREATIVITY?

The primary goal of assessing creativity in schools was expressed by Gowan (1977):

> Heretofore we have harvested creativity wild. We have used as creative only those persons who stubbornly remained so despite all efforts ... to grind it out of them .... If we learn to domesticate creativity—that is, to enhance rather than deny it in our culture—we can increase the number of creative persons in our midst by about fourfold. (p. 89)

The goal of assessing or identifying creativity in schools is not to generate creativity scores or to divide students into categories called "creative" and "not creative." Rather, it is to allow us to recognize creativity when it occurs and to create conditions that allow it to develop. It also can help us identify students such as Kenneth, whose exceptional creativity, as is any other special ability, should be nurtured and supported in school.

The following are some of the possible purposes Treffinger (1987) described for assessing creativity:

1. Helping to recognize and support the strengths of individuals as well as helping individuals to recognize their own strengths. Identifying students such as Kenneth as exceptionally creative not only allows us to understand and serve them better, but may allow them to understand themselves better. Kenneth's ability to see his unique points of view as evidence of creativity rather than strange behavior may be a source of comfort, strength, and motivation for him.

2. Expanding our understanding of human abilities, particularly knowing how creativity relates to traditional views of intelligence. If

we can learn how measures of creativity and intelligence are related or what kinds of tasks best predict creative performance, we will gain insight into the workings and relationships of these constructs.

3. Providing baseline data that may be used to diagnose student needs and plan instruction. If we understand students' strengths and weaknesses regarding creativity, we should be able to plan activities that are appropriate and challenging. Groups of students may differ in their abilities to use creative thinking skills and attitudes or to apply such skills to various domains. Understanding these patterns can help a teacher to plan effectively for individuals or groups of students.

4. Evaluating efforts to enhance creativity. At times, teachers or other individuals may implement programs or activities designed to increase creativity. How can we know whether these efforts make a difference if we have no way to compare performances before and after instruction? Various forms of assessment may be used as pre- and postinstruction data in such program evaluation.

5. Providing a common language for professionals wishing to discuss various aspects of creativity. One of the difficulties in reading research and theory on creativity is that the reader must constantly ask, "How is creativity defined?" or "What kind of creativity do they mean here?" Standardized measures allow for accuracy of communication as well as clarity in comparing research studies. If three studies identify personality characteristics associated with creativity but each defines creativity in a completely different way, it is difficult to make any generalizations regarding the studies. If all three use the same measures, comparisons will be easier.

6. Removing the concept of creativity from "the realm of mystery and superstition" (Treffinger, 1987, p. 104). If we view creativity as beyond our understanding, how can we encourage or support it? Assessing aspects of creativity, even some of them, can help us begin to see how creativity functions in some situations, adding to our understanding and motivation to explore further.

The type of assessment that is needed or appropriate varies with the purpose for which it is intended. In schools, the assessment of creativity is most likely to be used for planning instruction, for identifying students to be included in specific programs or opportunities (such as a summer arts program or school-based gifted and talented program), and occasionally for evaluating programs. If an assessment technique is to be used by a school or district to make decisions about educational opportunities for individual students, it must be the fairest and most accurate measure available. If a classroom teacher is using an assessment to plan class activities for her next unit, a more loosely constructed instrument may be acceptable. In many cases, teachers must use a combination of assessment tools to make valid judgments. The nature of creativity and the limitations of traditional forms of measurement provide challenges that can make any single form of assessment suspect.

Thinking About the Classroom

Think about the need for assessing creativity in your class or school. For what purposes might assessment be used? Compare your ideas with those of teachers in another building or district.

DIFFICULTIES ASSESSING CREATIVITY: THE NATURE OF THE BEAST

The most obvious difficulty in trying to assess creativity is lack of consensus on what constitutes creativity in the first place. Measuring something is extremely difficult if we are not sure what it is. Varying theories and definitions of creativity will support differing types of assessment. Are we trying to assess the type of creativity that allows an Einstein to change the nature of a discipline (sometimes informally called "Big C" creativity) or the more common creativity that might allow me to invent a new soup, play a new harp tune, or fix my leaky faucet without a washer (creativity with a "Little c")? A theorist interested in Rogers' self-actualizing creativity and an individual studying history's most creative musicians or scientists may wish to measure very different things. Researchers disagree on whether general creativity can be identified and measured or whether creativity must be subject specific. Some of the variations in assessment techniques reflect these differences and represent attempts to measure variables important to various theories. The more complex the theory, the more daunting the task of assessment. If, as some theorize, creativity is discipline specific, the measurement of generic creativity will be ineffective (Baer, 1993–1994). It is possible that each discipline will provide unique assessment opportunities (Sefton-Green & Sinker, 2000). If creativity is the same as divergent thinking, a single measurement will suffice. As more complex systems theories of creativity come to the forefront, attempts to measure any single factor become less appropriate. Kirschenbaum (1998) suggested that various aspects of creativity require diverse types of assessment. For example, assessing openness to experience may require different instrumentation than assessing appropriate self-evaluation of creative efforts. Attempts to assess creativity also are subject to difficulties related to the nature of measurement itself.

Measurement and the Usefulness of Instruments

The field of assessment is based on the assumption that the thing to be measured can be identified and quantified or judged. For these assumptions to be met, the instruments used for measurement must meet the tests of validity and reliability. At the most basic level, these two criteria mean that different observers can agree that they are measuring the thing they set out to measure and what the measurement is. For example, if I want to measure the length of the keyboard on which I am typing, I could use a ruler. If society in general has agreed on what length means and that a ruler, properly used, is an appropriate measure of length, my measurement can be considered valid. If I use a ruler, I can measure the variable I want to assess— length. To do so accurately, I must have a ruler that is consistent, or reliable. A standard ruler is reliable. If I measure my keyboard several times, I should get the same results. If someone else measures my keyboard with a standard ruler, he or she too should obtain the same measurement. If my ruler bent or stretched in hot weather, it would not be reliable. The measurements taken by that ruler would be essentially meaningless because they could differ with each attempt. I might never really know the length of my keyboard. Of course, dealing with reliability and validity in measuring abstract constructs such as creativity is more complex than determining the purpose and accuracy of a ruler.

Reliability. Reliability can be generally thought of as consistency. Reliability is the foundation of quantitative measurement. Without consistency in scores, measurements cannot be valid. The most easily recognized type of reliability is stability, or test–retest reliability. Just as I would hope that two measurements of my keyboard would result in the same number of inches, test–retest reliability ensures that an individual identified as highly creative today will also be identified as highly creative next week or next month. Assuming that no major changes in creativity occur, individuals should obtain relatively consistent scores on the same instrument if they are tested more than once. Without this type of reliability, test scores are useless. We would never know whether a given score is a true reflection of the variable being measured or whether the subject might obtain a totally different score on another day. Of course, test–retest reliability assumes that the variable being measured is relatively stable. If creativity actually changes from day to day or minute to minute, test–retest reliability—and most quantitative assessment—will be impossible.

Other types of reliability also are important in measuring creativity. Equivalent-forms reliability says that scores obtained on one form of an instrument should be about the same as scores obtained on any other form. This type of reliability is particularly important in the selection of instruments to be used for program evaluation. It is very common for evaluators to use one form of an instrument as a pretest and another form as the posttest, to avoid having students become familiar with the test itself. Without equivalent-forms reliability, scores on the various forms could not be compared in meaningful ways. Any differences found between pre- and posttest scores could be the result of differences in the tests rather than the effects of the program being evaluated.

A third type of reliability is interrater reliability. Interrater reliability is required for any instrument that relies on individual expertise or judgment for scoring. For it to be achieved, two raters scoring the same test or product have to produce similar scores. With commercial assessment instruments, interrater reliability often is affected by the level of detail in the scoring guide. If scorers are merely asked to designate scores on a 5-point scale, the scores are more likely to vary than if scorers are given examples and criteria for each level of the scale. This type of reliability clearly is an issue when creative products are being assessed. It would be unfair if students were judged to be creative or less creative depending more on who scored their product than on the merits of the product itself.

Perhaps the most commonly reported type of reliability is internal-consistency reliability. This type of reliability examines whether the items on a test instrument work together and seem to be measuring the same thing or whether different items are assessing different strengths. One way to test internal consistency is to correlate scores on odd-numbered items with those on even-numbered items, or to compare scores on the first and second halves of the test (also called split-half reliability). If the test is intended to measure one construct, such as creativity, internal-consistency reliability should be high.

When you examine commercial instruments for assessing creativity, you should find information on reliability in the documentation accompanying the test as well as in test reviews. Reliability scores generally are expressed as correlations, with a range from .00 (no reliability) to 1.00 (perfect reliability). Be sure to examine both the score itself and the type of reliability it expresses when determining the appropriateness of a particular instrument for a given purpose.

Validity. The types of reliability may occasionally become confusing, but the issues regarding reliability are actually pretty straightforward: Either a test produces consistent results or it does not; either two judges obtain similar scores or they do not. These results can be easily and clearly expressed in numerical scores. Validity offers no such clean assurances. In validity, we are concerned not with the consistency of the scores, but with their accuracy. Are we, in the end, measuring what we want to measure? Wonderfully consistent scores are of little value if they actually are measuring the wrong thing.

Scientists of the 19th century purported to have a wonderful measurement for assessing intelligence: brain weight. The reliability scores for that measure were excellent. Given an accurate scale, brain weights were extremely consistent if weighed at different times or by different evaluators. The only problem was that brain weight does not really measure intelligence. In examining measures of creativity, we must ask the same question: If the test measures something consistently and accurately, is that something creativity?

There are five types of validity that can be considered when we make judgments about assessment instruments. Content validity asks whether the content of the test items reflects the definition or theory of creativity we accept. In its simplest form it asks, "Do these tasks look as if they require creativity? Do they logically match creativity as we define it?" If our definition of creativity requires novel responses, the test should provide opportunities for novelty, and the scoring should reward novel responses. A multiple-choice test with specific correct responses probably would not be appropriate. If our definition also requires that responses be appropriate, the instrument should distinguish between responses that are unusual but fit the task and responses that are inappropriate.

Criterion-related validity asks whether the measure correlates with other measures of creativity. How do scores on a particular instrument relate to other standards previously identified for creativity? Criterion-related validity can be divided into two types: concurrent validity and predictive validity.

Concurrent validity examines whether a measure of creativity correlates with other current measures of creativity or assessments of creative productivity. It might ask whether individuals scoring high on a particular measure of creativity also score high on another creativity test, or if their writing is rated as more creative than the writing of those who score lower. Measures used to assess concurrent validity all are given to subjects during the same general period.

Predictive validity addresses a more difficult challenge. It asks not how measures correlate with other measures today, but how they may relate to activities tomorrow. Predictive validity examines whether scores on a measure of creativity predict creative performance at a later time. Are the students who score highest on a creativity test today most likely to be the creative writers, artists, or scientists of tomorrow? Developing an instrument with long-term predictive validity is a daunting task. Regardless of the power of the measure, an enormous number of factors outside the level of childhood creativity will affect whether a person is creatively productive in adulthood. School influences, values of the surrounding culture, family interactions, personal health, and politics in the field of interest are just a few of the forces that may shape an individual's opportunities for creative activities. Some theorists have reasoned that because any creativity test can measure such a limited segment of creative behavior and because the influences on creativity are so complex, expectations of long-term predictive validity for creativity tests are "unrealistic and inappropriate" (Treffinger, 1987, p. 109). Nevertheless, predictive validity remains an important goal of creativity assessments and can be a valid source of comparisons among measures.

Both concurrent and predictive validity are affected by what Treffinger, Renzulli, and Feldhusen (1971) called "the criterion problem" (p. 105). Briefly, the criterion problem is the difficulty in identifying external criteria against which to test the validity of creativity tests. If experts disagree on the nature and manifestations of creativity, how can they determine what standard to hold up for real creativity in order to evaluate assessments? Efforts at identifying criteria have included other standardized assessments, teacher and peer judgments, profiles of adult accomplishments, and assessment of creative products. Whereas the criterion problem is obvious in the attempt to predict future creativity, it is a factor in any determination of validity regarding creativity.

Like content validity, construct validity asks whether the tasks on an instrument match generally accepted characteristics of the construct being measured—in this case creativity. It also examines how the scores on an instrument relate to other measures of creativity. However, unlike either of the previously mentioned types of validity, construct validity also considers how the measure fits into the total pattern of theory surrounding the construct to be assessed. It is concerned not only with whether this test measures the same thing as other creativity tests, but also with whether we are sure it is creativity we are measuring. Could this test really be measuring intelligence, motivation, or some other construct related to creativity?

In determining construct validity you must examine scores on instruments attempting to measure the same variable as well as scores on measures of different but related variables. If I were to examine the construct validity of a new instrument designed to assess creativity, I might give my new instrument to a group of subjects, along with several other measures of creativity and intelligence. I would examine how my test correlates with the other measures of creativity and how highly it correlates with measures of other constructs—in this case, intelligence. If I have developed the test, I hope for high correlations with other creativity measures and low correlations with other tests. If the new test correlates more highly with measures of creativity than with measures of intelligence, that result would be evidence that it does tap into the construct of creativity. If not, my new test may not actually be measuring creativity, but may be measuring intelligence, persistence, or some other variable.

Each of these types of validity is important in our consideration of how creativity will be assessed. If educational decisions are to be based on such assessments, we must ensure that the tools being used are the most reliable and valid measures available. Unfortunately, as the following brief review of tests clearly shows, the reliability and validity of most instruments designed to assess creativity are limited. In some cases, the limitations are so severe that the instruments are inappropriate for educational decision making. In other cases, instruments, although limited, still may be the best available. Educators who are knowledgeable about the need for reliability and validity are in a better position to judge the value of assessment information and how it may be combined in a variety of ways to help make the best decisions possible with the available information. Without such knowledge, test users can be at risk of accepting scores as absolute truth—an assumption that is seldom, if ever, appropriate.

Thinking About the Classroom

Examine a standardized test manual for a test used in your district. Evaluate the types of reliability and validity information provided. Determine what types of information are given and what, if anything, is missing or unclear.

INSTRUMENTS FOR ASSESSMENT OF CREATIVITY

As you review some of the instruments that have been developed to assess creativity, you should again consider three perspectives from which the concept of creativity has been viewed: person, process, and product. Many assessment tools can be similarly categorized. Some instruments provide tasks that require individuals to use processes associated with creativity. They may require test takers to solve open-ended problems, pull together remote associations, or derive multiple responses for a particular question. Tasks are constructed to demand the types of thinking emphasized in the definition or theory accepted by the test constructor.

Other measures focus on the products of creativity. These assessments are less concerned with how a creative product came to be than in the quality of the product itself. Instead of presenting subjects with an artificial task, they may assess the products of wild, or at least authentic, creativity. Works of art, scientific experiments, pieces of writing, or other creative efforts can be evaluated. Although the emphasis with this type of assessment is on more real-world products, it is similar to the process-focused assessment in that the thing to be measured is the result of someone's creative effort.

Still other measures of creativity focus not on the processes or products of creativity, but on the creative person. Instead of asking individuals to complete specific tasks, these measures focus on biographical or personality traits tied to creativity. Individuals may be evaluated for their willingness to take risks, internal locus of evaluation, past creative efforts, or other traits or activities commonly associated with creativity. The assumption is that individuals who have a high number of the personal characteristics found in creative individuals may be creative themselves. Many times, these measures take the form of self-report surveys or observational checklists. This section reviews some of the more commonly used assessment tools in each of the three categories as well as some whose characteristics span or defy the categorization. In each case, it is important to remember what aspect of creativity is being measured and how that information fits into the complex construct of real-world creativity. Additional information on evaluation instruments can be found in Callahan (1991) and Puccio and Murdock (1999).

Assessing Creative Processes

The Torrance Tests of Creative Thinking. Many standardized creativity tests are based on the processes of divergent thinking identified by

Guilford (1967). The most widely researched and extensively used of these are the Torrance Tests of Creative Thinking (TTCT; Torrance, 1990, 1999). Because these tests are widely available and frequently used by both schools and researchers (Cramond, 1998), the following discussion describes them in some detail.

Torrance tests are available in both figural and verbal versions, each with an A and B forms. Both versions of the test ask the test taker to complete a series of open-ended tasks presented in test booklets. For example, the verbal test asks the individual to list all the questions he or she can think to ask about a given picture. Other test items require the test taker to list possible improvements for a product and unusual uses for common objects. The figural form asks the test taker to make as many different pictures as possible using a common shape (for example, a circle), and to make and label pictures using a series of abstract forms. All subtests are timed.

The tests are scored for fluency, flexibility, originality, and (in the figural tests) elaboration. The scoring procedures are described in considerable detail in the test manual, but the tests also may be sent to a scoring service. Fluency scores are simply a count of ideas listed or drawings completed. Flexibility scores reflect the number of categories of ideas represented. For example, using the figural version, student A may have completed 15 drawings using circles, all drawings of animals. Student B also may have completed 15 drawings, but may have included drawings of animals, vehicles, food, toys, and planets. Both students would have a fluency score of 15, but student A would have a much lower flexibility score than student B. Originality scores are determined by statistical infrequency. If an item or idea was rarely expressed by the students on whom the test was normed, it is considered to be original. Each idea is listed in a table and awarded 0, 1, or 2 originality points. The test scorer matches each idea or drawing with the closest approximation in the table and judges it for creative strength.

The open-ended nature of the tasks and multiple dimensions to be evaluated make scoring Torrance tests a time-consuming endeavor. However, the detail provided in the test manual helps ensure good interrater reliability. One caution was raised by Rosenthal, DeMars, Stilwell, and Graybeal (1983), who noted that although the correlations across raters were high, there still were significant mean differences across self-trained raters. That is, although the raters ranked the tests in approximately the same order, some judges gave generally higher scores than others. This discrepancy would mean that if Torrance tests are used to compare students or groups of students, the same scorer should evaluate all students, or adjustments should be made to compensate for differences in judges. In the same way, program evaluations using Torrance tests should use the same evaluator(s) for pre- and posttest scoring. Otherwise, any differences identified may be the result of a particular scorer's rating patterns rather than true differences among students or groups.

A new streamlined scoring technique was developed by Ball and Torrance (1980). It is designed to minimize scoring time and allow the scorer to assess additional dimensions of creativity, including emotional expressiveness and internal visualization. These additional dimensions are not norm referenced (i.e., they do not compare test takers with a standard degree of emotional expressiveness demonstrated by the norming population), but they allow scorers to make judgments in relation to specified criteria.

The predictive validity of the Torrance tests varies in different research studies. Torrance (1984) reported two longitudinal studies in which subjects' results on early versions of the TTCT were correlated with their accomplishments as adults after 12 and 20 years. Although the correlations were far from perfect (ranging from 0.43 to 0.63), they are as high as most predictive validity scores of achievement or intelligence tests. In 1999, Torrance reported similar findings after 40 years. Torrance and Wu (1981) found that students identified as highly creative in high school earned as many postgraduation degrees and honors as students identified as highly intelligent and surpassed the high-IQ students in adult achievement. Howieson (1981, 1984) also examined the predictive validity of Torrance tests, with less consistent results. He found that the verbal version of the TTCT did not predict adult creative achievement measured 23 years later at levels that were statistically significant. The verbal form predicted public and personally recognized achievements at levels ranging from 0.33 to 0.51. Interestingly, both Torrance and Howieson found that the tests were more accurate in predicting creative accomplishments for men than for women.

Perhaps the most important set of concerns regarding the Torrance tests comes from research suggesting that the conditions under which the test is taken can have a significant effect on the scores. Torrance (1988) listed 36 studies examining the results of varying testing conditions on TTCT scores. Of these, 27 studies found significant differences in scores on at least some test forms after changes in test conditions. The changes ranged from barren and enriched rooms to varying warm-up activities and differences in timing. Other differences have been related to whether the testing was preceded by an interesting or uninteresting activity (Kirkland, 1974; Kirkland, Kirkland, & Barker, 1976), whether conditions were testlike or gamelike (Hattie, 1980), and minor changes in test instructions (Lissitz & Willhoft, 1985). If students are to be compared using scores from Torrance tests, testing conditions should be consistent in as many details as possible. Reviews of the Torrance tests vary from the critical assessment that the tests are based on a "loosely formed" theory and best used for research and experimentation only (Chase, 1985, p. 1632) to their recommendation as "sound examples of instruments useful for research, evaluation, and general planning decisions" (Treffinger, 1985, p. 1634). Whatever their weaknesses, the TTCT remain the most widely used and researched assessments of creativity and, as such, often provide a standard against which other tools are measured.

Thinking Creatively in Action and Movement.   Another test developed by Torrance (1981), Thinking Creatively in Action and Movement (TCAM), examines fluency and originality as they are expressed in movement. Designed to be used with students as young as preschool age, the test asks subjects to move across the room in as many different ways as they can, to move in designated ways (e.g., like a tree in the wind), to put a paper cup into a waste basket in as many ways as possible, and to generate possible uses for a paper cup. The tests are not timed. They are scored for fluency (number of ideas) and originality using a scoring guide similar to the TTCT guide.

Short-term test–retest reliability and interrater reliability correlations for TCAM are high. Validity evidence is less well defined. Some efforts at establishing concurrent validity have compared scores on TCAM with scores on two other measures of fluency: the Multidimensional Stimulus Fluency Measure (Godwin & Moran, cited in Callahan, 1991) and Piagetian tasks identified by researchers as divergent (Reisman, Floyd, & Torrance, 1981). In both cases, scores correlated significantly. However, Tegano, Moran, and Godwin (1986) found significant correlations between the fluency scores on TCAM and both IQ and age. This finding raises questions about whether scores on TCAM reflect creativity or intelligence, and whether they might change significantly over time. Reviews have praised TCAM as an important contribution to the assessment of creativity in young children, but have noted its experimental nature and the need for additional research before it can be used with confidence in educational decision making (Evans, 1986; Renzulli, 1985; Rust, 1985).

Thinking Creatively With Sounds and Words.   Still another product of Torrance and his colleagues, Thinking Creatively With Sounds and Words (Torrance, Khatena, & Cunningham, 1973), uses recorded sounds to stimulate divergent thinking. The instrument actually comprises two tests: Sounds and Images and Onomatopoeia and Images. In the Sounds and Images test, test takers are presented with four abstract sounds. After each sound, the individual jots down the mental images he or she associates with each sound. The set of four sounds is presented three times. Subjects' ideas are evaluated for originality using a scoring guide similar to those in the two tests previously described. The Onomatopoeia and Images test is similar except that instead of abstract sounds, subjects are presented with 10 onomatopoetic words such as "boom" or "fizzy." The set of words also is repeated three times and scored as in the previous test. Both tests are available in A and B forms and with instructions designed for adults or children. As does TCAM, this test presents reasonable reliability data except for some weaknesses in alternate forms, but presents inadequate evidence of validity for it to be a major source in educational decision making (Houtz, 1985). Until further information on validity is available, the tests may be most useful as a source of interesting creative activities in varying domains rather than a means of assessment.

Guilford and the Structure of Intellect Assessments.   All of the tests assessing divergent thinking are built on the work of Guilford (1967, 1973, 1977). Based on his Structure of Intellect (SOI) model, Guilford's tests emphasized divergent production and transformations. Guilford's Creativity Tests for Children (1973) are made up of five verbal and five non-verbal divergent production tasks. They include generating names for stories, finding letters of the alphabet hidden in complex figures, and listing alternate uses for familiar objects. His Alternate Uses Test, which can be used for secondary students and adults, is a single task requiring test takers to list alternate uses for six common objects. The reviews of these tests have been critical. Concerns expressed by reviewers regarding the Creativity Tests for Children include low correlations with the Torrance tests and low reliability estimates (French, 1978; Yamamoto, 1978). The Alternate Uses Test was criticized for lack of interrater-reliability data, lack of correlation with other measures of divergent thinking, the influence of background experience on scores, and inadequate information in the test manual (Quellmalz, 1985). At this point, it appears that the second generation of divergent thinking tests (notably the TTCT) have outdistanced Guilford's original measures in estimates of reliability and validity.

Meeker also adapted groups of Guilford tests in a diagnostic–prescriptive model of instruction, the Structure of Intellect Learning Abilities Test (SOI-LA; Meeker, 1969; Meeker, Meeker, & Roid, 1985). Students are tested on various aspects of SOI (described in chap. 2) and provided with targeted remediation and instruction. Although not a creativity test per se, the SOI-LA does include a divergent thinking score associated with creativity. Unfortunately, like the Guilford's tests, the SOI-LA in general and the divergent thinking scores in particular have been seriously questioned by test reviewers. One reviewer suggested, "Maybe the SOI–LA represents an attempt to slice the intellectual pie too thinly" (Cummings, 1989, p. 790). Reviewers' concerns have included limitations in reliability of both test–retest and alternate forms, with divergent thinking scores particularly low. Certainly, limited alternate-forms reliability in divergent thinking scores would make the use of alternate forms for pre- and posttesting inappropriate (Clarizio & Mehrens, 1985; Cummings, 1989).

The Wallach and Kogan Tests.   Similar to the preceding tests, the Wallach and Kogan battery also is a series of tasks requiring divergent thinking. It includes five subtests: Instances (e.g., "Name all the things with wheels you can think of"), Alternate Uses, Pattern Meanings, Line Meanings (interpreting abstract designs or lines), and Similarities (e.g., "Tell me all the ways in which a cat and a mouse are alike"). The battery is not available from a publisher, but is reproduced in its entirety in *Modes of Thinking in Young Children* (Wallach & Kogan, 1965). Although it is not commonly used in schools, the Wallach and Kogan battery is important for at least two reasons: It is frequently used in research involving creativity, and it is conducted in a unique testing atmosphere. Wallach and Kogan (1965) believed that the formal test settings of most creativity tests are not conducive to creativity in young children, particularly if creativity requires a relaxed, playful state of mind. Consequently, their tests are designed to be given individually in an untimed, gamelike atmosphere. Their original research emphasized the relationship between tests of creativity and intelligence, a question of construct validity. In a study of 151 fifth-grade children, they found that the scores on the five subtests correlated strongly with one another, but not highly with measures of intelligence. This is one piece of evidence in the debate over the relationship between creativity and intelligence.

There is one unusual aspect to the scoring of the Wallach and Kogan battery. The tests are scored for fluency (the total number of ideas listed) and uniqueness (the number of ideas given that are not given by any other member of the group tested). Although this scoring variation may help to account for cultural differences (a response that might have been unique in a norming population used to create a scoring chart might be very common in another group), it causes scores to be heavily affected by the number of individuals taking the test. If I were to take the tests in a group of 10, it is much more likely that I would generate several unique ideas than if my responses were being compared with 500 others.

Because this test battery is published as part of a research study and not as a nationally distributed standardized test, the information on reliability and validity is not as extensive nor the sample as large as might be expected for other uses. There are some data suggesting that the battery may be more reliable for students scoring higher on standardized achievement tests (Runco & Albert, 1985), and that the verbal subtests correlate with self-reports of creative activities in students identified as gifted, but not in others (Runco, 1986). The relationship between Wallach and Kogan scores and general intellectual ability requires further investigation.

The Remote Associates Test.   The Remote Associates Test (RAT) was developed by Mednick (1967) as an assessment tool based on his theory of creativity. Recall from chapter 2 that Mednick believed creativity to be the result of mental associations. The more numerous and diverse the associations an individual can make, the more opportunities he or she has for creativity. The RAT attempts to assess the number of verbal associations at an individual's disposal by providing three stimulus words and asking the test taker to generate a word that can be associated with all three. For example, the words birthday, surprise, and line all can be associated with the response "party."

Some validity studies of the RAT have showed correlations between it and other assessments of creativity, whereas other studies have found no such relationships (Lynch & Kaufman, 1974; Mednick, 1962; Wallach, 1970). No validity data are available for the high school version of the test. Moreover, the validity of the RAT has been questioned on theoretical grounds. The nature of the test punishes novel or imaginative responses; an association is scored as correct only if it is the same association made by the test constructors. The test also has been criticized because studies of the processes used by individuals taking the test do not match those intended by the author (Perkins, 1981) and because scores on the RAT correlate highly with IQ scores (Ward, 1975). Another review also criticized the role of convergent production in the RAT and suggested that it "not be used for counseling or placement purposes at the present time" (Backman & Tuckman, 1978, p. 370). Finally, the RAT has been criticized for cultural bias because of its use of slang. The RAT is currently out of print.

The Creative Reasoning Test.   A more recent test from Midwest Publishers, the Creative Reasoning Test, contains 20 items designed to assess creativity using riddles. Unfortunately, at this point, even the most basic technical information on the test is unavailable. There are two versions of the instrument, but no information on alternate-forms or test–retest reliability is provided. There is no information on the groups on which the test was standardized, nor is there a comparison of scores on the Creative Reasoning Test with scores on tests of other potentially related constructs, such as IQ or critical thinking. Validity was assessed through a 0.70 correlation with the RAT. However, because the RAT also is convergent and correlates highly with IQ, this correlation leaves unanswered questions about the nature of the construct actually measured by this instrument (Drummond, 1992).

Process Tests Yet to Come. As theories of creativity continue to emerge, new assessment tools are being developed. Such tools often are more appropriate for research and test development activities than for educational decision making, but they can help us to consider the types of assessments that may be available in the future. For example, some researchers are experimenting with instruments that include the process of problem finding. Wakefield (1985, 1992) developed assessments of creativity that ask students to develop their own test items. In addition to responding divergently to patterns and lines from a test activity developed by Wallach and Kogan (1965), students were asked to create original designs and respond divergently to their own items. Divergent thinking scores for the standard items did not correlate significantly with another measure of creativity—the Group Inventory for Finding Creative Talent (GIFT; see later). However, there was a significant correlation between the GIFT and divergent responses to students' original items. These responses also correlated significantly with expert ratings of student drawings.

Smilansky (1984) also adapted existing tests to include the creation of original problems. High school students were tested with Series D and E of the Raven Progressive Matrices and asked to create a new problem for the test as difficult as possible to solve. Runco and Okuda (1988) followed similar procedures using adaptations of the Wallach and Kogan tests. They found that students generated significantly more responses to their own invented problems than to standard presented problems. Continuing research examines the relationship between the ability to solve problems and the ability to create them. It is possible that, in time, problem finding may become part of one or more standardized assessment techniques. It also is possible that other contemporary theories of creative processes may find their way into assessment.

Runco (1991b, 1993) and Runco and Chand (1994) suggested that an important dimension for assessing creative processes is evaluation. Creative producers, after all, must not only produce ideas, but also select those ideas worth pursuing. Judging an individual's ability to separate common from original ideas may provide another window to creative ability. This evaluation ability appears linked to divergent thinking and to attitudes that value divergent thinking, but not to evaluation as part of the Structure of Intellect (SOI) model. Runco (1991b) suggested that "the most important prediction [of creativity] would use evaluation skill, divergent thinking and problem finding ability, for all three are theoretically necessary for creative ideation" (p. 317).

Okuda, Runco, and Berger (1991) hypothesized that tests of divergent thinking might be more accurate in predicting creative behavior if the tests contained problems more similar to real-world situations. They examined students' performances with both presented and discovered real-world problems. In presented problems, students were asked to generate possible solutions to a problematic situation—for example, a friend who constantly talks in class. In discovered problems, students were asked to think of problems at home or school. Responses to the presented real-world problems were the best predictors of creative activities as measured by a self-report checklist.

Another possible adaptation in creativity testing is in the scoring procedures. To date, most tests of creative processes have examined divergent thinking, generally scored as fluency, flexibility, originality, and elaboration. However, there is considerable question as to whether these scores actually represent three different abilities. Callahan (1991) referred to fluency as a "contaminating factor" (p. 229) in the assessment of originality. Higher fluency scores accompany higher scores on originality. Similarly, higher fluency scores are associated with higher scores on flexibility. The concern about fluency as a contaminating factor has been echoed by other writers (Plucker & Renzulli, 1999; Plucker & Runco, 1998). It is possible that future research and test development may lead us to alternative scoring mechanisms for divergent thinking tasks. The streamlined scoring procedure for the Torrance Tests of Creative Thinking (TTCT; perhaps misnamed because it results in many more than four scores) is one effort in this direction. Other suggestions were made by Runco, Okuda, and Thurston (1987), who found that more valid scores could be obtained by summing divergent thinking scores or using a weighted fluency score. Runco and Mraz (1992) suggested that divergent thinking tests could be scored more easily and accurately by creating one score for the subject's entire output. In their research, judges assessed the entire pool of each individual's answers, giving one overall creativity score rather than separate scores for fluency, originality, and so on. Although it is not wise to add or otherwise adjust current creativity test scores contrary to the instructions of the test constructors, it is possible that future research will allow us to use scores in new and more effective ways.

Still other creativity tests to come may assess process factors not yet addressed in commercial measures. For example, a number of authors have examined the role of insight in creativity (see Sternberg & Davidson, 1995). Tests that attempt to measure insight, problem identification (Runco & Chand, 1994; Starko, 2000), or other process variables may one day add to our understanding of the creative process.

Assessing the Creative Person

Instruments focusing on the characteristics of the creative person include personality assessments and biographical inventories. These most often take the form of self-reports or observational checklists.

The Khatena–Torrance Creative Perception Inventory.   This two-part inventory includes the self-rating scales What Kind of Person Are You? (WKOPAY) and Something About Myself (SAM). It is designed to identify creative individuals ages 10 years and older (Khatena & Torrance, 1976, 1990). The WKOPAY is designed to "yield an index of the individual's disposition or motivation to function in creative ways" (Khatena, 1992, p. 134). It contains 50 forced-choice items that require the test taker to choose between items that may be socially desirable or undesirable, creative or noncreative. For example, one item might ask individuals whether they are more likely to care for others or have courage for what they believe. The scale yields five factors: acceptance of authority, self-confidence, inquisitiveness, awareness of others, and disciplined imagination.

The SAM is designed to reflect an individual's personality characteristics, thinking strategies, and creative products. Test takers review 50 statements such as "I like adding to an idea" or "I have made a new dance or song" and indicate which statements are true for them. This scale yields six factor scores: environmental sensitivity, initiative, self-strength, intellectuality, individuality, and artistry.

Reliability data for the inventory are satisfactory. Validity studies have shown moderate but significant correlations between SAM and tests of verbal originality and the Onomatopoeia and Images subtest of Thinking Creatively With Sounds and Words. Both scales correlated significantly with a measure of readiness for self-directed study (Kaltsounis, 1975;

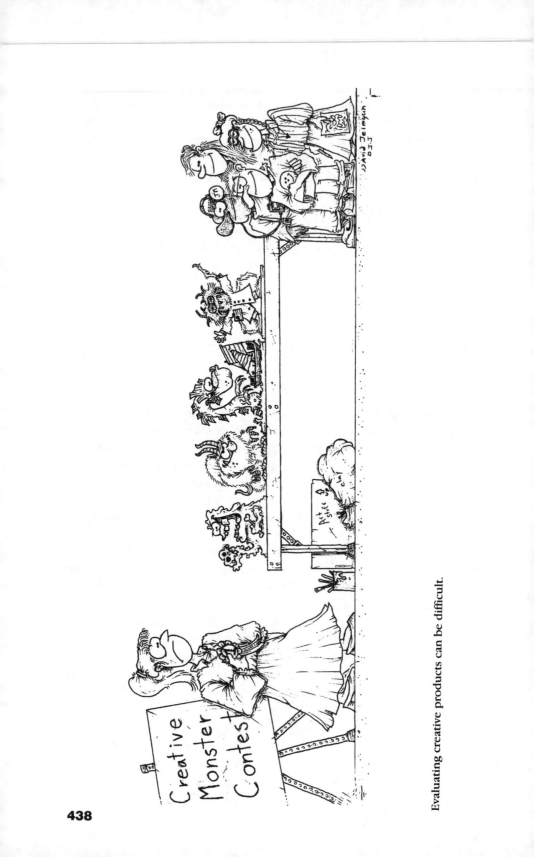

Evaluating creative products can be difficult.

Khatena & Bellarosa, 1978). At this point, there are no data on predictive validity for either scale.

Group Inventory for Finding Creative Talent.   The Group Inventory for Finding Creative Talent (GIFT) is a self-report form designed to assess the creative potential of students grades 1 to 6 (Davis & Rimm, 1980). Students respond "yes" or "no" to a series of statements designed to assess the traits of independence, flexibility, curiosity, perseverance, breadth of interests, and past creative activities and hobbies (Davis, 1992). They respond to statements such as "I like to make up my own songs," "I like to take things apart to see how they work," and "I like to do things that are hard to do." The GIFT instrument yields a total score and scores for three subscales: imagination, independence, and many interests. Tests must be scored by the publisher. Although publisher scoring ensures consistency, it can cause delays and makes it impossible to examine individual responses to analyze scores.

The split-half reliability (correlating one half of the scale with the other half) for GIFT is strong, but the test–retest reliability is only moderate. Validity studies have compared GIFT scores with teacher ratings of creativity and experimenter ratings of creative stories and pictures. The relationships were low to moderate (ranging from 0.20 to 0.54) and significant. Reviewers of the GIFT have stressed the need for additional validity data and more complete information in the test manual, but they have viewed the scale as a useful tool for decision making when used in conjunction with other types of assessment (Dwinell, 1985; Wright, 1985).

Group Inventories for Finding Interests (I and II).   The Group Inventories for Finding Interests (GIFFI) I and II are very similar to GIFT, but are designed for junior and senior high school students, respectively (Davis & Rimm, 1982). Their strengths and weaknesses are very similar to those of GIFT. Validity studies comparing scores on GIFFI with writing samples and teacher ratings have produced an average score of 0.45. The GIFFI has been criticized for cultural bias in some of the items (e.g, "I like to attend concerts"), which may undermine its effectiveness, particularly in multicultural populations (Weeks, 1985).

Creative Attitude Survey.   The Creative Attitude Survey (Schaefer, 1971) is designed to assess subjects' attitudes associated with creativity, including confidence in one's ideas, appreciation of fantasy, theoretical and aesthetic orientation, openness to impulse expression, and use of novelty. Validity information has come through the evaluation of two training programs in which elementary school children received creativity training over a period of weeks. The students who received the creativity training had increased scores on the Creative Attitude Survey, whereas the control groups did not. Twenty months later, the differences remained. At least one reviewer has suggested that this instrument may be effective for evaluating programs designed to increase creativity in elementary school–age children (McKee, 1985).

Biographical Inventory—Creativity.   The Biographical Inventory—Creativity (BIC; Schaefer, 1970) is based on the assumption that the best predictor of future activity is past activity—those who have been involved in creative activities in the past are more likely to be so involved again. The inventory consists of 165 items in which the test taker is asked whether he or she has participated in a given activity. It yields four scores: creative art for girls, creative writing for girls, creative math and science for boys, and art and writing for boys. Research on the BIC has indicated that the instrument successfully differentiated groups of high school students who had been nominated by teachers for scientific or artistic creativity from other students matched for school, grade, and grade point average (Anastasi & Schaefer, 1969; Schaefer, 1969; Schaefer & Anastasi, 1968). It is important to recognize, however, that significantly differentiating large groups is a different task from providing reliable and valid individual scores. Additional research is necessary regarding the appropriateness of the BIC for educational decision making for individuals.

As research on creative individuals continues, it is likely that other types of assessment instruments will emerge. For example, Selby, Treffinger, Isaksen, and Lauer (2002) have described a new instrument, VIEW, designed to assess problem-solving style. As we learn more about how creative individuals solve problems, we may discover multiple variations across individuals and domains.

Instruments Assessing Creative Products

With this type of assessment, an individual is faced with a creative product and asked to make a determination: "Is this creative?" or "To what degree is this creative?" Assessments of creative products are made every day by art, literary, and theatrical critics and editors of scientific journals. Using their knowledge of the forms, standards, and history of their discipline, these experts are able to determine where a work falls in the field at a given time. Assessments of creative products virtually always entail subjectivity, knowledge, and expertise. Packaging such assessments as standardized, easily purchased items is very difficult, but assessment of creativity must, ultimately, depend on the evaluation of its fruits.

Few empirical studies have attempted to identify the characteristics of a creative product (Besemer & Treffinger, 1981). One effort to develop a model for creative product analysis is the Creative Product Assessment Matrix (CPAM; Besemer & O'Quin, 1986). It suggests three dimensions for assessing creative products: novelty, resolution, and elaboration and synthesis. Novelty includes the originality of the product and its potential for generating further ideas and changes. Resolution entails how well the product serves its intended purpose, solves a problem, or fills a need. Elaboration and synthesis express stylistic attributes of the product and may include diverse complexity or simple elegance.

An instrument designed to assess students' creative products is the Student Product Assessment Form (SPAF; Renzulli & Reis, 1997). The SPAF is used to rate student products on nine factors (Fig. 8.1). Although not all factors are appropriate for every kind of product, item descriptions provide clarity in the judging of each factor and contribute to the reliability of this instrument. As efforts to create a concise model for assessing creative products continue, both CPAM and SPAF may provide general guidelines for those attempting to evaluate creative products.

Instruments such as these, designed to assist in the evaluation of creative products, generally are intended to bring consistency to the endeavor. If two movie critics give widely different reviews of the same movie, the disparity may be viewed as a legitimate difference of opinion. If a particular critic consistently reviews differently from the majority of his or her colleagues, he or she will be labeled a maverick or find a new career, but probably will not determine the fate of the films. If educational decisions are made on the basis of product evaluations, a maverick judge can affect children's opportunities in important ways. Therefore, although professional critics seldom sit down to review a product with a checklist in hand, such guidance may be appropriate in an educational setting.

The scoring rubrics for authentic assessment described in chapter 7 are a form of product assessment. Each is designed to provide a set of criteria along which complex products can be assessed. Similar patterns can be followed in the assessment of creative products, with consistent attention paid to the creativity expressed. Products to be assessed may be single items or a portfolio of creative efforts.

The concept of student portfolios to be used for planning and assessment gained in popularity during the 1990s, particularly in the area of

		NOT
FACTORS	**RATING***	**APPLICABLE**

Name(s) _____ Date _____

District _____ School _____

Teacher _____ Grade _____ Sex _____

Product (Title and/or Brief Description) _____

_____

Number of Months Student(s) worked on Product _____

FACTORS	RATING*	NOT APPLICABLE
1. Early Statement of Purpose	_____	_____
2. Problem Focusing	_____	_____
3. Level of Resources	_____	_____
4. Diversity of Resources	_____	_____
5. Appropriateness of Resources	_____	_____
6. Logic, Sequence, and Transition	_____	_____
7. Action Orientation	_____	_____
8. Audience	_____	_____
9. Overall Assessment	_____	_____
A. Originality of the Idea	_____	_____
B. Achieved Objectives Stated in Plan	_____	_____
C. Advanced Familiarity with Subject	_____	_____
D. Quality Beyond Age/Grade Level	_____	_____
E. Care, Attention to Detail, etc.	_____	_____
F. Time, Effort, Energy	_____	_____
G. Original Contribution	_____	_____

Comments:

Person completing this form:

_____

*Rating Scales: Factors 1–8   Factors 9A – 9G

   5 - To a great extent   5 = Outstanding   2 = Below Average

   3 - Somewhat   4 = Above Average   1 = Poor

   1 - To a limited extent   3 = Average

FIG. 8.1. Student project assessment form summary sheet. From "The Assessment of Creative Products in Programs for Gifted and Talented Students," by and J. S. Renzulli and S. M. Reis, 1985, *Gifted Child Quarterly, 35*(2), 130. Copyright © 1991 by Creative Learning Press. Reprinted with permission.

writing. Teachers and students collect samples of students' work throughout the year as a means of demonstrating student progress. Often, several
drafts of a work may be included to illustrate thought processes, self-assessment, and developing sophistication. Similar collections of work can
be made in other domains, such as science portfolios and math portfolios.
These may or may not be contained in physical folders. A student whose
oral history project or screenplay is best captured on videotape will need a
portfolio in a box.

Regardless of the subject areas, portfolios provide one strategy for organizing the assessment of creative products. If, for some reason (such as
participation in a particular school program), you need to identify exceptionally creative individuals in a given class or school, you may want to compile a separate creativity portfolio that documents creative activities in
multiple domains. It might contain photographs or originals of artwork,
creative writing, tapes or scores of original music, video of performances,
accounts of real-life problem solving, unusual responses to class assignments, records of science projects, invention notes, or any other documentation of creative activities. These can be assessed using a scoring rubric
developed as described in chapter 7. The rubric might include dimensions
for novelty, technical quality, depth or breadth of interests, or any other factor relevant to the selection need.

Thinking About the Classroom

Compile a creativity portfolio for at least one student. Include
evidence of creative activities in at least three areas. You may
want to share the information with the student's parents.

If creativity is to be evaluated, not for individual decision making, but as
part of general classroom assessment, a separate portfolio probably is not
necessary. One possible strategy is to examine the scoring procedures currently in place for any portfolio or other performance assessment currently
in use. Is there a dimension that gives credit for novelty in appropriate responses? If a writing portfolio provides numerous opportunities for teachers and students to examine proofreading and grammar skills, but few
chances to evaluate originality, imagery, or the use of metaphor, opportunities to evaluate and encourage creative products are being lost.

The products to be assessed may be naturally occurring—part of an individual's typical productivity—or they may be generated specifically for assessment. Both have their advantages. Products generated specifically for

assessment have the advantage of consistency and often are easier to rate relative to one another. Naturally occurring products are less likely to have been produced in a constrained amount of time and may be more likely to represent an individual's best work and genuine interests. A portfolio of creative work might include one or two items created specifically for assessment purposes, some regular class assignments, and some items created outside a school setting.

When student products are assessed, they should be judged in an appropriate context, with criteria suitable for students. If student products are judged by adult standards, few are likely to be viewed as highly creative. It is unlikely, for example, that a student will transform his or her discipline as did Martha Graham or Stephen Hawking. A publication of the Ohio Department of Education (1992) listed four types of products and how they might be manifested in adults and children. The products are theories, techniques, inventions, and compositions. Creative theories in adults include such developments as the theory of relativity or the theory of evolution. Students' theories include linking ideas and concepts in ways new to them. Creative techniques involve using materials or resources in new ways. In adults, this can be exemplified in the development of cubism or modern dance. In children, it can be manifested as novel uses of materials. Certainly, both children and adults are capable of creating new inventions, although adults may be more likely to generate inventions that are new to the world. In the same way, creative adult compositions may lead to great works of literature. Student compositions may share ideas in ways unique for the students' age or background. The four categories of theories, techniques, inventions, and compositions may provide guidance to those planning assessments of creative products. The categories might be used on a scoring rubric or as guidelines for materials that might be documented in a portfolio of student achievements.

There have been other efforts to develop standardized criteria for assessing student products. In addition to CPAM and SPAF described earlier, Parke and Byrnes (1984) reported on the Detroit Public Schools Creativity Scales, which include scales in art, music composition, music performance, drama, poetry, short story and novel writing, speech, and dance. Kulp and Tarter (1986) developed a rating scale for art products generated from five basic geometric figures. Although reliability and validity data on the scales are limited at this time, such instruments do represent a step forward in the assessment of student products.

In some cases, particularly with advanced students, teachers may feel they do not have sufficient expertise to assess creative products. For these situations, expert judges using Amabile's (1982, 1996) consensual assessment strategy may be most effective. In consensual assessment, expert judges rate creative products. If there is agreement among the judges as to the most creative products, usually at about 0.80, the judgments are considered sound. Because the judges are expert in the area being assessed, they are not provided with specific criteria for judgment, but are asked to make several global assessments such as evaluations of creativity, technical skill, and overall quality.

The following guidelines were offered to researchers using consensual assessment in research. They seem reasonable for others using expert judges as part of creativity assessment (Hennessey & Amabile, 1988).

1. Use experienced, knowledgeable judges. The judges need not all have the same level of expertise, but they should be knowledgeable in their domain. If creative products span several dimensions or domains, judges' expertise should be similarly broad. For example, if the art portfolios to be judged include sketches, paintings, advertising designs, and photographs of sculptures, a better panel would be judges whose expertise included several areas and techniques rather than those who all were landscape painters.

2. Have judges make their assessments independently. The correlations among judges become meaningless if judges have conferred. Each individual judge should bring his or her ideas of creativity to the task.

3. Make judgments of all dimensions at the same time. For example, if judges rate products on both creativity and technical expertise, it is easier to determine whether the judgments of creativity are related to, or independent of, technique.

4. Rate products relative to each other. It is important that judges be instructed to rate products in a student's own sphere rather than by the standards they might hold for adult colleagues. Although assessment according to adult criteria may be useful for older students, few useful purposes are served by observing that none of the elementary students' efforts meet adult standards.

5. Rate products in random order. Judges should not rate the products in the same order. Otherwise, assessment may relate more to order (e.g., specific comparisons or weariness of the judges) than to merits of particular products.

Assessment by experts might be appropriate for selecting highly creative students for advanced educational opportunities. Such processes are fairly familiar in the arts. For example, if students are to be nominated for a state-level summer art program, art students might be asked to compile a portfolio of their work. Portfolios could be judged by two or three professional artists whose combined scores could be used for decision making. Students can be taught to compile documentation of their creative efforts in other domains. They can keep records of science projects, musical compositions, writing, inventions, or historical research. Expert judges can assist in educational decision making and provide realistic feedback to older students about career opportunities.

Thinking About the Classroom

Work with colleagues to collect high-quality samples of student work in a particular domain. You may wish to focus on the work of secondary school students. Ask two or three expert judges to rate the samples separately for creativity, technical skill, and overall quality. See if your data provide support for consensual assessment as an evaluation tool.

Combinations and Other Types of Assessment

Some creativity assessment tools bridge the neat division into process, person, and product categories of creativity assessment.

Creativity Assessment Packet.   Williams' (1980) Creativity Assessment Packet (CAP) includes three tasks: the Exercise in Divergent Thinking, the Exercise in Divergent Feeling, and the Williams Scale. The Exercise in Divergent Thinking is almost identical to the picture completion subtest on the figural form of the Torrance Tests of Creative Thinking (TTCT). It includes 12 incomplete drawings that students are to complete and title. The drawings are scored for fluency, flexibility, originality, and elaboration. Titles are awarded from 1 to 3 points each, on the basis of length, complexity, creativity, and humor. The five scores are totaled for a creativity score. The Exercise in Divergent Feeling includes 50 items on which students are to rate themselves along a 4-point scale for such characteristics as curiosity and imagination. It yields scores for four subscales (curiosity, imagination, complexity, and risk taking) and a total score. The Williams Scale is a 48-item checklist to be used by a parent or teacher rating the child on creative characteristics and activities.

The combination of a divergent thinking measure, a self-assessment of characteristics associated with creativity, and a behavioral checklist would seem, at first glance, to be a logical and possibly winning combination. Unfortunately, the CAP has been criticized severely by reviewers. Concerns have included poor norming samples and unclear and inadequate reliability and validity data. Reliabilities are characterized as "in the sixties," and "validity scores" of 0.71 and 0.76 are given without any information as to what they mean or how they were obtained (Damarin, 1985). Two 1985 reviewers concluded that the limitations are so severe that the CAP cannot be recommended for use (Damarin, 1985; Rosen, 1985).

Creativity Behavior Inventory.   A second assessment tool that defies categorization is the Creativity Behavior Inventory (CBI; Kirschenbaum, 1989). The CBI is a teacher rating scale designed to measure four aspects of creativity: contact (amount and accuracy of reported details, and attraction to diverse aspects of the environment), consciousness (fluency and relevance of ideas and questions, and nonconformity in judgment), interest (perseverance), and fantasy (impact of images). Although reliability assessments show promise, reviewers did not recommend the CBI for educational decision making (Clark, 1992). The extensive review of the literature makes it clear that the instrument is theory based, but other validity data are limited and unclear unless the reviewer has an understanding of the Revolving Door Identification Model (Renzulli, Reis, & Smith, 1981), a model for the education of gifted children used in the validation study. The instrument was able to predict which above-average-ability students voluntarily engaged in a creative project with 8% accuracy. With further development, the CPI may become a useful tool for identifying students who may benefit from creative opportunities.

Behavioral Observations.   One common way of assessing creativity in schools is through the use of behavioral observations. Guided by a checklist or observation form, teachers identify students whose behaviors match descriptions of activities associated with creativity. One of the most commonly used tools for observation is the Creativity scale of the Scales for Rating the Behavioral Characteristics of Superior Students (Renzulli, Smith, White, Callahan, Hartman, & Westburg, 2002). This 9-item checklist describes behaviors such as imaginative thinking ability and "a non-conforming attitude, does not fear being different." Teachers use a 6-point scale to rate each student on each behavior. Both test–retest and interrater reliabilities data for this instrument are strong. In initial validity studies, the Creativity scale correlated significantly with verbal scores on the Torrance Tests of Creative Thinking (TTCT), but not with figural scores. The authors suggest that "this finding reflects a verbal bias in the Creativity Scale items and suggests that caution should be exercised in using this scale to identify students for programs that emphasize nonverbal creativity" (p. 9). The revised scales correlate with success in gifted programs for Grades 3–12.

Thinking About the Classroom

Use the Creativity scale of the Scales for Rating the Behavioral Characteristics of Superior Students to evaluate five randomly chosen students in your class. Do you feel the results of the scale accurately reflect the students' creative behavior in your class?

Another type of instrument, the Kingore Observation Inventory (KOI; Kingore, 1990), provides teachers with descriptions of target student behaviors on a large form to be kept on the teacher's desk. For several days, teachers jot a student's name next to a characteristic each time he or she demonstrates the behavior. Less commonly, teachers may plan a specific activity designed to elicit creative activity and make anecdotal records of student behaviors. The KOI is designed to identify young gifted children rather than to assess creativity. Although several of the categories of behavior may be associated with creativity (e.g., Perspective or Sense of Humor), the author has suggested that creative behaviors may be infused throughout any of the observations. No reliability or validity data are reported. The lack of reliability and validity data raises questions, and teachers wishing to assess creativity may want to use an instrument that targets key behaviors more specifically. However, the concept of observing designated behaviors over a designated period may prove fruitful as new observations are developed.

The subjective nature of most rating scales makes reliability and validity assessments difficult. In particular, school-specific homemade activities and scales are at risk of providing unreliable or invalid data. Yet observations of students' behaviors often can provide clues to strengths and abilities not accessed by written standardized tests. In addition, an observation of activities directly associated with the purpose of assessment (e.g., observations of activities in a high school industrial technology class in order to nominate students for a specialized program making creative use of technology) may provide appropriate information for particular circumstances. In no case, however, should instruments of questionable reliability and validity be the sole source of information for educational decision making.

ASSESSING CREATIVITY IN SCHOOLS

Schools and school districts have assessed creativity in a variety of ways, depending on their needs. If creativity is assessed outside a general classroom evaluation, it usually is for the purpose of identifying students with exceptional creative potential who may benefit from particular educational opportunities. If, for example, the school has a mentorship program in which community adults work with students in areas of mutual interest, all students could benefit from interaction with a concerned adult. However, it would be helpful if you could identify students who would benefit most from association with a creative cartoonist, scientist, or writer and match those students and mentors appropriately.

One model for performance-based assessment of creative thinking was proposed by the Ohio Department of Education (1992) (Fig. 8.2). It contains three levels: screening, referral, and identification. The model suggests that the type of assessment needed is based, at least in part, on teachers' knowledge and training in creative thinking strategies. Teachers with little knowledge in this area may be less likely to conduct classroom activities conducive to creative thinking and less able to identify manifestations of creative behaviors than teachers with extensive background in creativity.

At the screening level, information can come from several sources. Teachers may observe students' performance during regular classroom activities that promote creativity. They also may have students participate in a specific activity designed to elicit creative responses. Parents also may observe students' creative problem solving and activities outside school. A standardized assessment of creativity may be a part of this initial screening.

If students' activities at home or at school show an unusual degree of creativity in comparison with the activities of their peers, the students are referred for further evaluation. At the referral stage, a creativity portfolio or other documentation is submitted to a committee of evaluators for data review and possible nomination. The ultimate selection of students by the committee of evaluators is the identification stage.

In the hypothetical mentorship program, screening data might be gathered from parents, teachers, and classroom assessments. Students whose initial data indicate that they may be exceptionally creative would be referred to the selection committee. Students, teachers, or both would compile a creativity portfolio documenting evidence of the students' interests and creative activities. The committee then would suggest optimum mentor matches for particular students. Although this three-stage process is

Creative Thinking

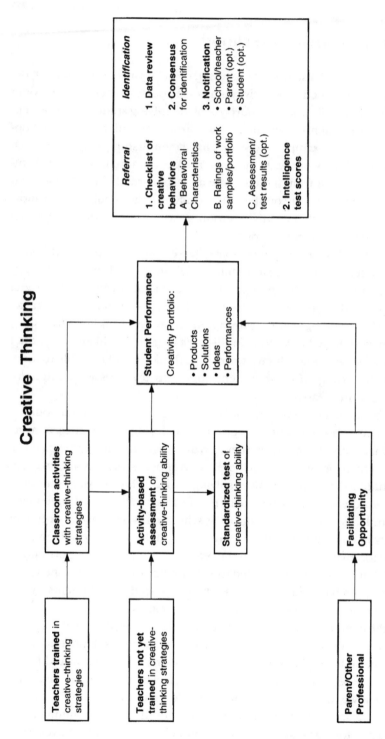

FIG. 8.2. Performance-based assessment for gifted identification. From *Model for the Identification of Creative Thinking Ability* (p. 22), by Ohio Department of Education, 1992, Columbus, OH: Ohio Department of Education. Copyright © 1992 by Ohio Department of Education. Reprinted with permission.

lengthy, it has the advantage of providing all students with the opportunity to demonstrate creative performance instead of beginning with an arbitrary test-score screen, and it does not rely on a single source of information for decision making.

CHALLENGES, LESSONS, AND RECOMMENDATIONS

Whatever the process, attempts to assess creativity are full of challenges. There is no universally agreed-on theory of creativity, no criterion for identifying creativity that satisfies all critics, and no standardized test that is free from concerns about some forms of reliability and validity. Although some instruments are stronger than others, there is no sure-fire no-fail test of creativity, no way to know for sure if a Bill Cosby, Michelangelo, or Hypatia are waiting in your classroom. Yet we are left with the feeling that although we may not be able to quantify creativity precisely, if we look for it, we may just recognize it when we see it. Furthermore, despite the difficulties, there are lessons to be learned from research on creativity testing that may add to our understanding of both assessment and creativity in general.

Lessons From the Research Front

Barron and Harrington (1981) carefully stated: "One can say that some divergent thinking tests, administered to some samples, under some conditions and scored according to some criteria, measure factors relevant to creativity criteria beyond those measured by indices of general intelligence" (p. 448). No measure of creativity—divergent thinking test, biographical inventory, or any other iteration—can take into account all the cognitive, affective, social, and cultural forces that ultimately shape an individual's creativity. However, even the small portion of creativity captured by tests of divergent thinking is affected by a variety of factors. These may provide clues to factors affecting the nature of creativity itself. A few of these possibilities include the following:

1. The conditions matter. Scores on tests of divergent thinking are affected both by the physical objects in the room and by the activities that precede the test. Students are more likely to generate fluent responses in a stimulus-rich than in a stimulus-poor environment (Friedman, Raymond, & Feldhusen, 1978; Mohan, 1971). They are less likely to produce creative responses if they are

interrupted from an interesting activity (Elkind, Deblinger, & Adler, 1970). If these trends carry into other kinds of creativity, consideration of the physical arrangements in the classroom and of transitions from one activity to another may affect students' creative performance. It is hard to imagine how students may be intrinsically motivated to be creative if an interesting discussion is cut short because the clock says it is time for art or creative writing.

2. The directions matter. Students are more likely to give original responses if they are told that original responses are desired. Runco (1986) compared the performances of students given tests from the Wallach and Kogan battery with and without explicit directions to give original ideas. With explicit directions, students gave fewer total ideas, but more ideas were original. Interestingly, explicit directions directing students to give original ideas increased originality scores more in students who had not been identified as gifted than in students who had been so identified. A similar phenomenon was observed by Friedman et al. (1978) and Mohan (1971). Although Mohan (1971) found that increasing the stimulation in the classroom increased scores, the increase came largely from the most creative students. Less creative students did not seem to use their environment to assist them. When Friedman et al. (1978) specifically cued students to look around them for ideas every 5 minutes, all students increased their scores. These studies suggest that if we want students to be creative, we should tell them so. If we are looking for fluency, originality, metaphor, or any other possible component of creative thinking, we are more likely to be find it if students understand that we desire and value such responses.

3. The types of stimuli matter. Scores on creativity tests are affected by the types of stimuli to which students respond. Verbal versus nonverbal and familiar versus unfamiliar stimuli may produce very different responses (Runco, 1986; Sawyers, Moran, Fu, & Milgram, 1983). If exercises designed to enhance creativity are structured around familiar or mundane stimuli, they seem less likely to stimulate original responses.

4. Some students are more affected than others by variations in the directions. Students who have been identified as gifted or highly creative may be less affected by changes in test directions than other students. Their test scores have sometimes been more reli-

able (perhaps suggesting they were less affected by other unintentional differences in test administration) than the scores of those not identified as gifted or highly creative. Although the relationship between creativity and intelligence remains somewhat unclear, it does appear that a variety of students may benefit from activities designed to enhance creativity, including students who may appear initially to be less able.

As research on assessment of creativity continues, additional insights into the workings of creative activity may emerge.

Recommendations

Runco (1991a) argued that with all their liabilities, tests of divergent thinking still may be considered "estimates of the potential for creative performance" (p. 185). Other estimates may be found in other assessments of creative processes, products, and personal characteristics. Although the limitations of standardized measurements of creativity can be discouraging, a few recommendations can be made.

First, match your assessment tools with both the definition or theory of creativity being used and the goals of your assessment. This recommendation, of course, presupposes that the school or district in which you are working has both a definition of creativity and a goal for any assessments being made. Unfortunately, my experience in schools suggests that these assumptions may be overly optimistic. If this is the case in your district, do your best to make sure that the decision-making process is carried out in a logical order.

If you are working in your own classroom only for the benefit of your general instruction, think about a definition and theory of creativity that make sense to you (perhaps using ideas from chaps. 1 and 2). Then think why you are interested in assessing creativity. Perhaps you plan to try some new activities and you want to see whether they affect students' creative thinking. Because this assessment is essentially for your own benefit and will be used only for general planning, you may wish to be fairly informal. Perhaps you might plan an activity that stimulates creative thinking and score it for various types of divergent thinking. After you have conducted your activities, you could use a similar measure. Your homemade measures would not have sufficient reliability or validity for assessing individual students, but they may give you a sense of how the class is progressing.

If, on the other hand, you are responsible for planning an assessment to be used for individual identification or large-scale screening, you will need much more reliable and valid measures. Make sure that before an assessment plan is devised, a definition is in place and a goal is in mind. (If there is no goal, you may rightly ask why you are assessing students in the first place!) With the preliminary decisions made, you can select reliable measures that match the opportunities for which students are being selected. For some opportunities, standardized creativity tests may be appropriate. For others, subject-specific assessments may make more sense. For example, an advanced music or acting program might be better served by having auditions with expert judges instead of using the most carefully planned set of standardized assessments.

Second, no one assessment has sufficient reliability or validity to be the sole determination of individual educational opportunities. If the creativity assessment is to be used for this purpose, it is important to have multiple sources of information. These could include standardized tests, performance assessments, and behavioral observations. In using multiple sources, it is best to examine each piece of data individually rather than create an artificial, summed creativity score. An individual who did not obtain a high score on a standardized creativity test but made an extraordinary creative product for which he or she earned a high score cannot be adequately described by a moderate-level score that attempts to combine the two.

Third, study all available information about the assessment tools to be used, looking particularly for information about reliability, validity, and potential bias. This review should include test reviews and research using the instruments. For example, Argulewicz and Kush (1984) found that Mexican American children scored lower than European American children on two of the three TTCT verbal scores. There were no differences between groups on the figural form of the test or on the Scales for Rating the Behavioral Characteristics of Superior Students (Renzulli et al., 1976). Any school with populations for which English is not the first language would want to take this information into account when selecting test instruments. Chen, Dong, Greenberger, Himsel, Kasof, and Xue (2002) found consistency in the consensual assessment technique used with Chinese and European American students. This provides some support for its use in multicultural settings in which judgment of individual student products is important.

Except for informal single-classroom assessments, standardized and researched scales probably have advantages over teacher-made instruments. Researchers with years of effort invested in the process have a difficult time producing tests or observation checklists with reasonable reliability and validity. It seems unlikely that any individual would do better in a first effort. The one exception to this rule may be assessment of creative products. As the technology for performance assessment develops, the time may come when reliable scales for assessing a variety of creative products are readily available. Until then, a consensus of expert judges or an evaluation with a clear scoring rubric designed for particular types of products may be the most reasonable path.

Fourth, be aware that assessments of creativity, particularly tests of divergent thinking, are affected by a variety of variables including the type of room, timing, and phrasing of the test instructions. To obtain reliable results and to be fair to all the students, you should make test administrations as uniform as possible.

Fifth, if the assessment of creativity is ongoing, collect a database of test information for your school. Examine how trends change over time and how scores vary among gender and racial groups in your area. Be aware that an instrument that works well elsewhere may not be right for your population. If you use performance assessment, consider using multiple raters and gathering reliability data on your rating scales. Think about saving the data and comparing them with those for other measures of creative performance in later years. This kind of effort can be invaluable in examining the validity and practicality of these measures.

Sixth, remember that teachers using observation forms or behavioral checklists need background information and instruction on the purpose and use of the forms. If a teacher is not sure what creative behaviors might look like or not aware that they might be manifested in positive or negative ways, it will be difficult for him or her to observe professionally. If you are part of any effort to gather information on creative behavior, try to ensure that those responsible for gathering data provide the time and opportunities for all teachers to learn the necessary observation skills before proceeding with the assessment.

Observations and assessments of creative activities in class must take place in an atmosphere that makes it possible for creative behaviors to emerge. In addition to the person, process, and product aspects of creativity, the influence of the creative environment is important. If a teacher encourages flexibility, motivation, originality, and independence every day, that teacher is more likely to observe students' creative behaviors than one whose only flexible activity is planned for the day of the observation. In some schools, the assessment of creativity may be better postponed until teachers have the opportunity to learn more about creativity and how to encourage it in students. Encouraging creativity, after all, is the goal—of assessment of creativity, of teaching creative thinking, and of this book.

BLIND MEN, ELEPHANTS, AND FAREWELL

As I worked on this book, I thought repeatedly of the story about the blind men and the elephant. In the fable, several blind men surround an elephant and explore him with their hands. Each man holds a portion of elephant's anatomy and is convinced he knows exactly what an elephant is like. The man holding the elephant's tail is certain that an elephant is very much like a snake. The one holding a leg assures him, no, an elephant is much more like a tree trunk. And so it goes, each man holding a little bit of knowledge, but no one able to comprehend the whole elephant.

Learning about creativity can be like the blind men and the elephant.

I think studying creativity is something like that. We examine patterns of divergent thinking or the characteristics of creative people or strategies for generating original metaphors and believe we are learning what creativity is about. The answer, I suspect, is that creativity is all those things and more. Creativity demands some kinds of divergent thinking and problem finding, persistence and intelligence, a willingness to take risks, task motivation, and more.

Fortunately, we can catch occasional glimpses of the elephant. When we listen to Mozart or Scott Joplin, when we look at Australian grave pole carvings or watch Samoan dances, we see the infinite variety of the human imagination at work. I believe we also can glimpse the elephant, perhaps at least a young one, as our students find and solve problems that are new to them, use ideas or materials in new ways, or connect ideas in patterns they have not seen before. In these activities, students are interacting with their environment in three-dimensional ways, encountering the unfamiliar, and exploring it in patterns that are at once as new and as old as human history. It is when we try to shield students from these complexities, to present neat, solvable problems and clean, clear solutions, that our view of creativity is muddied. The real world never comes in such neat packages. True creativity is about facing challenges, looking at the unknown, and trying to learn about things you do not totally understand. It is about learning to live.

The challenge I leave with you is to explore and to help your students explore as many aspects of this pachyderm, creativity, as you can. Knowing full well that no one piece makes the creature complete and understanding that we do not have all the answers, join the hunt with vigor. It is the search for the unknown that brings the wonder and excitement in discovering each new inch. If new paths cause occasional stumbles, they also bring adventure and understanding. Exploring them can make for schools of joy—and curious delight.

JOURNEYING AND JOURNALING

1. Examine some creativity tests and see how well you believe they reflect your own creativity. Take and score a Torrance Test of Creative Thinking (TTCT). You may want to try the new, streamlined scoring. Think about how the scoring process might work in a school with a large number of tests to evaluate.

2. Take one or both parts of the Khatena–Torrance Creative Perception Inventory. Compare the information obtained with that from

the TTCT. How was your creativity reflected? Did you get similar or different information from the two instruments?

3. Investigate whether students are evaluated for creativity in your district. If they are, examine the assessment procedure. Would you make any recommendations that might improve it?

4. By now you should have made considerable progress on your creative product. Devise a scoring rubric or other assessment procedure to assess products of the type you created. Use it to assess your product. Decide how well you believe your assessment procedure worked and how you felt evaluating your product.

REFERENCES

Amabile, T. M. (1982). Social psychology of creativity: A consensual assessment technique. *Journal of Personal and Social Psychology, 43,* 997–1013.

Amabile, T. M. (1996). *Creativity in context: Update to the social psychology of creativity.* Boulder, CO: Westview Press.

Anastasi, A., & Schaefer, C. E. (1969). Biographical correlates of artistic and literary creativity in adolescent girls. *Journal of Applied Psychology, 53,* 267–273.

Argulewicz, E. N., & Kush, J. C. (1984). Concurrent validity of the SRBCSS Creativity Scale for Anglo-American and Mexican-American gifted students. *Educational and Psychological Measurement, 4,* 81–89.

Backman, M. E., & Tuckman, B. W. (1978). Review of remote associates form: High school form. In O. Buros (Ed.), *The eighth mental measurements yearbook* (Vol. 1, p. 370). Highland Park, NJ: Gryphon Press.

Baer, J. (1993–1994). Why you shouldn't trust creativity tests. *Educational Leadership, 51*(4), 80–83.

Ball, O. E., & Torrance, E. P. (1980). Effectiveness of new materials developed for training the streamlined scoring of the TTCT, figural A and B forms. *Journal of Creative Behavior, 14,* 199–203.

Barron, F., & Harrington, D. M. (1981). Creativity, intelligence, and personality. *Annual Review of Psychology, 32,* 439–476.

Besemer, S. P., & O'Quin, K. (1986). Creative product analysis: Testing a model by developing a judging instrument. In S. G. Isaksen (Ed.), *Frontiers of creativity research: Beyond the basics* (pp. 341–357). Buffalo, NY: Bearly.

Besemer, S. P., & Treffinger, D. J. (1981). Analysis of creative products: Review and synthesis. *Journal of Creative Behavior, 43,* 997–1013.

Callahan, C. M. (1991). The assessment of creativity. In N. Colangelo & G. A. Davis (Eds.), *Handbook of gifted education* (pp. 219–235). Boston: Allyn & Bacon.

Chase, C. I. (1985). Review of Torrance Tests of Creative Thinking. In J. Mitchell, Jr. (Ed.), *The ninth mental measurements yearbook* (Vol. 2, pp. 1630–1632). Lincoln, NE: Buros Institute of Mental Measurement.

Chen, C., Dong, Q., Greenberger, E., Himsel, A. J., Kasof, J., & Xue, G. (2002). Creativity in drawings of geometric shapes: A cross-cultural examination with the consensual assessment technique. *Journal of Cross-Cultural Psychology, 33*(2), 171–187.

Clarizio, H. F., & Mehrens, W. A. (1985). Psychometric limitations of Guilford's Structure of the Intellect Model for identification and programming for the gifted. *Gifted Child Quarterly, 29,* 113–120.

Clark, R. M. (1992). Review of Creative Behavior Inventory. In J. J. Kramer & J. C. Conoley (Eds.), *The eleventh mental measurements yearbook* (pp. 249–250). Lincoln, NE: University of Nebraska Press.

Conoley & J. J. Kramer (Eds.), *The tenth mental measurements yearbook* (pp. 787–790). Lincoln, NE: University of Nebraska Press.

Cramond, B. (1998). The Torrance Tests of Creative Thinking: Going beyond the scores. In A. S. Fishkin, B. Cramond, & P. Olszewski-Kubilius (Eds.), *Investigating creativity in youth: Research and methods* (pp. 307–327). Cresskill, NJ: Hampton Press.

Cummings, J. A. (1989). Review of Structure of the Intellect Learning Abilities Test. In J. C. Damarin, F. (1985). Review of Creativity Assessment Packet. In J. Mitchell, Jr. (Ed.), *The ninth mental measurements yearbook* (Vol. 1, pp. 410–411). Lincoln, NE: University of Nebraska Press.

Davis, G. A. (1992). *Creativity is forever* (3rd ed.). Dubuque, IA: Kendall/Hunt.

Davis, G. S., & Rimm, S. (1980). *Group inventory for finding talent.* Watertown, WI: Educational Assessment Service.

Davis, G. S., & Rimm, S. (1982). Group inventory for finding interests (GIFFI) I and II: Instruments for identifying creative potential in the junior and senior high school. *Journal of Creative Behavior, 16,* 50–57.

Drummond, R. J. (1992). Review of Creative Reasoning Test. In J. J. Kramer & J. C. Conoley (Eds.), *The eleventh mental measurements yearbook* (pp. 250–252). Lincoln, NE: University of Nebraska Press.

Dwinell, P. L. (1985). Review of Group Inventory for Finding Interests. In J. Mitchell, Jr. (Ed.), *The ninth mental measurements yearbook* (Vol. 1, pp. 362–363). Lincoln, NE: University of Nebraska Press.

Elkind, D., Deblinger, J., & Adler, D. (1970). Motivation and creativity: The context of effect. *American Educational Research Journal, 7,* 351–357.

Evans, E. D. (1986). Review of Thinking Creatively in Action and Movement. In D. Keyser & R. Sweetland (Eds.), *Test critiques* (Vol. 5, pp. 505–512). Kansas City, MO: Testing Corporation of America.

French, J. W. (1978). Review of Creativity Tests for Children. In O. C. Buros (Ed.), *The eighth mental measurements yearbook* (Vol. 1, pp. 363–365). Highland Park, NJ: Gryphon Press.

Friedman, F., Raymond, B. A., & Feldhusen, J. F. (1978). The effects of environmental scanning on creativity. *Gifted Child Quarterly, 22,* 248–251.

Gowan, J. C. (1977). Some new thoughts on the development of creativity. *Journal of Creative Behavior, 11,* 77–90.

Guilford, J. P. (1967). *The nature of human intelligence.* New York: McGraw-Hill.

Guilford, J. P. (1973). *Creativity tests for children.* Orange, CA: Sheridan Psychological Services.

Guilford, J. P. (1977). *Way beyond the IQ.* Buffalo, NY: Creative Education Foundation.

Hattie, J. (1980). Should creativity tests be administered under testlike conditions? An empirical study of three alternative conditions. *Journal of Educational Psychology, 72,* 87–98.

Hennessey, B. A., & Amabile, T. M. (1988). The conditions of creativity. In R. J. Sternberg (Ed.), *The nature of creativity.* New York: Cambridge University Press.

Houtz, J. C. (1985). Review of Thinking Creatively with Sounds and Words. In D. Keyser & R. Sweetland (Eds.), *Test critiques* (Vol. 4, pp. 666–672). Kansas City, MO: Test Corporation of America.

Howieson, N. (1981). A longitudinal study of creativity: 1965–1975. *Journal of Creative Behavior, 15,* 117–135.

Howieson, N. (1984). *The prediction of creative achievement from childhood measures: A longitudinal study in Australia, 1960–1983.* Unpublished doctoral dissertation, University of Georgia, Athens.

Kaltsounis, B. (1975). Further validity on something about myself. *Perceptual and Motor Skills, 40,* 94.

Khatena, J. (1992). *Gifted: Challenge and response for education.* Itasca, IL: Peacock.

Khatena, J., & Bellarosa, A. (1978). Further validity evidence of something about myself. *Perceptual and Motor Skills, 47,* 906.

Khatena, J., & Torrance, E. P. (1976). *Manual for Khatena–Torrance creative perceptions inventory.* Chicago: Stoelting.

Khatena, J., & Torrance, E. P. (1990). *Manual for Khatena–Torrance creative perception inventory for children, adolescents, and adults.* Bensenville, IL: Scholastic Testing Service.

Kingore, B. (1990). *Kingore observation inventory.* Des Moines: Leadership Publishing.

Kirkland, J. (1974). On boosting divergent thinking scores. *California Journal of Educational Research, 25,* 69–72.

Kirkland, J., Kirkland, A., & Barker, W. (1976). Sex difference in boosting divergent thinking score by the context effect. *Psychological Reports, 38,* 430.

Kirschenbaum, R. J. (1989). *Understanding the creative activity of students.* Mansfield Center, CT: Creative Learning Press.

Kirschenbaum, R. J. (1998). The creativity classification system: An assessment theory. *Roeper Review, 21*(1), 2026.

Kulp, M., & Tarter, B. J. (1986). The creative processes rating scale. *The Creative Child and Adult Quarterly, 11,* 173–176.

Lissitz, R. W., & Willhoft, J. L. (1985). A methodological study of the Torrance tests of creativity. *Journal of Educational Measurement, 22,* 1–11.

Lynch, M. D., & Kaufman, M. (1974). Creativeness: Its meaning and measurement. *Journal of Reading Behavior, 4,* 375–394.

McKee, M. G. (1985). Review of Creativity Attitude Survey. In D. Keyser & R. Sweetland (Eds.), *Test critiques* (Vol. 3, pp. 206–208). Kansas City, MO: Test Corporation of America.

Mednick, S. A. (1962). The associative basis of the creative process. *Psychological Review, 69,* 220–232.

Mednick, S. A. (1967). *Remote associates test.* Boston: Houghton Mifflin.

Meeker, M. (1969). *The structure of intellect: Its use and interpretation.* Columbus, OH: Merrill.

Meeker, M. N., Meeker, R., & Roid, G. (1985). *Structure-of-intellect learning abilities test (SOI–LA).* Los Angeles: Western Psychological Services.

Mohan, M. (1971). *Interaction of physical environment with creativity and intelligence.* Unpublished doctoral dissertation, University of Alberta, Edmonton, Canada.

Ohio Department of Education. (1992). *Model for the identification of creative thinking ability.* Columbus: Author.

Okuda, S. M., Runco, M. A., & Berger, D. E. (1991). Creativity and the finding and solving of real-world problems. *Journal of Psychoeducational Assessment, 9,* 45–53.

Parke, B. N., & Byrnes, P. (1984). Toward objectifying the measurement of creativity. *Roeper Review, 6,* 216–218.

Perkins, D. N. (1981). *The mind's best work.* Cambridge, MA: Harvard University Press.

Plucker, J. A., & Renzulli, J. S. (1999). Psychometric approaches to creativity. In R. S. Sternberg (Ed.), *Handbook of creativity* (pp. 35–61). New York: Cambridge University Press.

Plucker, J. A., & Runco, M. A. (1998). The death of creativity measurement has been greatly exaggerated: Current issues, recent advances, and future directions in creativity assessment. *Roeper Review, 21,* 36–39.

Puccio, G. J., & Murdock, M. C. (1999). *Creativity assessment: Readings and resources.* Buffalo, NY: Creativity Education Foundation.

Quellmalz, E. S. (1985). Review of Alternate Uses. In J. Mitchell, Jr. (Ed.), *The ninth mental measurements yearbook* (Vol. 1, p. 73). Lincoln, NE: University of Nebraska Press.

Reis, S. M., & Renzulli, J. S. (1991). The assessment of creative products in programs for gifted and talented students. *Gifted Child Quarterly, 35,* 128–134.

Reisman, F. K., Floyd, B., & Torrance, E. P. (1981). Performance on Torrance's thinking creatively in action and movement as a predictor of cognitive development of young children. *Creative Child and Adult Quarterly, 6,* 205–210.

Renzulli, J. S. (1985). Review of Thinking Creatively in Action and Movement. In J. Mitchell, Jr. (Ed.), *The ninth mental measurements yearbook* (Vol. 2, pp. 1619–1621). Lincoln, NE: University of Nebraska Press.

Renzulli, J. S., & Reis, S. M. (1997). *The schoolwide enrichment model: A how-to-guide for educational excellence* (2nd ed.). Mansfield Center, CT: Creative Learning Press.

Renzulli, J. S., Reis, S. M., & Smith, L. H. (1981). *The revolving door identification model.* Mansfield Center, CT: Creative Learning Press.

Renzulli, J. S., Smith, L. H., Callahan, C., White, A., & Hartman, R. (1976). *Scales for rating the behavioral characteristics of superior students.* Mansfield Center, CT: Creative Learning Press.

Rosen, C. L. (1985). Review of Creativity Assessment Packet. In J. Mitchell, Jr. (Ed.), *The ninth mental measurements yearbook* (Vol. 1, pp. 411–412). Lincoln, NE: University of Nebraska Press.

Renzulli, J. W., Smith, L. H., White, A. J., Callahan, C. M., Hartman, R. K., & Westburg, K. (2002). *Scales for rating the behavioral characteristics of superior students* (Revised ed.). Mansfield Center, CT: Creative Learning Press.

Rosenthal, A., DeMars, S. T., Stilwell, W., & Graybeal, S. (1983). Comparison on interrater reliability on the Torrance tests of creative thinking for gifted and nongifted children. *Psychology in the Schools, 20,* 35–40.

Runco, M. A. (1986). Divergent thinking and creative performance in gifted and nongifted children. *Educational and Psychological Measurement, 46,* 375–384.

Runco, M. A. (1991a). *Divergent thinking.* Norwood, NJ: Ablex.

Runco, M. A. (1991b). The evaluative, valuative, and divergent thinking of children. *Journal of Creative Behavior, 25,* 311–319.

Runco, M. A. (1993, May). *Giftedness as critical and creative thinking.* Paper presented at the Henry B. and Jocelyn Wallace National Research Symposium on Talent Develop-ment, Iowa City, IA.

Runco, M. A., & Albert, R. S. (1985). The reliability and validity of ideational originality in the divergent thinking of academically gifted and nongifted children. *Educational and Psychological Measurement, 45,* 483–501.

Runco, M. A., & Chand, I. (1994). Problem finding, evaluative thinking, and creativity. In M. A. Runco (Ed.), *Problem finding, problem solving, and creativity* (pp. 40–76). Norwood: Ablex.

Runco, M. A., & Mraz, W. (1992). Scoring divergent thinking tests using total ideational output and a creativity index. *Educational and Psychological Measurement, 52,* 213–221.

Runco, M. A., & Okuda, S. M. (1988). Problem discovery, divergent thinking, and the creative process. *Journal of Youth and Adolescence, 17,* 211–220.

Runco, M. A., Okuda, S. M., & Thurston, B. J. (1987). The psychometric properties of four systems for scoring divergent thinking tests. *Journal of Psychoeducational Assessment, 5,* 149–156.

Rust, J. O. (1985). Review of Thinking Creatively in Action and Movement. In J. Mitchell, Jr. (Ed.), *The ninth mental measurements yearbook* (Vol. 2, p. 1621). Lincoln, NE: University of Nebraska Press.

Sawyers, J. K., Moran, J. D., Fu, V. R., & Milgram, R. M. (1983). Familiar versus unfamiliar stimulus items in measurement of original thinking in young children. *Perceptual and Motor Skills, 57,* 51–55.

Schaefer, C. E. (1969). The prediction of achievement from a biographical inventory. *Educational and Psychological Measurement, 29,* 431–437.

Schaefer, C. E. (1970). *Biographical inventory creativity.* San Diego, CA: Educational and Industrial Testing Service.

Schaefer, C. E. (1971). *Creative attitude survey.* Jacksonville, IL: Psychologists and Educators, Inc.

Schaefer, C. E., & Anastasi, A. (1968). A biographical inventory for identifying creativity in adolescent boys. *Journal of Applied Psychology, 52,* 42–48.

Sefton-Green, J. & sinker, R. (2000*). Evaluating creativity: Makng and learning by young people.* New York: Routledge.

Selby, E.C., Treffinger, D. J., Isaksen, S. G., & Lauer, K. (2002, January–March). VIEW assessment of problem solving style now available. *Creative Learning Today, 11*(1), 7–8.

Smilansky, J. (1984). Problem solving and the quality of invention: An empirical investigation. *Journal of Educational Psychology, 76,* 377–386.

Starko, A. J. (2000). Finding the problem finders: Problem finding and the development of talent. In B. Shore & R. Freedman (Eds.), *Talents unfolding: Cognition and development* (pp. 233–249). Washington, D.C.: APA Books.

Sternberg, R. J., & Davidson, J. E. (Eds.) (1995). *The nature of insight.* Cambridge, MA: MIT Press.

Tegano, D. W., Moran, J. D., & Godwin, L. J. (1986). Cross-validation of two creativity tests designed for preschool children. *Early Childhood Research Quarterly, 1,* 387–396.

Torrance, E. P. (1981). *Thinking creatively in action and movement.* Bensenville, IL: Scholastic Testing Service.

Torrance, E. P. (1984). Some products of 25 years of creativity research. *Educational Perspectives, 22*(3), 3–8.

Torrance, E. P. (1988). The nature of creativity as manifest in its testing. In R. J. Sternberg (Ed.), *The nature of creativity* (pp. 43–75). New York: Cambridge University Press.

Torrance, E. P. (1990). *Torrance tests of creative thinking.* Bensenville, IL: Scholastic Testing Service.

Torrance, E. P. (1999). Forty years of watching creative ability and creative achievement. *Celebrate Creativity: Newsletter of the Creativity Division of the National Association for Gifted Children, 10*(1), 3–5.

Torrance, E. P., Khatena, J., & Cunningham, B. F. (1973). *Thinking creatively with sounds and words.* Bensenville, IL: Scholastic Testing Service.

Torrance, E. P., & Wu, T. H. (1981). A comparative longitudinal study of the adult creative achievement of elementary school children identified as highly intelligent and as highly creative. *Creative Children and Adult Quarterly, 6,* 71–76.

Treffinger, D. J. (1985). Review of Torrance Tests of Creative Thinking. In J. Mitchell, Jr. (Ed.), *The ninth mental measurements yearbook* (Vol. 2, pp. 1632–1634). Lincoln, NE: Buros Institute of Mental Measurement.

Treffinger, D. J. (1987). Research on creativity assessment. In S. G. Isaksen (Ed.), *Frontiers of creativity research: Beyond the basics* (pp. 103–119). Buffalo, NY: Bearly.

Treffinger, D. J., Renzulli, J. S., & Feldhusen, J. F. (1971). Problems in the assessment of creative thinking. *Journal of Creative Behavior, 5,* 104–112.

Wakefield, J. F. (1985). Towards creativity: Problem finding in a divergent thinking exercise. *Child Study Journal, 15,* 265–270.

Wakefield, J. F. (1992, February). *Creativity tests and artistic talent.* Paper presented at the Esther Katz Rosen Symposium on the Psychological Development of Gifted Children, Lawrence, KS.

Wallach, M. A. (1970). Creativity. In P. Mussen (Ed.), *Carmichaels's manual of child psychology* (3rd ed., Vol. 2, pp. 1211–1272). New York: Wiley.

Wallach, M. A., & Kogan, N. (1965). *Modes of thinking in young children.* New York: Holt.

Ward, W. C. (1975). Convergent and divergent measurement of creativity in children. *Educational and Psychological Measurement, 35,* 87–95.

Weeks, M. (1985). Review of Group Inventory for Finding Interests. In J. Mitchell, Jr. (Ed.), *The ninth mental measurements yearbook* (Vol. 1, pp. 362–363). Lincoln, NE: University of Nebraska Press.

Williams, F. E. (1980). *Creativity assessment packet.* East Aurora, NY: DOK.

Wright, D. (1985). Review of Group Inventory for Finding Interests. In J. Mitchell, Jr. (Ed.), *The ninth mental measurements yearbook* (Vol. 1, p. 363). Lincoln, NE: University of Nebraska Press.

Yamamoto, K. (1978). Review of Creativity Tests for Children. In O. C. Buros (Ed.), *The eighth mental measurements yearbook* (Vol. 1, pp. 365–367). Highland Park, NJ: Gryphon Press.

Appendix
Problem-Finding Lessons

LESSON ONE: PEOPLE NEED PROBLEMS

Materials needed:

Two or three gadgets (vegetable peeler, pencil sharpener, etc.)

An assortment of catalogues

Picture of Chester Greenwood (optional, available in Steven Caney's Invention Book).

Opening

Have you ever heard anyone say, "Boy, I wish I had a problem?" What kind of a problem might someone want to have? We all know that there are some kinds of problems that no one wants to have, but there are other kinds of problems that can be important—and even fun. For the next few weeks we will be talking about why someone might look for an interesting problem and how they might do it.

Constructing Understanding

Let me start by telling you a story about a boy who found a problem and solved it. This problem started in a cold winter in Maine. A 15-year-old boy named Chester Greenwood had terrible trouble with his ears. Every time he went outside, even with his hat on, his ears were very cold. He tried wrapping a scarf around his head, but it was too uncomfortable. Finally, Chester made some loops out of wire and asked his grandmother to sew pieces of fur on one side and velvet on the other. Chester attached his fur-covered loops to a wire that went across his head. Chester Greenwood had invented the first earmuffs! In fact, Chester started an earmuff business and became a very successful inventor. *[Show a picture of Chester and his earmuffs.]*

What problem Chester did find? Do you think anyone else had ever had that problem? Why do you think no one else solved the problem the way Chester did? Sometimes one of the most important things that problem finders do is keep their eyes and ears open—they pay attention to the problems around them.

Another problem was solved more recently. A first-grade girl named Suzanna Goodin hated one of her chores at home. She hated feeding the cat! Now, Suzanna liked her cat and she wanted the cat to have food. There was only one thing wrong. She hated washing the cat food spoon. Every time she fed the cat, the spoon ending up covered with squishy, smelly cat food. It was disgusting to wash. Luckily, Suzanna was a good problem finder, much like Chester Greenwood. Instead of just complaining about the smelly cat food, she thought, "Aha! This is a problem I can solve." And she did. Suzanna invented an edible pet food spoon. The spoon is made of hard pet food, like a spoon-shaped dog biscuit. After you scoop the pet food out of the can, you can throw the spoon right in the bowl with the food. The cat or dog can eat it right up! For her invention, Suzanna won grand prize in that year's *Weekly Reader* invention contest.

Here is another invention. *[Hold up any convenient gadget. It may be a common object like a vegetable peeler or pencil sharpener, or something more unusual, like electric socks.]* What kind of problem might have caused someone to invent this? Why do you think they might have decided to work on that problem? *[Repeat with two or three inventions. Select from the discussion questions below as appropriate for your class.]*

Possible questions:

What made Chester or Suzanna a good problem finder?

Why do you think that some people notice problems and some don't?

Why do you think some people complain about problems and some people try to figure out how to solve them?

What inventions can you think of that solved a problem? Why do you think someone might have chosen to work on that particular problem.

Applying Understanding

Let's see if you can find examples of someone finding a problem and inventing something to solve it. Using these catalogs, find something that you think someone invented to solve a problem. Cut out the picture of the object you choose and paste it at the top of a piece of paper. Under the picture, describe what problem this invention solves and why you think someone decided to work on it. *[This activity may be completed individually or in pairs, as appropriate for your classroom.]*

LESSON TWO: INVENTORS LOOK FOR PROBLEMS

Materials needed:

Assorted Oreos or other multivariety snack foods (optional).

Opening

Yesterday we talked about inventors needing to find problems. Today we are going to act like inventors and find some problems to solve. Remember the stories of Suzanna Goodin and Chester Greenwood? What did they do that made them good problem finders? Chester and Suzanna:

1. Noticed things around them.
2. Decided to solve a problem instead of complaining about it.
   [List key points on the board or chart paper. Add other ideas from the class as appropriate.]

Constructing and Applying Understanding

Before we try to find some problems for ourselves, I need to tell you one more secret of being a good problem finder. A very famous scientist, Linus Pauling, once said that the secret of having good ideas is to have a lot of ideas. What do you think he meant by that? Finding a good problem to solve is like that. If you think of a lot of problems, you can pick an interesting problem to solve. If you think only of one problem, it might not be interesting or you might not be able to solve it. Your first idea (or problem) is practically never your best idea.

One way to find a problem to solve is to think about things that bug us. For example, it really bugs me when I'm trying to roll the TV/VCR into the classroom and I can't see over the TV to see where I am going. It bugs me when there's only a tiny bit of ketchup left in the bottle and I can't get it out or it squirts all over me. *[Substitute your own things that bug you here.]* Think about things that bug you at home, at school, or any place else you go. *[It probably will be necessary to clarify that we are not trying to think of people who bug us but things.]* Let's brainstorm as many things that bug us as we can. *[List ideas. This may be done as a class or in small groups.]*

Sometimes, problem finders don't find things that bug them, but things that can be improved or changed in some way. In this type of problem nothing is really wrong, but something could be different or better. For example, what are some of the ways Oreo cookies have been changed to make new products? *[Possibilities include Double Stuff Oreos, miniature oreos, giant Oreos, holiday Oreos, and reduced fat Oreos. You may wish to bring in examples of one or more of these.]* I don't think there was anything wrong with Oreos—Oreos probably didn't bug anyone—but someone thought of ways they could be changed or improved to make something new. Let's try to add to our list of problems by thinking of things that might be changed or improved. For example, is there anything in this classroom that could be changed to make it easier or more fun to use? *[Add to list.]*

Now we have LOTS of ideas to choose from, just as Linus Pauling suggested. If you were going to choose one of these problems to solve, which one would you choose? On a piece of paper, write one problem you think would be interesting to work on and why you'd like to work on it. You may choose one of the problems from our list or think of one of your own. If you decide to solve the problem, be sure to tell the class what you invent!

LESSON THREE: AUTHORS LOOK FOR PROBLEMS

Materials needed:

Two or three children's books by the same author
Berlioz the Bear by Jan Brett (1991), if possible.

Opening

We've been talking about how inventors find problems to solve or things to improve. What were some of the things good problem finders did? Yes, good problem finders:

1. Noticed things around them.
2. Thought of many possible problems.
3. Solved problems instead of complaining about them.

Today we are going to think about a very different kind of problem, one that can't be solved by an invention.

In the 1860s Louisa May Alcott wanted to be a writer. She wrote mysteries. She wrote romantic stories. She sent her stories to magazine publishers, but no one ever wanted to buy them. In fact, one editor told her she would never be able to write anything that had popular appeal. Louisa May Alcott didn't want to find a problem she could solve with an invention. What kind of problem did Louisa need? Yes, Louisa May Alcott needed to find a problem she could solve by writing. She needed to find something she could write about that would be interesting and allow her to tell a good story. Does anyone know how Louisa solved her problem? Louisa May Alcott decided to write stories about her family, especially about her life with her three sisters. Many of you may have read some of Louisa May Alcott's stories or seen a movie of her most famous book, *Little Women*.

Just as inventors need to find problems to solve with their inventions, authors need to find their own special kind of problems. An author looks for a problem he or she can solve with words—an interesting story to tell. One author I really enjoy is *[fill in a children's author you enjoy]. [The author]* writes books about *[give two or three examples]*. What do you think the author chose to write about?

Jan Brett, a children's author and illustrator, uses things around her to come up with ideas for her books. She tells the story of how she first started thinking of ideas for her story *Berlioz the Bear*. This is what she says in *Berlioz the Bear Newsnotes*.

I was listening to a Boston Symphony Orchestra concert. My husband Joe plays with BSO. While I was watching, Joe and all the double basses began to play loudly. I thought, "That is a large instrument, really huge. Something could fit right inside." Then I noticed the carved "F" holes in the front of Joe's bass. It would have to be a small something. A mouse? A caterpillar? Music does that. It leads one's thoughts to interesting places.

All this took place at an outdoor concert at Tanglewood, the Boston Symphony's summer home. Afterward the musicians were talking about their instruments. I asked Joe if his double bass changed with the weather. He looked concerned. "Jan," he said, "my bass is 100 years old. Sometimes the wood dries out and cracks. Then it makes a buzz." "A loud buzz" I asked, "that people can hear?"

At that moment I knew what kind of creature might live in a double bass, and my story had begun. (p. 1)

[You may want to share a few pictures from Berlioz the Bear *or ask if anyone knows what kind of animal Jan Brett wrote about. In the book, there is a bee inside the string bass.]*

Does anyone here have a favorite author or an author whose stories they especially like? How do you think that author decides what he or she is going to write about?

Applying Understanding

Today we are going to try to imagine why some of our favorite authors decided to write about the things they did. Maybe they wrote about their favorite places. Maybe they wrote about something they really had done, or maybe they wrote about something based on a favorite animal or object or dream. Pick a book you have enjoyed. Pretend you are the author. Write a paragraph explaining why you wrote the book and what first gave you the idea.

LESSON FOUR: LOOKING FOR INTERESTING OBJECTS

Materials needed:

A bag of miscellaneous small objects.

Opening

Today I want to tell you about another author who could not think of anything to write. The author's name was E. L. Doctorow, was a famous author of adult books. He already had one best-selling novel, *The Book of*

Daniel. But now he was stuck. He couldn't think of anything to write. Have you ever felt that way? Have you ever had journal time or a writing assignment and were not able to think of anything to write about? Well, that is exactly how E. L. Doctorow felt. Fortunately, E. L. Doctorow was a good problem finder. So, what do you think he did? He did many of the same things the inventors did when they were being good problem finders. He tried to think of many possible problems to solve and choose one of them to work on. Every day he sat down to write and tried to write something, even if he didn't think it was a very good idea. E. L. Doctorow knew that if he kept thinking of ideas, eventually he'd think of a good one. Where do you think he got his ideas? Where did the inventors get their ideas? Yes, they noticed things around them. E. L. Doctorow noticed things around him and tried to find ideas for his writing.

One day he couldn't think of anything to write about so he sat staring at a spot on the wall in front of him. He just kept thinking of more and more ideas. First, he just thought about the spot. Then he thought about the wall the spot was on. Thinking about the wall made him think about the house. Thinking about the house made him think about how old the house was. Thinking about how old the house was made him think about who might have lived there long ago and who might have been their neighbors. Thinking about that gave him an idea for a story about people who lived back when his house was first built. Eventually, after a lot of work and a lot more thinking, that idea grew into his next famous book, *Ragtime*.

Other authors sometimes get ideas from objects around them, too. Lawrence Yep, a Chinese American author, once got ideas for two mystery books by looking at some old coins. He thought the coins were interesting, so he thought about them until he had many good story ideas. If you are stuck and can't think of anything to write about, one thing you can do is try what E. L. Doctorow did. Pick something near you or something interesting and just let your mind wander. See if it leads to any interesting story ideas. Let's try a few. Sometimes asking questions about the object can help us. We'll choose an object from this bag to help us. *[Pull an item from the bag.]*

1. What is interesting about this object?
2. What interesting place might this object have been?
3. What interesting place might this object go?
4. Does this object remind you of anything interesting?
5. What story ideas does this object give you?
   [With the children, model the problem-finding process. It is not

necessary to come up with a full-blown story, just the general
story idea. For example, a wooden box might be interesting be-
cause of the designs on the lid or because we wonder what is in-
side. It might have been in someone's attic or on a bookshelf in a
fancy house. Maybe someone will hide it under a bed, using it to
hide a secret note from a friend. This could lead to ideas for a
story about a mysterious box in the attic, an artist who paints
magic boxes, or a friend with a secret she is afraid to share.]

Applying Understanding

Now it is your turn. Pick an object from the bag or choose another object in
the classroom. On your worksheet (Fig. A.1), answer the questions listed.
Try to come up with the most interesting story idea you can. Remember, you
probably will have to think of many different ideas before you choose the
idea you think is the most interesting. *[Do not assign students to write the*
story at this time. They may, of course, if they choose to do so.]

   Homework.   Tonight, look around you for an object that you think
might be interesting to think about. It must be something small enough to
carry to school. Bring the object to school tomorrow. *[At a convenient time,*
repeat the worksheet with the objects chosen by the students. This time, as-
sign students to choose their favorite idea and actually write about it.]

LESSON FIVE: LOOKING FOR INTERESTING CHARACTERS

Materials needed:

Two or three magazine photographs of faces.

Opening

[Hold up first photograph.] What do you think this person might be thinking? Where do you think the person might be? What might the person be doing? What kind of story about this person might be most interesting to tell?
[Make sure students generate several alternatives. Briefly repeat with a
second photograph. Use a third if you think it is necessary.]

Name _____ Date _____

What object did you choose?

What is interesting about this object?

What interesting places might this object have been?

What interesting places might this object go?

What does this object remind you of?

What story ideas does this object give you?

Put your best story idea here.

FIG. A.1.   Finding a story in an interesting object.

By now you can tell that good problem finders, whether they are inventors or authors, really have to keep their eyes and ears open. They notice the things around them, think of many possible problems or possible ideas, and then work on them. The last time we talked about finding writing possibilities by looking for interesting objects. Today we will talk about another way that problem-finding authors get their ideas—looking around for interesting characters.

Constructing Understanding

If you are going to be a problem-finding author, you will need to notice not just the objects around you, but the characters as well. Take out a piece of paper. On it, make a list of all the people you have seen today. You do not have to list every single name. Sometimes you might list a whole group of people at once like, "students in my class" or "people on the bus" or "my family." See how many people you can remember. Did you see a bus driver? A police officer? Someone driving a car?

Sometimes authors get ideas for characters by looking at the people around them. They might write about people they know, as when Louisa May Alcott wrote *Little Women* about her sisters. Laura Ingalls Wilder wrote about her family, too, in her Little House books. At other times, authors write about characters because someone they know is interesting and helps them think of interesting ideas. For example, remember how Jan Brett got the idea for *Berlioz the Bear* at a concert? She got the idea for her version of *Goldilocks and the Three Bears* a different way. Jan Brett met a girl named Miriam who was very, very curious. Miriam was very adventurous and spunky, and she made Jan think that she'd like to write about a little girl who was adventurous and spunky like Miriam. That is where her ideas for Goldilocks got started.

Look at your list. Think about the people you have seen today. Is there anyone on your list who has an especially interesting personality? Who do you think might be interesting to read about in a story? Pick two or three characters from your list who you think are the most interesting. Put a check mark by them.

Of course, characters are not always people. Jan Brett's ideas for her book *The First Dog* started when she tried to guess what her dog was thinking. Did you see any interesting animals today? Are there any animals in school that might make interesting characters? Add them to your list.

Name_____   Date _____

What character did you choose?

Why did you think that character was interesting?

List at least six words that describe your character.

List at least three places this character could go.

List at least three problems the character could have.

What story ideas does this character give you?

List your best story idea here.

FIG. A.2.   Finding a story in an interesting character.

Applying Understanding

Look at your list. Choose one character from your list. Use the worksheet (Fig. A.2) to help you think how that character might help you think of a story idea—a problem you can solve by writing a story. *[Again, do not require students to write the story at this time. They may, of course, if they wish.]*

Homework.   Tonight, look carefully at the people and animals around you. Try to find a character that might bring you interesting story ideas. Remember to think of many possibilities—your first idea is practically never your best idea. *[At a convenient time, have students repeat the worksheet with their chosen character. This time they should write at least a paragraph about their character.]*

LESSON SIX: SCIENTISTS LOOK FOR PROBLEMS

Materials needed:

Soap bubbles and wand

Hershey's Hugs or other candy with a hidden center, enough for each student to have one. If candy is not appropriate for your class, an unfamiliar fruit can also be used as long as it can be cut with a plastic knife

Plastic knives

Paper towels.

Opening

So far, we have talked about how inventors and authors both need to look for problems they can work on. Inventors look for problems they can solve through inventions. Authors look for interesting ideas or stories they can try to write. Today we will talk about another type of person who needs to find problems to investigate. Whom do you think that might be? *[Discuss student responses and acknowledge the many types of people who need to find things to investigate. Tell students that although many types of people need to find problems, today they'll be talking about scientists.]*

Constructing Understanding

Today I'd like to tell you about a scientist who made a very important discovery that saved many lives. Listen carefully and decide how you think this scientist is like the other problem finders we have talked about.

Alexander Fleming was working in the laboratory. He was doing an experiment for which he had to grow bacteria. One day in his lab he noticed something that probably did not make him very happy. Some of his petri dishes, in which he was growing the bacteria he needed, had mold growing on them. The mold had killed the bacteria, so his experiment was ruined. What do you think most people would have done with those moldy dishes? I suspect many scientists would have thrown them away. Luckily, Alexander Fleming did not do that. He wanted to know why the bacteria had died. Was there something about that mold that killed them? Now he had a new problem to investigate. The things Alexander Fleming learned from his moldy petri dishes led to the development of penicillin, an antibiotic that has saved many, many lives.

How do you think Alexander Fleming was like the other problem finders we've talked about? *[Make sure the discussion includes the ideas that he noticed things around him. He did not just complain about things he did not understand; he tried to understand them; and he thought of more than one problem he could investigate.]*

Scientists who are problem finders do many things, but three of them are especially important. Problem-finding scientists

1. Observe (notice) things around them.
2. Ask questions for which they don't have answers.
3. Try to find answers to their questions.

Today we are going to act like problem-finding scientists by practicing asking some of the kinds of questions scientists might ask. Alexander Fleming asked at least three questions. He asked,

"*What* happened in these petri dishes? *What* is growing here?" "*Why* did the bacteria die?" and "*How* did the mold kill the bacteria?" "What," "why," and "how" are three important words that many scientists (and other problem finders) use when they are asking questions. What, why, and how questions help us think about what we observe and why things happen the way they do.

Let's imagine we are scientists who have gone to the park one sunny afternoon. As we are sitting on a bench, we notice a child blowing soap bubbles. I'll pretend I'm the child and blow a few bubbles. *[Blow bubbles.]* You be scientists. What are some of the problems or questions we might think about if we saw these bubbles? Remember, scientists ask questions for which they do not have answers. Think about questions that begin with what, why, and how. *[Students should generate questions such as "What are the colors on the sides of the bubbles?" "Why do some bubbles end up bigger than others?" or "How do bubbles stick together?" If students ask obvious questions such as, "What are those?" or "What color is the bubble wand?" remind them that scientists ask questions for which they do not already have answers.]*

Those are interesting problems to think about. What other things might a scientist notice in a park that might lead to interesting questions? *[Spend a few minutes brainstorming other things that might be observed and how they might lead to questions or problems to be investigated.]*

Applying Understanding

Now, imagine that the scientist looked on the ground and saw one of these. *[Hold up a Hershey's Hug or other similar candy.]* Think about all the what, why, and how questions you could ask about this. I am going to give you each an object just like this one. Please examine it carefully. If you wish, you may use a plastic knife to help you. Be sure to put a piece of paper towel on your desk to protect it. As you observe your item, imagine that you are a scientist. Write down as many scientific questions about this object as you can. Try to use the words what, how, and why. The more carefully you observe, the more questions you will be able to ask. Circle the question you think is most interesting. *[After the activity is complete, let the students eat the candy!]*

LESSON SEVEN: MAKING COMPARISONS

Materials needed:

Scotch and masking tape.

Opening

The last time we talked about how scientific problem finders observe the things around them and ask questions. We talked about questions that started with three special words. What were the words we used? Yes, we thought of lots of questions that started with what, why, and how. Today I'd like to tell you a story about two groups of scientists who asked a different kind of question. Listen carefully and see if you can figure out how their questions were alike.

Both groups of scientists I will tell you about were elementary school children—in fact they were only 6 or 7 years old—but they found interesting problems to work on. The first group of students had a fish tank. What are some of the things the students might have wondered about the fish or the fish tank? *[Briefly brainstorm possible questions or problems. If you have an aquarium in your classroom, you may want to point it out.]*

Those are interesting problems to think about. In this class, the students became curious watching the bubbler that blew oxygen into the fish tank. They knew that fish in streams and ponds did not have bubblers to bring them oxygen. Most fish depend on plants to produce the oxygen they need. This made the students wonder if their fish would be healthier in a tank with a bubbler or in a tank with plants. They designed an experiment to find out. *[If your students are curious, you may explain that the class set up two fish tanks, one with a bubbler and one with plants. At set times of the day, they counted how many times the fish swam across the tank in 5 minutes, assuming that healthy fish are more active. The fish in the tank with plants were more active.]*

The second group of student scientists found a very different kind of problem. The weather was nice and many students had been playing jump rope on the playground. The problem-finding students observed the jumping and wondered whether older or younger students could jump rope longer. They thought that younger students, with more energy, might be able to jump longer than older students. They conducted an investigation into their problem and studied whether first- or fifth-grade students could jump rope longer. *[In this study, fifth-grade students did, much to the disappointment of the first-grade investigators!]*

Think about the questions these two groups of students wondered about—the problems that they found to study. The first group wondered, "Will fish be healthier in a tank with a bubbler (and no plants) or one with plants (and no bubbler)?" The second group wondered, "Who can jump longer, first graders or fifth graders?" How are these questions alike? *[In your discussion, help students determine that, although there are several possible similarities, one important one is that both questions are comparisons.]* Yes, both of these questions compare one thing with another. They ask which is healthier or better or longer. Comparisons are another type of question scientists ask. They might compare things and think about whether one thing is stronger, heavier, faster, or more efficient than another. They might wonder which antibiotic works best for a particular infection, which formula will create the bounciest ball, or which type of paper towel is most absorbent.

Applying Understanding

Look around the classroom. Imagine that you are a scientist looking for comparison problems to study. Think about what ideas you may discover just by looking at things around you. For example, looking at this tape might make me wonder if it is very sticky. I could write the comparison question, "Which is stickier, Scotch tape or masking tape?" When you have finished your list, circle the question you think would be the most interesting to investigate if you were a scientist and had a big laboratory. Put a star next to the question you think would be the most interesting to investigate in a school like ours. *[Do not require students to investigate the questions at this time. They may, if they choose to do so.]*

LESSON EIGHT: WONDERING WHAT WOULD HAPPEN

Opening

Have you ever done a real experiment? What did you do? Today we are going to talk about the kinds of problems that lead scientists to do experiments. I'm going to tell you about one more young problem finder who found a question that led to an interesting experiment and an unexpected difficulty.

This problem finder, named Alex, was studying plants in school. He had learned about things plants need. Can you guess some of the things Alex learned? Yes, Alex studied about how most plants need sun, water, and soil to grow properly. One day when Alex was thinking about plants growing, it made him think about the things he needed to grow. He didn't need soil to grow, but he did drink water. Thinking about how he drank water and the plants took in water gave Alex an idea. He knew that drinking milk helped him grow and develop strong teeth and bones. He wondered if he poured milk on plants instead of water whether the plants would grow stronger, too. Alex's question was a very important type of question that scientists ask. We have already talked about what questions, why questions, how questions, and comparison questions. Alex's question was a different type. He asked a "what if" question. What if questions lead to problems in which we investigate what would happen if we did something different from the things we usually do. In this case, Alex's question asked, "What if we put milk on the plants instead of water; what would happen?"

Alex was so interested in his problem that he did an experiment to find out. He used a group of bean plants. Half of the bean plants were watered every day, just as usual. Half of the bean plants received milk instead of water. After two weeks, Alex did not notice any difference in the beans, but he did notice something he had not expected—something he had not predicted before the experiment. See if you can imagine what it might have been. Imagine Alex pouring milk on the plants every day. Imagine those milky plants sitting in the warm sun on the window sill. After a few weeks, can you guess what happened? *[If no one guesses, tell the students that the soured milk began to smell horrible. It smelled so bad that no one wanted to go near the windowsill and they had to throw the plants away!]*

This story is a little silly, but it helps us think about three important things. First, it helps us think about what if questions and the interesting problems they can help us find. When George Washington Carver was a child, he asked what if questions about plants, too. He was always trying to find ways to help make sick plants healthy again. He grew up to be an important botanist. Perhaps Alex will, too. Second, it helps us remember that, because problem finders look for questions to which they do not already have the answers, problem finders sometimes run into unexpected results. When we find interesting questions or problems we never know exactly what will happen when we investigate them. That is what makes problem finding so exciting. But it also leads to the third important idea. If you find an interesting scientific problem, especially a what if question, you should always share your problem with an adult before you investigate it. Some investigations can be dangerous. All of us can think of lots of interesting problems that might be interesting to investigate. If we decide really to investigate them, it is important to tell an adult our plans before we conduct any experiments. Alex's unexpected results did not hurt anyone, but good scientists are careful scientists.

Applying Understanding

There are lots of ways to think of interesting what if problems. Sometimes, like Alex, we think of things we do and wonder what would happen if we did it differently. At home, I might look at a CD player and wonder whether students would do a better job on their homework with music playing or with no music playing. (Some sixth-grade students actually investigated that problem.) Sometimes we might look at something and wonder what would happen if we changed it in some way. For example, I might look at my flashlight and wonder if a flashlight with four batteries would shine brighter than one with two batteries. Or I might wonder if a colored filter on the flashlight make it easier or harder to see in the dark.

Today I'd like you to practice asking what if questions by thinking about how Bob and Sarah (Fig. A.3) spent the morning. Pretend you are Bob or Sarah, thinking about all the things you are doing and seeing. List as many what if questions as you can. Try to wonder about many interesting things. When you are finished, put a star by the problem that makes you the most curious.

LESSON NINE: TRAPPING YOUR IDEAS

Materials needed:

Pictures from Leonardo da Vinci's journals

Small notebook or pad of paper for each student.

Opening

We have talked a lot about different problem finders and some of the things they do. Today we will talk about something that all problem finders have to do, no matter what kinds of problems they are searching to find. Have you ever had a really good idea and then forgot what it was before you had a chance to do it? You might have thought, "Oh, no. I had an idea and now I can't remember what it was." Do you think that ever happens to the problem finders we have been talking about: to inventors or writers or scientists? It can, if they are not careful. That is why good problem finders have to be very careful to trap their ideas before they get away. What kind of trap do you think you might use to trap an idea? A mousetrap? Probably not. Many problem finders trap their ideas in a special problem-finding notebook.

Constructing Understanding

Just as there are many kinds of problems to find, there are many kinds of things to write in a problem-finding notebook. Inventors might keep an in-

Bob and Sarah's Morning

This morning Bob woke up to the sound of the alarm clock ringing at 7:30. Sarah woke up at 7:15, when her dog George jumped on her bed. Sarah and Bob both dressed warmly because it was a cold morning. They put on jeans, shirts and sweaters. After they were dressed, Sarah and Bob ate breakfast and fed their pets. Sarah ate cereal, milk and juice. She fed her dog, George, dry dog food and water. Bob ate cold pizza and milk. He fed his cat, Alex, a can of cat food.

After breakfast, Sarah and Bob left for school. Sarah put on her backpack and got on her bike. She rode next door to her friend Chris' house. Sarah and Chris rode their bikes to school together. They noticed that the snow had melted on the sidewalk and on the roads but not on the lawns. The snow on the lawns was still deep and was starting to look dirty and gray.

Bob walked to the corner to wait for the school bus. His friend Sam waited there, too. Bob and Sam got cold waiting for the bus to come. Bob wished he had a warmer hat. His Tigers cap did not keep his head very warm. When the bus came, Bob and Sam hurried to the back seat. They liked the way the back seat bumped when they rode over the railroad tracks.

When Bob, Sarah, and their friends arrived at school they walked down the hall to their classroom. Their feet sounded loud on the tile floor. They could hear children laughing and smell something good baking in the cafeteria. In the classroom they could see that their teacher had a big box on her desk. Maybe it was the pet snake she had talked about yesterday. Bob and Sarah hoped so! They went to their desks, took out pens and pencils, and got ready for the day.

Think about all the questions Bob and Sarah might ask about things they observe this morning. List all the questions or problems they might find. Use the back of this paper for more space. Put a star next to the question that makes you the most curious.

FIG. A.3. Bob and Sarah's morning.

ventor's log. In their inventor's log, they write down all the interesting problems they notice or ideas they get for inventions. They write down the ideas even if they don't plan to use them right away. Some day they may want to come back to an idea, and if the idea is trapped in a notebook, they will always be able to find it.

A very great problem finder named Leonardo da Vinci lived around the time of Columbus. He kept problem-finding notebooks that people still study today. Leonardo da Vinci recorded notes and drawings for many different kinds of problems. He made sketches for paintings he might paint someday and inventions he might want to build. He trapped ideas for different kinds of buildings. Leonardo da Vinci must have been a careful observer of the world around him. He certainly thought of many different problem ideas! *[Show pages from da Vinci's notebooks.]*

Writers also trap ideas. They might write down interesting ideas for characters, interesting places to write about, or titles they'd like to use some day. What other kinds of ideas might an author want to record? How about a scientist? What kinds of things might a scientist write in a notebook? Can you think of other kinds of ideas a different kind of problem finder might want to record? (For example, an artist might record interesting ideas for works of art, or a dancer might make notes about a new movement.)

Applying Understanding

Today you will be creating your own problem-finding notebooks. You may use a purchased notebook or pieces of paper stapled together. The important thing about a problem-finding notebook is not how elegant it looks, but how much you use it. Keep your problem-finding notebook with you so you can jot down ideas for different kinds of problems. You may want to divide your notebook into sections for different kinds of problems, or leave it all together. It is up to you. Tonight, see if you can record at least three interesting problems in your problem-finding notebook. *[Have students create their notebooks. Decorations may be as plain or elaborate as students choose. Effective problem-finding notebooks will easily fit in pockets or packs so that they are easy to transport.]*

LESSON TEN: WONDERING AND WONDERING

Opening

If I say something is a habit, what do I mean? What are some examples of habits you have? Have you ever heard the phrase "habits of mind?" What do you think habits of mind might be? Yes, habits of mind are ways of thinking that someone does over and over. Your habits of mind determine how you notice things and how you think about the world. Today I'd like to tell you about a few more problem finders. Think about them and about the other problem finders we've discussed and decide what kinds of habits of mind you think a good problem finder should have.

Constructing Understanding

The first problem finder I'd like to tell you about was named Charles W. Turner. Charles W. Turner was a very curious person. When he was young, he always wondered how ants could find their way home. He spent many hours on the ground observing ants, bees, and other insects. When he grew up, Charles became a naturalist, a person who studies nature. He discovered many things, including the finding that insects can hear and bees can see colors.

The second problem finder was named Vera Rubin. When Vera was growing up, she liked to look at the sky. Sometimes she would stay up all night looking at the stars and wondering what she saw. After she grew up and got married, she still wondered about the stars. Finally she decided she should study to become an astronomer. Vera Rubin studied galaxies far from our solar system. In fact, in 1979 she discovered the largest galaxy ever seen. It is 10 times larger than our Milky Way galaxy.

Langston Hughes found problems to solve with his writing. He loved the people and the sights and sounds of his neighborhood in Harlem. He found many ideas for poems there. Some of his most famous poems are about the things he saw and people he met in Harlem.

Edgar Degas found problems to solve with art. Degas was an artist who lived more than 100 years ago. He painted many things, but his most famous paintings and sculptures are of ballet dancers. Degas did not just paint the dancers while they were on stage dancing. He observed behind stage and in practice rooms, watching the dancers work. He watched carefully to find the most interesting moments. Those moments gave him ideas and problems to express with his art. Even when he grew older and his eyesight was failing, Degas continued to use his art to portray dancers through sculpture.

Think about Charles W. Turner and Vera Rubin, Langston Hughes and Edgar Degas. What kinds of habits of mind do you think they might have had? What about the other problem finders we've talked about; what kinds of habits of mind do you think they might have had? Do you think different kinds of problem finders have different types of habits of mind, or do you think inventors, writers, and scientists have some similar habits of mind?

Applying Understanding

[With the class, use the preceding discussion questions to help generate a list of "Rules for Problem Finding" or "What Makes a Good Problem Finder?" The rules should include such habits as observe things around you and think about what you see; think about things for a long time; think about many different ideas; don't give up; and think about any other ideas reasonably derived from this or previous lessons. Have students copy the list in the front of their problem-finding notebooks. Encourage students to continue to think like problem finders as they find interesting problems at home and at school.]

Author Index

A

Adata, P. M., 294, 352
Adler, D., 452, 459
Albee, E., 157
Albert, R. S., 102, 136, 434, 462
Allan, S. D., 394, 414
Allender, J., 163, 172
Amabile, T. M., 143, 165, 167, 168, 169, 172,
    261, 358, 362, 363, 364, 365, 366,
    368, 369, 370, 371, 415, 445, 458,
    460
Anastasi, A., 440, 458, 463
Anderson, C. W., 307, 313, 352
Apol, L. 284, 352
Argulewicz, E. N., 454, 458
Arlin, P. K., 162, 172, 173
Armeli, K. S., 56, 88, 363, 416
Aschbacher, P. R., 403, 416
Ashria, I. H., 39, 89
Atwell, N., 280, 352
Austin, G., 353

B

Backman, M. E., 434, 458
Baer, J., 82, 87, 131, 136, 189, 254, 371, 415,
    422, 458
Baer, D. M., 56, 89
Bagley, M., 240, 255
Bailey, C. T., 38, 87, 312, 355
Ball, O. E., 430, 458
Balta, V., 21, 26

Bandura, A., 168, 172
Bank, M., 294, 352
Barker, W., 430, 460
Barron, F., 89, 95, 96, 104, 113, 136, 256,
    451, 458
Basadur, M., 189, 255
Battista, M.T., 320, 352
Bedwell, R., 293, 352
Belenky, M. F., 130, 136
Bellarosa, A., 439, 460
Bennett, W. J., 17, 26
Berger, D. E., 436, 461
Besemer, S. P., 441, 458
Bingham, C., 309, 353
Bloom, B., 137, 143, 148, 151, 167, 171, 172,
    174, 363, 365, 370, 415
Boden, M. A., 69, 71, 73, 87, 223, 255
Bohm, D., 306, 353
Bollman, K. A., 20, 26, 316, 353
Borland, J. H., 111, 136
Bowers, C., 23, 26
Boykin, A. W., 38, 87
Bradbury, R., 183, 255, 282, 353
Brandt, R., 20, 26, 359, 418
Brandwein, P., 308, 353
Bransford, J. D., 15, 26, 253, 255, 322, 353
Brilhart, J. K., 197, 255
Brown, A. L., 322, 353
Brown, J. S., 20, 26
Brown, S. I., 329, 330, 353
Bruchac, J., 34, 87
Bruer, J. T., 359, 415
Bruner, J., 337, 353
Burns, D. E., 164, 172

Subject Index